Thomas Jefferson
and the
Education of a Citizen

THOMAS JEFFERSON (1743-1826).
Medallion engraving by
Charles Balthazar Julien Févret de Saint-Memin (1770-1852),
Washington, D.C., ca. 1804. Prints and Photographs
Division, Library of Congress, LC-USZC4-5179.

Thomas Jefferson
~ and the ~
Education of a Citizen

Edited by James Gilreath

Library of Congress

Washington

1999

Library of Congress
Cataloging-in-Publication Data

Thomas Jefferson and the education of a citizen / edited by James
Gilreath
    p. cm.
    Essays published here were selected from a conference, held at the
Library of Congress, May 13 to May 15, 1993; cosponsored by the
Library's Rare Book and Special Collections Division, the Center for
the Book in the Library of Congress, and the Institute of Early
American Culture at Williamsburg, Va.
    Includes bibliographical references and index.
    ISBN 0-8444-0965-0 (alk. paper)
    1. Jefferson, Thomas, 1743–1826—Views on citizenship—Congresses.
2. Citizenship—Study and teaching—United States—Congresses.
I. Gilreath, James, 1947- .
Z663.T425   1998
[E332.2]
973.4'6'092—dc21

Index: Victoria Agee

Contents

Preface

JOHN Y. COLE

ix

Acknowledgments

JOHN Y. COLE AND JAMES GILREATH

xi

Introduction

JAMES GILREATH

xiii

I.

The Public and Private Spheres

1

Citizens and Families: A Jeffersonian Vision
of Domestic Relations and Generational Change

MICHAEL GROSSBERG

3

Binding Ties: The Public and Domestic Spheres
in Jefferson's Letters to His Family

FRANK SHUFFELTON

28

Beyond Education: Thomas Jefferson's "Republican"
Revision of the Laws Regarding Children

HOLLY BREWER

48

Jefferson, the Family, and Civic Education

JAN LEWIS

63

II.

An Informed Citizenry

77

Jefferson and Literacy

DOUGLAS L. WILSON

79

Bulwark of Revolutionary Liberty: Thomas Jefferson's and
John Adams's Programs for an Informed Citizenry

RICHARD D. BROWN

91

Thomas Jefferson and Legal Education in Revolutionary America

HERBERT A. JOHNSON

103

"That Knowledge Most Useful to Us":
Thomas Jefferson's Concept of Utility in the Education
of Republican Citizens

JENNINGS L. WAGONER, JR.

115

Education and Democracy: Summary and Comment

BENJAMIN R. BARBER

134

III.
Influence of the Old and New Worlds
153

Thomas Jefferson and the Old World: Personal Experience
in the Formation of Early Republican Ideals
ELIZABETH WIRTH MARVICK
155

Why Slaves Can't Read: The Political Significance of Jefferson's Racism
JAMES OAKES
177

Thomas Jefferson's Dualistic Perceptions of Native Americans
DONALD A. GRINDE, JR.
193

The Old and the New Worlds: Summary and Comment
C. VANN WOODWARD
209

IV.
A Republic of Citizens
219

Citizenship and Change in Jefferson's Constitutional Thought
DAVID N. MAYER
221

Liberty and Virtue: Religion and Republicanism in Jeffersonian Thought
EUGENE R. SHERIDAN
242

Ward Republics: The Wisest Invention for Self-Government
SUZANNE W. MORSE
264

V.
An International Perspective
279

The Education of Those Who Govern

RALPH KETCHAM

281

Thomas Jefferson and His Conception of Happiness

LIU ZUOCHANG

295

Notes

307

Contributors

369

Index

373

Preface

The Library of Congress is one of Thomas Jefferson's principal legacies. In 1815 his personal library became the Library's core, and the wide range of his interests determined the universal and diverse nature of the Library's collections and services. Today's Library of Congress, which collects research material from throughout the world, epitomizes Jefferson's belief in the power of knowledge to inform citizens and shape democracy.

The Library has celebrated its Jeffersonian heritage in many ways: special events, exhibitions, lectures, symposia, and even the naming and renaming of its buildings.

The bicentennial of Jefferson's birth in 1943 was, in the words of Librarian of Congress Archibald MacLeish, "an occasion of the very greatest importance in the history of the Library of Congress." Exhibitions in different parts of the Library honored Jefferson, and Supreme Court Justice Felix Frankfurter delivered an address on "The Permanence of Jefferson." The Library removed the Declaration of Independence from its wartime storage site and displayed it in the newly opened Jefferson Memorial. The bibliographical reconstruction of Jefferson's personal library was begun, along with the microfilming of the Jefferson papers in the Manuscript Division. The Library published *The Declaration of Independence: The Evolution of a Text,* by Julian P. Boyd.

In 1976 Librarian of Congress Daniel J. Boorstin renamed the Library's Annex Building, calling it the Thomas Jefferson Building. The dedication ceremony included a symposium featuring Frederick R. Goff, chief of the Library's Rare Book Division, which is the home of Jefferson's library, and Jefferson scholars Dumas Malone and Merrill D. Peterson. In 1980, the Library's Main Building was named for Jefferson, and the former annex was christened the John Adams Building, honoring the man of letters and president of the United States who in 1800 approved the law establishing the Library of Congress.

The Library's commemoration of the 250th anniversary of Jefferson's birth in 1993 focused on its sponsorship, with other institutions, of "Jefferson at 250," a national lecture and discussion tour, and the symposium "Thomas Jefferson and the Education of a Citizen" described in these pages.

As the Library nears its own bicentennial in the year 2000, under the leadership of Librarian of Congress James H. Billington it is planning new activities and projects to honor its principal founder and renew its commitment to the knowledge-based society that Jefferson envisioned. The active, wide-ranging mind was central to Jefferson's concept of government, for both members of Congress and the citizens they represented. Jefferson believed that self-government depended on the free, unhampered pursuit of truth by an informed and involved citizenry.

In his preface to *Jefferson's Legacy: A Brief History of the Library of Congress* (1993), Dr. Billington concluded: "In a world of increasing physical restraints and limitations, it is only in the life of the mind and spirit that the horizons of freedom can remain truly infinite. We must rediscover what we should have known all along, that the pursuit of truth is the noblest part of Jefferson's legacy."

JOHN Y. COLE

Director, The Center for the Book
in the Library of Congress

Acknowledgments

The Center for the Book and the Rare Book and Special Collections
Division, the principal sponsors of the Library's commemoration of
Jefferson's 250th birthday in 1993, wish to express their thanks to several
organizations and individuals. The Institute of Early American History
and Culture in Williamsburg, Virginia, and the Library's James Madison Council, a
private-sector group, helped support the symposium described in these pages. We
are grateful also to the U.S. Department of Education for its help in funding this
publication and to the Library's Interpretive Programs Office, particularly Irene
Chambers and Andy Cosentino, for developing and presenting an exhibition,
"Jefferson and the Library of Congress," in conjunction with the symposium. Partial
funding also came from individual and corporate donors to the Center for the
Book, which was established in 1977 to stimulate public interest in books, reading,
literacy, and libraries.

Help in developing these and other Jefferson projects and publications also
came from Gerard Gawalt of the Library's Manuscript Division; Margaret Wagner
and Evelyn Sinclair of the Publishing Office; Anne Boni of the Center for the Book;
and Rosemary Frye Plakas of the Rare Book and Special Collections Division.
Finally, for advice and support, we wish to thank Daniel P. Jordan, director of the
Thomas Jefferson Memorial Foundation, Inc.; Merrill D. Peterson, who in the midst
of his many scholarly projects served as chairman of the Thomas Jefferson
Commemoration Commission; and Douglas L. Wilson, formerly of Knox College
and now director of the International Center for Jefferson Center at Monticello.

JAMES GILREATH AND JOHN Y. COLE

-cute it. in the purchase of books, pamphlets &c old & curious, or new & useful I shall ever keep you in my eye. whether I shall procure for you the books you have before desired at Philadelphia or Paris shall be decided according to circumstances when I get to Philadelphia, from which place I will write to you.

I have a tender legacy to leave you on my departure. I will not say it is the son of my sister, tho' her worth would justify my resting it on that ground; but it is the son of my friend, the dearest friend I knew, who had fate reversed our lots would have been a father to my children. he is a boy of fine dispositions, and sound masculine talents. I was his preceptor myself as long as I staid at home, & when I came away I placed him with mr Maury. on his breaking up his school I desired mr Short to dispose of him, but mr Short I expect will go with me to Europe. I have no body then but you to whose direction I could consign him with unlimited confidence. he is nearly master of the Latin, and has read some Greek. I believe he is about 14. years of age. I would wish him to be employed till 16. in compleating himself in latin, greek, french, Italian & Anglo-saxon. at that age I mean him to go to the college. I have written to my sister of the application I make to you & she will be very happy to have your advice executed, my steward Mr Key will furnish money to his tutors &c on your order. there is a younger one, just now in his Latin rudiments. if I did not fear to overcharge you I would request you to recommend the best school for him. he is about 10. years old, and of course ceteris paribus, of any two schools that nearest his mother would be most agreeable. you will readily understand I am speaking of the sons of mr Carr. —— I think Colo Monroe will be of the committee of the states. he wishes a correspondence with you; and I suppose his situation will render him an useful one to you. the scrupulousness of his honor will

Thomas Jefferson to James Madison, May 8, 1784. Before leaving for Europe as minister plenipotentiary, Jefferson wrote to his friend James Madison about the education of his two nephews Peter Carr and Dabney Carr, Jr., the sons of his sister Martha. (For a transcription, see *Letters of Delegates to Congress, 1774-1789* [Washington: Library of Congress, 1994], edited by Paul H. Smith, volume 21, pages 600-603.)

Introduction

Throughout 1993, the American nation celebrated the 250th anniversary of the birth of Thomas Jefferson with lectures, commemorations, publications, films, and dedications of various kinds. In large part these were not merely ceremonies but also educational events, something of which Jefferson would have approved; for he was a man who seems to have written something about nearly everything, and only after doing much investigation. Jefferson engaged in almost nothing that was not a studied effort in self-improvement and an attempt to improve the enterprise for others, whether it was gardening, architecture, reading, or even plowing, for he invented a new kind of plow. Education was, for Jefferson, not narrowly restricted to formal schooling; he considered all of life's activities to be instructional.

The articles in this volume are focused on citizenship and how members of society need to prepare themselves to be citizens of the American republic that Jefferson envisioned. The choice of this topic can be attributed to Jefferson himself. While reading through Jefferson's correspondence for another project, I noticed that Jefferson frequently mentioned the importance of citizens and the requirements of citizenship. I had not remembered reading anything about this subject in Jefferson scholarship and so turned to Frank Shuffelton's excellent bibliography, *Thomas Jefferson: A Comprehensive Annotated Bibliography,* for guidance. I found that little if anything had been written about the subject, either recently or throughout the twentieth century. Furthermore, I found very little about citizenship in all of recent American historical scholarship. In an effort to aid my own self-education, I organized a conference with John Y. Cole of the Center for the Book and Ron Hoffman of the Institute of Early American History and Culture entitled "Thomas Jefferson and the Education of a Citizen."

The essays published here were selected from this conference, held at the Library of Congress from May 13 to May 15, 1993, and cosponsored by the Library's Rare Book and Special Collections Division, the Center for the Book in the Library of Congress, and the Institute of Early American Culture at Williamsburg, Virginia. The conference was organized around several panels dealing with aspects of citizenship: "A Virtuous Citizenry," "The Family and Public Culture," "The Old and the New Worlds," "An Informed Citizen," and "Political and Ideological Bases of Citizenship." Members of each panel were assigned topics or proposed relevant ones, but instead of delivering their papers or summaries of their papers to the audience they submitted them to an eminent historian or political scientist who was not a Jefferson specialist but had written about the subject in a more general way. The commentator then presented a single paper at the conference, which aimed at tying the themes of the papers together and connecting them to broader and related issues. Each panelist then briefly replied to the commentator's remarks.

For the most part, this organization has been preserved in this book, though parts of two panels at the conference, "A Virtuous Citizenry" and the "Political and Ideological Bases of Citizenship" have been reformed under "A Republic of Citizens" and "An International Perspective" without commentators. The panelists' responses to their commentators have not been included in this book.

Jefferson grudgingly allowed that some form of central government was necessary but enthusiastically espoused the view that the real power resided in the citizens themselves who, he felt, had to be constantly vigilant so that those running the central government did not gradually accumulate for themselves more and more of the power of the citizens. For this reason and for the reason that Jefferson believed that citizens needed to make as many governing decisions as possible, he thought American citizens must be prepared and educated for power and that this education, as was Jefferson's own, needed to extend into all aspects of their lives. Raising a family was not only a private act but also had a dimension of public responsibility; a citizen must take care to be "informed" in the broadest sense of that word; and a citizen must be prepared to use the best of Old World and New World cultures for the benefit of the republic. Such preparation, in Jefferson's view, was not only a responsibility but a necessity if democracy was to work the way he hoped and was not to degenerate into oligarchy or some version of monarchy.

The papers presented here, with two exception, are written by American academicians, many with long and distinguished careers, who have tried in their writing to be accessible to as wide an audience as possible. The two exceptions to this academic slant are papers by Suzanne Morse and Liu Zuochang. Suzanne Morse is currently the executive director of the Pew Partnership for Civic Change, a national program funded by the Pew Charitable Trusts to encourage cooperation among private, public, and not-for-profit organizations to plan for the solutions of urban issues in smaller communities, and was formerly associated with the Kettering Foundation. Her essay is an attempt to bring someone actively involved with urban planners and those attempting to counter civic disengagement across the country to come to grips with Jefferson's ideas and ultimately to bring those ideas to the attention of an audience that may not habitually look to the eighteenth and nineteenth centuries for answers. Liu Zuochang teaches at Shandong Normal University, where he is translating Jefferson's works into Chinese—the first such attempt—and his essay is an opportunity for us to see how someone from a radically different culture views the third president's life and thinking. In a sense, it is more of a primary rather than a secondary source that may give clues about the direction of thinking of some elements of Chinese society.

There is a particularly interesting facet of Liu Zuochang's presentation to my mind. Garry Wills once said about foreign views about Jefferson that the further one got away from Jefferson the better he looked. Coming from China, Liu Zuochang is very far away indeed, and Jefferson looks very good to him, whereas American scholars, quite rightly from their own perspective, are quick to find gaps between his rhetoric and practice. I think this demonstrates two interesting aspects of Jefferson's thought. The first is that his rhetoric did exceed his grasp: he did write that all men were created equal, yet he did own slaves; he did discriminate in the education of the genders; and he did extol the manner in which American Indians governed themselves, yet advocated pushing them out of the way as the American empire moved westward. And though none who read this volume would want to be judged by the standards of two and a half centuries after our own time, as Jefferson is judged today, nonetheless the discrepancies between what he said and what he did undeniably exist.

As we learn in essay after essay in this volume, Jefferson ardently believed that the earth belongs to the living, and each generation not only can but must make its own compact with democracy and, as was his hope, move closer to the ideal. But the ideal must be envisioned and articulated, even when the reality is almost certainly doomed to fall far short of its lofty goal. It is because he expressed his principles in such a pure and unreserved manner that Jefferson's ideas are able to be tested 250 years after his death in a culture whose existence he could never have imagined.

JAMES GILREATH

I

The Public and Private Spheres

MICHAEL GROSSBERG

Citizens and Families:
A Jeffersonian Vision of Domestic Relations and Generational Change

"I set out this ground which I suppose to be self-evident, '*that the earth belongs in usufruct to the living*'; that the dead have neither powers nor rights over it," Thomas Jefferson declared in a famous 1789 letter to James Madison. Writing from France, Jefferson explained his theory of generational change with a critique of the law: "On similar ground it may be proved that no society can make a perpetual constitution, or even a perpetual law. The earth belongs always to the living generation. They may manage it then, and what proceeds from it, as they please, during their usufruct. They are masters too of their own persons, and consequently may govern them as they please. But persons and property make the sum of the objects of government. The constitution and the laws of their predecessors are extinguished then in their natural course with those who gave them being. This could preserve that being till it ceased to be itself, and no longer. Every constitution then, and every law, naturally expires at the end of 19 years. If it be enforced longer, it is an act of force, and not of right."[1]

Jefferson would repeat his theories of generational change many times in the future. Like so many of his most heartfelt declarations, his words have remained inspiring yet enigmatic. They have also been analyzed countless times. One way to try to understand them anew, and to ponder their implications from a new perspective, is to examine more closely the connection Jefferson himself made between generational power and law. Another often-studied subject, a product of the great collaboration between Jefferson and Madison, is a particularly revealing example of those connections. In 1785 Madison shepherded through the Virginia legislature statutory revisions that Jefferson had drafted several years earlier. Among the revisions were changes in inheritance that reveal how Jefferson tried to translate his theories of generational relations into law.

The future president took particular pride in the revisions abolishing entail and primogeniture and substantially revising the law of descent. Those changes, including within the latter a fundamental alteration in bastardy rules, constituted one of his most direct attempts to use law as a reform tool. In drafting the revisions,

Jefferson seized the unique opportunity afforded his generation by the revolutionary moment. Their options seemed vast because so much of their world, everything from markets to marriages, seemed open to change. The possibilities of that moment led them to engage in a far-reaching exploration of alternative routes for the improvement of their new society.

A new law of inheritance became one of Jefferson's major contributions to that search for a new order. It sprang from his conviction that meaningful change could occur only by altering the primal relationship between property rights and individual rights. He championed a revision of inheritance as a way to realize the egalitarian ideals at the heart of his political beliefs and of his generation's debate over the meaning of their revolution. Jefferson turned to legal reform to curb the influence of an artificial feudal hierarchy and an outdated code of family morality. Eliminating both of those would help create a republic based on demonstrated merit not on legally maintained inherited distinctions and would prevent parental sin from blighting a child's life prospects. By loosening the restraining grasp of the past over the intergenerational distribution of wealth and the meaning of individual equality, inheritance reform would make each generation responsible for its fate. As such, Jefferson's call to free the future from the past expressed his faith in progress. Reform would realize two of his cardinal beliefs: the proper relationship between government and the citizenry should be one of realization not restraint; and, the family should be a training ground for republican citizens. The connections between these two convictions also helped ensure their incorporation as fundamental assumptions about intergenerational responsibilities in an emerging Americanized law of the family being created in postrevolutionary America.[2]

Through the inheritance revisions Jefferson helped launch one of many debates over what the new republic would become under the tutelage of the revolutionary generation. As he and others surveyed the landscape of revolutionary America, they saw no single path to the future. Quite the contrary, at each bend in the road they battled over which fork to take. Their battles not only occupied themselves but have structured debate over the meaning of the revolution ever since. Clearly labeling Jefferson's voice in that debate has been difficult.

His role in inheritance reform suggests why. Like so much of what he did, Jefferson's deeds and words about intergenerational relations mingled the republican and liberal ideas that swirled about in the era to make his own idiosyncratic brew. They reveal him to be preoccupied with both republican concerns of civic obligation and community participation as well as with liberal causes of individual rights and antistatism.[3] In the end, however, through incorporation in family law Jefferson's inheritance reforms helped make liberal individualism a key tenet of American social ideology. Even so, his campaign for generational equity bequeathed a complex legacy of policies and possibilities to succeeding generations.

Revising Inheritance Law

Jefferson eagerly seized the unique opportunity to revise Virginia's laws provided by the revolutionary break from Britain. He recognized the possibilities of using law reform to jettison the lingering hierarchical organization of colonial society and create a new egalitarian order. To do so, Jefferson understood, meant that he and his fellow revolutionaries must insist, as Willi-Paul Adams has observed, "not only that everyone enjoy equality before the law or have an equal voice in government but also that everyone have an equal share in the fruits of the common enterprise."[4] Those goals could be realized only through reforms that directly altered the inherited distribution of power and authority between as well as within generations.

To realize the possibilities of the revolutionary moment, in September 1776, Jefferson left the Continental Congress, refused appointment as a minister to France, and took a seat in the Virginia legislature. He was ready to draft legal reforms that would institutionalize the ideals he had just advocated so passionately in the Declaration of Independence. As Joyce Appleby has argued in her attempt to document Jefferson's liberalism, his commitment to the use of government in the protection of the natural rights of self-fulfillment and his corresponding denial that government existed to protect vested interests, led him to amend Locke's natural rights to "life, liberty and property" to make the Declaration instead affirm the natural rights to "life, liberty and the pursuit of happiness."[5] Jefferson would make clear the implications of his revision of Locke in his own revision of inheritance law. "I knew," he recalled in his 1821 autobiography written at age seventy-seven, "that our legislation under the regal government had many very vicious points which urgently required reformation, and I thought I could be of more use in forwarding that work."[6]

At the heart of his approach to law reform lay the subordination of property evident in the new phrase that would henceforth always be identified with him. Property in Jefferson's view was not a natural right at all, "but one which is established by and subject to civil power," and as such decidedly subordinate to the natural and inalienable right to pursue happiness.[7] "*Bonheur*, happiness, is man's *telos*,"[8] Richard Matthews contends in his radical reading of Jefferson. "Rights—property and other—are mere instruments to aid men in their pursuit of happiness. And governments must either be structured or dissolved and restructured so that all men will have access to this pursuit."[9] Jefferson wanted to alter the structure of power by compelling Virginians to use their newfound power to transform the rules governing intergenerational transfers of wealth. He compiled a package of changes that used inheritance reform as a means of ensuring that the inevitable demise of one generation would liberate its successor. Redefined intergenerational property rules, he believed, would help make the family a creator of self-reliant republican citizens.

The revisions sprang from Jefferson's critique of the Anglo-American inheritance laws his generation had inherited and that had recently been systematically presented in Sir William Blackstone's *Commentaries on the Laws of England.* The law remained dominated by remnants of its feudal and dynastic origins. As English legal historian Frederic Maitland complained late in the nineteenth century, it "is in the province of inheritance that our medieval law made its worst mistakes. They were natural mistakes. There was much to be said for the simple plan of giving all the land to the eldest son. There was much to be said for allowing the courts of the church to assume a jurisdiction, even an exclusive jurisdiction, in testamentary[10] causes. We can hardly blame our ancestors for their dread of intestacy[11] without attacking their religious beliefs. But the consequences have been evil. We rue them at the present day, and shall rue them so long as there is talk of real and personal property."[12]

The rules Maitland would bemoan and Jefferson would revise had several key features all premised on the assumption that the family was a corporate institution and the preservation of its property was the central responsibility of its members and the state. The rules focused on the disposition of male property. Upon a patriarch's death, the law provided for transmission of his property either to those he designated in his will—*testamentary disposition*—or, in the absence of a valid will, to his heirs according to a statutory scheme of distribution—*intestate succession.* The latter must, English authorities decreed, proscribe a policy that accorded with the dynastic priorities assumed to be the desire of all family heads. English men long enjoyed the power to devise personal property by will, and acquired a similar power to dispose of real property with the passage of the Statute of Wills in 1540. This legislation established substantial liberty of testament in England and, significantly, also established substantial freedom for alienation of property before death, although dower, curtesy, the rule against perpetuities, and certain other doctrines limited actions of the testator.[13]

Emblematic of the priorities of English inheritance law were the doctrines of entail and primogeniture and the denial of significant testamentary rights to women. Entail enabled a testator to rule from the grave by restricting the power of the designated recipients of his real property to alienate it during their own lifetimes. When a decedent had died intestate, primogeniture dictated that his lands descended to his eldest son, though his personal property went in equal shares to his children with a dower portion reserved for his widow. Dower constituted the major inheritance right of married women. Under the English law of coverture, a wife did not exist at law and had no testamentary power. By enshrining these policies in intestate rules, English authorities had devised a practical plan—and a symbolic endorsement—for the corporate preservation of the family estate as the central responsibility between generations.

English inheritance law also included a particularly revealing silence. It excluded illegitimate children altogether. For property conscious common lawyers, inheritance cemented domestic bonds by creating a common interest in preserving the family heritage and resources. English law denied inheritance rights to bastards—designated *filius nullius,* the child of no one—in an attempt to discourage illegitimacy and premarital intercourse and the threats they posed to the perpetuation of the family. Blackstone endorsed the policy by singling it out as a basic difference between the common and the civil law. On the continent, he declared disparagingly, "a bastard was likewise capable of succeeding to the whole of his mother's estate, although she was never married; the mother being sufficiently certain, though the father is not. But our law, in favor of marriage, is much less indulgent to bastards."[14] This lack of indulgence was evident not only in inheritance law but also in marriage rules that increased the chances of a child becoming a bastard. Besides children born out of wedlock, those born to parents who later married or to parents whose marriage was declared legally void also became illegitimate.

As Jefferson well knew, English inheritance law granted a man of property immense power over present and future generations. He could dispose more or less freely of his property by will, while at the same time the provision for intestate succession made sure that the family estate survived the failure to write a will. A highly developed system of contractual family settlements, trust creations, and similar nontestamentary arrangements further complicated inheritance law. Nevertheless, the intergenerational transmission of wealth remained dominated by "a narrow unilateral system with great individual freedom for family heads."[15]

The American colonists followed the general spirit of the English law of inheritance, although statutory and judicial innovations occurred in every colony.[16] The most significant modifications altered primogeniture, especially in the New England colonies, which generally opted for partible inheritance of testate estates, frequently reserving a double portion for the eldest son. Entail, however, operated in all the colonies, as did the denial of inheritance rights to illegitimates. Despite their complications and feudal origins, the colonists refused to abandon the basic inheritance policies and priorities of their English ancestors. The colonists' slavish replication of English rules governing generational wealth transmission—particularly "primogeniture, the testamentary freedom to will property outside of the lineage, and married women's lack of property rights—were among the biggest surprises encountered by immigrants from Europe. Many had come from Old World villages where a customary bilateral system of inheritance prevailed, one which incorporated a broader notion of lineage."[17]

Jefferson's Virginia followed the general pattern. There had been some tinkering such as a 1705 statute making it impossible to break an entail without obtaining a special act of the assembly and thus blocking the use of the traditional and relatively painless English mode of terminating entails by fine and recovery. And even though subsequent legislation restored the right of docking for small estates and allowed the leasing of entailed land, entail remained as a dynastic tool to control the actions of later generations.[18] John Orth has explained the consequences quite vividly: "the message communicated by these colonial statute books was plain: Just as primogeniture was the rule for inheritance and entailment was available if desired, so disentailment was an exceptional remedy, requiring time, expense, and specific justification. Young Virginia or North Carolina planters needed the concurrence of their social peers gathered in their respective colonial assemblies before they could sell or break up the family estate."[19]

Jefferson hoped to break that stranglehold of the past on the present with a revolutionary revision of inheritance law. He found inspiration not only in the anti-patriarchalism of the revolution itself, but perhaps, as Kenneth Lockridge has argued, in his own rage at finding himself under the control of his mother after his father's death.[20] Generational independence had come to have personal as well as political meanings for the Virginian.

Prodded by Jefferson, in October 1776, the Virginia legislature authorized the creation of a committee to revise the commonwealth's laws. In a preamble to the act, Jefferson championed revision as a republican necessity to renovate the existing laws, "many of which are inapplicable to the powers of government as now organized, others are founded on principles heterogeneous to the republican spirit, others which, long before such change, had been oppressive to the people, could yet never be repealed while regal power continued, and others, having taken their origin while our ancestors remained in Britain, are not so well adapted to our present circumstances of time and place, and it is also necessary to introduce certain other laws, which though proved by the experience of other states to be friendly to liberty and the rights of mankind, we have not heretofore been permitted to adopt."[21] Years later in his autobiography, he amplified the point with a reiteration of the republican creed that had animated his actions: "our whole code must be reviewed, adapted to our republican form of government, and, now that we had no negatives of Councils, Governors, and Kings, to restrain us from doing right, it should be corrected, in all it's parts, with a single eye to reason, and the good of those for whose government it was framed."[22]

Under his proposal, a five person committee would be given "full power and authority to revise, alter, amend, repeal or introduce all of any of the said laws, to form the same into bills, and report them to . . . the General Assembly." In November, the legislators voted Jefferson, Edmund Pendleton, George Wythe, George Mason, and Thomas Ludwell Lee onto the committee.

At the first committee meeting, in January 1777, the revisors agreed on the basic principles that would guide their work. Revision, not wholesale transformation would occur. In an 1809 letter, Jefferson recalled that "the question was discussed whether we should attempt to reduce the whole body of law into a code, the text of which should become the law of the land? We decided against that, because every word and phrase in that text would become a new subject of criticism and litigation, until its sense should have been settled by numerous decisions, and that, in the meantime, the rights of property would be in the air. We concluded not to meddle with the common law, *i.e.,* the law preceding the existence of the statutes, further than to accommodate it to our new principles and circumstances; but to take up the whole body of statutes and Virginia laws, to leave out everything obsolete or improper, insert what was wanting, and reduce the whole within as moderate a compass as it would bear, and to the plain language of common sense, divested of the verbiage, the barbarous tautologies and redundancies which render the British statutes unintelligible. From this, were excepted the ancient statutes, particularly those commented on by Lord Coke, the language of which is simple, and the meaning of every word so well settled by decisions, as to make it safest not to change words where the sense was to be retained."[23] The decision to revise not revolutionize the commonwealth's code put the limits on the possibilities of change even before the committee began its serious work.

The committee then agreed on a working plan. Jefferson again recalled that "Colonel Mason declined undertaking the execution of any part of it, as not being sufficiently read in the law. Mr. Lee very soon afterwards died, and the work was distributed between Mr. Wythe, Mr. Pendleton, and myself. To me was assigned the common law, (so far as we thought of altering it,) and the statutes down to the Reformation, or end of the reign of Elizabeth; to Mr. Wythe, the subsequent body of the statutes, and to Mr. Pendleton the Virginia laws. This distribution threw into my part the laws concerning crimes and punishments, the law of descents, and the laws concerning religion." After they had each worked separately on their tasks, he remembered going over the first and second parts "weighing and correcting every word, and reducing them to the form in which they were afterwards reported." Pendleton had not completed his task, however, leaving it to Jefferson and Wythe.[24] In the end, Jefferson explained in his 1782 *Notes on the State of Virginia*. "The common law of England . . . is made the basis of the work. It was thought dangerous to attempt to reduce it to a text: it was therefore left to be collected from the usual monuments of it. Necessary alterations in that, and so much of the whole body of the British statutes, and of acts of assembly, as were thought proper to be retained, were digested into 126 new acts, in which simplicity of style was aimed at, as far as was safe."[25] The task, however, had taken two and a half years and included innumerable delays, modifications, and separate enactments before the legislature received the final results on June 18, 1779.[26]

During those years, Jefferson had been Virginia's principal advocate for legal reform. Taking an active role in the legislature, he championed revision and vigilantly tried to rebuff any attempts to perpetuate the old regime. Success came in a spate of specific enactments as well as in his continued role in comprehensive revision. Failure had propelled his efforts at law reform. During the summer of his triumph in Philadelphia, the Virginia Convention of 1776 ignored his proposed constitution. Thwarted, Jefferson turned to revising the law in a second attempt to recast his state's basic laws. He would transfer from his constitutional proposals to legislative revisions not only specific clauses but the determination to use legal reform as "a system by which every fibre would be eradicated of antient or future aristocracy; and a foundation laid for a government truly republican."[27] Indeed, Julian Boyd argues that Jefferson's three draft constitutions not only "foreshadowed much of his legislative reforms of 1776—1777," but contained "most if not all of the leading principles to which Jefferson's entire career was dedicated."[28]

Jefferson's proposed constitutional strictures on inheritance underscore Boyd's point. Jefferson called for the abolition of entail by mandating that "all lands shall [be] held in fee simple [and] shall descend in future," but he stipulated a radical alteration in the line of descent beyond even the abolition of primogeniture: "Descents, instead of being to the eldest son, brother, or other male cousin of the ancestor, shall be to all his [heirs] as directed by the laws heretofore[;] shall be to all brothers & sisters of the sd. heir at law who shall be of the whole blood of the ancestor, each of whom shall have an equal portion with the heir at law, but where lands shall have been given by such ancestor to any one of the sd. co-heirs it shall be brought into hotchpotch or such heir [or] coheir not entitled to any further share of the inheritance."[29] In later drafts, perhaps to curry more support, Jefferson altered both provisions. He simply proposed that "Lands heretofore holden of the crown in fee simple and those hereafter to be appropriated shall be holden of no superior by him in full & absolute dominion of no superior whatever." The clause on descents was also severely truncated: "Descents shall go according to the laws of Gavelkind, save only that females shall have equal rights with males."[30]

Jefferson explained the intent of his constitutional proposals in an August letter to Pendleton, president of the Virginia Convention. "The opinion that our lands were allodial[31] possessions is one which I have very long held," he told Pendleton, "and had in my eye during a pretty considerable part of my law reading which I found always strengthened it. It was mentioned in a very hasty production, intended to have been put under a course of severe correction, but produced afterwards to the world in a way with which you are acquainted." Despite Pendleton's known aversion to major changes in the legal regulation of property, Jefferson would not beat a retreat: "This opinion I have thought & and still think to prove if I should ever have time to look into books again. But this is only meant with respect to the English law as transplanted here. How far our acts of assembly or acceptance of grants may have converted lands which allodial into feuds I have never considered." Yet he wanted Pendleton to know that his interest lay more in the need to seize the revolutionary moment than in legal history: "This matter is now become a mere speculative point; & we have it in our power to make it what it ought to be for the public good."

Trying to make land reform enticing, Jefferson urged his fellow Virginian to consider the benefits that would flow from conversion of land into fee simple tenure. Undoubtedly with quit-rents in mind, those heinous taxes based on assertions of crown ownership of the land, he reminded Pendleton that such policies had been universally condemned in Virginia and warned him that if changes did not occur and the revolution was lost those same land taxes and restrictions would reappear. More pointedly, he compiled yet another long train of abuses to demonstrate the dire effects of maintaining restrictive land controls like entail; he wrote: "was not the separation of the property from the perpetual use of lands a mere fiction? Is not its history well known, & the purposes for which it was introduced, to wit, the establishment of a military system of defense? Was it not afterwards made an engine of immense oppression? Is it wanting with us for the purpose of military defence? May not its other legal effects (such as them at last as are valuable) be performed in other more simple ways? Has it not been the practice of all other nations to hold their lands as their personal estates in absolute dominion? Are we not the better for what we have hitherto abolished of the feudal system? Has not every restitution of the antient Saxon laws had happy effects? Is it not better now that we return at once into that happy system of our ancestors, the wisest & most perfect ever devised by the wit of man, as it stood before the 8th century."[32] Jefferson's questions, whether rhetorical or otherwise, did not convert Pendleton. "Bitterly disappointed over the Convention's failure to remold Virginia society in accord with republican principles," Boyd argues, "Jefferson then set about, as he later declared, to reframe the whole body of law, to achieve by legislation what he had not been able to accomplish in the framing of a constitution."[33]

Jefferson was so determined to rid Virginia of entail that he introduced "A Bill to Enable Tenants in Fee-tail[34] to Convey Their Lands in Fee-simple"[35] even while campaigning for the creation of the law revision committee.[36] Banishing entail simply could not wait, as Jefferson made clear in a preamble: "Whereas the perpetuation of property in certain families by means of gifts made to them in fee-tail is contrary to good policy, tends to deceive fair traders who give a credit on the visible possession of such estates, discourages the holder thereof from taking care of it and improving the same, and sometimes does injury to the morals of youth by rendering them independent of, and disobedient to, their parents; and whereas the former method of docking such estates by tail by special act of assembly formed for every particular case employed very much of the time of the legislature, was burthensome to the public, and also to the individuals who made application for such acts." To end these abuses, he proposed that the legislature unilaterally convert all estates and other property, including slaves and trusts, held in fee-tail into fee-simple.[37] Through such a conversion the revolution would fulfill part of its republican promise by freeing the present generation from ancestral constraints and granting it full ownership rights. Property could then be used however its present owners chose; their fate would be in their hands. The act represented Jefferson's opening attack on the foundations of an aristocracy of wealth designed to "make an opening for the aristocracy of virtue and talent."[38]

The bill also reignited Jefferson's now running feud with Pendleton. Opposed to the abolition of entail, Pendleton tried to water down the reform through amendments that would have made fee simple only an option for landowners conveying property. This time, however, Jefferson carried the day. His first attempt to reorder the intergenerational transfer of wealth passed the Assembly on October 23, 1776.[39]

Before the Senate took up the bill, wealthy planter Landon Carter tried to rouse the opposition. In a letter to George Washington, Carter interpreted the movement against entail as an attack on the "right to do as we please with our property," which he regarded as the "very basis of the American contest." Despairing that few of his fellow planter elite would openly fight the measure, he complained:

> It is called docking all entails; but is it not entailing one they cannot dock? The curses of posterity on them who must in that very contest for liberty entail a load of debts upon those who are able to come, after they have robbed them of their very estates to pay that debt from, by overturning the very principles of justice on which they built their claim of freedom. This is what I call sowing the seeds of contention, which must spring up sooner or later, and all from the poisoned seed of popularity.

Fearing popular excess and political leaders who played to the masses, Carter specifically denounced Patrick Henry and Jefferson. He could attribute the latter's actions only to the possibility of his being a drunkard. Even so, he declared, "[i]t is not usual for the those who are against a bill to be the bearers of it, and this bill (as cursed in its nature as the removal of a neighbor's landmark, his will and pleasure in giving his own property away) borne about by the famous T. J—n!" The object of that tirade, however, continued to push the bill through the legislature despite the opposition of a "half-dozen aristocratical gentlemen, agonizing under the loss of pre-eminence" in the shift from monarchy to republic. It passed the Senate on November 1.[40]

On the same day that the Assembly voted to abolish entail, the legislators had also authorized the creation of the legal revision committee. After the initial committee meetings in early 1777, Jefferson went to work on his sections.[41] Two years later he produced his inheritance law revision. He was now Virginia's governor, while Pendleton and Wythe had become state judges. Jefferson's proposal contained a complete set of inheritance rules, but the clauses abolishing primogeniture and granting illegitimates inheritance rights captured the spirit and intent of his approach to generational property reform.

Jefferson demanded the abolition of primogeniture and adoption of partible inheritance in equal shares to all the children of a decedent. Henceforth, he wrote, when a Virginian died intestate, his estate "shall descend and pass in parcenary to his kindred male and female" according to the formula approved by the committee in 1777.[42] Once again, however, Pendleton had opposed changing the law governing family property. In his autobiography, Jefferson recalled the conflict: "I proposed to abolish the law of primogeniture, and to make real estate descendible in parcenary to the next of kin, as personal property is by the statute of distribution. Mr. Pendleton wished to preserve the right of primogeniture, but seeing at once that that could not prevail, he proposed that we should adopt the Hebrew principle, and give a double portion to the elder son. I observed that if the eldest son could eat twice as much, or do double work, it might be a natural evidence of his right to a double portion; but being on a par in his powers and wants, with his brothers and sisters, he should be on a par also in the partition of the patrimony, and such was the decision of the other members."[43]

No similar controversy apparently arose over Jefferson's attempt to alleviate the plight of illegitimates. These star-crossed children received two legal assists. First, their inheritance rights were to be enlarged. "Bastards," Jefferson proposed, "also shall be capable of inheriting or of transmitting inheritance on the part of their mother, in like manner as if they had been lawfully begotten of such mother." Second, he urged modifications of age-old Anglo-American marriage law principles that would reduce the chances of a child being labeled illegitimate: "Where a man having by a woman one or more children, shall afterwards intermarry with such woman, such child or children if recognized by him shall be thereby legitimated. The issue also of marriages deemed null in law shall nevertheless be legitimate."[44]

Jefferson cataloged his inheritance changes as Bill no. 20 among the 126 revisions the committee presented to Virginia legislature. Wartime uncertainties prevented a wholesale debate on all the bills. Only a few passed immediately, those primarily dealing with the organization and operation of the government. The rest languished awaiting the outcome of the war. In the meantime, Jefferson reached an initial verdict on legal reform when compiling his *Notes on the State of Virginia* in 1781 and 1782. After describing the general organization and intent of the revisions, he listed "remarkable alterations proposed." Bill 20's attempt to "change the rules of descent [so as to introduce equal partition]" was one of these. The proposal won a similarly exalted place in his subsequent comments on the revision.

Finally, in June 1784 Madison began to shepherd the revisions through the legislature. In November of the following year the inheritance bills won easy approval. Early in 1786, Madison reported to Jefferson, now in Paris as the new republic's minister to France, that he had found sentiment in favor of the revisions stronger than he had anticipated and "we went on slowly but successfully, till we arrived at the bill concerning crimes and punishments." But the differences over those proposals did not stymie Jefferson's lieutenant, and in a December 1786 letter he chronicled his success in getting many of the bills, including the law on descents, through both houses of the legislature. It had not been easy, though: "This business has consumed a great deal of the time of two Sessions, and has given infinite trouble to some of us. We have never been without opponents who contest at least every innovation inch by inch."[45] Indeed, the fights over revision would continue into the next legislative session and into the 1790s. But the inheritance changes were now law.[46]

The difficulties and delays, however troubling to Madison, did not quench Jefferson's enthusiasm for the possibilities of change promised by revising the rules of intergenerational transmission of wealth. He invested great rhetorical significance in the new inheritance laws. By the time he wrote his autobiography, the now elder statesman would declare of the bills to abolish primogeniture and entail, establish religious freedom, and create a general system of education:

> I consider 4 of these bills, passed or reported, as forming a system by which every fibre would be eradicated of antient or future aristocracy; and a foundation laid for a government truly republican. The repeal of the laws of entail would prevent the accumulation and perpetuation of wealth in select families, and preserve the soil of the country from being daily more and more absorbed in Mortmain. The abolition of primogeniture, and equal partition of inheritances removed the feudal and unnatural distinctions which made one member of every family rich, and all the rest poor, substituting equal partition, the best of all Agrarian laws.[47]

He had held similar hopes at the time as well. In a 1785 letter to Madison discussing property and natural rights, Jefferson shared a telling anecdote. He explained that while walking in the countryside he had rewarded a poor woman for acting as his guide, and that her effusive gratitude for his small offering had led him "into a train of reflections on that unequal division of property which occasions the numberless instances of wretchedness which I have observed in this country and is to be observed all over Europe." Logic drove him to envision the immense benefits of a massive redistribution of wealth, but he acknowledged to his more cautious friend: "I am conscious that an equal division of property is impractical, but the consequences of this enormous inequality producing so much misery to the bulk of mankind, legislators cannot invent too many devices for subdividing property, only taking care to let their subdivisions go hand in hand with the natural affections of the human mind." Family affection and individual equality dominated his thoughts as they did his revisions.

Undoubtedly thinking of the new inheritance laws as one means of a more limited redistribution, Jefferson declared: "The descent of property of every kind therefore to all the children, or to all the brothers and sisters, or other relations in equal degree, is a politic measure and a practical one. Another means of silently lessening the inequality of property is to exempt all from taxation below a certain point, and to tax the higher portions of property in geometrical progression as they rise. Whenever there is in any country, uncultivated lands and unemployed poor, it is clear that the laws of property have been so far extended as to violate natural right." And once more he linked redistribution with generational responsibilities by arguing that the "earth is given as a common stock for man to labor and live on. If, for encouragement of industry we allow it to be appropriated, we must take care that other employment be furnished to those excluded from the appropriation. If we do not, the fundamental right to labor the earth returns to the unemployed."[48]

In suggesting that property originated as a means to an end and that property rights must be contingent on the responsibility to provide employment for those excluded from ownership, Jefferson brought the redistributive possibilities of the inheritance revisions to the surface.[49] Like other property rights, he wanted inheritance rules judged by their results. They must fulfill the state's primary role of creating a society that allowed individuals to realize their own goals. Once the remnants of aristocratic controls had been repudiated by a republican revision, Jefferson's argument contained an implicit liberal anti-statist assumption of distinct public and private realms and a priority on private action. Changes like the inheritance revisions implied that the state acted properly not by ordering society and individuals' lives from above, but by providing the underlying structures which made it possible for individuals to order society themselves. In that vein, Matthews has argued that Jefferson's radical conception of the pursuit of happiness had public and private meanings. "Public happiness," he argues, "specifically refers to the citizen's right of access to the public realm where he can be free, can be seen, and can be, as Jefferson puts it, 'a participator in public affairs.'" However, Matthews contends, "Jefferson also believes in the pursuit of happiness in the private realm, outside of the public gaze, 'in the lap and love of my family, in the society of my neighbors and my books, in the wholesome occupations of my farm and my affairs.' The pursuit of happiness, in its dual interdependent facets, can provide a fully human life; but the pursuit of either at the neglect or expense of the other will lead to personal perversion in the individual and to social decay in the corporate body."[50] A faith in individual self-reliance and autonomy and in participatory government led him to champion state-sanctioned generational freedom as well as revealing how he combined liberal and republican ideals. And his faith in the linkage of family and property was evident in a bill drafted in 1778. He proposed that every freeborn Virginian who married and resided in the state for one year be given "seventy five Acres of waster or unappropriated Land." The policy would promote "the more equal Distribution of Lands" and "encourage Marriage and population."[51] The bill failed, but, as his letter to Madison indicated, Jefferson dreamt of a state-sponsored redistribution of wealth that would guarantee that each generation started anew.

In this manner, the revisions in primogeniture, entail, and illegitimacy were component parts of common assumptions. They used public authority to banish the inequity of inherited hierarchy and the illogic of inherited morality. Equity and affection would take their places as guides to the transmission of generational wealth. The reforms would make the family a primary institution for creating a republican society by ensuring that birth actually provided a new start for every member of each generation. And in that manner they promoted an emerging ideal of the family as a collection of autonomous individuals bound together by affection not a corporate enterprise linked by dynastic commitments. Out of the republican family would come virtuous republican citizens ready to participate in public affairs.

The relationship between these goals and the elimination of primogeniture and entail was clear. Jefferson believed that the changes would prevent a previous generation from using property controls to shackle the next and thus perpetuate an artificial aristocracy based on birth and birth order. By curbing the intergenerational transmission of wealth he hoped to bar the aristocratic accumulation of property. He also saw the changes as unleashing the natural affection parents had for all their children, not merely the eldest son. Each generation and each member of a generation would then, he hoped, enter the world unfettered by the dead hand of the propertied past and be able—indeed compelled?—to make his or her own place. A natural aristocracy would then be bred to earn a place based on merit not inherited privilege. The twin bills represented, as Dumas Malone has argued, Jefferson's "implacable hostility to artificial privilege of every sort."[52]

A similar implacable hostility led Jefferson to champion rights for illegitmates. Along with limits in the transmission of intergenerational wealth, he wanted to limit the transmission of intergenerational morality. His campaign illuminates the words in his famous 1816 letter to Samuel Kercheval:

> But I know also, that laws and institutions must go hand in hand with the progress of the human mind. As that becomes more developed, more enlightened, as new discoveries are made, new truths disclosed, and manners and opinions change with the change of circumstances, institutions must advance also, and keep pace with the times. We might as well require a man to wear still the coat which fitted him when a boy, as civilized society to remain ever under the regimen of their barbarous ancestors.[53]

Jefferson translated that desire to be rid of inherited morality into revisions that tried, in what would become the watchword of bastardy reform, to prevent innocent children from being punished for the sins of their parents. He challenged the legitimacy of this form of intergenerational power just as vehemently as he did the other. In the 1770 case of *Howell v. Netherland,* Jefferson failed in an attempt to win freedom for a mulatto slave. But in arguing over the meaning of the province's bastardy rules, the future legal reformer recorded in his case notes: "It was observed that the purpose of the act was to punish and deter women from that confusion of the species, which the legislature seems to have considered an evil and not to punish their innocent offspring."[54] Jefferson wanted the revolution to produce a new morality that freed illegitimates from the stain of their birth. The changes he sponsored in marriage law narrowed the possibility of bastardy and used inheritance rules to give illegitmates a recognized place in the line of succession. Most significantly, he channeled his faith in the family and his society's faith in the redemptive power of republican mothers into the creation of a new household, the illegitimate child and its mother, and bound them together like other households by ties of inheritance. Property rights and maternal tutelage, he assumed, would give these star-crossed children a chance to rise on their own merits like the second sons, daughters, and other victims freed from the vices of English aristocratic morality.[55]

By promoting reform of inheritance law, Jefferson helped create a new baseline for generational relations in the new republic. Yet, its meaning for families remained unclear. Despite his radical rhetoric, limits were already apparent. The logic of Jefferson's indictment of the unequal distribution of intestate property might well have led him to call for the total abolition of inheritance, as would be called for shortly in France.[56] Similarly, his defense of illegitimates might well have led him to call for the total abolition of bastardy. He did neither. Nor did he deviate from the age-old English linkage of generational power and inheritance rights. Yet, as Stanley Katz has argued of Jefferson, "it is significant that at least one influential Revolutionary American perceived that the logic of republican revolution pointed toward radical reevaluation of the law of inheritance."[57] The new law of descent, and especially Jefferson's rhetoric in its support, contained a radical redistributive potential. But the potential could only be realized in the process of incorporating the inheritance reforms into the social ideology and family practices of the new republic.

Incorporation and the Limits of Inheritance Reform

Just how much of a new start each new generation would receive from the newly codified republican inheritance laws became an issue for postrevolutionary Americans. Jefferson emerged as an acknowledged leader of a national movement. State after state abolished entail and primogeniture, extended the testamentary power of daughters, and enlarged the inheritance rights of bastards.[58] In many jurisdictions, the statutes merely codified the end to long-discarded policies. But the widespread adoption of inheritance reform, as Jefferson had always insisted, made an important statement about the character of generational relations. It reinforced anti-aristocratic forces in the new republic. And in an era when many Americans died without writing wills, the changes carried practical as well as symbolic value.[59]

Equally important, the Jeffersonian approach to inheritance became incorporated into an emerging American law of the family. It provided the rules of domestic relations with fundamental tenets about intergenerational relations and individual responsibility. The inheritance reforms reinforced the emergence of the freely contracting, autonomous individual as the fictional ideal of domestic relations law. As Sir Henry Maine pointed out in a central postulate to his evolutionary theory of the movement of societies from status to contract, the individual was "steadily being substituted for the family as the unit of which civil laws take account."[60] That could occur only through changes such as the new inheritance rules that dismantled the legal concept of the family as a corporate patriarchal preserve and replaced it with one of the household as a collection of distinct individuals. Yet, just as Jefferson's thought wavered between republicanism and liberalism, the transition of family law to liberal individualism was never complete. The emerging domestic relation law continued to proclaim a commitment to an idealized vision of household unity even though its policies like inheritance often encouraged domestic fragmentation through the creation of separate legal identities within the nation's home.[61]

Most critically here, incorporation into family law moderated the revolutionary inheritance reforms. Their redistributive potential dimmed as the newly enacted inheritance laws helped establish and legitimate a primal family law principle: American egalitarianism promised equal opportunity not equal status. In part, this was the doing of Jefferson and other reformers. Despite his occasional flights of redistributive rhetoric, neither he nor any other inheritance law reformer ever demanded that the new states directly legislate equality. Indeed, Madison and many of his other correspondents resisted Jefferson's radical redistributive schemes whenever he broached them.[62] As a result, the statutory reforms in Virginia and other states tended more to destroy the props of inherited privilege and to challenge the legitimacy of inherited morality than to achieve equality among children. As Isaac Kramnick has argued, "[d]esigned to limit concentrations of landed property and to end the political dominance of a landed elite, the American statutory reforms removed devices of compulsory inequality, but stopped short of requiring equality." Consequently, the reforms encouraged American families to breed new generations not of equals but of children equipped as fully as possible to enter, in Kramnick's telling phrase, the "race of life."[63]

The critical implications of that new family role became clear as the inheritance reforms became part of American domestic relations law early in the nineteenth century. Jefferson himself never returned to the fray. Instead, just as he had depended on Madison to shepherd the reforms through the Virginia legislature, so now he had to rely on others to translate his inheritance reforms into policies that would guide generational relations.

The reformist career of one self-styled Jeffersonian, St. George Tucker, is a revealing example of the process of incorporation. A Bermudian by birth, twenty-two-year-old Tucker arrived in Virginia in 1772 to seek his fortune. After successfully studying law with Jefferson's mentor and fellow code reviser George Wythe and skillfully negotiating a marriage with a wealthy widow, Tucker launched what would be a very distinguished legal career. Appointment as Wythe's successor as the Professor of Law and Police Policy at William and Mary capped his rapid rise. Tucker also served as a local judge and as a member of a committee on legal revision that pushed a final comprehensive package of postrevolutionary changes through the legislature in the early 1790s.[64]

The bitter political wars of the 1790s made Tucker a committed Jeffersonian. He not only shared the growing animus of his fellow Virginian toward the Federalists and their high-handed statist acts like the Alien and Sedition Acts, he also joined Jefferson in denouncing the Tory influence of Blackstone on American law and lawyers. Jefferson's aversion to Blackstone dated almost from first appearance of the *Commentaries* in America, but his strongest denunciation came in a letter to Madison written only months before his death. In discussing the selection of a law professor for the University of Virginia, Jefferson recalled that his own training, like most of his generation's, had been based in part on reading the words of the great seventeenth-century common lawyer Edward Coke: "You remember also then our lawyers were all whigs. But when his black-letter text, and uncouth but cunning learning got out of fashion, and the honied Mansfieldism of Blackstone became the student's hornbook, from that moment, that profession (the nursery of our Congress) began to slide into toryism, and nearly all the young brood of lawyers now are of that hue. They suppose themselves, indeed, to be whigs, because they know no longer what whiggism or republicanism means. It is in our seminary that the vestial flame is to be kept alive; it is thence it is to spread anew over our own and sister States."[65]

Tucker agreed with this indictment, and he acted. In 1795, he began negotiating with printers to publish an Americanized version of *Blackstone's Commentaries*. Based on his lectures at William and Mary, the edition would mix an exact reprint of the British jurist's words with footnotes and appendixes that demonstrated how Americans had successfully challenged toryism. Tucker had his own hopes for generational freedom. He wanted his Americanized version of the *Commentaries* to help present and future law students, practitioners, and judges recognize and resist the Tory ideas of Blackstone.[66]

The first volume of Tucker's *Blackstone* appeared in May 1803, and the American editor proclaimed his commitments in a lengthy preface. "Perhaps because he was a confirmed Jeffersonian, writing at the zenith of Jeffersonianism," Robert Cover explained in a review of a 1969 reissue of the volumes, Tucker fell outside the conservative consensus of most postrevolutionary and antebellum legal commentators. Instead, he stood out "as a notable exception to the rule. His work exudes a reformist and libertarian vitality unthinkable in a Kent, a Story, or a Dane."[67] In his attempt to translate Jeffersonian political theory into law, the Virginia lawyer warned his readers that in their haste to understand the law they should not be seduced into accepting Blackstone as a reliable guide to American law. On the contrary, the break with Britain "produced a corresponding revolution not only in the principles of our government, but in the laws which relate to property, and in a variety of other cases, equally contradictory to the law, and irreconcilable to the principles contained in the *Commentaries*." Blackstone could only instruct them on what "*the law had been*"; to discover "*what it now is*" required a republican legal education. Reading his edition of the *Commentaries,* with special attention to the footnotes and appendices, would, he promised, render Blackstone "a *safe*" guide to law in Virginia and other states.[68]

Like his political leader, Tucker singled out the inheritance reforms as examples of the revolutionary spirit and substance of an American law. "But independent of those alterations in the system of our jurisprudence to which local circumstances might be supposed to have given birth," he explained in making a case for the commonalties of postrevolutionary law reform, "there are a great number which appear to be merely the suggestions of political experiment, or a desire to conform to the newly adopted principles of republican government; among these we reckon the ABOLITION of *entails;* of the right of *primogeniture;* of the preference heretofore given to the *male* line, in respect to real estates of inheritance; and of the *jus accrescendi,* or right of survivorship between *joint-tennants;* the *ascending* quality communicated to real estates; the *hereditability* of the *half-blood;* and of *bastards;* the *legitimation* of the latter, in certain cases; and many other instances in which the rules of the COMMON LAW, or the provisions of a statute, are totally changed." And he wanted lawyers and laypeople alike to understand the connections between the law and citizenship: "In a government founded on the basis of equal liberty among all its citizens, to be ignorant of the law and the constitution, is to be ignorant of the rights of the citizen."[69] In the text, he spelled out the details of inheritance law to ensure that his fellow Americans understood how much their revolution had changed the legal relations between generations.

In volumes two and three, *The Law of Persons* and *The Rights of Things,* Tucker pockmarked Blackstone's text with footnotes that approvingly listed the statutory revisions of English inheritance law. The impact of the 1785 statutory revision had been immense. Readers learned how thoroughgoing had been its egalitarianism in countless corrections to aristocratic English law: all formerly crown land had become allodial; posthumous children inherited along with those living at the time of a father's death; the law of hotchpotch had been adopted, thus instituting the pudding-like legal idea of blending together all of an intestate's lands and dividing them equally among daughters; half-bloods inherited like those of whole blood; and bastards could be legitimated by parental marriage and would remain so despite a marital annulment.[70]

Tucker took pains to explain and endorse the most significant changes. He heralded the abolition of entail by declaring that "when the revolution took place, a different mode of thinking succeeded; it was found that entails would be the means of accumulating and preserving great estates in certain families, which would, not only introduce all the evils complained of in England, but be utterly incompatible with the genius and spirit of our constitution and government."[71] And not only had primogeniture been abolished and equality established among all children, but "[n]o preference whatsoever, is now given to males, among the lineal descendants, or collateral heirs of the intestate, over the females. They come into the inheritance at the same time, and take equal portions." And yet, he had to admit, a male preference did remain: "where, for want of issue, the inheritance is directed to ascend, the nearest male ancestor, shall be preferred to the female ancestors, and collateral relations in the same degree."[72] Tucker then returned to his chronicle of reform to report that bastards had become "capable of inheriting or transmitting an inheritance, on the part of their mothers, as if they had been lawfully begotten: and if the father of a bastard marry the mother, and afterwards recognize the bastard as his child, he is thereby legitimated, and consequently capable of inheriting as if born in lawful wedlock."[73] In a long footnote denouncing rapacious creditors intent on robbing children of family estates, Tucker captured the spirit of the inheritance reforms: "But surely the laws ought so far to interfere in behalf of an infant child, not yet arrived at years of discretion, and consequently, incapable of giving just cause of offence, as to prevent his parent from disinheriting him, either by deliberate and diabolical cruelty, or by indiscretion."[74]

The reforms, however, had not sought to shackle testamentary rights. Instead they relied on parental affection and responsibility to govern generational relations. And to make sure that his readers understood the depth and scope of the reforms, Tucker added a "Discourse Concerning the Several Acts Directing the Course of Descents, in Virginia" to the appendix of volume three. In it, he detailed the revisions of English law and offered illustrative examples first tried out in his William and Mary law lectures. Amid the detail, however, lay the fundamental comparison he wanted understood:

> Thus, these two primary rules, or canons, which may be considered as the ground-work and foundation of the two systems of law, established in England, by immemorial usage on the one hand; and in this country, by the mature consideration of the most eminent sages of the law, and confirmed by the deliberate voices of the legislature on the other, are found in no one instance whatsoever agreeing, but, on the contrary, in continual and diametrical opposition to each other. The former being the offspring of feudal barbarism and prejudice, the latter the dictates of enlightened reason, following the course which nature herself seems to have marked in the human breast, and endeavouring to obliterate the traces and memorials of the former, wheresoever they could be discerned.[75]

Tucker's *Blackstone* quickly became a staple of the antebellum bar. Law students were weaned on it, established practitioners relied on it. Jefferson himself consistently recommended Tucker's version of the *Commentaries* to all would-be law students.[76] And with its steady use, the Jeffersonian message of proper generational relations embedded in inheritance law was broadcast throughout the republic.

The message, however, had been muted. Just as had Jefferson's first inheritance reform surrogate, so his second championed the intent but not the full spirit of Jefferson's own hopes for generational liberation. As Madison had argued in the

Virginia legislature, so Tucker used his Americanized *Commentaries* to promote the inheritance changes as critical legal devices to create a society opposed to aristocratic privilege and inherited distinctions yet committed to filial equity, testamentary freedom, and enlightened morality. Jefferson's latent vision of radical redistribution through generational change slipped further and further from the debate over the intergenerational transfer of wealth and power, and as it did, inheritance law fast became a source for the conviction that egalitarianism in the new republic meant equal opportunity. Despite the words he penned in his letters, Jefferson himself did nothing to challenge this tenet of an emerging American social ideology.

Tucker's role in incorporating his version of Jeffersonianism into American law did not end with the publication of the *Commentaries*. It took a different and equally revealing turn after 1804. In that year, the transplanted Bermudian realized his deepest judicial ambitions when the legislature appointed him to the state's highest tribunal, the Court of Appeals. He immediately faced a case that challenged his commitment to the Jeffersonian inheritance reforms he had championed in Americanizing Blackstone.

Stones v. Keeling began before the passage of the 1785 act, when William Keeling married Arthalia Arbuckle. She had been married before, though she no longer lived with her first husband or even knew his whereabouts. It turned out, however, that he was still living at the time that Arbuckle married Keeling. The Keelings had two daughters; and William had a son from his first marriage. Keeling died after his son. An inheritance fight then broke out between the daughters and his son's widow, centering on the legitimacy of the two girls, whose mother's prior marriage was still valid at the time that she had wed Keeling. Tucker, writing a concurring majority opinion reversing the widow's lower court victory, championed the daughters' cause. He urged that the 1785 act be understood as having eliminated previous bars to inheritance and their feudal dynastic priorities: "in that light, the law ought to receive the most liberal construction; it being evidently the design of the legislature, to establish the most liberal and extensive rules of succession to estates, in favour of all, in whose favour the intestate himself, had he made a will, might have been supposed to be influenced. And here there can be no doubt that these daughters would have been the first objects of his care."

Tucker's fellow judge, Spencer Roane, issued an even more eloquent endorsement of Jefferson's reforms. He held out the daughters' plight as "a strong case to show the sense of the legislative, that the turpitude, or guilt of the marriage, should not break upon the heads of their innocent offspring." Roane rejoiced that "the general policy of our law" proved to be "much more favourable to bastards, than the law of England." On the contrary, the judge argued that the new American policy "considered as most worthy the claims of those who stand nearest in the affections of the last occupant, (and it is clear that the affections of a parent toward his child, do not at all depend upon the legal validity of his marriage)." He dismissed the contention of the widow's attorney that the act only encouraged bigamy and reduced the inducements to marry. In fit Jeffersonian form, Roane insisted that the fate of the generations be separated. Parents and children must be treated differently. The legislature, he argued, "certainly meant not to encourage fornication, or incestuous marriages, and yet it has expressly legitimated the offspring of both."

The Court of Appeals' translation of Jeffersonian generational ideals into legal doctrine contained a caveat, however, that modified inheritance and every other family law rule. In response to an assertion that the 1785 statute would legitimate the children of an illegal (and thus void) interracial marriage, Roane assured his fellow white citizens that the racially blind terms of Jefferson's revision were to "be construed and understood in relation only to those persons to whom that law relates; and not to a class of persons clearly not within the idea of the legislature when contemplating the subjects of marriage and legitimacy."[77]

In illegitimacy, as in the other inheritance reforms, opinions like *Stones v. Keeling* set a pattern for the spread of Jeffersonian inheritance law throughout the nation. Some states, like Kentucky in 1796, had simply enacted the Virginia statute in toto; other states adopted the changes piecemeal as a part of a complex process of legal diffusion.[78] But controversy remained, and Jefferson's revisions ensured that Virginia continued to be a critical forum in a debate that increasingly focused on the difficulties of balancing the twin commitment to collective egalitarianism and individual liberty embedded in Jefferson's reforms. Once again, conflicts in bastardy law arc particularly illustrative.

Jefferson's determination to use inheritance law to bind a mother to her bastard offspring stirred numerous legal challenges. The reform created a new legal family unrecognizable to corps of common lawyers trained by memorizing Blackstone. In 1820 the staunch Federalist Supreme Court justice Bushrod Washington tried to constrain the breadth of this new family in a case from Ohio that required an interpretation of the 1785 Virginia statute. *Stevenson's Heirs v. Sullivan* involved the inheritance rights of children legitimated by the subsequent marriage of their Virginia parents. The offspring claimed the estate of a sibling born after the marriage and thus legitimate from birth. Concerned about claims by mothers who demanded the estates of their illegitimate offspring and by similar claims from maternal lineal and collateral heirs, Justice Washington interpreted the 1785 statute to mean that bastards could not inherit from their siblings and mothers could not receive the estates of their illegitimate issue. Despite the reforms, he insisted, illegitimate children remained "bastards." They had "neither father, brother, or sister." The only alteration in their rights he found irrefutable was the right to maternal estates obviously created by the act. Beyond that, bastards remained outside the legal sphere of their mothers' families.[79]

Other state and federal judges also tried to limit the reforms and in the process undermined Jefferson's attempt to use inheritance to free illegitimate children from bearing the sins of their parents.[80] But the reforms continued to structure the debate. Not surprisingly, Tucker had tried to pass on his Jeffersonian views not only to the profession but also to his own children. Like his mentor, Tucker had to offer his offspring blunt counsel as a result of both his strong convictions and the press of debt. Having squandered much of the fortune he had built through a life as a lawyer and planter, Tucker warned his children, the "consequence, my dear boys, must be obvious to you—your sole dependence must be on your own personal abilities & Exertions."[81] One son took both messages to heart.

In 1837, ten years after his father's death, Henry St. George Tucker sat on the Virginia Court of Appeals. Along with his two brethren, the junior Tucker rejected Washington's narrow reading of the Jeffersonian reforms in the *Stevenson* case. He argued that the Federalist jurist had misunderstood Virginia's postrevolutionary spirit and had cleaved too closely to the repudiated English common law. "After the termination of the revolution," Tucker declared, "when a revision and radical change of much of our system of jurisprudence became indispensable, other counsels prevailed as to the law respecting bastards as well as in relation to inheritances generally." The elimination of primogeniture and the creation of inheritance rights for bastards became part of the nation's family law, he asserted in words that echoed his father's, because "our law of descents was formed in no small degree upon the human affection; and the legislature very justly conceiving that the object of laws of descent was to supply the want of a will, and that it should therefore conform in every case, as nearly as might be, to the probable current of those affections which would have given direction to the provision of such will." Tucker and his fellow judges agreed that the reforms had intended bastards to become members of their maternal families, fully sharing in property as well as in household affairs. Indeed, he went out of his way to endorse the faith in maternalism that permeated the reform: "I can see, indeed, much *reason* for restoring the filial tie between the mother and her spurious child." And in doing so, Tucker added another voice to the chorus singing the praises of mothers as republican caretakers and, as Jan Lewis has argued, used inheritance law to help make women's roles symbols for the affective values and social solidarity being abandoned by a masculine liberalism.[82] The intent of the law, Tucker concluded, had been to "abolish this distinction, to a certain extent, between legitimate and illegitimate children; and to endow the latter with inheritable blood on the part of the mother."[83]

Though far less litigated than the bastardy law reform, similar comments peppered judicial discussion of the other inheritance changes. The imprint of the Jeffersonian reforms was clear. A Virginia judge made the point directly in a 1925 inheritance dispute. The state's revolutionary era intestate rules had, he argued, rejected the English determination to place the protection of a family estate over the equal treatment of family members: "This principle is in a measure feudal and is akin to the law of primogeniture. It had its origin in a society saturated with aristocratic rather than democratic traditions; the underlying purpose being the conservation of the estate for the preservation of the family, and is reinforced by the fact that we should not overlook the claims upon us of those for whose being we are responsible."[84] It was precisely such a sense of generational responsibility that Jefferson had succeeded in injecting into American family law.

And despite occasional objections like Justice Washington's, Jefferson's inheritance revisions had become the widely accepted base for the legal regulation of intergenerational property relations. Since the revolutionary days of the 1770s, their incorporation into family law had produced a meaning for the reform that won the support not only of Jeffersonians like the Tuckers but also of the heirs of very different revolutionary political traditions. New Englander Noah Webster had endorsed the changes by declaring that their "principles of descent" were "essential to the continuance of republican governments."[85] Latter-day Whig Daniel Webster made the same point in his celebrated Plymouth Oration of 1820. After praising the New England settlers for jettisoning feudal property rules, he told an attentive throng that republican government could not be "brought about solely by written political constitutions, or the mere manner of organizing the government, but also by the laws that regulate the descent and transmission of property."[86] A few years later, in his own legal commentaries, die-hard Federalist James Kent synthesized such endorsements by broadcasting the now orthodox meaning of the changes as necessary legal props for American liberal individualism and its fundamental tenet of equal opportunity: "Entailments are necessary in monarchial governments, as a protection to the power and influence of the landed aristocracy; but such a policy has no application to republican establishments, where wealth does not form a permanent distinction, and under which every individual of every family has his equal rights, and is equally invited by the genius of the institutions, to depend upon his own merit and exertions."[87]

Perhaps the most effusive endorsement came from the pen of French sojourner Alexis de Tocqueville. He highlighted the changes in *Democracy in America* and declared that "the law of inheritance was the last step to equality." Tocqueville insisted that "the law of equal division exercises its influence not merely upon the property itself, but it affects the minds of the heirs and brings their passions into play." In what might be read as a tribute to Jefferson's attempt to achieve generational change through law reform, the French social critic concluded: "When the legislator has once regulated the law of inheritance, he may rest from his labor. The machine once put into motion will go on for ages, and advance, as if self-guided, toward a point indicated beforehand."[88] Tocqueville, however, may have captured only Jefferson's legislative intent and not his redistributive dreams.

By the time Tocqueville wrote, the distant point he envisioned had become clearer. The inheritance changes had not only been diffused throughout the new republic, they had acquired a dominant meaning. Embedded in the new American

law of the family, the inheritance changes had given a central meaning to generational responsibility: provide as equal a start as possible for each member of every
new generation. The various possibilities of revolutionary egalitarianism had come
to mean liberal equal opportunity.

The implications of that ideological development emerged in another insight of
Tocqueville. His newly coined word *individualism* described precisely the new goals
of American inheritance law. It characterized Americans as "apt to imagine that
their whole destiny is in their own hands."[89] Soon social ideals like the self-made
man would further direct the egalitarian legacy of the revolutionary era into the
safer channels evident in the moderation of inheritance reform. Liberal individualism assumed a public ethic that individuals were of equal worth and should have an
equal opportunity for material advancement. Inheritance law made the family one
more means to that end.

Shorn of Jefferson's redistributive dream of generational liberation, incorporation had made inheritance reform a source of the pervasive individualism that soon
dominated American society. Far from Jefferson's intent, this view helped foster an
often illusionary generational independence as a "race for life" that every son and
daughter must enter even though few could ever hope to win. Without legislative
intervention to dilute constraints such as race, class, gender, and, despite the reform,
illegitimate birth, the race always began with many of the runners hobbled by debil-
itating handicaps. Ironically, at the same time, the liberal ideal of equal opportunity as a fairly run race for life had itself become a barrier to a far more extensive egalitarianism of status. Despite its origins in an attempt to eliminate aristocratic privilege, the fate of inheritance reform suggests why equal opportunity became, as
Kramnick persuasively argues, "a theory not really of equality but of justified and
morally acceptable inequality."[90]

Coda: A Jeffersonian Legacy

Throughout his life, Jefferson remained committed to the cause of generational liberation. And though he expressed that commitment in many ways, his inheritance
reforms remain his most determined attempt to free the future from the dead hand
of the past. They institutionalized his belief that each generation deserved the right
to start life anew. A similar reform impulse swept through the other states of the
newly independent republic and helped embed the changes as a baseline of generational responsibility in a newly emerging American law of the family. Thanks to
Jefferson and his revolutionary generation, American inheritance law represented
both a symbolic and an actual break from the past. They helped make liberal individualism and its central corollary, equal opportunity, primary tenets of American
social ideology. The declaration of David Williams, an English dissenting minister
and friend of Jefferson, aptly summarized those beliefs: "All men should start from

equal situations and with equal advantages, as horses do on the turf. Afterwards everything is to depend on ability and merit."[91]

Despite the common chord of change, however, Jefferson's defense of generational liberation left a more complex legacy than is readily apparent in either the statutory rules and common law doctrines of inheritance law or the majoritarian social ideology of individualism they helped promote. His words, if not the actual content of the legal changes he sponsored, held out the promise that even greater change could occur by refusing to encumber new generations with the baggage of those that had departed. He made the connection between social policy and social possibilities clear many times, but perhaps most passionately in his famous 1813 letter about natural aristocracy to John Adams. After denouncing an "artificial aristocracy, founded on wealth and birth, without either virtue or talents," he declared: "The natural aristocracy I consider as the most precious gift of nature, for the instruction, the trusts, and government of society. And, indeed, it would have been inconsistent in creation to have formed man for the social state, and not to have provided virtue and wisdom enough to manage the concerns of society. May we not even say, that that form of government is the best, which provides the most effectually for a pure selection of these natural *aristoi* [aristocrats] into the offices of government? The artificial aristocracy is a mischievous ingredient in government, and provision should be made to prevent its ascendancy."[92] His inheritance reforms had been designed to do just that, and in doing so his words had held out the promise not just of an egalitarianism of opportunity but of a more utopian vision wherein each generation is able to create its own version of a just and fair society.

It is that vision that constitutes the most inspiring legacy of Jefferson's attempt at generational liberation. His remains a legitimating voice from the past for those who would renew the struggles over generational change and the law. The poet Mary Jo Salter is one of the most recent to find inspiration in his words. She concludes "The Hand of Thomas Jefferson, Philadelphia 1776" with the couplet:

"The earth belongs to the living," he would write—
out of his hands, henceforth into ours.[93]

FRANK SHUFFELTON

Binding Ties:
The Public and Domestic Spheres in Jefferson's Letters to His Family

During the presidential campaign of 1992, spokespeople for the Republican Party attempted to make a campaign issue out of what they called family values. Although this strategy failed to elect their candidate, both the support they received and the vigorous criticism of their definition of family values indicated that they had touched a sensitive spot in the late-twentieth-century American public consciousness. If the vision of a nuclear family, headed by a working father and a homemaker mother, churchgoing and middle class in the generous American sense of the term, seemed anachronistic or unrealistic to many, to others it seemed to describe the moral foundation of American society, albeit a foundation seriously threatened. In no small degree the anxiety raised by the appeal to family values reflected the awareness on all sides of an increasing diversity of family configurations that diverged from the traditional perception of the happy family, the central fiction of the family values campaign. Census Bureau figures indicated that 56 percent of American women over the age of fifteen were in the work force, and that only 25.9 percent of American households consisted of married couples with children. The August 1992 issue of *Playboy* featured sixteen pinup housewives, suggesting a rather different version of family values than implied by the platforms of either of the major political parties.[1]

Before the summer of 1992, however, concern for the moral and social integrity of the family had been ritually expressed at the highest national levels for years. In 1977 Christopher Lasch had described the way in which the nineteenth-century notion of the family as a "haven in a heartless world," a private, intimate bulwark against "a world from which pity and tenderness had fled in horror," has been undermined by the modern intrusion of social and therapeutic expertise.[2] Lasch's analysis of the threat to the contemporary family made his book a best-seller and brought an invitation from President Carter to the White House that expressed a symbolic commitment to the idea of family. Lasch's depiction of family integrity undermined by the mystification and intrusion of educational, social, and medical professionals must receive a sympathetic reading from those worried about government involvement of all phases of private life, and his portrayal of the nineteenth-century bourgeois "glorification of private life" struck a nostalgic chord for many late-twentieth-century readers who shared a suspicion that society was "something alien, impersonal, remote, and abstract."[3]

This conception of the family as a privileged site for affective, personal relationships arose, most scholars agree, in the years between the American Revolution and about 1830. Carl N. Degler, for example, traces the emergence of what he called "the modern American family" to this period, and he contends that the characteristic elements of this family idea still persist in the second half of the twentieth century. Because Degler holds that a basic feature of the modern family is "the doctrine of the separate spheres," an ideological division between male work outside the home and a female domestic sphere, the apparent erosion of this doctrine in recent decades may indicate an imminent transformation of the long dominant conception of family in America.[4] If this is indeed true, a nostalgic attempt to preserve the family as an insulated domestic sphere may be critically and historically less useful than a careful examination of the variety of family systems that Americans have at one time or another actually inhabited. The period between the Revolution and about 1830 that saw a major transformation of family systems and family styles is thus particularly interesting today: in a time of radical social change and far-reaching destabilization of ideologies and institutions, the challenge for families to reinvent themselves must be familiar to many.[5] In the early republic the conditions and terms in which such challenges presented themselves were of course vastly different from those today, but then as now some people struggled under the banner of an egalitarian ethic to work out a relationship between public and private life that did not simply oppose them. Shaped by a still influential republican ideology, these Americans attempted to socialize their children with the understanding that public, civic life was worth the concern of every citizen; moved by late eighteenth-century currents of sentimentalism and romanticism, they also sought to make the family a place which could nurture the child's emotional and affective identity.

One Possible Family

One of the most interesting and potentially instructive of all these attempts was that of Thomas Jefferson, who simultaneously worked to build a nation and a home but who often seemed hard put to reconcile these domains of public and private life with each other or with his own egalitarian principles. The years between his marriage to Martha Wayles Skelton in 1772 and his death at Monticello in 1826 span the period which Degler and other historians of the American family see as that of a major social transformation. The possessor of an archival imagination unmatched in his generation, Jefferson preserved a body of correspondence that offers an unusually full record of his conduct of his family. His letters are more than a simple mirror of his family life, however, for he used his correspondence to construct and regulate his family by schooling his children and grandchildren in the moral practice of communication. Jefferson conceived of moral behavior not as a following of mere rules or legalisms but as a sort of moral conversation, an internalized process of thinking about life that both reflected social practices of interpersonal communication and supported them. He attempted to use letter writing as a method to foster, in conditions of intimacy and affection, the younger generation's emotional and intellectual engagement with the world. At the same time his family letters, tangled in issues of freedom and control, reflect the contradictions present elsewhere in his life even as they show him trying to resolve the tensions between the demands of public and private life. If his cultural authority as the spokesman in the Declaration of Independence for principles of liberty and equality seems tarnished by the apparent contradictions of those principles in his private life, particularly in the matter of keeping slaves, the troubled Jefferson who emerges in these letters may be to people torn between hope for a better society and desire for a lost intimacy a more useful figure of contemplation than the traditional patriotic icon.[6]

Several important qualifications and considerations intrude themselves at this point. First, if Jefferson's family life parallels the great transformation in family systems that occurred in the decades around 1800, we should not generalize the specific instance of Jefferson's family into a larger category of Jeffersonian families or even *the* republican family. As Stephanie Coontz warns, "there is no such thing as 'the' family in any given society," but Jefferson's family as one possible family can be of interest to those resisting the imposition of a universal family model, of a single set of family values that will fit everyone.[7] Second, because we will be looking at Jefferson's family life primarily from the point of view of his correspondence with his children and grandchildren, we should remember that our subject is less the family per se than Jefferson's view of it and his management of it on the level of exchanged texts. Each member of a family has a different role in it at any given moment, a role often in conflict with those played out by other family members, and consequently her or his view of the family will be unique.

Finally, since Jefferson's life at the head of his own family extended more than half a century, we should remember that family roles change as members move through the course of their lives. Father Jefferson faced different circumstances than Grandpapa Jefferson did, and the vigorous sixty-year-old president of the United States was a different figure from the declining and nearly bankrupt eighty-year-old.[8] In an impressive study of the changing social understanding of Virginia's gentry between 1750 and 1830, Jan Lewis has described Jefferson as a transitional figure, suggesting that he bridged two historical eras and shared values with each. His transitional understanding of family, however, is not merely a static position but a continuously evolving experience.[9] If there are consistent patterns in Jefferson's understanding of his family, there are also changes in his experience of family and consequent changes in the expression of that experience which reflect his continuously shifting circumstances.

Practicing Fatherhood

Jefferson in his family only emerges into historical view after he has ceased being son and husband; he apparently destroyed any correspondence with his mother sometime after her death in 1776 and later did the same with letters to and from his wife after she died in September of 1782. The earliest surviving letter we have between Jefferson and a member of his immediate family was written to his older daughter, Martha, on November 28, 1783, over a year after the death of his wife. Martha Wayles Jefferson's death had been deeply traumatic for Jefferson, throwing him into "a stupor of mind" that made him seem for almost three weeks "as dead to the world as she was whose loss occasioned it." Tales of Jefferson's grief circulated, some reporting that he swooned away whenever he saw his children.[10] This event marked a crucial moment in Jefferson's life, a moment when public rationality was overwhelmed by private grief, but it is also a threshold between a family life that has receded into silence and the privacy of his own heart and a family life that was enacted for the historical record in his correspondence. Taking on the primary responsibility for three young daughters, he had to reinvent himself as a parent and reconstruct his image of his family.

This reinvention of parenthood does not take place as a simple commitment to the domestic sphere. Smarting from criticism of his role as governor of Virginia and anxious for his wife's health, he had told James Monroe in a famously bitter letter of May 20, 1782, that he wanted to live out the rest of his life in "mental quiet" as a private citizen, to attend to his family unburdened by any public employment.[11] After his wife's death, however, private life was less a scene of mental quiet than a theater of woe and barrenness. In the first intimate, personal letter he appears to have written after his wife's death, he told his sister-in-law, Elizabeth Wayles Eppes, "This miserable kind of existence is really too burthensome to be borne, and were it not for the infidelity of deserting the sacred charge left me, I could not wish it's continuance a moment."[12] Shortly after he had begun to come out of his "stupor of mind," therefore, he found an excuse to absent himself from Monticello, taking his children to Archibald Cary's Ampthill in order to be inoculated against smallpox, and in November Congress appointed him as one of the ministers for negotiating peace in Paris. He readily accepted, took himself and daughter Patsy (as Martha Jefferson was known) off to Philadelphia in late December, and entrusted baby Lucy and four-year-old Mary to Elizabeth Eppes.

In the end Jefferson did not sail for France, although he was in no hurry to return home, but his taking up the call to public employment once again began a period of twenty-five years when he would spend more time away from his children, his "sacred charge," than he would with them. It also initiated a pattern that would manifest itself in later episodes of emotional distress or threats to his "mental quiet." The letter to Monroe embracing private life reflected hurt feelings about the official inquiries into his conduct as governor of Virginia, and his readiness to leave Monticello was apparently a similar desire to flee an emotionally painful scene. Jefferson's polarization of private and public life, evident in the letter to Monroe and elsewhere, led him to seek recourse in one sphere when he was distressed in the other, but this meant that he needed to maintain the possibilities of each sphere in order to make the other supportable.[13] In spite of his occasional rhetoric, he never abandoned his commitment to both public and domestic life, and he bridged the gap between them with letters that purported to bring private concerns to his public friends and public involvement to members of his family.

As if slowly learning his new role as the bearer of a "sacred charge," Jefferson wrote few letters to the Eppes family when they had custody of his youngest daughters, and it is not until March 4, 1783, that it seemed to occur to him to close a letter to Francis Eppes with a desire to "Present my love . . . to the little ones."[14] It might have been about this time that Jefferson acquired his copy of Dr. John Gregory's *A Father's Legacy to His Daughters,* a best-seller of the 1770s and 1780s that offered a model for the moral education of daughters. Gregory, a professor of medicine at Edinburgh University, was, like Jefferson, a widower, but he was particularly moved to write because of his fear of his own death. *A Father's Legacy* was first published in 1774, the year after his death, and was widely and frequently reprinted on both sides of the Atlantic; Jefferson owned a 1779 London edition that he later included in the library sold to Congress in 1815. When his daughter Martha was pregnant with her first child, he sent her another title by Gregory, his *Comparative View of the State and Faculties of Man with those of the Animal World,* noting "that she will find in it a great deal of useful advice for a young mother."[15] He might conceivably have looked into Gregory for possible guidance on the duties of a father, undoubtedly putting it, though, to the same critical reading as he did almost everything else.

Gregory's *Legacy* passed on the spirit of John Locke's treatise on education as modified by the sentimental benevolence of the Scottish philosophers of common sense. Like Locke he feared that "the minds of children [are] as easily turned this or that way as water itself," and he wished to inculcate moral habits that could withstand the subversive pressures of an immoral world. Gregory, perhaps not unrealistically, saw the world as particularly threatening to young women and advised a policy of extraordinary emotional and intellectual self-restraint that was one of the building blocks for the notion of a separate domestic sphere. He advised his daughters, "Be ever cautious in displaying your good sense. It will be thought you assume a superiority over the rest of the company. But if you happen to have any learning, keep it a profound secret, especially from the men who generally look with a jealous and malignant eye on a woman of great parts, and a cultivated understanding."

In public life they might meet with men who "will complain of your reserve. They will assure you that a franker behavior would make you more amiable. But trust me, they are not sincere when they tell you so."

Only in the long chapter on "Friendship, Love, and Marriage" does he consider the possible situations for self-revelation and self-expression: "If you have the good fortune to meet with any who deserve the name of friends, unbosom yourself to them with the most unsuspicious confidence." The most likely place to find such deserving friends, however, turns out to be within the family itself; brothers and sisters make the best confidants, and ultimately one's spouse ought to be such as well. Gregory's portrayal of a threatening public sphere that demands self-repression as part of the necessary bargaining for advantage expresses a Lockean heritage that encouraged Jefferson almost always to conceal his own emotional life, but his presentation of the domestic sphere as place where "an open temper, if restrained by prudence, will make you, on the whole, much happier" foreshadowed Jefferson's privileging of Monticello as thc site for feeling and affection.[16]

When it came to advising his own daughters, however, Jefferson did not exactly follow Gregory's implicit polarization of public and domestic spheres. In the earliest surviving letter he wrote to one of his children, he told Patsy, "The acquirements which I hope you will make under the tutors I have provided for you will render you more worthy of my love, and if they cannot increase it they will prevent it's diminution" (19). He was more forceful and explicit in a letter written to hcr while she was attending school in Paris: "The more you learn the more I love you, and I rest the happiness of my life on seeing you beloved by all the world" (30). What seems to us an almost shocking bit of emotional blackmail was in many ways a rather conventional pedagogic maneuver at the time, a sentimentalized form of Locke's recommendation to make children "conceive that those that are commended and in esteem for doing well will necessarily be beloved and cherished by everybody, and have all other good things in consequence of it."[17]

Jefferson came back again and again to this strategy for controlling and directing the education of the children in his family; in 1811, for example, he wrote to his grandson Francis Wayles Eppes, "be industrious in advancing youself in knolege, which with your good dispositions, will ensure the love of others, and your own happiness, and thc love and happiness of none more than of Yours affectionately, Th: Jefferson" (402). Offering parental love as the ultimate reward and the danger of losing it as a threat could cover other injunctions Jefferson laid upon his children, but typically Jefferson connected the promise of parental affection to the acquisition of knowledge for both children and grandchildren.[18] He went beyond Locke in advocating learning less for the "good things" it could bring than for the good responses it might evoke. In encouraging children to measure their personal happiness in terms of a social happiness, he implied a more complex relationship between private and public life than the oppositional spheres imagined by Gregory.

Jefferson's pedagogic linking of affection and learning was embedded in the Scottish moral sense philosophy of his time, but it departed both from the common understanding of moral behavior as the ultimate expression of filial gratitude and also from attempts to make the separate domestic sphere a unique moral center based upon Hutchesonian sentimentality. Francis Hutcheson had described moral action as resulting from a disinterested feeling of benevolence, the moral sense, that is natural to every person. Although moral sense theory was central for Jefferson's understanding of human nature, he eventually went beyond Hutcheson's definition of the moral sense as an internal guide in order to understand its function in the social world.[19] Thus, his 1786 admonition to Martha to learn more in order to increase his love for her is augmented and enclosed by the desire of seeing her "beloved by all the world." The acquisition of learning finds more significant motivation in the emotional and affectionate responses from others, in their judgments, than it does in the mere self-approbation of a good done to them, of a Hutchesonian benevolence.

In this regard Jefferson is closer to the opinions of Adam Smith, Hutcheson's student and successor as Professor of Moral Philosophy at the University of Glasgow. He had recommended Smith's *Theory of Moral Sentiments* for the library of Robert Skipwith, and his letters frequently show traces of Smith's particular development of moral sense theory. Both Hutcheson and David Hume had given prominence in their ethical theories to the role of a spectator who could represent the disinterested character of the moral standpoint, but in his *Theory of Moral Sentiments* Smith's notion of an impartial spectator went beyond his predecessor's to argue that the conscience is a product of social relationship.[20] "The chief part of human happiness arises from the consciousness of being beloved," claims Smith, and it is the desire "to deserve love and to deserve reward [that] are the great characters of virtue . . . But all these characters have an immediate reference to the sentiments of others." We accordingly develop our consciences through complex acts of moral imagination that put us in place of observing others even as we have to imagine those others in our place. "We begin . . . to examine our own passions and conduct, and to consider how these must appear to [other people], by considering how they would appear to us if in their situation. We suppose ourselves the spectators of our own behaviour, and endeavour to imagine what effect it would, in this light, produce upon us." Or as Jefferson wrote to a grandson, "Under temptations and difficulties, I could ask myself what would Dr. Small, Mr. Wythe, Peyton Randolph do in this situation? What course in it will ensure me their approbation?"[21](363).Smith distinguished between crude desire for the applause of the world, for the approbation of mere public opinion, and the approbation of that imagined impartial spectator that could enable a person to, "in some measure, despise the censure of the world."[22] Approbation, the expression of public esteem, was a frequent and worrisome concern in Jefferson's reflections upon his public life, but his appeal to the respected figures of his own young manhood, given presence and voice in his own imagination, helped him to substitute the judgments of conscience for the often troubling voices of public criticism and party dispute. Jefferson's construction of a socialized conscience that he imposed on himself seemed to authorize him in turn to impose it upon others; spoken to, he could speak in turn. His advice to a grandson presented a model of conscience as a moral conversation, even if it was intended more immediately as an encouragement to meet figures of learning and virtue—Jefferson Randolph was attending lectures at the University of Pennsylvania at the time—who could be reimagined as his own internal voices.

If Jefferson certainly wished to be a figure whose approbation mattered to his children and grandchildren, his concern for their moral development led him to encourage them to look beyond the narrow circle of family for other impartial spectators with whom they might correspond. He cited not one voice but three, the conversation of a small society, in modeling the moral sense for Jeff Randolph, and if Smithian moral theory made public judgment internal and private, it also required personal engagement in the larger society. The development of a moral guide conceived as an internalized impartial spectator is, according to Smith, natural to all humans, since sympathy always involves the ability to imagine ourself in someone else's place, but it also requires social, communicative experience. "Were it possible that a human creature could grow up to manhood in some solitary place, without any communication with his own species, he could no more think of his own character, of the propriety or demerit of his own sentiments and conduct, of the beauty or deformity of his own mind, than of the beauty or deformity of his own face. . . . Bring him into society, and he is immediately provided with the mirror which he wanted before."[23]

Communication thus becomes a primary form of moral activity, and for Jefferson and his contemporaries letter writing could embody the reflecting glass of society, making present those who were distant and putting the voice of the writer and the imagined voice of the recipient in dynamic play with each other.

The Education of Young Women and Men

Smith's moral sense theory with its internalized imagined voices and its theatricalized impartial observers was in fact a philosophy for the republic of letters. The notion of the republic of letters, an ancient idea given new energy in the eighteenth century, projected an imagined, egalitarian community parallel to the privileged and politically authoritative sphere of the state. It was participatory community of the literate (thus perhaps more egalitarian in theory than in experience), and one earned citizenship in it by entering into exchanges of fact and opinion with others interested in extending the reach of learning.[24] More important, the republic of letters constituted a part of a public sphere that was identical with neither the private, intimate realm of family nor the public world of authority and power. The public sphere in this particular sense was constituted by private people coextensively with the public world of the sovereign, the realm of the "police" as Jürgen Habermas has called it.[25] The republic of letters and the public sphere in this sense formed a third space distinct from those oppositional private and public spheres that, according to Carl Degler and others, defined the nineteenth-century family. As such a third space, it provided a means of negotiating between public and private realms and a position from which to criticize them.

The institutions of the republic were the magazine and the learned society, which made their correspondents' private knowledge public, but its model of literate exchange informed basic eighteenth-century notions of epistolary activity. The republic of letters offered not only a means by which the learned could publish knowledge that might change the world but also a system of moral reform. Participants in this community of discourse sought authorization for their own understanding of the world by gaining the approval of other participants, who were thought of less as possessors of expert knowledge than as impartial rational observers. In science as in religion, said Jefferson, "Reason and free enquiry are the only effectual agents against error."[26] When he corresponded with the American Philosophical Society and when he wrote to his children and grandchildren, he offered information different in kind and level of sophistication, but the process of exchange and approbation enacted by the writing was similar. If his letters to his children were a means by which he furthered their moral development, they were also a means by which he disciplined his own moral sense as a parent by imagining their spectatorship of the world.

If Jefferson's letters sometimes functioned as small sermons for his family, he also intended them to evoke reports to his learned world from the world of their learning. He wished his children and grandchildren to commit themselves to the discipline of correspondence to which he had submitted himself. In the first letter to his daughter Martha he had given her a plan of studies and told her to write him every week: "Inform me what books you read, what tunes you learn, and inclose me your best copy of every lesson in drawing" (19-20). It was not enough that she correspond only with him, however, and he instructed her to write an additional letter a week to one of her aunts or to her sister. Martha's correspondence as her father envisioned it complemented her participation in society. She was to discuss her plan of studies with Mrs. Thomas Hopkinson, her Philadelphia caretaker, in order to see if she approved of it, in effect enlarging the circle of friends who were active spectators of her moral development. Two months later he advised, "With respect to you meeting Mr. Simitière at Mr. Rittenhouse's, nothing could give me more pleasure than your being much with that worthy family wherein you will see the best examples of rational life and learn to esteem and copy them"(23).[27] Seeing and being seen, receiving instruction and passing on the fruits of her learning, Martha

Jefferson was being taught how to be "beloved by all the world" by taking part in the conversation of that world. Despite an occasional paternal scolding for not writing, she seemed to learn her lesson well, especially pleasing her father in the winter of 1784 with a letter written in French.

Relatively few family letters survive from the years Jefferson spent in Paris as minister to France. Martha accompanied him, and although he sent her to the boarding school at Panthémont, she was apparently close enough for visits. She informed him of her studies, asked whether he wished her to dine at the abbess's table, and complained of the difficulties of Livy. His few long letters to her came from his two-month excursion through the south of France, giving his observations of that larger world and simultaneously encouraging her to develop internal resources. From Aix he objected, "I do not like you saying that you are unable to read the antient print of your Livy, . . . We are always equal to what we undertake with resolution. . . . It is a part of the American character to consider nothing as desperate; to surmount every difficulty by resolution and contrivance. In Europe there are shops for every want. It's inhabitants therefore have no idea that their wants can be furnished otherwise. Remote from all other aid, we are obliged to invent and to execute; to find means within ourselves, and not to lean on others"(35). He sent a list of places he had been, telling her to "take your map" and trace them out "In order to exercise your geography"(40). He described the canal of Languedoc and the fountain of Vaucluse with its Petrarchan associations and told her, "The object most interesting to me for the residue of my life, will be to see you both developing daily those principles of virtue and goodness which will make you valuable to others and happy in yourselves, and acquiring those talents and that degree of science which will guard you at all times against ennui, the most dangerous poison of life"(41). After Mary Jefferson arrived in Paris during the summer of 1787 and joined her sister at Panthémont, visits apparently took the place of letters between Jefferson and his children.

After Jefferson's return to America and his taking on the duties of secretary of state in 1790, the tone, and in some ways the strategy, of the family letters evolved because of important changes in the structure of his family and in his own situation. Shortly after the family's return to Virginia, Martha married her cousin Thomas Mann Randolph, Jr., an event that Jefferson thought ought to signal a new era in which she ceased to be a dependent child and became an independent person with her own interests, a conversational equal in the republic of letters.[28] On April 4, 1790, he wrote, "The happiness of your life depends now on the continuing to please a single person. To this all other objects must be secondary; even your love to me, were it possible that that could ever be an obstacle"(51). If this letter shows his awareness of Martha's independence from himself, its injunction to focus on the approval of her husband reveals disturbingly conventional attitudes about gender roles that undercut Jefferson's earlier advice that she ought to strive to be beloved by all the world. Recognizing her independence makes her an epistolary equal, but this letter also consigns her to the narrow world of wife in which only one spectator really counts for anything.

Replying nearly three decades later to a query about the education of women, Jefferson confessed,

> A plan of female education has never been a subject of systematic contemplation with me. It has occupied my attention so far only as the education of my own daughters occasionally required. Considering that they would be placed in a country situation, where little aid could be otained from abroad, I thought it essential to give them a solid education, which might enable them, when become mothers, to educate their own daughters, and even to direct the course for sons, should their fathers be lost, or incapable, or inattentive. My surviving daughter accordingly, the mother of many daughters as well as sons, has made their education the object of her life.[29]

Jefferson never resolved the contradictions attendant between encouraging his daughters to acquire knowledge in order to be beloved by all the world and making their attainments subject to the approbation of a society that maintained traditional notions of woman's roles, notions he himself largely accepted. Even though he had taken on himself some maternal responsibilities after his wife's death, his conventional notions of gender roles and his basically instrumental ideas about education kept him from clearly thinking through the consequences for his daughters and granddaughters of his own advice. For instance, he told his favorite granddaughter, Ellen, "if you continue to learn as fast, you will become a learned lady and publish books yourself," even though he immediately qualified that prospect by hoping, "you will at the same time continue to be a very good girl, never getting angry with your playmates nor the servants, but always trying to be more good humored and more generous than they"(214). A few months later, however, he wrote a single letter to grandchildren Anne, Jeff, and Ellen, with the traditional advice undifferentiated by gender considerations: "the more that you are all advancing in your learning and improving in good dispositions the more I shall love you, and the more everybody will love you"(218). When moved to a "systematic contemplation" of the education of daughters, Jefferson reinscribed conventional notions of the republican family, but in the actual practice of the family letters he suggested different, more egalitarian possibilities.

The presence of Jefferson's son-in-law also revised the possibilities of the family as an epistolary community. Thomas Mann Randolph had earlier sought Jefferson's advice about his own education and he shared his interests in agriculture and natural history. Jefferson encouraged the Randolphs to live at Edgehill, a farm only a few miles from Monticello, and whenever he was at home, Martha and her family moved over to take up residence with him. He also changed the pattern of his correspondence and attempted to put it on a systematic basis that reflected the new structure of the family. "I write regularly once a week," he told Martha, "to Mr. Randolph, yourself, or Polly, in hopes that it may induce a letter from one of you every week also"(54). As this scheme suggests, he regarded his new son-in-law as one of his family and incorporated him into its network of correspondence, although years later Randolph would withdraw into silence and melancholy.[30]

He shaped each letter to the interests of the particular recipient, discussing the health of Martha's children, the progress of Mary's reading, and farming and politics with Randolph, but he also used them to pass on information and news that might be interesting to others in the family. Thus, on May 16, 1790, his letter to Martha enclosed newspapers for Mr. Randolph that contained some of John Adams's "Discourses on Davila"; the letter of May 23 to Mary urged her to continue reading *Don Quixote* and to apply herself to her music, and the letter of May 30 discussed meteorological observation, books Randolph should read if he wished to study law, and the latest political news.[31] Jefferson clearly intended the correspondence to take a conversational shape—at least with the older correspondents; Mary still came in for a few sermons. At the same time, however, his mention of enclosures indicates that the newspapers he sent along, the enclosed letters to and from others, and the poems he later sent to his granddaughters were a part of the whole communicative act that is the letter. It is easy to overlook the significance of these enclosures because editions of Jefferson's writing do not print them, but they surely supported his continuing strategy of engaging family members in an epistolary conversation with the public world.

As the minister to France, Jefferson was an ocean away from those whose approbation mattered to him, but during the later years in which he was near or at the center of national government, he found himself involved in party disputes and the subject of criticism and vilification. Complaints about his periodical migraines are most frequent in the letters to his family between 1790 and 1808, and other signs of stress appear as well. He often complained about not receiving letters from his family, as in December 1790: "This is a scolding letter for you all. I have not recieved a scrip of a pen from home since I left it which is now eleven weeks. I think it so easy for you to write me one letter every week, which will be but once in three weeks for each of you, when I write one every week who have not one moment's repose from business from the first to the last moment of the week"(67). Improvements in the post would bring letters to him more regularly, but as partisan contentions with Hamilton and others grew, he longed to return home and began to sentimentalize his image of the family. The more exposed he became to attacks in the press and in pamphlet warfare, the more he envisioned the family as an escape into unqualified affection.

Thus in January of 1793 he noted his "agitation of mind which I scarcely ever experienced before, produced by a check on my purpose of returning home at the close of this session of Congress." He felt unable to leave office "just when I had been

attacked in the public papers" because "The only reward I ever wished on my retirement was to carry with me nothing like a disapprobation of the public"(110).
During his term as vice president the political climate was far more contentious,
and his polarization of the public and domestic spheres sharpened. "Environed here
in scenes of constant torment, malice, and obloquy, worn down in a station where
no effort to render service can aver any thing," he wrote to Mary in February 1799,
"I feel not that existence is a blessing but when something recalls my mind to my
family or farm. This was the effect of your letter, and it's affectionate expressions
kindled up all those feelings of love for you and our dear connections which now
constitute the only real happiness of my life"(173-74). As he waited for the House of
Representatives to decide the election of 1800, he complained, "Worn down here
with pursuits in which I take no delight, surrounded by enemies and spies, catching
and perverting every word which falls from my lips or flows from my pen, and
inventing where facts fail them, I pant for that society where all is peace and harmony, where we love and are loved by every object we see"(195).[32] He was thus
tempted to imagine the family as a utopian sphere for the unstinted exchange of
love because he thought of it as a system in which words could make distant affection present and a place in which suppressed intention could find candid expression. This notion of the family, however, depended upon a conception of the world
beyond the family as fundamentally alien and censorious, and Jefferson was not
ready to make this judgment.

    He continued to urge upon members of his family the necessity of a rational
engagement with the larger world, since unqualified flight into the harmonious circle of the family would leave standing the alienation from the impartial observers of
the public sphere. "Tranquillity is now my object," said Jefferson, but Adam Smith
had observed, "Society and conversation . . . are the most powerful remedies for
restoring a mind to its tranquillity, if, at any time, it has unfortunately lost it." "Men
of retirement and speculation," he noted, "seldom possess that equality of temper
which is so common among men of the world."[33] When Martha was unable to bring
her family from Edgehill in March 1797, Jefferson had complained, "The bloom of
Monticello is chilled by my solitude"(142). Five years later, when Mary was reluctant
to visit him in Washington because "so little accustom'd to be in so much company
as I should be in there" (217), he admonished her, "I think I discover in you a willingness to withdraw from society more than is prudent. I am convinced that our
happiness requires that we should continue to mix with the world, and to keep pace
with it as it goes; and that every person who retires from free communication with
it is severely punished afterwards by the state of mind into which they get, and
which can only be prevented by feeding our sociable principles"(219). Referring to
his years at Monticello between his career as secretary of state and his term as vice
president, he commented, "I felt enough of the effect of withdrawing from the
world then, to see that it led to an antisocial and misanthropic state of mind, which

severely punishes him who gives in to it: and it will be a lesson I never shall forget as to myself"(219). No matter how strongly Jefferson seemed to wish to separate the public and domestic spheres, his belief in the importance of "our sociable principles" always reasserted itself.

Under fire from political enemies, Jefferson tended to oppose the family and the world of politics in terms of their sentimental economies: "When I look to the ineffable pleasures of my family society, I become more and more disgusted with the jealousies of this scene and lament my having ever again been drawn into public view"(146). There seemed to be little possibility of exercising sociable principles across such a distinction, but by redefining the public sphere in terms of the republic of letters, he could find a grounds of conversation and correspondence. He wrote to Martha in February 1800, "Politics are such a torment that I would advise every one I love not to mix with them. I have changed my circle here according to my wish; abandoning the rich, and declining their dinners and parties, and associating entirely with the class of science, of whom there is a valuable society here"(184). If the members of the American Philosophical Society became a substitute for the consolations of family at Monticello, it is not entirely surprising that Jefferson would try to reconstitute the social circle of home in terms of that more public world.

His preference for a philosophical conversational circle in Philadelphia reflects his project of improving the conversational level of Albemarle County by persuading congenial spirits to take up residence there. A month previous to this letter he had opened a correspondence with Joseph Priestley, regretting that he had not settled in Virginia and asking, "Will not the arrival of Dupont tempt you to make a visit to this quarter?" He was more successful in persuading two Philadelphia acquaintances, Hore Browse Trist and William Bache, to take up residence nearby, and he made similar efforts in later years to develop the conversational possibilities of his neighborhood.[34] Further, his expressed preference for associating with "the class of science" is also an early indication of an increasingly important theme in his letters to his family, particularly to the youngest members.

Jefferson encouraged the children in his family to practice elementary forms of scientific and learned exchange in their letters to him, although not always with success. He asked daughter Mary in 1791 "to note every appearance animal and vegetable which indicates the approach of spring, and . . . communicate them to me. By these means we shall be able to compare the climates of Philadelphia and Monticello"(74). When she failed to report a killing frost, however, he lamented, "I find I have counted too much on you as a Botanical and zoological correspondent"(79). He found the correspondent he desired in his oldest granddaughter, Anne Cary Randolph; he requested, "I must pray her to become my correspondent" because "It will be useful to her, and very satisfactory to me"(242). His next letter instructed her in the sort of information he desired: "What sort of weather had you from the 6th to the 10th. Here we had frost, ice, and snow, and great damage in the garden and orchards"(245-46). The sort of information that could be supplied by a twelve-year-old granddaughter would hardly be the stuff of a report to the Philosophical Society or the Agricultural Society of Albemarle, but Jefferson was inculcating the habits of observation that might qualify a person to write such a report.[35]

Letters to other grandchildren encouraged other learned interests and suggested likely material that could fill their letters to him. Like the letters written twenty years earlier to his children, these looked to the contents of his grandchildren's letters as a record of what they were learning, but unlike those earlier letters, they seem much more interested in stimulating the form of letter-writing as a sociable and intellectual process. Responding to Ellen Wayles Randolph's complaint that there was little of interest to report from the country, President Jefferson argued, "you have a great advantage as to matter for communication. You have a thousand little things to tell me which I am fond to hear; for instance of the health of every body, and particularly of your dear Mama, everything relating to her being of the first concern to me: then what you are reading, what are your other occupations, how many dozen Bantams you have raised, . . . &c. &c. &c."(295).[36] Taking him at his word, she later tells "My dear Grandpapa" that she "will relate to him what passes among us which though dull and uninteresting to another will serve to show him that rather than not write at all I will this"(333). Jefferson answers that "With great news I am more than surfieted from other quarters" and informs her that among his books at Monticello "is a copy of Madame de Sévigné's letters, which being the finest models of easy letter writing you must read"(333).

One by one as the older grandchildren learned to write they were welcomed into the culture of letters: "I congratulate you my dear Cornelia," he wrote in the last months of his presidency, "on having acquired the invaluable art of writing. How delightful to be enabled by it to converse with an absent friend, as if present. To this we are indebted for all our reading, as it must be written before we can read it. To this we are indebted for the Iliad, the Aeneid, the Columbiad, Henriade, Dunciad, and now for the most glorious poem of all, the tarrapiniad, which I now enclose you"(373-74). He encouraged his grandchildren's thoughtful responses to their reading and experience, and thus after sending Cornelia a copy of Maria Edgeworth's *Moral Tales for Young People,* "seeming better suited to your years than to mine," he comments, "I have not looked into them, preferring to recieve their character from you after you shall have read them"(401). All this time Jefferson had been regularly communicating with their parents, and these grandchildren grew up with the notion that corresponding to the Grandpapa absent in the public world was a normal and desirable activity. In 1793, fondly using Anne Cary Randolph's baby talk, Martha reported that her daughter was "at present busily employed *viting* [i.e., writing] to you, a thing she has never missed doing whenever her health has permitted her"(109). Children who could not yet form their letters imitated their elders;

Jefferson asked Ellen to thank younger sister Mary for her letter, "but tell her it is in a cypher of which I have not the key"(296).

During the years of his presidency, letter-writing was a central strategy in Jefferson's ongoing construction of his family life that affirmed the connection he saw between it and the public world. Jefferson's correspondence with family members strengthened him against the threatening sentimental economy of the political world on the one hand, and on the other it domesticated the manners and virtues of the larger world by imagining society, the mirror that Smith had seen as the moral remedy for solitude, as the model for the family system. One small sign that Jefferson had some sense of his family as a reflection of America at large might lie in the names given to the Randolph grandsons. Thomas Jefferson Randolph had younger brothers named James Madison, Benjamin Franklin, Meriwether Lewis, and George Wythe Randolph, almost as if they were living equivalents to the busts of famous men scattered about Monticello. Both house and family in their own ways mirrored and were mirrored by the public world of art, learning, and politics.

Family as Philosophic Conversation

To imagine the family as defined by its negotiation with public life is one thing, however, and to lead children to commit themselves to participate in that public life is another. Jefferson's grandsons did not enter the public sphere of politics and learning in anything like the way in which their grandfather or fathers had. Their relative obscurity is not really surprising; the publicly active generations of Adamses and Rockefellers are exception rather than the rule. Jefferson discounted simplistic assumptions about eligibility for public office based upon ancestry, and he was ultimately more concerned about the morality of his grandchildren than in their accomplishments. His grandsons' failure to follow his example in the public sphere to any significant degree suggests that reinventing the family as if it were a system in the republic of letters did not ensure its continuity on that basis. Constant engagement with children's writing was necessary in order to turn them into young *philosophes,* and the grandchildren of Jefferson's who seem most thoroughly given over to the shadows of private life are those too young to have been drawn into his network of correspondence. Home from Washington at last, Jefferson complained of the burden of letter writing and did not submit the younger Randolph grandchildren, including those grandsons with their iconic public names, to the epistolary discipline he had imposed on their older siblings.

Moreover, letter-writing in the world of learning was a discipline, demanding rigor of observation and argument that in family correspondence could be subverted by the affectionate relationship that bound the writers. There was always a tension between the authority of learning, mentorship, and parenthood that gave superiority to one correspondent over the other and the sentimental and intellectual assumptions of epistolary equality they shared. The charm of the letters full of grandchildren's babytalk—their first efforts at writing, their responses to children's literature—threatened to draw Jefferson's inscription of his family into the private world of sentiment and to undermine his desire to engage the family with society. The pleasures of intimate family life always threatened to subvert Jefferson's role as a mentor who could lead them into participation in the public sphere. Affection could be more attractive to him than discipline, and the enjoyment of family intimacy might seem preferable to conducting a school for public life, particularly within the context of new attitudes about family emerging in the latter half of his life. The changing self-understanding of society both in Virginia and in the nation at large was increasingly defined by a cult of sensibility that privileged the family as a uniquely private and intimate space.[37]

With his two oldest grandsons he resisted the attraction of family sentiment by reasserting the disciplinary purpose of letter writing in a specifically educational context. When Jefferson Randolph, for example, attended lectures on medicine in Philadelphia in the autumn of 1808, his grandfather advised him to "commit to writing every evening the substance of the lectures of the day. . . . Then, if once a week you will, in a letter to me, state a synopsis or summary view of the heads of the lectures of the preceding week, it will give me great satisfaction to attend your progress, and it will further aid you by obliging you still more to generalize and to see analytically the fields of science over which you are travelling"(353). A year and a half later, he wrote to Jeff, now studying in Richmond with Louis Hue Girardin, "I would advise you as an exercise, to write a letter to somebody every morning, the first thing after you get up. As most of the business of life, and all our friendly communications are by way of letter, nothing is more important than to acquire a facility of developing our ideas on paper; and practice alone will give this"(397). Jefferson was certainly interested in inculcating self-discipline into a grandson whose mother had already suggested that he might show a bit too much of the impulsive, irritable "Randolph character"(360). At the same time, he was clearly speaking in a disciplinary voice as one of those impartial spectators whom the young man was to internalize as a control over his tempestuous "Randolph character." These letters seemingly intended to encourage the recipient's independence also dictated the terms on which it could be won.

No stranger to unresolvable dialogues between the head and the heart, Jefferson chose his letters to his grandchildren in the years after his presidency to maintain the balance between public and private life, between reason and sentiment, by assuming that the sentimental and intellectual economy of the family, since it was based on a universal moral sense, could be extended to larger systems not defined by kinship. He tried to relocate the family discourse into his projects for a college in Virginia, arguing in the Rockfish Gap Report that "The affectionate deportment of father and son, offers in truth the best example for that of tutor and pupil."[38] This final reinvention and extension of family, however, would expose the limitations of the republican epistolary family, and they would reveal themselves precisely over an issue of discipline.

If he could reimagine his family on the model of the republic of letters, using his correspondence to turn the family into a never-ending seminar with Professor Jefferson, then why could he not design a university as a modification of the philosophical family? In addition to his attempts to lure congenial neighbors to Albemarle, Jefferson had regularly invited young men among his family and acquaintances interested in reading for the law to come Monticello and use the resources of his library. These symbolic augmentations of his family prefigured the ultimate scheme of the academical village he had proposed as early as 1810, and family and university each came to be imagined as systems in the republic of letters.[39] Because Jefferson saw the play of reason that disciplined the republic of letters as a universal truth, he failed to recognize the degree to which the public sphere of his youth had been transformed. Ironically, his plan for a university preserved the possibilities of the republic letters for American society by defining it as a public space, potentially open to all impartial observers, at the same time the republic's disciplinary power was surrendering to the charm of sentimental relationships within the family.[40]

Even if Jefferson thought of both as affectionate philosophical conversations, the family and the university were very different enterprises, a point made abundantly clear by the student disorders in the first year of the university's operation. When insubordinate students rampaged on the Lawn and defied the faculty in 1825, it was clear that Jefferson's "hope that much of self government might be trusted to the discretion of the students" was misplaced. Ranged against his hope in an institution "based on the illimitable freedom of the human mind to explore and to expose every subject susceptible of it's contemplation" was "the rock which I most dread . . . The insubordination of our youth."[41] In destroying the illusion of the affectionate bonds between tutors and students, the campus disorders demonstrated that a family and an academical village could not operate on equivalent terms in the republic of letters.

In fact, they never were really equivalent, because without quite recognizing it, Jefferson had transformed the republic of letters' conditions of knowledge when he established the university. In his letters to his family he had encouraged the children and grandchildren to pursue knowledge on the basis of their own observation and reasoning, but despite his intentions to make the university provide its students the freedom to participate in similar ways in their own educations, he designed a place where knowledge would be consumed rather than produced. When grandson Francis Wayles Eppes, waiting for Central College to begin operation, attended the College at Columbia, South Carolina, he objected to its insistence on students following a prescribed course of studies. Jefferson sympathized, responding, "This will certainly be the fundamental law of our University to leave every one free to attend whatever branches of instruction he wants, and to decline what he does not want"(436). If Jefferson's ideal student enjoyed the freedom of inquiry that characterized both the republic of letters and present-day American higher education, he also became the course-shopper, the consumer of the university's wares. In the epistolary family individual members were required to take an active role in the philosophical conversation of the family, but at the university students should accept discipline and acquire, as he advised Jeff Randolph, "an absolute power of silence" over their sentiments (369).

In a further irony, Jefferson's transformation of the conditions of knowledge in the university was an important aspect of its particular modernity. The republic of letters and its encompassing public sphere was collapsing for a variety of reasons, and not least among them was the evolution of a culture-consuming society out of what Habermas calls a "culture-debating" society.[41] Jefferson's design for the university had placed the library in the dominant position occupied by the Rotunda, and he had always implicitly assumed that his own library at Monticello was an authoritative resource to which he might variously send students of law or granddaughters in quest of information about Aristotle's Adsatick cock. The genuine authority at Monticello, however, was his own letter-writing as an exemplary and stimulating activity. The university replaced the epistolary illusion of conversing "with an absent friend, as if present"(373) with the silence of reading, replaced participatory correspondence with consumption in the library. In doing so it was merely reflecting changes in the larger society that were displacing the epistolary, manuscript culture of Jefferson's youth with the print culture of the nineteenth century. The University of Virginia was a powerful example for American education because it preserved many values of the republic of letters as it accommodated them to the emerging modernity of American society.

The changes reflected in Jefferson's university also indicated unwitting changes in his ongoing reimagination of his family. As late as 1810 he could inform Jefferson Randolph that "our views in giving you opportunities of acquiring sciences" were ultimately intended "to enable you, by the possession of knolege, to be happier and more useful to yourself, to be beloved by your friends, and respected and honored by your country"(396). A decade later he wrote to Francis Eppes, "It either is, or ought to be the rule of every collegiate institution to teach every particular student the branches of science which those who direct him think will be useful in the pursuits proposed for him, and waste his time on nothing which they think will not be useful to him"(436). Usefulness is the criterion in each recommendation, but it is inflected in a very different way by dropping the consideration of being "respected and honored by your country." Allowing his own correspondence with his grandchildren to lapse, Jefferson implicitly reconceived his family as consumers of culture rather than producers of it, as a group that read news from the larger world without feeling the need to respond to it beyond the level of the neighborhood.

When Jefferson died, the family seminar ended, but the example of his epistolary conduct of family relationships survives. It does not provide any easy model for
late twentieth-century citizens in search of family values, unless they seriously think
all young people will enthusiastically take up the study of Livy and Tacitus. In any
case, Jefferson's reinvention of the family as philosophic conversation was in many
ways a unique phenomenon, and even in his own family others did not necessarily
perceive it as such. Certainly as a scheme for disciplining emotional disturbances it
was unable to counter the disappointment and melancholy of Thomas Mann
Randolph or whatever drove Charles Bankhead, granddaughter Anne's husband, to
alcoholism and wife abuse. Nevertheless, we might profit from a serious consideration of Jefferson's attentiveness to the emotional and intellectual welfare of his family and of his insistence that the charms of family life not be gained by the repudiation of society. His encouragement of learning in order to be beloved by all the
world, although it is probably an appeal that can no longer be made in those terms,
can still speak to the necessity of nurturing our children, for self-esteem is perhaps
more a matter of confidence in the value of one's knowledge than of feeling alone.
Above all, we can always benefit from the generosity of spirit that led him to advise
his daughter, "Every human being, my dear, must thus be viewed according to what
it is good for, for none of us, no not one, is perfect: and were we to love none who
had imperfections, this world would be a desart for our love. All we can do is to
make the best of our friends: love and cherish what is good in them, and keep out
of the way of what is bad: but no more think of rejecting them for it than of throwing away a piece of music for a flat passage or two"(61). Of course, even more generous would have been the admission of young women such as his daughters and
granddaughters to his university, but Thomas Jefferson was not prepared for that
unthinkable act.

HOLLY BREWER

Beyond Education:
Thomas Jefferson's "Republican" Revision of the Laws Regarding Children

D uring the Revolutionary War Thomas Jefferson not only wrote a draft for a new Virginia Constitution but participated, with Edmund Pendleton and George Wythe, in an attempt to revise and update Virginia's entire code of laws. His purpose in the "revisal of the laws" was not only to "remove from our book shelves about twenty folio volumes of statutes [of England and early Virginia] retaining all parts of them which either their own merit or the established system of laws required," but also to eradicate "every fiber of antient or future aristocracy" and to lay "a foundation . . . for a government truly republican."[1] These passages point to the close interconnection between political ideas and laws, a connection that some recent historians have challenged.[2] Jefferson himself acknowledged this connection explicitly: "Every political measure will for ever have an intimate connection with the laws of the land; and he who knows nothing of these will always be perplexed and often foiled by adversaries having the advantage of that knoledge over him."[3]

An examination of Jefferson's philosophical perspectives and his revision of Virginia's laws reveals some of the tensions that existed between the theory of republican government and the practice thereof, as well as the philosophical tensions that existed within republican ideology itself.[4] These interconnections and tensions emerge as we examine the implications for children of the political discourse of the New Republic. Jefferson, who held some of the more revisionist ideas espoused by Virginians or in the new republic as a whole, proposed significant legal reforms that affected the status of children. At the center of Jefferson's ideas about the state's regulation of children was the public education of children, but Jefferson also advocated other revisions in the codes of laws and upheld older laws even though, in a few cases, they had become inconsistent, philosophically, with his reforms. These revisions and reembodiments are important if we are to understand how children were defined and also the ways in which republican political theory was understood in the late eighteenth century. The separate space Jefferson allocated to children—indeed, the extension of that space—reveals the tensions within political theory, tensions engendered by the inequalities that remained within a theory of equality.

Children in Republican Political Thought

Children and childhood hold a central place in any discussion of eighteenth-century political thought because even more than women, blacks, or Indians, they were explicitly classified as the nonrational in Enlightenment writings. Most eighteenth-century republican political theorists assumed that reason formed the foundation of human nature and that only adult men had the capability to exercise reason. Most also qualified these assertions by arguing that reason needed to be cultivated from infancy or by arguing that men in positions of power needed to be prevented from having their reason corrupted. Ultimately, the character of the government they advocated rested to a significant degree on whether they believed that human reason was innate, acquired, or impossible and unnecessary for most to acquire. The lack of reason (because some group of people had not yet—or could not—acquire it) became an excuse for excluding people from having a political voice or political power. Inequalities based on age were built into Jefferson's legal reforms and were justified within Jefferson's political philosophy: children were distinctive because they were not reasonable.

The reigning political theory at the time of the founding of the first English colonies was patriarchalism, and it was this theory that republican theorists and Jefferson argued against. Patriarchal theory, as espoused by such thinkers as Sir Robert Filmer in the seventeenth century, compared the king's power over his people to a father's power over his children. Both the responsibilities and the privileges of the king were the same as those of a political father. Filmer wrote "[i]f we compare the natural rights of a father with those of a king, we find them all one . . . as the father over one family, so the king, as father over many families, extends his care to preserve, feed, clothe, instruct, and defend the whole commonwealth."[5] The only difference between a father's power and the king's power was that the king gained his right by primogeniture. The king's position was based on inherited status, not on his production of offspring. Filmer echoed earlier patriarchal ideas such as those expressed by James I in 1598 and gave them a more rigorous justification. In *The Trew Law of Free Monarchies,* James I claimed that "the King towards his people is rightly compared to a father of children," and the people must behave dutifully toward their king. The people do not consent to the king's government. Rather, the king's right is based only on his being "their heritable overlord, and so by birth . . . comes to his crown . . . [as] the nearest and lawful heir." No matter how "wicked" any king's actions, he was king by the will of God, and it should be left to God, not the people, to judge his actions.[6]

Although patriarchal theory as such received its most rigorous justification in the early seventeenth-century attempts by the Stuarts and Royalists to justify absolutism, two of its basic premises had formed key elements of medieval political thought. First, the description of the king as a temporal "Father" of his people was a direct analogy to the spiritual "Father" God and his spiritual earthly representatives in the church.[7] Second, the rules of primogeniture served as the primary means of granting authority.

Thomas Jefferson's political ideas can only be fully understood when it is realized that many of the books that influenced him were written as reactions to the royalist Sir Robert Filmer and to patriarchal absolutism. In fact, two of the philosophers whom Jefferson most admired, John Locke and Algernon Sidney, wrote their political treatises directly in response to Filmer. The following sketch of Thomas Jefferson's political ideas draws not only on his own writings but also on the writings of Sidney and Locke.[8] Although some modern historians have found a dichotomy between Sidney and Locke, and thus have seen Jefferson as torn between two opposing schools of thought, Lockean Liberalism on the one hand and Classical Republicanism on the other, this difference has been drawn too rigidly and rests partly on an overemphasis on the place of liberty in John Locke's thought and a corresponding underemphasis on the place of liberty, equality, and consent in Classical Republican thought.[9] Focusing on reason in the thought of Jefferson, Locke, and Sidney illustrates that conflicts between two opposing schools of thought can be seen instead as tensions within a single paradigm.

In Jefferson's America, students of Locke read both of his treatises of government as well as his *Some Thoughts Concerning Education* and his *Essay Concerning Human Understanding*.[10] Any careful reading of the documents in conjunction, or even a reading of *The Second Treatise of Government* that highlights Locke's consideration of the status of children, illustrates that Locke did not perceive humans as asocial, nor did he believe that human beings should not learn self-discipline and virtue, or that humans should or could have perfect liberty. For Locke, liberty and equality come only with control over the passions and the exercise of reason. John Locke's writings formed probably the strongest philosophical argument for the formal education of children in eighteenth-century England and his *Some Thoughts Concerning Education* and *Essay Concerning Human Understanding*, in particular, resulted directly in the appearance in England and America of a literature, the first of its kind, directed specifically toward children.[11] In many ways, what Pocock described as the emphasis on virtue in republican writings is similar to the emphasis on education in Locke's writings. Public virtue in classical republican theory, according to Pocock, meant, in part, the gaining of independent, rational thought and control over the passions, a self-control that was the same focus of Locke's education.[12]

Writing in the early 1680s, nearly forty years after Filmer, John Locke claimed in his *Two Treatises of Government* that paternal authority is not the same as political authority, that most citizens are not children but are adults who can reason and should be able to consent to their own government. At the same time, however, Locke distinguished adults who could reason from the children who could not: "Children, I confess, are not born in this full state of equality, they are born to it. Their parents have a sort of rule and jurisdiction over them. . . ." Locke referred to children as "weak and helpless, without knowledge or understanding." The parents' task is to "govern the actions of their yet ignorant nonage, 'til reason shall take its place." This power belongs to parents in particular because the child is dependent on the parent—to feed and clothe it and care for it.[13] He elaborated on these ideas in *Some Thoughts Concerning Education* and *An Essay Concerning Human Understanding,* both of which described the lengthy process a child undergoes in order to develop reason, what Locke called "reflection," or the ability to "abstract" generalizations from particular observations to develop complex ideas. The chief end of developing the understanding is to discover, and follow, morality. He held that these abilities were essential to participatory citizenship.[14]

Thus although Locke, as most scholars have emphasized, advocated equality and made consent the basis of legitimate authority, he excluded some from having a political voice because they did not have reason. He also upheld key elements of Filmer's patriarchal theory, particularly the power of parents over children. Locke limited parental authority more than Filmer because Filmer held that the father had the power of life and death over his children while Locke held that only the state had that power. Still, Locke never held that parental authority should originate in consent but rather that parents legitimately exercised authority because children were dependent and lacked reason.[15]

Writing at the same time as John Locke, Algernon Sidney did not emphasize formal education to the same degree and wrote more about "virtue" and "wisdom" than the "reason" that Locke explicitly emphasized.[16] Yet he attacked Filmer's ideas at precisely the points as did Locke; he objected to primogeniture as a system for the allocation of power and to the link that Filmer had established between familial and state power. For Sidney, people should be advanced to leadership positions by merit of their experience, wisdom, and virtue, not by birth. The fact that children—who lacked wisdom and experience and could more easily be corrupted—could be advanced to leadership positions represented, for Sidney, the best proof of the problems with monarchy in particular and with a feudal as opposed to a republican system. Sidney began his *Discourses* with an attack on primogeniture, a system of government that allocated power on the basis of inheritance rather than reason, merit, and virtue.[17] He mocked Filmer's defense of primogeniture by describing its consequences. While Filmer acknowledged that with primogeniture, "it comes to pass that many a child, by succeeding a king, hath the right of a father over many a greyheaded multitude, and hath the title of Pater Patriae,"[18] Sidney made this right seem ridiculous. For Filmer, primogeniture with respect to kings is the

Royal Charter granted to kings by God. They all have an equal right to it; women and children are patriarchs; and the next in blood, without any regard to age, sex, or other qualities of the mind or body, are the fathers of as many nations as fall under their power. We are not to examine whether he or she be young or old, virtuous or vicious, sober minded or stark mad; the right and power is the same in all.[19]

Although the lack of age and reason are not the only characteristics by which Sidney mocked Filmer's claim that kings were patriarchs (clearly Sidney held that a disregard to sex was suspect as well) the fact that a person could be the leader of a nation who had neither age nor reason nor virtue formed the crux of his argument against Filmer. The text of Sidney's *Discourses Concerning Government* is devoted to demolishing Filmer's argument for an inherited authority based on primogeniture, or a government based upon status. The fact that a child could be king represented the most ludicrous aspect of monarchy.[20]

Thomas Jefferson, like Locke and Sidney, believed that in order to be a participatory citizen, a person needed to be able to exercise reason. A simple statement perhaps. Yet it hides layers of assumptions and creates, by definition, a two-tier system of equality, one in which children, in particular, were defined as the nonreasonable. That those who could participate in government should be able to exercise reason was the key theoretical formulation underpinning Jefferson's plan for public education and his statute on religious toleration. It also affected a range of public policies that served to define and limit children's participation. Jefferson, like Locke and Sidney, still advocated equality: the fact that there were differences in who could participate did not mean that equality was merely a fiction.[21] Rather, equality needs to be understood within the context of this emphasis on reason. Equality was clearly an important element of Jefferson's thought and provided the basis for some of his legal reforms. Indeed the other two reforms—in addition to public education and religious toleration—that Jefferson regarded as the key elements of his "republican revisal" both sought to erase a system of inheritance that had favored one child because of birth: they did away with entail and primogeniture. In other words, Jefferson's thinking, like that of many reformers whose political ideas developed in the crucible of the American Revolution, reflected shifting political priorities that moved away from an emphasis on inherited status and toward an emphasis on merit, with that merit defined, largely, through a person's or a group's ability to exercise reason.

Like both Locke and Sidney, Jefferson in some passages seemed to imply that humans possessed free will and were equal in that freedom as soon as they had been created. "All men are *created* equal," he wrote in the *Declaration of Independence,* "they are endowed by their creator with certain unalienable rights; that among these are life, liberty and the pursuit of happiness." In his manuscript for *A Summary View,* published in July 1774, he wrote similarly that "The God who gave us life, gave us liberty at the *same time:* the hand of force may destroy, but cannot disjoin them."[22] In the original published version of his *Bill for Establishing Religious Freedom,* Jefferson wrote that he (and the Virginia Legislature) were "[w]ell aware that Almighty God hath *created* the mind free, and manifested his supreme will that free it shall remain by making it altogether insusceptible of restraint."[23]

A closer examination, however, reveals what kind of limits he set on that equality and that freedom. The sentence that follows "life, liberty and the pursuit of happiness" in the Declaration of Independence is, "to secure these rights, governments are instituted among men, deriving their just powers from the *consent of the governed.*" Did Jefferson believe that all should consent? The restrictions on voting that Jefferson proposed in his draft of a Virginia Constitution, written in the same year, reveal that he did not.[24] Are the governed, then, the same group as could consent? No. Are the governed the same group who had a right to life, liberty, and equality? Although the answer to this question is more complicated, it to some extent matches the first, particularly with respect to "liberty" and "equality." In his *Bill for establishing Religious Freedom,* Jefferson explained how he thought people came to have "opinions and belief" that made them able to consent. "The opinions and belief of men depend not on their own will, but follow involuntarily the evidence proposed to their minds . . . the holy author of our religion . . . chose . . . to extend it by its influence on reason alone."[25]

For Jefferson, then, what humans believe is shaped by reason filtered through experience. Not until humans gain reason, through both experience and (possibly) a formal education, are they actually entitled to the freedom to which they were born. "To render a child independent of its parents," Jefferson wrote on the question of leaving money to grandchildren, "is to ruin it's education, it's morals, it's reputation and it's fortune."[26] John Locke had developed this argument further, linking together what sometimes seem to be contradictory statements within Jefferson's writings. Just after claiming that all men are equal, Locke equivocated: "Children, I confess, are not born in this full state of equality, they are born to it."

> Thus we are born free, as we are born rational; *not that we have actually the exercise of either:* age, that brings one, brings with it the other too. And thus we see how natural freedom and subjection to parents may consist together, and are both founded on the same principle. A child is free by . . . his father's understanding, which is to govern him till he hath it of his own. The freedom of a man at years of discretion, and the subjection of a child to his parents, whilst yet short of that age, are so consistent, and so distinguishable . . ." [my italics].[27]

Thus for Jefferson, as for Locke, until children attained reason, or roughly speaking, until they gained the appropriate age, they should be dependent on their parents and subject to their will.

Yet the gaining of reason did not come merely with age for Jefferson. Although in a letter to Madison of 1786 he implied that men could and should form their own opinions,[28] in general he made it clear that some measure of formal education was necessary in order to adequately nurture reason. Although Jefferson fluctuated he generally emphasized formal education, rather than just experience, as the key to wisdom: reason was learned deliberately; it was not innate to all those who had accumulated a certain amount of experience or lived a certain length of time.

Thus, although reason and education do not necessarily accompany one another, for Jefferson they were usually allied. The content of education was to teach a method of analysis and to learn about the range of human experience. For Jefferson as for Locke, education was a mixture of experience and a program of formal education. Jefferson thought that a more formal education served three functions: It gave people the strength of purpose to resist mental vassalage to others; it was a prerequisite for "rightful" informed consent; and it provided equality of opportunity. The first two goals of education relied on an education that taught reason; the third goal generally aimed at educating children in a trade, such that those who inherited no land at least had a means to subsist.[29]

Jefferson strongly promoted public education as a means of inculcating public reason—that is, teaching people to think for themselves so they could be less easily duped by unscrupulous rulers. The purpose of public education was to "enlighten" the public and to help them exercise their reason. In 1786, in a letter to George Wythe about the far-reaching changes in the legal code of Virginia, he wrote: "I think by far the most important bill in our whole code is that for the diffusion of knowledge among the people. No other sure foundation can be devised for the preservation of freedom, and happiness." Afraid that without education the mass of the people in America would become, like the peasants in France, the victims of unscrupulous overlords, he cautioned his friend Wythe:

> Preach, my dear sir, a crusade against ignorance; establish and improve the law
> for educating the common people. Let our countrymen know that the people
> alone can protect us against these evils [kings, nobles, and priests], and that the tax
> which will be paid for this purpose is not more than the thousandth part of what
> will be paid to kings, priests and nobles who will rise up among us if we leave the
> people in ignorance.[30]

If people were left ignorant, they would not realize when governments or religious organizations threatened their interests.

Education was also a prerequisite for "rightful" informed consent. Jefferson elaborated on this aspect of education in January 1787, in a letter giving his response to news of Shays' Rebellion in Massachusetts. Instead of endorsing the military force which was in fact used Jefferson warned that "to punish [the] errors [of the people] would be to repress the only safeguard of the public liberty." He told Edward Carrington not to "be too severe upon their errors but *reclaim them by enlightening them*"[my italics].[31] Almost thirty years later, in 1816, he reinforced the same message: "I know no safe depository of the ultimate powers of society but the people themselves; and if we think them not enlightened enough to exercise their control with a wholesale discretion, the remedy is not to take it from them, but to inform their discretion by education." Here in particular Jefferson acknowledged that the "unenlightened" should not have a political voice. But unlike John Adam's and Gouverneur Morris's solution, which was simply to exclude those who could not exercise reason, Jefferson's solution was to educate them.[32]

Jefferson's 1801 inaugural address made a similar distinction: "that although the will of the majority is in all cases to prevail, that will, to be rightful, must be reasonable."[33] Although Jefferson was describing the general character of the people's consent he was also, by implication, commenting on the qualifications of the electors. He was not excluding the unreasonable adult. Clearly Jefferson felt that the people, uninformed by reason, should be granted some limited political authority, if only to restrain those in power from becoming tyrants. Yet Jefferson did argue that only with an informed electorate could the will of the people be "rightful," or correct. In other words, the people would not perceive wholly their own good, or the good of the country, until they had reason.

Thus, although it could be argued that Jefferson modified a conservative interpretation of Locke and inclined more toward Sidney, who did not emphasize a formal education and held that most male adults had reason, it is also clear that Jefferson believed that formal education of the people was critically important to "rightful" government.[34] Jefferson's comments on the power of parents or teachers contain a similar tension. In his letter to John Banister he suggested that parents should act more as friends than as authorities toward their children: "The post which a parent may take most advantageous for his child is that of his bosom friend. I know your way of thinking too well to doubt your concurrence in this."[35] Indeed, his letters to his daughters, while persuading them to be good and study hard, are full of love and affection and certainly not strictly authoritarian.[36] His letter to Peter Carr telling him to obey his tutor, however, implies that he thought a teacher should have a great deal of authority and should be obeyed. "Do not be misled by others into an opinion that to oppose a tutor and to set him at defiance is shewing a laudable spirit, on the contrary nothing can be more blameable and nothing will discredit you more in the opinion of sensible men."[37] The passage quoted above, wherein Jefferson showed that he thought too much independence in a child would render it impossible for the child to be properly educated, shows that he thought, at the very least, that the structure of authority should exist, even if parents or tutors did not always choose to act upon it. "To render a child independent of it's parents is to ruin it's education, it's morals, it's reputation and it's fortune." Even his letters to his daughters reveal that while he might extend a hand of friendship and love, he does it partly to bolster his authority.[38]

Ultimately, as the laws Jefferson outlined make clear, he relied upon a somewhat simple equation between reason and age, with age serving as a marker for intellectual development, to set the qualifications for obtaining personal and political power. Some age distinctions were already partly built into the common law, but Jefferson helped to solidify legal distinctions based on age: to strengthen parents' powers over children until children had achieved "the age of reason" and to decrease children's legal abilities by increasing age requirements for various citizenship rights and responsibilities. Jefferson's advocacy of these reforms hinged on the same conception of an elongated childhood that underlaid his emphasis on formal education and experience.

Legal Reform to Limit Children's Authority

Particularly in the practical laws he wrote, Jefferson showed clearly that he did not indeed believe that all people, even all men, were equal from birth. More than some of his contemporaries, he gave a great deal of freedom to youth—once they came of age. He advocated that a constitutional convention be held every generation so that as each group of young men came of age they need not be bound by their father's consent to their new government, but could be bound by their own. In some ways Jefferson had a vision of America as a young nation, and he thought that a seal of the United States should have an image of a father presenting his son with a bundle of rods.[39] Yet Jefferson explicitly altered many laws to give increased power to parents while their children were young and lengthen the legal dependency of childhood. He made these alterations to coincide with republican political theory. They included the abolishing of entail and primogeniture, plans for public education, minimum age requirements for those elected, such as members of the Virginia Senate, and stronger parental control over marriage choices. Other elements of the laws, which Jefferson might have chosen to change (and indeed which were changing gradually during this period), he apparently did not choose to dramatically alter. Among them were poor law policy and various regulations relating to children and contracts and children as witnesses.

Primogeniture and entail were parts of the English common law relating to inheritance. Entail, in layman's terms, was a process by which some ancestor wrote in a will, "I leave this to my son and to the *heirs* of his body after him." This coded legal passage then prohibited the man who inherited the property from choosing to whom the property would descend: it automatically followed general rules of primogeniture and went to his eldest son, and if he had no son, to his daughter, or if he had no daughter, to his brother, and so on. The property could descend to daughters as long as the entail did not specify male heirs, which it sometimes did. This practice gave very little manipulative control to parents over children: children would inherit what they would inherit. Jefferson consciously described this lack of control as a problem. In the preamble to his bill abolishing entail, he wrote that one of the evils of entail was that it could do "injury to the morals of youth, by rendering them independent of and disobedient to their parents."[40] Whereas earlier historians had concluded that entails were not common in Virginia and thus that these reforms were unimportant, my recent work has shown that entails exerted a powerful grip over Virginia and that thus getting rid of them was a very significant change in Virginia's law and institutions.[41]

Primogeniture also referred specifically to the system of inheritance where a person possessed of nonentailed real property died without a will, or intestate. In this case, the estate would be distributed as though it had been entailed. With this looser type of primogeniture, the testator had control over how his or her property was distributed if he or she chose to leave a will—although there might well have been a residual tendancy to transmit all property to one priviliged heir so that a plantation would remain in the family without having to be broken up. The changes Jefferson proposed abolished both systems (entail and general primogeniture) and divided estates among all children (females as well as males) where a man died intestate. Otherwise, the testator had complete discretion over the disposal of his estate and the education of his children, a change that increased the father's power. These bills concerning "wills" and the "course of descents," both known to have been written by Jefferson, he regarded as cornerstones of "the foundation . . . for a government truly republican."[42] They were doubly so: not only did they increase equality of opportunity for the younger generation, but they increased fathers' powers over their children by increasing their control over inheritance. By itself the abolition of entail reveals the tension between control and liberty, equality and inequality, within Jefferson's political and legal thought.

This tension is also illustrated in Jefferson's discussion of children as citizens. Were children citizens and at what age did they become participatory citizens? Bill 55 of the revision of the Virginia laws, attributed by the editors of his papers to Jefferson, stated that all were citizens who either were born within the territory of "this commonwealth" or who migrated there and swore allegiance, including "all infants [children under twenty-one] wheresoever born, whose father, if living, or otherwise, whose mother was a citizen at the time of their birth" or whose parent(s) migrate to Virginia.[43] On the one hand this discussion argued that a child is a citizen regardless of age. On the other, it argued that the citizenship of the child was determined by the parent (and the child could not choose it) until it arrived of age (although Jefferson did note that children who migrated to [the United States?] of their own accord could be considered citizens.) A discussion of property rights modified this point: According to Jefferson, an adult citizen of America could not inherit property from a relative in Britain, because the American citizen would be an alien in Britain. A child, however, could inherit property, even though living in America (as long as he or she was born in Britain or in the colonies before independence), because he or she would not be of age to choose their citizenship.[44] The child being both citizen and not citizen went beyond the mere question of property. Jefferson, Pendleton, and Wythe in the revision of the laws directed in several places that normal statutes of limitations would not begin for children until they reached the age of twenty-one.[45]

With respect to active citizenship—voting, jury service, and militia service— Jefferson either approved or increased age requirements. Age requirements for voting had been set in Virginia in 1699, following the addition of age requirements (to property requirements) in England in 1695; both set twenty-one as the minimum age to vote or to be elected. These age requirements were set just after the Glorious Revolution, and the addition of age to property requirements probably reflected the influence of John Locke, if not Sidney (although his *Discourses* was not published until 1699), and of Whig pamphleteers such as Henry Care who railed against the practice of "minors" being elected in the 1680s.[46] Jefferson upheld the age of twenty-one in his various writings on suffrage requirements, and suggested thirty-one as the age at which a man could be elected to the Virginia Senate, or six years older than the age requirement in the Virginia Constitution.[47] Age requirements increased in two other areas of citizenship in the years after the Revolutionary War: jury service and military service. The minimum age for jury service was fourteen in Virginia until 1792 when the Virginia legislature increased it to twenty-one; the age minimum for military service in Virginia, although it changed sporadically over the eighteenth century, was raised from sixteen to eighteen in 1784. Jefferson's precise role in these raises in age limits is unclear, but they fit in with a larger pattern of republican principles. With so much emphasis on reason, and children being given as examples of the unreasonable, it was logical to exclude them from participatory citizenship.[48]

The exclusions that Jefferson chose to leave in place, minimal property qualifications, twenty-one years of age, male gender, and sanity, all reflect a concern with the reason and the independence of the voter. Independence was not merely a vague consideration, as Richard Bushman and Edmund Morgan have pointed out: bribery and "dependence," in the form of being an employee or a renter, might in fact influence a person's vote.[49] Reason and mental and physical independence were in fact closely linked in political theory, and indeed implicitly by Jefferson himself, although, as argued above, Jefferson tended to shy away from the dependence argument as it related to adult males.[50] Rather than just excluding unenlightened, unreasonable, or otherwise dependent adult white males, Jefferson sought to include them by educating them.[51]

Jefferson also strengthened parental power in critical respects, partly, perhaps, because he saw girls and boys under twenty-one as unable to make their own decisions and the parent as their best, and most loving, counselor. Jefferson can be partly credited with Bill 86, which would have revised Virginia marriage law, although he probably did not write it. Wythe, Pendleton, and Jefferson met and discussed the revisions *in toto*. Bill 86 strengthened the power of parents by making the marriages of those under twenty-one void unless their parents had consented: "And a marriage between any persons whatsoever unless it be with such license [that contains the father's or guardian's consent], and, moreover if both or either of the parties not having been married before, be under the age of twenty one years, with such consent, as herein after directed, shall be *null.*"[52]

This voidability presented a dramatic strengthening of Virginia marriage law. In eighteenth-century Virginia, ministers were merely fined if they had performed marriages without having the parent's, generally the father's, signature on a license or without having published banns (presumably the parents could dissent after hearing the banns). Making these marriages void would have given much more legal weight to parents, although this portion of the law was not ultimately passed.[53] This change had been adopted in 1753 in England in a law that attempted to prevent "clandestine" marriages, and had resulted in a flurry of pamphlets about whether girls between the ages of twelve and twenty-one and boys between the ages of fourteen and twenty-one could in fact consent at all to the marriage contract if the parents' consent was also necessary. In other words, they should either be able to make that decision or not able, since it was they, not their parents, who would have to spend the rest of their lives in that relationship.[54] In fact the law in England and Bill 86 of the Revision of the laws in Virginia represented dramatic attempts to strengthen parental control over marriage. Under the Catholic church before the reformation in England and in the Anglican ecclesiastical courts, it is clear that the agreement to marry, in the future, between two people, unmarried, of opposite genders and over twelve for girls and fourteen for boys, if proven, represented a binding promise in the eyes of the ecclesiastical law. The punishment for teenagers who disobeyed their parents might be a loss of inheritance, but nothing more. Although early American colonists instituted laws that strengthened parental power by restraining the ability of ministers to officiate over the marriages of minors without parental consent, they never sought to actually invalidate marriages once they had occurred.[55]

Yet Jefferson's refusal to reinstate the English law on statutory rape in his bill on crimes and punishments challenges the idea that Jefferson did not think children could consent to sex. According to a statute passed during the reign of Queen Elizabeth, a statute that appeared in early Virginia guides to justices of the peace, which were basic guides for how the law should be enforced, sexual relations with a girl under the age of ten was rape whether or not the girl consented, based on the idea that a girl under ten had no ability to consent. Jefferson's reasoning against statuatory rape rested on an argument that this law was not part of the common law. He ultimately chose to dismiss this statute passed during the reign of Queen Elizabeth because it was a statute, and thus, he argued, not part of the common law, and because Blackstone, in his *Commentaries*, did not discuss it.[56] Yet ultimately, this statute had been in force so many years and had been recognized as valid by enough people that Jefferson could easily have chosen to accept it based upon a common law argument or to accept it as a revision that he thought beneficial. Perhaps Jefferson thought that statutory rape should not be a crime because it assigned blame to only one person — the adult male — for an act of consensual sexual intercourse.[57] Both Jefferson's dismissal of statutory rape and his revision of the marriage law involve a child's or young adult's consent to sexual relations. That these two policies in some ways contradict each other suggests that Jefferson did not think through the entire context of his reforms. On the one hand, with regard to parental consent to marriages, he seemed to greatly strengthen parental power and undercut a young adult's abilities to consent, and on the other, he seemed to accept that girls, even under ten, had enough reason to give valid consent to sex—or at least that they could be partly to blame. Jefferson, on neither point, was accepted: marriages without parental consent were not voided, and the rape and abduction of young girls continued to be punished by Virginia law and codified statutes were introduced as part of a continuing revision (in which Jefferson probably had no part) by an abduction law of 1789, and a statutory rape law of 1792.[58]

Jefferson displayed reciprocity, however, in his revision of intrafamilial murder law, a reciprocity that in some ways undercut parental power. His opinions in this respect display some of his reasons for strengthening parental power in other respects: Jefferson felt that natural parents were unique and had strong ties of affection to their children, bonds which made them the most appropriate and natural overseers of their children. Although according to common law it had been "petty treason" for a child to kill a parent and only murder for a parent to kill their offspring, with the punishment for petty treason being worse than the punsishment for murder, Jefferson imposed the same punishment on a parent who killed a child as a child who killed a parent, "death by hanging, and his body be delivered to Anatomists to be dissected." The dissection was an interesting variant on the previously more horrible death imposed on those who committed treason of any kind, whether high or petty, which had been, if male, to be first "drawen" (disembowelled while alive) and then hanged, or, if female, to be burned alive.[59] Jefferson also eliminated an old law that presumed an unmarried woman guilty of murder if her child was stillborn or died soon thereafter and she had concealed the birth. This law had argued that the concealment itself signified an intent to kill the child. Jefferson challenged this: "If shame be a powerful affection of the mind, is not parental love also? Is it not the strongest affection known? Is it not greater than even that of self-preservation? While we draw presumptions from shame, one affection of the mind, against the life of the prisoner, should we not give some weight to presumptions from parental love, an affection at least as strong, in favor of life?"[60]

Jefferson also might have intended to reinforce the natural bonds between parent and child through a pension plan for the families of soldiers involved in the Revolutionary War. Under the poor law as it was administered in Virginia, when families could not support themselves, the children were almost always removed from their families and bound out as apprentices by the overseers of the poor. This temporary pension plan, which gave food and other supplies to families who were poor and who had a father or son fighting in the Revolutionary War, began in fall 1779, during Jefferson's first term as governor.[61] It had the effect of reducing the rate of children removed from their natural parents and apprenticed, a removal process usually based on the poverty of the parents. Analysis of data collected from Frederick County, Virginia, reveals that the rate of children apprenticed dropped from 7.3 percent to 3.9 percent of all children between 1751-60 and 1781-90. Thus many more children were able to remain with their natural parents, particularly with their natural and legitimate mothers.[62] This would certainly fit in with Jefferson's emphasis on parental love and with the emphasis, explicit in Locke and Sidney and implicit in Jefferson's political thought, that parental power was separate from state power.

The poor law, as it had existed in Virginia and in England, had operated under the aegis of *parens patriae,* or the state as parent. Jefferson did not altogether dismember the old poor law in his revision of the laws. Indeed, that would have been an expensive step: for without apprenticeship, assuming that the state should not let these children starve, a system that let many children remain with their parents would have meant substantial transfer payments from the parish or county or the commonwealth of Viriginia to each family. Jefferson, instead, supplemented and found substitutes for the older policy, adding provisions for all apprentices to be able to attend the public schools that he was developing and adding the pension plan discussed above. He still, however, directed that every orphan who could not be maintained out of the estate which they were to inherit should be bound out, as well as mulattos and the children of the those who received poor relief.[63] The pension plan did not completely reform the poor law, yet in providing avenues for children to remain with their natural parents—when these were the children of soldiers fighting for their country—the pension law increased the separation between the powers of parents and the powers of the state, putting the responsibility for children ever more fully into the private familial domain.

The core of Jefferson's revision of the laws with respect to children, in his own eyes, was his Bill for the More General Diffusion of Knowledge, in which he provided three years of public education for all free children, male and female. For Jefferson, a formal education that included reading, writing, common arithmetic, and "Graecian, Roman, English and American History" was critical for making a republic work. Education helped the populace to protect its own exercise of natural rights, prevented tyranny, and encouraged the most "wise and honest," the most endowed with "genius and virtue," to rise to positions of leadership without regard to inequalities based on inherited wealth. Thus, for Jefferson, education, or the process of "illuminat[ing], as far as practicable, the minds of the people at large," granted people the reason necessary to make their government function properly, based on their consent and their participation.[64]

People should be promoted based upon their wisdom and virtue, not based on the abstractions of birth; and children should be excluded from positions of power. They were the unreasonable. They had not learned virtue and had not yet gained wisdom. They should not reach positions of power through "the accident of birth," that Sidney railed against, and they lost some of the legal privileges they had previously exercised. Childhood became extended because there was more emphasis on that development. And parents gained more power over their children as children lost some autonomy, and state power became more separated from parental power.

Conclusion

Jefferson himself did not always make clear what was new in his revision of the laws; regarding children, indeed, he was caught in broader changes. Given the tendency of the common law to conceal change because every alteration is based upon "precedent," it is sometimes hard to know whether Jefferson recognized the extent to which he was a part of changes that were being incorporated into the common and statute laws of England and America.[65] These changes grew out of the political theories that originated in England during the two revolutions of the seventeenth century, theories that were adopted and reinforced by Americans during our Revolutionary War. Broader changes included statutory changes in the initial requirements for a voting age that appeared in England and Virginia soon after the Glorious Revolution; also the shift in the minimum age for jury service which occurred in Virginia in 1792, but in England in 1694, the year before minimum age limits were attached to voting and being elected; and the shift in military service from sixteen to eighteen in Virginia in 1784. Aside from these statutory changes in Virginia, other changes occurred within the supposedly unchanging common law. Children lost the ability to testify as witnesses during the seventeenth and eighteenth centuries, part of a broader reform of the laws of evidence, a change also linked to the rise in age for jury service; and children's consent ceased to be requisite for trade apprenticeship contracts. I discuss these changes elsewhere.[66] They are linked to the distinction in political theory between the rational adult and the irrational child and occurred in the context of debate over who was reasonable and independent enough to fulfill citizenship rights, a debate in which age became increasingly relied upon as a gauge of reason and independence. The place of children in republican political theory and in Jefferson's revision of the laws illustrates some of the tensions within republican political theory itself. Whatever Jefferson might have felt about these other issues that affected the legal status of children, it is clear that Jefferson legally sought not to liberate children themselves, at least not until they became adults: he thereby set liberty and equality in the context of a theory of human development.

Jefferson, the Family, and Civic Education

Those who want to consider the place of "the family and public culture" in Thomas Jefferson's views on education face a daunting task. Because this is a topic that Jefferson himself did not treat systematically or formally in the way that he did such subjects as equality or nature or even slavery, those who want to examine it must do so indirectly. The index to the fine collection of Jefferson's writings that Merrill Peterson has compiled for the Library of America has no listing for "family," nor does the earlier Modern Library edition.[1] This apparent lacuna in the corpus of Jefferson's thought is something of a puzzle.

Contemporary scholars have noted that the American revolutionaries often used the language of the family to describe the relationship between America and Great Britain, comparing the king to an unfeeling parent and the colonies to a misused child.[2] Although Jefferson described the British as "unfeeling brethren" in a passage excised from the final version of the Declaration of Independence,[3] he did not usually write in the familial idiom. Perhaps the explanation is in part biographical: Jefferson's father died when he was fourteen, he was married for only ten years of his very long life, and his only son died before he could be given a name. For most of his life Jefferson presided over a household whose inhabitants were primarily his female kin. The family, as lived experience, would have been somewhat different for Jefferson than it was for most of his contemporaries.[4]

These facts noted, however, we would be doing both Jefferson and the tradition in which he wrote a grave disservice were we to argue that Jefferson's own family experience did anything more than shade his political thought. As both Holly Brewer and Frank Shuffelton point out, when Jefferson did happen to write about the family, he did so in terms that were part of a discourse shaped by such European thinkers as John Locke, Algernon Sidney, Francis Hutcheson, and Adam Smith. The greater puzzle is why Jefferson, whose mind ranged widely, did not examine the family and its relationship to public culture in a systematic or sustained way. It is the achievement of Holly Brewer, Michael Grossberg, and Frank Shuffelton that they have been able to tease out of Jefferson's family correspondence and legal papers, as well as the more familiar body of his writings, very specific notions about the relationship between the family and public culture. And these notions are all the more interesting for having been buried, as it were, in discussions ostensibly about other issues.

Considering that Jefferson's discussions of the family are generally oblique and that they are enveloped in his writings on other topics, it is significant that Brewer, Grossberg, and Shuffelton have found common threads running through those discussions. For example, they all have focused upon parent-child relations, which may also be generalized as the relationship between the current generation and the one that will follow. In so doing, they faithfully reflect Jefferson's concerns. While others of the revolutionary generation may have been interested in the metaphorical possibilities in marriage or brotherhood as representations of the bonds between relative equals,[5] Jefferson was drawn to the inherently unequal relationship between parents and their children.

The objective of Jefferson's practices and policies that treated the family was, as Brewer, Grossberg, and Shuffelton each point out, to tighten the mutual bonds between parents and children. As Holly Brewer shows, Jefferson thought the penalty for murder of one's child should be as severe as that for murder of one's parent. He also worked to eliminate a law that presumed that mothers who concealed the birth of their illegitimate children were guilty of murder if that infant was later found dead. It seemed to him that parental affection—"the strongest affection known"—was likely to prevail over the shame such women might feel at the birth of bastard children, so that there should be no presumption of guilt.[6] Jefferson also advocated a temporary pension for veterans of the Revolution, which would enable children to be cared for at home, by their parents, instead of being apprenticed to other families. Brewer suggests that here Jefferson was implicitly rejecting the doctrine of the state as parent upon which the poor law rested: For Jefferson, the blood family and not the state was the most appropriate parent.

Yet, as Grossberg points out, Jefferson was doing something more than shifting the balance of power between the state and a corporate family that could be as overbearing to the individuals who constituted it as any form of government. Grossberg sees in Jefferson's attempts to reform the aspects of the Virginia legal code that applied to the family a manifestation of Jefferson's egalitarianism. Grossberg presents us with a Jefferson who was first and foremost an egalitarian who recognized, in the words of Willi-Paul Adams, "'not only that everyone [must] enjoy equality before the law or have an equal voice in government but also that everyone have an equal share in the fruits of the common enterprise.'" In reforming the laws of inheritance, Jefferson would compel his fellow Virginians to "alter the structure of power" itself. Jefferson took aim at the English common law heritage as codified by Blackstone, which assumed "that the family was a corporate institution and the preservation of its property was the central responsibility of its members and the state." By enabling families to entail their estates, and pass them on to the eldest son, as well as by denying illegitimate children the right to inherit any portion of the parental estate, "English authorities had devised a practical plan for and issued a symbolic endorsement of the corporate preservation of the family estate as the central responsibility between generations."

In revised form, most of Jefferson's proposals were adopted, and many years later, the aged statesman would list their passage as among his life's greatest achievements: They formed "a system by which every fibre would be eradicated of antient or future aristocracy; and a foundation laid for a government truly republican." Implicitly, then, Jefferson considered the corporate family a vestige of aristocracy and the oppressive form of government it sustained. Grossberg, somewhat like Daniel Boorstin in his seminal work *The Lost World of Thomas Jefferson,*[7] suggests that Jefferson was much better at describing what he hoped to get rid of than outlining a program for the future. In the case of the family, this approach meant that Jefferson assumed that, once freed from unnatural and arbitrary restraint, the family would function in the way that nature had intended. Grossberg suggests that this vision of the family was not only similar to Jefferson's laissez-faire economics but was also, in fact, an important component of that political economy.

As Grossberg explains it, Jefferson's radical goal of "silently lessening the inequality of property" notwithstanding, "once the remnants of aristocratic controls had been repudiated by a republican revision" of the laws, "Jefferson's argument contained an implicit liberal antistatist assumption of distinct public and private realms and a priority on private action." On the one hand, a "state sponsored redistribution of wealth" would free each generation to start anew, writing a new constitution every nineteen years. On the other hand, when Jefferson imagined each family bequeathing equal shares of the parental estate to each child, male and female, he was creating a new form of family, "a collection of autonomous individuals bound together by affection." One of the objects of Jefferson's inheritance law reforms, then, was to unleash "the natural affection parents had for all their children." In the end, Grossberg suggests, this authorization of the affectionate family would work to limit the more radical possibilities inherent in Jefferson's theories of generational relations. Jefferson would not, after all, advocate the abolition of inheritance altogether.

The implications of this limitation upon Jefferson's radicalism is most clear in the writings of the following generations. Jefferson's vision of a radical redistribution of property would slip away, as revolutionary egalitarianism increasingly came to mean equality of opportunity. By the time that Henry St. George Tucker was adjudicating cases—in the 1830s—Jefferson's reforms had been codified in the law of the nation, which is another way of saying that inheritance law reform was interpreted, even by Jefferson's heirs, as pertaining not to the redistribution of wealth or power but to affection within the family. As Tucker put it, "our law of descents was

formed in no small degree upon the human affection; and the legislature very justly conceiving that the object of the law of descent was to supply the want of a will,
and that it should therefore conform in [e]very case, as nearly as might be, to the
probable current of those affections which would have given direction to the provision of such a will." Such propositions became so unexceptionable that even arch-
Federalists such as Daniel Webster and James Kent could subscribe to them.

"Shorn of Jefferson's redistributive dream of generational liberation," Grossberg
concludes, codification "had made inheritance reform a source of the pervasive
individualism that soon dominated American society. Far from Jefferson's intent, it
helped foster an often illusory generational independence as a 'race for life' that
every son and daughter must enter even though few could ever hope to win." The
family, then, sustains an unequal economic order, and it performs this task materi-
ally—by keeping property more or less intact from one generation to the next—and
ideologically, by making it appear that such an order is "natural," as natural as the
bonds of affection within a family.

It is somewhat startling to see Jefferson in this light. To be sure, a number of
scholars have identified Jefferson with the liberal individualism that would come to
prevail in America in the nineteenth century,[8] and the connections between liberal
individualism and the affectionate family, cut off from the wider society, have been
analyzed since Alexis de Tocqueville first noted them more than a century and a half
ago.[9] But Jefferson himself is usually associated with an older, almost Augustan family form, not the sentimental family of the Victorian period. On the one hand,
Jefferson adopted for himself and advocated for others a strict discipline over the display of emotion, and, on the other, he devoted most of his life to public service. He
was, as Jay Fliegelman has recently noted, a model of self-effacement.[10]

To be sure, Grossberg does not say that Jefferson imagined, sought, or would
have been pleased by the modern family that is isolated from the wider world and
works to perpetuate its inequalities. Grossberg sees Jefferson as a radical; the residue
of inequality perpetuated by the family is what was left when Jefferson's most radical impulses were frustrated or stripped away. Holly Brewer's essay, "Beyond
Education: Thomas Jefferson's 'Republican' Revision of the Laws Regarding
Children," suggests that those limitations in the Jeffersonian vision were intrinsic,
and hence, the relationship that would emerge in the nineteenth century between
the family and American society and politics is one that might have been anticipated, even if it had not been fully planned.

Brewer uses her discussion of Jefferson's proposed revision of the law to reveal
the limits of his egalitarianism. In a strikingly original formulation, she turns the
very premises of Jefferson's theories on education upside down and inside out. We
are, with good reason, accustomed to thinking of Jefferson as an advocate of education; indeed, it is the very premise of this conference. Throughout his lifetime,
Jefferson worked to establish systems of public education, and the crowning

achievement of his life was the creation of the University of Virginia. In both Jefferson's mind and the minds of his contemporaries, education was one of the requirements for the sort of democratic society that they hoped to create and sustain. This connection between democracy and education, which is premised upon reason, is so fundamental that it has been almost unquestioned.

Brewer begins by asking a very simple question, one that might appear almost rhetorical. Why, she wants to know, did children require education? It was because they were not yet reasonable. As Locke put it in *Two Treatises of Government*, children were "weak and helpless, without knowledge or understanding." As a consequence, they were incapable of granting the informed consent upon which government was supposed to rest. And if children could not consent to be ruled, even less were they capable themselves of ruling. Algernon Sidney—another political thinker whose influence on Jefferson is well-known—could find no better way of exposing Filmer's defense of monarchy than by pointing out that under it, blood heirs to the throne "all have an equal right to it; women and children are patriarchs; and the next in blood, without any regard to age, sex, or other qualities of the mind or body." Rule was supposed to be based upon consent, and rulers to be chosen for their merit, that is, their superior reason.

Here we are at the heart of the democratic tradition, with its critique of hereditary monarchy and its insistence that legitimate government rest upon the consent of the governed. And this is where Brewer finds "the inequalities that remained within a theory of equality," for if children could be excluded from civic life and placed under paternal authority, so could all others who appeared to be deficient in reason: women, as Sidney suggested, and later in America, Africans and Indians as well. Because the domination of children seemed so natural—and generally seems so even today—it was the pattern from which all other subjugations could be cut. Brewer's aim is not to provide an intellectual foundation for the contemporary children's rights movement, although her work certainly seems relevant to it,[11] but rather to draw our attention to a fundamental limitation in theories of democratic government. Even at their inception, these theories recognized and legitimated certain exclusions. "Liberty and equality were contextualized," Brewer concludes, "and linked to a theory of human development."

Hence we find Jefferson, the apostle of liberty, equality, and independence, advocating dependence for children. "To render a child independent of its parents," Jefferson wrote, "is to ruin it's education, it's morals, it's reputation and it's fortune." As Brewer shows, this perspective also clarifies a number of Jefferson's proposals, such as the elimination of primogeniture and entail, thereby simultaneously increasing "equality of opportunity for the younger generation"—Grossberg's point—and expanding "fathers' power over their children by increasing their control over inheritance." Several other proposals, such as raising the minimum age for election to the Virginia Senate, participation in the militia, and service on juries, also reveal what Brewer calls "the tension between control and liberty, equality and inequality, within Jefferson's political and legal thought." Once we recognize that Jefferson's commitment to equality and liberty was not unqualified, we can begin to understand how certain inequalities and exclusions—ones that applied not simply to children, but to women and racial minorities as well—could be woven into the fabric of American democratic liberalism.

To be sure, Jefferson never thought of himself as providing an ideological basis for perpetuating dependence and inequality within an egalitarian system. Nor did he aim specifically to strengthen adult control of children; rather, as Brewer suggests, his objective was to tighten the mutual bonds between parents and children. "The post which a parent may take most advantageous for his child is that of his bosom friend," Jefferson had written John Banister. Once again we see that the affectionate family, one in which, in true Lockean fashion, parents would play the part of friends, more than rulers, could sustain an unequal social order.[12] And although Grossberg is more impressed by Jefferson's radicalism than is Brewer, once again we find that this outcome was not the one that Jefferson intended. Instead, Jefferson assumed and sought to encourage a family bound by affection rather than force; but, as Frank Shuffelton suggests too, such a family, rather than remaking the world, would eventually retreat from it.

Much like Grossberg, Shuffelton discerns in Jefferson the best of intentions that collapse, finally, into an inward-turned modern family that has withdrawn from an increasingly competitive and consumerist world. "The Public and Domestic Spheres in Jefferson's Letters to His Family" is a careful reading of Thomas Jefferson's family correspondence. Shuffelton recognizes that during Jefferson's lifetime, "the family, like the nation, was in a period of transition." Jefferson, however, did not intend that the family would become a refuge from the world; instead, he believed it should be a training ground for participation in a vigorous public life. As Shuffelton puts it, Americans such as Jefferson "struggled under the banner of a professed egalitarian ethic to work out relationships between public life and private that did not simply oppose public and domestic life. Shaped by a still influential republican ideology, they attempted to socialize their children with the understanding that public, civic life was worth the concern of every citizen; moved by late eighteenth-century currents of sentimentalism and romanticism, they also sought to make the family a place which could nurture the child's emotional and affective identity."

Both Grossberg and Brewer examine Jefferson's ideas about the family; Shuffelton looks closely at the particularities of Jefferson's relationship with his own family. Jefferson constructed his family through a set of "exchanged texts," the letters that he exchanged with his daughters and grandchildren. These texts were both the substance and emblem of family life for Jefferson, the means by which he structured and imagined his family as well, trying to make it conform to his ideal of a family-in-society. Family life for Jefferson was a form of communication—among family members, between the family and society—for which the exchange of letters served as the best form of training. Although Jefferson tended to "polarize" public and private life, he "never abandoned his commitment to both public and domestic life, and he bridged the gap between them with letters that purported to bring private concerns to his public friends and public involvement to members of his family."

If, then, in his more categorical statements about the family, Jefferson did indeed polarize public and private life—and this is where Grossberg and Brewer lead us—in his epistolary interactions with his own kin, Jefferson tried to bridge that gulf. Even Jefferson's most manipulative letters to his daughters—for example the 1780 one to Patsy in which he told her that "the more you learn the more I love you, and I rest my happiness in life on seeing you beloved by all the world"—are interpreted in the light of a Lockean pedagogy. "What seems to us an almost shocking bit of emotional blackmail," Shuffelton observes, "was in many ways a rather conventional pedagogic maneuver at the time, a sentimentalized form of Locke's recommendation to make children 'conceive that those that are commended and in esteem for doing well will necessarily be beloved and cherished by everybody.'" Adam Smith's influence, Shuffelton suggests, is equally clear. Conscience, then, for Jefferson, was a sort of "moral conversation," not only among the members of the family, but with other "impartial spectators" with whom one might correspond, and communication was "a primary form of moral activity . . . making present those who were distant and putting the voice of the writer and the imagined voice of the recipient in dynamic play with each other."

Applying the theories of Jürgen Habermas, Shuffelton suggests that at the same time that Jefferson was constituting the family as a realm of warmth and affection, he was using correspondence to draw his young charges out into the public sphere, a "republic of letters." Shuffelton acknowledges that, especially when he was "under fire from political enemies, Jefferson tended to oppose the family and the world of politics in terms of their sentimental economies." We are all probably familiar with the letters in which Jefferson contrasted the bitterness of political life with the harmony of Monticello,[13] but Shuffelton seems to suggest that at the same time that Jefferson was constructing a private world into which he could retreat and lick his wounds, he was also struggling to maintain the connection between the private and public worlds. It is important to note—and here Shuffelton may offer a something of a corrective to Brewer and Grossberg—that Jefferson's fundamental commitment was to the public world. After all, we are celebrating Jefferson's 250th birthday because of his extraordinary accomplishments in the public sphere, not the private.

Shuffelton concludes by asking how well this strategy worked, but he is inclined to blame what he perceives as its deficiencies—none of the grandsons, for example, fulfilled the expectations entailed upon them by their heroic names—on changes extrinsic to the Jeffersonian vision. By the time that Jefferson's Randolph grandsons—Thomas Jefferson, James Madison, Benjamin Franklin, Meriwether Lewis, and George Wythe, not to mention the granddaughters, one of whom bore the name of the legendary Roman mother Cornelia—reached maturity, a "cult of sensibility that [was privileging] the family as a uniquely private and intimate space" was too powerful to resist.

Shuffelton implies that Jefferson would have wanted to resist this force that was transforming the relationship between the family and the public sphere. The best that Jefferson could do, according to Shuffelton, was to shift his focus to the University of Virginia, an extrafamilial institution that he conceived along familial lines, casting teacher and student in the roles of father and son. Yet even this effort was doomed to failure. The university, almost from its inception, was marked by student rebelliousness and a consumerist approach to the acquisition of knowledge, not the active engagement with and creation of letters that formed the basis for Jefferson's idealized image of the family. And as he allowed his correspondence with his grandchildren to lapse, "Jefferson implicitly reconceived his family as consumers of culture rather than producers of it, as a group that read news from the larger world without feeling the need to respond to it beyond the level of the neighborhood."

Hence with Shuffelton, as with Brewer and Grossberg, we end up in much the same place, as each of these scholars has traced the line that connects Jefferson's views on the family to a modern world in which the family appears to have withdrawn from the wider society, only to perform, from its position of isolation, the ideological work of legitimating the modern social, political, and economic order. Of course, Jefferson did not write about the family in precisely this way; indeed, Jefferson spoke and seemed to think about the family in terms of affection rather than power. The family, for Jefferson, was a natural unit ruled by love; it could be trusted to govern itself. This view of the family was implicit in Jefferson's First Inaugural, where he defined a "good government" as one that, after restraining men from "injuring one another, . . . shall leave them otherwise free to regulate their own pursuits of industry and improvement."[14]

Although Jefferson's view of government was strikingly negative, for he was acutely aware of its power to do harm, he was not himself setting up an opposition between a harmonious social and familial order and a dangerous and corrupt public sphere. He did not see the family as a refuge from the world or a counterweight to it; rather, he saw society—of which the family was a part—as the only world that mattered. In other words, I believe that Jefferson would have recoiled from the thought of a modern social, economic, and political order that stood outside of the domestic realm and in opposition to it. After all, that was what he had seen in Europe; America was supposed to be different. Yet if Brewer, Grossberg, and Shuffelton are right, that the outcome of Jefferson's views on the family was indeed a smaller social space for the family, but an increased ideological function—in some ways the exact reverse of Jefferson's vision—we must ask why Jefferson's presumed goals were so easily frustrated.

Part of the problem may lie in what Joyce Appleby has recently called Jefferson's "complex legacy."[15] Jefferson spoke in general and evocative terms whose implications could be altered by changing historical circumstances. Moreover, and perhaps somewhat surprising for a man who thought so carefully about so many matters, some elements of Jefferson's social and political thought remained undeveloped. Brewer, Grossberg, and Shuffelton show how Jefferson's views on the family can be teased out of Jefferson's plans for legal reform and his correspondence with his daughters and their children. Jefferson's ideas about the relationship between the family and the wider world may be even harder to put together. As Shuffelton has noted, Jefferson sometimes seems to have assumed a dichotomy between the public and private spheres, yet it is not always clear just which institutions Jefferson considered public and which private. Or, to be more precise, the family, surely, was in the private sphere, and government in the public, but where, in this scheme, did Jefferson situate society?

As Shuffelton notes, the public sphere represented a middle space, in between the family and the state. These are Habermas's terms, and they are quite useful in analyzing Jefferson's thought, but they are not precisely the ones he would have used. What Habermas calls the public sphere is essentially what Jefferson termed "society," but its antithesis was not so much the private realm of the family as government (which Habermas called the "state").[16] This was a distinction that Paine observed in *Common Sense* when he pronounced that "society is produced by our wants, and government by our wickedness; the former promotes our happiness *positively* by uniting our affections, the latter *negatively* by restraining our vices. . . . Society is in every state a blessing, but government even in its best state is but a necessary evil."[17] Jefferson's First Inaugural, in which he also asked his countrymen to "restore to social intercourse that harmony and affection without which liberty and even life itself are but dreary things,"[18] was premised upon the same political sociology.

Shuffelton is quite correct, I believe, when he argues that Jefferson wanted to draw his daughters and their children out into this public realm, that he intended to educate them, boys and girls both, for social life, a sphere much more extensive than that of the household or family. Yet at the same time, other of his writings, especially the letters written to his daughters when he was frustrated with his role as a public servant, suggest that Jefferson thought of the family as the epitome of the private sphere. Hence in 1798 he would tell his daughter Martha that the seat of government represented "every thing which can be disgusting" and "Monticello and my dear family . . . every thing which is pleasurable."[19] Yet several years later, when Martha herself became frustrated by the intrusion of the public into what she thought was the private familial sphere of Monticello, her father equivocated; the public could be barred from Monticello only "by a revolting conduct which would undo the whole labor of our lives."[20] Indeed, as Shuffelton notes, Jefferson had long encouraged a number of his friends to move near him in Albemarle. "With such a society," he told one of them, "I could once more venture home and lay myself up for the residue of life, quitting all its contentions which grow daily more and more insupportable. . . . Life is of no value but as it brings us gratifications. Among the most valuable of these is rational society."[21] One of the chief labors of Jefferson's life was the establishment of just this sort of rational society, which seems to me to be something more than than "symbolic augmentations" of the family. Jefferson could not imagine that his family alone could sustain him.

Jefferson, then, spun out two threads of social analysis simultaneously. One posed the family and the government as opposites, and the other gave the antipode of "government" the name "society." Jefferson was always clear about which side of happiness government might be found on; the precise relationship between society and the family, however, he never worked out. From the terms in which he described them, however, we may discern that for Jefferson the family was, ideally, a realm of pure affection and society, one of rational discourse. Still, because Jefferson, as something of a sentimentalist,[22] did not sharply distinguish between affection and intellect, this distinction cannot be a clear one. Instead, it was a matter of emphasis, as when Jefferson described home as "the only scene where, for me, the sweeter affections of life have any exercise."[23] But here, the contrast was not to society but to the world of politics.

Perhaps Jefferson felt no need to clarify the relationship between the family and society because that distinction probably would have been of pressing interest only to women. This, essentially, was the clarification his daughter Martha had demanded when she asked why they had to entertain so many visitors at Monticello, but it was a clarification her father was unable to make. Having described the public realm as one in which he was "surrounded by enemies and spies," in contrast to home, "where all is peace and harmony," Jefferson could not very well turn around and insist that the claims of the public sphere outweighed those of the home. Instead, Jefferson claimed that the visitors were "evidences of the general esteem which we have been able all our lives trying to merit,"[24] as if everyone came to the home of the man who was soon to become president simply to honor him, and not to do the nation's business. The home, unlike society, was a place where, by definition, political work could not be done.

Jefferson was, of course, an extraordinary public servant who disparaged the realm of politics, and just as he had difficulties in describing the role of government in positive, rather than negative terms, so also was he almost incapable of describing political life in a way that rendered it as honorable or appealing. It was only the individual public servant—he who merited "general esteem"—not public political life, that was worthy. And that worthiness was born and renewed within the family because, finally, that was the place where politics could not enter.

Surely we must take this rather ambivalent attitude toward political life into consideration when we try to understand the role that Jefferson imagined for the family in civic education. It may explain, for example, both the reach and the limitations of Jefferson's vision of the "republic of letters" as a form of civic education. Perhaps Shuffelton's analysis may serve as a corrective or balance to the misogyny that is sometimes imputed to Jefferson.[25] Indeed, Shuffelton makes a valiant effort to persuade us that Jefferson wanted to draw the women in his family, and by extension all women, out of the confines of the home into the public sphere of letters. Surely his correspondence with his daughters and granddaughters and, as Shuffelton has shown elsewhere, with Abigail Adams did just that.[26] The republic of letters could embrace literate women; and that may be the extent of its reach— marking its outer bounds, as well. For we must be careful not to conflate the republic of letters with the republic itself, that is, with the realm of politics.

Jefferson was eager to draw his female kin out into society, the realm that "unite[s] our affections." He could imagine no place for them, however, in the realm of politics itself. As he wrote Anne Willing Bingham from Paris in 1788, "All the world is politically mad. Men, women, and children talk nothing else, & you know that naturally they talk much, loud, & warm. Society is spoilt by it, at least for those who, like myself, are but lookers on. —You too have had your political fever. But our good ladies, I trust, have been too wise to wrinkle their foreheads with politics. They are contented to soothe & calm the minds of their husbands returning ruffled from political debate. They have the good sense to value domestic happiness above all other, and the art to cultivate it beyond all others. . . . Recollect the women of this capital, some on foot, some on horses, & some in carriages hunting pleasure in the streets, in routs & assemblies, and forgetting that they have left it behind in their nurseries; compare them with our own countrywomen . . . and confess that it is a comparison of Amazons and Angels."[27] Jefferson disparaged politics and imagined women as its antidote, yet we must not forget that the political sphere was the world in which he achieved his well-deserved and lasting fame.[28]

There is a gap, then, between Jefferson's experience as a political leader and his ability to characterize those activities in positive terms. Likewise, there is a discrepancy between his formal and theoretical consideration of female education and the attention he devoted to it in his own family. In 1818 he admitted to Nathaniel Burwell that "a plan of female education has never been a subject of systematic contemplation with me. It has occupied my own attention so far only as the education of my own daughters occasionally required."[29] This admission from a man who thought systematically about virtually everything else is quite amazing. Jefferson's confession suggests that when he made provision for three years of education for every free female child in his "Bill For the More General Diffusion of Knowledge"— the minimum that would be offered all free male children[30]—he had not given this portion of his plan very much thought.

Nonetheless, Jefferson's daughter Martha and several of her daughters must have been among the best educated women of their day. Shuffelton describes the way in which Jefferson cultivated his daughters' and granddaughters' intellects: He gave them books, told them to read them, and engaged them in conversation about them. Years later, one of his granddaughters would reminisce, "My Bible came from him, my Shakespeare, my first writing-table, my first handsome writing-desk . . . ."[31] He encouraged his female charges to observe the natural world around them and to describe for him what they saw. After his retirement, when he would retreat to Poplar Forest, he would often take several of his granddaughters with him; all of them would spend much of their time in study. Jefferson described these young women as "the severest students I ever met with."[32] We can get some notion of the nature of these young women's studies when we note that Ellen would name her twin sons Algernon and Sidney.[33] There is also significant evidence from Grossberg's paper that Jefferson was aware of and sensitive to some of the injustices that women had suffered; his drafts of revisions in the inheritance laws specified again and again that estates should descend equally "to all the children, or to all the brothers and sisters" . . . . "females shall have equal rights with males." If, as Grossberg suggests— rather convincingly, I should add—that these provisions in favor of partible inheritance would foster equality of opportunity, we must wonder what sort of opportunities for women Jefferson imagined.

I believe that Shuffelton, Grossberg, and Brewer are essentially correct in subsuming Jefferson's attenuated discussions about gender under their analyses of his thought on the family and public culture. As we have noted, Jefferson was much more interested in intergenerational relations than in those between women and men. When Jefferson did think about women, particularly in connection with politics or education, he could not help locating them in the family. When Nathaniel Burwell asked Jefferson for some comments about female education, Jefferson replied that his daughter would be "a better judge of the practical part than myself."[34] That Jefferson never thought systematically about the education of women even in the company of the severest students he ever met with surely tells us how unimportant he considered this topic to the welfare of the republic.

There are two apparent contradictions, then, in Jefferson's thinking about the family and civic education; or more precisely, there are gaps between his practice and his precepts. Jefferson disparaged political life, and, hence, the life that he, for most of his years, led. He was unable to represent that world as meaningful or valuable even to his daughters. At the same time, Jefferson ignored the question of female education, even though he equipped his daughters and his granddaughters too with extraordinary educations. When Jefferson thought of "a plan for . . . education," he thought primarily in the terms he had laid out in the "Bill for the More General Diffusion of Knowledge," whose objective, of course, was civic education. Holly Brewer's work suggests that this exclusion of women from the political sphere may have been inherent in Jefferson's political thought. Like children, women may have—in theory that is—lacked reason, and that deficiency, as much as their ability to "soothe and calm the minds of their husbands" may have dictated their exclusion from politics. However it was, when Jefferson spoke about women and politics, he fell into, or perhaps he invented, clichés—enemies and spies, amazons and angels. Gone was the realm of society where educated and polite individuals of both sexes could meet on a common ground, uniting in their affections. It was society that Jefferson craved, and it was society—the "harmony and affection" of "social intercourse"—that was a blessing, but Jefferson could not find a means to integrate it into his sociology.

The legacy for us diminishes politics and the family both, robbing the one of the capacity for morality and meaning, and the other of a meaningful connection to the world beyond the home. That Jefferson did not intend these outcomes seems clear, yet that these were the logical results of his thinking about the relationship of the family to civic education seems just as evident, as the fine work of Holly Brewer, Michael Grossberg, and Frank Shuffelton shows. More troubling still is that Jefferson's own experience in government and the family both contradicted what is, finally, his clichéd depiction of both realms. That Jefferson either could not or would not attempt to think about these problems systematically is a disappointment to those of us who revere so much of the body of his thought.

Rather than concluding on that solemn note, however, let me seek to recover a portion of the Jeffersonian legacy. It is something that I cannot fully explain, for it is in some measure inconsistent with Jefferson's occasional musings on women and education. It is the part of Jefferson that enabled him to take his granddaughters, those severe students, on educational retreats to Poplar Forest, where they whiled away the hours, all of them lost in their books until "the twilight of the evening" when they would "sally out" onto the terrace to exercise and perhaps discuss what they had read.[35] That this extraordinary man who thought so carefully about almost everything that came to his attention could not incorporate the implications of this exquisite family tableau into his political theories or even into his systematic thinking on education does not mean that we cannot complete the task.

II

An Informed Citizenry

DOUGLAS L. WILSON

Jefferson and Literacy

In common with many of the founders of the American republic, Thomas Jefferson subscribed to the Ciceronian ideal, the belief that persons of privilege had an obligation to cultivate their advantages and gifts and to employ them for the good of their country. But whereas most of his fellow founders and people in fortunate circumstances generally tended to be wary and mistrustful of the general populace and doubtful about their capacities, one of the things that set Jefferson apart was a radical faith in the ability of ordinary citizens to arrive at responsible decisions, political as well as moral. To put such faith in the great unwashed seemed to some of his contemporaries naive, to others foolhardy, and to those who distrusted Jefferson's motives, it appeared an expression of a demagogic wish to promote himself politically with a large number of potential voters. But Jefferson persisted in his belief, and over the course of a long life, he never changed. If anything, he became even more convinced.

In the hindsight of history, the misgivings about Jefferson and his faith in the ordinary citizen may appear ill-founded, and reservations on the subject of democracy may seem uncharitable or undiscerning, or both. But this would be to underestimate the degree to which Jefferson's very attitudes and opinions have helped shape America's developing culture. Jefferson's firmly held belief in the judgment of the ordinary citizen may be explained partly as an outgrowth of the moral sense philosophy he embraced, which held that the sense of right and wrong is inborn in every human being and does not need to be taught. But I wish to suggest that it also had to do, in large part, with his experience as a reader and his ideas about literacy.

Literacy is not Jefferson's word for the subject at hand; it is ours. But what we call literacy and see today as a prime issue in education, Jefferson understood very well. And his extraordinary faith in its potential, like his faith in the judgment of ordinary people, derived in part from his belief in the transforming power of reading and the written word. From an early age, Jefferson showed a propensity for study and a love of learning. He maintained all his life that he was constitutionally ill-suited for politics and public life, and in his declining years he insisted that he would never have involved himself in governmental affairs had not the times he lived in demanded it. Certainly he made the most of his opportunities, for he somehow contrived, in an unusually busy life, to read and absorb more than most could manage in a lifetime of leisure.

He was bookish almost to a fault. His biographer, Merrill D. Peterson, affirms that "Jefferson was dependent on books, tended to take his knowledge from them rather than from direct experience, and approached the world with studied eyes."[1] Reading was not only Jefferson's principal source of information; it was apparently his principal source of pleasure as well. "Those, which depend on ourselves," he once wrote, "are the only pleasures a wise man will count on: for nothing is ours which another may deprive us of. Hence the inestimable value of the intellectual pleasures."[2]

Jefferson's belief in the efficacy of literacy is at least partly traceable to the times and traditions in which he was raised. David D. Hall has called attention to the urgency with which literacy was pursued in colonial New England, and he has shown that what he calls the "uses of literacy" were primarily religious. For these early Americans, Hall says, "Literacy and religion were inseparable. So everyone assumed, and especially those in charge of the civil state. According to the Massachusetts school law of 1647, the very future of the Protestant religion was bound up with knowing how to read."[3] This reminds us that one of the principal and most persistent issues of the Protestant Reformation centered on the reading of the Bible and that America in the seventeenth and eighteenth centuries was largely a Protestant outpost.

At the height of the Stamp Act crisis in 1765, when Jefferson was still a student, John Adams published an attack on the arbitrary authority of kings and established churches, which he described as the principal reason the New England forefathers had emigrated to America. Such people, he argued, have always understood that the kings and churchmen are the enemies of knowledge, as well as of freedom. "Wherever a general knowledge and sensibility have prevailed among the people," he wrote, "arbitrary government and every kind of oppression have lessened and disappeared in proportion."[4] Americans, he pointed out, have instituted common schools and encouraged education because knowledge is the enemy of tyranny and the means of freedom. In this context, Adams writes: "A native of America who cannot read and write is as rare an appearance as a Jacobite or a Roman Catholic, that is, as rare as a comet or an earthquake."[5]

Jefferson was not the militant and combative Protestant that Adams was, but following the lead of his intellectual hero Voltaire, he regarded the established church—Roman or Anglican—as the enemy of freedom, and he shared Adams's view that promoting the ability to read among the citizenry generally was an effective weapon against tyranny. This was certainly behind his determined effort to secure legislation to ensure religious freedom in Virginia, the drafting of which he ever regarded as one of his proudest achievements. At the same time, and as part of the same general effort to put the new state of Virginia on the road to progress, Jefferson drafted legislation to establish a public school system that he called A Bill for the More General Diffusion of Knowledge (1779). The language of the prologue is especially revealing. It declares that the best means of resisting tyranny is "to illuminate, as far as practicable, the minds of the people at large, and more especially to give them knowledge of those facts, which history exhibiteth, that, possessed thereby of the experience of other ages and countries, they may be enabled to know ambition under all its shapes, and prompt to exert their natural powers to defeat its purposes."[6]

Here Jefferson strikes a note that he would sound over and over again in his writings—an affirmation of the crucial role of history, especially ancient history, in education for citizenship. With Charles Rollin, the compiler of the most widely read history of the ancient world in the eighteenth century, Jefferson believed that "history may properly be called the common school of mankind, equally open and useful to great and small."[7]

Universal Education

Jefferson's Bill for the More General Diffusion of Knowledge failed to pass in the revolutionary era, but he kept pushing it. He wrote John Adams years later, "I have great hope that some patriotic spirit will, at a favorable moment, call it up, and make it the key-stone of the arch of our government."[8] Another of his ideas that did not at first catch on in Virginia, but which he kept encouraging there and elsewhere, was a provision for public libraries. It is clear from an explanation of his basic idea made in 1809 that his rationale, like that given for public schools, was conceived in political terms.

> The people of every country, are the only safe guardians of their own rights, and are the only instruments which can be used for their destruction. And certainly they would never consent to be so used where they not deceived. To avoid this they should be instructed to a certain degree. I have often thought that nothing would do more extensive good at small expense than the establishment of a small circulating library in every county, to consist of a few well-chosen books, to be lent to the people of the country under such regulations as would secure their safe return in due time. These should be such as would give them a general view of other history, and particular view of that of their own country, a tolerable knowledge of geography, the elements of Nature, Philosophy, of Agriculture, and Mechanics.[9]

For Jefferson, a direct correlation obtained between literacy and successful self-government; the one was necessary to ensure the future of the other. Unlike the New England Puritans and their descendants, Jefferson's religion was enlightenment, and he believed it came—the way faith came to a Protestant—to all who opened their minds and hearts to it. With literacy came knowledge and discernment, and with these came the means of safeguarding self-government and independence. Thus the link between literacy and successful citizenship was unambiguous and direct. Such was his devotion to forging this link that when he heard of a proposed provision in the Spanish constitution to withhold citizenship from people who could not read and write, he endorsed it enthusiastically as a wise innovation, apparently without considering that it may have been intended to screen from the governmental process the very people he wanted to bring in.[10]

Like a number of Jefferson's hopeful ideals, his belief in the necessary connection between basic literary and an informed citizenry eventually took its place in the nation's creed, but in our own time, like so much of what was once taken for granted, it has come in for critical reexamination. In the past twenty-five years, the concept of literacy has been widely investigated, and its historical role in our national life has been searchingly reassessed. Simply what literacy is or means has been the subject of considerable dispute. The educational historian Carl Kaestle observes that "Although at first glance the term 'literacy' seems straightforward, it proves very slippery. It can refer to a wide range of reading and writing skills, and historians' definitions vary."[11] Nor are historians of literacy agreed on the historical significance of literacy. Some have seen literacy as "liberating and enlightening," as having a role in "widening mental horizons and bolstering rationality," whereas others "have seen literacy as an ideology of middle-class schooling, in keeping with the trend in revisionist educational history to view schooling as an imposition."[12]

Jefferson was assuredly a wise man, but he was not all-wise. His thinking had the limitations inherent in his own ideas. He began with the notion that a basic and general literacy, combined with the solid common sense which he believed to be the natural possession of ordinary people, would make for an intelligent and reliable citizenry, who could be depended upon to make responsible decisions for themselves and their communities. But it is doubtful that he could have had in mind the more comprehensive notion of cultural literacy that is currently being urged as essential for effective citizenship in our own times. Jefferson seems to have believed that the more sophisticated determinations based on a broad cultural knowledge would remain the domain of the more gifted and better educated class of citizens, who would act in behalf of the general population.

But the notion that Jefferson's beliefs and efforts, in promoting universal schooling for all citizens, male and female, were part of a conservative force serving conservative, rather than liberating ends is problematical, to say the least. Kaestle notes that "Literacy can serve many purposes, sometimes traditional and constraining, sometimes innovative and liberating."[13] Jefferson's record as an innovator in social and political matters and his ardent commitment to individual liberty would seem to defy any attempt to construe his intentions as conservative or constraining.

But if schooling was for literacy, what was literacy for? Cathy N. Davidson addresses this question in a provocative book on reading in the early national period and makes the point that the debate over literacy has ideological implications, as well as historiographic ones. "Literacy," she allows, "is not simply the ability to decode letters upon a page, the ability to sign a name instead of making a mark.

Literacy is a *value.* In a democracy especially, literacy becomes almost a matter of principle, a test of the moral fiber of a nation. Revolutionary societies often proclaim their validity by boasting of improving literacy levels, and John Adams's insistence on universal literacy implicitly asserts a vision of a fair and equitable nation."[14] What is interesting here is that Davidson goes on to criticize Adams for having motives other than "a fair and equitable nation" in advancing the cause of universal literacy. Adams, she says, "suspecting that social divisions were fixed in human nature, did not believe that public education would amalgamate the lower orders into the higher, but that education would bring the unprivileged into a more compliant attitude toward authority and would foster 'the Virtues and Talents of the People' and even help quell the 'affrays and Riots' that plagued Boston during the post-revolutionary era."[15]

However accurate this might be with respect to Adams, it will not do for Jefferson. Submissiveness among the citizenry was the opposite of what he had in mind. Especially when young, Jefferson took pleasure in the self-assertion of ordinary citizens and even their rambunctiousness in standing up to authority. The man who advocated universal schooling in Virginia was the same man who believed in the armed resistance to authority and thought a revolution every twenty years might be a good thing.

Literacy and Self-Government

Jefferson saw at the time of his 1779 education bill—and continued to see and say clearly—that self-government depended on widespread literacy. This doctrine is strikingly evident in one of his most famous and most quoted remarks, which is usually rendered thus: "Were it left to me to decide whether we should have a government without newspapers, or newspapers without a government, I should not hesitate a moment to prefer the latter." But like so many sound bites that are plucked from their contexts, the full resonance of Jefferson's meaning in that passage is muted by its isolation. Jefferson was writing from his diplomatic post in Paris and reporting to a friend back home on the European reaction to Shays' rebellion. He had a real sympathy for the plight of the insurrectionary Massachusetts farmers who were facing ruin as a result of the financial after-effects of the American Revolution, and this comes out in his letter to Edward Carrington:

> I am persuaded myself that the good sense of the people will always be found to be the best army. They may be led astray for a moment, but will soon correct themselves. The people are the only censors of their governors: and even their errors will tend to keep these to the true principles of their institution. To punish these errors too severely would be to suppress the only safeguard of the public liberty. The way to prevent these irregular interpositions of the people is to give them

full information of their affairs thro' the channel of the public papers, and to contrive that those papers should penetrate the whole mass of the people. The basis of our governments being the opinion of the people, the very first object should be to keep that right; and were it left to me to decide whether we should have a government without newspapers, or newspapers without a government, I should not hesitate a moment to prefer the latter. But I should mean that every man should receive those papers and be capable of reading them.[16]

E. D. Hirsch, Jr., has noted that "Jefferson's last comment is often omitted when the passage is quoted, but it's the crucial one."[17] One may agree that the frequent omission of the admonition about everyone receiving and being capable of reading the newspapers is regrettable and distorting, but I would argue that what is even more important in understanding Jefferson's meaning is the surrounding context. Rather than the horrifying spectacle of the people turning treacherously on their own government, what Jefferson sees in Shays' rebellion is the phenomenon of ordinary citizens defying and attempting to chastise their governors for the harmful effects of bad government. "The people are the only censors of their governors," he says "and even their errors will tend to keep these [that is, the governors] to the true principles of their institution." Therefore, he argues, "To punish these errors too severely would be to suppress the only safeguard of the public liberty."

The only way of ameliorating the situation, according to Jefferson, is to provide full information to keep public opinion—the very basis of democratic government—on the right track. And this is where newspapers and the importance of universal literacy come in. An informed public, Jefferson is saying, is the superior of its government, which is why an informed people without a government is preferable to a government with an ignorant public. Perhaps no other passage in his writings so perfectly exemplifies Jefferson's deeply ingrained belief in the necessary connection between literacy and self-government, and indeed, the sense in which he sees self-government, for most of mankind, as self-preservation.

The Experience of Reading

Jefferson's views on the direct connection between literacy and citizenship are indeed important and repay study, but I want to propose that Jefferson's deep-seated belief in the power of literacy, in its efficacy for an expanding and more durable democracy, went beyond his Enlightenment presuppositions and his progressive vision of human affairs. Commingled with the idealism of the visionary there was, in Jefferson, an abiding practicality as well. To give him his due, we must acknowledge that he based his ideas not only on the hopes and promises of theory but on the concrete evidence of actual practice and his own personal experience. In this connection, we must bear in mind that in his own life, nothing had proven so important and consequential from his earliest years as the experience of reading, and, in the long run, nothing directed and shaped his developing consciousness so significantly as his early attachment to books.

Merrill Peterson's remark that Jefferson was dependent on books and that he "tended to take his knowledge from them rather than from direct experience" may raise the question of the extent to which he could be out of touch with the world of affairs. But if one grants the truth of this characterization, it is clear that Jefferson's personal experience as a reader was more than that of one who wished to broaden himself and supplement his knowledge of the world; for Jefferson, the activity of reading was more fundamental than that, and more profound.

Jefferson virtually began life as a reader. The tradition in his family is that he had read all the books in his father's modest library by the time he was five, but even if this tradition were off by five years, it would still point to a remarkable and indicative circumstance. We know that Jefferson regarded his love of reading as the outcropping of a natural disposition and that it persisted unabated from his childhood to the very end of his life. At the age of seventy-five, he confessed to John Adams that he still possessed "a canine appetite for reading."[18] As such, his love of reading cannot be said to have been the product of a calculated, rational program for self-improvement, though the discipline that he imposed on his busy life to allow ample time for reading certainly was. But one important result of Jefferson's early career as a devoted reader was surely his discovery, through his own experience, of the transforming power of reading.

One of the things that has puzzled generations of Jefferson students has been the apostrophe to fiction he included in his famous letter to Robert Skipwith in 1771. There he argues that the reader's encounter with fictional representations of moral or immoral acts engages, and thus exercises and strengthens, the reader's innate moral sense. What is remarkable about his contention that "the entertainments of fiction are useful as well as pleasant" is that he does not himself seem to have been a reader of novels. At least part of the puzzlement is resolved when we recognize two things. The first is that the theory of the moral utility of fiction expounded so eloquently in the Skipwith letter belongs not to Jefferson but to one of his intellectual heroes, Lord Kames, and that Jefferson was trying out on Skipwith the ideas and terminology he had been reading in Kames's *Elements of Criticism.*[19] The second is a matter that underlies Jefferson's defense of fiction in the Skipwith letter and presumably was more important—an acknowledgment and confirmation of the power of reading itself to directly affect human attitudes and behavior.

Evidence abounds that Jefferson regarded the experience of reading as revolutionary, as having the power to subvert one's understanding and uproot even the most deeply imbedded beliefs. Reading David Hume's history of England as a young man, he would later testify, had cost him dearly: "I remember well the enthusiasm with which I devoured it when young," he wrote nearly fifty years later, "and the length of time, the research and reflection, which were necessary to eradicate the poison it had instilled into my mind."[20] Reading Lord Bolingbroke's *Philosophical Works* at about the same age seems to have had an equally decisive effect on the young Jefferson's attitudes toward orthodox Christian doctrines, though he apparently experienced no regret at this development.[21] In fact, he probably had in mind the example of the subversion of his own orthodox beliefs in advising his nephew, Peter Carr, to read the Bible as he would Livy or Tacitus. "Do not be frightened from this inquiry by any fear of it's consequences . . . Your own reason is the only oracle given you by heaven, and you are answerable not for the rightness but the uprightness of the decision."[22] Reading could be disruptive, but the disruptions authorized by reason were necessary, purposeful, and creative.

For a person who habitually troubled himself with the problems of society and its prospects for amelioration and advancement, such an insight had notable implications. If reading can affect readers and, of itself, alter their behavior, it follows that it might be the agent of real and potentially dramatic change. Changes in the world of human affairs must, of course, find their way beyond the imaginations of readers and issue in concrete actions, but reading could be a meaningful precipitant as well as an engine of augmentation. In a democratic climate of openness and possibility, the spread of literacy thereby takes on an added importance that potentially equals or even surpasses that of assuring an informed and responsive citizenry. This dimension of Jeffersonian literacy, with its capacity for disruption and revolutionary results, might be called "liberation." Some historians of literacy in America have argued that, statistically at least, "literacy's efficacy in improving individual life chances was a 'myth,' "[23] but I should like, in what follows, to cite two divergent but telling examples that put Jefferson's faith in the liberating power of literacy in a different light.

A Liberating and Transforming Force

Jefferson was aristocratic in many ways, certainly in his tastes and his style of living, but he recognized as few did the wellspring of natural talent and ability that issued from even the poorest and least fortunate segments of society. This is, of course, the basis of his idea of a "natural aristocracy" that he enunciated in his famous exchange on the subject with John Adams. In his letter, Jefferson had occasion to speak of the way that science, or knowledge, had "liberated the ideas of those who read and reflect."[24] Such liberation might be genuinely ameliorative, as in the case of the European readers Jefferson had reference to, but the actual example of others suggest it could also be truly transforming.

In recent years, the extraordinary case of Frederick Douglass teaching himself to read and thus deliberately unfitting himself for slavery has become more familiar, but it bears retelling in the present context, if only to make clear the radical extent to which the transforming power of literacy might reach. Taken from a Maryland plantation as a child and installed as a servant in a Baltimore family, Douglass was taught his ABCs and the rudiments of reading and spelling by his kindly mistress. But his master soon put a stop to these lessons, with an explanation that Douglass was fortunate enough to overhear: "if you teach that nigger (speaking of myself) how to read, there would be no keeping him. It would forever unfit him to be a slave." These words came to the young slave as a "special revelation, explaining dark and mysterious things, with which my youthful understanding had struggled, but struggled in vain. I now understood what had been to me a most perplexing difficulty—to wit, the white man's power to enslave the black man . . . From that moment, I understood the pathway from slavery to freedom."[25]

Douglass's recognition of the liberating potential of literacy and his tenacious struggle to teach himself to read is a classic example of self-liberation. Nothing in his remarkable *Narrative* is more memorable than his depiction of his resourceful efforts to become literate, such as trading bread to street urchins for reading lessons, and experiencing, in his success as a reader, alternating measures of joy and agony. He thrilled at the discovery of a wider and more wondrous world but found, at the same time, "that learning to read had been a curse rather than a blessing. It had given me a view of my wretched condition, without the remedy. It opened my eyes to the horrible pit, but to no ladder upon which to get out."[26] But because of the revolution in his outlook occasioned by his reading, Douglass did succeed in getting out and, of course, went on to make a profound difference in the ultimate demise of slavery.

The memorable episode of teaching himself to read has come to be regarded as more than a mere autobiographical anecdote in Douglass's *Narrative*. According to Dana Nelson Salvino, in a study of race and literacy in antebellum America, recent students of the *Narrative* consider that "the most important message in the work is that literacy leads to freedom, that literacy *constitutes* freedom." Salvino goes on to say that these students "reflect a powerful view held throughout the Western world, and especially in America: knowledge is freedom. Particularly, knowledge begins with literacy, and freedom is constituted by the possibility of moral, economic, and social advancement."[27] A more unmistakably Jeffersonian idea is hard to imagine.

Like Frederick Douglass's, Abraham Lincoln's rise to a position of great consequence in American history might be described as literacy-related and even literacy-driven. In spite of the fact that his parents were barely literate, Lincoln became an ardent reader at an early age and in this way acquired his education almost entirely through his own efforts. Though Lincoln's boyhood reading has ascended in the American imagination to the level of myth, the evidence reveals that his actual feats of reading were worthy of the legend. Growing up in a house with very few books except for the Bible, he seems to have borrowed and read every book in the surrounding neighborhood that he could lay his hands on. After he left home at age twenty-two, he settled into a program of disciplined study, teaching himself such things as grammar and elocution, mathematics, and history.[28] In his maturity, Lincoln talked and wrote very little about the process of self-education that had been so important to his rise, and when forced to comment on it, he was frankly disparaging, as when he described his education in a biographical questionnaire for congressmen with a single word: "defective." Yet he emerged from this process as a person not only sufficiently educated to practice a profession with a rare degree of proficiency, but even more significantly, as a master of language.

Though their backgrounds and experience were vastly different, there is a propitious linkage between Jefferson and Lincoln. Lincoln's admiration for Jefferson's political principles and his championing of the Declaration of Independence are well known, and there is little doubt that Lincoln consciously drew on Jefferson's example to focus his own political thinking and to give it expression. Moreover, Lincoln's rise from obscurity to greatness seems to bear out Jefferson's faith in the power of a democratic system to summon forth talent and ability even from the least advantaged segments of society.

In a letter to John Adams, Jefferson focused attention on conditions in Europe in terms of the irreversible effects of printing on human culture. "The light which has been shed on mankind by the art of printing," he wrote to Adams, "has eminently changed the condition of the world. As yet that light has dawned on the midling classes only of the men of Europe. The kings and the rabble of equal ignorance, have not yet recieved it's rays; but it continues to spread. And, while printing is preserved, it can no more recede than the sun return on his course."[29] By an interesting coincidence, Abraham Lincoln's only surviving public lecture, "Discoveries and Inventions," deals with the same subject and bears strikingly on the issues at hand.

Although Lincoln was a skilled platform speaker who could hold and even transfix an audience, his 1859 lecture seems not to have been well received and was generally accounted a failure. The testimony of his close friend Joseph Gillespie may help to explain why, for Gillespie noted that in endeavoring "to trace out the source and development of language," Lincoln "was surprised to find his investigations in that direction so interesting and instructive to himself."[30] In working up his lecture, Lincoln apparently became so deeply interested in his subject that he uncharacteristically lost sight of the need to make it entertaining for his audience.

The lecture begins with a consideration of the activity that precedes printing: "Writing, the art of communicating thoughts to the mind, through the eye—is the great invention of the world." Writing deserves this primacy, according to Lincoln, because it enables us "to converse with the dead, the absent, and the unborn, at all distances of time and space."[31] Printing, he goes on to say, is "but the other half—and in real utility, the better half—of writing; and . . . both together are but the assistants of speech in the communication of thoughts between man and man. When man was possessed of speech alone, the chances of invention, discovery, and improvement, were very limited; but by the introduction of each of these, they were greatly multiplied."

Here was at least one great discovery by a man who rose to prominence through his ability with the spoken word: that the written word had vastly more power and potential by virtue of its ceaseless availability and potential utility to succeeding generations.

> When writing was invented, any important observation, likely to lead to a discovery, had at least a chance of being written down, and consequently, a better chance of never being forgotten; and of being seen, and reflected upon, by a much greater number of persons; and thereby the chances of a valuable hint being caught, proportionably augmented. By this means the observation of a single individual might lead to an important invention, years, and even centuries after he was dead.[32]

Needless to say, this insight proved invaluable to Lincoln, whose career had been built on his superior ability as an extemporaneous speaker but by 1859 was marked by a calculated reliance on painstakingly crafted pronouncements, drawn with an eye toward publication. In fact, after being elected president, he avoided impromptu speeches and concentrated on the written word in a masterful series of speeches, letters, and state papers that will probably never be equaled. And in the case of the Gettysburg address, it can be argued that he was consciously attempting to take a page directly from Jefferson's own book and set down something aimed not just at the present but at posterity. For just as Lincoln had concluded in the 1850s that the preamble of the Declaration had been inscribed by its author and endorsed by the founders not so much as a description of the current reality but as the statement of an ideal to guide succeeding generations, so in the Gettysburg address he pointedly framed the underlying national purpose in the optative mood, so to speak, as a common dedication to a single irreducible proposition—that all men are created equal.

Like Jefferson before him, Lincoln saw a clear connection between the advancement of printing, which widens the circle of literacy, and the rise of democracy. He went on in his lecture:

> It is very probable—almost certain—that the great mass of men, at that time, were utterly unconscious, that their *conditions*, or their *minds* were capable of improvement. They not only looked upon the educated few as superior beings; but they supposed themselves to be naturally incapable of rising to equality. To immancipate the mind from this false and under estimate of itself, is the great task which printing came into the world to perform.[33]

Thomas Jefferson could hardly have said it better. The liberating power of literacy was here acknowledged to be of consequence as it affected individual readers, heightening their sense of themselves and their own capabilities, and truly momentous in terms of the historical transformations that it made possible. Emancipating the mind from a false underestimate of itself is a strikingly Jeffersonian precept. It could aptly be used to describe what had happened to Frederick Douglass in Baltimore, or what had happened to Abraham Lincoln in southwestern Indiana and New Salem, but on a larger scale it could also encompass the revolutionary rise of democratic institutions.

Jefferson's emphasis on literacy as a liberating and transforming force in the world is both a key to his thinking and a gauge of the character of his most enduring contributions. Increasingly criticized in our own day for his shortcomings when measured by modern standards, Jefferson survives as an ineluctable force in cultural history precisely because he constantly concerned himself with the ongoing process of human liberation. Untrammeled by considerations of race, class, or gender, his preoccupation with literacy serves to bring this into sharp focus and to underscore, 250 years after his birth, the continuing relevance and importance of his ideas.

RICHARD D. BROWN

Bulwark of Revolutionary Liberty: Thomas Jefferson's and John Adams's Programs for an Informed Citizenry

The origins of the idea of an informed citizenry lie in the Renaissance era and in the political contests of seventeenth-century Britain. But it was during the American war for independence that reformers first asserted that the creation of an informed citizenry was primarily a state responsibility, and that the state must create institutions to maintain such a citizenry on a permanent basis. Thomas Jefferson and John Adams were two of the key actors in this reform, and if their proposals for Virginia and Massachusetts were not wholly original, they were both emblematic and influential. Grounded in Radical Whig and Enlightenment traditions, their proposals combined diverse strands of secular and religious ideology and practice under the rubric of public education.

By the middle of the eighteenth century, even before the imperial conflict began between Britain and her American colonies, Radical Whigs and others had articulated the idea of an informed citizenry in various ways. Moreover, such widely supported ideals as free speech and press and religious liberty, together with the general Enlightenment belief that an increase in knowledge was progressive and beneficent, reinforced the notion of an informed citizenry. Faith in social hierarchy remained powerful—as did the sense that society, like nature, must be stratified—but the Mandevillean argument that social peace required keeping the lower classes ignorant found few spokesmen. To bring the light of learning, including the knowledge of the Gospel, to all Englishmen was a goal commanding general assent.

From a political standpoint, however, the idea of an informed citizenry remained inconsequential in the American colonies as well as in Britain. The central preoccupations of Georgian politics lay elsewhere—in the tensions between Crown and Parliament, in debates over balanced government, and in the pronounced concern over corruption that was associated with Robert Walpole's parliamentary regime. Moreover the meanings of all the high principles that surrounded the informed citizen ideal—free speech and press, religious liberty, and belief in the general expansion of learning—were contested. Learning and popular literacy were defended by high churchmen as measures promoting moral improvement and piety, whereas secular voices wanted learning to erase superstition and mindless credulity among common folk.

Understandings of the concept of religious liberty were even more vexed. To secular-minded Deists it meant the total separation of church and state and an end to centuries of tax-supported religion. For the established Anglican clergy, religious liberty carried no such implications whatsoever; it merely meant that no one would be forced to worship contrary to the dictates of conscience and that Christian worship of all varieties might be freely permitted. Among Protestant sectarians no single viewpoint ruled, and some were ready to endorse church taxes, provided they were distributed according to the taxpayer's religious preference.

The meaning of free speech and press, a principle that was interwoven with the idea of an informed citizenry, was similarly controversial. After Britain's licensing law for publications lapsed in the 1690s, freedom of the press came to mean the absence of continental methods of prior censorship. Publishers could print anything they wished; afterwards, however, they might be sued punitively for libel by individuals or punished by officials of the state and the church for the crimes of seditious or blasphemous libel. By mid-century, in New York at least, the Zenger case had advanced the proposition that publishing the truth was protected, even against prosecution for seditious libel. And although Radical Whigs on both sides of the Atlantic believed that some kinds of false and malicious speech should be prohibited, they were moving toward a more extended view of a free press than merely no prior censorship. But there was no agreement as to where the limits of free speech and press ought to lie. Like religious liberty, freedom of speech and press were among the celebrated rights of Englishmen, and they supplied a grounding for the idea of an informed citizenry. But it was a rather uncertain foundation, because all of these ideas were ambiguous, indefinite, and fluid.

Still, sentiment by mid-century broadly favored some vague idea of an informed citizenry. Indeed, Britain was dotted with scores if not hundreds of charitable endowments that helped to support schools and colleges and assisted in the education of well-connected, talented, but needy boys. But the creation and maintenance of an informed citizenry was not a public responsibility. The Church of England was expected to promote "Christian knowledge"—priests should catechize their flocks—but otherwise the education of children and youth was the purely private responsibility of families. As with other potentially marketable skills for which British parents purchased their children's apprenticeships, instruction in reading, writing, arithmetic, or any other subject was a private matter.

Conditions in the American colonies generally reflected patterns in Britain, although from the perspective of Enlightenment ideals there were some discouraging differences. Charitable endowments were rare in America; and, in addition, there were hundreds of thousands of African slaves and Native Americans who could not be included in social calculations regarding free speech and press, religious liberty, or an informed citizenry. Indeed, to many masters of slaves, the Mandevillean belief in the social necessity of keeping the laboring class ignorant still made sense. Slavery, moreover, was an established institution in every colony.

On the other side of the balance, however, there were the exceptional practices of Puritan New England, that is, Massachusetts and Connecticut. In these colonies, contrary to every other political jurisdiction in the British Empire except Scotland, public authorities laid taxes to support free schools for all free boys.[1] The objective of these seventeenth-century policies had been essentially religious—an ignorant people were sinful, unconverted, and would provoke God's wrath—but by the mid-eighteenth century there were secular and civic justifications as well. Moreover, the results, which were equally connected to New England's broad diffusion of property and its literate heritage, struck many observers. In 1765 the young Massachusetts attorney John Adams boasted "that all candid foreigners who have passed through this country, and conversed freely with all sorts of people here, will allow, that they have never seen so much knowledge and civility among the common people in any part of the world."[2]

New England's Puritan legacy, observers agreed, gave the region a more educated common standard than other colonies, but the differences were matters of degree rather than kind. In New York City a gentleman complained in the 1750s at "how common it is to see a Shoemaker, Taylor, or Barber, haranguing with a great deal of Warmth on the public Affairs." Though armed only with "Knowledge from the News-Papers," a tradesman would "condemn a General, Governor, or Province with as much Assurance as if he were of the Privy council."[3] To a British gentleman the effrontery of such a tradesman was more striking than his information, but these remarks suggest that the common citizenry in New York was, at least in its own eyes, informed politically.

The observations of the Anglican clergyman Jacob Duché of Philadelphia supply further evidence that in regions where there was no New England-style school establishment ordinary men valued being informed and often saw themselves as informed citizens. "The poorest laborer upon the shore of the Delaware," Duché reported, "thinks himself entitled to deliver his sentiments in matters of religion or politics with as much freedom as the gentleman or scholar." Deferential manners, Duché said, were diminished, for "cringing servility" was not the regional style. And although Duché believed "literary accomplishments here meet with deserved applause," he pointed out that "such is the prevailing taste for books of every kind, that almost every man is a reader; and by pronouncing sentence . . . upon the various publications that come in his way, puts himself upon a level, in point of knowledge, with their several authors."[4] Farther south, learning was said to be less widespread among common white men. Yet a 1762 North Carolina statute held masters accountable for the literacy of even their colored apprentices and, in Virginia, justices of the peace had "consistently held parents and masters responsible for the education of their children and servants."[5] As in Britain, schooling was generally "used as a vehicle for personal advancement."[6] Though John Adams was speaking of white New Englanders in 1765 when he asserted that "a native of America who cannot read and write . . . is as rare as a comet or an earthquake,"[7] and the literacy levels of colonial women lagged behind those of men, scholars agree that American literacy rates surpassed those of England, attaining levels comparable to those of Presbyterian Scotland.[8] This cultural foundation, which joined widespread literacy and property-holding with unusually broadly expressed feelings of empowerment among ordinary householders, gave special cogency to the idea of an informed citizenry in colonial America.

Institutions of Public Education

But when it came to implementing the idea after independence, Revolutionary leaders possessed no generally accepted, clearly understood models to imitate. If American leaders were going to lay the institutional foundations for an informed citizenry, they would have to innovate. The rhetorical creation and valuation of the Republican Wife and Mother offered a new approach that enhanced the public significance of family life. The freeing of religious sects by the state legislatures was an even more radical and problematic innovation, which encouraged Protestants to pursue salvation and virtue according to their own lights and so might promote a net increase in public virtue. Neither of these innovations required public expenditures. Nor did the widening state adherence to the doctrine of free speech as a means for assuring an informed citizenry. They freed Americans to follow republican ideals. Another innovation of far-reaching significance was, however, potentially costly: the statutory commitment to public education by means of schools and colleges.

The fiscal implications of what was called public education in the revolutionary era were unclear. In Britain, public schools and colleges were open to the public for admission, but they were financed wholly out of student tuitions, fees, and private endowments, not tax revenues. In a strict sense, that was all that public education meant in 1776. Indeed, when one considers the Pennsylvania and North Carolina constitutions of that year, it appears that their provisions for public schools and universities meant public in the British sense and that neither state intended to raise tax revenues to supply free education for its inhabitants. Rather, they encouraged the formation of an extensive, tuition-based educational system.

But there was also a New England public school model available for consideration, and its meaning was different. In Connecticut and Massachusetts tax revenues and public lotteries as well as tuition charges and student fees paid for the public education regime. Colony statutes required towns to lay taxes to support schools, and though towns did not always comply, in most communities the public taxed itself so as to supply tuition-free elementary education for boys and, increasingly, girls as well. At the same time, however, parents bore the responsibility of maintaining the schoolhouse, providing it with firewood, and supplying their children's textbooks. The public defrayed the capital cost of erecting a school building, normally a cheap wooden structure, and also paid a teacher's salary, but the rest was up to the parents. At the next higher level of the grammar school, where elements of Latin were taught and where a boy might prepare for college, actual public provisions fell far short of statutory claims. Fewer than half of the towns which were required to support grammar schools with tax revenues did so (in 1765, 65 out of 144 did so), and many boys prepared for college in private tutorial with a local clergyman, as John Adams had in the 1740s.[9] At the college level, both Harvard and Yale received some capital funds and operating expenses from their colony legislatures, but they also relied on tuitions, fees, gifts, and endowments. With the exception of a few charity scholars, the students paid for the operating costs of education. This New England model, in which "public" meant spending tax revenues, would prove influential over time as states in other regions adopted some of its elements.

Concerned with enabling legislation, Thomas Jefferson proposed the most dramatic revision of the New England arrangement for Virginia in the 1779 Bill for the More General Diffusion of Knowledge. This bill was part of a comprehensive revision of state law and institutions designed to make Virginia a model republic. For Jefferson and James Madison, its principal advocates, the permanent establishment of an informed citizenry was the central purpose of the proposal. To his old mentor, the widely respected attorney and judge George Wythe, Jefferson declared that this was "by far the most important bill in our whole code." "Preach, my dear Sir," he entreated Wythe, "a crusade against ignorance; establish and improve the law for educating the common people."[10] This law originated in Radical Whig fears concerning the seductive, deceitful paths that tyrants used to seize unlawful power, as well as the Enlightenment faith in reason and knowledge as agents for human improvement.

The first objective was to block the rise of tyranny; and the bill asserted that an informed citizenry was ultimately the only effective barrier against despotism. The bill proposed to "illuminate . . . the minds of the people at large, and more especially to give them knowledge of those facts, which history exhibiteth, that, possessed thereby of the experience of other ages and countries, they may be enabled to know ambition under all its shapes." Thus informed, common people would be "prompt to exert their natural powers" so as to repel tyranny. A further goal was to secure "publick happiness," a goal requiring laws that were "wisely formed and honestly administered."[11]

Because common people could not make and implement laws on their own, they needed the guidance of men possessing natural "genius and virtue," whose "liberal education" rendered them worthy to rule. For that reason the bill called for a two-tier school system leading to college, whereby the ablest and most virtuous youths might be brought forward "without regard to wealth, birth or other accidental condition." As in New England, the whole system was to be supported financially by a combination of taxes and tuitions. At the elementary level "all the free children, male and female," should have three years of schooling at public expense. The subjects of instruction were basic, reading, writing, and arithmetic; but they would do double service because textbooks in these subjects should simultaneously "make them acquainted with Graecian, Roman, English and American history."[12] This secular education for girls as well as boys, without either Bible or catechism, would establish the foundation for the republican commonwealth of Virginia.

To supply republican leaders, the bill provided for higher levels of training. Grammar schools located on one-hundred-acre lots at intervals throughout Virginia would be not mere log cabins, but instead physical emblems of the permanent commitment to an informed citizenry. Each one would be constructed at state expense out of "brick or stone" with "a room for the school, a hall to dine in, four rooms for a master and usher, and ten or twelve lodging rooms for the scholars."[13] The curriculum would include Latin and Greek, English grammar, geography, and the higher parts of arithmetic such as decimals and cube roots.[14] Most of the students here would pay their own way; but each year one boy with at least two years of training would be selected from each of the local elementary schools to attend his region's grammar school at state expense if his "parents are too poor" to pay tuition.[15] Such gratis scholars would be progressively weeded-out over a six-year period so that at the highest level each grammar school would have only one gratis "senior" student. One of these gratis seniors, "of the best learning and most hopeful genius and disposition," was then to be sent for three years to the College of William and Mary to complete his education at public expense.[16] To ensure that the college itself would be adequate to the new demands of leadership, Jefferson also prepared a bill to revamp the college's constitution, finances, and curriculum so as to include eight secular professorships in ethics and fine arts, law, history, mathematics, anatomy and medicine, natural philosophy and history, ancient languages, and modern languages.[17] Radical Whig ideology and Enlightenment learning were joined in the Virginia scheme.

At the same time Jefferson's plan aimed to unite mass popular education with the perpetuation of elite, albeit enlightened, rule. "The best geniuses will be raked from the rubbish annually," Jefferson explained, thereby gaining for the state "those talents which nature has sown as liberally among the poor as the rich, but which perish without use, if not sought for and cultivated." As for those possessed with merely common abilities, the public schooling would develop their political understanding: "it will avail them of the experience of other nations; it will qualify them as judges of the actions and designs of men; it will enable them to know ambition under every guise it may assume; and knowing it, to defeat its views."[18] Overall, the statutes would create a broad base of discerning, watchful citizens who would be qualified to choose wisely among their liberally educated leaders. In a state whose citizens had already selected such leaders as Thomas Jefferson, Richard Henry Lee, James Madison, George Mason, and George Washington among others, the reforms did not so much point to any radical change in the character of politics as to a regular process to institutionalize the nascent republican order, and guard against future despots and demagogues.

In New England, where means for informing and educating the inhabitants were well developed, Radical Whigs were confident that the informed citizenry had already proved itself in the crises of 1775 and 1776. Virtually no one believed that major reform, such as Jefferson proposed for Virginia, was necessary, because the system had so recently demonstrated that it was not broken. Yet, there were new concerns that went beyond Radical Whig attention to citizens as politically informed defenders of liberty. The empowerment of common men at the moment of independence did not necessarily encourage respect for the best informed, most learned citizens, or respect for men who believed in elite republican rule according to New England models or the principles of the Virginia reform.

In New Jersey there was "a Prejudice against liberal Education" among the people, and John Adams reckoned that "there is a Spice of this every where." Elite snobbery was partly to blame, Adams thought, and he admonished "Gentlemen of Education to lay aside Some of their Airs, of Scorn, Vanity and Pride." "Gentlemen," Adams warned, "cannot expect the Confidence of the common People if they treat them ill, or refuse hautily to comply with some of their favorite Notions."[19] But this antagonism between men with common education and those few possessed of greater learning cut deeper than issues of style. There was "a Jealousy or an Envy taking Place among the Multitude" which was aimed at "Men of Learning." The short-term practical result of this jealousy "in various Parts of these States" including New England, was "a Wish to exclude them [men of learning] from the public Councils and from military Command."[20]

From a long-term perspective this tendency was even more ominous, since it would lead to rule by parochial, self-interested demagogues. To revolutionary leaders who believed that a republic, above all other forms of government, needed the guidance of disinterested men of enlarged learning and vision, the jealousy Adams identified was poisonous.[21] Day-to-day necessities in 1776 would push aside the worries of the Massachusetts delegate to the Continental Congress, but his fear "that human Nature will be found to be the Same in America as it has been in Europe, and that the true Principles of Liberty will not be Sufficiently attended to" would not only activate Virginia reformers to propose a new foundation for republican institutions but would motivate New Englanders as well.[22]

In Massachusetts, Radical Whig and Enlightenment ideas were interwoven with the Puritan legacy and clerical influence for laying the foundation of republican society. As in Virginia, the informed citizenry was seen to be crucial. According to the patriot clergyman who preached the 1778 election sermon, "knowledge and learning will be considered as most essentially requisite for a free, righteous government, . . . a certain degree of knowledge is absolutely to be diffused through a state for the preservation of its liberties and the quiet of government."[23] Here the Radical Whig defense of liberty merged with the Puritan and clerical concern for order. But there were also larger Enlightened aspirations: "A republican government and science mutually promote and support each other." Underlying these calls to support learning were the fears John Adams had earlier expressed. The election homily of 1778 asserted:

> Every kind of useful knowledge will be carefully encouraged and promoted by the rulers of a free state, unless they should happen to be men of ignorance themselves; in which case they and their community will be in danger of sharing the fate of blind guides and their followers. The education of youth, by instructors properly qualified, the establishment of societies for useful arts and sciences, the encouragement of persons of superior abilities, will always command the attention of wise rulers.[24]

Were the Massachusetts legislators "wise rulers," or were they "men of ignorance?" When the preacher delivered these lines he was treading carefully, since he knew very well that most of his audience had never attended college. Yet he drew on a common social vision that was rooted in colonial experience.

Two years later the new Massachusetts Constitution, drafted by John Adams, formalized the admonitions of this 1778 sermon. Recasting the mission of government in broad republican rather than Puritan terms, the Constitution of 1780 proclaimed a comprehensive public responsibility, not merely for education at all levels, but for an advanced, enlightened, knowledgeable and progressive society. Like the Virginia reform proposals of the previous year, the new Massachusetts Constitution was designed to enable republican principles and institutions to endure. Only in the custody of a virtuous and informed citizenry, could they survive.

The Constitution emphasized the fundamental importance of the Radical Whig ideal, and furnished institutional means for its support. In the opening section, the "Declaration of the Rights of the Inhabitants" called for "the public worship of God" because public happiness and civil order required "public instructions in piety, religion and morality." Significantly, this religious establishment was justified in secular rather than sacred terms; the republican state was interested not in salvation but in order and ethical behavior. Religious instruction was said to supply social benefits, and for that reason "the support and maintenance of public protestant teachers of piety, religion and morality" were required in every locality within the state. "Attendance upon the instructions of the public teachers," sermon-going, was also enjoined unless such attendance violated an individual's religious scruples.[25] The chief purpose of all these institutional arrangements was to maintain a citizenry sufficiently informed in Christian principles to embrace morality and so to embrace civic virtue. Being morally informed was an essential part of the prescription for republican citizenship.

Political information, however, was equally important; and as in Virginia, the same declaration of rights also guaranteed the "liberty of the press," which the constitution declared to be "essential to the security of freedom in a state."[26] In addition to a free press, all of the other means that had been employed by patriots to inform the people from 1765 onward would be protected in perpetuity: "to assemble to consult upon the common good; give instructions to their representatives and to request of the legislative body, by way of addresses, petitions, or remonstrances, redress of the wrongs done them, and of the grievances they suffer."[27] These general guarantees of free press and assembly were widely adopted by the states in their revolutionary constitutions, drawn as they were from the Radical Whig repertoire of requirements for the preservation of a free state.

In Massachusetts these passages in the declaration of rights recalled the English heritage of the recent past; whereas the provision for a religious establishment—so contrary to the letter and spirit of the Virginia reforms—blended elements of the Puritan legacy with the Anglican conservatism that linked piety and order and referred to citizens as "subjects of the commonwealth." To combine these distinct, even conflicting, traditions—Radical Whig, Puritan, and Anglican—to promote a coherent political order was problematic. Later it would generate divisions, but in the short term the combination sustained the revolutionary coalition.

The fifth chapter of the Massachusetts constitution, devoted to "The University at Cambridge, and Encouragement of Literature &C," was even more innovative. It expressed a whole new enlightened vision of an informed and cultivated citizenry, a vision that would be elaborated by leaders throughout the United States for two generations and would ultimately have major institutional consequences. Here John Adams went way beyond the themes he articulated in 1765 in his *Dissertation on Canon and Feudal Law* and drew on cosmopolitan Enlightenment ideas to articulate a new mission for government.

The constitutional provisions for Harvard were in themselves ordinary. Chiefly, the constitution guaranteed Harvard's property and its system of governance. In addition, however, the state extended the purpose of the university far beyond its original Christian and civic missions. "The encouragement of arts and sciences, and all good literature," the constitution proclaimed, "tends to the honour of God, the advantage of the christian religion, and the great benefit of this and the other United States of America."[28] Here Massachusetts was assigning a broad range of secular objectives to the university, objectives whose fulfillment would enrich the state and the nation.

What was remarkable, however, was not the portion dealing with the university: the ideal of an informed elite, after all, reached back to the Renaissance. It was the next paragraph, titled "The Encouragement of Literature," concerning the information and education of common people that was revolutionary. Here earlier Puritan and Radical Whig traditions were transformed into an Enlightenment ideal of comprehensive education that would ensure a society that was not only Christian and free but also just, humane, and progressive. According to the commonwealth's constitution:

> Wisdom, and knowledge, as well as virtue, diffused generally among the body of the people, being necessary for the preservation of their rights and liberties; and as these depend on spreading the opportunities and advantages of education in the various parts of the country, and among the different orders of the people, it shall be the duty of legislatures and magistrates, in all future periods of this Commonwealth, to cherish the interests of literature and the sciences, and all seminaries of them; especially the university at Cambridge, public schools, and grammar schools in the towns; to encourage private societies and public institutions, rewards and immunities, for the promotion of agriculture, arts, sciences, commerce, trades, manufactures, and a natural history of the country; to countenance and inculcate the principles of humanity and general benevolence, public and private charity, industry and frugality, honesty and punctuality in their dealings; sincerity, good humor, and all social affections, and generous sentiments among the people.[29]

Adams's tribute to universal education, embracing all productive and illuminating fields of endeavor, carried Massachusetts well beyond Radical Whig notions of an informed citizenry as a bulwark against tyranny. The objective was more than a defense of liberty; it was the positive creation of a progressive, enlightened, and virtuous society.

For Adams and Jefferson, indeed the entire generation of revolutionary leaders, the success of liberty and of republican government and society rested on the crucial equation of virtue and knowledge. As they saw it, Rousseau's notion of a virtuous (and ignorant) savage was absurd, a benighted, uninformed people could not be virtuous, just as a virtuous people could not be ignorant. Within this consensus, the principal differences among patriots concerned the place of religion. According to Evangelical formulations, people who came to know Christ embraced His message and became unselfish, virtuous citizens.[30] Mainstream protestants, too, linked good citizenship to knowledge of religious truth. According to Benjamin Rush, a Pennsylvania Presbyterian who signed the Declaration of Independence, "a Christian cannot fail of being a republican." In Rush's mind the two were conflated, inasmuch as "Republicanism is a part of the truth of Christianity."[31] To the latitudinarian president of Yale College, Ezra Stiles, the idea that "all should be taught to read the scriptures" was axiomatic. At the same time Rush, a scientist and college-founder, concluded that "without religion I believe learning does real mischief to the morals and principles of mankind."[32] Knowledge, after all, was linked to sin in the Garden of Eden, and the Devil himself was a knowledgeable fallen angel. To many revolutionary leaders the idea of raising a wall of separation between

Christianity and the new republican states seemed self-contradictory and ill-advised if the merger between knowledge and virtue was to flourish.

Not so for Thomas Jefferson and his Virginia constituents. In principle, Baptists argued, religion was a private not a public matter; and besides, pragmatists pointed out, religious establishments led to sectarian wrangling and infringements on freedom of worship. Both Adams and Jefferson shared an essentially secular orientation, looking to Christianity chiefly for ethical standards, not personal theological truth; but they disagreed over the relationship between organized religion and the state. Adams, whose outlook was shaped by his Massachusetts constituency, saw the need for a religious establishment; whereas Jefferson came to the conclusion that religion must be separate from the state, and proudly championed a law to that end, the Virginia Statute of Religious Liberty, which echoed Milton in its claim "that truth is great and will prevail if left to herself, that she is the proper and sufficient antagonist to error."[33] On both sides, however, revolutionary leaders agreed that republican states bore a central responsibility for guaranteeing their own survival by making provisions to ensure an informed citizenry.

Widening Circles of Information

Before the movement for independence began, the idea of an informed citizenry was already an established part of the Whig and Radical Whig ideologies. But it was the mobilization of colonial opposition to imperial reform that made it relevant to everyday politics and led revolutionary leaders to invest it with more urgent importance than ever before. So long as colonial political opposition was confined to legislative and council chambers, the extent of political information among the population at large could be overlooked, as had long been the case in every colony. The plantation and village parochialism of farmers who seldom needed to look beyond their dungheaps had long made popular engagement in province or imperial politics an occasional event, rather than a routine staple of colonial public life. But now the widening circles of opposition to British measures, and the intensification of protests gave new meaning to the idea. Concern for the kind of information, its mode of presentation, and its political content stimulated a new consciousness of being informed or ignorant. Indeed, as being informed assumed heightened importance among common men and women, pamphlets, newspapers, and formal public oratory gained larger, more diverse audiences. A more socially comprehensive conception of the informed citizenry emerged, together with the sense that a more active, critical role belonged to common people. When British government was swept away between 1774 and 1776, it was immediately apparent that old customs and institutions were not fully equal to meeting republican needs for an informed citizenry. Now the need to be informed was constant, not episodic, and public engagement in the revolutionary cause was essential to its survival.

So in 1776, and later, revolutionaries turned to the state as a principal agency to form and perpetuate an informed citizenry. Two kinds of approaches were adopted simultaneously. The first, drawing on Radical Whig prescriptions for a free state, focused on liberating the channels of information: free speech, free press, and freedom of assembly and petition. Connected to this movement, as well, was the liberation of religious sects—freedom of religion—which meant that the state would no longer interfere with the several pathways to virtue. Indirectly, freedom of religion promoted the formation of an informed citizenry by releasing religious energy to encourage virtue, just as free speech and press enhanced the circulation of information.

The second approach, using the state in a positive way to support the institutions required by an informed citizenry—schools, colleges and universities, libraries, and learned societies—represented a substantially new departure. In the case of Massachusetts, secular public institutions were intended to complement the long-standing role of churches and clergymen in promoting knowledge and virtue. To the south, in Virginia, reformers sought to bypass the old Anglican establishment, and create new, secular educational institutions. Everywhere there was confidence that the state could play a positive role in establishing the foundations of an informed citizenry.

Revolutionaries were optimistic, even visionary in the cases of Thomas Jefferson and John Adams, when they looked into the future, even though there were signs of hostility to cosmopolitan learning and its supporters from the outset. This incipient populist resistance to higher learning proved to be only one of many complications prompted by the idea of actively creating an informed citizenry. For as the idea of being informed was enlarged beyond the Radical Whig notion of knowing one's rights and some political history—and now came to embrace a multitude of useful and speculative Enlightenment and Christian topics—forming a consensus as to what being informed really meant became elusive. The difficulties that Christians found agreeing on doctrine offered a foretaste of the problem of reaching an agreement about what being informed ought to mean.

Revolutionary leaders, even the most far-sighted like Adams and Jefferson and Rush, were even more limited than the common man by their culture and historical context in that they did not suspect the dynamic impact of the Revolution on the concept of citizenry itself. They could not seriously entertain the idea that the political meaning of *citizen* as "freeholder" might in a generation or two be challenged. The idea that propertyless men, white or black, might be candidates for equal political rights appeared truly radical in the 1770s, and the notion of women, propertied or not, as political actors was almost unthinkable. For revolutionary leaders, an informed citizenry was more finite and tightly linked to virtue than the future would prove it to be.

HERBERT A. JOHNSON

Thomas Jefferson and Legal Education in Revolutionary America

Professor James Landis and then Professor Felix Frankfurter, while writing their *Business of the Supreme Court,* observed that "Old political institutions like low forms of organism have tenacious vitality."[1] The comment might well be applied to American legal education. Although one type of training might predominate at a given historical period, the brethren of the long robe have hesitated to clean house and eliminate older methods. For example, clerkship, the prevailing method of the colonial period, barely survived into the twentieth century, but its modern successor, clinical legal education, is very much with us. It is important that legal education be seen as a field of pedagogy in which there are several layers of historical development. At the same time there are some fairly stable requirements for the training of would-be lawyers, and these have remained remarkably constant over the course of American history.

First, the practical, craftsmanlike training of clerkship is needed to produce an attorney who is diligent and effective in the daily routines of practice. Second, would-be lawyers must be accomplished at finding the law, analyzing its content, and preparing written and oral presentations of their client's legal position. Third, they must be competent to try cases, both before juries and before judges sitting without juries. Fourth, they must be educated in a wide variety of subjects and capable of learning new materials rapidly and accurately. Because the American bar traditionally has been undifferentiated into the ranks of barrister and solicitor, each lawyer's education must provide him or her with minimum training to meet each of these requirements.[2]

Historically, American legal education has moved from clerkship as the preferred colonial method, to legal training in the colleges during the Revolutionary War and until 1800, to the era of the private law school stretching from 1790 to 1825, and then to the establishment of the modern law school, affiliated with a university but providing an independent faculty and a curriculum separate from the liberal arts. Thomas Jefferson's connection with this process was in the integration of legal education into the modified liberal arts curriculum of early nineteenth-century America.

The third president played a significant role in launching the reform of higher education that took place in American colleges during the five decades between the Declaration of Independence and his death in 1826. When he was wartime governor of Virginia, Jefferson, by virtue of his office, was rector of the William and Mary board of visitors. This placed him in an ideal position to initiate a curriculum reform that abandoned the traditional classical studies for more utilitarian course offerings in the modern languages, mathematics, moral and political philosophy, and in the natural and physical sciences. The establishment of the professorship of law and police as part of that overall curricular reform, was the first American effort to introduce the study of law into colleges.[3]

Jefferson and the Clerkship Model

Jefferson's lifelong interest in legal education was shaped by his early experiences with the law, as a student and as a practitioner. Singularly blessed in his own legal education, he benefited from a leisurely five-year apprenticeship to George Wythe, then one of the most prominent attorneys in practice before the higher courts of Virginia.[4] During the colonial period and the early republic Virginia's bar was divided into two categories—those lawyers who practiced in the General Court and Chancery Court, which met in Williamsburg, and those who elected to practice in the county courts, where most of the civil and criminal cases were tried.[5] Consequently as Wythe's clerk, Jefferson was exposed to the most challenging practice of the day, far removed from the more routine and tedious debt cases and minor assaults that occupied lawyers practicing in the trial courts. There he would have been involved in the most important land litigation of the day, felony trials, and numerous civil appeals, all of which constituted the business of the General Court. In addition he dealt with those complicated equity matters reserved for determination in the Court of Chancery or heard on appeal there. Appellate counsel in the higher courts carried a much lighter caseload and enjoyed adequate time to prepare their cases. Their clerks had the distinct advantage of working on important and complex matters with a minimum of those clerical duties or scrivener's tasks that dominated the daily routine of clerks to county court practitioners.

Yet, it was not only the quality of Wythe's practice that was of value to his clerk. Wythe was an unusual lawyer whose prominence at the bar did not deflect his attention from classical study and scientific experimentation. Those interests enriched the experience of his clerks who lived in his household. Even more significant was Wythe's devotion to the education of his apprentices. Wythe's biographer, Father Bob Kirtland, describes him as an Enlightenment man who possessed the patience of temperament and the enthusiasm for learning that mark a great teacher.[6] Jefferson's mentor taught for the simple joy of imparting information, and it is documented that he refused to accept compensation for taking young men into his household for instruction in law. Indeed Wythe's joy in the teaching function is shown by his willingness to instruct the young even during the course of a brief encounter. Kirtland relates the childhood experience of Nathaniel Beverly Tucker, who happened to meet Wythe in front of his house on the Palace Green. Wythe took him into the house for a look at the interior of a beehive, visible through a window, and provided the youngster with a thorough explanation of the activities of bees. Tucker never forgot the adventure, nor did he fail to recall the lawyer's enthusiasm in explaining the hive to him.[7] All of Wythe's law clerks established lifelong friendships with their master. In Jefferson's case it has been suggested that Wythe occupied the place in his life left vacant by the premature death of his father many years before.[8] Whether or not this is true of the personal relationship, there is no doubt that for Jefferson clerkship with Wythe was studying law in the very best of circumstances.

By way of contrast most American lawyers trained by clerkship found the experience unpleasant and dreary at best. Beginning law clerks were assigned to tedious copying of pleadings, contracts, wills, land deeds, and other legal documents in a clear and legible hand. They served and filed their master's writs and judgments, and performed countless other menial and clerical tasks needed in a frantically busy office, where there was little time for instruction in substantive law.[9] As clerks gained in knowledge and maturity their duties expanded to maintenance of fee books and court calendars. Only upon completion of these tasks were they free to attend motion days in the courts where points of law were argued by counsel and decided by the judges. Should longer periods of time become available clerks might witness jury trials at common law or hearings in equity. Only the short hours of evening sunlight remained available for study of the lawbooks in the master's library.[10]

As often as not the lawyer was absent on trial or other business, leaving the apprentices to pore over the complexities of Coke on Littleton and of early case reports in Law French without any guidance or explanation. Future law teacher Peter Van Schaack expressed his frustration at such neglect, "how many hours have I hunted, how many books turned up for what three minutes of explanation from any tolerable lawyer would have made evident to me! It is vain to put a law book into the hands of a lad without explaining difficulties to him as he goes along."[11] Thomas Jefferson was fully aware of the haphazard education that most clerkships offered, and advised young men that serving a clerkship frequently impeded, rather than aided, progress in legal study.[12] In 1796 he observed that most lawyers took advantage of their clerks because: "We are all too apt by shifting on them our business, to incroach upon that time which should be devoted to their studies. The only help a youth wants is to be directed what books to read and in what order to read them."[13]

In dismissing out of hand the value of a practitioner's advice, Jefferson naively assumed that others had his gift for solitary learning. This was obvious in his attitude toward the writings of Sir William Blackstone, which he denounced for being superficial. For him Sir Edward Coke's *Institutes* and *Reports* were the true fountain of the law,[14] but for most of his contemporaries, as well as for modern readers, Coke provides a rather bitter drink of water!

Clerkship produced lawyers who were accomplished at the detailed work of their profession. Thoroughly familiar with litigation and conveyancing forms, they were more haphazard in their mastery of substantive law. Lawyers trained by clerkship were aware of the many local variations from English common law that characterized their provincial law, but it was unlikely that their horizons had been elevated to consider Roman and European law, canon law, or the great issues of constitutional law that dominated the history of seventeenth-century England. They were hypercritical of errors in transcribing legal documents. As Peter Van Schaack wrote to a colleague in practice, "the deed drawn in your office was rather slovenly copied, and by its alterations afterward looked rather out of the way. . . . Excuse the freedom of these hints; but we cannot be too attentive to matters of this kind. A lawyer's reputation, like a woman's, is often lost by one error."[15] Important as accuracy and chastity may be, such an attitude can deaden creativity—and in legal study, it can reduce law practice to a trade rather than a learned occupation. Working with George Wythe, Thomas Jefferson lost out on some of the practical training deemed so precious by clerkship-trained lawyers, but he gained a more generous understanding of law and its impact upon society.[16]

Jefferson was also fortunate in the timing of his first acquaintance with the law. Although Coke's *Institutes* remained the central portion of a law clerk's reading, the abridgments of Bacon and Viner[17] provided easier access to law reports and in some cases supplied summaries of cases not yet available in Virginia. Increasingly colonial lawyers snapped up newly published case reports and treatises as soon as they were available from booksellers. This reflected the increased affluence and professional sophistication of the colonial bar.[18] Like Jefferson many of the new generation of law clerks had already received a thorough education in the liberal arts, with a resultant taste for the classics, philosophy and the sciences.[19]

As a public man Jefferson was frequently asked for advice concerning legal studies. He recommended not only "black letter law" in the treatises, statutes, and case reports, but also insisted that such reading be interspersed with more general study.[20] In 1786 he told Thomas Mann Randolph that a lawyer's education should commence with the study of languages (particularly French) followed by mathematics; a second stage of preparation should include astronomy, physics, natural history, anatomy, botany, and chemistry, for "every science is auxiliary to every other."[21] While these specific subjects were being mastered, the neophyte should proceed with a regimen of historical reading, one of the "lighter occupations" which "exercises principally the memory."[22] Of course historical works should whenever possible be read in the ancient languages or, in more recent studies, in the language of the author. Finally, historical reading should be unhurried, and form the subject of lifetime attention.

Jefferson's ideal legal education, described in part in his advice to neophytes, and reflective of his own experiences as a law clerk to George Wythe, represented a marked departure from the clerkship model. Admittedly it built upon the growing tendency of the bar to insist that applicants for clerkship have at least some training in the liberal arts before their professional training began. But with Jefferson and Wythe the study of law was coordinated with other studies designed to place the law in context with the emerging social science disciplines, and to give the future lawyer a broader view of law as an instrument of public policy.

This American development may have mirrored English academic developments in 1761 when Sir William Blackstone was appointed Vinerian professor of law at Oxford. Previously only Roman law, European civil law, and canon law had been taught at English universities, and training in the common law and equity was left to the Inns of Court and Inns of Chancery in London. Over the centuries the Inns had lost any pretense at serious pedagogy, and by the eighteenth century their vestigial educational program demanded only that students eat a certain number of meals and attend certain lectures and moots before their admission to practice would be granted.[23] As a consequence it was difficult to secure an adequate legal education, either in the mother country or in the colonies, except by clerkship. And it was the clerkship model that was to be modified by the new format suggested by Jefferson and first instituted at the College of William and Mary under Wythe.

Admitted to the Virginia Bar in 1767, Jefferson almost immediately began practice in the General Court. According to Frank Dewey, a careful student of his law practice years, there is no evidence that he had any cases in the county courts.[24] Cases in the higher courts were slow in coming to a new practitioner, and when they did clients were even slower in paying their attorney fees. Calendar delays meant that only by having cases referred by other attorneys might Jefferson hope to take a case to trial.[25] He was not very successful financially.[26] He did, however, show evidence of being broadly based in the law and overly diligent in the preparation of his cases for argument. Anticipating the need to present a divorce petition to the legislature, he prepared an exhaustive brief dealing with rules of natural law, civil law, Jewish biblical law, and Christian principles from the New Testament. Among his proposed miscellaneous arguments were references to Montesquieu's *Spirit of the Laws*, David Hume's essay on polygamy and divorce, and the writings of John Locke. Alas this virtuoso display of learning was rendered useless when the client died![27] Later in life, shortly after leaving the presidency, Jefferson expended even greater effort and preparation upon a book-length brief on the Batture controversy.[28] The time and effort expended upon these briefs may perhaps go far to explain his lack of financial success in law practice, for academic research does not always yield victory in litigation and frequently destroys profits. These efforts do illustrate, however, the high intellectual plane upon which Jefferson believed litigation should be conducted. It was this view of law practice as an extension of academic learning which dominated Jefferson's approach to legal education.

The Study of Law within the Context of the Arts and Sciences

Understandably the professorship of law and police established at William and Mary in 1779[29] and first occupied by George Wythe, represented a substantial departure from clerkship training. Among Wythe's first students in the summer of 1780 was a young army veteran named John Marshall. It is clear from Marshall's notebook that Wythe turned him loose on making notes from Matthew Bacon's *New Abridgment of the Law*.[30] He also attended moot courts and model legislatures, as well as lectures on natural philosophy by the Rev. James Madison, president of the college but not the United States.[31]

Although no evidence exists concerning the content of Wythe's instruction, the published lectures of Associate Justice James Wilson,[32] delivered in the 1790s at the University of Pennsylvania, provide some idea of what a professor of law and police was expected to teach. According to Wilson's plan, set forth in his first lecture[33] and followed throughout the series, the lectures began with general principles of law and obligation and the law of natures and of nations. The focus then shifted to man, both in the state of nature and in society, followed by the nature of government. Under government, some mention was made of the common law, but Wilson devoted the main part of this discussion to the fundamental (that is normative and constitutional) aspects of the common law, rather than discrete subtopics within the scope of common law.[34] Among "black letter law" the sole topic given individual attention was that of evidence, although here also, Wilson expounded upon the theory of evidence and epistemology rather than specific rules of evidence for trial at common law or in equity.[35] Justice Wilson's coverage of property law was limited to a few brief comments under the general category of "natural rights."[36] The lectures paid some attention to the rights and status of husbands and wives in marriage, but the complexities of strict settlements and antenuptial trusts to protect married women's property are not mentioned. Rather Wilson moved on to consider marriage in Anglo-Saxon times.[37] Perhaps in response to widespread interest in reform of the criminal law, Wilson spent all ten chapters of part 3 dealing with various types of crime and suggested punishments. These sections of his lectures are notable for their detailed coverage typical of the standard English law treatises, although there are interspersed references to the laws of ancient Egypt, Rome, and Europe.[38]

The young man who was preparing for the bar would gain a great deal of history, political theory, and philosophy from Wilson's lectures but find himself ill-prepared for a bar examination or the mundane situations encountered in everyday practice. Yet much of the learning displayed in Wilson's lectures fell into that catch-all category of the science of government that the eighteenth century referred to as "police." This included public law and jurisprudence as well as smatterings of what today would be classified as group psychology, sociology, economics, and political science. Consequently the lectures provided broad general knowledge for those lawyers, judges, and legislators who would shape the future of American law.

Professor McCloskey, who edited Wilson's lectures, suggests that they were "nothing less than the presentation of a complete political theory, grounded on theology and psychology and leading to a philosophy of American law."[39] James Wilson would have agreed that his lectures were to delve into the philosophical constructs from which law emerged, but at the same time he would have insisted that law was a subject in which all educated men should take an interest, and not be limited to the narrow professional concerns of the practitioner and judge. "The science of the law," he stated, "should in some measure, and in some degree, be the study of every free citizen, and of every free man. Every free citizen and every free man has duties to perform and rights to claim."[40] In a subsequent lecture Wilson delineated his goal: "let my humble task be to select and make such observations concerning our powers, our dispositions, and our habits, as will illustrate the intimate connexion and reciprocal influence of religion, morality and law."[41]

He was lecturing at an interdisciplinary level, using methods future generations would call comparative and historical. Such single-minded attention to jurisprudence and its place within the broader disciplines of the social sciences was very new and exciting in American legal education. Although Wilson's lectures provide the best surviving example of this broadly based intellectual approach to legal education, the origin of this new direction unquestionably was the William and Mary curriculum reform sparked by Thomas Jefferson and effectuated by George Wythe.

Lacking the text of Wythe's lectures, we cannot be certain how closely they paralleled James Wilson's 1790 curriculum at the College of Philadelphia. When Marshall studied with Wythe in 1780, his notes were taken from Matthew Bacon's *New Abridgment of the Law,* but during the course of his professorship in the 1780s Wythe switched to using Blackstone's *Commentaries* as his major text. When St. George Tucker succeeded Wythe at William and Mary in 1790, he continued to use Blackstone.[42] The outline of Wilson's lectures at Philadelphia demonstrates some similarity to the topical outline of Blackstone's *Commentaries,* from which we may surmise that the work had become the standard for organizing legal education by 1790. Superimposed on the Blackstonian outline was the more extensive coverage that American teachers gave to constitutional law subjects applicable to the American states and federal union, coupled with references to non-Anglo-American sources.

St. George Tucker's law students were expected to meet the requirements for a liberal arts academic degree while they completed their legal studies at William and Mary. The reading assignments were extremely demanding. Rising with the sun, students read law until eleven in the morning, at which time Tucker began three hours of lecture. Following the lectures they returned to their books, had dinner, and read until darkness descended.[43]

The more academic aspects of Tucker's professorship concentrated upon the internal organization of a political unit—the control and regulation of the comfort, health, morals, and safety of society.[44] Tucker ranged broadly in his selection of lecture materials—Locke, Vattel, Rousseau, Thomas Paine, DeLolme, Montesquieu, Burlamaqui, and of course, Thomas Jefferson's *Notes on the State of Virginia*.[45] These same sources appear on his reading list, supplemented by many others, including Rutherford's *Institutes of Natural Law*, Grotius on *War and Peace*, Justinian's Institutes, edited by Harris, Adam Smith's *Wealth of Nations*, the marquis de Beccaria's *Crimes and Punishment*, works by Joseph Priestley and Thomas Paine, the text of the *Federalist*, and virtually all published English reports.[46]

Student and parental reactions to Tucker's course varied greatly. Thomas Watkins of Petersburg was sufficiently impressed with the curriculum that he sent his son to study with Tucker rather than to a traditional clerkship. Joseph S. Watson rebelled at the heavy emphasis upon law in Tucker's teaching and curriculum, asserting that "Law, though called a liberal profession, is surely one of the greatest enemies of liberal learning."[47] The most rebellious student, Garritt Minor, left Tucker's lecture hall to clerk in a Fredricksburg law office, arguing that:

> It is impossible by any reading to obtain a competent, even a clear knowledge of
> the practice of law. In gaining this knowledge you gain also a portion of the theory
> of law. Of the two, it is preferable to know the practice. This you must allow can-
> not be learnt in a professor's chamber.[48]

Although Minor considered the professor to be too much involved with "antiquarian civilians" such as Bacon, Selden, Rolles, Plowden and Coke,[49] he nevertheless retained a great respect for Tucker's learning and character.[50]

The law professorships at William and Mary and the College of Philadelphia were augmented in 1794 by the selection of young James Kent to be professor of law at Columbia College in the City of New York.[51] Kent's inaugural lecture shows that he shared the dream of Jefferson, Wythe, Tucker, and Wilson—the study of law was to be added to the course of collegiate education, where it would help prepare young men to assume political office when their state and nation called them.[52] Because of the unique situation of the American union and states, a lawyer in the new republic needed a thorough grounding in constitutional law.[53]

> A lawyer in a free country, should have all the requisites of Quintillian's orator. He
> should be a person of irreproachable virtue and goodness. He should be well read
> in the whole circle of the arts and sciences. He should be fit for the administration

of public affairs, and to govern the commonwealth by his councils, establish it by his laws, and correct it by his example.[54]

Such attributes were gained by the reading the best Greek and Roman authors, and this was to be supplemented by study of the Roman civil law. Logic and mathematics were indispensable training for the close reasoning needed in law practice and should be supplemented by reading in moral philosophy.[55] Kent thought that a student's education was to be on a high plane.

> This [*i.e., Columbia College*] is not the proper place to prescribe a system of rules for the mere mechanical professor of our laws. The design of this institution, is undoubtedly of a more liberal kind. It is intended to explain the principles of our constitutions, the reason and history of our laws, to illustrate them by a comparison with those of other nations, and to point out the relation they bear to the spirit of representative republics.[56]

Needless to say the lectures contained little more black letter law than those offered by Justice Wilson in Philadelphia. Like Wilson's effort, Kent's venture into the higher levels of jurisprudence was lost upon his audience by the end of the first year and attendance dropped precipitately. A certain leveling influence brings even the most scholarly law professor down to earth—student demands that legal education prepare them for the actual practice of the law. In the retrospect of history it seems clear that, even though the professorship at William and Mary endured, it was being subjected to severe criticism.

More importantly, the lectureships at colleges had proved inadequate for bar examination preparation, and young men began to find their way to the private law schools that united the practical knowledge gained from clerkship with education in substantive law private law. The establishments of Tapping Reeve at Litchfield, Connecticut, and Peter Van Schaack at Kinderhook, New York, are only the best known of many similar enterprises that began in the postwar years of the 1780s and persisted into the third decade of the nineteenth century.[57]

Professionalism in Legal Education

These private law schools developed from the earlier apprenticeship tradition, in the sense that the students were trained by one lawyer (or in the case of Litchfield, by two instructors), and were given access to the teacher's library. They were, however, not based upon clerkship duties but rather involved the students in full-time study, consisting of lectures and participation in moots and periodic oral examinations.[58] The methods of instruction were not substantially different from those used by Wythe. The course content, however, was markedly different. Rather than dealing with Roman or European law, the work at Litchfield emphasized mastery of private law in the English and American systems of common law.[59] Among those topics covered by Reeve and James Gould at Litchfield are: Municipal Law, Master and Servant, Parent and Child, Fraudulent Conveyances, Bailments, Assumpsit, Writs of Error, Insurance, Charter Parties, and Devises and Real Property.[60] Modern lawyers may well wonder if these two were not responsible for creating most of the categories in the West Publishing Company's digests of the law![61] What was conspicuously absent was the treatment of constitutional law and other topics of public law that received such extended treatment in college lectures.

A comparison of Litchfield's course of study with that undertaken by George Wythe and others as professors of law and police provides a clearer perception of Thomas Jefferson's contribution to American legal education. As we have already suggested, Jefferson and the university lecturers were interested in law study as an instrument for citizenship training.[62] They ranged widely in their coverage but maintained a fixed focus upon uniquely American aspects of public law. Liberal education demanded consideration of all forms of government, ancient and modern, unitary and federal, English and continental. Operating within liberal arts guidelines, Wythe and his contemporaries sought to exercise the minds of their listeners and produce new modes of thinking about political and governmental processes. Ironically, the most outstanding exemplar of this training would be Thomas Jefferson's *bête noire*, Chief Justice John Marshall.

Admittedly Marshall had been exposed to Wythe's lectures for only a short time, but his subsequent career as a lawyer and judge evidenced the very qualities of mind fostered by such an education. Marshall exercised clear and precise analysis of public law issues, tempered with an appreciation for the economic and social impact of political and legal decisions. He gained expertise in the construction of statutes and constitutional provisions; he was adept at the explication of the meaning of words, and in the application of logic to legal problems. On the other hand, his opinions lack the classical allusions so popular in his day and are not speckled with citations to English and American precedents. It is documented that in a number of fields of the law, he relied heavily upon the erudition of at least two Supreme Court colleagues, Bushrod Washington and Joseph Story.[63]

The continuance of university lectureships in law, as conceived by Jefferson, was challenged by the advent of the first private law school at Litchfield in 1784. There, and at similar schools throughout New England and the Middle Atlantic states, instruction centered upon private law subjects. Unabashedly, Reeve and his colleagues undertook the training of professional technicians who would win cases for their clients without elaborate citation to historical or foreign practices. Professor McKenna writing about Litchfield suggests that "Despite its narrow technicalism, or perhaps because of it, Litchfield's form of legal training caught on."[64] After 1830 even the successful university law schools had to accommodate their goals to incorporate this emphasis upon professionalism.[65]

This ground swell of support for professionalism in university legal education followed shortly after Thomas Jefferson's last venture into the field. This involved the establishment of a course of study for the University of Virginia, chartered in 1819 primarily through the efforts of the former president and Joseph C. Cabell. Jefferson's 1814 draft of a proposed course of study allocated law (both municipal and foreign) to a professional school. This was to serve two groups, (1) those who were entering the legal profession as a means of earning their livelihood and (2) the wealthy who aspired to share in conducting the affairs of the nation.[66] Ten years later, with the charter secured and funds appropriated, Jefferson and Cabell began a search for professors to fill the chairs at the new university. The former president put special emphasis upon the legal professorship, for it was there that heresies might be introduced. "It is our duty to guard against the dissemination of such principles among our youth," he wrote to Cabell,[67] but it was difficult to find a politically correct Jeffersonian in the legal profession who would work for the stipend being offered.

In an effort to snare William Wirt, Jefferson and Cabell tendered him the presidency of the university to supplement the salary of a professor, but the offer was refused. Earlier they considered offering a judge a supplementary appointment as a district chancellor in the Virginia court system if he would accept the professorship, but they were unsuccessful.[68] Two months before he died, Jefferson was relieved to learn that John T. Lomax, a Fredricksburg lawyer of "strict construction" views, had accepted appointment as professor of law at the University of Virginia.[69] For Jefferson's peace of mind on his deathbed, it was just as well that he was unaware that although he had won the battle for political orthodoxy, he had lost the war for broadly based legal education. As early as 1829 there were complaints that law teaching at Charlottesville failed to prepare young men for practice. Lomax and his successors found it necessary to devote their instruction to the more practical needs of students with professional goals.[70] Otherwise they could not compete with the private law schools and the revised curriculum then being implemented by Justice Joseph Story, the Dane Professor of Law at Harvard.

Following Story's 1829 appointment, he successfully blended Jefferson's concept of public law training for citizenship with Reeve's emphasis upon private law. Story had been trained by clerkship after completing the traditional Harvard College curriculum with its emphasis upon the classics. Years of practice followed by seventeen years on the Marshall Court provided Story with a broad and comprehensive view of all legal systems, augmented by professional expertise in the common law and its method. His classes were never empty. Rather than teaching through lectures he held recitations, sparked by an impish sense of humor and quick recall of precedent. Like many a modern law professor, he was occasionally led into diverting monologues by the questions of mischievous students. He and his colleagues combined a vigorous study of private law topics with close attention to American public law matters.[71] For Story the law was "a science, in which there is no substitute for diligence and labour."[72] Yet, theoretical approaches to law and government were dangerous:

Great vigilance and great jealously are . . . necessary in republics to guard against
the captivations of theory, as well as the approach of less invidious foes.[73]

Many of our most illustrious statesmen have been lawyers; but they have been
lawyers liberalized by philosophy, and a large intercourse with the wisdom of
ancient and modern times.[74]

In his teaching Story emphasized the common law, both as preparation for professional life and as a study worthy of scholars and gentlemen who wished to obtain
a broad knowledge of the precepts of law.[75] Abstract theory was an object of suspicion, and Story taught his charges to rely upon experience rather than reason. He
proclaimed that the end of all true logic was "the just application of principles to
the actual concerns of human life."[76]

Story's appointment to the Dane Professorship was the most significant event in
American legal education since Jefferson's 1779 reform of the William and Mary
curriculum. Within a relatively short period of time Justice Story succeeded in syn-
thesizing the public law emphasis of Wythe, Wilson, and Kent with the professional training of Reeve, Van Schaack, and others. Emphasis upon the need for experiential learning was a forerunner of the future case method and may be derived in
part from Van Schaack's method of having students read the record of cases. Putting
the students through formal recitations may be viewed as Story's humane prototype
of the more vigorous Socratic method still very much in vogue today. The foundations for the modern law school were laid by Story's tenure at Harvard from 1829 to
his death in 1844.

It was the cruel fate of Thomas Jefferson to live to see the day when his concept
of legal education would languish and die at Pennsylvania and Columbia. It survived only precariously at William and Mary, and by 1825 had gained only a tenu-
ous foothold at Virginia. Yet, the Jeffersonian ideal of training for citizenship was
one of the two major streams—university lectures and private law school training—that give rise to the modern law school. Perhaps it was just as well that
Jefferson did not live to see Story, his political adversary, undertaking this synthesis
of legal education!

The separation of professional legal education from liberal arts studies has
remained characteristic of the United States in the twentieth century, but Jefferson's
ideal of law as education for citizenship is still with us. The proliferation of legal
studies programs in American colleges during the past decade indicates growing
student and faculty interest in integrating law into the undergraduate curriculum.
At the same time law schools have sought to provide students with social science
and humanities perspectives. These courses are designed to expand the ways in
which professional lawyers think about law and its relationship to society. Where
humanists once felt isolated by the utilitarianism rampant in law faculties,[77] they
now find themselves welcomed. Today, perhaps more than ever before in the history of legal education, we are closer to realizing Jefferson's dream of educating citizens through legal training.

JENNINGS L. WAGONER, JR.

"That Knowledge Most Useful to Us": Thomas Jefferson's Concept of Utility in the Education of Republican Citizens

While serving as minister to France in 1785, Thomas Jefferson received a letter from John Banister, Jr., an American seeking his advice regarding "the best seminary for the education of youth in Europe." Jefferson dutifully replied with commentary on the relative merits of Geneva and Rome, which at the time he considered the most desirable European centers of learning. Rather abruptly, Jefferson then diverted his correspondent's attention to a more fundamental question: "But why send an American youth to Europe for education?" Jefferson asked. "What are the objects of an *useful* American education?"[1]

What indeed were to be the "objects" or aims of education for citizens of the new republic? Why should it matter what young Americans studied or whether they were educated at home or abroad? What, to Jefferson's way of thinking, was the relationship between the content and context of "an useful education" and the conduct and character of American youth? We shall argue here that Jefferson's responses to these questions are central to an understanding of his evolving concept of the form and manner of education most useful for republican citizens. We will consider as well the charge that Jefferson's emphasis on utility in education has contributed directly to the uncritical and conservative nature of American education.

The rationale Jefferson presented in 1785 in reply to his fellow countryman's inquiry provides an important, if somewhat circumscribed, beginning point in our search for Jefferson's depiction of "that knowledge most useful to us." It is with that response and the events and influences that shaped that response that our exploration must begin.

The Education of Republican Citizens: Content and Context

Thomas Jefferson both respected and resented Europe's claims of superiority in cultural matters. He had undertaken his mission to France with some concern that he might be perceived as "a savage from the mountains of America." He found himself dazzled and charmed by the gracious manners and refinement of the French elite, among whom, he said, "it seems that a man might pass a life without encountering a single rudeness." He marveled at the heights that had been achieved in the arts and opened his heart to one correspondent by declaring:

> Were I to tell you how much I enjoy their architecture, sculpture, painting, music, I should want words. It is in these arts they shine. The last of them particularly, is an enjoyment the deprivation of which with us, cannot be calculated. I am almost ready to say, it is the only thing which from my heart I envy them, and which, in spite of all the authority of the Decalogue, I do covet.[2]

As captivated as Jefferson was by European artistic and literary attainments, he was appalled at the misery and squalor that he observed among the masses in France. In the same letter in which he confessed envy of the status of the arts in Europe, he observed that "the general fate of humanity here [is] most deplorable." Jefferson asserted that "the great mass of people are suffering under physical and moral oppression," and he contended that even among the aristocracy there was less happiness and domestic tranquility than was enjoyed by the general population of America. Jefferson's experiences in Europe prompted him to give thanks repeatedly for the fact that a great ocean separated the fledgling American republic from the contamination of European conditions and conventions.[3]

In light of Jefferson's ambivalent assessment of European society, it is not surprising that, in his reply to Banister, he was brief not only in his treatment of the question regarding the best seat of learning in the Old World, but also in his mention of the studies he thought most appropriate for youth in the New World. He recommended a knowledge of the classical and modern languages, especially French, Spanish, and Italian. He also listed mathematics, chemistry, agriculture, botany, and other branches of science, as well the study of history and ethics. Studies such as these Jefferson considered the bare essentials, the core areas of knowledge that should be in the possession of any American who sought enlightenment.

In numerous other letters and documents written both before and after his exchange with Banister, Jefferson elaborated in some detail on the value of these and other fields of study, as we shall see. In this letter, however, he deemed a mere listing to be sufficient. Jefferson in this instance was intent on engaging an issue that he considered more pressing than that of the textual substance or content of education. The value or usefulness of education, Jefferson reasoned here, is determined by context as well as by content. To Jefferson, the kind of education most valuable for republican citizens was one that could be acquired more surely and more safely in the raw towns and villages of the new American nation than in the ancient and revered capitals of Europe.

Writing from Paris, a metropolitan center of renowned sophistication and refinement, Jefferson invited Banister to consider the disadvantages of sending

American youth to Europe. He pointed to only a few of the many snares awaiting, for to enumerate them all, said Jefferson, "would require a volume." Jefferson reflected first on the questionable pastimes to which a lad would be exposed if sent to England to study. He listed "drinking, horse racing, and boxing" as the chief amusements of the youth of that nation. In that country and elsewhere abroad an American student would likely acquire a "fondness for European luxury and dissipation, and a contempt for the simplicity of his own country," Jefferson warned. Moreover, wrote Jefferson, the youngster quite likely would become fascinated with the grand lifestyle of European aristocrats and look with scorn upon the advance of equality in his native land. In passages that would stir the imagination if not the emotions of youth (and, as one psychohistorian has suggested, that may have reflected Jefferson's own yearnings), he warned also of the lure of the "voluptuary dress and arts of the European women" that would arouse the desire for "female intrigue." Yielding to this, the "strongest of all the human passions," Jefferson said, would lead to infidelity and the ruination of both health and marital happiness.[4]

Jefferson set forth yet another consideration directed even more pointedly to the perils of foreign study. A young man educated in Europe, he cautioned, would form friendships that would be useless and temporary, while at the same time he would miss out on forming bonds with fellow countrymen that under proper conditions would be of "the most faithful and permanent" kind. Educated as a foreigner in terms of his affections, values, tastes, and even in style and manner of writing and speaking, an American abroad, Jefferson concluded, would become alienated and lost. He would lose, said Jefferson, "in his knowledge, in his morals, in his health, in his habits, and in his happiness."

Although Jefferson confessed to Banister that his zeal as an American may have led to a bit of hyperbole in his description of European dissipation and dangers, he nonetheless appealed to Banister's own experience as an American: "Cast your eye over America: who are the men of most learning, of most eloquence, most beloved by their countrymen and most trusted and promoted by them? They are those who have been educated among them, and whose manners, morals, and habits, are perfectly homogeneous with those of the country."[5]

In this and many other letters written from France, Jefferson revealed at once a pride in his homeland and a keen sense of the frailty of the embryonic nation. Convinced that enlightened Americans needed to attend consciously and deliberately to the serious work of educating the body politic, Jefferson sought to distance his countrymen from the social and political traditions that he believed contrasted so markedly with the conditions that should emerge and prevail in the new nation that was forming. Jefferson's letter to Banister was thus an appeal to a rising American consciousness. It also highlighted an important facet of his concept of utility in education: republican citizens must themselves be educated *in* the new republic.

Toward the More General Diffusion of Knowledge

Jefferson had not long been in the public arena before he turned his attention to the pressing question of the relationship between education and liberty. Dumas Malone, the premier biographer of Jefferson, contended that throughout Jefferson's life, "liberty was his chief concern, and his major emphasis was on the freedom of the spirit and the mind." Merrill Peterson has more recently commented that "Jefferson's faith in freedom and self-government was at bottom a faith in education, which therefore became a paramount responsibility of the state." Jefferson himself set forth in unmistakable terms the essential linkage between liberty and education in a letter to George Washington in 1786:

> It is an axiom in my mind that our liberty can never be safe but in the hands of the people themselves, and that too, of the people with a certain degree of instruction. This it is the business of the state to effect, and on a general plan.[6]

To Jefferson then, liberty depended on education, an education that would ensure that the inalienable rights recently proclaimed and fought for in the Revolution would in fact be realized by his and future generations. The need, quite simply, was for an education that would be useful for republican citizens. This conviction led Jefferson, a member of a special legislative committee that had been formed in late 1776 to revise Virginia's laws, to draft Bill 79, a Bill for the More General Diffusion of Knowledge. This bill, composed in 1778, and two companion proposals, one recommending changes in the constitution of the College of William and Mary and another providing for the establishment of a public library in Richmond, were presented to the legislature on June 18, 1779.[7]

Jefferson had high hopes for his education proposal. Before the bill's fate had been decided, Jefferson wrote to his friend and colleague George Wythe that "the most important bill in our whole code is that for the diffusion of knowledge among the people. No other sure foundation can be devised for the preservation of freedom, and happiness."[8]

Had Jefferson's education bill been adopted, it would have provided for publicly supported elementary and secondary schools and access to the College of William and Mary for a limited number of the best and brightest young men "raked from the rubbish annually." Malone suggested that had the bill been successful, Jefferson would have probably listed it along with his statute for religious freedom as among his greatest achievements. Jefferson was denied that possibility, however. When finally brought to a vote in late 1786, Bill 79 was defeated, the cost of the measure being cited as the main deterrent. Jefferson's disappointment can be gauged in part by an appeal he had made to Wythe a few months earlier:

> Preach, my dear Sir, a crusade against ignorance; establish and improve the law for educating the common people. Let our countrymen know . . . that the tax which

will be paid . . . is not more than the thousandth part of what will be paid to kings, priests, and nobles, who will rise up among us if we leave the people in ignorance.[9]

Jefferson, who in his own words was "not a friend to a very energetic government," considered popular education as a preferable alternative to a strong government. Although governmental power should be limited, in one sphere its activity was, he thought, quite legitimate. Providing for the education of the people, he wrote to James Madison in the winter of 1787, was "the most legitimate engine of government." Echoing a familiar refrain, Jefferson reminded Madison that an educated populace would see the advantage of preserving peace and order and would be, in fact, "the only sure reliance for the preservation of our liberty."[10]

We need not detain ourselves here with numerous points of detail concerning Jefferson's bill. What does invite our attention, however, are questions of utility: what was the practical aim of Jefferson's plan? In what way did the system he outlined and the studies he proposed promise to enhance republican citizenship? In exploring the contours of Jefferson's mind regarding these matters, we move into a deeper understanding of the mode and content of education that he thought not only useful but essential in a republican society.

In the preamble to the 1779 education bill, Jefferson addressed squarely the overarching purpose of his proposed legislation. Noting that even under the best forms of government those entrusted with power are tempted to pervert it into tyranny, Jefferson asserted that the most effective means of preventing this would be "to illuminate, as far as practicable, the minds of the people at large." This he proposed to do through the creation and public support of a statewide system of elementary schools to which all free children, male and female, would be granted admission without charge.

The curriculum Jefferson outlined for pupils at this level appears at first glance to be rather conventional: reading, writing, and arithmetic. Jefferson proposed, however, that the books used to teach reading "shall be such as will at the same time make them acquainted with Grecian, Roman, English, and American history." History was to play a special role in the basic education of republican citizens. It would be through the study of history, Jefferson maintained, that the young would gain knowledge of events in other ages and other countries and, so informed, would be able to recognize or "know ambition in all its shapes" and thus be motivated to "exert their natural powers to defeat its purposes." In a society in which the governed were to be the guardians of their own liberties, no other study could be of comparable importance. The value or utility of history, as Jefferson conceived it, makes more understandable his assertion decades later that there is "no safe depository of the ultimate powers of the society but the people themselves," and his corollary that, "if we think them not enlightened enough to exercise their control with a wholesome discretion, the remedy is not to take it from them, but to inform their discretion by education."[11]

However limited Jefferson's proposed elementary curriculum might appear to those of a later age, his objectives for education at this level suggest a degree of usefulness and range of competencies that would challenge the best efforts of teachers of any era. Years later, in drafting "The Rockfish Gap Report" that led to the establishment of the University of Virginia, Jefferson enumerated the aims of education appropriate for republican citizens. His listing of the objectives of primary or elementary education in that document merits quotation in full:

> To give every citizen the information he needs for the transaction of his own business;
> To enable him to calculate for himself, and to express and preserve his ideas, his contracts and accounts, in writing;
> To improve, by reading, his morals and faculties;
> To understand his duties to his neighbors and country, and to discharge with competence the functions confided to him by either;
> To know his rights; to exercise with order and justice those he retains; to choose with discretion the fiduciary of those he delegates; and to notice their conduct with diligence, with candor, and judgment;
> And, in general, to observe with intelligence and faithfulness all the social relations under which he shall be placed.[12]

If the mass of the population were so instructed, Jefferson reasoned, the odds of the continued survival of the society would be greatly increased. Jefferson was equally certain that, without the widespread diffusion of knowledge, the future of the republican experiment was in doubt: "If a nation expects to be ignorant and free, in a state of civilization," he wrote, "it expects what never was and never will be."[13]

It is significant to note that Jefferson made no mention of the "fourth R," religion, in his 1779 proposal. His own upbringing and schooling certainly had included inculcation in the general precepts of Anglicanism, and, for all his anticlericalism and skepticism on many points of Christian doctrine in later life, he considered religion as "too important" and "the consequences of error . . . too serious" for that realm to be ignored.[14]

There were others during the revolutionary era and beyond who, like Jefferson, expressed great concern regarding the moral fiber and religious convictions of citizens in the new republic. Benjamin Rush, for example, a signer of the Declaration of Independence and probably the best-known American physician of his day, argued that "the only foundation for a useful education in a republic is to be laid in RELIGION." Rush reasoned that without religion, "there can be no virtue, and without virtue there can be no liberty, and liberty is the object and life of all republican governments." Believing then that the safety, happiness, and well-being of civil government necessitated that American children be indoctrinated in the doctrines and disciplines of their families' *Christian* faith, Rush in effect equated Christianity with republicanism:

A Christian ... cannot fail of being a republican, for every precept of the Gospel inculcates those degrees of humility, self-denial, and brotherly kindness which are directly opposed to the pride of monarchy and the pageantry of a court. A Christian cannot fail of being useful to the republic, for his religion teacheth him that no man "liveth to himself." And lastly, a Christian cannot fail of being wholly inoffensive, for his religion teacheth him in all things to do to others what he would wish, in like circumstances, they should do to him.[15]

If the irony of Rush's invocation of the Golden Rule and his admonition that Christianity should be the preferred if not the established religion of the Republic escaped him, Jefferson was more attuned to the tension. No less than Rush, Jefferson also valued the moral teachings of Christianity in terms of their effect on public virtue and individual happiness. He also perceived an intimate connection between religion and morality. Jefferson, however, maintained that morality, while rooted in religion, was independent of the dogmatic teachings of specific religious sects. "On the dogmas of religion, as distinguished from moral principles," Jefferson said, "all mankind, from the beginning of the world to this day, have been quarreling, fighting, burning, and torturing one another, for abstractions unintelligible to themselves and to all others, and absolutely beyond the comprehension of the human mind." The points on which religious groups divide, Jefferson concluded, had little or nothing to do with moral action. Having no doubt that the practice of morality was necessary for the well-being of society, Jefferson also believed that "the interests of society require the observation of those moral precepts only in which all religions agree (for all forbid us to murder, steal, plunder, or bear false witness)."[16]

Although Jefferson mentioned morality as an explicit aim of elementary education, he implicitly consigned specific religious instruction to the private sphere of family and church. Moreover, Jefferson deemed religion a complex and highly rational affair, a matter that required intensive study and contemplation. This was beyond the reach of young children. Peter Carr, Jefferson's nephew, was seventeen years of age when Jefferson advised him that he was then mature enough to "fix reason firmly in her seat, and call to her tribunal every fact, every opinion" regarding the existence of God and other religious teachings.[17]

Jefferson's advice to his nephew certainly did not mean that moral or ethical teachings should wait until one's reasoning powers were fully developed. Jefferson, who believed that "true religion is morality," also believed that the Creator had implanted in human beings a common or shared "moral sense." He referred to this moral instinct as "the brightest gem with which the human character is studded." This conscience or sense of right and wrong, said Jefferson, "is as much a part of man as his leg or arm. It is given to all human beings in a stronger or weaker degree, as force of members is given them in a stronger or weaker degree." Thus, like bodily muscles, the moral faculty might be strengthened by exercise. To Jefferson, it was therefore not so much the content of the moral law that needed attention, but rather the process of making moral decisions.[18]

In the Jeffersonian approach to moral development, the task of the school, along with the family, was to use every opportunity to help the young develop virtuous habits. In part this would be done by encouraging young people to reflect on the consequences of decisions made in everyday life and to heed the promptings of conscience. Judicious reading could also aid in the moral reasoning process. Although generally contemptuous of novels as being a "mass of trash" and a waste of time, Jefferson nonetheless contended that carefully selected works of fiction could be of some value in terms of teaching values. Authors who modeled their narratives on the incidents of real life were sometimes able, he suggested, to provide "interesting and useful vehicles of a sound morality." Books that described situations closely similar to those of life in which the characters confronted moral choices had a special utility. Jefferson maintained that "everything is useful which contributes to fix in us the principles and practice of virtue." Reading of acts of charity may stimulate "a strong desire in ourselves of doing charitable and grateful acts, also." By the same token, Jefferson contended, "when we see or read of any atrocious deed, we are disgusted with its deformity and conceive an abhorrence of vice." These vicarious lessons, Jefferson believed, could stimulate and exercise moral feelings and thereby strengthen the habit of thinking and acting virtuously.[19]

If fiction could be instructive in strengthening morality, factual knowledge held even greater potency. Jefferson's conviction that history offered lessons that could serve to prevent the reappearance of tyranny was tied to his belief that the study of the past presented limitless opportunities for calling the moral sense into play. He observed in his *Notes on the State of Virginia:*

> Instead therefore of putting the Bible and Testament into the hands of the children, at an age when their judgments are not sufficiently matured for religious enquiries, their memories may here be stored with the most useful facts from Grecian, Roman, European, and American history. The first elements of morality too may be instilled into their minds; such as, when further developed as their judgments advance in strength, may teach them how to work out their own greatest happiness, by shewing them that it does not depend on the condition of life in which chance has placed them, but is always the result of good conscience, good health, occupation, and freedom in all just pursuits.[20]

For Jefferson, then, the utility or value of moral development was that it contributed directly to the happiness and well-being of the republican citizen and to the harmony of the republican state. The useful citizen was the moral citizen, respected and admired by his countrymen. "Above all things," Jefferson advised his nephew, "lose no occasion of exercising your dispositions to be grateful, to be generous, to be charitable, to be humane, to be true, just, firm, orderly, courageous, &c. Consider every act of this kind, as an exercise which will strengthen your moral faculties *and increase your worth.*"[21]

Although Jefferson's plan of 1779 provided for the education of girls through the elementary grades, he did not envision public support for the education of women beyond that point. He did, however, favor the continuing education of women and was clearly utilitarian in his motives. Reflecting the accepted definition of the "woman's sphere" in the early American social order, Jefferson reasoned that, as future mothers and wives, young women needed instruction in household economy as well as in other realms. In properly ordered households, most of the guidance and instruction of girls naturally would rest with the mother.

Jefferson, who after ten years of marriage became a widower left with the responsibility of three young daughters, was acutely aware of the fact that one could not assume the existence of a "typical" family or take for granted that young girls would consider domestic skills to be of great importance. He nonetheless thought it imperative that girls be given the instruction they would need in order to become good wives, mothers, and, if necessary, even paternal surrogates. Advice on these matters he frequently gave his daughters, while much of their actual instruction and care, especially during his years abroad, was of necessity provided by relatives.[22]

Jefferson accounted "the order and economy of a house [as being] as honorable to the mistress as those of the farm to the master." He was persistent in urging his surviving daughters, Martha and Mary, to practice their domestic skills. "Tell me," he wrote to his daughter Mary in a rather typical letter, "how many hours a day [do] you sew? . . . [Do] you know how to make a pudding yet, to cut out a beefsteak, to sow spinach? or to set a hen?" In a letter to Martha, he wrote of needlework as a valuable skill and a useful activity that could help her pass the time when forced to endure dull weather or dull company. He added that a plantation mistress could not direct the work of her servants if she lacked the skills herself. Domestic proficiency, Jefferson insisted, was of absolute necessity if a woman were to perform her duties as a responsible wife and mother.[23]

There were other responsibilities and duties women faced that required education of a more formal sort. Jefferson thought it essential that his own daughters be given a "solid education," one which would enable them to educate their daughters and even to direct the course of their sons' education, "should their fathers be lost, or incapable, or inattentive." Jefferson gave serious thought to the possibility that his daughters' husbands might not be able or willing to carry out their responsibilities toward their children. Jefferson once calculated that the odds were about fourteen to one that a daughter might marry a "blockhead" and thus have to survive by her own wits! It was obvious to Jefferson that women as well as men needed a useful education.[24]

Although Jefferson once stated that "a plan of female education has never been a subject of systematic contemplation with me," he in fact did give the matter considerable thought, as his letters to his daughters, to his granddaughters, and to others testify. Jefferson had definite ideas regarding the education of women in a republican society, at least for those whose circumstances might enable them to continue in self-improvement beyond the level of elementary schooling that he hoped would be made available to the entire citizenry.

Jefferson encouraged his own daughters and granddaughters to gain proficiency in French, Spanish, and Latin as well as in English, and directed their reading in history and carefully selected works of literature. He coaxed them with assurances that the more they progressed in their studies, the more worthy of his love they would become. Jefferson was unrelenting in his prodding and planning in their behalf. "I am anxious to know what books you read, what tunes you can play, and to receive specimens of your drawing," he wrote to Martha. She was eleven years old when her father laid out a plan of studies that detailed how she might most profitably spend each hour of the day: music practice from eight to ten o'clock; dancing or drawing (on alternating days) followed by letter writing from ten to two; French from three to four; music again from four to five; and five until bedtime, "read English, write, &c." He admonished her to take care to never spell a word wrong in her correspondence, for a lady who always spells correctly will earn "great praise." She should attend meticulously to her appearance, giving care to dress herself in such a manner that "you may be seen by any gentleman without his being able to discover a pin amiss, or any other circumstance of neatness wanting." These and countless similar admonitions that filled Jefferson's letters to his daughters and grandchildren convincingly demonstrate that Jefferson's expectations were demanding and often quite detailed. Admitting this in a letter to Martha, he added that his expectations were "not higher than you may attain. Industry and resolution are all that is wanting."[25]

Jefferson's most explicit directives on the education of women were presented in a letter to Nathaniel Burwell in 1818. As noted earlier, Jefferson urged caution regarding fiction, except for novels known to have redeeming moral qualities. Poetry he thought of little value for women, although he did concede that some works by Pope, Dryden, Shakespeare, or Molière, among others, might be useful in terms of forming style and taste and therefore might be read "with pleasure and improvement." Jefferson informed Burwell that French was "an indispensable part of education for both sexes." He recommended dancing lessons as a desirable "ornament," as a source of healthy exercise, and as a necessary accomplishment for young women who would be expected to participate "without awkwardness" in the circles of festivity. Jefferson entered a caveat regarding dancing, however. The value of dancing was of short duration, he said, noting that he subscribed to the French "rule" that "no lady dances after marriage." More than mere decorum lent support to this custom, for as Jefferson explained to Martha, the prohibition "is founded in solid physical reasons, gestation and nursing leaving little time to a married lady when this exercise can be either safe or innocent."

Jefferson thought drawing of some value in the education of girls: "an innocent and engaging amusement, often useful, and a qualification not to be neglected in one who is to become a mother and an instructor." He suggested that music was invaluable in furnishing escape from the cares of the day and was a source of enjoyment that would last throughout life. Ever practical, however, Jefferson bluntly offered his opinion that if a child does not have an ear for music, no attempt should be made to provide instruction.[26]

With the exception of the stress laid on domestic skills, Jefferson's advice regarding the education of girls is remarkably similar in kind, if not degree, to the education recommended for boys. Certainly the general themes are the same: an emphasis on morality, health, and practical knowledge that would enable one to become self-reliant and able to be of service to others. Jefferson easily could have been writing to a nephew or grandson, rather than to his daughter, when he admonished:

> The object most interesting to me for the residue of my life, will be to see you both developing daily those principles of virtue and goodness which will make you valuable to others and happy in yourselves, and acquiring those talents and that degree of science [knowledge] which will guard you at all times against ennui, the most dangerous poison of life. A mind employed is always happy. This is the true secret, the grand recipe for felicity.[27]

For the daughters as well as the sons of republican citizens, then, education should equip one for the pursuit of happiness in the broadest sense. Happiness was to be found in virtue, in useful service, and in an active mind. It was on this foundation that the structure of the "good life" and the scaffolding of the new nation should be built.[28]

Educating Republican Leaders

The general object of Jefferson's educational scheme was to provide instruction "adapted to the years, to the capacity, and the condition of every one, and directed to their freedom and happiness." In 1814 he wrote to a mature Peter Carr that every citizen needed "an education proportioned to the condition and pursuits of his life." For the average citizen who in Jeffersonian terminology belonged to the "laboring" class, a basic level of elementary education as outlined in his 1779 Bill for the More General Diffusion of Knowledge would suffice. For those citizens who gave evidence of belonging to "the learned" class, however, elementary education was to serve as a foundation for further study. Those boys "whom nature hath endowed with genius and virtue" required more advanced preparation in order to qualify them for their varied pursuits and duties in a republican society.[29]

Jefferson's 1779 bill (and a later version written in 1817) called for public support of poor but talented boys who could survive the periodic screenings that would thin the ranks of the scholarship students (or "public foundationers," as Jefferson called them) in the grammar or secondary schools. A select few of these, "chosen for the superiority of their parts and disposition," would pursue, at public expense, the most advanced education then available by matriculating at the College of William and Mary. Other students, less talented but whose parents or guardians were able to pay tuition fees, could, as always, continue with their schooling as long as they wished.[30]

Jefferson had laid out the basic rationale for his differentiated system of education and made clear its utilitarian orientation in his initial education bill. In that proposal he stated that people are happiest "whose laws are best, and are best administered." The wise formation and proper administration of the laws in turn depended upon wise and honest public servants. Jefferson therefore contended that "it becomes expedient for promoting public happiness" that the best and brightest students should be prepared by education to "guard the sacred deposit of the rights and liberties of their fellow citizens." Leadership should be determined by merit "without regard to wealth, birth, or other accidental condition or circumstance." Since the parents of many children "whom nature hath fitly formed and disposed to become useful instruments for the public" could not afford to educate their offspring, Jefferson concluded that "it is better that such should be sought for and educated at the common expense of all, than that the happiness of all should be confined to the weak or wicked."[31]

Theoretically, at least, Jefferson's educational scheme would seem to have been both democratic and meritocratic. Equality of opportunity for all at the foundation of the system was to be converted into the advancement of the talented few as the most able students progressed toward the top of the educational pyramid. It has been argued with some justification, however, that Jefferson's vision was obstructed by the fact that he failed to take into account the ability of the wealthy to maintain their edge by providing any and all of their children with the advantages of education, regardless of their ability. Merle Curti points out, for example, that the landed gentry "could enrich the lives of even the more mediocre of their children" and could, through their ability to pay tuition, enable them to advance far beyond the average child of the poor who would be permitted only three years of elementary education at public expense.[32]

That Jefferson was unable to resolve a feature of American social life that persists to this day ought not be allowed to diminish an appreciation for the boldness of his proposal in the context of eighteenth-century Virginia. His plan, which might be said to represent a modest compromise between private and public education, was a radical departure from the conventions of the day. Moreover, his belief that citizens of superior talents ought to serve in positions of leadership was not at all antithetical to his belief that "every government degenerates when trusted to the rulers of the people alone." Convinced that the people had to be the ultimate guardians of their own liberty, he not only held it imperative that the children of *all* citizens should receive a basic education in the rights and duties of citizenship, but he insisted that those who would become the representatives of the people should be properly prepared for their solemn responsibility. The part of his plan that provided for the identification and support of the most talented youth from among the laboring population was clearly designed "to avail the state of those talents which nature has sown as liberally among the poor as the rich." These citizens of demonstrated ability were to make themselves available for public office, not as rulers, but as servants; they were to become "useful instruments for the public."[33]

In an exchange of letters with John Adams late in life, as the two former political foes were trying to bridge the years and ideological gulf that had separated them, Jefferson commented on several bills he had prepared for the Virginia legislature in the late 1770s in his effort to lay "the axe to the root of pseudo-aristocracy." He specifically mentioned his education bill and asserted that, had his proposal been adopted, "worth and genius would thus have been sought out from every condition of life, and completely prepared by education for defeating the competition of wealth and birth for public trusts." Jefferson confided to Adams:

> For I agree with you that there is a natural aristocracy among men. The grounds of this are virtue and talents. . . . There is also an artificial aristocracy, founded on wealth and birth, without either virtue or talents. . . . The natural aristocracy I consider as *the most precious gift of nature,* for the instruction, trusts, and government of society. . . . May we not even say, that that form of government is best, which provides the most effectively for a pure selection of these natural aristoi into the offices of government?

Jefferson added: "The artificial aristocracy is a mischievous ingredient in government, and provisions should be made to prevent its ascendancy." This could be done, Jefferson suggested to Adams, by free elections in which an *educated* populace could separate the natural from the artificial aristocracy, as wheat could be separated from chaff. Clearly, as Jefferson wrote to Adams, in the republican society for which both men had long labored, education had to become "the keystone of the arch of our government."[34]

In any assessment of Jefferson's education prescriptions, one must keep in mind Merrill Peterson's observation that Jefferson's ideas "were in constant motion and seldom abstracted from immediately practical objectives." This caution applies with special force when considering the ordering of studies in Jefferson's various writings on secondary and higher education. His views as expressed in legislative proposals and private correspondence reflected the constraints and opportunities of the moment as well as the maturing of his thought over time. Thus, for example, his ideas in the late 1770s regarding curricular reforms at William and Mary, or his advice to Peter Carr in 1814 regarding the transformation of the lifeless Albemarle Academy into Central College, or his later recommendations regarding the offerings of the University of Virginia were not altogether consistent in detail. There was, however, a very definite consistency in purpose and function. As he repeatedly stressed in correspondence, the institution envisioned as the apex of his educational system should be so constituted that *"every branch of science, useful at this day, may be taught in its highest degree."* However the various subjects were ordered or categorized in this or that proposal, always the focus was on useful knowledge of the highest level.[35]

In 1800, long before Jefferson was able to give sustained attention to the academical and architectural design of the University of Virginia, he had written to Joseph Priestley of his ambitions for his state:

> We wish to establish in the upper country, and more centrally for the State, an University on a plan so broad and liberal and *modern,* as to be worth patronizing with the public support, and be a temptation to the youth of other States to come and drink of the cup of knowledge and fraternize with us.

Jefferson observed that the courses of study in this modern university should be judiciously selected, for "in an institution meant chiefly for use, some branches of science, formerly esteemed, may now be omitted."[36]

Jefferson ventured a hasty listing of useful courses in his letter to Priestley, and fourteen years later, in writing to Carr, provided a much more thoughtful and detailed sketch of studies he thought appropriate for each tier in a complete system of education. A listing of university-level courses appeared as well in Jefferson's 1817 attempt to have the state of Virginia establish a comprehensive system of public schools. It was in Jefferson's 1818 curricular design for the University of Virginia, however, that he laid out in sharpest relief the programs of study and statements of purpose that should define the nature of the higher learning. It is to that document, "The Report of the Commissioners Appointed to Fix the Site of the University of Virginia, &c."—more generally referred to as "The Rockfish Gap Report"—that we now turn our attention.[37]

Consistent with his lifelong rejection of the notion that his or any generation should "tread with awful reverence in the footsteps of our fathers," Jefferson declared in the Rockfish Gap Report his belief in progress and his conviction that education was the key to progress. "Education," he wrote, "engrafts a new man on the native stock, and improves what in his nature was vicious and perverse into qualities of virtue and social worth." He noted further:

> And it cannot be but that each generation succeeding to the knowledge acquired by all those who preceded it, adding to it their own acquisitions and discoveries, and handing the mass down for successive and constant accumulation, must advance the knowledge and well-being of mankind, not *infinitely,* as some have said, but *indefinitely,* and to a term which no one can fix and forsee.[38]

Indefinite progress, however appealing as a concept, was much too abstract to stand undefined as the ultimate purpose of advanced education. Jefferson had in view a university that would contribute directly to the betterment of mankind in clearly defined ways, a university in which each set of offerings would be immediately tied to the needs of the society. He made explicit his vision of the ends the new university should serve by stating that its purposes were:

> To form the statesmen, legislators and judges, on whom public prosperity and individual happiness are so much to depend;
>
> To expound the principles and structure of government, the laws which regulate the intercourse of nations, those formed municipally for our own government, and a sound spirit of legislation, which, banishing all arbitrary and unnecessary restraint on individual action, shall leave us free to do whatever does not violate the equal rights of another;
>
> To harmonize and promote the interests of agriculture, manufactures and commerce, and by well informed views of political economy to give a free scope to the public industry;
>
> To develop the reasoning faculties of our youth, enlarge their minds, cultivate their morals, and instill into them the precepts of virtue and order;
>
> To enlighten them with mathematical and physical sciences, which advance the arts, and administer the health, subsistence, and comforts of human life;
>
> And, generally, to form them to habits of reflections and correct action, rendering them examples of virtue to others, and of happiness within themselves.[39]

Jefferson's listing of the objectives for the University of Virginia made necessary a wide range of advanced studies in the arts, the sciences, and the professions. When setting forth his proposed curriculum, Jefferson grouped what he then considered to be the most useful branches of knowledge into ten categories, each with various subspecialities. Departing significantly from the conventional collegiate practice of holding all students to a common curriculum rooted in the classics, Jefferson proposed that each student be permitted to elect the lectures or courses of study of most interest to him. Provision was made for the ancient languages, but Jefferson's expectation was that students who entered the University of Virginia would come having already acquired a solid foundation in classical language and culture. At the university, "their classical learning might be critically completed, by a study of the authors of highest degree," said Jefferson. If unable to attain this level, he added, they should not be admitted to the university.[40]

Jefferson's advocacy of modern languages emphasizes in bold relief the utilitarian orientation of his curriculum. Jefferson contended that French was "the language of general intercourse among nations" and declared that "as a depository of human science, [it] is unsurpassed by any other language, living or dead." Spanish was important, said Jefferson, because it was the language spoken by a large portion of the inhabitants of the New World and much of early American history could be obtained only in that language. Italian literature abounded with valuable works, he explained, many of which provided excellent "models of the finest taste in style and composition." And, if at the moment France had the lead in some areas of scholarship, Germany "now stands in a line with the most learned nations in richness of erudition and advance of the sciences." That language, too, was of immense value.

The uniqueness of the Jeffersonian curriculum was especially evident in his insistence that Anglo-Saxon was a "modern language" worthy of study. Understanding the evolution of the English language not only would offer insight, Jefferson maintained, into the derivation of words and their usage, but also would provide a deeper understanding of ancient common law on which the American system was based. Our native language, Jefferson asserted, "already fraught with all the eminent science of our parent country, the future vehicle of whatever we may ourselves achieve, and destined to occupy so much space on the globe, claims distinguished attention in American education."[41]

Jefferson's ambitions for medical study at the University of Virginia were much more modest than his claims for other realms of useful knowledge. Considering medicine as occupying the shadowy realm between science and charlatanism—and lacking prospects for the establishment of a hospital in Charlottesville which would be necessary for clinical study and surgical practice—Jefferson commended the historical and theoretical study of the field as an aspect of general culture. Studies in the history of medicine, anatomy, and pharmacology—the last an applied aspect of courses in botany, mineralogy and chemistry—would at least, he reasoned, enable students to gain a better understanding of the extent and limits of medicine's contributions to human life and health.[42]

If Jefferson considered medicine as a sort of charlatanism of the body, he was clearly even more suspicious of theology and its theorists, the charlatans of the mind. In keeping with his dedication to the principle of maintaining a wall of separation between church and state, Jefferson insisted that there should not be a professor of divinity at the state university. He did take care to emphasize, however, that the historical, moral, and literary aspects of religion would be taught as a component of the study of ancient languages and in lectures on ethics. As he had noted on other occasions and in other contexts, Jefferson maintained that in the teaching of ethics, the emphasis should be placed on those moral obligations on which all sects agree. His stance assumed the emergence over time of a common—and thereby useful—faith uniting Americans in a general religion that would reflect the reason of the "author of all the relations of morality." Giving credence to the endless sectarian divisions and doctrinal disputes that had subverted the essence of Christianity, however, he considered as anything but useful.[43]

Jefferson's belief in a common religion was not shared by religious sectarians of his day and fears of a "godless university" gained currency early on. By 1822 Jefferson concluded that, without compromising his or the Constitution's principles, a way might be found to provide his religious critics with some reassurance. He reported that there had been no intention of making the University of Virginia in fact or in appearance indifferent to religion. To the contrary, Jefferson contended, "the relations which exist between man and his Maker, and the duties resulting from those relations, are the most interesting and important to every human being," and should indeed be the object of the most serious study and investigation. Jefferson then proposed that the various sectarian bodies establish seminaries or divinity schools "on the confines" of the university. Jefferson astutely pointed out that the existence of these schools, while independent of the university and of each other, would make it possible for university students to participate in religious exercises with seminarians of their faith. No doubt of greater importance to Jefferson, however, was his contention that students in the divinity schools could have access to the scientific lectures of the university. This, he hoped, would have the effect of elevating the level of religious discourse to a higher, more scholarly plane. Moreover, by bringing the sectarian religionists together and mixing them with the mass of other students, the university community could "soften their asperities, liberalize and neutralize their prejudices, and make the general religion a religion of peace, reason, and morality."[44]

The political nature of Jefferson's proposal is obvious, and his strategy proved effective. Jefferson's point-man in the state legislature, Senator Joseph Cabell, informed him that the seminary proposition was warmly received by that body. That no seminaries were established near the university is perhaps beside the point. At least the charge of godlessness at the institution that had not yet even opened had been muted somewhat by Jefferson's assertion that the existence of these religious institutions "would complete the circle of useful sciences" embraced by the university.[45]

A Conservative or a Liberating Legacy?

"The circle of useful sciences," although Jefferson's own phrase, seems much too circumscribed and limiting to be in harmony with his dynamic concept of knowledge. Knowledge to Jefferson, like his original design of the "academical village," was open-ended, expansive, and forward looking. In a statement characteristically bold, optimistic, and defining of his ideal for the university, Jefferson proclaimed that "This institution will be based on the illimitable freedom of the human mind. For here," he said, "we are not afraid to follow truth wherever it may lead, nor to tolerate any error so long as reason is left free to combat it."[46]

To Jefferson, the unending path to "truth" was the unending path to useful knowledge. Knowledge that was static, that was bounded by time or space, was of little or no value. And yet, there was little that Jefferson found useless—except, perhaps, for the mysticisms of Platonic philosophy and the babel of Christian orthodoxies that had been erected upon those illusive forms.

Although Jefferson refused to be bound by the dead hand of the past, he nonetheless discovered value and utility in history. The rise and fall of former civilizations, he contended, held important lessons for present and future generations. He found in ancient languages models of style as well as ethical and moral teachings of enduring relevance, just as he advocated the study of modern languages for their value in broadening scientific understanding, extending commerce, and developing amiable relations with foreign countries. For one of Jefferson's disposition and curiosity, knowledge by its very definition was utilitarian. (Metaphysical or theological speculations, by contrast, dealt with the unknowable and thus were not useful or of genuine concern.)

That Jefferson stressed utility—an education that would equip republican citizens with the understandings and skills that would enable them to pursue happiness individually and as a people—would not seem to be at issue. As we have noted throughout this essay, Jefferson measured the value of every study and activity by its contribution to the happiness and prosperity of the living generation. Yet, it has been argued that this very feature of Jeffersonian educational theory has contributed to the entrenchment of an educational tradition that has served conservative rather than liberal (or liberating) ends.

This position has been articulated by, among others, Daniel Boorstin in his insightful study of the Jeffersonian quest for useful knowledge, *The Lost World of Thomas Jefferson*. Boorstin contends that Jefferson and others in his enlightened circle, dedicated to utilitarian ends as they were, promoted the push toward "vocationalism" in American education. Boorstin further charges that Jefferson and those who shared his views assigned to educators a largely conservative task, "namely to adjust men to their present roles in society." Striking directly at what he considered the Achilles heel of Jeffersonian educational theory, Boorstin asserts:

> Despite all that had been said about distributing educational opportunities in the proportions in which the Creator had distributed talents among men, the large outlines of the Jeffersonian educational system were designed to prepare each individual for the practical tasks assigned him by his present place in the social hierarchy. . . . [T]he Jeffersonian demand that education give men implements immediately and obviously useful, has surely helped establish the American tradition, which combines enthusiasm for education with an insistence that education be uncritical and conservative.[47]

Boorstin's allegations are uncomfortable, perhaps even uncharitable, but not completely unjustified. One cannot study the history of American education—or reflect on the current malaise in American society—without recognizing the persistence of class structures, inequality, and the complicity of schools in the maintenance of the social and economic status quo. Indeed, a growing body of literature and disaffection on the part of increasingly larger segments of society suggest that schools are much better at selecting and sorting (or "reproducing") children in patterns remarkably similar to their parents' socioeconomic background than they are at "raking geniuses from the rubbish." Nor can we assert two centuries after Jefferson began his crusade against ignorance and tyranny over the mind of man that the "artificial aristocracy" has been replaced by some sort of pure "natural aristocracy."

All this being granted, one might argue that it is much too great a leap to saddle

Jefferson (or "Jeffersonians") with the burden of coconspiracy, consciously or otherwise, in a system of social repression or resignation. Boorstin is surely correct in observing that Jefferson's educational hierarchy (and his lack of sustained attention to the marginal status of women, Native Americans, and African Americans) paralleled the existing social inequalities of his era. But he is also correct in his observation that the orientation of Jefferson's philosophy was futuristic. The conditions of the moment were not to be the conditions of the future. As Boorstin himself puts it, "Since the hope and the fact were not yet one, the Jeffersonians had a sense of living at the beginning of history." The America that might be, that could be, is still an America yet to be.[48]

Jefferson's insistence that education that is valuable must also be useful invites a definition of utility that transcends the moment and the mundane. To "pursue happiness" in the grandest meaning of that concept, Jefferson would have us understand, requires attention to the moral, civic, and aesthetic dimensions of life as well as to the immediately useful. In ways that Jefferson himself may not have wholly appreciated and never fully articulated, his own life underscored the fact that education is more than a *means;* it can also properly be an *end* in itself. Although Jefferson tended to measure the value of all his studies and activities on the basis of functional utility, his intellectually active mind, aesthetic sensibilities, and notions of virtue, service, and the progress of mankind all provide a remarkable example of a life that was both useful and beautiful. Stephen Bailey frames this point with notable clarity:

> [Jefferson] failed to see what his brilliant life emphasized; that beyond facilitating direct service to others, an educated life is itself a thing of beauty, a hosanna to the Almighty, and, coming full circle, by its very example, a supreme indirect service to the happiness of the entire human race.[49]

Perhaps the most appropriate summation of the usefulness and necessity of education for citizens in a republic may be to allow Jefferson, once more, to speak for himself. "If the condition of man is to be progressively ameliorated, as we fondly hope and believe," Jefferson wrote in 1818, education is to be "the chief instrument in effecting it."[50] There is nothing uncritical or conservative in this conception of "that knowledge most useful to us."

BENJAMIN R. BARBER

Education and Democracy: Summary and Comment

As it became professionalized and vocationalized in the years following World War II, education was increasingly decoupled from the life and practice of democracy. Today, education is widely discussed, but with a focus on performance, standards, global competition, and outcomes that has largely eclipsed its link to citizenship. Yet civic pedagogy and public schooling have always been crucial to those who advocate democratic forms of governance. Nowhere is this more evident than in the thought of Thomas Jefferson, in whose account of democratic practices the nurturing of education often seems more crucial than the nurturing of politics. Dumas Malone has noted the relationship that exists between political liberty and the cultivation of the spirit in Jefferson, and Merrill Peterson has argued that Jefferson's faith in freedom and self-government was at bottom a faith in education.

From the time of the Greeks, who spoke of the educational and cultural practices around which a just and republican society rooted in the demes could alone be established, the very meaning of citizenship has been informed by reference to particular understandings of civic education and the transformation of ordinary private human beings into citizens. The citizen, it has been argued, is the calculating egoist educated to public judgment; the citizen is the corrupt merchant induced to virtue, the bigoted individual conditioned to tolerance, the impulsive actor trained to deliberateness, the adversary taught to seek common ground with her opponent. The standards will vary, but all traditional political theory—liberal, republican, and democratic—insists that citizens are created rather than born, products not of nature but of educational artifice. As human beings we may be born free, but civil liberty is an acquisition for which we need education. It is not democratic theorists but only their inattentive detractors who have asserted that democracy is the rule of the mob and citizens but self-interested individuals operating in the political arena.

For democratic theorists, education has defined not merely citizenship but democracy itself. Where is the apostle of democracy who advocates the unbridled governance of masses? More even than the critics of democracy, the proponents have worried about the fitness of the people to govern themselves. That it is their natural right does not in itself capacitate them to do so. The right is not the ability. The normative claim of democracy is disclosed by the phrase "government of, by, and for the people," but its effective operationalization depends on government by, of, and for citizens—a people educated in the arts of liberty.

Without education, democracy may mean little more than the tyranny of opinion over wisdom. From Plato to Alexander Hamilton and Allan Bloom, critics of democracy have complained that to empower the people is to elevate ignorance to the throne. Indeed, many Federalist founders distrusted popular government (if not central government) to a point where they were willing to exercise quite extraordinary constitutional ingenuity in circumventing the popular sovereignty nominally undergirding their new republic. Representative government can be seen as their compromise between natural republican aristocracy, in which the best govern a sovereign people whose sovereignty is limited to accountability, and democracy, in which the subjects and the rulers are one and the same and in which all citizens partaking regularly in the affairs of government govern themselves. The compromise of representation (sometimes called Madisonian) permitted the many to choose the few, but vested governing power in the few, thereby filtering out the passions and prejudices of the many. With its astonishing panoply of institutions—the college of electors, the indirect election of the president and Senate, state nominating conventions—representative government was meant to guarantee excellence without violating the spirit of popular sovereignty. Its multiple filters insulated the people from their prejudices by separating the prejudiced from the rulers, the best from the rest, ensuring a government of natural excellence in a setting of popular sovereignty.

Now Thomas Jefferson was no less exercised by the possibility that democracy might enthrone ignorance than his fellow Virginians. He too sought a system of filtration by which government might be insulated from passion. His appeals to elective aristocracy have been duly noted by critics of direct democracy. But Jefferson's discriminating "filters" were to be installed within rather than between men. Rather than separate men from government, he wished to school them in government. People in power are often indiscreet, for power breeds indiscretion in the wise as well as the foolish.

> Cherish therefor the spirit of our people and keep alive their attention. Do not be
> severe upon their errors, but reclaim them by enlightening them. If once they
> become inattentive to public affairs, you and I and Congress and Assemblies,
> judges and governors, shall all become wolves.
> (Thomas Jefferson to Edward Carrington, January 16, 1787.)

The trick was, however, not to take from the people a power that was rightfully theirs (and which, in other hands, would be vulnerable to still more dangerous abuses); not to withdraw a power they might use indiscreetly, but rather to "inform their discretion."[1] Jefferson never imagined that the common birthright of liberty meant the actual equality in talent and ability of all those born free. The birthright of freedom was a study in immanence, and the actualization of liberty required much more than just getting born. While no less devoted to the idea of a natural aristocracy of talent than any founder, Jefferson believed that popular sovereignty entailed popular government, and popular government could transcend popular ignorance only by way of popular education. In this knowledge, he drafted the 1779 Virginia "Bill for the More General Diffusion of knowledge" and made the founding of a public university in Virginia the primary work of his post-presidential years. On his gravestone he memorialized not his presidency but his role as the university's founder.

Precisely because he saw in democracy a test of discretion and judgment, he made education the keystone of the governmental arch. To filter the passions by filtering the potentially passionate out of government not only risked error—who could ensure that it would not be the wealthy or the privileged (the artificial aristocracy) rather than the wise and judicious (the natural aristocracy) who found their way into service?—but it violated the fundamental logic of democracy. If men could not be trusted to govern themselves, how on earth could they be trusted to govern others?

> . . . the people, especially when moderately instructed, are the only safe, because the only honest, depositories of the public rights, and should therefore be introduced into the administration of them in every function to which they are sufficient.
> (Thomas Jefferson to A. Coray, October 31, 1823)

To put it simply, Thomas Jefferson preferred education to representation as democracy's guarantor. In his case, this choice was a necessity, because he did not think a democracy could survive rooted solely in indirect governance and in that version of original consent which for many members of the founding generation was sufficient to establish a liberal republican constitution. Like Rousseau, Jefferson worried that representation forced people to alienate their liberty. If one took seriously the claim that liberty was inalienable—the central claim of the social contract tradition—then a form of representative government in which liberty was alienated to representatives risked the destruction of the self-evident rights on which the constitution rested. In a Kantian language that was certainly not Jefferson's, but one he might nevertheless appreciate, we might say that autonomous principles first agreed on by unanimous consent (the social contract itself as a founding covenant) quickly become heteronomous when passed on to subsequent generations. The laws of usufruct applied to precepts as well as produce: ownership of principles belongs to those who use and embrace them rather than to those who merely inherit them. Thus, Jefferson insisted, constitutions were not to be looked upon with "sanctimonious reverence" but had to be reinvoked, reembraced, reinvigorated generation by generation—if necessary by blood struggle.

In Jefferson's take on liberty, one senses a certain kinship between democracy and revolution. The democratic will had to reassert itself spontaneously in each generation and within each citizen. The birthright of liberty as potential came alive only in the practice of liberty. Whereas champions of the social contract reasoned that the original consent of founders coupled with the tacit consent of those who subsequently obeyed its precepts sufficed to legitimize a government as democratic, Jefferson understood democratic legitimacy to reside in a series of ongoing choices made afresh by each generation of citizens.

To understand the place of revolutionary ardor in Jefferson's perspective on democracy, we need to look at the spirit associated with political spontaneity—that sense of fresh ownership that each generation brings to a constitution or political order through its participation in the political process. Jefferson was hardly a model for Trotsky, but there was a sense in which he embraced the idea of permanent revolution. For his object was in a certain sense to make revolution commonplace, a permanent feature of the political landscape rather than just a founding mechanism for a new more legitimate politics of stasis. Democracy's chief guarantor was not accountability but participation, not representative but local government. The cry "divide the country into wards" with which Jefferson liked to conclude letters and speeches during one phase of his career was a reminder to the young republic that devolving power into the hands of citizens was a surer way to protect against the abuse of power than to insulate the power-holders from popular prejudice by means of representative institutions.

Following Rousseau's insight that liberty represented was liberty lost (at least with respect to the fundamentals of the sovereign will), Benjamin Rush had reminded would-be democrats that though in the American system "all power is derived from the people, they possess it only on the days of their elections."[2] Jefferson, who loved "dreams of the future more than the history of the past,"[3] had a special sensitivity to the centrality (and fragility) of revolutionary zeal. He warned against looking "at constitutions with sanctimonious reverence, and deem(ing) them like the arc of the covenant, too sacred to be touched,"[4] and he is known famously for his insistence that "the tree of liberty must be refreshed from time to time with the blood of patriots and tyrants. It is its natural manure."[5] These sentiments were linked both to his conviction that constitutions must change with the times,[6] and to his belief that "the earth belongs in usufruct to the living" and "that the dead have neither powers nor rights over it."[7] But it was finally the preservation of the revolutionary spirit itself that was at issue: a "little rebellion now and then," he had argued, was a "good thing" in and of itself.[8] In later life, he certainly distanced himself from the specifics of the French Revolution whose spirit he had rather naively celebrated at the outset of the event, but he never ceased to believe in the need for a refreshing of principle and a reembracing of founding precepts as a condition for the survival of democracy.[9]

There is of course a paradox here, since a revolution is always a founding (and thus a foundation) as well as the kindling of a certain spirit of spontaneity hostile to foundationalism. As Hannah Arendt has observed, in America the revolutionary spirit founded a constitution at odds with that spirit—as social contracts and fixed laws are always likely to be at odds with the spirit of innovation that creates them.[10] Jefferson saw democracy itself, more particularly ward government and active participation by citizens in self-governance, as the remedy to the ossification of the democratic constitution founded on an original compact which successor generations could only approach as an ancient artifact in a spirit of abstract loyalty. Like Rousseau before him and Robert Michels after him, Jefferson worried that representative government could swallow up a people's liberties and lead to an "elective despotism," the worse for being legitimized by a social contract rooted in the very notion of direct voluntary consent being violated by representation. He preferred the internal filter of education to the external filter of representation in part because as we have seen he feared that in representation the distancing of individuals from their prejudices was won only at the cost of distancing them from the responsibilities that defined and gave life to their liberties.

The call for ward government and full participation by citizens "not merely at an election one day in the year, but every day"[11] was to Jefferson a way of critiquing representation as well as a way of advocating participation. Ward government not only secured negative liberty by decentralizing the sovereign power of that state to the neighborhoods, it secured positive liberty by turning right into an affirmative participatory principle in which freedom was not merely preserved but also exercised—in which rights were recoupled with the responsibilities that alone could make rights more than parchment parapets (as Madison had it) from which to defend liberty. The lesson taught by Jefferson is that the celebrated principle of original consent as derived from the foundational principles of natural right (the essence of social contract reasoning) is wholly inadequate to the democratic mandate.

It is in this Jeffersonian mood that I have spent so much of my career trumpeting the benefits of strong, participatory democracy. For according to this Jeffersonian logic, it is not just foundationalism but foundings themselves that imperil the democratic orders they establish. The tension between constitutional order and the revolutionary spirit has been the subject of two recent books that pointedly capture the contradictions between founding and democracy: Gordon Wood's *The Radicalism of the American Revolution*[12] (winner of the 1993 Pulitzer Prize in History) and equally suggestively Bruce Ackerman's *We the People*, volume 1, *Foundations.* Ackerman offers an account of what he calls "dualist democracy" in which in which "Rights Foundationalists" face advocates of the actual exercise of popular sovereignty in a contest over the meaning of democracy and of the revolution that made it. Ackerman sees in historical moments like the Founder's rejection of the Articles of Confederation (and the procedural principles the Articles mandated), or Roosevelt's New Deal, revolutionary emblems of the nation's true democratic spirit. "Americans have not been 'born equal' through some miraculous act of immaculate conception," Ackerman argues. "To the extent that we have gained equality, we have won it through energetic debate, popular decision, and constitutional creativity." His conclusion is Jefferson's: "Once the American people lose this remarkable political capacity, it is only a matter of time before they lose whatever equality they possess—and much else besides."[13]

Gordon Wood also treats the American founding, understood in terms of the Revolution more than in terms of the Constitution, as far more than a rejection of the previous monarchial constitutional order. It did not simply refound a social contract on the basis of popular sovereignty and thereby create a republic, "it actually reconstituted what Americans meant by public or state power and brought about an entirely new kind of popular politics and a new kind of democratic officeholder."[14] The American founding was more than a legitimizing event: it was the beginning of a self-renewing and self-perpetuating process whose legitimacy depended less on its origins than its on-going character and the objects after which it strove. In this sense the Declaration of Independence and subsequent founding documents defined not a point of origin but destiny; not a naturalistic starting point but an artificial ideal; not something to be built upon but something to be brought into being and accomplished over time. James MacGregor Burns thus has it exactly right in the title of his book on "the pursuit of rights."[15] Rights are what the American political system was designed to pursue and bring into being. They may be celebrated as constitutive of a founding moment, but their realization depends on a permanent democratic politics that secures them "for all" only through painful struggle over a long period of time.

Recent critics of Jefferson have reveled in what they deem his overarching hypocrisy. The democrat who boasts on his gravestone about his authorship of the Declaration of Independence and pronounces all men born equal, is in truth not merely a slaveholder who in his latter penurious days comes to depend on slavery for his economic security, but a racist persuaded of the generic inferiority of the African race. To Connor Cruse O'Brien, Jefferson is a hypocrite and a mountebank posturing as the defender of liberty even as he profits from the American caste system.[16] Yet Jefferson's democratic politics and his devolution to a progressive political process are what save him from his institutional and period prejudices. He may have despised the Negro race (if not individual Negroes) but he embraced a participatory politics that opened the way to a struggle for rights within rather than against the political system. He may have hypocritically excluded from inclusion in the vaunted rights of the Declaration and the Bill of Rights the rights of people of color (as well as Native American Indians and women about whom he also expressed himself in extraordinarily derogatory terms), but he set those rights in a context of revolutionary expectations that allowed abolitionists in the 1850s and women in the 1890s and again civil rights marchers in the 1960s to organize under their banner and fight not for the overthrow of the system but for inclusion within it.[17]

Democrats and egalitarians owe him a debt less as a historical figure than as a devotee of an anti-foundationalist participatory politics of the present and the future that allowed what might have become a stultifying system of stasis to become a revolutionary instrument each new generation of Americans could employ in their own struggle for enfranchisement and rights. In short, it is not so much Jefferson's principles in the Declaration but the practical politics and civic education those principles justified to which egalitarians ought to pay tribute. The critics have called his integrity into question by contrasting his principles with his practices as a slave-holder: but the whole point of the principles in question was to subject all practices to constant criticism. Jefferson's great utility to modern democrats was his recognition of the most essential (and paradoxical) of all democratic principles: that politics always trumps principle. In the short term, this may dismay upholders of the "right" principles (such as the principles of right). But in the long run, it is the only hope for both principles and for rights. We need not engage in Jeffersonian hagiography to acknowledge this and give Jefferson his due.

Democratic foundationalism, Jefferson recognized, although it represents an authoritative establishing of the credentials of democracy, may undermine democracy. Representation can successfully distance government from popular passion but it can also erode popular responsibility and destroy active citizenship. Michael Oakeshott once said rationalists are "essentially ineducable," by which he meant that, wedded to formal models of truth and cognition, they were closed to the evidence of their senses about the here and now, and the common sense conversation of those around them.[18] Citizens, on the other hand, are defined by their civic educability: they are not only eminently educable, but they are constituted by that capacity, which is part of the meaning of republican civic virtue. Democracy enjoins constant, permanent motion—a gentle kind of permanent revolution, a moveable feast that affords each generation room for new appetites and new tastes, and thus allows political and spiritual migration to new territory. Yet for this radical version of democracy to work, the citizens upon whom the burden of its success rests must be fit for their responsibilities. Which brings us back to the crucial role of education in Jefferson. The logic of the arguments offered here suggest that it was precisely Jefferson's commitment to autonomous, participating citizens, his distrust of representation, and his belief in the necessity of revolutionary ardor in vitalizing everyday democracy that made civic pedagogy and public education central to his political philosophy.

There are of course some critics who have suggested not only that Jefferson was a bigot and a racist, but that his attachment to natural aristocracy and his distrust of central government made him a less fervent ally of radical democracy than enthusiasts like some of us allow. Gordon Wood has made this kind of argument in our deliberations here, suggesting that Jefferson would have inevitably been caught up in the distrustful temper of the times. Yet a careful reading of the letters proves again and again that, as Bernard Bailyn has said, although Jefferson distrusted central power, he did not distrust either republicanism or government by the people. He had none of that liberal fear of the unwashed masses that typified so many of his peers. Indeed, it is precisely this faith in the populace of France (and America) that has exercised his critics. They take for granted that his enthusiasm for the French Revolution is prima facie grounds for distrust. But of course it was not just revolution in the abstract he endorsed; he also defended real rebels of the kind who had unnerved the young country in Shay's Rebellion. "I like a little rebellion now and then," he had written to Colonel William Smith, for it helps "keep alive" that valuable "spirit of resistance" on which popular government depends.[19]

There is then no convincing way to enlist Jefferson in the battles of those modern anti-democrats whose "liberalism of fear" (bred by Europe's twentieth-century holocausts) begins with a deep suspicion of popular government. Europe's teeming cities may have given their governors a reason to fear the malcontent urban mob, but to apply their lessons to "the independent, the happy, and therefore orderly citizens of the United States" was to do them a grave injustice (Jefferson wrote in a letter to John Taylor in 1816). Jefferson refused the politics of anxiety. Well after his supposedly youthful flirtation with the French Revolution, he still wrote to Samuel Kercheval (July 12, 1816): "I am not among those who fear the people." On the contrary, he tells the Marquis de Lafayette (November 4, 1823), it was "the sickly, weakly, timid man" who "fears the people" and who was thus a "Tory by nature. The healthy, strong and bold, cherishes them." Nor did Jefferson, like so many of the Founders, prefer property to the people. To John Taylor (in 1816) he wrote to excoriate the arrangements that excluded "like Helots, from the rights of representation" that "one-half of our brethren who fight and pay taxes . . . as if society were instituted for the soil and not for the men inhabiting it."

There was to be sure a certain American naivete in Jefferson's earliest and most ardent embrace of European revolutionaries that was to be rehearsed again in succeeding generations by Walt Whitman (see his "To a Foiled European Revolutionnaire") and made transparent in Melville's brilliant account in "Benito Cereno" of the innocent American ship captain Delano who cannot fathom the corruption and evil that confront him when he boards a Spanish slave ship that has been seized by its human cargo. Jefferson misjudged and underestimated the appetites for slaughter of the French revolutionaries (though not much more than the critics of the Jacobins misjudge and overestimate the tolerance and good will of the established ecclesiastic and secular hierarchies against whom the revolutionaries acted). His later retreat from his encomiums was not however a retreat from his belief either in democracy or in democratic education—celebrated to the very end in the epitaph he composed for himself.

It remained clear to Jefferson to the end of his life that a theory of democratic life that is rooted in active participation and continuing consent by each generation of citizens demands a civic pedagogy rooted in the obligation to educate all who would be citizens; and, since the reverse was also true, to make citizens of all who are educated—another eventual Jeffersonian-style justification for the abolition of slavery in the face of educated men like Frederick Douglass. (Douglass overheard an overseer comment "if you teach that nigger how to read, there would be no keeping him. It would forever unfit him to be a slave." And, we need only add, fit him to be a citizen.) The spirit of new world democracy destined the people to govern themselves and Jefferson's radicalism insisted democracy had to mean self-government. Under such circumstances, there was no alternative to educating citizens; and then no other choice but to enfranchise the educated.

Citizen education was then neither a concern merely contingent to Jefferson's politics, nor a narrow obsession arising out of his involvement in educational curricula at the College of William and Mary and the University of Virginia. It was the central, defining moment of his political and moral philosophy: everything else turned on it. When he peered through his telescope mounted on the hill above Charlottesville where his blessed Monticello rested and looked down at the university whose buildings he had designed and whose curriculum he had written, whose faculty he had helped appoint, it was not merely as its parent but as the father of democracy, which he understood as a process dependent on education. The juxtaposition on his tombstone of two founding documents of rights and the founding of America's first public university evinces the forceful logic by which Jefferson grounded liberty's claims inscribed on two pieces of parchment in education, thereby giving to rights a living meaning and a defensible reality. Education makes citizens; citizens make bills of rights; rights make democracy. There is no democracy without citizens, no citizens without public education. The questions raised by this logic confront crucial democratic controversies of our own time no less than Jefferson's: how much democracy, and for whom? What kind of democracy—egalitarian or liberal—and at what price to reason? Who should be educated and how, and to what end?

*   *   *   *

I offer these remarks as preface to some more specific comments on the scholarly papers that are a part of this volume. I trust they help throw into sharp relief the crucial role played by democratic theory and practice in understanding Jefferson's work, and make clear that citizen education—the theme around which we gathered for a Library of Congress colloquium—was also his core theme.

What the four superb essays I have the pleasure of responding to make clear is that while Jefferson's commitment to civic education is indisputable, what was entailed by civic education may be a good deal more controversial. The four papers complement one another in that each focuses on complementary but differential dimensions of civic education: Douglas Wilson's on the fundamental role of basic literacy in forging the crucible of civic capacity; Jennings L. Wagoner's on the "utility" of civic education—utility understood here both as practical usefulness and "utility" in the narrow, technical sense; Richard D. Brown's on substantial education programs (using Massachusetts and Virginia—and Jefferson and John Adams—as complementary foils for one another); and Herbert A. Johnson's on legal education—the training of lawyers in citizenship and of citizens in the law as a prerequisite of a free society founded on laws.

While sharing the democratic, civic frame I have outlined in my introductory remarks, the four propose not only different roads to citizenship but distinctive conceptions of the citizen and different interpretations of Jefferson's putative democratic radicalism. I will probably outrage all four authors in saying so, bit it seems to me that the focus on literacy and general education (Wilson and Brown) cast Jefferson as more of a radical democrat, whereas the focus on utility and law (Wagoner and Johnson) permit him to emerge in more conservative dress. I will sketch very briefly what I take to be their arguments and then comment critically on each of them. I hope to draw some conclusions from their careful analyses as well as from my own reading of Jefferson as a civic pedagogue that will have some bearing on the modern debates about education and democracy.

Douglas Wilson

Douglas Wilson offers us a portrait of Jefferson as a Ciceronian advocate of natural excellence who in contrast to many of his countrymen nonetheless believed that everyman could be educated to an excellence sufficient to the tasks of self-government. This was not a whim but, as Wilson writes, a belief in which Jefferson persisted "over the course of a long life . . . . If anything, he became even more convinced."[20] If education was the keystone in the arch of democratic government, literacy was for Jefferson the keystone in the arch of education. As an ardent lover of books and a man with a powerful "belief in the transforming power of reading and the written word," Jefferson saw books as the chief instruments of popular education. Judicious citizenship required not just specifically civic training but a "general knowledge and sensibility among the people." Where these prevailed, Jefferson was sure, "arbitrary government and every kind of oppression have lessened and disappeared in proportion."

When in 1778 Jefferson comes to draft legislation to establish a public school system in Virginia, "A Bill for the More General Diffusion of Knowledge," he urges "illumination" as the cure to tyranny. History was "the common school of mankind, equally open and useful to great and small," and bookishness was thus the paradoxical route to usefulness. Jefferson combined a faith in book-learning (Wilson does not dispute Merrill Peterson's claim that Jefferson "tended to take his knowledge from books rather than from direct experience") with an "abiding practicality" that made book-learning a road to (and road map for) real life experience, and this rich if not wholly tension-free mixture was reflected in all his educational proposals. Libraries are for Jefferson not reclusive monasteries to which men flee when tired of society but windows on society that facilitate judicious participation in it. For this reason, Wilson rightly devotes some significant attention to Jefferson's attachment to them.

Nor do bookishness and the appeal to history suggest for Wilson a conservative Jefferson on the model of Hume or Burke. Although Cathy Davidson and others have charged that postrevolutionary uses of literacy by John Adams and his countrymen were a legitimation device meant to enforce popular compliance and quiescence, such a view of Jefferson simply "will not do. Submissiveness among the citizenry was the opposite of what (Jefferson) had in mind." Self-assertion and standing up to authority were precisely what Jefferson was looking for in educated citizens. Wilson seeks support for this radical interpretation in Jefferson's sympathetic view of Shay's rebellion and his insistence that people have a right even to their errors, since these too "will tend to keep (the governors) to the true principles of their institutions." Error is in any case best addressed by information, not punishment.

Wilson completes his argument by alluding to the examples of Frederick Douglass teaching himself to read and thus "purposely unfitting himself for slavery" and Abraham Lincoln, who in Wilson's view rose to power in a fashion that was "literacy-related and even literacy-driven." Wilson notes also the interest shared by Jefferson and Lincoln in printing, the artful science through which the gift of literacy became accessible to all. The same science, though Wilson does not mention it, democratized first Christianity (direct access to the Word by Protestants bypassed the priests and subverted the authority of ecclesiastic hierarchies) and then government. Lincoln thus proclaims, in Wilson's well-chosen citation: "To immancipate the mind from (a falsely demeaning) underestimate of itself is the great task which printing came into the world to perform." Hand-maiden to literacy, printing helped give birth to democracy and became for Jefferson the foundation of literacy and thus of democratic citizenship.

Richard D. Brown

Douglas Wilson's focus on fundamental literacy roots democracy deeply in education but does not enjoin distinctions between basic education and civics. Reading and writing would almost seem to be the only arts of liberty necessary to citizens.

Richard D. Brown's comparative study of the complementary educational projects for an informed citizenry developed by Jefferson for Virginia and John Adams for Massachusetts is concerned more explicitly with political values and political education and with the policies required to make literacy a universal possession of citizens. Brown explores the birth of public education in America from "Radical Whig and Enlightenment traditions," which were combined in the New World with "diverse strands of secular and religious ideology," and goes on to show how publicly funded education became the instrument by which the ideal of an "informed citizenry" was to be realized.

This civic ideal had been relatively unimportant during the colonial era both in Georgian England, where politics confronted tensions between crown and parliament, questions of balanced government, and the dominant issue of corruption, and in colonial America, which more or less reflected English patterns. Indeed, the colonies seemed worse off, knowing no charitable institutions and steeped in slavery. Yet even before the Revolution, there were the "exceptional practices of Puritan New England (Massachusetts and Connecticut), where taxes were levied to support free schools for all free boys, and it was this that allowed John Adams to boast in 1765 that nowhere in the world could one see "so much knowledge and civility among the common people" than in his Massachusetts—where, Adams avowed, "a native who cannot read and write is as rare as a comet or an earthquake." Indeed, a 1762 statute cited by Brown "held masters accountable for the literacy of even their colored apprentices."

Meanwhile, in Virginia justices of the peace had "consistently held parents and masters responsible for the education of their children and servants." Still, these patterns where checkered, and following independence there were "no generally accepted, clearly understood models to imitate." As in the case of their new constitution, revolutionary leaders would have to invent the kind of public education they thought the ideal of an informed citizenry would require. The most significant (and costly) innovation would be the "statutory commitment to public education by means of schools and colleges" for which the New England public school provided a model.

The Virginia Bill for the More General Diffusion of Knowledge proposed a similar model, even as it represented Jefferson's effort to mount a first line of defense against the rise of tyranny. Education alone could permit men to "know ambition under all its shapes" and prompt them to "exert their natural powers" against it. The Virginia Bill (which never passed) called for establishing grammar schools throughout the state at one-hundred-acre-lot intervals and building brick or stone—that is, permanent—schoolhouses with lodgings for selected scholars and their teachers. These schools would offer access to all on the basis of ability alone ("The best geniuses will be raked from the rubbish annually" Jefferson wrote, in that amazing Jeffersonian rhetoric that at once celebrated and demeaned equality!) The state would, in other words, make scholarships available to the poor. One gratis scholar from each grammar school would be sent for three years to William and Mary at public expense. (This probably sealed the fate of the bill, publicly funded education being an alien notion to eighteenth-century Americans.) John Adams indicted the ignorance which democracy potentially empowered as the enemy of virtuous government, but like Jefferson was inclined to think that educating the ignorant was the appropriate remedy in a Whig Republic. Adams thus managed to persuade his Massachusetts brethren to enact as legislation the suggestions of his 1778 homily calling for the public encouragement of all "useful knowledge."

The Massachusetts Constitution of 1780 thus recast traditional Puritan language as a "broad republican" call "for comprehensive public responsibility, not merely for education at all levels, but for an advanced, enlightened, knowledgeable and progressive society." This went well beyond radical Whig concerns with citizens as defenders of liberty, and actually seemed to dare to "empower" common men, although it risked agitating the learned who, jealous of their privileges, assailed the multitude for their "envy" and their supposed desire to keep the wise from power and thus encourage demagoguery. The founding tendency to distrust democracy and interpose representative "filters" between the voters and their government was here made manifest, and prompted many of the elite to oppose both participation and public education. Yet the very same arguments, inverted, served to support the call for popular education—Jefferson's internal filter for passions and prejudices. As Jefferson said, the appropriate response to the indiscretion of an ignorant citizenry in power is not to remove their power but to inform their discretion. If Republican institutions "could survive only in the custody of a virtuous and informed citizenry," then institutions had to be found that would educate it to virtue and knowledge. In Massachusetts, public religion was thus encouraged, and Harvard was given special responsibilities that went far beyond its original Christian and civic missions. As Jefferson has linked the Virginia Statute of Religious Freedom and the establishment of a public university, the Commonwealth of Massachusetts's new constitution made "wisdom and knowledge, diffused generally among the body of the people" indispensable to "the preservation of their rights and liberties."

The imperative to ensure an educated citizenry in whose hands democracy would be safe led leaders to regard the state as an appropriate instrument of public education. Schools, colleges, libraries, and learned societies—true to the spirit of the Enlightenment—became tools of state policy. Although the idea of citizenship obviously did not yet extend to propertyless men, either white or of color (although Brown might want to look at Pennsylvania's constitution for a bolder line here), institutions were being set in place that would in time facilitate an ever-widening access to citizenship by the voiceless and dispossessed. Jefferson was no universal egalitarian and circumscribed the precious circle of citizenship in ways utterly unacceptable to moderns, but he still made a powerful case for the education of all who qualified as citizens and so was a friend of radical democracy as conditioned by his times.[21]

Herbert A. Johnson

Unlike Wilson and Brown, Herbert A. Johnson is not concerned generically with the education of an informed citizenry that makes Jefferson a radical but with his concrete commitments to legal education (and thus the rule of law—or the rule of lawyers!), where he looks a good deal more conservative. Count the lawyers who people postwar Congresses and postwar Cabinets, including Bill Clinton's, and it will be apparent how completely we have become a nation governed by lawyers.

In a fascinating account of how the "stable requirements for the training of would-be-lawyers" were differently refracted through the very different lenses of clerkship in the colonial era, colleges in the period between the Revolution and the constitutional founding, private law schools from about 1790 to 1830, and emerging models of modern professional law schools thereafter, Johnson manages not only to illuminate legal training, but to link it to the issues of literacy, citizenship, and civic virtue raised in the other papers. The through-line in the changing debates about what constituted proper legal education from 1750 to 1850 was the need to balance technical legal training and the kinds of liberal education associated with Enlightenment learning and informed citizenship.

Jefferson was himself trained in the law and his early leisurely apprenticeship of five years with George Wythe exposed him both to the "blue ribbon" practices of the General Court and Chancery Court in Williamsburg where Wythe practiced and the scientific and humanistic studies to which, as an Enlightenment man, Wythe was devoted. These two poles, theoretical and practical, set the parameters for Jefferson's own attempts to merge law studies and legal education—to introduce classical studies into law training, and to introduce the law into liberal education.

If Jefferson erred in striking the balance, it was on the side of law as a learned occupation rather than law as a trade. While "working with George Wythe," Johnson notes, he might have "lost out on some of the practical training deemed so precious by clerkship-trained lawyers, [but] he gained a more generous understanding of law and its impact on society." Having never practiced in the mundane county courts—then as now, the forward trenches of the legal infantryman—when asked for advice on legal studies, as he often was, he recommended books! That is, he proposed a course of studies which at first glance might have seemed remote from the law: languages and mathematics and all of the sciences, along with a very heavy dose of history. As in other things, Jefferson valued books over experiential practice—one reason perhaps why he was never too successful as a litigator.

In pursuing the evolution of law studies in young America, Johnson necessarily moves beyond Jefferson's career and views, looking briefly at a number of other lawyers and law professors from Wythe and one of Wythe's first students after he had occupied the new professorship of law and police at William and Mary in 1779, John Marshall, down to Associate Justice James Wilson, whose Philadelphia College law lectures offered nothing less, in Professor Robert McCloskey's words, "than the presentation of a complete political theory, grounded on theology and psychology and leading to a philosophy of American law" and which saw in the science of the law "the study of every free citizen, and of every free man."[22] This language is repeated again and again by Jefferson no less than by his Federalist enemies Marshall and Marshall's associate Joseph Story, who eventually took the Dane Professorship of Law at Harvard and who not long after Jefferson's death wrote in a surprisingly Jeffersonian tone: "many of our most illustrious statesmen have been lawyers; but they have been lawyers liberalized by philosophy and a large intercourse with the wisdom of ancient and modern times."

Jefferson had worried about the narrowness and parochialism of the legal education offered by the private schools at Litchfield, Connecticut, and Kinderhook, New York, and had spent the last decade of his life trying to establish and then find a candidate to occupy a professorship of law at the University of Virginia, and working to integrate legal curricula into liberal arts education. Johnson is attentive to the rupture in Jefferson between the demands of professional legal training and the civic requirements of liberal education, but although he appears to capture the force of the cleavage, he underestimates its polarizing impact. After all, the pedagogical strategies of practical law and civic virtue diverge almost immediately, as Jefferson grasps when he directs law students to classical studies and the natural sciences. Johnson himself cites Joseph S. Watson's rebellious characterization of St. George Tucker's William and Mary law curriculum as too legalistic. "Law," Watson charged, "though called a liberal profession, is surely one of the greatest enemies of liberal learning."

Johnson here returns us to the question of Jefferson's radicalism: can the radical proponent of a little revolution every generation, of an autonomy and spontaneity inseparable from classical liberal learning, really be assimilated to a relatively conservative and parochial reading of the law. Is Jefferson Hume or Burke? I argued above in citing the passage from Hannah Arendt about the paradoxical character of the American founding, that law itself is from a certain radical democratic perspective an adversary of autonomy, impressing itself on the will of the people with an indelible stamp inimical to true freedom. In the heart of every zealous liberal lives an anarchist. The lawyer's job is after all to enforce convention; the citizen's is to challenge and reinvent it. Can their education be identical? Is a nation of lawyers and a nation of citizens really the same thing? Are the talking skills of lawyering and the listening skills of citizenship inculcated in the same fashion? Johnson would like to believe that Jefferson's compromise between legal training and liberal learning satisfactorily reconciles the two, and that the modern law school has achieved a comfortable synthesis of professionalism and humanism. "Where humanists once felt isolated by the utilitarianism rampant in law faculties," he writes in his conclusion, "they now find themselves welcomed. Today, perhaps more than ever before in the history of legal education, we are closer to realizing Jefferson's dream of educating citizens through legal education."

Perhaps it speaks to the exceptional humanism of the University of South Carolina's Law School where he teaches that Johnson can be so sanguine. But in most university law schools, the model of Litchfield and Kinderhook has prevailed, with technical legal training in torts, corporations, property, civil and criminal law not merely taking precedence over philosophy, history, and social science but driving them wholly out of the curriculum. It is not too much to say that many law schools today aim at "deprogramming" liberal arts students by surgically removing their reflective and critical faculties and replacing them with a legal (and lethal) logic whose foundations are rendered incontestable or at least invisible and thus impossible to challenge. Law Board scores that can be improved substantially by LSAT courses do not suggest a way of thinking that is deeply critical. Yes, critical legal studies at Harvard, legal and political philosophy at Yale, constitutional studies at Virginia do acknowledge the limitations of legal method, but they do not alter the fact that legal training for the vast preponderance of American lawyers consists of technical training, technical training, and more technical training on a vocational scale that make Litchfield and Kinderhook look like Aristotle's Lyceum.

I see in Jefferson's attempts to innovate in the field of legal education an attempt to radicalize the law and remove it as an obstruction from the path of citizenship. He did not err in privileging theory over practice and classical studies over legal studies: he made a conscious choice to take law away from lawyers and return it to citizen philosophers who both knew its limits and, by making it their own, could free themselves from its hold over them. To think otherwise is to make Jefferson a far more conservative and legalistic thinker than is warranted by every other fact of his intellectual biography: his prior devotion to literacy, to civic education, to public schooling, and to the maximal public spread of knowledge.

Jennings L. Wagoner, Jr.

In the final paper on this subject, Jennings Wagoner offers an extended analysis of the notions of usefulness and utility in Jefferson's approach to the education of citizens. His almost biographical take is both the most politically engaging and the most politically problematic of the four. He takes his theme from a letter from John Banister, Jr., to Jefferson while Jefferson was a minister to France in 1785 that posed the question (in connection with why an American youth might usefully be sent to Europe to be educated), "what are the objects of an American education?" The story Wagoner tells on the way to answering this query takes him and us on a whirlwind tour of the vices of Old World education and the virtues of New World education, and explores the Bill for the Diffusion of Knowledge and the Rockfish Gap report that lead to the establishment of the University of Virginia. He also treats Jefferson's views on the comparative utility of education for women as well as for men and for the laboring as well as the learned class. Wagoner completes his journey by returning to the theme of Jefferson's politics and whether they are to be seen as radical or conservative.

The deep belief in the power of education in early America is nowhere more evident than in Jefferson's Bill for the More General Diffusion of Knowledge, where he insists that "providing for the education of the people" is "the most legitimate engine of government"—strongly reenforcing Brown's claim that public expenditure for general education is the New World's most radical innovation. Jefferson's observations on moral education and moral development, less persuasive to me than those of Rousseau in his *Emile*, are sharply delineated by Wagoner, who helps establish Jefferson's belief in the secular uses of moral reasoning. To Wagoner, "the utility or value of moral development (to Jefferson) was that it contributed directly to the happiness and well-being of the citizen and to the harmony of the republican state."

I have difficulty only with the latter part of Wagoner's paper, where he takes up meritocratic education and the education of women. As happens with Johnson's reading of Jefferson's compromise between technical legal education and classical liberal studies, Wagoner's reading of Jefferson's compromise between the education of the natural aristocracy and the education of the common man turns out to cast Jefferson in a more conservative light than seems consistent with his work generally. Now there can hardly be a doubt that Jefferson both recognized and celebrated what he understood to be the natural aristocracy of talent in human beings and that he inaugurated what almost appears as a scientific argument for the inferiority of women and people of African ancestry. But it is less evident to me than to Wagoner that Jefferson "underestimated" the artificial aristocracy of wealth and birth or that his view on the education of natural aristocrats defined the whole of the purposes of civic education for him.

The limits of Jefferson's democratic radicalism appear to me rather to arise out of the boundaries he posits between the body of citizens and others who are not citizens rather than boundaries within the body of citizens—say those between the natural and artificial aristocracy, or white male property holders who are learned and those who are foolish. For it is the virtue of Jefferson's radicalism that education not only makes the naturally wise more judicious but makes the naturally foolish more wise. Education may create the conditions for the progress of the whole species but its most important political use is its capacity to train for citizenship those Jefferson deemed qualified.

When we turn to the education of those who are not part of "we the people," however, Jefferson looks as dimly undemocratic as any of the New York bankers he regularly condemns. He not only excoriates blacks and assimilates native American Indians to the new country's bountiful flora and fauna, but treats women with a paternal dismissiveness that reads as misogynist even in his own not yet modern times.[23] Wagoner's comments on education for women make one wish he had relegated that subject to the domain of silence. He has somehow persuaded himself that Jefferson's remonstrations to his daughters to be neat and learn how to please their husbands, to learn how to spell and dance (though only before marriage, after which "gestation and nursing leave little time to a married lady when this exercise can be either safe or innocent"), demonstrates that Jefferson's "expectations were high." High? Because he held girls up to high standards of spelling? Such claims hardly persuade me that "Jefferson's advice regarding the education of girls is remarkable similar in kind, if not degree, to the education recommended for boys." Perhaps Wagoner has been carried away by the "practicality" called up by his focus on the "utility" of education. Since Jefferson calls on both men and women to be practical, Wagoner deems their treatment as commensurate; since both sexes are urged to be moral and to find happiness, he regards them as equals in Jefferson's eyes.

The practical education that fosters efficient home economics and the practical education that fosters an efficient legal practice or responsible citizenship are worlds apart in terms of liberty and power and the fact that both are practical is inconsequential. Being "serviceable" to others—something Wagoner says men and women have in common in Jefferson's scheme of education—means serving the community of equals for male citizens; but for women it means serving men, not quite the same thing. Jefferson treated his slaves and his women with the respect a civilized gentleman offers useful (even beloved) inferiors, but radical democracy, which is to say, liberty, clearly ended for him at the frontiers of citizenship and citizenship was forever circumscribed by race and gender.

Finally, if commentators like Dumas Malone and more recently Jennings L. Wagoner, Jr., give too little attention to Jefferson's unsavory treatment of Native Americans, slaves, and women, Wagoner for one seems to give too much credence to Daniel Boorstin's claim that Jefferson's educational program was vocationally directed and that Jefferson himself had set a "largely conservative task" for education. The notion that Jefferson's commitment was to an education that was uncritical and conservative is gainsaid by everything he wrote and did about the role of education in cultivating a new "new world" democracy, and indeed seems controverted by some of the argument in Wagoner's own paper.

Conclusion

In any case, the issue today seems to me to be more elementary: for our society has pretty much abandoned the notion that education is above all a training ground for citizenship, the place where we acquire the arts of liberty. On the contrary, we train for job competition and we train for the vocations, and occasionally we uphold ivory tower intellectualism as an end in itself, but we do not educate for citizenship and we seem neither to try nor to care. The responsibility of the state to provide for public education is acknowledged neither by taxpayers unwilling to fund schools equitably nor by many politicians who argue for the privatization of schooling via vouchers, as if the "public" in public education was an accident of infelicitous speech. There has been a great deal of discussion about the paltry condition of American democracy today: is it possible that the problem arises directly out of the paltry condition of education? Surely Thomas Jefferson would have thought so, as he watched us ignore his principles in the name of an obsession with his unsavory practices, all the better to promote unsavory practices of our own.

III

Influence of the Old and New Worlds

Thomas Jefferson and the Old World: Personal Experience in the Formation of Early Republican Ideals

When Thomas Jefferson disembarked in France on the last day of July 1784, he brought with him conceptions of the Old World, formed over more than forty years, that were deeply colored by his Virginian rearing, education, and experience.[1] He had traveled little in his own country and spent little time outside an area of his state within a circumference of one hundred miles.[2]

When he left France for good in October 1789, Jefferson had experienced a deeper, if not wider, exposure to European social, cultural, and physical reality than almost any American of his day. That exposure had included intimate links with leaders of a revolution developing in France that would change the political face of the western world. One might expect that such an experience would have profoundly affected Jefferson's perspectives on that world. Yet the consensus of Jeffersonian scholarship is that he emerged from his European stay with his view of the world essentially unchanged.

Whether or not this conclusion is generally correct, it is important to know *how* Jefferson assimilated the "scene of Europe" to his own experience. What is at issue is not the official performance of Jefferson as a diplomat.[3] It is our understanding of his personality as he coped with a setting unfamiliar to him. As Bernard Bailyn has said of Boyd's presentation of the problems of Jefferson's personality during these years, "the way in which these problems appeared and the way in which they worked themselves out are not merely passages in an important biography; they are elements in our national history."[4]

The problems that have made Jefferson's personality puzzling to so many scholars over the years have to do with an apparent duality in his behavior and commentary that seems altogether exceptional. The attitudes and policies that Jefferson affirmed in the French context, like his attitudes and policies before and after his European experience, had an ambiguous aspect that has been noticed by almost everyone who has inquired into the character of the third president. For Gilbert Chinard it was a "partitioning" between theory and practice: "Far from being a single-track mind, his was decidedly a double-track intellect, with two lines of thought running parallel without any apparent contradiction."

Gilbert Chinard is one of the many admirers of Jefferson who have attempted to reconcile these dual "lines of thought." He postulates a distinctively American— or "Anglo-Saxon"—tolerance for discrepancy between theory and practice. Jefferson's political behavior represented a synthesis of the two in what he calls "practical idealism."[5]

Yet for every scholar who has attempted to resolve this duality in Jefferson's favor, there are others, like Robert Tucker and David Hendrickson, who see Jefferson as having lived a "life of paradox" characterized by "ambivalence and con-tradiction" and who reject Chinard's solution as a futile "marrying of opposites."[6] The charge of hypocrisy, raised so often by Jefferson's enemies, has been echoed down through many generations by those who have studied Jefferson's sometimes conflicting words and contrasting deeds in his personal conduct and in the many fields of public policy that he touched.

William Short, a young man with a Virginian background, education, and fam-ily links very like Jefferson's, became his secretary, factotum, and so-called "adoptive son" in France.[7] He is one of the few who took a balanced view of these contrasts. Writing to a nephew in 1816, Short thought that Jefferson's "opinions may be often erroneous, as he is a man and therefore subject to err, but I believe his opinions are always honest, at least as much so as political opinions generally are." Although he might be "more extolled by his friends & more blamed by his enemies than he deserves . . . [and] . . . much and often calumniated, he has also been often extolled beyond what he was entitled to."[8] Calm detachment like this was rare among those who had been close to Jefferson.

The fact that Short came to know Jefferson most intimately during the Paris years suggests that close study of the future president during that period is likely to be particularly helpful in gaining insight into the paradoxes presented by his per-sonality. At a time when Jefferson was still a relatively unimportant figure in the public eye, he was challenged by an unfamiliar assignment in an environment that he had only imagined. His persona was not yet as fully fashioned as it would become as secretary of state. His privacy was less well protected. As Bailyn has put it, the contrasting elements in his character at this time showed only a "weak inte-gration." A cautious analysis might thus yield more insight than it would later in Jefferson's life.[9]

Jefferson's Vision and Scenes of France

Jefferson's correspondence and notes include few comments on the impressions made upon him by his first sight of France. Accompanied by his thirteen-year-old daughter and a male slave, he set off, following an itinerary that led the travelers through Rouen with its flamboyant cathedral, Vernon, a garden spot on the Seine, Mantes, where Jefferson notes visiting the church, the town of Saint-Germain-en-Laye, dominated by its spectacular Renaissance palace, and the château of Marly, whose architecture was supposedly important to Jefferson later.[10] At the time he merely noted paying to see the Marly waterworks.[11]

He did affirm to Monroe, however, soon after his arrival in Paris, that on that first trip he had seen farming country "than which nothing can be more fertile, better cultivated or more elegantly improved."[12] Martha Jefferson was more expansive on her first impressions of the physical aspect of France. It was the "most beautiful country I ever saw in my life . . . a perfect garden," she wrote a friend. She mentions also the magnificence of the churches seen on the way and their stained glass windows.[13] Both Jefferson and his daughter remarked on the many beggars that crowded around their carriage at the stops on their journey—until then their experience with heavily concentrated populations had been slight.

Jefferson arrived in France with his *Notes on the State of Virginia* in his baggage. One of its themes was that the new American nation—its physical aspects, as well as its culture and society—had been ignorantly, if not maliciously, belittled by French writers. His book is in part devoted to description of the natural assets of Virginia and stresses the vigor and size of its flora and fauna[14] and the distinctiveness and attraction of some of its geographical features. His reaction—or lack of it—to some of the scenes encountered on his first European journey becomes more understandable if it is seen in the light of the country he had left behind him. For this we may turn to what travelers of the era, visiting America or Virginia for the first time, had to say about the sights that had met them.

Count Volney, for example, would say of his own transfer from France to America in 1783 that he "left a country of peace and plenty, to go live in a country of barbary and poverty," and painted an especially bleak picture of rural life in the United States.[15] As for Virginia, almost all visiting strangers commented on the sparsity of population, the primitive state of the dwellings they encountered, and the disorder of the countryside. A visitor to Charlottesville as late as 1839 would comment on how inferior was the "travelling in the South in every respect to that in the North." In Virginia he found "bad horses, bad vehicles, . . . roads . . . public houses, bad bedding, dirty miserably clothed negroes . . . nothing wearing the appearance of comfort or neatness; even in the little villages . . . every thing bears the aspect of the want of comfort and tidiness and finish, the houses unpainted, no glass in the windows."[16]

Jefferson's granddaughter, who married a Bostonian, commented in a letter written after her move North on the contrast of the prosperous New England countryside with that of her former Virginian home, despite the "immense advantages of soil and climate which we possess over these people." A contrast with the view from Monticello is implied when she continues, in words that echo her mother's report from France forty years before: "From the top of Mount Holyoke . . . the whole country as you look down upon it, resembles one vast garden."[17]

That Jefferson, too, saw France, at least at first, against the background of his native Virginia partly accounts for his comparative silence on features that were certainly entirely new to him. Instead of the sights all around him, he stresses, in letters home, the moral disadvantages of France compared to his own country. He writes to Monroe that a trip to Europe is worth while only to make one appreciate home: "the pleasure of the trip will be less than you expect . . . [it] will make you adore your own country, its soil, its climate, its equality, liberty, laws, people and manners." Later in the summer he has come to like the French people, but he is still sure that misery is the lot of more than nine-tenths of them.[18]

When, in early 1787, he set out on a tour of the south of France he at first mixed positive evaluations only sparingly into his comments on the country. At the beginning he is sure there is "extreme poverty" in Champagne, for the sight of women and children engaged in heavy outdoor labor is an "unequivocal" sign of it. If he sees "few beggars" it is probably "the effect of a police." If the people in Burgundy are well clothed, it may be because it is Sunday. They have only "the appearance of being well fed"—perhaps deceptive?

As he proceeds southward, he sees more in the natural scenery to admire. A part of the Beaujolais is the "richest country I ever beheld"; prospects are sometimes "charming." "On the whole," scenes in the Rhone valley are "romantic, picturesque." Nevertheless the people of the Beaujolais and Burgundy are subject to all the "oppressions" of their various governments. Curiously, Jefferson is sure they are "less happy and less virtuous" gathered in the villages in which he finds them than they would be were they "insulated with their families on the grounds they cultivate"—his model for living at Monticello.[19]

His language in reporting to Lafayette is less enthusiastic than in his notes or his letters to William Short. He writes to the marquis that the peasants he encountered in the Midi were in "a less degree of physical misery" than he had expected. They were better clothed and had plenty to eat, although they were perhaps "over worked." He found Champagne and Burgundy to have soil "more universally good" than expected—comparing better than "generally admitted" with England, which he had visited briefly the year before.

Indeed, a considerable portion of the positive remarks Jefferson makes on all aspects of the French scenery, economy, culture, and people are to the disadvantage of their British counterparts.[20] Among the few counts on which English assets have the advantage are the more copious use of manure and the creation of pleasure gardens.[21]

As for French art, most of his enthusiasm is reserved for ancient structures. He is not appreciative of the architecture of Paris, with the exception of the new, neo-classical Hôtel de Salm, which, in a letter to a French woman friend, he reports contemplating at length from the Tuileries gardens.[22] It is rather startling to read, in a letter from Aix to William Short, that in his trip from Paris—which had taken him through Sens, Dijon, Beaune, Lyon, Tournus, Mâcon—the "only thing in sculpture" that he has found "worthy of notice" is a work at a château in the Beaujolais by a certain René "Michel-Ange" Slodtz.[23] Jefferson saw one painting of which he approved in Lyon, but "in architecture nothing anywhere except the remains of Antiquity."[24] Rice remarks upon the fact that, in a later visit to Strasbourg, the only thing Jefferson seemed to find interesting about the cathedral was the height of its steeple.[25]

Gilbert Chinard remarks "how little of European culture . . . penetrated his American mind, how carefully he preserved himself from the contamination of European manners and ways of thinking . . . [He] remained very narrow and provincial, and almost a Philistine in his outlook." He attributes this to a typically American puritanism, a belief or feeling of moral wrongness in the enjoyment of purely aesthetic values. Chinard thinks he took "wicked pleasure in denying himself the disinterested joys of the artist and philosopher."[26]

Yet Jefferson's cosmopolitan tastes often laid him open to charges of amoral hedonism—his love of music, his connoisseurship of fine wines and food, his openness to the cuisine of southern France, his eagerness to acquire works of art, or copies of them, his declared love of classical architecture.

In considering Jefferson's apparent imperviousness to certain sights of Europe it is noteworthy that he attempted in some way to take possession of many, if not most, of those art objects that he admired. Marie Kimball attributes certain perversities of Jefferson's taste to a contemporary American perspective that failed to distinguish between objects of curiosity—collectibles in today's terminology—and works of art.[27] In fact, almost every object Jefferson liked became an object for collection. Over the years, for example, he would try to incorporate neoclassical features of the Hôtel de Salm, and its one-storied facade, into the design of Monticello. Indeed, he was willing to sacrifice the comfort of his second-story bedrooms there to this end, and, if Madison had allowed it, those of the Madison family as well.[28]

The length of impracticality to which he was willing to go to express his liking for the design of the dome of the Paris grain market, which he supposed to be like that of the Roman Pantheon, is well known in its effects on Monticello, the United States Capitol, and the University of Virginia, as is the effect of the Maison Carrée of Nîmes on the capitol of his own state. Whatever this may say for his taste, it scarcely bears out the concept of Jefferson the Philistine Puritan, for whom nonutilitarian aesthetic values inspired guilty feelings.[29]

Instead, it seems that his appreciation of objects of art, as also of objects of utility, depended on his ability to incorporate them, to make them his own, or to imagine them an part of what belonged to him. Hence the irrelevance of the great cathedrals of France, the stained glass of the Sainte Chapelle, Renaissance palaces, and other masterpieces that integrated complexly detailed artistry with flamboyant goth-ic or baroque design.[30] Imagination could not integrate such objects with Jefferson's idea of Virginia, nor his mode of existence in it. By contrast, he thought the dimen-sions and orders of the villas and temples of antiquity could be exactly replicated, and they were consonant with his conception of the Virginian way of life.[31]

This acquisitiveness may also help account for the unusual "rapture" afforded him by the olive and orange groves of Provence. Unusual too is his appreciation of the city of Aix-en-Provence: "one of the cleanest and neatest I have ever seen in any country." The sun ("my almighty physician") and climate of the region revived him after a northern winter, and seemed close enough to that of his native Virginia to make emulation of provençal assets possible at home. His notes on his journey show his interest in importing the means to cultivate or reproduce almost all the growing things he appreciated, except the oranges.[32]

Jefferson's possessiveness extended even to natural scenery he admired. In a flir-tatious letter to the artist Brigitte de Tott, he imagines her with him, painting sights surrounding him around Marseilles. In this way he seems to take possession both of the lady and of the scene. To Maria Cosway, the Anglo-Italian painter with whom he had a brief romance, he writes a letter with a similar theme, imagining her engaged in painting the Natural Bridge near his Virginia home—a piece of proper-ty that he did actually own, and "our own dear Monticello."[33]

In the same context may be considered his insistence on remodeling and revis-ing the living arrangements he chose for himself in France. In October of 1785, after he had been designated Benjamin Franklin's successor as Minister to France, he moved into his third residence, the Hôtel de Langeac, a new and magnificent house, designed by the architect of a mansion on today's Place de la Concorde and of the newer tower of the church of Saint-Sulpice. Situated above the city, on the kind of "sightly eminence" that Jefferson loved,[34] possessed of fine gardens, elegant recep-tion rooms, and amenities as modern and convenient as piped running water and upstairs water closets, the dwelling was luxurious, "even for Paris," as his daughter noted.[35] Jefferson, however, found it deficient in important ways, for he set about hiring workmen to remodel it.[36] He had already complained to an American corre-spondent that a "capital housejoiner . . . cannot be got here," presumably on the basis of his experience altering his house in the cul-de-sac Taitbout. "Nothing can be worse done than the house-joinery of Paris," was his judgment.[37] By the begin-ning of 1787 he was also dissatisfied with the quality of the gardening service and discharged the gardener provided by the landlord.[38] When he returned to America he had planted an experimental garden. He was beginning to live, as he would have counseled French farmers, "insulated . . . on the grounds they cultivate."

Jefferson described his lifelong practice of building, remodeling, and recon-structing as "one of my favorite amusements." By "putting up, and pulling down," as he called it,[39] he seems to have made objects, or his idea of them, peculiarly his own.

The Political Culture

Jefferson had felt obliged to decline two previous diplomatic appointments in France, in September 1776 and in August 1781. On the second occasion he professed deep regret at being unable to take advantage of the offered opportunities. When, in 1784, he was finally able to set sail, with the mission to join John Adams and Benjamin Franklin in the negotiation of commercial treaties favorable to the United States, he had at last the prospect of "combining public service with private gratification, of seeing countries whose improvements in science, in arts and in civilization it has been my fortune to admire at a distance but never to see."[40]

Jefferson seemed to be eager to visit in person the scenes of the sources of American culture, but France had not been his focus. As many have stressed, his formation had been that of an English lawyer. His early papers show unambiguously that his basic intellectual furniture was supplied by a classical education in the English tradition. To him, the "three greatest men that have ever lived" were Englishmen—Bacon, Newton, Locke—not French luminaries like Montaigne, Descartes, Montesquieu, Rousseau, or Voltaire.[41] In his bill of 1778 for the reform of the Virginian educational system, a radical plan of primary education for all free children prescribed teaching of "Graecian, Roman, English and American history." Modern continental Europe was not in the picture.[42] Even after two years of residence in France he advised his future son-in-law to read "particular" histories of England, whereas only a "general history of the principal states of Europe" was necessary for a well-rounded education. As for modern languages, Jefferson had studied French and Italian, and perhaps Spanish, enough to acquire some reading proficiency in them. He once admitted to having no capacity at all in German.[43]

That Jefferson had some negative initial views of the contemporary French intelligentsia is affirmed by one theme of the *Notes on the State of Virginia*. Drafted in 1781 and 1782, in response to an inquiry from François Barbé-Marbois, secretary of France's legation in Philadelphia, it challenges comparisons of the Old and the New Worlds made by the renowned French naturalist Buffon and the ideas of the abbé Raynal are treated with righteous indignation as a "wretched philosophy."[44]

This unfavorable orientation to certain French ideas about America[45] may be considered with more generally negative expectations Jefferson seems to have held, when he first set foot in Normandy, of the reception he would meet in French society. Writing to an American friend two years after his arrival in France he declares, "We have no idea in America of the real French character." In reality, he continued, he had found that the French are people who wish "to make one happy—a people of the very best character it is possible for one to have." Presumably the idea of the French he had shared with his correspondent before his departure was more pessimistic.[46]

Whatever doubts Jefferson may at first have held concerning the French desire to "make one happy" must have been largely dispelled as he apprehended the great good will toward all things American then prevailing in the capital. As early as 1782, the wife of an American diplomat in Paris wrote to a friend in Virginia, "It is now very much the fashion to wish to go to America, many of the young Nobility are soliciting it as a great favour." In that year the marquis de Lafayette, who had left America shortly after the Yorktown victory, had just rejoined his wife in Paris. The American letter-writer continues, "I am quite delighted with the Marquise; she . . . says that I must look upon her as an American, for her heart is entirely so."[47]

By the time Jefferson arrived in France, the vogue for America was still mounting. After a stay of two years it seemed to him that it was a nation "the whole mass of which is penetrated with an affection for us."[48]

Jefferson's own career at home had not yet been such as to attract much notice in France. Although to a few he was known as an author of the Declaration of Independence, general fascination with American news had commenced with the alliance of France and the new republic in 1778. Jefferson's later activity as governor of Virginia had been short and rather undistinguished, and his service in the Congress of the Confederation, though impressive to his colleagues on committees, was almost invisible, even to the American public.

For the French in 1784 the heroes of the moment were their own American Revolutionary leaders, Rochambeau and Lafayette. Most admired from afar was the imposing persona of George Washington.[49] Rochambeau himself described Washington's extraordinary status among the French in a letter urging his former American counterpart to visit France: "Be well assured," he wrote, "that although you are not a king, you will be as well received here as though you were"—an extraordinary assurance from a general serving a monarch whose divine authority had not yet been seriously challenged.[50] Lafayette himself, though lionized throughout Parisian salon society, owed his lofty reputation in considerable part to having been the favorite, and "companion in arms" of the American commander in chief. In the elegant town house of his father and mother-in-law, duke and duchess d'Ayen, a "handsome portrait" of America's founding father had place of honor near the mantelpiece.[51]

In their midst since 1776 was another popular American hero who knew well how to dramatize his self-presentation. He was Benjamin Franklin, minister of the United States to France and head of the commission which Jefferson joined. In all the social circles that welcomed Americans, Franklin's reputation as scientist, philosopher, and moral embodiment of rustic American virtue gave him a celebrity almost as great as that held by Voltaire, of recent Parisian memory.[52]

In Franklin's long residence abroad he had learned to speak French fluently and wittily, though often incorrectly. Jefferson's initial misgivings concerning his French hosts may have been compounded by his own incapacity in spoken French. As a Virginian aristocrat, he was accustomed to depending on the service of others for filling many of his needs,[53] but the novelty of depending on others as interpreters was an unfamiliar, and probably painful, intellectual dependency. It is not clear how much his conversational capacity improved during his five-year stay, but Short writes that after "more than twelve months in France" Jefferson's "progress in French" was "scarcely perceptible." Short, who had immersed himself in the language in the heart of a French family claimed that he was by then able "to converse with tolerable ease," although, at about the same date, Jefferson wrote to a relation, "Short and myself are scarcely better at it [speaking French] than when we landed."[54] How much he disliked such an incapacity is suggested not only by his inclusion of Short in it, but by a letter to Madison not long after this, in which he surely embroiders reality in describing himself as striking up conversations with strangers in the countryside around Fontainebleau.[55] It is shown by the terms he uses to commiserate with Madame de Brehan who has gone to America, and who is, he supposes, like him in France, troubled by "the perplexities of a foreign language, the insulted state in which it places us in the midst of society and the embarrassment it occasions when speaking or spoken to."[56]

Sponsored by Franklin and Adams, who were already well-initiated into Parisian society, Jefferson was drawn into a circle that required little facility in the language of the country. Intellectually it was centered around two distinguished French aristocrats, the duchesse d'Enville, heir to the great estate of her father, the late duc de La Rochefoucauld, and her son, Louis-Alexandre d'Enville de La Rochefoucauld, heir to his grandfather's dukedom by special order of Louis XV. La Rochefoucauld, about Jefferson's age, was a scholar and scientist and his mother, who had remodeled her father's famous library into a "well-organized studious retreat" of eight thousand volumes, was herself a well-educated person who had won the distinction of John Adams's favorable notice for the good sense of her remarks. Both were powerful patrons of the sciences and literature and champions of liberal causes. The duke was influential in court politics and his mother given to "useful and serious" good works in her duchy and elsewhere.[57]

Through their salons in the country and in Paris passed a good number of Europe's foremost politicians and intellectuals. Among these were a group dubbed "les américains" because of their liberal sympathies with the new republic. The marquis de Chastellux, who had visited Jefferson at Monticello a few years before, and La Rochefoucauld himself, were among these and, along with the abbé Morellet, were expert translators from English and apparently anglophones, as were several of the women in the group, known for their admiration of English literature. The young daughter of John and Abigail Adams regretted that more conversations in which she took part were not in French.[58]

As long as Franklin and Adams remained in Paris, Jefferson's status was junior, and his responsibilities almost invisible to the public. During these months his rather peripheral role in French social life was mediated by an old acquaintance, the multilingual Geneva-born Charles Williamos, who lived with the newly arrived diplomat, accompanied him almost everywhere, and whose relationship with him was at this time one of "warm friendship and mutual confidence,"[59] a description that could then perhaps be applied to no other friend of Jefferson except Madison.

In the spring of 1785 Jefferson was sworn in as minister plenipotentiary to France. Shortly afterward the Adamses departed for London. Franklin sailed for America in mid-July. At just this time Jefferson broke off his close relationship with Williamos.[60] By then the new minister was in a good position to forego the support of his Swiss acquaintance; he had deepened and strengthened with the twenty-eight-year-old marquis de Lafayette a relationship of far greater personal and social importance than that with Williamos had ever been. The quality and significance of Jefferson's association with Lafayette in France show much about the interaction of Jefferson's personality with his political environment.

Lafayette had returned to France in January of 1785 after a visit to the United States marked by official and popular triumph. Reports of his great success in America contributed to his greatly augmented popularity in France. As a vanquisher of British forces in the American revolution and the reported favorite of that revolution's greatest hero, his destiny in France as a political star seemed clear. As possessor of a great fortune and vast properties, he had, through his wife's connections as well as his own, unrestricted access to the highest circles at court and, according to many, unbounded ambition to wield influence. He has been called "one of the first 'celebrity politicians' to appreciate the importance of image promotion and media manipulation."[61] Lafayette's acquaintance with Jefferson began during his wartime assignment in Virginia in 1781. Jefferson was now one of the first with whom he renewed contact in France.

Not all American leaders who had observed the young marquis were eager for him to play an important part in Franco-American relations. In 1783 Congress instructed American foreign representatives to consult with Lafayette on important decisions, a policy that John Adams thought "an humiliation" that would diminish respect for the new nation. He was frank about his misgivings in a letter from Paris to a congressman friend: "I see in that youth the seeds of mischief to our country if we do not take care." Lafayette, he thought, was possessed of "unbounded ambition," and he could foresee the time when "this mongrel character of French Patriot and American patriot" could be used by the French court to "break our Union." He thought it essential that ministers' consultation with him be at their own discretion, and that American ministers take credit for "their own measures . . . of doing your service."[62] James Madison had similar misgivings which he confided to Jefferson before Lafayette arrived that in addition to the young man's "considerable talents" he showed "a strong thirst of praise and popularity."[63]

Jefferson, on the other hand, seems from the first to have welcomed the closest interaction with the popular nobleman, although, knowing Madison's sentiments, he was careful to express to him reservations he had about the young man's "canine appetite for popularity and fame."[64] Lafayette himself was more than ready to accept guidance from the American diplomat. Early orphaned, politically inexperienced, and, according to Louis Gottschalk, "fundamentally insecure and timid," Lafayette communicated to Jefferson at this time a surprising willingness to do his bidding in court circles on behalf of the American republic. The filial devotion he expressed in letters home to George Washington seems to have been extended to the imposing person of America's emissary in France.[65]

Jefferson, for his part, had predispositions to slip easily into the role Washington had played for the young man. He himself was closely connected to the American commander by ancestral links, personal acquaintance, and political collaboration. Aside from the historic and circumstantial affinities between the two Virginians, Jefferson seems early to have felt a certain identity of perspectives between himself and his older countryman. He had already been convinced on at least one occasion that (contrary to other evidence) Washington shared his view that the Society of the Cincinnati should be dissolved.[66] He would later affirm to William Short his intuitive knowledge of the general's wishes (again contrary to probability).[67] As Jefferson's career unfolded in Washington's footsteps the younger man would more than once express his feeling of commonalty with the first president, despite the widening political division between them in Washington's last years.[68]

But if Lafayette was more than willing, in Jefferson's phrase, to "drive Jefferson's nails" on behalf of American interests, Jefferson showed himself equally willing to lend himself to Lafayette's ambitions. Whether his judgment on these was based on sensitive intuition or on actual confidences from the marquis, Jefferson geared his advice to the assumption that Lafayette would eventually hold a preeminent political position in France. In 1787 he writes his young friend from the Midi counseling him to prepare himself for his future great role by following Jefferson's example of familiarizing himself with the life of the people. He should come to the region, "where I believe you have not been," and, like Jefferson, "loll" in the beds of peasants to judge their comfort, test their wines and sample their potages, to prepare himself for the day to come when he will be able to improve their lot.[69]

Others have traced Jefferson's covert, but highly active role in attempting to steer the course of the French revolution by means of Lafayette. The written record shows Jefferson's influence at every critical point in Lafayette's political activity. It has only recently come to light that Jefferson's highly uncharacteristic letter to Madison speculating that "the Earth should be held in usufruct for the Living," was actually drafted to suggest rationalizations Lafayette might offer to the Constitutional Assembly in favor of fundamental constitutional change. Jefferson's care to disguise the political purpose of this document, like his later concealment of his authorship of a Charter of Rights that Lafayette presented to the king, and his private role as adviser and editor of Lafayette's proposed Declaration of Rights, exemplify the indirect technique which Jefferson usually preferred to use in influencing policy in his native country.[70] In France, communication problems exaggerated the difficulties Jefferson often had in using open, direct persuasion. Lafayette's unusual docililty in his older friend's hands more than offset these limitations of Jefferson's.

Julian Boyd seems to suggest that personal ambition made it natural that the author of the Declaration of Independence of America should also wish to be the author of the Declaration of Rights of France.[71] But the quality of personal interaction between Lafayette and Jefferson makes a different motivation plausible: Jefferson had made Lafayette's career his own to the extent that he imagined himself in his place.

When, in May of 1789, Lafayette was acting as a delegate of the Auvergne nobility to the meeting of the Estates General, Jefferson urged him to disregard his instructions and take at once that "honest and manly stand" with the Third Estate, "which your own principles dictate." Such advice (Jefferson adds, "You must not consider this as advice"!) speaks of many hours of social intercourse during which Jefferson gained a sense that Lafayette's principles were the same as his own. To encourage his young friend he tells him that the course he advises will "be approved by the world which marks and honours you as the man of the people." So far does Jefferson identify with the role the marquis is playing that he warns him against treachery from those Frenchmen Lafayette knows best: "The Noblesse . . . especially . . . of Auvergne will always prefer men who will do their dirty work for them . . . They will therefore soon drop you." By then, he foresees, it may be too late to get taken up by "the people."[72]

Jefferson himself had never traveled in the Auvergne and it is not likely that he had had much personal acquaintance with its nobility, except through what Lafayette had told him, and what he had imagined on the basis of other reports.[73] But his ability to construct Lafayette's perspective for him, to make it his own, and to elaborate upon it provides an object lesson in the techniques with which Jefferson enlisted many young followers throughout his career.

Concerning Lafayette, Jefferson's adaptivity extended even to adopting French forms of sentimental self-expression. In one notable letter he tells his French friend of his affection for him in terms unlike any he would use toward members of his most intimate American circle.[74]

Jefferson's feeling of oneness with Lafayette was never to be ruptured. Chinard notices that after Jefferson's return to the United States, he changed, in writing a letter to Short, "suddenly from *I* to *We* in speaking of the marquis."[75] Gottschalk and Margaret Maddox point out that toward the end of his life Jefferson's recollection of Lafayette's stand on the demand that Louis XVI approve a charter of rights actually confused the position that the Frenchman had held with his own.[76] During his stay in France Jefferson had, in truth, felt that their lives and fortunes were profoundly linked.

Parisian Social Circles and Jefferson's Politics

Of all the challenges to Jefferson's adaptive abilities that France offered, none was more formidable than the position of women in the society into which he was introduced.

In America, Jefferson's early relations with women of his own class had been a mixture of mysogyny, awkward admiration, diffidence, ardor, and dependency.[77] In none of these modes, however, had there been any place for intellectual exchanges based on parity. For such exchanges his happiest experiences were entirely male. Their model had taken form in his Williamsburg student days when he was welcomed into a "partie carrée," completed by three older men, George Wythe, Governor Fauquier, and William Small. It was a "truly Attic" society, as he recalled it later, unsurpassed in its quality of conversation by any culture.[78]

In the Paris of the 1780s, however, "Atticism" was the attribute of brilliant gatherings organized and led, in large part, by middle-aged women. In this early "golden age of the revolution, French salons experienced one of the liveliest and most brilliant phases of their history,"—a history in which women had always been prominent.[79] The "*atticisme*" characteristic of these salons at this golden moment, wrote Sainte-Beuve, required a "light touch" in familiar intercourse in both spoken and written words. "In France," he continued, "women of a certain age are better at this type of perfection than men, or the youngest women."[80]

Among the leaders of these gatherings, besides the duc de La Rochefoucauld and his mother, were Madame Necker, Madame Helvétius, well-to-do widow of the philosopher and high functionary, and Madame de Tessé. The salon of the first centered around the political ambitions of her husband, during Jefferson's stay twice recalled to serve as finance minister in Louis XVI's government.[81] In suburban Auteuil, where Madame Helvétius presided with bohemian manners and a careless toilette that disgusted Abigail Adams (and must have been alarming to Jefferson), Benjamin Franklin had been the irreplaceable star.[82] The comtesse de Tessé, of the powerful house of Noailles and wife of a high, but self-effacing court and military official, ran a salon in which the only requisite article of belief was in the supreme qualities of the marquis de Lafayette, husband of her niece. In the nearby village of Sannois, Sophie de Lalive d'Houdetot, formerly beloved of Rousseau and currently patroness and sponsor of St. John de Crèvecoeur, was hostess to leading artists, writers, scientists, and politicians. She too had worshipped at the shrine of Franklin's reputation.[83]

Jefferson enjoyed the hospitality of all these women and from some of them he gained much. He had been happy of an entry to Madame d'Houdetot's assembly, because, as he wrote John Adams, he hoped thereby to become acquainted with leading "literati" who frequented her group.[84] But central to his social life in Paris and most important in his correspondence was the welcome extended to him by the comtesse de Tessé. As friend to her beloved Lafayette and representative of the popular new American government he was received by her without reservation.

The circles with which Jefferson became familiar were, of course, those in which Anglo-Saxon culture was admired and liberal ideals defended. Sociability among devout partisans of the Church was carried on separately, although it overlapped considerably as well—for instance, in the person of Adrienne de Lafayette, whose indomitable belief system was impervious to her husband's skepticism. There were a number of leading intellectuals who did not often appear at such gatherings and socially and intellectually important women who did not sponsor any. One of the latter was the learned marquise de Créquy, whose intelligence and wit was compared with Montaigne's.[85] Her nephew was married to Madame de Tessé, whom she respected for her noble manners, witty conversation, and intellectual finesse, but whose lack of religion she deplored.[86]

Créquy was contemptuous of the leveling tendency of Madame de Tessé's salon, but found her to have a "good head and a great soul." In this society Jefferson, with his linguistic limitations, could not have cut much of a figure, but, Créquy remarks of her relation, "so powerful was her influence" that those who were deficient in social skills "were able to acquire in her salon the distinction that they lacked." Chinard, indeed, concludes that Jefferson owed to this hostess much of the social grace with which he was able to operate in Parisian society.[87] The letters he wrote to her on his southern trip in 1787, though in an English of a contrived style, are evidence of considerable effort to turn compliments in what he must have conceived to be a French manner.

At the time of Jefferson's arrival in France, most of these salons were not primarily political in nature. Although they may have revolved around a particular political figure—Choiseul, Turgot, and, in Jefferson's time, Necker and Lafayette—literature, art, natural science, and philosophy were the primary objects of attention. When the pace of political change began to quicken with the summons of the Assembly of Notables in 1787, however, politics was increasingly the preoccupation of these aristocratic women, as well as of their men.

From Jefferson's Virginian perspective, a concern with political matters was entirely unsuitable for women. This remained his unalterable view in his communications with American women. When he solicited more letters from his Philadelphia friend, Eliza Trist, he asked that she not write of politics, but of everyday gossip and human interest stories.[88] Writing to the beautiful Anne Willing Bingham, who had recently returned from Europe to preside, with her rich husband William Bingham, over the haut monde of Philadelphia, Jefferson rejoiced that American women provided a chaste refuge and solace for their menfolk from the sordid necessity to toil in the workshops of commerce and politics.[89]

In view of what was apparently a real aversion, it is remarkable that Jefferson quickly recognized that what he considered taboo in his own country was taken as a matter of course in France. He learned to take part in conversations with his hostesses on political matters close to his personal concerns as well as to theirs. We have infrequent hints about his conversations with women on these subjects, but correspondence does sometimes disclose what their substance was. Madame d'Houdetot wrote Jefferson to congratulate him after she had learned from Crèvecoeur, who was consul in New York, of the ratification of the Constitution by Virginia in 1788. Clearly, the progress of the ratification movement had been a subject of discussion at her home in Sannois.[90]

In a letter to Jefferson after his return to the United States, Madame d'Enville recalls, at the height of the Terror, a conversation she had had with him "at the beginning of our revolution." His reassurances had then "calmed her" concerning the political changes taking place. As matters had developed, of course, she had been more prescient than he concerning the *suites funestes* of the events of 1789.[91]

Jefferson's correspondence shows that he was usually able to adapt himself effectively to the interest and competence of French women in political matters. During the months that Lafayette was occupied with the Assembly of Notables, for example, Madame de Tessé sent Jefferson, who was traveling in the south, a concise account of the proceedings and the prospects of their success. Jefferson responded with comments on her observations and expressed opinions of his own that seem to be intended to be passed on as advice to Lafayette.[92]

With Madame d'Houdetot, too, Jefferson carried on a correspondence that included political subject matter about which she was exceptionally well informed, not only from French sources, but from American correspondents like Crèvecoeur, and Franklin himself. In response, Jefferson gives her what appears to be confidential information concerning European affairs that he learned in the course of his diplomatic duties.[93]

There are signs, however, that his adjustment to these French feminine customs was felt by him as an effort of diplomacy, instead of, as with his adaptation to Lafayette's style and aims, a mingling of interests. Most significant of his real feelings, perhaps, is a letter to Anne Willing Bingham in which he depicts the typical French noblewoman in a harsh light as vain, pretentious, ignorant, and indolent. Ostensibly, the letter is intended to flatter her virtuous, industrious, and self-sacrificing counterpart, the American woman. In this case, however, he seems to have been a poor judge of his correspondent's state of mind. Mrs. Bingham replied with indignation on behalf of her French friends, whom she knew to be grossly misrepresented by Jefferson's satire. Moreover, she took offense at the fact that Jefferson, in accordance with his conception of her chief role as an ornament, had sent her news of Paris fashions instead of material on the current literary and musical scene, which, she said, she would be more interested in receiving.[94]

Jefferson was still more averse to the political influence exercised by French women of his time. The same aristocratic women who had befriended him were accustomed to taking an important part in influencing appointments to office. Jefferson knew of some of these interventions. Madame d'Houdetot, for example, successfully lobbied high personages at court to obtain a diplomatic appointment for Crèvecoeur.[95] Madame de Tessé had informed herself through contacts with the minister of war on the chances of a military post for a friend.[96] Madame de Créquy frankly acknowledged to Sénac de Meilhan that she dispensed appointments to the Académie Française.[97]

To Jefferson this feminine pressure was "unbelievable." He wrote to Washington that in France women were an "extraordinary obstacle to the betterment of things," since they "visit alone persons in office, solicit in defiance of laws and regulations."[98] As far as his French women friends were concerned, it is likely that he concealed his intolerance of such influence. After he became American secretary of state, the respected duchesse d'Enville was not afraid to write to him to beg for the appointment of William Short as minister to France.[99] We do not know how Jefferson responded to his old acquaintance except that Short continued to be denied the job.

Jefferson was less restrained, during his stay in France and afterward, about the case of a woman with whom he was not personally acquainted. According to him, the worst example of female interference in French politics was that of the most highly placed woman in France—Marie-Antoinette, the queen. During the early months of revolutionary activity he tended to be indulgent toward Louis XVI himself. He hopes, in a letter to Lafayette, that the king, "who means so well," will agree to necessary constitutional reforms on the British model. To George Washington he predicts that the king will champion the people's cause against "nobles and priests." To Madame de Tessé he writes that Louis is a "good and young king." In an encoded letter to Madison three months later he believes still that the king "loves justice," but is "limited in his understanding and "too much governed" by his queen who is "capricious," under the thumb of her brother, the Emperor Joseph II of Austria, and "devoted to pleasure and expence."[100]

Jefferson's plan of persuading the king, through Lafayette, to grant a Charter of Rights failed, and Jefferson returned to the United States as the revolutionary momentum escalated. From there he received Short's alarming reports on the growing violence in France. The secretary of state reproached his former secretary for his apparent hostility to the progress of the revolution. There had been, Jefferson assured him, no possibility that the king would consent to reasonable demands.[101] But toward the end of his life Jefferson returned to the view that the king would have agreed to a "wise constitution." The problem had been the queen who had "absolute sway" over him. Her "inflexible perverseness" was the cause of the course the revolution had taken. "Had there been no Queen, there would have been no revolution."[102] Thus, in retrospect, the obstacle to his and Lafayette's plan for the "betterment of things" in France was indeed the one of which he had warned Washington years before—undue intervention of women in politics.

Jefferson between Two Worlds

To be a Virginian—and one with political ambitions in America—imposed certain constraints on Jefferson's adaptation to the French milieu in which he lived, more and more at ease and increasingly happy, from 1784 to 1789. Political sentiments among his French friends, particularly when they concerned America, often took account neither of Jefferson's personal needs and inclinations nor of the realities with which he would have to come to terms when he returned home.

First, there was the question of slavery. The perniciousness of slavery, and the need for its abolition, for example, was one issue on which nobles and intellectuals who made up the liberal circle to which Jefferson belonged tended to be of one mind. So prominent was French abolitionist sentiment during Jefferson's stay that the issue of the slave traffic was a major topic in Necker's opening address to the assembly of the Estates in 1789.

Jefferson became known in Paris as an enemy of slavery from the publication of 200 copies of his *Notes on the State of Virginia* there in 1785. He distributed copies to a good many French intellectuals, but his chief concern seems to have been to put them in the hands of students at William and Mary in Williamsburg. At the same time he worried about this plan. He wrote Madison for advice on the idea. Before he received an answer he wrote again, saying "I am anxious to hear from you on the subject of my Notes." He feared a poor reaction from the passages on slavery. Madison confirmed his apprehension, advising him that it would be more prudent to make the book available in the William and Mary library, rather than to risk parental backlash from direct distribution to the young men. Presumably, Jefferson took the advice.[103]

Early in 1788 the journalist Brissot invited Jefferson to attend an organizing session of the proposed Société des Amis des Noirs. Ending the slave trade was to be discussed. Jefferson declined the invitation, saying "those whom I serve having never yet been able to give their voice against this practice, it is decent for me to avoid too public a demonstration of my wishes to see it abolished." But he took advantage of the opportunity to declare his wish to see "an abolition not only of the trade but of the condition of slavery: and certainly nobody will be more willing to encounter every sacrifice for that object."[104]

In fact, Jefferson's wish to be known as an abolitionist was in conflict not only with his hopes for a political future at home but also with his private situation. In Paris he could speak of sacrifice for the sake of righteousness, but he would find, after his return to Virginia, that he was in deep financial trouble. His difficulties were such that not only was he not prepared to abolish the "condition" of slavery in his own household, but he found it necessary to raise money by remortgaging a portion of the most liquid asset in his possession. One hundred and fifty slaves who had already been mortgaged to various of his friends became collateral for a new personal loan for $2,000 from Nicholas Van Staphorst & Company, Dutch bankers who had done public business for the United States while Jefferson was in Paris.[105]

Second among realities confronting him was the Constitution. On American constitutional issues, too, Jefferson was subjected to conflicting pressures from French opinion. He had at first been doubtful about the merits of radical constitutional reform in America, expressing the view that all that was needed was to give the United States a single voice in foreign policy. In France, however, intellectuals of his acquaintance were enthusiastic for a change that would institutionalize a firm authority in the new American nation. Early in 1787, moreover, publicity in Paris about Shays' Rebellion confirmed them in their views.[106]

Jefferson's suspicions of centralizing institutions were not dispelled once he had seen the document. He commented regretfully that all that was good in it could have been couched in "3 or 4 new articles" keeping "the good old and venerable fabric which should have been preserved even as a relic."[107]

But he could not have been unaffected by the status in France of Washington, who had been a sponsor of the Constitution and was obviously to be leader of the government under its provisions. Veneration of "le grand Washington" in France had probably encouraged Jefferson to try to link himself, more than he had in the United States, to the persona of Washington, with whom, indeed, he had much in common.

Although in principle Jefferson could not support what he feared might become an executive-centered federal government, he finally conceded the necessity of ratification. He accepted the Constitution although he still stood for changing the provision for reeligibility of the president, "should the majority change their opinion" but not before "we can avail ourselves of the services of our great leader . . . [who is so] peculiarly necessary to get the government underway . . . that it may afterwards be carried on by subordinate characters."[108]

Perhaps Jefferson would never have adopted such language to denote Washington had he not seen all around him in France evidence of the powerful appeal of the general, not least from Lafayette. The young marquis faithfully followed Jefferson's lead in agreeing that "Those presidential powers seem to me too great," but he had confidence that General Washington, once he assumed the office, would remedy the matter.[109] Subjected to such evidence in France of faith in Washington and to increasing pressure from partisans of the Constitution in America, by the end of the year Jefferson was writing to the prospective president that he had seen, "with infinite pleasure, our new constitution accepted by 11 states."[110] During his stay in France he was even to lend himself to projects for Washington's embodiment in monuments. It was Jefferson who took responsibility for commissioning Houdon's statue of Washington for the Virginia capitol, a project which eventually required subsidizing a trip to the United States for the sculptor himself.

The Church was a third issue. Another source of constraint between Jefferson's French and his Virginian personae derived from the pleasant adaptation he had made to a privileged niche in a society that was, as he would on occasion write, "oppressed by priests and nobles." However much he might avert his eyes from the church architecture all around him, and however proudly he might claim credit from his French friends for his authorship of the Virginia Bill for Religious Freedom,[111] he found himself enjoying important benefits that Catholic France had to offer in ways that might have appeared strange in Richmond.

We may notice, for example, his reassurance to his sister that his daughters' school, the Abbaye Royale de Panthemont, is "altogether the best in France," that it had no more Catholic than Protestant pupils, and that "not a word is ever spoken to them on the subject of religion."[112] Martha's sponsor in gaining admission to this convent school was a niece of the abbess herself, the comtesse de Brionne. Chastellux, announcing to Jefferson that he has secured this lady's promise to sponsor Martha, mentions that there are other foreigners among the pensioners, but says nothing about religion.[113] The institution itself was "among those few most exclusive convents reserved for the royal princesses of France and the daughters of the highest-ranking nobility."[114] Early in her tuition at the convent, Martha, together with her father and the Adams ladies, witnessed the ceremony of two young women taking the veil. The Adams's daughter Abigail reports that on this occasion "the priest in his sermon invited all the others who were present to follow the example of these nuns."[115]

If this example of proselytizing was really exceptional at Panthemont, there was nevertheless a powerful force exerted for Catholicism by softer influences. Jefferson claimed that the school had the best masters in France. One of them, Claude Balbâtre, a well-known composer and church organist who would later become organist of Notre Dame de Paris, was reported to have been very sorry at Martha Jefferson's departure. Martha, who assured an American friend that all her teachers were excellent (exempting only the drawing master) seems to have had a flirtation with one of them, a certain curé called (nicknamed?) Athée. An English schoolmate's letter mischievously reminded her that priests cannot marry.[116]

According to Ellen Randolph Coolidge's memory, Jefferson withdrew both his daughters from Panthemont when Martha announced her interest in becoming a nun, but this is not certain. Jefferson's last payment for the girls' pension seems to have been made in April 1789, probably near the end of the term, when he was already preparing to return home with his family.[117]

Jefferson himself was much attracted by the comfortable solitude of Catholic monastic life. According to his daughter, he took refuge in the Hermitage of Mont

Calvaire on Mont Valérien (between Nanterre and Suresne) and his account books show that he "took possession" of an apartment there on September 5, 1787. Members of the order visited him in his house in town as well.

Martha recalls mistakenly that Mont Calvaire was a Carthusian monastery. The only such monastery was the Chartreuse de Paris, a notable establishment adjacent to the Luxembourg palace on the still countrified edge of the faubourg Saint-Germain. Described in detail in the guidebook used by Jefferson and his Paris contemporaries, its extensive group of buildings occupied an "immense terrain" of which the kitchen garden alone was larger than most palace grounds.[118] Its important collection of paintings included a large group by Eustache Lesueur, a seventeenth-century artist Jefferson seems to have admired, since he bought a copy of one of his works, "The Sacrifice of Lystra," for Monticello.[119]

This monastic establishment, no longer standing, was notable not only for its lavish collection of paintings and works of art, but also for a vast experimental horticultural nursery, dating back to the house's foundation in the thirteenth century. It therefore seems likely that it too was visited by Jefferson during his stay, and that his daughter's memory of his contact with the convent of this order reflects time spent there, as well as at Mont Valérien.[120]

Back to Virginia

On his departure from France, and many years later, in often-quoted terms, Jefferson avowed his warm appreciation of the people and culture of France.[121] There is no doubt that his personal experience there had given him deep satisfaction.

Officially, Jefferson's return to the United States in 1789 was not definitive. It is not clear, however, whether he really expected to resume his duties as minister after a home leave. He did not know, of course, until he reached Norfolk, of Washington's desire to have him serve as secretary of state, but his correspondence with Short in 1789 and 1790 shows that they had speculated together on "the place to be offered" before Jefferson left France.[122]

One piece of evidence that he intended to return to France is his invitation to Jonathan Trumbull, a young painter from Connecticut, to become his secretary in Paris if William Short decided to return home. This proposition is of interest because he had recently written Short, in emphatic, paternal terms, of the dangers to the younger man's career and personal life of remaining in Europe. If, after making his way in the law and marrying in the United States, Short should wish to return, Jefferson advised, "You could come back as a diplomat." But, he continues, "I think you will never wish to return to Europe . . . the happiness of your own country is more tranquil, more unmixed, more permanent."[123] Short, who was at the time attending to American financial matters in The Hague, had for some time been involved in a love affair with the young duchesse de La Rochefoucauld and was seriously thinking of making a life in France. From Jefferson's first weeks in France he had anticipated the danger of unsuitable liaisons with French women, "difficult for young men to refuse . . . where beauty is a begging in every street." He had written then of the hazard to an American youth "of forming a connection . . . which he might be unwilling to shake off when it shall be proper for him to return to his own country."[124] Now, to Trumbull, Jefferson declares that he does not know what Short's decision will be, and that he has not presumed to advise him. He tells him, however, that as a painter Trumbull might be judged, unlike Short, to have a professional reason to remain abroad.[125]

Jefferson's warning to Short about the dangers to young American men of succumbing to the lures of Europe echoes similar strictures Jefferson dispensed to his nephew, Peter Carr, and to a friend, John Banister, Jr., who was interested in sending a son abroad for his education. As for a European education, after only three months on France's soil "inspection" confirmed Jefferson in the disapproval he had always had "from theory" of a European education for an American youth. Indeed, Jefferson declared at that early date, "I know not one good purpose on earth which can be effected by a young gentleman's coming here."[126] A year after his arrival in France, Jefferson has expanded his idea of the hazards to youthful Republican ideals of a European sojourn. A young American man "acquires a fondness for European luxury and dissipation and a contempt for the simplicity of his own country; he is fascinated with the privileges of the European aristocrats, and sees with abhorrence the lovely equality which the poor enjoys with the rich in his own country."[127]

Is not Jefferson here describing temptations of which he himself had felt the force, and had not always rejected? More than any other practice of Jefferson, his habit of admonishing young people to shun indulgences that he allowed himself and directing them to follow regimens that were more austere than he himself had been able to follow in comparable situations have laid him open to the charge of hypocrisy in personal as well as political conduct.

If Jefferson actually had considered returning to Europe for another tour of duty after home leave in 1789, he must have given up the idea very soon after his embarkment for America. That he had some regrets at losing the life he had led in France is perhaps suggested by the fact that some years later he added two or three years to the time he remembered spending there.[128]

In the event, Short did not return to his own country for several years. Jefferson, given to making statements he hoped would be self-confirming, might have been reminded of the assurance he had given to the young Monroe several years earlier: "No man now living will ever see an instance of an American removing to settle in Europe and continuing there."[129]

C. Vann Woodward has described the particularly fierce war that ambitious Virginians had to wage against self-indulgence and sloth.[130] Jefferson showed in a famous letter to Chastellux that he saw a tendency of Southerners to be "voluptuary, indolent, unsteady," and of the Virginian character to be "aristocratical, pompous, clannish, indolent, hospitable, and . . . thoughtless in their expences."[131] Jefferson had found some of these temptations immeasurably enhanced in Europe, and he had mostly overcome them. But the danger they held for him personally may have caused him to extend the battlefield of the campaign not only to the struggle against his own impulses, but also to their control in others whom he felt as most important to himself, particularly to young people.

At a time when he was enjoying the "raptures" of the lush Midi in the splendid comforts at the spa of Aix, he wrote a humorless reply to his daughter's confession of problems with her schoolwork. He warned, "Of all the cankers of human happiness, none corrodes it with so silent, yet so baneful a tooth, as indolence." As an American she is specially obliged to conquer the temptation to be lazy and dependent: "It is a part of the American character . . . to surmount every difficulty by resolution and contrivance. . . . Remote from all other aid, we are obliged to invent and to execute; to find means within ourselves, and not to lean on others."[132]

After five years in Europe he managed to turn his back on its un-American lures.[133] There he had also learned better strategies, more refined tastes, and new skills that would enable him vastly to extend his powers from his intimate circle to his fellow citizens, even to future generations. Writing to Madison of his hopes eventually to give a new constitution to Virginia he had once said, "What we have to do, I think, is . . . to keep alive the idea that the present one is but an ordinance, and to prepare the minds of the young men."

Why Slaves Can't Read:
The Political Significance of
Jefferson's Racism

"Mr. Jefferson's" speculation that blacks were inherently inferior to whites in the endowments of body and mind "has in truth injured us more, and has been as great a barrier to our emancipation as anything that has ever been advanced against us." So David Walker argued in his scathing indictment of Thomas Jefferson's *Notes on the State of Virginia.* "Mr. Jefferson's remarks respecting us have sunk deep into the hearts of millions of whites," Walker added, "and never will be removed this side of eternity."

The son of a slave father and a free mother, Walker published this *Appeal* in 1829, only four years after Jefferson's death, thereby leaving posterity to consider an especially painful irony of our history: one of the first sustained attacks on slavery written by an African American was framed as a blistering critique of Thomas Jefferson, a man remembered chiefly for his commitment to freedom and equality and who himself professed an abiding hatred of the "peculiar institution."[1]

More than a dozen times in the first half of his pamphlet Walker attacked "Mr. Jefferson" and cited his *Notes* in support of the *Appeal's* central thesis. Simply put, Walker argued that American blacks were the most brutally oppressed people in the history of the world, not so much because they were subjected to uniquely barbarous treatment—although in some ways be believed they were—but because unlike all other oppressed peoples, past and present, American blacks were denied their basic humanity thanks to an ideology of inherent racial inferiority. Native Americans, the Irish, the Jews—all were oppressed, Walker noted, and yet all "are called *men,* and of course are, and ought to be free." Even the ancient Egyptians, for all their cruelty, never argued that the Israelites "were not of the human family."[2] Yet for Walker this was precisely what Jefferson seemed to have said: that the ignorance of American blacks was rooted in nature rather than circumstance, and that as such they could never live as free men and women within the borders of the United States.

Walker did not dispute the ignorance of American blacks; he merely argued that it was the product of a racist environment in which whites not only denied blacks educational opportunities but actively feared the prospect of educated blacks. "[F]or the Africans to acquire learning in this country, makes tyrants quake and tremble on their sandy foundation," Walker declared. "Why," he asked pointedly, "what is the matter? Why, they know that their infernal deeds of cruelty will be made known to the world. . . . The bare name of educating the coloured people, scares our cruel oppressors almost to death."[3] Yet blacks were also to blame, Walker argued. Whites kept slaves in ignorance because they understood what most blacks apparently failed to see: that ignorance was the handmaiden of tyranny, and that so long as blacks remained ignorant they would remain oppressed. It was therefore up to blacks themselves to refute Jefferson, he concluded, by rigorously educating themselves and in the process demonstrating that their ignorance was not a product of an inherent racial inferiority.

Walker's was a ruthlessly honest and unusually astute intelligence, yet even he seemed more conscious of the racist ideology he struggled against than of the political culture within which he himself wrote. He was undoubtedly correct to cite Jefferson's *Notes* as the veritable fountainhead of American racism. By contrast, Walker made no mention at all of John Trenchard, Thomas Gordon, or like-minded radical Whigs whose works passed so readily from England to America in the decades after 1720. Yet they were among the first authors published in the colonies to equate ignorance with slavery—an equation that both Walker and his readers could take for granted a hundred years later. In *Cato's Letters,* for example, Trenchard and Gordon insisted that "Ignorance accompanies Slavery, and is introduced by it." Everywhere, they argued, "we . . . find Tyranny and Imposture, Ignorance and Slavery, joined together."[4] Among minds steeped in the Enlightenment the equation of freedom with education was a cherished maxim, the logical corollary of which was the equation of slavery with ignorance.

African American leaders quickly adopted this line of reasoning. Since the late eighteenth century they had been pointing out that among the "dreadful Evil[s]" of slavery was "that of holding us in gross Ignorance."[5] In 1808 the Boston African Society complained that "Slavery hath ever a tendency to spread ignorance and darkness, poverty and distress in the world."[6] By the 1820s the equation of slavery with enforced ignorance was commonplace among black abolitionists. In many cases they fused their attacks on the enforced ignorance of the slaves with their Protestant commitment to the vernacular Bible. Denying slaves the ability to read meant, of course, preventing them from reading the scriptures on their own. "Nearly three millions of your fellow-citizens are prohibited by law . . . from reading the Book of Life," Henry Highland Garnet pointed out in 1843. "Your intellect has been destroyed as much as possible, and every ray of light they have attempted to shut out from your minds."[7] Enlightened Protestants were thus doubly offended by the laws making it a crime to teach a slave how to read.

The classic anecdote in this tradition tells of a Baltimore master named Hugh

Auld who, sometime around 1825, chastised his wife for having taught one of their slaves the alphabet and the rudiments of spelling. "A nigger should know nothing but to obey his master—to do as he is told to do," the slaveholder told his wife. "Learning would *spoil* the best nigger in the world . . . It would forever unfit him to be a slave. He would at once become unmanageable, and of no value to his master. As to himself, it could do him no good, but a great deal of harm. It would make it discontented and unhappy." Sophia Auld had indeed made a fateful error. She had taught Frederick Douglass how to read.[8]

Clearly the Whig tradition to which David Walker appealed in 1829 had not entirely lost its radical edge. Quite the contrary. As his militant prose circulated throughout the South it provoked a storm of protest from the slaveholders. The governor of Georgia reportedly demanded that the mayor of Boston suppress Walker's pamphlet. Insurrectionary plots across the South were attributed to the insidious influence of the *Appeal,* including Nat Turner's spectacular uprising in Southampton County, Virginia, in the summer of 1831. Indeed, having persuaded themselves of the direct link between Walker's *Appeal* and Turner's rebellion, slave-holders began to question the wisdom of allowing slaves to read. "Is there any great moral reason," the *Southern Presbyterian* asked, "why we should incur the tremen-dous risk of having our wives slaughtered in consequence of our slaves being taught to read incendiary publications?"[9]

The answer was perfectly clear to southern legislators. They responded to the Turner rebellion by passing an extraordinary series of laws formally restricting slave literacy. In Alabama and Louisiana the statutes endured for a generation; in four other states—Virginia, North and South Carolina, and Georgia—the statutes long outlasted the fallout from Turner rebellion and remained on the books through the Civil War. The laws varied in severity as well. In some states (Virginia, Maryland, and Missouri, for example) individual slaves could be educated but assemblies of slaves could not. Elsewhere owners could be fined for teaching any slave to read.[10]

In many ways these laws tell us more about the state of mind of the slaveholders at a critical moment in their history than they do about the day-to-day realities of the slave regime in the antebellum South. In practice there were always literate slaves, and always masters who depended on such literacy. Jefferson himself wrote out instructions to some of his slaves, and he was far from unique. Nor is it clear that Mrs. Auld violated any laws when she taught Frederick Douglass how to read. Yet the master's reaction, and the significance Douglass attributed to it, suggest that the laws themselves, however, erratically enforced, reflected the masters' belief that slaves were most docile when they were most ignorant. "We have as far as possible closed every avenue by which light may enter their minds," one Virginia slavehold-er explained. "If we could extinguish the capacity to see the light, our work would be completed."[11] The traditional equation held up in the antebellum South: slavery and ignorance went hand in hand.

Here, if nowhere else, David Walker could see eye to eye with the most reactionary proslavery racist. But where the masters feared that literate slaves, under the sway of abolitionist propaganda, would rise up against their owners, Walker believed that only the vast ignorance of the slave population could account for their failure to rebel more often than they did. Whatever else they argued about, therefore, slave and slaveholder, abolitionist, and proslavery ideologue worked from the common assumption that to be a slave was to be kept in ignorance. Unfortunately, this assumption was—and remains—so commonplace that its historical peculiarity has been effectively obscured.

In fact the laws restricting slave literacy are astonishing, however erratically they were enforced in practice. In the entire history of American education there is nothing comparable. There have been arguments against higher education for women, but never were there laws making it a crime to teach a woman to read. Confronted by millions of uneducated immigrants, nativists were more likely to legally require than to prohibit literacy training for foreigners. Only in the antebellum South, and only with regard to black slaves, was it ever illegal for one American to teach another how to read. And if such laws have no parallels in the history of American education, they have no obvious parallels in the history of slavery either. No matter how modern scholars define slavery—as unfree labor, as brutal exploitation, as social death—nothing in their definitions can explain why so many southern states passed laws restricting the literacy of slaves. In other slave societies such restrictions were unknown. Enforced ignorance was not a feature of slavery in ancient Greece. In Rome slaves often taught Greek literature, philosophy, mathematics, and history to the children of the upper class. Not only were there no laws against teaching slaves to read, there was no assumption whatsoever that slavery had anything to do with the ability to read or write. In short, illiteracy is not one of the defining features of slavery.

Jefferson's Views of Innate Human Traits

No one understood this better than Thomas Jefferson. He set about methodically to distinguish the intellectual achievements of ancient slaves from the ignorance of their modern counterparts. In Rome, he pointed out, slaves often ranked among their society's best artists. They "excelled too in science." Some of Rome's greatest philosophers, "Epictetus, Terence, and Phaedrus, were slaves." This was so, Jefferson insisted, despite the fact that ancient slavery was far more severe that American. What might account for the superior intellectual achievements of Roman slaves? "They were of the race of whites," Jefferson explained. Hence his famous conclusion regarding African American slaves: "It is not their condition then, but nature, which has produced the distinction."[12] Blacks could never be educated to the level of whites, not because they were slaves but because they were black.

In precisely which ways were blacks intellectually deficient? "Comparing them by their faculties of memory, reason, and imagination," Jefferson explained, "it appears to me that in memory they are equal to the whites; in reason much inferior, as I think one could scarcely be found capable of tracing and comprehending the investigations of Euclid; and that in imagination they are dull, tasteless and anomalous."[13] No one else of Jefferson's generation felt so compelled to specify the dimensions of black inferiority and to explain them in biological terms.[14]

This was not an easy argument to make. Jefferson had no IQ tests to substantiate the claim of black intellectual inferiority—no Shockley or Jensen or Herrnstein to provide a scientific veneer for his racist convictions, no E. O. Wilson to substantiate his belief in the inheritance of traits otherwise thought to be socially determined. Yet where Jefferson bent over backward to defend the intellectual capacities of Native Americans, he leaned the other way to argue that the degraded condition of Africans was not a product of enslavement but of "real distinctions" in nature. For some reason it mattered a great deal to Jefferson that black intellectual inferiority be placed beyond the reach of environmental improvement, that it be reckoned an innate trait, one that no amount of conditioning could alter.

About this Jefferson never changed his mind. Over the course of his life he had shifted positions in a number of critical ways. Having initially opposed the development of American manufactures, he argued later in life that they were necessary for the security of the American republic. As the spirit of democracy spread after the Revolution, Jefferson abandoned his earlier support of property qualifications for voting and office holding, adopting instead the principle of universal white manhood suffrage. But until the day he died, Jefferson never repudiated the speculations he had made in the early 1780s regarding black inferiority. On more than one occasion Jefferson expressed an unsurpassed desire to see demonstrative proofs of black equality. But as far as he was concerned no such proof was available. On the contrary, whenever he was confronted with substantial evidence of black intellectual achievement—whether the poetry of Phillis Wheatley, the calculations of Benjamin Banneker, or the writings of Ignatius Sancho—he dismissed it as either inconclusive or intellectually inferior. A few notorious paragraphs in the *Notes on the State of Virginia* therefore stand as Jefferson's first and last word on the subject of black inferiority.

Historians have pored over those paragraphs with a good deal of care, recovering their logic, exposing their inconsistency, pointing to the crudeness of Jefferson's sentiments and to the apparent squeamishness with which he expressed them. For some scholars Jefferson's remarks are full of equivocations and qualifications that mitigate their author's culpability. For others Jefferson's racism is blatantly offensive, one of the most extreme arguments that had ever been made for the innate inferiority of blacks. Intellectual historians have traced in detail the origins of Jefferson's racism. They have placed it in a variety of cultural and historical contexts.

They have subjected it to psychohistorical analysis, linking it to Jefferson's most intimate obsessions. They have examined its long-range consequences for American culture as a whole.

Notwithstanding all of this attention, there is still reason to go back to the *Notes* and look very carefully at some of the striking distinctions that appear in Jefferson's own words. For all the crudeness of his language, Jefferson was anything but indiscriminate. On the contrary, he managed in the space of a few pages to make precise calculations of the ways in which he thought whites and blacks different, similar, superior, and inferior. Consider what else he *might* have said, but did not. Disciplined work mattered a great deal to Jefferson, but he never argued that blacks were inferior to whites in their capacity to work hard. He was convinced that sociability was one of the defining characteristics of humanity, suggesting that it was a trait innate to all men and women, black and white alike. He believed in the importance of a moral sense, but he never argued that blacks were less capable than were whites of drawing proper moral conclusions. Why, then, did Jefferson argue for innate differences of intellectual capacity between whites and blacks? What, in short, was the political significance of Jefferson's racism?

The powerful equation of literacy with freedom—an equation popularized in the eighteenth century and persisting well into the nineteenth—points toward an answer. Free people, in particular free men, were not merely allowed to read; the connection was much more profound. Literacy was a constitutive element of freedom; to read was to be free. For to be free in America was to think rationally, to reflect on issues public and private, to weigh arguments, to enter into reasoned discourse. Literate slaves were therefore a dual threat. Specifically, they could read incendiary literature that would make them difficult to control if not openly rebellious. But more generally a literate slave was an oxymoron, a contradiction in terms. You might as well talk of a free slave—there was no such thing. In the United States of America, a slave who could read was a slave who would be free.

And for Thomas Jefferson, black freedom was the heart of the matter. It was not that the alleged intellectual inferiority of blacks made them uniquely suited to enslavement but that it rendered them unfit to live as equals in free society. Jefferson sincerely believed it immoral to hold any human being in slavery, yet he recoiled in horror from the prospect of freeing black slaves to live among whites as equals. He thus constructed his racism as a justification for colonizing the freed slaves beyond the borders of the United States. But what kind of argument would it take to pronounce blacks unsuited to live as equals among whites? The answer depends on how Jefferson thought about freedom, for the traits in which he deemed blacks inferior were determined by the traits he valued most in those who were free.

Jefferson believed blacks were "inferior to the whites in the endowments both of body and mind." Bodily inferiority was a broadly aesthetic judgement embracing several distinct features of Jefferson's racism. Most clearly, Jefferson found blacks physically repulsive: their hair, their complexions, their physiognomy all contrasted unfavorably with Jefferson's white ideal. Blacks tended to sweat too much. They smelled. They were sexually attractive to apes. Invoking what he presumed were transcendent standards of beauty, Jefferson declared that blacks were literally ugly. Moreover their aesthetic inferiority was internal as well as external, Jefferson thought, mental as well as physical. Indeed it is not always easy to separate the endowments of the body from those of the mind in Jefferson's writing. If blacks failed to measure up to absolute standards of beauty, so were they incapable of appreciating the beauty that approached Jefferson's exalted ideals. And they most certainly could not produce such beauty. Poems written by African Americans were "below the dignity of criticism" in Jefferson's eyes; African music was simplistic and crude by the standards of western harmonics. Thus culture and biology conspired to render blacks aesthetically inferior to whites: African Americans could neither produce nor appreciate beauty, and this seemed somehow connected to their own inherent ugliness.[15]

Jefferson was somewhat more ambiguous about the moral sense. In theory a moral sense was a sign of humanity itself, and nobody ever seriously argued that Africans were not human beings. Blacks were therefore endowed with a moral sense that allowed them to tell right from wrong. Until Garry Wills made his strong case in the 1970s, few historians appreciated the significance of moral sense philosophy in eighteenth-century America. Wills argued that Jefferson's racism was substantially tempered by his conviction that blacks and whites were equally endowed with a moral sense. But the issue was further complicated by Morton White's persuasive argument that during the eighteenth century there were two competing schools of thought about the moral sense. One held that it was utterly independent of human reason; the other saw reason as the guide and check for the moral sense. And Jefferson, White demonstrated, belonged to the latter school.[16] Thus Jefferson spoke repeatedly of the important role education played in the cultivation and strengthening of the moral sense. To some extent, therefore, the blacks' capacity to use their moral senses depended on the power of their rational faculties—a subject on which Jefferson was rather less ambiguous.

Consider the issue of memory. Jefferson believed that blacks and whites were equally endowed on this score, and at first glance this seems encouraging. But Jefferson associated memory with intellectual immaturity. The memory should be exercised chiefly in those early years, between the ages of eight and sixteen, before the more mature faculty of reflection was fully developed. At this young age "the mind, like the body, is not yet firm enough for laborious and close operations," Jefferson explained. "The memory is then most susceptible and tenacious of impressions." This was the ideal time to focus on the study of foreign languages, which, "being chiefly a work of memory, it seems precisely fitted to the powers of this period."[17] So in pronouncing blacks and whites equal in the faculty of memory,

Jefferson was at best offering a back-handed compliment. At worst, he was simply restating the intellectual superiority of white men, among whom the rigorous exercise of memory was but an adolescent phase on the way toward mature rationality.[18]

Although Jefferson believed that blacks and whites were equally endowed with a moral sense and with the capacity of memory, he reserved his most enduring faith in the inequitably distributed faculties of reason. On a few occasions, most famously during his brief infatuation with Maria Cosway, Jefferson argued for the primacy of the heart over the head. "An honest heart being the first blessing," he wrote in 1785, "a knowing head is the second."[19] But as Dumas Malone and others have pointed out, these unusual outbursts pale beside the overwhelming evidence of Jefferson's nearly unswerving commitment to the rule of reason. "Your own reason," he once explained to Peter Carr, "is the only oracle given to you by heaven."[20] Jefferson held everything up to the scrutiny of reason: law and religion, kings and people. He had revised the statutes of Virginia, he explained in his autobiography, "with a single eye to reason."[21] In 1787 he advised Carr that his "reason is now mature enough" to examine the subject of religion. "Fix reason firmly in her seat, and call to her tribunal every fact, every opinion. Question with boldness even the existence of a god; because, if there be one, he must more approve the homage of reason, than that of blindfolded fear."[22] The implications of Jefferson's racism depend therefore on what he meant by "reason" and the political significance he attributed to it.

Jefferson went beyond John Locke's assumption that reason was an innate human characteristic. As Daniel Boorstin argued some time ago, Jefferson and his circle had a pronounced tendency to naturalize a plethora of traits—moral sense, sociability, taste—that are better understood to be socially constructed. "Nature hath implanted in our breasts a love of others, a sense of duty to them, a moral instinct," Jefferson explained in 1814. "The Creator would indeed have been a bungling artist, had he intended man for a social animal, without planting in him social dispositions."[23] It is certainly true that Jefferson and his friends spoke of characteristics such as sociability as though they were inherited physical traits. But the issue was more complicated than Boorstin allowed.[24]

Jefferson emphasized the critical interaction of inherited characteristics with the social and cultural environment. Inherited dispositions would rarely manifest themselves automatically. Thus the moral sense was like a muscle—a genetic inheritance common to all human beings but one that had to be developed and exercised so as to be kept in good working order. Strictly speaking Jefferson was neither exclusively environmentalist nor exclusively naturalist. Consequently, he swerved back and forth between environmentalist and naturalist logic. Depending on the circumstances or the issue involved, he could stress one pole or the other.

Jefferson never claimed that inherited traits were impervious to environmental influences. For example, he posited the existence of a Natural Aristocracy—"the most precious gift of nature"—yet he also believed that society had to devise means for isolating and cultivating the wise and virtuous lest nature's gifts go to waste.[25] As with wisdom and virtue, so, too, with stupidity: it was both an inherited weakness and a cultivated flaw. In a slashing critique of monarchy written in 1810, Jefferson offered an explanation for the idiocy of European royalty that is almost Lamarckian in its suggestion that acquired traits can subsequently be inherited. "Now, take any race of animals, confine them in idleness and inaction, whether in a stye, a stable, or a state room, pamper them with high diet, gratify all their sexual appetites, immerse them in sensualities, nourish their passions, let every thing bend before them, and banish whatever might lead them to think, and in a few generations they become all body and no mind. . . . Such is the regimen of raising Kings." After centuries of inter-marriage, Jefferson concluded, their stupidity was hopelessly inbred. The king of England was "a cypher;" the king of Sardinia "a fool;" the queen of Portugal "an idiot by nature. And so was the King of Denmark." The king of Prussia was "a mere hog in body as well as in mind." Gustavus of Sweden, and Joseph of Austria, were "really crazy."[26] For Jefferson these mental deficiencies were as much a product of royal nature as of royal nurture.

Jefferson spoke in nearly identical terms about characteristics as varied as taste, morality, and sociability. Each was an inherited trait; each was strongly influenced by the environment. As he explained to Robert Skipwith as early as 1771, "dispositions of the mind, like limbs of the body, acquire strength by exercise. But exercise produces habit," Jefferson went on, "and in the instance of which we speak, the exercise being of the moral feelings produces a habit of thinking and acting virtuously."[27] The rational faculty was no different. A genetic endowment, reason nonetheless required the discipline of sustained education and proper socialization before it could mature. If the critical years of early life are "suffered to pass in idleness," Jefferson warned, "the mind becomes lethargic and impotent, as would the body it inhabits if unexercised during the same time."[28] The most impressive intellectual endowment could atrophy if not carefully cultivated.

The same was true of entire societies. They, too, developed and matured in their rational capacities. They, too, were differentiated between the more and less reasonable. Jefferson feared the immigration of Europeans because they came from places where the rule of reason was suppressed and were therefore unfit to participate as equals in American public life. "If all the sovereigns of Europe were to set themselves to work to emancipate the minds of their subjects from their present ignorance and prejudices . . .," he explained in 1786, "a thousand years would not place them on that high ground on which our common people are now setting out." Again appealing to vaguely Lamarckian rhetoric, Jefferson located the distinctive rationality of the American people in their having been "separated from their parent stock and been kept from contamination, either from them, or the other people of the old world, by the intervention of so wide an ocean."[29] For Jefferson, then, reason was a social as well as an individual trait, an innate capacity and an acquired characteristic.

So when he argued that blacks were intellectually inferior to whites, Jefferson was invoking a distinction that he applied in a variety of ways. Blacks were indeed inferior to whites, but women were also the intellectual inferiors of men. European societies were less rational than American. Monarchies produced idiots for leaders, whereas republican democracies would give rise to natural aristocrats. And in each case, Jefferson linked the distinction to the capacity for self-government. "It is a blessing . . . that our people are reasonable," he wrote Caesar Rodney in 1810, "that they are kept so well informed of the state of things as to judge for themselves, to see the true sources of their difficulties."[30] In fact, it would be hard to understate the political significance Jefferson attached to the people's capacity for reason.

Most of his faith in the future of freedom and democracy depended upon that capacity. "It rests now with ourselves alone to enjoy in peace and concord the blessings of self-government, so long denied to mankind: to shew by example the sufficiency of human reason for the care of human affairs and that the will of the majority, the Natural law of every society, is the only sure guardian of the rights of man . . . Let us then, my dear friends, for ever bow down to the general reason of the society. We are safe with that." In his more optimistic mode, Jefferson could delight in the "spreading . . . influence of reason and liberty over the face of the earth."[31] Over and over Jefferson linked "reason and liberty" in precisely this way. "I have so much confidence in the good sense of man, and his qualifications for self-government, that I am never afraid of the issue where reason is left free to exert her force."[32] What would reason look like when so unleashed upon the world?

It would appear, first, in the rejection of arguments from authority. Nothing was true simply because the king, the pope, or any other authority said so. The age of reason was, for Jefferson, an age of reasons: truths were established, policies were made or abandoned, only after their merits and demerits had been thrashed out in public discussion, the reasons for and against them thoroughly and freely aired. Here was "the unforced force of the better argument" that the German social philosopher, Jürgen Habermas, defines as the utopian goal of the bourgeois public sphere.[33] Without freedom of inquiry, therefore, the "habit of testing everything by reason" could never become ingrained and the government "of reason and truth" could never develop.[34] Jefferson sometimes spoke of the "freedom of language,"[35] foreshadowing John Stuart Mill's definition of democracy as government by discussion.

Jefferson's model for discussion was scientific inquiry. "Freedom," he once explained, was "the first-born daughter of science."[36] Elsewhere he reversed the parentage and pronounced liberty "the great parent of science and of virtue . . . a nation will be great in both," he added, "always in proportion as it is free."[37] On such occasions Jefferson came close to equating freedom with the Enlightenment ideal of methodical inquiry. How else could "public opinion"—a discovery of the eighteenth century—do its work? The "great honor of science and the arts," Jefferson wrote to John Adams in 1816, is "that their natural effect is, by illuminating public opinion, to erect it into a Censor, before which the most exalted tremble."[38] This "effect," once set in motion, was all but irreversible—for knowledge, once known, cannot be un-known.

At times Jefferson grounded his argument in technology: "The light which has been shed on mankind by the art of printing has eminently changed the condition of the world."[39] The "American mind is already too much opened," he explained in 1799, "and while the art of printing is left to us, science can never be retrograde; what is once acquired of real knowledge can never be lost. To preserve the freedom of the human mind then & freedom of the press, every spirit should be ready to devote itself to martyrdom; for as long as we may think as we will, & speak as we think, the condition of man will proceed in improvement."[40] The fortunes of freedom were therefore linked, in Jefferson's mind, to society's capacity to produce and reproduce the accumulated wisdom of the ages.

Jefferson sometimes likened this intellectual accumulation to a force of nature, the inevitable consequence of the primary proposition that "Almighty God hath created the mind free."[41] Wherever this God-given freedom is allowed to flourish, he explained, "truth" will prevail, for "she is the proper and sufficient antagonist to error, and has nothing to fear from the conflict unless by human interposition disarmed of her natural weapons, free argument and debate." Errors, he concluded, cease to be dangerous when truth "is permitted freely to contradict them." To Richard Price, Jefferson rehearsed his argument for the self-correcting tendency of enlightened public opinion. "[W]herever the people are well informed they can be trusted with their own government . . ., whenever things get so far wrong as to attract their notice, they may be relied on to set them to rights."[42] For Jefferson, then, the capacity to reason was the prerequisite to freedom and human progress.

Hence the centrality of education in Jefferson's vision. When he proposed that every free child in America be taught to read and write, that they all learn the basic lessons of their own history, Jefferson had no intention of rendering them fit for worthwhile employment or setting them on the road to upward mobility. Jefferson's goals were straightforwardly political: he saw the cultivation of rational faculties through universal education as the greatest bulwark of democracy and enlightenment against the forces of feudalism and darkness. In passing references and in extended arguments, Jefferson repeatedly contrasted feudalism and aristocracy with enlightenment and education. He spoke of the "seigniorial powers and practices" of the French aristocracy as inconsistent "with reason and right." In his autobiography Jefferson listed universal education among the four major reforms that would eradicate "every fibre . . . of antient or future aristocracy."[43] From Paris he wrote to George Wythe urging a crusade against ignorance. "No other sure foundation can be devised for the preservation of freedom, and happiness. . . . [E]stablish and improve the law for educating the common people. Let our countrymen know that . . . the tax which will be paid for this purpose is not more than the thousandth part of what will be paid to kings, priests and nobles who will rise up among us if we leave the people in ignorance."[44]

Fearful that the people might actually be "deceived" into destroying their own rights, Jefferson argued, "they should be instructed to a certain degree." Even libraries served this political purpose, by circulating "a few well-chosen books" among the people.[45] And what was true of libraries was even more true of public schools—they would provide the people with the education they needed to protect themselves in their liberty. A carefully developed system of universal education, he wrote to John Adams in 1813, "would have raised the mass of the people to the high ground of moral respectability necessary to their own safety, and to orderly government." Indeed, only an educated people would be competent "to select the veritable aristoi, for the trusts of government," to discern among themselves those most fully endowed with the natural capacity to rule.[46]

Thus for Jefferson education served two distinct purposes. On the one hand it trained the great mass of people to participate as equals in a political democracy. On the other hand, it cultivated the natural aristocracy, training it to various degrees for service at the appropriate levels of government. Public education would thereby prepare the rulers and the ruled in a complementary fashion: the former to assume their proper positions of authority, the latter to hold such authority in check.[47] "This requires two grades of education," Jefferson explained. One would afford to "every member of society" the capacity "to read, to judge & to vote understandingly on what is passing."[48] The other grade would prepare the "few subjects in every State, to whom nature has given minds of the first order." This would be the training ground for the natural aristocracy.

To be sure, Jefferson saw more of value in education than simply the destruction of feudalism and the defense of democracy. In his "Report of the Commissioners for the University of Virginia,"[49] he reckoned the benefits of mass literacy rather more broadly. It would give all citizens the tools they needed to transact their business, including the ability to enter into written contracts having clearly calculated and expressed their interests. Education would improve their moral faculties; it would help them understand and meet their obligations to the community and the nation. Through education citizens would come to know their rights and understand how to exercise them. They would be competent to select with discretion those they hire and to judge the adequacy of their performance. In short, universal education would facilitate the development of a bourgeois society in which social relations were grounded in contract rather than ascription.

Higher education served even more explicitly political ends: "To form statesmen, legislators and judge. . . . To expound the principles and structure of government, the laws which regulate the intercourse of nations, those formed municipally for our own government, and a sound spirit of legislation, which, banishing all arbitrary and unnecessary restraint on individual action, shall leave us free to do whatever does not violate the equal rights of another." Beyond this, higher education was designed to promote the general well being by developing "informed views of political economy," cultivating "the reasoning faculties of our youth," enlightening them in the arts and sciences, and more generally making them fit objects of emulation by others.

The Author of the Declaration of Independence

Here, in the broadly political purposes Jefferson assigned to education, lay the spectral shadows of his incipient racism. For by arguing in very particular ways for the intellectual inferiority of blacks, Jefferson raised—implicitly but inescapably—a series of troubling questions about their capacity to participate as equals in American public life. Could education make blacks into fit statesmen, effective legislators, or wise judges? Could blacks ever develop "informed views of political economy," ever contribute great works of art, ever appreciate the intricacies of science and technology? Would they ever understand their rights as fully as educated white people? Could they be trusted to identify, much less empower, society's natural aristocrats? Would any amount of education render them fit to participate as equals in American public life?

Apparently not. With precise logic Jefferson laid out his case for the ineducability of blacks—ineducable not in the sense that blacks could learn nothing, but in the sense that they could never be educated to the levels that whites could. To make his case, Jefferson had to confront powerful environmentalist explanations for black inferiority. He did so with considerable determination, systematically attacking the claim that African ignorance could be explained either by centuries of life in backward civilizations or by the more recent degradations of New World slavery. He put forward four varieties of evidence. First, he disputed the claim that blacks had suffered by their isolation from the benefits of a superior white civilization. On the contrary, Jefferson argued, many blacks in America were "so situated" that they had in fact been the beneficiaries of extensive conversations with whites. Many more were trained in artisanal skills that once again put blacks and whites into close association. Still others were "liberally educated." And all African Americans, Jefferson pointed out, "have lived in countries where the arts and sciences are cultivated to a considerable degree, and all have had before their eyes samples of the best works from abroad."[50]

Notwithstanding such wide and close exposure to the achievements of white civilization, black inferiority persisted. "[N]ever yet could I find that a black had uttered a thought above the level of plain narration; never saw an elementary trait of painting or sculpture." Indeed, the finest black author Jefferson knew of, Ignatius Sancho, scarcely measured up to the standards of his white contemporaries. "[W]hen we compare him with the writers of the [white] race among whom he lived . . .," Jefferson argued, "we are compelled to enroll him at the bottom of the column." Thus did Jefferson begin to whittle away the environmental explanation for the alleged intellectual inferiority of blacks.[51]

In a second line of reasoning Jefferson turned the tables on those who blamed black ignorance on slavery. The indisputable degradations of bondage notwithstanding, Jefferson argued, slavery did not stifle many of the emotions that so often inspire impressive artistic achievement. In some ways it heightened such emotions. "Misery is often the parent of the most affecting touches of poetry. Among the blacks there is misery enough, God knows," Jefferson argued, "but no poetry." Love inspires poetry among whites, he continued, but among blacks "it kindles the senses only." Not even religion could "produce a poet" among blacks.[52]

Jefferson carried his war on environmentalism further still by comparing American slaves unfavorably to the indigenous peoples of North America. Native Americans, Jefferson argued, had none of the advantages of liberal education or proximity to whites that so many African Americans enjoyed. Yet Indian artistic efforts revealed "a germ in their minds that only wants cultivation," a germ presumably missing from blacks. Similarly, Native Americans "astonish you with strokes of the most sublime oratory," suggesting once again an imaginative endowment that blacks simply lacked.[53]

And finally, of course, Jefferson trumped the environmentalists by pointing to the impressive achievements of the slaves of ancient Rome. They had suffered appalling degradations—degradations unknown to their counterparts in North America. Roman slaves were systematically stripped of a family life, cruelly discarded in their old age, and subjected to a hideous variety of barbaric tortures. "Yet notwithstanding these and other discouraging circumstances among the romans, their slaves were often their rarest artists," Jefferson declared. Roman slaves excelled in the sciences, tutored their masters' children, produced some of their most respected philosophers. "But," Jefferson explained, "they were of the race of whites."[54]

The point was clear enough: No amount of education would bring blacks to the level of whites. And since the survival of democracy depended on an educated citizenry, the inference to be drawn from the presumed fact of black ineducability was just as clear: in a free society blacks and whites could not live together as equals. For Jefferson this did not mean that blacks should remain enslaved. "[W]hatever be their degree of talent it is no measure of their rights," he insisted.[55] For all his equivocations, his silences, the pusillanimous rarity of his public statements on the subject, Jefferson never abandoned his conviction that slavery was a monstrous violation of the fundamental right to liberty. "Nothing is more certainly written in the book of fate than that these people are to be free," he wrote in his autobiography.

"Nor is it less certain," he quickly added, "that the two races, equally free, cannot live in the same government. Nature, habit, opinion has drawn indelible lines of distinction between them."[56] Here was Jefferson's famous dilemma: he believed, simultaneously, that the slaves should be freed and that they could not live with whites as equals. Indeed, at several points in the course of his life he predicted that if blacks and whites were somehow forced to live together in freedom, an apocalyptic race war would erupt, ending only with the complete extermination of either the whites or the blacks.

Jefferson believed that equality was the precondition for rational communication. If aristocratic hierarchy, with its corrupting interdependencies and ingrained condescension, made free and open communication virtually impossible, so did racial inequality. To prove this case was the great burden of Jefferson's racism. A veritable spokesperson for the enlightened liberalism of eighteenth-century America, Jefferson was deeply committed to the idea of an educated citizenry. He could not separate democracy from the public sphere wherein issues were resolved by recourse to arguments and reasons rather than authority and status. Under the circumstances, Jefferson's claim that blacks were "in reason much inferior" to whites amounted to an argument for keeping blacks out of the public sphere. Lacking the requisite rational faculties, blacks could never engage as equals in the reasoned discourse of American public life. Jefferson concluded, therefore, that the slaves should be freed and thereafter removed—colonized—beyond the borders of the United States.

But this was not the inevitable conclusion—there are few inevitable conclusions in the history of ideas. On the contrary the political significance of Jefferson's racism extends to the multiple and contradictory inferences that so many Americans drew. Countless whites shared Jefferson's carefully considered assumption that freedom and enlightened reason went hand in hand. At least as many agreed that blacks were intellectually inferior and therefore unsuited to participate in free society as the equals of whites. But the conclusion they drew from these assumptions was rather different from Jefferson's. For most of those who believed that blacks and whites could never live together as equals, the evident conclusion was to maintain blacks in slavery and in ignorance. Were they embracing or repudiating Jefferson's legacy?

For David Walker the slaveholders were Jeffersonians *par excellence.* In his view, Thomas Jefferson's *Notes on the State of Virginia* had by 1829 assumed the status of holy writ among those who justified the continued enslavement and oppression of American blacks, slave and free. Like Jefferson, Walker equated slavery with ignorance and freedom with enlightenment. And both saw slavery as a straightforward violation of the fundamental right to freedom. But in asserting the capacity of blacks and whites to live together as equals, in demanding emancipation without colonization, and above all, in asserting the fundamental equality of blacks and whites, Walker distanced himself from Jefferson as much as any proslavery ideologue ever did.[57]

The irony is appalling. Thomas Jefferson believed it immoral to hold human beings in slavery, yet by arguing that blacks were unsuited to live in freedom as the equals of white men, he constructed for his intellectual heirs the moral foundations of proslavery ideology. Buried deep within those laws making it a crime to teach a slave to read were a host of Jeffersonian assumptions equating blackness with unreason, and unreason with slavery. The masters who passed such laws were convinced that a literate slave was a dangerous slave; they were men for whom the equation of education with freedom remained very much a living principle. With Jefferson, they believed blacks were unfit to participate in public life as the equals of white men. But they carried Jefferson's reasoning to tragic yet logical conclusion: by enforcing black ignorance, they made his racism a self-fulfilling proposition.

Shall we conclude, then, with slaveholders invoking Jefferson and abolitionists assailing him? It is a disquieting way to end, because it is not quite right.

David Walker understood as much, though he seemed reluctant to admit it. In the closing passage of his *Appeal* he wondered whether the greatest oppressors in history had "ever treated a set of human beings, as the white Christians of America do us, the blacks, or Africans." And yet these were the "very American people" who swore their devotion to the Declaration of Independence. "Hear your language proclaimed to the world," Walker demanded, "July 4, 1776—'We hold these truths to be self evident—that *ALL* MEN ARE CREATED EQUAL!'"[58] Having attacked Jefferson—by name—so often and so mercilessly in the first half of his *Appeal,* Walker ended without making any reference at all to the authorship of the Declaration. Yet surely it matters that David Walker's best witness against Thomas Jefferson on racial hierarchy turned out to be Thomas Jefferson on human equality.

DONALD A. GRINDE, JR.

Thomas Jefferson's Dualistic Perceptions of Native Americans

"Societies . . . as among our Indians . . . [may be] . . .
best. But I believe them inconsistent with any great
degree of population."

—Thomas Jefferson to James Madison,
January 30, 1787[1]

Thomas Jefferson's perceptions of American Indians illuminate the ambiguities and curiosity that Euroamericans have held over time about the native peoples of the Americas. A survey of Jefferson's writings reveals that he was, at once, scholarly, imaginative, informed, and full of contradictions. Vernon L. Parrington, Dumas Malone, Merrill Peterson, and Julian P. Boyd have provided us with scholarly treatments of Jefferson that represent him as a heroic voice of freedom. Conversely, Leonard W. Levy's work on Jefferson has delved into his darker, more dictatorial side.[2] In a similar vein, Winthrop Jordan pointed out that Jefferson sounded the rhetoric of antislavery while maintaining that African Americans were inferior.[3] Yet, Jefferson's views of American Indians have never been fully examined and remain enigmatic.

Since American Indians acted autonomously in North America, the Sage of Monticello's ideas about them were even more circumspect than his ideas about African Americans. As a result of the intellectual debates of his era, Jefferson often found himself compelled to assert that American Indians were mentally and physically equal to whites, arguing against the environmental degeneracy thesis advanced by the comte de Buffon and others. Upon stepping out of the intellectual arena, Jefferson often abandoned his views on the equality of American Indians to confront the political realities of nurturing the conquest state in America. In striving to impart the benefits of Christianity, education, and private property to Native Americans, Jeffersonian philanthropy had largely negative effects on American Indian lives even when the discourse about Native American cultures was superficially positive.[4] In assessing Jefferson's interests in the political structures of American Indians, Richard K. Matthews adds that the "study of American Indians . . . helped to convince Jefferson that man was a social, harmonious, cooperative and

193

just creature . . . who could live happily in a community that did not need the presence of Leviathan."[5] Indeed, Matthews observes that whereas Hamilton and
Madison had their ideal of the "market man, Jefferson has the American Indian,
who provides the empirical model for his political vision."[6] Matthews concludes
that Jefferson's knowledge of American Indians provided his "scientific mind with
the concrete evidence that he needed so that he could erect a solid democratic political theory."[7] Matthews's analysis, although praising American Indian societies and
Jefferson's appreciation of them, does little to address Jefferson's dualistic approach
to American Indian people.

Like Matthews, Julian P. Boyd recognized the enormous impact of Native
American people on the Europeans who encountered them. A generation ago, Boyd
asserted that the "Indian was . . . a factor of enormous importance in the 18th century, far out of proportion to his actual numbers."[8] He argued that Native American
influences on colonial and European thought was extensive and that Native
American ways inspired Montesquieu's "*Spirit of Laws* and from the same sources
emerged Rousseau's *Social Contract*. . . . [T]he French Revolution was but another
link in the chain of influence that has stretched from the western frontiers to the
capitals of Europe."[9] Similarly, the political and legal theorist Felix Cohen has
stated that American Indian political ideas influenced Rousseau, Montaigne, and
Jefferson so much that

> it is out of a rich Indian democratic tradition that the distinctive political ideas of
> American life emerged. Universal suffrage for women as well as for men, the pat-
> tern of states within a state that we call federalism, the habit of treating chiefs as
> servants of the people instead of their masters, the insistence that the community
> must respect the diversity of men and the diversity of their dreams—all these
> things were part of American life before Columbus landed.[10]

Despite these varied observations during several generations of scholarly analysis,
the impact of Native Americans on Jefferson and on the political nature of America
remains unexamined for most American historians. Some contemporary scholars
like Neal Salisbury have attributed this neglect to the stereotypes of "heathen savages" and "civilized Europeans" that persist in scholarly discourse. In surveying the
historical literature, Salisbury observed that such racist terms have persisted among
"contemporary scholars supposedly emancipated from the religious and racial
superstitions of the past."[11] Thus, the inherent problems in examining Jefferson's
often contradictory scholarship on American Indians are compounded by some of
the same dualistic motivations within the historical profession itself.

Dualism, Jefferson, and the American Indian

An analysis of Jefferson's assertions about American Indians reveals two often
contradictory perceptions. Jefferson often admired Native Americans for their nat-

ural sagacity and yet reproached them for what he perceived as their primitive culture and stubborn resistance to European forms of civilization. In Jefferson's discourse, American Indians could be an intellectual foil against the environmental degeneracy arguments of a Buffon and then, almost in the same breath, these same American Indians could become the focus of Jefferson's extermination efforts for resisting the westward movement of American settlers.

Jefferson's own accounts demonstrate that his entire life was rich in positive associations with the native peoples of America. His father, Peter Jefferson, was an avid naturalist who introduced young Thomas to American Indian sachems and visitors who lodged at the family home on their way to and from official business in Williamsburg. Toward the end of his life, in a series of published letters that reconciled the political differences of the two retired presidents, Jefferson wrote to John Adams that he believed his early contacts with Native Americans were an important influence on his development:

> Concerning Indians, in the early part of my life, I was very familiar, and acquired impressions of attachment and commiseration for them which have never been obliterated. Before the Revolution, they were in the habit of coming often and in great numbers to the seat of government *where I was very much with them.* I knew much the great Ontassete, the warrior and orator of the Cherokees; he was always the guest of my father, on his journeys to and from Williamsburg [emphasis added].[12]

Jefferson's "attachment" to Indians took many forms throughout his life. It could be personal, as in his writings to his daughter Martha, where he recounts a conversation in 1792 with a Peoria chief in Philadelphia whom he had known earlier.

> One of the Indians chiefs now here, whom you may remember to have seen at Monticello a day or two before Tarlton drove us of[f], remembers you and enquired about you. He is one of the Pioria nation. Perhaps you may recollect that he gave our name to an infant son he then had with him and who, he now tells me, is a fine lad.[13]

Jefferson's personal contacts with American Indians also helped him in his observations of their manners and customs. Often, his political life gave him opportunities to see things like the burial practices of American Indians.

> I believe you knew Otchakity, the Indian who lived with the Marquis Lafayette. He came here lately with some deputies from his nation, and died here of a pleurisy. I was at his funeral yesterday. He was buried standing up according to their manner.[14]

As a result of his many personal and public contacts, Jefferson frequently voiced his respect for Native Americans. For example, in 1785 he wrote, "I am safe in affirming that the proofs of genius given by the Indians place them on a level with the whites . . . I have seen some thousands myself, and conversed much with them. . . . I believe the Indian to be in body and mind equal to the white man."[15]

But when American Indians opposed the expansion of the United States, Jefferson could also be quite harsh and negative in his judgments of them. As the War of 1812 began, he wrote this to John Adams: "the backward [Indians] will yeild, and be thrown back. These will relapse into barbarism and misery. . . , and we shall be obliged to drive them, with the beasts of the forest into the Stony Mountains."[16] Clearly, Jefferson's positive perceptions of American Indians coupled with his willingness to serve the interests of the planter class made his scholarship and politics vis à vis Indians inconsistent and opportunistic.

As an American, Jefferson bristled at any suggestion that nature had dealt the New World environment an inferior hand. Under the guise of science, so-called degeneracy theories had gained some currency in Europe during the late eighteenth century.[17] This particular school of pseudoscience was pressed into service as a justification for colonialism in much the same way that craniology, which linked intelligence to the relative size and volume of skulls among the races, would be used a century later.[18]

Jefferson's *Notes on the State of Virginia* was, in part, a refutation of the assertions of the comte de Buffon of France and others that the very soil, water, and air of the New World caused plants and animals including human beings to grow less rapidly and enjoy less sexual ardor than their Old World counterparts. The ongoing controversy over the innate intelligence of American Indians was also factored into this debate. Essentially, Buffon and others championed the theory of inherent and environmental Native American and transplanted European inferiority in North America. Countering the degeneracy theorists, Jefferson maintained that native peoples of America enjoyed mental abilities equal to Europeans. In his *Notes on the State of Virginia,* he quoted the eloquent speech Logan delivered after Euroamericans had massacred his family as evidence that American Indians had a full measure of intelligence and compassion.[19]

At every opportunity, Jefferson and his contemporaries sought to turn degeneracy theorists on their heads. Jefferson was fond of relating a conversation that took place at a dinner, attended by Benjamin Franklin, a few other Americans, and several French degeneracy theory advocates, when Franklin was representing the new nation in France. Franklin listened politely as Abbé Raynal, a well-known proponent of American degeneracy, described how even Europeans would be stunted by exposure to the New World; Franklin then simply asked the Frenchmen to test their theory "by the fact before us." "Let both parties rise," Franklin challenged, "and we shall see on which side nature has degenerated." The table became a metaphorical Atlantic Ocean as the Americans, on one side, rose to their feet and towered over the French on the other. The Abbé, "himself particularly, was a mere shrimp," Jefferson smirked.[20]

In order to combat the degeneracy theorists, Jefferson and others were forced to uphold the equality of American Indians to maintain their own equality in the environment of North America. To further this line of reasoning, Jefferson's analysis of native political systems was enhanced in some editions of his *Notes on the State of Virginia* by Charles Thomson, who served as secretary to the Continental Congress from 1774 to 1787. As a young man, Thomson was adopted into the Delaware Nation and received the name Wegh-wu-law-mo-end or "the man who tells the truth." He also witnessed a Delaware and Mohawk Condolence Ceremony two decades before the American Revolution. With this kind of background, Thomson confidently wrote detailed descriptions of American Indian customs and political structures for Jefferson's *Notes on the State of Virginia*.[21]

But Jefferson's respect for American Indians and his philanthropic attitudes toward them were always clouded by the ominous threat of extermination. On August 28, 1807, Jefferson wrote to General Henry Dearborn that "if we are constrained to lift the hatchet against any tribe, we will never lay it down until that tribe is exterminated."[22] Jefferson added that "[I]n war, they will kill some of us; we shall destroy all of them."[23]

Thus, Jefferson could pursue the study of American Indian languages and cultures as an academic curiosity, but, in reality, autonomous American Indians resisting white domination were to be ruthlessly destroyed when they opposed frontier expansion. When "noble savages" imbued with qualities equal to the white man attended to their own political and military interests, they became ``children'' that the presidential Jefferson addressed as ``my son'' and admonished to take ``the advice then of a father'' and avoid the white man's quarrels.[24] Jefferson also believed that American Indian nations and their leaders were to be dealt with in an opportunistic manner when necessary. He stated to William Henry Harrison on February 27, 1803, that ``[W]e shall . . . be glad to see the good and influential individuals among them run in debt, because we observe that when these debts get beyond what the individuals can pay they become willing to lop them off by a cession of lands."[25]

And yet, Jefferson the slaveholder could sometimes transcend the dualistic contradictions through his belief in the universal morality of mankind. From a practical and intellectual standpoint, Jefferson was quite capable of acknowledging and promoting intermarriage with native peoples in order to create a "continental family." In January 1802, Jefferson told an American Indian delegation that "[y]our blood will mix with ours, and will spread, with ours, over this great island."[26] Although these inconsistent aspects of Jefferson's views are a product of his era, we should be grateful to Jefferson for his frank observations about American Indian customs and traditions. He seemed to comprehend that reporting the events of his time was often more important than understanding them.

Although visitors to Monticello were greeted in the Great Hall or entryway with a striking array of American Indian artifacts, Jefferson's attitudes toward American Indians were not genuinely egalitarian. Undeniably, Thomas Jefferson was a lifelong student of the origins, languages, cultures, philosophies, prehistory, history, and politics of American Indians. Whereas many European observers discussed Native Americans from afar, using travel accounts and occasional encounters in Europe with Native Americans, Jefferson's sustained and significant contacts with American Indians made him an important firsthand observer of their ways. Jefferson viewed American Indian societies as a window to a premonarchial world that had ceased to exist in Europe with the advent of feudalism. It would be a mistake, however, to think that Jefferson was seeking a noble savage as was Jean-Jacques Rousseau. Whereas Jefferson's studies of American Indians were detailed empirical exercises to support his arguments about their virtues and shortcomings, Jean-Jacques Rousseau and others waxed eloquent about natural law in Native American societies in a metaphorical sense.[27]

For his time, Jefferson's *Notes on the State of Virginia* was the most knowledgeable statement about North American Indian societies and their peoples. Jefferson's observations about Native Americans in *Notes on the State of Virginia,* with the knowledge supplied by Charles Thomson for the manuscript, also give us a concise portrayal of the new American nation's thoughts about American Indians. In the late eighteenth and early nineteenth centuries, Jefferson's opinions on American Indians held special weight at home and abroad. As the author of *Notes on the State of Virginia,* president of the American Philosophical Society, and correspondent with individuals throughout the world, Jefferson was both a scholar of American Indians and a leader in forging an intellectual consensus on their nature.[28]

For Jefferson, the study of the origins of American Indians was more than an academic pursuit. If American Indians were to "intermix and become one people" with Euroamericans, they had to be acceptable biologically and intellectually for the civilizing process.[29] Jefferson thus accepted the universalizing penchants of his era and embraced, as axiomatic, the basic unity of human origins. For Jefferson, such an assumption would not deny American Indians a full place in the human family. Jefferson's acceptance of the Asian origins of American Indians was not uncritical, because he criticized the Jesuit Joseph François Lafitau's 1724 work that slavishly drew parallels between ancient civilizations and American Indians. In a letter to John Adams, Jefferson asserted that Lafitau had "a preconceived theory on the mythology, manners and institutions and government of the ancient nations of Europe, Asia and Africa, and seems to have entered on those of America only to fit them into the same frame."[30] Jefferson also points out the selectivity of Lafitau's scholarship since he presented "all the facts, and adopts all the falsehoods which favor his theory, and very gravely relates such absurdities as zeal for a theory could alone swallow."[31] Jefferson also reveals his critical reading of Lafitau by stating that although he was a missionary among Canadian Indians for five years, he collected "his matter much more from the writings of others, than from his own observation."[32] Although Jefferson's criticism of Lafitau is far from unique, it demonstrates that he had read and thought a great deal about American Indian origins and Lafitau's ideas.[33]

As an informed student of the literature of the period, Jefferson also examined three of the folio volumes of Theodor de Bry. Jefferson observed that in these volumes, "fact and fable are mingled together, without regard to any favorite system. They are less suspicious therefore in their complexion, more original and authentic, than those of Lafitau and Adair."[34] Jefferson believed that de Bry's very early published accounts of American Indian and European contact were a truer representation of American Indian manners and customs than some of the later accounts that had an axe to grind about Native American origins. He took pride in his having one of the few copies of some of the de Bry volumes in the United States.[35]

In his commentary to Adams, Jefferson leveled a more judicious critique of James Adair's work *History of the American Indians* (1775). Jefferson maintains "Adair too had his kink. He believed all the Indians of America to be descended from the Jews: the same laws, usages; rites and ceremonies . . . and . . . almost the same religion."[36] However, Jefferson points out that Adair's book "contains a good deal of real instruction" about American Indians if the reader is "constantly on his guard against the wonderful obliquities of his theory" about the alleged Hebrew origins of American Indians. He notes that Adair "was personally acquainted" with the southern Indians (Cherokee, Creek, Chickasaw, Choctaws, and Catawbas).[37] Jefferson, in dispensing with the some of the more speculative scholarship on American Indians, felt that "the question of Indian origin, like many others, pushed to a certain height must receive the same answer, 'Ignoro.' "[38]

In his scholarship, Jefferson cast aside comparisons of customs in the fathoming of Native American origins, and it is clear that he believed that language could lead to very concrete conclusions about American Indian origins. Writing on August 4, 1787, from Paris, Jefferson thanked his friend Benjamin Hawkins for some Indian language vocabularies that he wished to study. He stated "[T]his is an object I mean to pursue, as I am persuaded that the only method of investigating the filiation of Indian nations is by that of their languages."[39]

In 1791, Jefferson indulged his interest in American Indian languages with his companions James Madison and General William Floyd.[40] For thirty years, in fact, Jefferson studied American Indian languages and during his presidency he resolved to put the results in print, but a new set of western American Indian words gathered by Meriwether Lewis stopped him from completing the work during his presidency. Although when he left the presidency in 1809, he looked forward to getting to the task of publishing his linguistic studies, all Jefferson's labors were to be lost. In preparing to leave Washington, he put his language materials into a trunk to be shipped by water. En route up the James River the trunk was torn open and looted by a thief. Some of the tattered and muddy remnants of his notes floated ashore and were salvaged, but most were never recovered. The fragmentary remains of his American Indian vocabularies and notes were shipped to the American Philosophical Society, where they testify to his diligence and commitment to this intellectual pursuit. Although he wanted to retrace his research, Jefferson never rededicated himself to the task.[41]

Ironically, Jefferson drew one conclusion from his lost research that supported Native American contentions about their antiquity in America. Drawing from memory, Jefferson postulated in 1816 that the diversity of Native American languages was such "that the tribes speaking them could not probably understand one another." From this linguistic observation, he intimated that Native Americans had lived long enough in the Americas to even be the parent stock of Asian peoples![42]

Jefferson was also fascinated by the archaeological discoveries of a Native American mound-building culture in the Mississippi Valley. In addition to large puzzling earthen rectangular structures, burial mounds were noted that were similar to the burial mounds on the Rivanna River that Jefferson had depicted in *Notes on the State of Virginia*.[43] Exaggerated speculation that the mounds were the original home of the Aztecs made Jefferson counsel the American Philosophical Society to obtain "exact descriptions of the monuments . . . and insert them naked in their transactions. . . . Patience and observation may enable us in time to solve the problem."[44] Although many observers of the time believed that the mound builders were a superior culture descended from Asians or Europeans, Jefferson maintained that the mound builders were the ancestors of modern day American Indians. His was a minority opinion during his life, but Jefferson's cautious powers of observation and avoidance of theoretical flights of fancy served him well in his analysis of the origins of the earthen mounds in the Mississippi Valley.[45]

In dealing with the customs, languages, and prehistory of Native Americans, Jefferson's emphasis on the value of detailed observation and his ability to divorce theorizing from fact made his speculations and conclusions about Native Americans more tentative than those of some of his contemporaries. In retrospect, he seemed to have a very modern understanding of the fundamentals of American Indian societies.

Jefferson and American Indian Political Theories

While Jefferson maintained a critical attitude toward the basic aspects of American Indian cultures, he also used Native American ways to enhance his political discourses and occasionally to provide him with an alternate identity. Julian Boyd, the editor of Jefferson's papers, recognized this process not only in the mind of Jefferson but also in the thinking of many other Euroamericans and Europeans:

> In the realm of political thought, the Indian probably had a greater influence over civilized society than any other savage race. . . . Marc Lescarbot, Gabriel Sagard, and the authors of the great Jesuit Relations began in the 16th and 17th centuries by describing Indian society and ended by praising it with a praise that carried an implied criticism of the European political system. From this it was an easy step to

put in the mouth of an American savage a blunt criticism of civilized political organization.[46]

In his observations of France, Jefferson sometimes cloaked himself in what might be called a savage identity to contrast American and European social structures. As American ambassador to France, Jefferson admired that nation's neat cultivated fields and the beauty of the music of the continent, but he reacted with a kind of smug horror when beggars gathered around his carriage nearly every time it stopped in a European town or city. "Behold me at length on the vaunted scene of Europe," he wrote to Charles Bellini. "You are perhaps curious to know how this new scene has struck a savage from the mountains of America. Not advantageously, I assure you. I find the general state of humanity here most deplorable. The truth of Voltaire's observation offers itself perpetually that every man here must be the hammer or the anvil."[47]

Indeed when Jefferson first arrived in Paris, the city was the largest in the Christian world, with a population of about six hundred thousand. A fifth of the city's adult population was unemployed, a number larger than the combined populations of New York, Boston, and Philadelphia; tens of thousands more were only marginally employed. In this environment, Jefferson observed: "Of twenty millions of people supposed to be in France, I am of the opinion that there are nineteen millions more wretched, more accursed in every circumstance than the most conspicuously wretched individual of the whole United States."[48]

Too much government and law bred tyranny, Jefferson reasoned. When comparing the governments of France and Britain to those of the American Indians, Jefferson left no doubt which he favored: "As for France, and England, with all their preeminence in science, the one is a den of robbers, and the other of pirates, as if science produces no better fruits than tyranny, murder, rapine and destitution of national morality. I would rather wish our country to be ignorant, honest and estimable as our neighboring savages."[49] Obviously, Jefferson equated corruption with modern European governments and saw virtue in American Indian ways. He sometimes argued adamantly against British traditions in American government. Through such insights, Jefferson and many of his contemporaries asserted an independent identity for America and Americans that sometimes verged on the messianic. Thomas Paine enthused, "We see with other eyes; we hear with other ears; we think with other thoughts, than those we formerly used."[50] As a student of government and the Europe of his day. Jefferson found the political landscape of England full of ideas he wished to change, not emulate. Writing to John Adams, he asserted that force or corruption had been "the principle of every modern government, unless the Dutch perhaps be excepted."

> I am sure you join me in the detestation of the corruption of the English government that no man on earth is more incapable than yourself of seeing that copied among us, willingly. I have been among those who have feared the design to intro-

duce it here, and that has been a strong reason with me for wishing there was an ocean of fire between that island and us.[51]

Writing to Edward Carrington in 1787, Jefferson, in explaining the role of public opinion in government, also linked freedom of expression to the right to happiness and cited American Indian societies as an example.

> The basis of our government being the opinion of the people, our very first object should be to keep that right; and were it left to me to decide whether we should have a government without newspapers or newspapers without a government, I should not hesitate for a moment to prefer the latter . . . I am convinced that those societies [as the Indians] which live without government enjoy in their general mass an infinitely greater degree of happiness than those who live under European governments.[52]

"Without government" could not have meant without social order in Jefferson's eyes. Jefferson knew native societies too well to argue that Native Americans functioned without social cohesion. He and many of his contemporaries had experience with native leaders as treaty negotiators, which was a peer relationship. Throughout the American Revolution and into the early years of the United States, relations with the major native nations that were adjacent to the United States were a primary focus of the nation's statecraft. It was clear that the Iroquois, for example, could not have organized a confederacy with alliances spreading over much of eastern North America "without government." No matter how much the American Indian conceptions of government differed from the European standard, its non-European alternatives were what Jefferson appreciated and studied in order to factor natural law and natural rights into his political designs for the United States. Jefferson so emphatically stressed the importance of public opinion among American Indian polities that he was willing to abandon all government to maintain such a right.[53]

Jefferson provided a description of American Indian governance, which in some respects resembled the government that the United States was then constructing. The pattern of states within a nation, which the founders called federalism, was delineated by Jefferson.

> The matters which merely regard a town or family are settled by the chief and principal men of the town; those which regard a tribe . . . are regulated at a meeting or a council of the chiefs from several towns; and those which regard the whole nation . . . are deliberated on and determined at a national council.[54]

His use of the word *men* passed over the fact that women also played an important role in many native nations, but in analyzing the nature of Native American polities, Jefferson rather accurately described the deliberations of native national councils; his observations could have been drawn from many of the New England tribes—the Iroquois, Hurons, Cherokees, or Choctaws—but were probably generalizations drawn from the Indian nations he knew. Each Indian nation had its meetinghouse for government business, where

[in] council, it is common for the chiefs of the several tribes to consult thereupon with their counsellors, and when they have agreed, to deliver the opinion of the tribe at the national council; and, as their government seems to rest wholly on persuasion, they endeavor, by mutual concessions, to obtain unanimity.[55]

In his analysis, Jefferson was sophisticated enough to deny reports that Indian sachemships were inherited. "The sachem or chief of the tribe seems to be by election" rather than passed down in the tradition of European royal titles.[56] However, he tended to ignore the subtleties that distinguished the passage of power in native societies from either pure election or pure inheritance. Iroquois women, for example, elected male sachems from within the bounds of the clan or extended family, who held in common the traditional inherited titles. In essence, Iroquois men served in leadership positions but could not vote whereas women elected the leaders but could not serve in leadership positions.[57] Jefferson, however, comprehended only imperfectly the powerful role of women in American Indian societies. His *Notes on the State of Virginia* describes the role of American Indian women in this way.

> It is civilization alone which replaces women in the enjoyment of their natural equality . . . Were we in equal barbarism, our females would be equal drudges. The man with them is less strong than us, but their women stronger than ours; and both for the same obvious reason; because our man and their woman is habituated to labor and formed by it.[58]

Jefferson perceived that American Indian women's powers were based on their economic contributions to their societies. Of course, he completely misperceived the role of American Indian men in their societies since men worked just as hard as women to gain the resources necessary to sustain their societies.[59]

Jefferson also placed value on the study of American Indian societies as a formal academic pursuit. He complained that traditional university curricula, which were based on European precedents, did not pay enough attention to the natural history and cultures of the Americas and Africa. So, when he designed a curriculum for the University of Virginia, he included traditional European subjects as well as courses in American Indian cultures and languages.[60] In his opinion, the control of educational content was just one more way in which British imperialism sought to dominate and often exterminate native peoples—from Ireland to Africa to America to "wherever Anglo-mercantile cupidity can find a two-penny interest in deluging the world with human blood."[61]

Because Jefferson held such ideas, he did not seek to transplant England's political system to America intact. Rather he argued that the United States was a combination of Old and New World ideological materials: "Every species of government has its own specific principles. . . . Ours perhaps is more peculiar than any other in the universe. It is a composition of the freest principle[s] of the English constitution, and others derived from natural right and natural reason."[62] American Indians and their societies figured into the conception of "life, liberty, and happiness" as understood by Jefferson, who wrote the phrase in the Declaration of Independence. Franklin had operated in many ways as Jefferson's revolutionary mentor. So the two founders' descriptions of American Indian societies played a provocative role in a major debate of the time, which erupted when the word "happiness" was substituted for "property."[63]

Jefferson called up the same images in his *Notes on the State of Virginia* in a section that was inserted into the 1787 edition while the Constitutional Convention met. The Native Americans, wrote Jefferson, had never "[s]ubmitted themselves to any laws, any coercive power and shadow of government. Their only controls are their manners, and the moral sense of right and wrong. . . . An offense against these is punished by contempt, by exclusion from society, or, where the cause is serious, as that of murder, by the individuals whom it concerns. Imperfect as this species of control may seem, crimes are very rare among them."[64]

The lesson here seemed clear to Jefferson. "Insomuch that it were made a question, whether no law, as among the savage Americans, or too much law, as among the civilized Europeans, submits man to the greater evil, one who has seen both conditions of existence would pronounce it to be the last."[65] Jefferson's observations and ideas on the political system of the Iroquois Confederacy were accessible to many influential people, including the marquis de Lafayette, James Madison, and Franklin, through his *Notes on the State of Virginia,* which ran through several editions, was quickly translated into French, and proved popular enough to be pirated.[66] The book was read in the United States at the time of the Constitutional Convention, a period that the author himself spent in France.[67]

Even though Jefferson's ideas about American Indian societies might be less than accurate by contemporary scholarly standards, his desire to find fresh alternatives to European and British governmental systems made studies of the American Indian important in the forging a new political reality after the American Revolution. It was also Jefferson who wrote that American Indians had far less government than Europeans: "Our Indians are evidently in that state of nature which has passed the association of a single family, and not yet submitted to authority of positive laws, or any acknowledged magistrate."[68]

In disputing proposals to enlarge the size of states to be admitted to the union, Jefferson used Native American political theories to further his arguments that smaller governmental units are the most responsive. Feeling that Americans were contentious, often intractable, and prone to lengthy public debates that eventually led to consensus, Jefferson believed that creating new large western states reversed "the natural order of things. A tractable people may be governed in large bodies but, in proportion as they depart from this character, the extent of their government must be less. We see into what small divisions the Indians are obliged to reduce their societies."[69]

Jefferson summed up his views on the nature of American government in his letter to John Rutledge (one of the delegates from South Carolina) as Rutledge was finishing the first draft of the Constitution in August of 1787. Jefferson objected to discussions of a monarchy in America because the "effect of kingly government . . . is to produce the wanton sacrifice . . . of the people." He concluded his analysis by stating that some people characterized "our's a bad government. The only condition on earth to be compared with ours, is that of the Indians, where they still have less law than we. The European, are governments of kites over pigeons."[70] Clearly, Jefferson saw European governments as predatory and corrupt and felt that Americans had created governments that were similar to American Indian polities. However, Jefferson's views on the "Indian" or Non-European characteristics in American government were not extreme. As in other things, he worked toward a consensus in his discourses.

For various reasons, some of the founders of American government rejected ancient and modern European models. At the end of the American revolution, European scholars such as the marquis de Chastellux reflected on American independence and hoped that its leaders would not look to the "old maxims of the Greeks and Romans . . . but follow the wise counsels" of Franklin, the Adamses, and the Schuylers.[71] Chastellux might wish to ignore ancient European traditions in creating a new political structure for America, but Charles Pinckney of South Carolina in 1788, delegate to the Constitutional Convention, rejected European traditions completely when he described the process of constitution-making in this way.

> From the European world no precedents are to be drawn for a people who think they are capable of governing themselves . . . Much difficulty was expected from the extent of country to be governed. All the republics we read of, either in the ancient or modern world, have been extremely limited in territory—we know of none a tenth so large as the United States. Indeed, we are hardly able to determine . . . whether the governments we have heard of under the name of republic really deserved them, or whether the ancients had any just or proper ideas on the subject.[72]

Pinckney's sentiments were also echoed by Jefferson and others at a state banquet in New York City in 1790. On August 2, 1790, the Sons of Saint Tammany acknowledged the country's debt to the Iroquois for providing notions of unity and federalism to the founders. This banquet was attended by many prominent members of the Tammany society—Secretary of State Thomas Jefferson, Chief Justice of the Supreme Court John Jay, and Secretary of War Henry Knox—along with a delegation of Creek Indians. The assembled members and guests were reminded that the Tammany society had been established in order to "cherish—to spread abroad, and to maintain the love of freedom." According to tradition, their two great leaders, Tammany and Columbus, directed the society in all of its proceedings from "a world of the spirits in great harmony." The Caucasian Tammany sachems, cloaked in American Indian garb, pointed out that the Creek Indian chief Alexander M'Gillvray was both European and Indian; therefore, both they and the Creeks were "altogether children of one father."[73] A copy of the Constitution was presented to M'Gillvray and it was described in Iroquois symbolic terms and imagery, asserting "we are all children of the same soil, let one tree of peace shelter us with its branches of union."[74]

This political analogy using the Iroquois tree symbol as a metaphor for American government was more than casual verbiage for the sake of diplomatic protocol. Many more American Indian images were used that evening. President George Washington was toasted as "the beloved sachem of the 13 fires." Hence, in the presence of Jefferson and other dignitaries, the Tammany society rejoiced about the transference of Iroquois political theory to the new American government in New York City during the final stages of the Constitution's ratification. In the eyes of some observers, Americans had not only forged a new identity but had also created a new political structure that some felt was a synthesis of the European and Native American worlds.[75]

Indeed, David Ramsay—physician, politician, and one of the first chroniclers of the American Revolution—believed that geography and the American environment, in which American Indians were definitely an integral part, were very important elements in shaping the American character. His opinion was that "the natural seat of freedom" was "among the high mountains and pathless deserts . . . of America." Ramsay further noted:

> The distance of America from Great Britain generated ideas in the minds of the colonists favorable to liberty . . . Colonists growing up to maturity, at such an immense distance from the seat of government perceived the obligation of dependence much more feebly, than the inhabitants of the parent isle, who not only saw but daily felt, the fangs of power.[76]

Ramsay also believed that principles of government were radically altered during the American Revolution. In 1802, he stated, "the political character of the people was also changed from subjects to citizen . . . [A] citizen is [by definition] a unit of a mass of free people which collectively possess sovereignty . . . and each] . . . contains within himself by nature and the constitution as much of the common sovereignty as another."[77] In essence, Americans were no longer subjects to a sovereign king, but now retained sovereignty over themselves. This new attitude in government was, in part, derived from the Jeffersonian discourse on Native American polities. Often, American Indian alternatives were examined when the British system of government seemed lacking, and Jefferson was an integral part of this political and intellectual process.

Jefferson could proclaim that American Indians were "formed in mind as well as in body, on the same module with the '*Homo sapiens Europaeus*.'"[78] He could also vilify and minimize them when they hindered westward expansion and opposed assimilation into American society. Certainly, the political concepts of Native

Americans held a great fascination for Jefferson and many of his contemporaries. Often, the historical record reveals that Jefferson referred to his perceptions of Native American society in his intellectual discourses and his investigations into the linguistic and prehistoric origins of Native Americans. These references served his intellectual needs since he often used his knowledge of Native Americans to parry the thrusts of a degeneracy theorist like a Buffon or an Abbé Raynal.

Furthermore, an examination of Jefferson's writings demonstrates that he often felt free to discuss the nature of American Indian governments. Some observers of the time, such as Pinckney and Franklin, believed that all European governments were not appropriate to North America. By advancing these kinds of arguments, Jefferson and others of his era were engaged in a time-honored tradition of criticizing European societies by comparing them to non-European societies. *The New Cambridge Modern History* remarks that the use that Montesquieu and other thinkers "made of a . . . noble savage to point a criticism of European conditions was an indication of how much the impact of other civilizations was affecting European ways of thought."[79] For Jefferson, American Indians were the readiest foil available to defend America against European environmental degeneracy theories. The fact that he had firsthand knowledge of American Indian societies made his arguments even more effective.

If the American Indian was an important facet in Jefferson's and his contemporaries' education, then why has it been neglected? Native American historians such as Jack Forbes have asserted that too often our history has been overly Eurocentric, providing us with interpretations that assume that everything begins in Europe and "the history of Overseas Europeans [in America] is the central or only theme." Forbes adds that although the scholars that advocate such themes are also Americans, they often ignore their native roots when they study the intellectual and cultural dynamics of the Euroamerican colonial system. Forbes and other Native American scholars assert that such a viewpoint alienates American history not only from American Indians but also from the entire American public by ignoring the fundamental role that America's native people played in the development of the United States.[80]

To say that America helped shape Europe and that Europe shaped America is obvious; few today doubt the material gifts America provided Europe or ignore the fact that many Europeans became Americans. To assert, however, that America and its native societies helped to fundamentally shape our ideas is controversial, despite mounting evidence that the example of American Indian confederacies were important to the evolution of democratic thought. The debate over the impact of Native American democratic theory on American thought is difficult, because it enters the intellectual and academic discourse often through non-Western conceptual and evidentiary avenues.[81]

Although Jefferson felt that American Indians retained some very important premonarchial characteristics in their societies, ultimately he placed American

Indians in an unequal position. In 1824 at the end of his life, Jefferson codified his stage theory of human evolution:

> Let a philosophic observer commence a journey from the savages of the Rocky Mountains, eastwardly towards our seacoast. These he would observe in the earliest stage of association living under no law but that of nature.... He would next find those on our frontiers in the pastoral state.... Then succeed our own semi-barbarous citizens, the pioneers of the advance of civilization, and so on in his progress until he would reach his, as yet, most improved state in our seaport towns. This, in fact, is equivalent to a survey, in time, of the progress of man from the infancy of creation to the present day.[82]

In Jefferson's mind, when American Indians were no longer needed to defend the essential equality of the American environment, American Indians became children or people in "the infancy of creation." According to Jefferson, they became impediments in the way of "the advance of civilization."[83] Winthrop Jordan and other commentators about Jefferson place American Indians above African Americans in the hierarchy of Jefferson's mind, but a more cogent observation would be that Jefferson used American Indians in the environmental degeneracy debate and in the critique of European political theories and then had little use for them. Unlike African Americans, American Indians were not useful to the yeoman settler state that Jefferson envisioned and so assimilation or ethnocide was advanced as a hallmark of United States Indian policies. Failing to achieve assimilation, Jefferson and others were perfectly willing to resort to the extermination of the Native American. American society needed African Americans for practical economic reasons; it did not desire or need independent Native American peoples. They were, in Jefferson's mind, a hindrance to "progress."[84]

The result of Jefferson's ideas and those of his contemporaries was to conquer native peoples in North America in the name of a superior civilization and place the few surviving American Indians in economic, social, and political environments that fostered their cultural and often physical destruction. Jefferson might theorize about the survivability of American Indian governments, as a practical matter, but he believed that American Indians should remain outside the pale of white society, as they do today. Jefferson ambiguously asserted that American Indians might be assimilated into American society as individuals, but he allowed no room for American Indians to survive as a distinct group, even in "the Stony Mountains." Obviously, Jefferson studied and used American Indian prehistory, languages, and political theories in his scholarship and rational debates; but such abstract and intellectual pursuits meant little, ultimately, to Jefferson the politician and planter.

The Old and the New Worlds: Summary and Comment

Through all three papers that I undertake to summarize there runs a common theme, a theme that not only gives coherence to the individual papers but unwittingly links the three interpretations together. Had our three gifted historians met and conspired in advance in order to give the session unity and simplify my task of summary and comment, I do not see how they could have done better. I believe it was consensus rather than coincidence or conspiracy, but I am even more grateful for it, and I do not for a moment believe that the consensus lacked foundation in fact. The common theme of the three authors is the duality of the Jeffersonian mind and personality—two Jeffersons in one man from three points of view.

I begin with the paper by Elizabeth Wirth Marvick, entitled "Thomas Jefferson and the Old World." As her subtitle indicates she explores Jefferson's personal experiences of five years in France, 1784—89, as they relate to early republican ideals. He probably knew more about contemporary Europe than any American of his time. She begins right off on the theme of duality and quotes the French scholar Gilbert Chinard, a Jefferson admirer, as saying "his was decidedly a double-track intellect, with two lines of thought running parallel without any apparent contradiction."[1] She then readily admits that many other scholars who share Chinard's perception of duality refuse to resolve it in Jefferson's favor and call it "contradiction" or "paradox" or "ambivalence," and even "hypocrisy." For some of them duality is tantamount to duplicity. We will find all these views reflected in some degree in the papers at hand.

Ms. Marvick leans to the more charitable view of Jeffersonian duality, attributing it in large measure to changes in circumstance and experience. The young Virginian arrived in France with copies of the first small printing of his *Notes on the State of Virginia* in his baggage. Written in part to refute some absurd notions of European Enlightenment philosophers like Buffon and Raynal about the inferiority and degradation of all things American, it expressed the author's defense against such attacks and his own attack on European culture and claims of superiority. At first he appeared to see, or at least to admit seeing, few aspects of French culture or institutions worthy of his praise and much that provoked his scorn. Among the latter were the misery of the common people and the arrogance of the elite and privileged.

For one thing, as Ms. Marvick points out, "his basic intellectual furniture was supplied by a classical education in the English tradition." His heroes were Bacon, Newton, Locke—not Montaigne, Descartes, or Voltaire. But that was not the only explanation. In addition to the English or Scottish orientation and his egalitarian convictions there was more than a suggestion of provinciality. Even his admirer Chinard could remark that he was "very narrow and provincial, and almost a philistine in his outlook" and in "how carefully he preserved himself from the contamination of European manners and ways of thinking."

Two years after his arrival, however, Jefferson could write home that the French were people who wish "to make one happy—a people of the very best character it is possible for one to have." In the meantime he had discovered how out-of-date was the anti-Americanism of the old French philosophers he had come to refute, and how pro-American the French people had since come to be. Fashionable Parisian opinion had it that America was a new start for mankind, a model for revolution, a revival of antique virtue, a golden age of present, past, and future—in short the best of all possible worlds. A group of French intellectuals dubbed "*les américains*" because of their liberal sympathies could hardly find words to express their enthusiasm for the new republic and embarked for a pilgrimage there as soon as they could. French heroes were those of the American Revolution: Lafayette, Rochambeau, and most of all George Washington. And now they discovered in their midst the author of the famous Declaration of Independence.

Jefferson willingly and affectionately took young Lafayette under his wing and found him useful not only in promoting American interests in France, but in advancing Jeffersonian ideas for fundamental reform in the Constitutional Assembly and steering the French Revolution in the direction he favored. It has been suggested that the author of the American Declaration of Independence may have aspired to become the author of the French Declaration of Rights. In all this so far, if I understand Ms. Marvick correctly, she sees development rather than duality in Jefferson.

Hints of duality do appear in Jefferson's indulgence of his cosmopolitan tastes, love of music, art, fine wines and food that made him a target for charges of hedonism. Some critics found inconsistency in the pleasure he took in the salons of aristocratic women where politics was the leading subject of discussion in the golden age of the French revolution. He delighted particularly in the salon of Madame de Tessé, who held advanced ideas of equality. Such conversations with women over politics and ideas were, of course, taboo in Virginia, and Jefferson expressed reservations about the influence of women in French politics. He especially deplored the "capricious" influence of Queen Marie-Antoinette over King Louis XVI, whose good instincts and intentions Jefferson tended to trust. He went so far as to say that but for the queen "there would have been no revolution."

In spite of his egalitarian views and his love of freedom, Jefferson felt obliged to use caution in expressing his ideas publicly not only because of his ambition in American politics but also because of his personal problems. He declined a French invitation to attend a meeting to promote abolition of the slave trade because he must "avoid too public a demonstration of my wishes to see it abolished." Not only would open avowal of abolition end his political future, but he owned one hundred and fifty slaves himself, mortgaged as collateral for loans he desperately needed. Another inconsistency was his misgivings about the need of drastic constitutional reform in America, however much he thought it needed in France.

In the fall of 1789 Jefferson returned to his native land with much warmer feelings toward France than those with which he arrived there in 1784. Ms. Marvick takes pains to point out that although Jefferson himself at times indulged in some of the European luxuries he deplored (the duality theme again), he never ceased to deplore them, to reject and denounce aristocratic privilege and monarchical institutions, and to champion the cause of common folk.

In his paper, the third presented here, Donald Grinde announces his purpose to "address Jefferson's dualistic approach to American Indian people." He finds the Virginian's views both "scholarly" and "informed" as well as "enigmatic and often contradictory." Jefferson both admired and reproached the native culture. Mr. Grinde believes that "the sage of Monticello's ideas about American Indians were even more circumspect than those about the black man." In his debates with the Enlightenment philosophers over the inferiority of America he repeatedly held the native people to be mentally and physically equal to whites. Knowing them and their chiefs personally and observing their communal life first hand, he was no Rousseau dreaming of imaginary noble savages. His father had put American Indian chiefs up in his home. Jefferson knew many of them and made elaborate studies of their languages with the intention, never fulfilled, of publishing them. He found in their institutions of tribal government much to admire and regard as examples and models.

Yet for all his admiration and respect for native culture and institutions, he firmly put Native Americans aside when faced with the political realities and demands of his own people, committed to the conquest of a continent. Jefferson the president in 1807 declared that "if we are constrained to lift the hatchet against any tribe, we will never lay it down until that tribe is exterminated." As Mr. Grinde succinctly describes the "reality" of the situation, "American Indians resisting white domination were to be ruthlessly destroyed when they opposed frontier expansion." When they complied with white demands Jefferson addressed them as his "children," referred to a chief as "my son," and spoke of himself as their "father."

But then in the same years and later, he could resume the role of scholar, benevolent moralist, and believer in the moral equality of mankind. In 1802 he told a visiting delegation of Indians that "your blood will mix with ours, and will spread, with ours, over this great island." He was capable of promoting intermarriage between the two peoples, who would "intermix and become one people," thus creating a "continental family." He welcomed the influence of Indian political culture upon white government in America and compared it with European corruption, wretchedness, and oppressive governments. He was convinced, he said, that the native people "enjoy in their general mass an infinitely greater degree of happiness than those who live under European governments."

Among the several elements of native government and culture Jefferson admired, he cited the election of chiefs or sachems as against European reliance upon inherited titles, and the chiefs' role as servants rather than masters of their people. He was also struck by the role of women, who elected the chiefs but were disqualified from serving as chiefs. He appreciated the powerful place of women in Indian society and thought "their women stronger than ours." Mr. Grinde is careful to point out some misunderstandings of Indian culture on the part of Jefferson.

In spite of shortcomings in his scholarship, Jefferson is credited with providing for his time "the most knowledgeable statement about North American Indian societies and their people." As author of *Notes on the State of Virginia,* as president of the American Philosophical Society, and in his voluminous correspondence, he was, as Mr. Grinde says, a "leader in forging an intellectual consensus on the nature of American Indians." In planning the curriculum for the University of Virginia, its founder included along with traditional European subjects courses in Indian culture and languages.

For those academic reformers of the present day who are persuaded that a multicultural curriculum is the means of correcting injustice to minorities and the political path to reforms that achieve those ends, Jefferson's curriculum for his university offers cold comfort. By that time the Sage of Monticello himself had come to believe that Indians were people in "the infancy of creation," and had become impediments to "the march of civilization." Failing to meet the test of "assimilation," Indians were pushed ever westward by white settlers and eventually into segregation or extermination.

With the paper by James Oakes on the racism of Thomas Jefferson, we come finally to the cruelest and most intractable dualities of all—those involved in Jefferson's views of the black race and those on slavery. Mr. Oakes has no difficulty whatever in adducing evidence that Jefferson held views regarding black Americans that would now be called "racist," a term unknown in his time. As a race black Americans in their present state of development were "inferior to the whites in the endowments both of body and mind," according to Jefferson. And further in their physical appearance and appeal he considered them inferior to the Indians as suited for intermarriage and integration with whites.

The first inconsistency that might come to mind would be that between one of those truths in the Declaration proclaiming it to be "self-evident, that all men are created equal," and his views on racial inequality just quoted. Mr. Oakes concedes on this point that some scholars now contend that "Jefferson's racism was substantially tempered by his conviction that blacks and whites were equally endowed with a moral sense," but that debate on that point continues. His own view is that Jefferson was "somewhat more ambiguous about the moral sense." His further contention in a footnote that Jefferson's views on black inferiority "coincided neatly with his liberal ideology" would seem to require more elaboration and linguistic clarification than the limits of the paper allow.

A clearer if more difficult duality of Jefferson on race was that between attributing inferiority to nature or to environment, whether mental capacity was fixed and limited by heredity and biology or could be improved and increased by "environment," education, training. Sometimes Jefferson "leaned one way, sometimes the other, depending on the circumstances," as Oakes puts it. "Strictly speaking," he continues, "Jefferson was neither exclusively environmentalist nor exclusively naturalist. Consequently, he swerved back and forth between environmentalist and naturalist logic." Sometimes the one, sometimes the other.

But it should be emphasized that the choice between these alternative and contradictory views is of prime significance for Mr. Oakes's treatment of the laws and customs keeping slaves in ignorance and illiteracy and forbidding the teaching of them to read. If the "naturalist logic" prevailed and ignorance was biologically determined, then the black slave's mind was impervious to improvement and the laws could have made little difference. It is obvious, however, that they were held to be necessary by those who made them.

Jefferson's writings from early until late in his life make it clear that he held the institution of slavery to be an abomination and its practice to be immoral. He hated slavery. No passages he wrote on the subject are more moving or more poignant than those in his *Autobiography* denouncing slavery, predicting that "these people are to be free," and then declaring it to be no less certain "that the two races, equally free, cannot live in the same government." As Oakes says, "The irony was appalling." What Jefferson was saying was that an institution he held to be immoral was essential to the survival of a form of government he held to be superior to all others and worth revolution to establish. Self-government and democracy were possible only in a government whose citizens were educated and enlightened to a degree that the black people were then incapable of attaining. While Jefferson believed that the slaves should and would eventually be freed, he was convinced that they could not live with whites as equals and would have to be colonized to maintain peace and avoid racial war. The author is aware, I am sure, that Lincoln took virtually the same position in 1854.

Mr. Oakes's declared purpose is to disclose the political significance of Jefferson's racial views. He finds what he believes to be the answer "in the multiple and contradictory inferences that so many Americans drew" from the assumptions

Jefferson made. He adds, however, that "the conclusion they drew from these assumptions was rather different from Jefferson's," though he does not specify just how and to what degree they differed. And he leaves unanswered his question, "Were they embracing or repudiating Jefferson's legacy?" And perhaps that is understandable, for there are no easy answers, and his time was limited.

The time was also limited for my brief and inadequate summaries of these three excellent papers. The complaints of their authors will deserve your sympathy. In the meantime I am allotted a few minutes for my own reflections on some of their ideas.

I begin by picking up on their common theme of Jefferson's duality, which I find so congenial. My favorite and most cherished example is his famous dialogue between the Head and the Heart. It is contained in a very long love letter that Jefferson wrote Maria Cosway, a gifted and beautiful young woman, after she left him in Paris to return with her husband to England. The letter makes evident the anguish of the lover, and his dialogue between Head and Heart is written in his most exquisite eighteenth-century prose. But it is written with both the tenderness of emotion and the subtlety of cool reason. The mixture left Maria Cosway completely baffled. And to this day Jefferson scholars still disagree over which prevailed in the dialogue, the Head or the Heart.[2]

In addition to this duality and those over New World and Old World pictured by Marvick, over native Indians by Grinde, and over race and slavery by Oakes, there are many others. Enough perhaps to justify Chinard's characterization of Jefferson as "a double-track intellect, with two lines of thought running parallel, without any apparent contradiction." We may well hold reservations about the "apparent contradiction," but in assessing this troublesome duality we should take pains to weigh the alternative of a single-track intellect for Jefferson. Would we have had our Virginia patriot democrat frozen in a stiff puritanical and provincial resistance to all the charms of Paris in the golden age of the Enlightenment? Or a music lover plug his ears to the outpouring of Mozart's genius in his most brilliant years? Or require him to spurn fine wines, elegant cuisine, and charming women?

Granted Jefferson's dualities over the native American race and the African slaves and their rights and future are harder to handle. But I think it is due his reputation to remember that he was not a full-time closeted philosopher-scholar on a Virginia mountain but a fully engaged public figure up to his ears in politics—local, state, national, and international—from the 1770s to the 1820s. His major purpose was to preserve the republic. I think it only fair to consider the cost of consistency between his scientific and moral convictions on the one hand and his public policies on the other. There were few quicker and surer ways to stop a political career in its tracks in Jefferson's time than to oppose white conquest of western lands in the name of Indian rights or to advocate the abolition of slavery, even with colonization of those emancipated. The price Jefferson would have had to pay is clear.

Then there is the price the new American republic would have paid: a

Revolution, a Bill of Rights, a President Jefferson, and a Jeffersonian legacy without his towering figure? Especially when we think of the possible alternatives who might have attempted to fill his shoes. Like many others, of course, I feel the temptation to cry "moral consistency at any price," to confuse duality with duplicity, and to spit upon all sordid compromises of politics and expediency. Nevertheless, I think Jefferson was right. If that makes me a Machiavellian, so be it.

But there are still other matters to consider. I am sure that my colleagues, sound and experienced historians all of them, would agree that one of the rules of our craft forbids holding the past to the standards, modes, fashions, styles, expectations, and convictions of the present and judging it thereby. They would as readily agree perhaps that the rule is as much honored in the breach as in the observance, but that it is still a rule they honor, teach, and try to practice. And furthermore I believe they could be persuaded to agree that the founding fathers—and Jefferson in particular—have of late been frequent victims of breaches in the rule.

The fathers of the republic present tempting targets for those revisionists more noted for the breach than the observance of the rule just noted. They are often revisionists with lessons to teach—to teach not so much to the present as to the past about its shortcomings and its failures to live up to standards of the present. And this despite all the monuments erected to them, the honors accorded them, and their use as models for the morals of posterity—for us. One test of such revision is to turn the tables and imagine the past sitting judgment on the present—on us. What would Thomas Jefferson have to say about American life in our own time— the homeless, the jobless, the fatherless, the poverty, the drug addicts, the gangsters, the gang wars, the gun-play of children, the homicide in school rooms, and the horrors of street violence, the random drive-by murders, and the race wars rehearsed in one metropolis after another and feared by many to become nationwide. And at the root of all that a disgraceful public education system and years of incompetent and often corrupt government that has left the future and our children burdened with problems so immense they may prove insuperable.

But although the sins of the present help to put those of the past in perspective, they do not absolve the past of its own sins. And so we return to what Mr. Oakes has aptly termed "the spectral shadows" of Jefferson's views on race and slavery. He was not born with them, nor did he arrive at all of them simultaneously. His original draft of the Declaration of Independence contained a passage roundly denouncing King George for perpetuating the slave trade. It was rejected by his fellow revolutionists, but Jefferson made sure it was preserved by making numerous copies of it and including it in his *Autobiography*. He also drafted several model constitutions for Virginia prohibiting slavery, and all of which were rejected by the constitutional convention of the state, which reaffirmed the legality of the institution. In explaining his failure to press his opposition against hopeless odds he resorted to a defense he was often to use later: the time was not ripe; to act prematurely was to weaken his case and destroy his influence. A shorter term for it was expediency. So also with the slaves in his own possession, some one hundred and fifty of them, twenty inherited, the majority acquired by a heritage of his wife. His explanation for failure to free them could hardly be described as a justification. State law required any slaveholder freeing his slaves to take them out of Virginia and provide them with means of supporting themselves. His financial plight not only prevented that but obliged him to mortgage his slave property to friends in order to finance his debts. Again a pragmatic rather than a principled position.

In *Notes on the State of Virginia* Jefferson cautiously ventures his views on the racial inferiority of blacks to whites as "a suspicion only," one requiring much scientific study.[3] But the "suspicion" grows upon him without the study, and he gives expressions to opinion and prejudice about black inferiority of mind and body, talent and imagination that would amply justify the modern term *racism*. We may well wish he had never expressed them and that he had shared the supposedly superior morals we profess. But there they undeniably are. Since racism in present usage is a term even more devastating to respect and reputation than *abolitionism* was in its time, I think it is due Jefferson to record some of the modifications and ambivalences he entertained about the subject.

Our colleague Richard Matthews has ably assembled relevant examples. Among them is a letter of 1785 to the marquis de Chastellux in which Jefferson advances the hypothesis that in time, with equal opportunities, blacks could become fully equal to whites. In another to the marquis de Condorcet years later and a third to Henri Grégoire, he commented on outstanding achievements of black people, one as a mathematician and others as writers. He devoutly hoped, he said, "to see a complete refutation of doubts I have myself entertained and expressed on the grade of understanding allotted to them by nature." He had always believed it "self evident" that their endowment of "moral sense" was equal to that of any other race. He repeatedly expressed his abhorrence of slavery and his conviction that the enslaved were to be free. It was this conviction that he expressed most movingly and passionately in a familiar passage: "Indeed I tremble for my country when I reflect that God is just: that his justice cannot sleep forever."[4]

It is a mistake to forget in all this that Thomas Jefferson was a revolutionist, in fact a participant in two revolutions. Not only was he a central figure in one, but a keen witness to the coming and opening phase of a second, a consultant and adviser of key figures in the early stage of the French Revolution, and he rejoiced in the fall of the old regime. But here we return once more to the "double-track" duality of Jefferson: the defender (and conserver) of one revolution and the eventual critic of another that took a very different turn in the hands of revolutionists of "single-track" mentality. Under control of the single-trackers, the French Revolution became a police state and the perpetrator of atrocities of unbelievable horror. One of them was the cold-blooded massacre of at least fourteen hundred helpless prisoners. That one was defended by Danton as necessary to appease the people of Paris. Another blood bath with even more barbarities, the slaughter of six hundred a month earlier was praised by Robespierre as "the most beautiful revolution that has ever honored humanity."[5] Comparison of single-track with double-track revolutionists inspires some respect for duality in the matter.

Lest my emphasis on the duality thesis seem to rob Jefferson of his credentials as a radical let me call to witness two recent books by respected colleagues on this symposium: Gordon S. Wood's reassessment of the American Revolution, and Richard Matthews's work on the radicalism of Thomas Jefferson, already mentioned. Mr. Wood demonstrates that "only if we measure radicalism by violence and bloodshed" can the French Revolution be held more radical than the American. When judged by the explosive transformation of society they brought, however, the American Revolution outstrips the French in radicalism.[6] Mr. Matthews reminds us of Jefferson writing Madison to quiet his alarm over the Shays' rebellion: "I hold it that a little rebellion now and then is a good thing." He thought one every twenty years would be about right. That incidentally conformed with his idea of a "fresh start" for each new generation every nineteen years embodied in his words, "The earth belongs always to the living generation," words carved around inside the rotunda of his memorial. Since he rejected any "perpetual constitution, or even a perpetual law," he suggested a new national constitution as well as new state constitutions for each new generation. This together with the rewriting of all codes of law, and the cancellation of all debts and property rights of the dead.[7] If this does not meet the standards of the neoradicals currently engaged in discrediting Jefferson's reputation, let them seek something more radical in presently fashionable or recently discredited dogma. I doubt they will find it in either category.

Meanwhile we might remember just where this symposium was held and whose personal library, whose sixty-seven hundred volumes, in eleven wagonloads driven up from Monticello to Washington, were the first in the Library of Congress after the British burned the original collection that was less than half that size. And when we leave the Library of Congress and make our way to National Airport along the Mall past one monument after another to a national figure we might recall on passing the one to Lincoln his tribute to Thomas Jefferson: "who was, is, and perhaps will continue to be," he said, "the most distinguished politician of our history."[8] Then on over the bridge, to the right of which, a few hundred yards from the Lincoln memorial, there stands in its rotunda a towering figure in bronze.

IV

A Republic of Citizens

DAVID N. MAYER

Citizenship and Change in Jefferson's Constitutional Thought

No single aspect of his constitutional thought more distinguished Jefferson's approach from that of his contemporaries than did his attitude toward constitutional change.[1] From the early 1780s until the end of his life, Jefferson was generally a consistent and frequent advocate of such fundamental change at both the state and the national level. Constitutional conventions held no terrors for him; indeed, in his later years, he favored both a new convention in Virginia and a new federal convention. As Julian Boyd has observed, Jefferson "anticipated that forms of government would come and go, being changed as often and as drastically as changing circumstances required." To him, "the danger to be feared was not so much imperfection in the fabric as a failure in the people to discern the nature of the imperfection and to demand its remedy."[2]

Jefferson's favorable attitude toward constitutional change, moreover, may be regarded as the capstone of his constitutional theory. As I have argued elsewhere, Jefferson's constitutional thought is best understood as Whig, federal, and republican, in the sense that Jefferson meant each of those terms—a fairly precise sense, the full meaning of which has become obscured in our day. Put simply, Jefferson viewed constitutions primarily as devices by which governmental power would be limited and checked, to prevent its abuse through encroachment on individual rights (the Whig aspect of his thought). His preferred system for doing this was one in which governmental power was divided into distinct spheres (the federal aspect), each of which was in turn subdivided into distinct branches (legislative, executive, and judicial) equally accountable to the "rightful" majority will of the people (the republican aspect). In the interrelationships—and, at times, tensions—between these three essential elements of Jefferson's constitutional thought, his response to the particular constitutional issues and problems of his time are best explained.[3] His favorable attitude toward constitutional change is perhaps the one aspect of his thought that most clearly reveals how the Whig foundations of Jefferson's philosophy of government were shaped by his evolving theories of federalism and republicanism.

In discussing Jefferson's views regarding constitutional change and citizenship, I will first trace the evolution of Jefferson's favorable attitude toward constitutional change, showing that it paralleled the development of his constitutional thought. As Jefferson's constitutionalism became more republican, his advocacy of constitutional change correspondingly became more strident. Second, I will focus on Jefferson's proposals concerning citizen education and participation in the process of government, including his support for the principle of rotation in office, what we today generally regard as term limitation. These proposals, I argue, were the prerequisites for the successful implementation of his ideas about legal and constitutional change, as well as the successful realization of his theory of republican government. It is in his theory of constitutional change and the associated assumptions that Jefferson's most distinctive contributions to Anglo-American constitutional thought were made.

"Hand in Hand with the Progress of the Human Mind":
Constitutional Change and the Evolution of Jefferson's Thought

The impulse toward constitutional reform and innovation was not original with Jefferson, nor was it—as one might assume it was—solely a product of Enlightenment thought. Rather, the basis for this impulse may be traced to the ideas of certain radical Whig writers on government who called themselves "Real Whigs." These writers included not only such mid-eighteenth-century constitutional reformers as James Burgh and John Cartwright, but also seventeenth-century republican philosophers of government, particularly Algernon Sidney.[4] Indeed, it was Sidney whom Jefferson echoed in 1816 when he observed, "We might as well require a man to wear still the coat which fitted him when a boy as civilized society to remain forever under the regimen of their barbarous ancestors." Sidney, whose *Discourses Concerning Government* Jefferson consistently recommended as an elementary text on the subject, had likewise asked, "If men are not oblig'd to live in Caves and hollow trees, to eat Acorns, and go naked, why should they be forever oblig'd to continue under the same form of Government that their ancestors happen'd to set up in the time of their ignorance?"[5]

Behind both Jefferson's and Sidney's observations was the basic idea expressed by the Real Whig writers on government: that government was an artificial contrivance, erected by the people of a society and deriving its powers from their consent. As one of these Real Whig writers, James Burgh, argued in his *Political Disquisitions* of 1774, "All lawful authority, legislative and executive, originates from the people." "Power in the *people* is like light in the sun, native, original, inherent, and unlimited by any thing human," whereas the power of government "may be compared to the reflected light of the moon; for it is only borrowed, delegated, and limited by the intention of the people, whose it is, and to whom governors are to consider themselves responsible, while the people are answerable only to God."[6] Burgh's criticisms of Parliament—chiefly, its excessive duration and its unrepresentative composition, criticisms that led him to the conclusion that Parliament had no power to tax the American colonies—followed from this basic premise that the legitimate powers of government were founded on the people's consent.

Burgh went further to suggest that it was a defect in the English constitution that it could not be changed by the constituent power of the people, except in extraordinary circumstances such as the so-called Glorious Revolution of 1688-89. As Burgh wrote, "happy is that people, who having originally so principled their constitution, that they themselves can without violence to it, lay hold of its power, wield it as they please, and turn it, when necessary, against those to whom it was entrusted, and who have exerted it to the prejudice of its original proprietors." The latter idea had been expressed ninety years earlier by Sidney, who had written that "Good Governments admit of Changes in their Superstructures, whilst the Foundations remain unchangeable." Burgh followed Sidney's suggestion, and anticipated American constitutionalism, when he proposed that

> In planning a government by representation, the people ought to provide against their own *annihilation.* They ought to establish a regular and constitutional method of acting by and from *themselves,* without, or even in opposition to their *representatives,* if necessary. Our ancestors therefore were provident, but not provident enough. They set up parliaments, as a curb on *kings* and *ministers;* but they neglected to reserve to themselves a regular and constitutional method of exerting their power in curbing *parliaments,* when necessary.[7]

Also behind the idea of the necessity of constitutional change was the Whig premise that power corrupts, even in the best constituted governments. Indeed, to writers such as Sidney and Burgh, the notion that there existed a perfect constitution was absurd. "All human Constitutions are subject to corruption, and must perish, unless they are timely renewed, and reduced to their first principles," wrote Sidney. Although the abhorrence of "corruption," both as the notion apparently was held by Sidney and as it has been interpreted by modern scholars, was essentially a conservative impulse, motivated by a reverence for the existing constitution and a desire for its preservation, it also provided a rationale for change:

> Corruptions slide in insensibly; and the best Orders are sometimes subverted by malice and violence; so that he who only regards what was done in such an age, often takes the corruptions of the State for the institution, follows the worst example, thinks that to be the first, that is the most ancient he knows; and if a brave People seeing the original defects of their Government, or the corruption into which it may be fallen, do either correct and reform what may be amended, or abolish that which was evil in the institution, or so perverted that it cannot be restor'd to integrity, these men impute it to sedition, and blame those actions, which of all that can be performed by men are the most glorious.

"We are not therefore so much to inquire after that which is most antient, as that which is best, and most conducing to the good ends to which it was directed," Sidney concluded. And as government was instituted to obtain justice and to preserve liberty, "we are not to seek what Government was the first, but what best provides for the obtaining of Justice, and preservation of Liberty. For whatever the Institution be, and how long soever it may have lasted, 'tis void, if it thwarts, or do not provide for the ends of its establishment."[8]

The "resort to first principles" to which Burgh, Sidney, and other writers referred was an idea derived originally from Machiavelli, but it was taken far beyond the ideological confines of classical republicanism by some of the Real Whigs of the late eighteenth century and their American counterparts.[9] Despite their frequent references to an ideal Anglo-Saxon constitution that they sought to preserve against the corruptions of the modern English system of government, many of these Whigs, like Sidney in the passage quoted above, took reason rather than antiquity as their standard. The "first principles" to which they sought to return were not merely those that identified an idealized Anglo-Saxon, or "Gothick" constitution, but included the fundamental principles of popular sovereignty and government by consent of the governed: principles that underlay all forms of free government. The process of reverting to these principles, moreover, could involve both frequent elections and popular tumults; as Sidney pointed out, either could remedy the insolence of office and the corruptions of power. Jefferson's complacent reaction to Shays' Rebellion, for example, can be best understood in this context. As he wrote to Edward Carrington and to James Madison in 1787, such "tumults" or "irregular interpositions of the people" would keep the governors of society "to the true principles of their institution." Hence "a little rebellion" now and then was a good thing, "as necessary in the political world as storms in the physical" and "a medicine necessary for the sound health of government."[10]

Jefferson nevertheless saw as a strength of American republican government the fact that such extralegal resort to first principles was not really necessary. That was so because the American constitutions had institutionalized the process of reverting to first principles, in two ways. The first, for which nearly all the early state constitutions provided, involved devices such as frequent election and rotation in office, devices that the Real Whig parliamentary reformers had advocated so earnestly in the 1770s and 1780s.[11] The second, and far more innovative, way involved further devices such as the amending process and the constitutional convention, by which "the people might recurr to first principles in a Regular Way, without hazarding a Revolution in the Government."[12]

The idea of orderly constitutional change through the devices of the constitutional convention and the amendment process was invented in America during the decade or so after 1776. It did not develop easily, however; as Merrill Peterson has observed, "there was a good deal of fumbling and stumbling before the idea of institutionalized constitutional change was clearly grasped." Of the eleven original early state constitutions, nine contained no provision for amendment, seven no provision for change by way of a convention, and five contained neither provision. A typical provision, that of the Pennsylvania constitution of 1776, created a Council of Censors to be elected and to meet every seven years, to determine whether the constitution has been preserved, where and how it had failed or been violated, and whether a convention should be called for the purpose of making corrective amendments. As Peterson has observed, the purpose of such a provision was not to innovate or to adapt the constitution to changes in circumstance but to preserve inviolate the original constitution; it was a provision still within the classical republican paradigm of decline.[13]

Jefferson's early ideas about constitutions, however, were not limited by the confines of classical republicanism; and in his reading of Sidney, Burgh, and other radical Whig writers on government he was quick to grasp the implications of popular sovereignty with respect to constitutional change. Jefferson regarded as the "more favorable ground" on which the American Revolution rested to be the opportunity that it gave Americans to devise new forms of government, based not on the "musty records" of the past but on the light of reason. Yet he was aware that the American experiments with making constitutions were indeed experiments and that the constitutions created in 1776 and the years following were far from perfect. He was well ahead of his contemporaries in making provision for progressive constitutional change in his draft constitutions for Virginia, although he too did not immediately hit upon the device of a provision for regular amendments to the constitution. His final 1776 draft contained an unprecedented provision permitting "repeal or alteration" of the provisions of the constitution "by the personal consent of the people." Under Jefferson's plan, the legislature would propose changes that would be submitted to the people, meeting in their respective counties and all voting on the same day; approval by two-thirds of the counties would be necessary for the changes to be effective.[14] His 1783 draft contained a provision permitting a convention, authorized by the government and elected by the people, to be called "for altering this Constitution or correcting breaches of it," although—despite the recent example of the Massachusetts constitution of 1780—he did not provide for popular ratification.[15]

Jefferson's *Notes on the State of Virginia* elaborated his criticisms of the Virginia constitution of 1776, among them, that the constitution may be altered by the ordinary legislature; it was in the context of this criticism that he first called for a constitutional convention "to fix our form of government."[16] His 1783 plan was printed as an appendix to *Notes on the State of Virginia* and thus may be regarded as representative of Jefferson's position with respect to constitutional change in the mid-1780s.

It was this position that James Madison attacked in *The Federalist* number 49 in 1788, in a rare instance of public disagreement with his friend. Madison first recognized that Jefferson's provision for periodic change through conventions elected by the people followed from the logic of popular sovereignty: "As the people are the only legitimate fountain of power, and it is from them that the constitutional charter, under which the several branches of government hold their power, is derived; it seems strictly consonant to the republican theory, to recur to the same original authority, not only whenever it may be necessary to enlarge, diminish, or new-model the powers of government; but also whenever any one of the departments may commit encroachments on the chartered authorities of the others." But, Madison continued, there were "insuperable objections" against such a recurrence to the people "as a provision in all cases for keeping the several departments of power within their constitutional limits." Among the objections cited by Madison was that too frequent appeals to the people to "new-model" government would "in great measure deprive the government of that veneration, which time bestows on every thing, and without which perhaps the wisest and freest governments would not possess the requisite stability." The reason of man might be a sufficient reliance in "a nation of philosophers," but in an ordinary nation, something more is required to maintain the necessary reverence for the laws. Another objection put forward by Madison was that a frequent reference of constitutional questions to the decision of the whole society raised "the danger of disturbing the public tranquility by interesting too strongly the public passions."[17]

If, as Merrill Peterson has suggested, Jefferson and Madison had aired their disagreement on this issue during earlier discussion of a new Virginia constitution,[18] it marked the beginning of a line of development in Jefferson's constitutional thought that would take it rather far afield from the thought of Madison and most of his other contemporaries. Jefferson's apparently easy embrace of the idea of periodic change in the constitution, not only for the purposes of correcting abuses but also for making substantive changes in the fundamental plan of government, shows that by the late 1780s he had taken to its logical conclusion the Real Whig notion of recurrence to first principles. The constitutional convention became, to Jefferson, the American solution to the problem perceived by Burgh and Sidney—the need for some "regular and constitutional method" by which the sovereign voice of the people could be heard—transforming from the realm of pure theory to the real world of practical politics the notion that government was founded on the consent of the people.

Jefferson's praise for the new federal Constitution—praise that focused more on the process by which the form of government was changed than on the substance of the changes themselves—provides added evidence of his acceptance of the idea of constitutional change. He was applauding not only the fact that change had been accomplished peaceably, without bloodshed, but also that it had come through the will of the people having been heard. Initially he had been ambivalent about the Constitution: although he generally admired the document (and concurred wholeheartedly in its strengthening of the national government's powers over commerce and foreign affairs), he had qualms about two "defects" that he perceived in it. The first was the absence of a bill of rights, which was corrected by the addition of the first ten amendments to the Constitution—a development in which Jefferson played a critical, albeit indirect, role through his correspondence with Madison during the years 1787-89.[19]

The second defect in the Constitution that concerned Jefferson at this time was what he characterized as "the abandonment of the necessity of rotation in office," namely, the perpetual eligibility of the president for reelection. "Experience concurs with reason in concluding that the first magistrate will always be re-elected if the constitution permits it," he maintained. He therefore feared that this would make the president an officer for life, essentially an elective monarch—an evil in itself, and but one step away from a return to hereditary monarchy.[20] He also feared the possibility of foreign intervention in American elections, observing, "The importance to France and England to have our government in the hands of a Friend or foe, will occasion their interference by money, and even by arms. Our President will be of much more consequence to them than a king of Poland."[21]

Jefferson grudgingly acquiesced in the perpetual eligibility of the president, despite his firm belief that it could lead to monarchy, when he realized that it had excited virtually no objection in America. "After all, it is my principle that the will of the Majority should always prevail," he wrote Madison. Noting that Americans' "jealousy" was "only put to sleep by the unlimited confidence" they had in Washington, whom everyone expected to be elected president, he concluded that amendment of the Constitution to correct this flaw would have to wait until "inferior characters" succeeded Washington in that high office and "awaken us to the danger which his merit has led us into." Amending the Constitution, would be necessary sooner or later, Jefferson urged, because "if it does not take place erelong, it assuredly never will. The natural progress of things is for liberty to yeild and government to gain ground."[22]

The notion that government was inevitably threatening to liberty was part of the radical Whig tradition in which Jefferson's early intellectual life was steeped. What he added to this tradition in the late 1780s— as he contemplated not only the new United States Constitution but also the possibilities for a new French constitution, possibilities brought into being by the Revolution that he witnessed during his final months in Paris—was the doctrine of natural rights, which, when tied to the notion of popular sovereignty, provided the underlying rationale for not only constitution-making but also frequent constitutional change. As circumstances change—as new possibilities emerge for government to threaten liberty—it was not only essential (from the Whig standpoint) but also right (from the standpoint of natural rights theory) that constitutions change to meet these new threats.

It was in a letter that Jefferson wrote to Madison from Paris in September 1789 (and redrafted early in 1790) that he developed the theory that furnished the basis for his advocacy of frequent constitutional change, the theory of "the sovereignty of the living generation"—the theory otherwise identified by the expression Jefferson used in his letter, that "the earth belongs to the living."[23] From this proposition he concluded that "no generation can contract debts greater than may be paid during the course of it's own existence," not only because this would violate the basic principle, by making the earth belong to the dead and not the living generation, but also because generations have no superiors, no laws of the society, governing them. Rather, "by the law of nature, one generation is to another as one independent nation is to another."[24]

Similarly, he argued—and here he reached the most important implication of the principle—"no society can make a perpetual constitution, or even a perpetual law." He concluded then that every constitution, and every law, "naturally expires at the end of 19 years," the period of time he calculated as the average lifetime of a generation. "If it be enforced longer, it is an act of force, and not of right."[25] Jefferson regarded the principle that the earth belongs to the living as one "of very extensive application and consequences," in France and in the United States; but in submitting it to Madison's consideration in early 1790, he ostensibly directed it to the matter of public debts, which was occupying Madison's attention as a member of Congress. He urged Madison to establish the principle in the first law for appropriating the public revenue, declaring against the validity of long-term debts. He also suggested that the duration for rights in the law to be passed for protecting copyrights and new inventions be nineteen, rather than fourteen, years.[26]

Madison's reply to Jefferson's letter was polite—noting that the idea was "a great one" that suggested many "interesting reflections to legislators," particularly with respect to public debts—yet firm in raising some practical objections to the application of the doctrine to a constitution. He reiterated objections he had raised to the provision for change in Jefferson's 1783 draft constitution for Virginia: that a "Government so often revised" might become "too mutable" to be venerated or might "engender pernicious factions." With respect to laws that might bind succeeding generations, Madison asked whether "the *improvements* made by the dead form a debt against the living who take the benefit of them." Debts may be incurred, observed Madison, for purposes that benefit the unborn as well as the living; indeed, they may be incurred principally for the benefit of posterity, as may be the case for the United States debt. If benefits can be passed from one generation to the next, equity demands the descent of obligations from one to another; and "all that is indispensible in adjusting the account between the dead and the living is to see that the debits against the latter do not exceed the advances made by the former." Finally—in perhaps the most devastating part of his reply to Jefferson's proposal—Madison argued that there was no way the theory could be applied practically. Noting that "all the rights depending on positive laws, that is, most of the rights of property," would be subject to redefinition at the end of the term, he foresaw "the most violent struggles . . . between those interested in reviving and those interested in new-modelling the former state of property." Anarchy, the depreciation of property values, and discouragement of industry would be among the other ill effects.[27]

The only escape from the difficulties of Jefferson's theory, both theoretical and practical, that Madison could see was "the received doctrine that a tacit assent may be given to established Constitutions and laws, and that this assent may be inferred, where no positive dissent appears." Jefferson had anticipated the implied consent, or tacit assent, argument in his letter to Madison, arguing that the power of repeal was not an equivalent because under no form of government could the will of the majority always be obtained fairly and without impediment and that, therefore, "a law of limited duration is much more manageable than one which needs a repeal." Madison did not directly respond to this argument, but instead raised the question, "whether it be possible to exclude wholly the idea of tacit assent, without subverting the foundation of civil Society?" He noted that the voice of the majority binds the minority, not under a law of nature—which would rather require unanimity— but rather under this principle of tacit assent. Although he said he did not mean to impeach "either the utility of the principle in some particular cases, or the general importance of it in the eye of the philosophical Legislator," he concluded that Jefferson's theory was not likely to sway many members of Congress: the "spirit of philosophical legislation" was not in fashion, and "our hemisphere must be still more enlightened before many of the sublime truths which are seen thro' the medium of Philosophy, become visible to the naked eye of the ordinary Politician."[28]

Jefferson did not persist in pushing his radical doctrine, largely because he soon found that more urgent challenges posed throughout the 1790s—first by the Bank of the United States and other aspects of Hamilton's financial program and later by other Federalist measures such as the Alien and Sedition Acts—dictated his stance, in contending for the preservation of the federal Constitution. He nevertheless continued to voice his support for the idea of constitutional change by applauding the fact that the American constitutions were capable of adapting to changed circumstances when such adaptation was necessary.[29]

Throughout the decade of the 1790s Jefferson sought not to change the Constitution, either through the amendment process or through implicit change by way of construction or interpretation. Indeed, he strongly opposed the latter means of change, advancing instead the theory of strict construction of federal powers that is evident in his 1791 opinion on the constitutionality of the bank bill.[30] Not until the electoral crisis of February 1801, when the tie in electoral votes between Jefferson and Aaron Burr placed the contest for the presidency in the House of Representatives, did Jefferson suggest that a second constitutional convention might be necessary to reform the Constitution. The threat that the Federalists might succeed in preventing the constitutional election of the president raised, in

Jefferson's mind, the specters of the dissolution of the government and rebellion—evils that could be obviated by the immediate calling of a convention, which Jefferson and his friends proposed to do if it proved necessary. The crisis ended with Jefferson's election on the thirty-sixth ballot; nevertheless, looking back on these events just shortly after his inaugural, he observed that "a convention, invited by the Republican members of Congress . . . would have been on the ground in eight weeks, would have reformed the Constitution where it was defective, and wound it up again." He also said that "this peaceable and legitimate resource, to which we are in the habit of implicit obedience, superseding all appeal to force, and being always within our reach, shows a precious principle of self-preservation in our composition."[31] As in his reaction to the adoption of the federal Constitution, he was again applauding constitutional change by way of a convention and popular ratification as a peaceable alternative to the resort to force.

Eventually the addition of the Twelfth Amendment to the Constitution resolved the "defect" in the mode of choosing a president that had given rise to the crisis of 1801. Amazingly, this was the last amendment to the United States Constitution in Jefferson's lifetime; indeed, over sixty years would pass before the addition of the Thirteenth Amendment. This was not as Jefferson would have liked it; several times during and after his presidency he urged amendments to the Constitution.

Only in one respect was Jefferson, while president, apparently loathe to propose amendments to the Constitution: he resisted demands put forward by some of the more radical members of his own party, the so-called Old Republicans, that he do so at the beginning of his administration. John Randolph expressed the feelings of these ardent Virginia Republicans when he observed, "In this quarter we think that the great work is only begun: and that without *substantial reform,* we shall have little reason to congratulate ourselves on the mere change of *men.*"[32] Edmund Pendleton, in an essay entitled "The Danger Not Over," published in the Richmond *Examiner* on October 20, 1801, proposed a series of constitutional amendments designed to institutionalize the "revolution of 1800," as it was understood by the Old Republicans. Pendleton's suggested amendments provided, among other things, that the president's duration in office be restricted to a single four-year term, that senators serve a shorter term and be removable by their constituents, that judges be appointed by Congress and removable by vote of both houses, that members of Congress and judges be prohibited from receiving appointments while in office, and that limitations be placed on the power to borrow money. Although Jefferson was probably sympathetic to these pleas, the policy of moderation and conciliation that he followed as president prevented him from supporting the Old Republicans.[33]

While he was president, Jefferson did propose amendments to the Constitution to sanction the Louisiana Purchase and to permit Congress to appropriate money for internal improvements projects. Indeed, Jefferson's qualms about the constitutionality of the Louisiana treaty prompted him to draft an ad hoc amendment that would have permitted it, retroactively; but, as with the Old Republican demands for comprehensive constitutional change, practical political considerations mitigated against the effort.[34] In his letter to Wilson Cary Nicholas in September 1803, at the height of the Louisiana crisis, Jefferson warned that loose construction would make the Constitution "a blank paper" and also presented his rationale for change. "Nothing is more likely," he noted, than that the original enumeration of federal powers was "defective," for this was "the ordinary case of all human works." He then suggested, "Let us go on then perfecting it, by adding, by way of amendment to the Constitution, those powers which time and trial show are still wanting."[35]

It was after his retirement from the presidency that Jefferson was most explicit in calling for constitutional change on both the federal and state levels. Although he wrote to one correspondent in 1813 that the Republican party was "steady for the support of the present constitution"—and that having "obtained at its commencement all the amendments to it they desired," they were "perfectly reconciled to it"—he nevertheless noted that some Republicans, perhaps himself included, sought "to popularize it further, by shortening the Senatorial term, and devising a process for the responsibility of judges, more practicable than that of impeachment."[36] What was most significant in prompting Jefferson to desire amendments to both the Virginia and United States Constitutions during his later years was his full realization of the implications of republicanism.

When Jefferson used the term *republicanism,* he did not use it in the classical, civic republican sense that several modern scholars have described.[37] He used it, rather, in the modern sense, as synonymous with representative democracy, stressing the importance of popular control of all branches of the government. "The equal rights of man, and the happiness of every individual, are now acknowledged to be the only legitimate objects of government," and "the only device by which these rights can be secured," he wrote in an 1823 letter, was "government by the people, acting not in person, but by representatives chosen by themselves":

> With us, all the branches of the government are elective by the people themselves, except the judiciary, of whose science and qualifications they are not competent judges. Yet, even in that department, we call in a jury of the people to decide all controverted matters of fact, because to that investigation they are entirely competent, leaving thus as little as possible, merely the law of the case, to the decision of the judges. And true it is that the people, especially when moderately instructed, are the only safe, because the only honest, depositories of the public rights, and should therefore be introduced into the administration of them in every function to which they are sufficient; they will err sometimes and accidentally, but never decidedly, and with a systematic and persevering purpose of overthrowing the free principles of the government.[38]

Jefferson's fullest articulation of his theory of republican government appeared in a series of letters written in the year 1816. He defined republicanism, variously, as "the equal right of every citizen in his person and property, and in their management"; or as "action by the citizens in person, in affairs within their reach and competence, and in all others by representatives, chosen immediately, and removable by themselves"; or as "a government by its citizens in mass, acting directly and personally, according to rules established by the majority."[39] Under these definitions, and particularly the last, the American constitutions proved wanting. "The full experiment of a government democratical, but representative, was and is still reserved for us," he observed; it had not been "pushed into all the ramifications of the system, so far as to leave no authority existing not responsible to the people." His "earnest wish," he said, was "to see the republican element of popular control pushed to the maximum of its practicable exercise."[40]

The most significant of the letters he wrote in 1816 was a famous letter in which he declared his enthusiastic support for constitutional change. "Some men look at constitutions with sanctimonious reverence, and deem them like the arc of the covenant, too sacred to be touched. They ascribe to the men of the preceding age a wisdom more than human, and suppose what they did to be beyond amendment." As a member of the revolutionary generation, he "knew that age well," but he also knew that "forty years of experience in government is worth a century of book-reading." He therefore declared "preposterous" the idea that constitutions ought to remain unchanged, despite changes in circumstances and the greater political wisdom that a society gains through experience. "I am certainly not an advocate for frequent and untried changes in laws and constitutions," he wrote, observing that it was possible to accommodate oneself to "moderate imperfections" and to find "practical means of correcting their ill effects." "But," he added, "I know also, that laws and institutions must go hand in hand with the progress of the human mind," and that "as that becomes more developed, more enlightened, as new discoveries are made, new truths disclosed, and manners and opinions change with the change of circumstances, institutions must advance also, and keep pace with the times." To his correspondent Samuel Kercheval, author of a pamphlet advocating the calling of a convention to write a new constitution for Virginia, Jefferson expressed his support. Let Virginians follow the example of people in their sister States and "avail ourselves of our reason and experience, to correct the crude essays of our first and unexperienced, although wise, virtuous, and well-meaning councils," he concluded. And, he added, "let us provide in our constitution for its revision at stated periods," suggesting again nineteen or twenty years as the appropriate period, revealed by mortality tables as the average lifetime of a generation.[41]

In this letter he stressed the "mother principle" of republicanism—that "'governments are republican only in proportion as they embody the will of their people, and execute it'"—and, on that basis, criticized the first American constitutions as having "no leading principles in them." As in the 1780s he again was extremely critical of the Virginia constitution of 1776, explaining its defects by observing that

Americans in 1776 were novices in the science of government. Similarly, as he had written to another correspondent in 1816, he regarded the federal Constitution also as exhibiting only various "shades" of republicanism, depending on how far each of its departments were from the direct and constant control by the citizens. He found the House of Representatives "mainly republican" but the Senate "scarcely so at all" because of its longer term and choice by the state legislatures, rather than by the people directly. The president was "more republican than the Senate," because of a shorter term and, in effect, more popular election. Finally, he found the federal judiciary, too, to be quite unrepublican, since lifetime appointment made judges "independent of the nation." "If, then, the control of the people over the organs of their government be the measure of its republicanism . . . it must be agreed that our governments have much less of republicanism than ought to have been expected," he concluded.[42]

To Kercheval, Jefferson proposed a series of amendments to the Virginia constitution. These included almost universal white male suffrage; equal representation in the legislature; popular election of the governor, judges, and sheriffs; and division of the counties into wards. He also urged periodical amendments of the constitution: "Let us provide in our constitution for its revision at stated periods," suggesting nineteen years as the period shown by mortality tables as the average life of a generation. These "loose heads of amendment," he said, he was throwing out for consideration; their object was "to secure self-government by the republicanism of our constitution, as well as by the spirit of the people; and to nourish and perpetuate that spirit." With much understatement Jefferson added, "I am not among those who fear the people."[43] He then went on to observe that he believed that "laws and institutions must go hand in hand with the progress of the human mind." He also noted that the present generation had the right "to choose for itself the form of government it believes most promotive of its own happiness; consequently, to accommodate to the circumstances in which it finds itself, that received from its predecessors."[44]

In the 1816 letter to Kercheval, Jefferson thus presented a rationale for constitutional change that combined all the principles upon which his advocacy of change had rested: the idea that the earth belongs to the living, the idea of progress, and republicanism. In a subsequent letter to Kercheval he added an additional justification. Although expressing his determination not to "intermeddle" in the question of a constitutional convention, which he said had become "a party one," and his willingness to live under the present constitution if a majority of his fellow Virginians preferred it, he declared his conviction that "for the sake of future generations (when principles shall have become too relaxed to permit amendment, as experience proves to be the constant course of things) I wish to have availed them of the virtues of the present time to put into a chaste & secure form, the government to be handed down to them."[45] This was reminiscent of his observation in *Notes on the State of Virginia* that the time to secure the liberties of the people was when the revolutionary spirit was still high: an awareness of practical considerations that was rather inconsistent with his notions of frequent, continuing amendment. On balance, however, Jefferson in 1816 was continuing to take a position that was quite distinct from that taken by Madison, who had warned that frequent change would lessen the people's veneration of the constitution and lead to social turbulence. Jefferson, as he said, did not fear the people; nor did he fear the prospects of public controversy over constitutional questions, although he personally preferred to stay out of the fray.[46]

With respect to the federal Constitution, Jefferson voiced support for several amendments, the general thrust of which was to preserve the Constitution in the federal, republican form that Jefferson believed constituted its "true theory." One of his most explicit statements favoring amendments to the Constitution appeared in a letter he wrote rather late in life, when he declared that "the real friends of the constitution in its federal form, if they wish it to be immortal, should be attentive, by amendments, to make it keep pace with the advance of the age in science and experience." He proposed three "great amendments": "the limitation of the term of presidential service"; "the placing the choice of president effectually in the hands of the people"; and "the giving to Congress the power of internal improvement, on condition that each State's federal proportion of the monies so expended, shall be employed within the State."[47]

One other amendment that he supported during his retirement years was some provision to make the federal judiciary more accountable to popular will. Exactly what provision Jefferson desired is unclear. In his autobiography he suggested submitting the judges to "some practical & impartial controul," compounded of "a mixture of state and federal authorities."[48] At about the same time he indicated his support of proposals to appoint judges for fixed terms, with reappointability at the approbation of Congress.[49] Earlier he had indicated his support of proposals to make the judges removable by the president in conjunction with both houses of Congress. Clearly, following the failed effort during the first term of his presidency to impeach Supreme Court Justice Samuel Chase, Jefferson considered impeachment an ineffective device.

Perhaps more important than Jefferson's advocacy or support for particular constitutional amendments was his advocacy of the general principle that constitutional problems ought to be resolved not through ingenious construction—whether through executive prerogative, as in the Louisiana Purchase, or through judicial interpretation, as in Chief Justice Marshall's opinion in *McCulloch v. Maryland*—but rather through appeals to the people. He envisioned either an informal process, of having the will of the people "reintegrated" into the Constitution through the electoral system, or the formal process of constitutional conventions and amendments.

Late in life, during the years following his retirement from the presidency,

Jefferson returned to the idea that the earth belongs to the living, reiterating the argument that he had presented to Madison—but with two important differences. He no longer referred to nineteen years, or any other time period, as the lifetime of a generation; and he apparently accepted the tacit assent argument that Madison had made in 1790. Noting that although society had found it "more convenient to suffer the laws of our predecessors to stand on our implied assent," he noted that nevertheless "this does not lessen the right" of new generations to repeal old laws if they wish. Without abandoning the basic principle that the earth belongs to the living, Jefferson softened the doctrine somewhat, transforming it from a rationale for periodic, radical change into a rationale for change whenever the will of the majority or circumstances call for it. Similarly, in a letter written to John Cartwright in 1824, he again affirmed the basic idea that the earth belongs to the living, arguing that "a generation may bind itself as long as its majority continues in life; when that has disappeared, another majority is in place, holds all the rights and powers their predecessors once held, and may change their laws and institutions to suit themselves." This is the context in which he concluded, "nothing then is unchangeable but the inherent and unalienable rights of man."[50]

In the early 1820s, during the Virginia campaign against the claim that the United States Supreme Court was the ultimate arbiter of constitutional questions,[51] Jefferson emphasized the position that he had earlier claimed in the Kentucky Resolutions, that the ultimate arbiter was the people themselves. As he stated to Justice Johnson in 1823, "The ultimate arbiter is the people of the Union, assembled by their deputies in convention, at the call of Congress, or of 2/3 of the states."[52] Or, as he wrote to another correspondent a few years earlier, as the *Cohens* case was before the Supreme Court, "I know no safe depository of the ultimate powers of the society but the people themselves; and if we think them not enlightened enough to exercise their control with a wholesale discretion, the remedy is not to take it from them, but to inform their discretion by education. This is the true corrective of abuses of constitutional power."[53]

"The True Corrective of Abuses of Constitutional Power":
An Educated and "Jealous" Citizenry

The necessity of popular participation in government was confirmed in Jefferson's mind by his fundamental conviction that government inevitably threatened liberty; or, as he put it to Madison in 1789, "the natural progress of things is for liberty to yeild and government to gain ground." His experience as American minister to France had persuaded him that this was the danger from all governments, republican as well as monarchical. He was an advocate for republicanism because he believed that the people's "jealousy," together with structural constitutional safeguards (primarily, the division of governmental power), could minimize the danger.

He put it best in his draft of the Kentucky Resolutions of 1798, where he wrote, "Free government is founded in jealousy, and not in confidence; it is jealousy and not confidence which prescribes limited constitutions, to bind down those whom we are obliged to trust with power. . . . In questions of power, then, let no more be heard of confidence in man, but bind him down from mischief by the chains of the Constitution."[54]

Jefferson thus retained great confidence in the people, even when his contemporaries did not. For example, he reacted with relative calm to news of Shays' Rebellion, the uprising of farmers and debtors in Massachusetts in 1786-87. News of such "tumults in America" did not shake Jefferson's confidence or pride in American republicanism. Although he said that he considered the citizens' resort to arms "acts absolutely unjustifiable," he benignly concluded that such turbulence was the price that America paid for its republicanism. Weighed against the oppression of monarchy, it "becomes nothing," he noted, adding that he was not at all discouraged: the rebellion in Massachusetts was the first in the thirteen American states after eleven years of independence, which he calculated to amount to "one rebellion in a century and a half for each state." "What country ever existed a century and a half without rebellion?" he asked. Thus he even cited the rebellion as evidence showing that the American "experiment" would be successful in proving to the world that "men may be trusted to govern themselves without a master."[55]

Two of Jefferson's letters commenting on Shays' Rebellion early in 1787 are especially deserving of mention. To James Madison he expressed the hope that the governmental authorities in America would not act too harshly in putting down such turbulence because it "prevents the degeneracy of government, and nourishes a general attention to the public affairs." Thus, he concluded, "a little rebellion now and then is a good thing, . . . a medicine necessary for the sound health of government." Two weeks earlier, in a letter written to Edward Carrington, Jefferson similarly urged tolerance. "The people are the only censors of their governors; and even their errors will tend to keep these to the true principles of their institution. To punish these errors too severely would be to suppress the only safeguard of public liberty." Jefferson also contrasted America with Europe, arguing that societies without governments (such as that he believed the American Indians had) enjoyed greater happiness than those, like most in Europe, where under the pretext of governing, one class of people preyed upon another, like "wolves and sheep." He urged his correspondent, "Cherish therefore the spirit of our people, and keep alive their attention. Do not be too severe upon their errors, but reclaim them by enlightening them. If once they become inattentive to the public affairs, you and I, and Congress, and Assemblies, judges and governors shall all become wolves."[56]

The notion that the control by the people over their government, according to their own "wholesome discretion," informed by education, constituted the "true corrective" of abuses of power is distinctively Jeffersonian. Indeed, the emphasis that Jefferson placed on popular participation and control—making the people themselves a vital element in constitutionalism—was the preeminent hallmark of Jefferson's constitutional thought.[57] None of his contemporaries, with perhaps the exception of John Taylor of Caroline, so emphasized this element. It in fact underlay many of the other aspects of his constitutional thought. As I have shown in my study of Jefferson's constitutional thought, both the pure theory of separation of powers as well as the theory of federalism that Jefferson espoused were ultimately derived from his thoroughgoing republicanism. With each branch of the federal government, and with each state in the Union, determining constitutional questions, potentially in conflict with one another, some common ground was necessary; and that common ground—in effect, the glue that held Jefferson's constitutional system in place—was in fact the active participation of the people in constitutional questions.

Jefferson regarded it America's great mission to prove to the world the efficacy of republican government. As he explained in a letter written early in his presidency, America was in an advantageous situation:

> Our people in a body are wise, because they are under the unrestrained and unperverted operation of their own understandings. Those whom they have assigned to the direction of their affairs, have stood with a pretty even front. If any one of them was withdrawn, many others entirely equal, have been ready to fill his place with as good abilities. A nation, composed of such materials, and free in all it's members from distressing wants, furnishes hopeful implements for the interesting experiment of self-government; and we feel that we are acting under obligations not confined to the limits of our own society. It is impossible not to be sensible that we are acting for all mankind; that circumstances denied to others, but indulged to us, have imposed on us the duty of proving what is the degree of freedom and self-government in which a society may venture to leave it's individual members.[58]

Thus he indicated what he perceived as a prerequisite, or precondition, of his system of republican constitutionalism: that the people be wise, by being "under the unrestrained and unperverted operation of their own understandings." The emphasis on education is a recurrent theme in Jefferson's political writings. While in France, he wrote to George Wythe back in Virginia, admonishing him to "preach, my dear Sir, a crusade against ignorance; establish and improve the law for educating the common people."[59] Many years later he observed, "If a nation expects to be ignorant and free, in a state of civilization, it expects what never was and never will be."[60] And, in one of his more poetical expressions of his confidence in the education of the people as a means of preserving liberty, he wrote, "Enlighten the people generally, and tyranny and oppressions of body and mind will vanish like evil spirits at the dawn of day."[61]

An important element of Jefferson's proposals for republican reform of Virginia's laws during the Revolution was the establishment of a system of public education. The purpose for his "Bill for the More General Diffusion of Knowledge," as he explained it in *Notes on the State of Virginia,* was that of "rendering the people the safe, as they are the ultimate guardians of their own liberty." "Every government degenerates when trusted to the rulers of the people alone. The people themselves therefore are its only safe depositories. And to render even them safe their minds must be improved to a certain degree."[62]

Jefferson's bill sought to do this through a two-tier system of publicly support-ed education. All citizens would receive a basic schooling in reading and writing at the hundred schools; there they would also learn "the most useful facts" from ancient and modern history. The emphasis on historical education was quite delib-erate, Jefferson explained: "History by apprising them of the past will enable them to judge of the future; it will avail them of the experience of other times and other nations; it will qualify them as judges of the actions and designs of men; it will enable them to know ambition under every disguise it may assume; and knowing it, to defeat its views." Beyond this basic schooling, the best students would receive advanced training suitable to prepare the "natural aristocracy" for public service: by this means, "those persons, whom nature hath endowed with genius and virtue, should be rendered by liberal education worthy to receive, and able to guard the sacred deposit of the rights and liberties of their fellow-citizens, and that they should be called to that charge without regard to wealth, birth, or other accidental condition or circumstance."[63]

Ensuring that "genius and virtue," not accidental circumstances such as wealth and birth, should be the foundations of the republic's leaders—in other words, ensuring that the natural, not the "pseudo" aristocracy should lead the republic—was one important reason for public support of education. Another, as Jefferson explained later in connection with his proposal for a national university, was to ensure that all sciences necessary to the improvement and preservation of the nation be nourished.[64] Most fundamentally, however, Jefferson regarded education as too important to be left to chance; the very survival of republican government depended on it.

In later years Jefferson coupled education with one other proposal, which he considered equally necessary to the preservation of republicanism: his proposed system of local government by wards. These "little republics," he said, would be the main strength of the greater ones.[65] Jefferson's proposal was to divide the counties into wards of such size that every citizen can attend, when called on, and act in per-son. The government of each ward would take care of "all things relating to them-selves exclusively": a justice, a constable, a military company, a school, the care of the poor, the care of local public roads, the choice of jurors, and so on. Such a system, he maintained, would not only relieve the county administration of most of its business, but would do it better; moreover, "by making every citizen an acting mem-ber of the government, and in the offices nearest and most interesting to him, will attach him by his strongest feelings to the independence of his country, and its republican constitution." These wards, like the townships of New England—or, one might add, the hundreds of Anglo-Saxon England as described by Whig historians—have proved themselves "the wisest invention ever devised by the wit of man for the perfect exercise of self-government, and for its preservation." He envisioned the marshaling of government into four levels: first, "the general federal republic, for all concerns foreign and federal"; second, the state, for what relates to its own citizens exclusively; third, "the county republics," for the duties and concerns of the county; and finally, "the ward republics, for the small, and yet numerous and interesting concerns of the neighborhood." By this system of division and subdivision, Jefferson maintained, "all matters, great and small, can be managed to perfection."[66]

Jefferson similarly explained the rationale for the ward system in a letter to Joseph Cabell in 1816:

> The way to have good and safe government, is not to trust it all to one, but to divide it among the many, distributing to every one exactly the functions he is competent to. Let the national government be entrusted with the defence of the nation, and its foreign and federal relations; the State governments with the civil rights, laws, police and administration of what concerns the state generally; the Counties with the local concerns of the counties; and each Ward direct the interests within itself. It is by dividing and subdividing these republics from the great national one down through all its subordinations, until it ends in the administration of every man's farm and affairs by himself; by placing under every one what his own eye may superintend, that all will be done for the best.

"What has destroyed liberty and the rights of man in every government which has ever existed under the sun?" Jefferson asked. "The generalizing and concentrating all cares and powers into one body." The "secret" of maintaining freedom, he suggested, was to make the individual alone "the depository of the powers respecting himself, so far as he is competent to them, and delegating only what is beyond his competence by a synthetical process, to higher & higher orders of functionaries, so as to trust fewer and fewer powers, in proportion as the trustees become more and more oligarchical." The system of republics thus described would accomplish this and thereby itself become a vital element of constitutionalism. "Where every man is a sharer in the direction of his ward-republic, or of some of the higher ones, and feels that he is a participator in the government of affairs, not merely at an election one day in the year, but every day; when there shall not be a man in the State who will not be a member of some one of its councils, great or small, he will let the heart be torn out of his body sooner than his power be wrestled from him by a Caesar or a Bonaparte," he also observed. Emphasizing the importance with which he viewed the subject, he noted that "as Cato then concluded every speech with the words 'Cathago delenda est,' so do I every opinion with the injunction 'divide the counties into wards.'"[67]

One further advantage would be gained by the ward system, of immediate importance to the problem of resolving constitutional questions. "A general call of ward meetings by their wardens on the same day through the State, would at any time produce the genuine sense of the people on any required point, and would enable the State to act in mass," as New Englanders do in their town meetings, Jefferson noted.[68]

Jefferson thus envisioned, as a vital element of constitutionalism—indeed, as the most effective check on the abuse of governmental power—the active involvement of citizens in the government itself. In the wards citizens would gain practical education in government that, together with the education they received through formal schooling, would constitute the "two hooks" upon which "the continuance of republican government hung."[69] An educated, actively involved citizenry would be simultaneously self-reliant, managing directly those affairs to which individuals were alone competent, and vigilant, keeping a close watch over their elected officials to whom they had entrusted all other affairs, and making certain that they did not turn into wolves.

Jefferson's proposed ward system also gives added meaning to his support for the principle of rotation in office. As is evident in the modern debate over various proposals to limit the terms of state legislators and members of Congress, one of the goals of rotation in office is to increase the level of popular participation in government by mandating turnover. Thus, as the proponents of term limitations argue, the virtual monopoly that incumbent, professional politicians hold on some offices may be broken, and the way created for a return to the citizen-politician model of the nineteenth century. The appeal of term limitations to modern-day Jeffersonians is exactly the same as their appeal to Jefferson himself: they enhance the possibility that each citizen may become, in his words, "a participator in the government of affairs, not merely at an election one day in the year, but every day."

A full understanding of Jefferson's ideas regarding constitutional change—and indeed, of his constitutional thought generally—must take into account Jefferson's dual emphasis on education and participation. The essentially negative view of politics that Jefferson held thus ultimately influenced his constitutional thought in a profound way.[70] He regarded as truly modest the achievements of his generation, believing that subsequent generations, learning from additional experience, would improve on the founders' handiwork, with the problem of maintaining a free government becoming far simpler as subsequent generations hit upon better and better solutions. Hence he recommended that every generation create anew their constitutions—a recommendation that reveals both his assumptions that constitution-making was a relatively simple matter and that the people, as a whole, were fully competent to the task. Although a preeminent member of what Dumas Malone has called the "great generation," Jefferson disclaimed its greatness.[71]

Jefferson's view of constitutionalism, in the final analysis, was one which placed less emphasis on mechanics—the written enumeration of powers, division of powers, checks and balances, and so on—than it did on the character of the people themselves. "Where is our republicanism to be found? Not in the constitution, but merely in the spirit of the people."[72] Or, as Jefferson put it more rhapsodically by quoting a poem:

> What constitutes a State?
> Not high-raised battlements, or labor'd mound,
>   Thick wall, or moated gate;
> Not cities proud, with spires and turrets crown'd;
>   No: men, high minded men;
>   Men, who their duties know;
> But know their rights; and knowing, dare maintain.
>   These constitute a State.[73]

EUGENE R. SHERIDAN

Liberty and Virtue:
Religion and Republicanism
in Jeffersonian Thought

Thomas Jefferson's personal religious views and his commitment to the establishment of a lasting republican order in America are two subjects that have generally been studied in isolation from each other. Without in any way trying to deny the predominantly secular character of Jefferson's republican vision, this essay explores some crucial points of intersection between Jefferson's rationalistic religious beliefs and his republicanism. In Jefferson's view, the protection of liberty and the promotion of virtue were two of the most vital prerequisites for ensuring the stability of a republican regime in America.

At two critical points in Jefferson's career his religious views intersected with his republican ideology to affect significantly his approach to liberty and virtue. Both points reflected crucial stages in the development of his religious opinions. Whereas the first involved his struggle to achieve religious freedom and separation of church and state in Virginia, the second involved his effort to preserve republican virtue in the face of a rising tide of liberal individualism in the United States.

"Fix Reason Firmly in Her Seat":
The Rejection of Christian Orthodoxy

The central theme in the evolution of Jefferson's religious views was the clash between the spirit of critical analysis and the doctrines of traditional Christianity. Peter Gay and other historians have identified the clash as one of the distinguishing features of the Enlightenment, a crucial turning point in Western intellectual history, of which Jefferson was perhaps the finest American exemplar. It marked a decisive shift, at least among key sectors of the educated elite in Europe and America, from a predominantly theological to a fundamentally secular world view.

Inspired by the striking successes of the Scientific Revolution, weary of a long succession of bloody religious wars and inconclusive doctrinal disputes between Catholics and Protestants, excited by perceptible signs of sustained economic growth and improved standards of living, and provided with a compelling alterna-

242

tive system of humanistic values through the Renaissance's rediscovery of classical culture, enlightened thinkers scorned metaphysical and theological speculation as a vain and useless enterprise. Instead, with reason as their guide, they embarked upon the investigation of nature and the reform of society, with the avowed aim of improving humanity's lot in this world rather than preparing souls for the life to come, emphasizing the pursuit of happiness in the here and now rather than the pursuit of salvation in the hereafter.

The rationalistic spirit of the Enlightenment inevitably brought it into conflict with Christian orthodoxy, whose emphasis on the continuing validity of supernatural revelation, tradition, and ecclesiastical authority prompted many enlightened thinkers to insist that religion was only valid insofar as it accorded with human reason and was socially useful. The Enlightenment critique of religion was less prominent in America than in Europe because of the generally high degree of religious tolerance the colonies enjoyed under British rule and the even higher degree of religious freedom the new American nation enjoyed after the Revolution. But in this respect the highly cosmopolitan Jefferson was more attuned to the critical spirit of the European Enlightenment than most Americans. Indeed, to a large extent Jefferson was almost a perfect embodiment of Gay's compelling portrait of the typical philosophe as a modern pagan whose intellectual development can be summarized as a dialectical progression from a rejection of Christianity to an embrace of classicism to a pursuit of modernity.[1]

The Enlightenment's demand for the rationalization and demystification of religion was reflected in Jefferson's youthful rejection of his ancestral Anglican creed in favor of natural religion and classical ethics. Unable "from a very early part of my life" to accept the core Christian doctrine of the Trinity because of the "difficulty of reconciling the ideas of Unity and Trinity" in the godhead,[2] Jefferson subjected the rest of Christianity to rational analysis and concluded that its basic doctrines were contrary to human reason and thus unacceptable to an aspiring young philosophe. "Fix reason firmly in her seat, and call to her tribunal every fact, every opinion," he later advised one of his nephews in the course of a disquisition on the proper approach to religion, no doubt reflecting his own experience.[3]

In the course of investigating the claims of Christianity, Jefferson was heavily influenced by the philosophical writings of Lord Bolingbroke, the libertine Tory leader and champion of Deism whose works constitute a veritable encyclopedia of rationalistic criticism of revealed religion. In fact, the specific grounds for Jefferson's rejection of orthodox Christianity can be traced through an analysis of the passages from Bolingbroke's works that he entered into his *Literary Commonplace Book* in 1765-66, three years after finishing his education at William and Mary and while he was still studying law with George Wythe. Running to almost sixty pages in manuscript and constituting the longest single entry in the *Literary Commonplace Book*, the extracts from Bolingbroke, echoed as they were in Jefferson's later writings, show that the young Virginian thoroughly embraced the Deist critique of Christianity and its corollary assumptions about the sufficiency of human reason, the goodness of man, the benevolence and transparency of God, and the unacceptability of mystery in religion.[4]

Thus, Jefferson rejected the Bible as the inspired word of God, because divine inspiration was an empirically unverifiable phenomenon and because, in his opinion, scripture contained "gross defects and palpable falsehoods" that "no man who acknowledges a supreme all-perfect being can beleive to be his word."[5] Instead, he regarded the Bible as a mere work of history, to be judged as one would judge the works of Livy or Tacitus—and not a very edifying history at that. In his view, the Old Testament was the record of the barbarous dealings of a barbarous God with a barbarous people, and the New Testament was suspect because its miracle stories contradicted his understanding of the inviolability of the laws of nature.[6] He likewise objected to the Christian scheme of salvation, because it postulated that for centuries the one true God had restricted knowledge of himself to a small nation on the eastern rim of the Mediterranean—a nation, moreover, which, to Jefferson's way of thinking, was antisocial in its ethical principles and degraded in its concept of the deity. He found the Christian plan of redemption equally offensive, because he did not believe that a just God would have allowed his innocent son to be sacrificed on the cross to satisfy his divine anger at sinful humanity and because the doctrine of original sin was inconsistent with his notion of an essentially just and benevolent deity.[7]

In fact, Jefferson decided, God had not sent his only son to redeem the world because, in his judgment, Jesus was not divine. In his view, the miracles Jesus worked were figments of the imaginations of his superstitious followers; the moral principles he taught were incomplete and not rationally derived from the laws of nature; and the development of Christian doctrine after his death forced one to assume that he had imperfectly executed his divine commission.[8] Far from being the son of God, therefore, Jesus was merely, in Jefferson's later words, "a man of illegitimate birth, of a benevolent heart, enthusiastic mind, who set out without pretensions to divinity, ended in believing them, and was punished capitally for sedition by being gibbetted according to the Roman law."[9] Moreover, if Christian orthodoxy was intellectually unacceptable to the rationalistic Jefferson because its fundamental doctrines were mysteries that could not be comprehended by human reason, he also had grave doubts as to its social utility. For when he viewed the history of Christianity, he saw, as he subsequently wrote in *Notes on the State of Virginia,* not the glorious unfolding of the kingdom of God on earth, but a gloomy chronicle of misguided efforts to impose doctrinal uniformity, which had stifled free thought, led "Millions of innocent men, women, and children" to be "burnt, tortured, fined, imprisoned," and made "one half the world fools, and the other half hypocrites."[10]

Like many other adherents of the Enlightenment, Jefferson turned to natural

religion after discarding his inherited Christian faith and rejecting supernatural revelation and ecclesiastical authority as valid sources of religious truth. John Calvin
"was indeed an Atheist, which I can never be; or rather his religion was
Daemonism," Jefferson asserted late in life, thereby revealing both the limits of his
religious skepticism and a certain lack of theological sophistication.[11] Convinced
that human reason was the sole arbiter of religious truth and heavily influenced by
the ancient argument from design that the orderly structure of the cosmos proved
the existence of God, Jefferson firmly believed in a supreme being who created a
strictly material universe, continued to sustain it by means of mathematically precise natural laws, and like the universe itself was also material—a being Jefferson
variously described as the "God of justice," "Creator of the Universe," "benevolent
governor of the world," "Sovereign Disposer of all human events," "Author of morality," and "Infinite Power."[12] Disdaining to interrupt the workings of his laws through
miraculous interventions in human affairs or through special revelations to chosen
people, this just and benevolent God revealed himself to all men at all times and in
all places through the natural wonders of his created universe and was thus infinitely superior to the arbitrary, jealous, mysterious, and vindictive tribal deity the
youthful Jefferson perceived in the Old and New Testaments. Nor did this God simply set the universe in motion and then remain aloof from human affairs. For, without pretending to understand its exact contours, Jefferson assumed that there was a
general providential design at work in history whose ultimate goal was the expansion of human liberty, a design, however, in which human agency, not divine intervention, was the main operative factor.[13]

　　In addition to substituting the God of nature for the God of revelation, Jefferson
also found a new basis for morality to replace the Christian emphasis on the essential corruption of human nature through original sin and man's consequent need
for saving grace. Under the influence of the writings of the Scottish philosopher
Lord Kames, Jefferson concluded that Nature's God had endowed virtually everyone with an innate faculty for distinguishing right from wrong known as the moral
sense. Using social utility as its standard, the moral sense performed this function
by making virtuous acts pleasing and vicious acts displeasing to men. Nature,
Jefferson rejoiced, "implanted in our breasts a love of others, a sense of duty to
them, a moral instinct in short, which prompts us irresistibly to feel and succour
their distresses."[14] But for the moral sense to work best, it had to be instructed by
education and example to incline its possessor toward right conduct. In order to
cultivate and nurture his own moral sense, the youthful Jefferson turned to the ethical precepts of the classical Epicurean and Stoic philosophers. Under their guidance, he sought to achieve the Epicurean ideal of a tranquil and virtuous life free
from pain by adhering to the stern self-discipline enjoined by the Stoics. For at this
point in his life he wholeheartedly agreed with Bolingbroke that the ethical precepts
of these classical mentors were "more entire, more coherent, and more clearly

deduced from unquestionable principles of knowledge" than those of Jesus of Nazareth—a judgment he later revised.[15]

In the course of rationally examining the claims of Christianity, Jefferson acquired a lasting aversion to clerical authority. Deistic writers commonly faulted Christianity and other revealed religions on the grounds that throughout history their priestly castes had deliberately fabricated mysterious or supranational doctrines so as to fortify their position as indispensable mediators between God and man and thereby enhance their power over the laity. In keeping with his own insistence on the need to rationalize and demystify religion, Jefferson fully accepted the justice of this criticism. While respecting the right of others to submit to clerical authority if they freely chose to do so, he himself remained intensely anticlerical for the rest of his life; and even though he nominally belonged to the Anglican Church until his death, he refused to be attended by one of its ministers on his deathbed.[16]

Jefferson's early rejection of Christian orthodoxy and his espousal of natural religion left him with a lifelong commitment to religious freedom and the primacy of morality over dogma in religion. Each person, he decided, had a natural right to worship—or not to worship—God as he pleased. Under the influence of John Locke, he regarded the very essence of religion as being the free assent of the human mind to what it deemed to be the truth about God and man's relation to him. Consequently, no one could be forced to believe what his reason rejected, for coercion produced hypocrisy rather than conviction and was thus an affront to man and his creator alike. At the same time, he concluded that the most important aspect of religion was the moral standards it instilled in its adherents rather than the theological doctrines it taught. In his view, dogma dealt with matters that were beyond human understanding and had therefore been needlessly productive of bitter strife throughout history— nowhere more so than in Christian societies. In contrast, morality regulated human relations in the social world to which men had been destined by their creator and thus had the potential to generate harmony in society—a key element in the Jeffersonian hierarchy of values. Jefferson's religion was therefore relentlessly moralistic in emphasis, as befitted one whose controlling purpose in life was the improvement of man and society in this world rather than the preparation of souls for salvation in the next. With its stress on reason and morality, its rejection of supernatural revelation and ecclesiastical authority, its denial of the need for any mediators between man and God, it was, in a certain sense, a secularized version of the Protestant doctrine of the priesthood of all believers.[17]

"The Holy Cause of Freedom": The Commitment to Republicanism

In keeping with Peter Gay's model of the typical philosophe, Jefferson, having rejected Christianity for natural religion and turned to classical philosophy for ethical guidance, embarked in earnest upon a pursuit of modernity by embracing republicanism during the final throes of the imperial crisis that led to the disruption of the First British Empire in 1776. Thereafter the creation of an enduring republican social and political order in America became the central purpose of Jefferson's life, and the quasi religious fervor with which he pursued this quest was truly remarkable. For Jefferson, republicanism was nothing less than the "Holy Cause of Freedom." Its supporters adhered to the "holy republican gospel," remained true to the "good old faith," and held aloft for all the world to see the "sacred deposit," the "holy fire," the "sacred fire" of liberty.[18] In contrast, those who defected from this "political creed" were "apostates" whose "heretical" doctrines threatened to corrupt the "orthodox" doctrines of republicanism.[19] Fortunately, political ostracism was the worst fate Jefferson ever conceived for these erring brethren. Otherwise, on the rhetorical level at least, there were times when this transference of categories of traditional religious discourse to the political realm brought Jefferson eerily close to the harshly driven ideological world of Robespierre and the Republic of Virtue.

Jeffersonian republicanism was a dynamic blend of Lockean liberalism and civic humanism that simultaneously looked to the future and took heed of the past. It was a potent constellation of ideas and attitudes that entailed the rejection of all vestiges of monarchy and hereditary privilege. Instead it sought to promote liberty, advance enlightenment, and unleash the creative energies of the American people within the framework of limited government, popular sovereignty, and an agrarian society guided by a natural aristocracy based upon virtue and merit rather than birth and wealth. In keeping with the precepts of Lockean liberalism, Jefferson eloquently defended the philosophy of natural rights and the contractual theory of government. Each person, as he stirringly proclaimed in the Declaration of Independence, was endowed by God with certain natural and inalienable rights, including but not limited to the sacred trinity of life, liberty, and the pursuit of happiness, and he went to great lengths to emphasize the ultimately religious basis of these rights. For, as he asked in *Notes on the State of Virginia,* "can the liberties of a nation be thought secure when we have removed their only firm basis, a conviction in the minds of the people that these liberties are the gift of God? That they are not to be violated but with his wrath?"[20] The object of government was to protect these rights, so as to leave people free "to regulate their own pursuits of industry & improvement, and . . . not take from the mouth of labor the bread it has earned."[21] In order to ensure that government respected the natural rights of man, Jefferson believed that it was necessary sharply to limit its powers and make it strictly accountable to the people by means of written constitutions, fundamental guarantees of basic rights, checks and balances among the different branches of government, and frequent elections. With government thus checked and the liberties of the people secure, Jefferson looked forward with hope to a general expansion of liberty, enlightenment, and prosperity that "must advance the knowledge and well-being of mankind, not *infinitely,* as some have said, but *indefinitely,* and to a term which no one can fix and foresee."[22]

But for Jefferson the survival of republicanism in America depended less upon the structure of the American government than the character of the American people. In accordance with the ideological presuppositions of civic humanism, Jefferson believed that in the last resort a republic could only survive among a virtuous people who were independent, frugal, temperate, industrious, ready to take up arms in defense of liberty, and willing when necessary to subordinate their private interests to the public good. Republican virtue was ultimately based upon personal independence, and personal independence depended upon the ownership of property: hence Jefferson's idealization of yeomen farmers as the backbone of American republicanism. As long as America remained a basically agrarian society, Jefferson was reasonably confident that republican liberty would endure. For as society moved from the agrarian to the commercial to the manufacturing stages of development, it was marked by the growth of increasing webs of economic and social dependency that would ultimately undermine the personal independence upon which republican virtue rested and destroy the republic itself. To maintain agrarian dominance in American society for ages yet to come, Jefferson sought new foreign markets to absorb the surplus production of American farmers and supported trans-Mississippi territorial acquisitions in the belief that expansion across space would delay the corruption over time to which republics were inevitably subject.[23]

Jefferson's emphasis on the need for republican virtue among the people was informed by his civic humanist reading of history. For Jefferson and for many other members of the revolutionary generation, human history was a constant struggle between power and liberty. In this epic contest, power, always active and ever aggressive, was forever striving to stifle liberty, ever fragile and always vulnerable. Because of this ceaseless tension between power and liberty, republics were never immune to corruption and decay. Of all the Founding Fathers, as Paul Rahe has recently contended, Jefferson was the one most sensitive to the ravages with which power constantly threatened liberty.[24] Once the people "become inattentive to the public affairs," once they ceased to care about their rights, he warned, "you and I, and Congress and Assemblies, judges and governors shall all become wolves."[25] He was particularly alert to the dangers of what he perceived to be British forms of corruption—a strong central government, standing armies, excessive public debt, high taxes, undue executive influence over the legislature, and government patronage of a monied interest. But looking at the longer sweep of history, beyond the English Financial Revolution that had brought these forms of corruption in its wake and that Hamiltonian finance threatened to replicate in America, Jefferson was also concerned about the union between church and state, for to his mind this had been one of the most effective forms of tyranny, stifling political liberty and free thought alike. In order for a republic to survive, therefore, power had to be limited, decentralized, made subject to strict popular control and accountability. Power had to be checked by liberty, and liberty had to be buttressed by virtue. Else the American republic would go the way of republics in the past and succumb to corruption, decay, and degeneration, with power once again triumphing over liberty.[26]

Active citizenship in the Jeffersonian republic was subject to strict racial, gender, and ethnic limitations. Jefferson completely excluded blacks from his republican vision, not only because as slaves they were inherently dependent on their masters, but also because deep-rooted racial prejudice on his part made him unable to accept the possibility of blacks and whites living together peacefully on terms of liberty and equality in America. Hence his tortured insistence that the abolition of slavery in the United States had to be accompanied by the colonization of the freed slaves in Africa or the West Indies. He also excluded women, again not simply because they were dependent on parents or husbands, but also because he regarded them as generally frivolous outside their proper domestic sphere. He excluded as well servants and minors, because they clearly were marked by those indelible qualities of dependence that automatically disqualified anyone from active republican citizenship. Finally, despite his eloquent defense of expatriation as a natural right, Jefferson had grave doubts about the desirability of allowing America to serve as a haven for large numbers of immigrants from monarchical lands, lest they corrupt the American republic with monarchical principles. In brief, for Jefferson, the fate of the American republic rested largely on the shoulders of white, adult, male, predominantly Anglo-Saxon farmers, planters, merchants, artisans, and craftsmen—those who possessed the requisite personal independence to exercise republican virtue.[27]

"The Most Inalienable and Sacred of All Human Rights": Religious Freedom and Republican Liberty

Jefferson's religious beliefs and republican principles both conspired to impel him to play a leading role in the struggle to achieve religious freedom and separation of church and state in Virginia. The successful completion of this struggle marked a decisive turning point in what has since become a general repudiation of what one might call the Constantinian Period in Western history—that is to say, the era marked by the deeply ingrained and widely institutionalized assumption that civil enforcement of religious solidarity (or at least civil supervision of religious tolerance) was a necessary precondition for the maintenance of social and political order. In contrast, for Jefferson religious freedom was "the most inalienable and sacred of all human rights,"[28] and he believed that it could only be assured by drawing a strict institutional line of demarcation between the sacred and the secular realm. In the course of Jefferson's long career in public life, there were any number of key issues on which political necessity forced him to backtrack, waver, or compromise. But he remained unflinchingly consistent in his advocacy of complete freedom of religion through strict separation of church and state. And if one seeks the source of this consistency, one finds that his stance was governed by his rationalistic religious principles as well as by two basic republican imperatives. For in the universe of Jeffersonian republicanism, religious liberty promoted intellectual freedom and enlightenment, thereby fostering a spirit of personal independence among the citizenry that was an essential pillar of republican liberty, and separation of church and state prevented a potentially dangerous concentration of clerical and magisterial authority, thereby depriving power of what historically had been one of its most effective weapons in its eternal struggle with liberty.

Jefferson clearly combined religious rationalism and republican ideology in the arguments that he publicly articulated in favor of establishing freedom of religion and separating church and state in Virginia. These arguments appear in his notes for a speech to the Virginia House of Delegates, which he prepared late in 1776, and in his chapter on religion in *Notes on the State on Virginia*, which he wrote on the basis of these notes five years later. Thus, despite the guarantee of religious freedom contained in the Virginia Declaration of Rights of 1776, Jefferson maintained that Virginians still lived in a potential state of "religious slavery" because under common law and acts of the colonial assembly they were subject to various civil and criminal penalties for sundry acts of apostasy, heresy, recusancy, popery, and profanity. He conceded that at the moment these acts were dead letters because "happily the Spirit of [the] times [is] in favor of [the] rights of Conscience."[29] But, ever alert to the fragility of liberty, he warned that it was not enough to rely on the continuation of such a liberal spirit. The "spirit of the times may alter, will alter," he warned, revealing his deepest fears about the susceptibility of republics to corruption and degeneration. "Our rulers will become corrupt, our people careless. A single zealot may commence persecutor, and better men be his victims."[30]

To prevent this latent state of "religious slavery" from ever becoming fully actualized in Virginia, Jefferson argued that it was necessary to move beyond the Virginia Declaration of Rights and establish by law complete freedom of religion and strict separation of church and state. Repudiating one of the most basic presuppositions of Western culture for well over a millennium, he proclaimed that, in the area of religion, government had no legitimate authority over the "operations of the mind" but over "such acts only as are injurious to others."[31] In his view, freedom of religion was one of the natural rights of mankind, and his own rationalistic conception of religion precluded any state interference with it. The essence of religion was the free assent of the human mind to the evidence offered to it concerning the proper relationship between God and man. True religious belief was uncoerced, freely given, a private affair between each individual and God, one in which the state had no rightful authority. He readily conceded that government had the right to intervene when religious beliefs gave rise to actions that threatened public order, but it had no right to favor, promote, or support one system of religious beliefs over another. "God requires every act according to *Belief*,"[32] and true belief presupposed a genuine inner conviction that could never be imposed on the minds of men by external authority. "Reason and free enquiry are the only effectual agents against error," he warned, in an eloquent epitome of his rationalistic approach to religion. "Give a loose to them, they will support the true religion, by bringing every false one to their tribunal, to the test of their investigation. They are the natural enemies of error, and of error only."[33]

But if liberty was an essential precondition for true religion, any alliance between church and state was a clear and present danger to liberty, especially for a people who had chosen to commit themselves to republicanism. Thus, Jefferson brought to bear a wide array of arguments to contest the still widely held assumption that civil encouragement of Christianity through some form of union between church and state was necessary to preserve the fabric of society. Training his sights on the quest for religious uniformity that underlay all such unions, he contended that the goal was not worth the social costs involved. Religious uniformity could only be achieved by stifling the spirit of free inquiry that was responsible for "all improvements in Religion or Philosophy,"[34] by subjecting men to levels of coercion that would merely produce outward conformity and inner hypocrisy among many, and by enabling fallible magistrates to exercise tyrannical powers over the minds of men. Appealing to the experience of the Constantinian Period in Western history, he argued that it proved the essential futility of efforts to achieve uniformity in religion. "Is uniformity attainable? Millions of innocent men, women, and children, since the introduction of Christianity, have been burnt, tortured, fined, imprisoned; yet we have not advanced one inch towards uniformity. What has been the effect of coercion? To make one half the world fools, and the other half hypocrites. To support roguery and error over all the earth."[35] And, citing the counterexamples of Pennsylvania and New York, he pointed out that a religious establishment was not needed for religion and social order to flourish. In light of this record, Jefferson concluded, the grave danger that the union between magisterial and clerical authority naturally posed to republican liberty could only be averted by erecting a strict wall of separation between church and state. Although Jefferson did not use this metaphor until after his election to the presidency, it accurately captured the essence and the spirit of the church-state relationship he sought to achieve in Virginia.[36]

The same mix of rational religion and republican principles suffused Jefferson's epochal Virginia Statute for Religious Freedom. Beginning with the rationalistic premises that God had created the human mind free and insusceptible of restraint, and that all opinions and beliefs involuntarily followed the evidence offered to the mind, Jefferson also justified the relegation of religion and government to institutionally separate spheres by denouncing the long train of abuses that the union of church and state had produced in history. Thus, he arraigned this unholy alliance between priestly and magisterial power for begetting "habits of hypocrisy and meanness" in society, for endowing "fallible and uninspired men" with a tyrannical dominion over the human mind, for maintaining "false religions over the greatest part of the world," for corrupting the "very religion it is meant to encourage," and above all for violating man's natural right to religious freedom. Declaring that civil rights were independent of religious beliefs and that government had no jurisdiction over such beliefs except when they led to overt acts "against peace and good order," he therefore provided for full freedom of religion and a rigid separation of church and state, thereby creating yet another bulwark for republican liberty in its age old contest with power.[37] Or, as he remarked after the Virginia legislature passed this act in 1786, "it is comfortable to see the standard of reason at length erected, after so many ages during which the human mind has been held in vassalage by kings, priests, and nobles; and it is honorable for us to have produced the first legislature who has had the courage to declare that the reason of man may be trusted with the formation of his own opinions."[38]

In place of the traditional alliance between church and state to maintain a Christian society in the Old Dominion, Jefferson proposed an innovative union between the state and public education to help secure the emerging republican order in revolutionary Virginia. In his celebrated Bill for the More General Diffusion of Knowledge, presented to the Virginia legislature in 1779 but never approved, Jefferson sought to achieve two objectives that he regarded as vitally necessary for the preservation of a republican polity and society in his native state. On the one hand he hoped to create an enlightened citizenry by providing all white children in the state with three years of primary education at public expense in order to make them aware of their rights and sensitive to the dangers that power had historically posed to liberty. On the other hand he wished to establish a natural aristocracy based on virtue and merit, instead of birth and wealth, to guide the fortunes of the republican ship of state by offering a more advanced education for a select group of young white Virginia males, including a chosen number of the most promising sons of poorer families whose continued schooling would be funded by the public. In pursuit of these objectives and in keeping with his insistence on drawing a sharp line of demarcation between the sacred and the secular realm in a republican society, Jefferson strongly emphasized the primacy of history over theology in the education of a republican citizenry. While excluding biblical studies from his proposed curriculum, he gave pride of place to the study of ancient and modern history as the primary intellectual means of reinforcing the commitment of revolutionary Virginians and their descendants to republicanism. For, noting the overriding importance of "rendering the people the safe, as they are the ultimate guardians of their own liberty," Jefferson argued, once again revealing his fears about the vulnerability of republics to corruption, that history "by apprising them of the past will enable them to judge of the future; it will avail them of the experience of other times and other nations; it will qualify them as judges of the actions and designs of men; it will enable them to know ambition under every disguise it may assume; and knowing it, to defeat its views."[39]

"The First of Human Sages":
The Quest for the Historical Jesus

If within the parameters of this essay the keynotes of the first half of Jefferson's career were his rejection of Christian orthodoxy and his embrace of natural religion, coupled with his efforts to preserve republican liberty through his struggle for religious freedom and separation of church and state in Virginia, then the keynotes of the last half of his career were his acceptance of what the great German theologian Rudolph Bultmann might have called a demythologized form of Christianity and his growing conviction that it could serve as one anchor for republican virtue in the face of the increasing salience of liberal individualism in America. In his masterpiece of analytical scholarship, *The Quest of the Historical Jesus,* Albert Schweitzer brilliantly surveyed the efforts made by a succession of German scholars from the late eighteenth to the early twentieth century to study the Jesus of history as opposed to the Jesus of faith, so as to ascertain the relationship between the historical facts about Jesus that could be rationally extracted from the New Testament and the dogmas that traditional Christian theology had formulated about his person and mission.[40] If Schweitzer had cast his scholarly gaze across the Atlantic, he would have had to reckon with the protean figure of Jefferson. For Jefferson was the first person in American history to embark upon a quest for the historical Jesus. In the course of this quest he subjected the New Testament to rational analysis and extracted two compilations of extracts from the Gospels that to his mind represented the genuine teachings and deeds of Jesus, *The Philosophy of Jesus* in 1804 and *The Life and Morals of Jesus* in 1819-20, after first having set forth his own estimate of Jesus's general historical significance in his 1803 "Syllabus of an Estimate of the merit of the doctrines of Jesus, compared with those of others."[41] Although in part a personal search for an ultimate meaning in life, Jefferson's quest for the Jesus of history, which led him to accept a demythologized version of Christianity based upon his conception of Jesus as "the first of human Sages,"[42] was also part of his broader encounter with the gradual transformation of the United States from a republican to a liberal society.

Jefferson embarked upon his quest for the historical Jesus in response to four factors that converged during the crisis of American republicanism that began during the 1790s. To begin with, Jefferson was deeply troubled after 1790 by what he perceived to be a breakdown of the new American nation's fundamental consensus on republican values and a concomitant threat to its basic social harmony, both of which he regarded as vital for ensuring the success of the American experiment in republicanism. As the country divided along Federalist and Republican lines, Jefferson became convinced that the very future of republican government and the very existence of a republican society in the United States were at stake. The establishment of the Hamiltonian fiscal system and its accompanying panoply of what Republicans regarded as British forms of social and political corruption, the adoption of a foreign policy that appeased aristocratic Britain while affronting republican France, the use of military force to suppress popular discontent during the Whiskey Rebellion, the creation of a large standing army during the XYZ crisis, and the use of the Sedition Act to silence Republican criticism of the Adams administration—all these things portended nothing less to Jefferson than a settled Federalist design to monarchize American government, anglicize American society, and accentuate American dependence on Britain.[43]

In addition to Federalist policies that threatened to destroy his vision of a virtuous agrarian republic, Jefferson was also concerned that political differences between the two parties were becoming so acrimonious in the late 1790s that they threatened to undermine the social harmony and civility which he considered to be essential for preserving a republican form of government. "You & I have formerly seen warm debates and high political passions," he complained from Philadelphia shortly after assuming the office of vice president to a former associate in the Continental Congress. "But gentlemen of different politics would then speak to each other . . . It is not so now. Men who have been intimate all their lives, cross the streets to avoid meeting, & turn their heads another way, lest they should be obliged to touch their hats."[44] In a political climate like this Jefferson feared that American society would be irrevocably divided into hostile classes and interests, with each one striving to achieve its own selfish ends instead of cooperating harmoniously to achieve the elusive republican goal of the common good. Since Jefferson believed that the preservation of social harmony and civility was partly a matter of personal morality and character, it is not surprising that he became interested in a system of morality that would be more efficacious for this purpose than the one provided by the classical philosophers who had hitherto been his primary ethical guides.

Jefferson's growing concern during the 1790s with the Federalist threat to fundamental republican values and the need to preserve social harmony in the face of accelerating political polarization coincided with his adoption of a more sympathetic attitude toward Christianity than he had previously manifested. This change in attitude was heavily influenced by his reading sometime after 1793 of Dr. Joseph Priestley's *An History of the Corruptions of Christianity*. In this work the noted English chemist, Unitarian theologian, and friend of Jefferson's set forth a highly demythologized version of Christianity which so impressed Jefferson that he adopted key parts of it and later praised the work itself as the "groundwork of my view of this subject" and as one of the bases of "my own faith."[45] Priestley argued that Christianity was originally a simple religion that had been corrupted by the early church fathers in a misguided effort to make it intellectually respectable to pagan philosophers and by later churchmen for the less edifying purpose of subjecting the laity to their control. The essence of true Christianity, Priestley insisted, could be briefly summed up in a few plain propositions. There was but one, non-Trinitarian God, who had given Jesus a special mission to reveal his true nature to the world and to teach men how to live virtuous lives on earth so that they would be rewarded with bliss in the life to come. Jesus was not a member of the godhead, nor did he ever claim to be, but God had signified his approval of Jesus's teachings by empowering him to perform miracles and by raising him from the dead. As a result, apart from the injunctions to worship the one true God and follow the moral precepts of Jesus, everything else in orthodox Christianity was a perversion of the primitive purity of the original Christian message, which had to be purged of its corruptions and restored to its pristine simplicity so as to be made acceptable to modern enlightened men.[46]

Priestley's work deeply impressed Jefferson. It convinced him that the early Christians had a Unitarian concept of God and that therefore an anti-Trinitarian like himself could be a true Christian. It persuaded him that Jesus had never laid claim to divinity, which made Jesus more credible to him as a great moral teacher, Jefferson having previously tended to regard him as a somewhat misguided Galilean enthusiast. It increased his appreciation of Christian morality by convincing him that the dogmas that had led him to reject Christianity as a young man were actually perversions of the original Christian message. Still rejecting on rational grounds the possibility that Jesus had performed miracles or risen from the dead, Jefferson nevertheless accepted Priestley's basic contention that true Christianity was essentially a simple religion whose original emphasis on monotheism and the primacy of morality over dogma had been corrupted over time by the development of metaphysical and theological doctrines that were beyond human understanding and by the introduction of forms of worship that were degrading to a rational man. Thus, by presenting Jefferson with a demystified form of Christianity that comported with his rationalistic world view, Priestley made it possible for him to regard himself as a genuine Christian and helped to launch him on his quest for the authentic teachings of Jesus.

As Jefferson's view of Christianity began to change under the impact of Priestley's writings, he was impelled to consider the relationship between republicanism and Christianity by that importunate Philadelphia physician and social reformer, Dr. Benjamin Rush. Although Jefferson and Rush were both convinced republicans, they had sharply differing perceptions of the ultimate significance of America's republican destiny. Whereas the philosophically rationalistic Jefferson regarded republicanism as an essentially secular movement that was designed to improve humanity and reform society by securing the natural rights of man and expanding the scope of self-government, the theologically universalist Rush viewed it as basically a religious movement that was part of a divine plan to bring about the kingdom of God on earth by freeing mankind from the burdens of royal and ecclesiastical oppression. Convinced that Jefferson's secular outlook on life was blinding him to the most vital dimension of America's republican experiment, the zealous Rush characteristically took it upon himself to convince the erring Virginian that the progress of Christianity and republicanism must go hand in hand to achieve the millennium he so confidently expected.

Thus, in a series of private conversations in Philadelphia in 1798-99 and in subsequent correspondence, Rush pressed this view of the matter on Jefferson and urged him to articulate his religious beliefs. In the course of these conversations, according to Rush's account, Jefferson expressed admiration for Jesus, without conceding his divinity, and expressed his belief that men would be rewarded or punished in a life after death. In the end, of course, Jefferson remained immune to Rush's extravagant millennial hopes. But by forcing him to confront the question of the relationship between Christianity and republicanism at a time when his attitude toward a demythologized version of the former was growing more favorable, Rush was undoubtedly instrumental in helping to persuade Jefferson that Christian morality could serve as a stabilizing force for America's republican experiment by promoting social harmony among the American people.[47]

The final factor that launched Jefferson on his quest for the historical Jesus was the sustained attack Federalists unleashed on his religious views—an assault that Jefferson viewed as part of an unholy Federalist effort to reunite church and state in order to crush freedom of thought in politics and religion. Beginning with an anonymous letter to President Washington in 1792 accusing Jefferson of atheism and continuing during the election of 1796 with a pamphlet by the South Carolina Federalist William L. Smith charging that he was an infidel, these attacks reached a crescendo during Jefferson's second run for the presidency four years later with a barrage of Federalist pamphlets urging voters to reject him as a known enemy of Christianity.[48] Because Jefferson himself had kept his private religious views from the public, Federalist critics made use of selected passages from *Notes on the State of Virginia* to make their case. To this end, they charged that Jefferson's refusal to concede that a "universal flood" was a sufficient explanation for the presence of shells high atop the Andes was a covert attack upon the biblical account of the flooding of the world, which made the author a party to that "war upon revelation [in which] infidels have levelled their batteries against the miraculous *facts* of the scripture: well knowing that if its historical truth can be overturned, there is an end to its claim of inspiration."[49] They cited his "suggestion" that blacks might have been created as a distinct race as proof of his rejection of the scriptural account of the creation of man and alleged that he thereby meant to imply that the "history of the bible, which knows of but *one* [race], is a string of falsehoods from the book of Genesis to that of Revelation; and the whole system of redemption, predicated on the *unity* of the human race, is a cruel fiction."[50] They construed his remark about farmers being the chosen people of God "if ever he had a chosen people" to signify his rejection of the providential role of the Jews in the Christian scheme of salvation. They argued that his refusal to include biblical instruction for children in his proposed system of public education for Virginia indicated that he opposed religious education in general.

But by far the worst part of Jefferson's only published book, in the eyes of Federalist critics, was the argument that the state should refrain from interfering with religion because "it does me no injury for my neighbour to say there are twenty gods or no god. It neither picks my pocket nor breaks my leg."[51] Instead of demonstrating Jefferson's respect for religious diversity, they insisted that this statement betrayed a level of religious indifference that threatened to produce disturbing social consequences. "Let my neighbor once persuade himself that there is no God," a New York minister proclaimed, "and he will soon pick my pocket, and break not only my *leg* but my *neck*. If there be no God, there is no law, no future account; government then is the ordinance of man only, and we cannot be subject for conscience sake."[52] In light of this evidence, Federalist pamphleteers warned, Jefferson was an atheist, an infidel, or at best a Deist whose election would call down the wrath of God on the American people and lead to social chaos. While disdaining as a matter of principle to reply to critics of his religious views, Jefferson deeply resented their efforts to equate his rejection of Christian orthodoxy with a generalized hostility to religion. Ironically, by impelling Jefferson to reexamine his own religious views, these attacks played a part in leading him to accept a variant of the very religion to which Federalists charged he was unalterably opposed.

Under the impact of these four factors, Jefferson embarked upon a quest for the historical Jesus that led him to embrace a demythologized Christian faith—one which rejected all mythic, mysterious, and miraculous elements in Christianity and sought to return to what he understood to be the primitive purity and simplicity of the original Christian message. The cornerstone of Jefferson's demythologized faith was an unshakeable belief in a monotheistic God, the creator and sustainer of the universe, the ultimate ground of being, who revealed himself through the natural wonders of his rationally structured cosmos and not through any special revelation directly imparted to man and written down in sacred scripture. Jefferson lavishly praised Jesus for making the one true God worthy of human worship insofar as he took "for his type the best qualities of the human head and heart, wisdom, justice, goodness, and adding to them power, ascribed all of these, but in infinite perfection, to the supreme being."[53] But he continued to believe that the one true God mankind ought to worship and adore was not the triune deity of orthodox Christianity, for to him trinitarian doctrine was a contradiction in terms, a relapse into polytheism, the worst of all the alleged corruptions of Christianity.[54]

Next in importance to the unity of God were the moral teachings of Jesus.

Jefferson's examination of the New Testament convinced him that Jesus had not formulated a complete system of morality, because he died before reaching full intellectual maturity, because he never set down his teachings in writing, and because of
the intellectual shortcomings of the disciples who first wrote them down many
years after his death. Yet Jefferson was equally convinced that the fragmentary teachings of Jesus that did survive constituted the "outlines of a system of the most sublime morality which has ever fallen from the lips of man."[55] Jefferson continued to
admire the classical Epicureans and Stoics for teaching mankind the art of self-discipline, but he now found them seriously deficient because of their failure to instill
"peace, charity, and love to our fellow men" or to embrace "with benevolence, the
whole family of mankind."[56] Classical ethics, in short, were insufficient for guiding
the moral sense of a republican nation dedicated to the common good as well as the
individual pursuit of happiness. In contrast, Jefferson now esteemed Jesus for offering an unsurpassed system of morality inasmuch as it took account of individual
motivation when judging the morality of any act and more importantly because it
instilled "universal philanthropy, not only to kindred and friends, to neighbors and
countrymen, but to all mankind, gathering all into one family, under the bonds of
love, charity, peace, common wants, and common aids."[57] In short, Christian morality was well suited to temper the pursuit of private interests with a concern for the
overriding common good and thereby promote republican virtue among the
American people.

Belief in the one true God and adherence to the moral teachings of Jesus would
lead, Jefferson assumed, to some sort of reward in a life after death. He especially
praised Jesus for preaching the doctrine of a life in the hereafter in order to encourage virtuous behavior in the here and now. In addition to the obvious social utility
of this doctrine, Jefferson also embraced it for an intensely personal reason: a long-
ing that grew stronger as he grew older for reunion with his departed relatives and
friends. Jefferson strongly rejected the Christian doctrine of hell, apparently because
the concept of eternal punishment was inconsistent with his notion of divine
benevolence, and therefore presumably agreed with the Universalists that in time
everyone would be reconciled with the deity.[58]

Jefferson's quest for the historical Jesus led him to revere the founder of
Christianity as the greatest moral teacher in history. He did not believe that Jesus
was the son of God, nor did he think that Jesus had ever claimed such an exalted
rank in the cosmic hierarchy. He conceded that Jesus believed himself to be divine-
ly inspired, but he excused such an unfortunate lapse from grace as the inevitable
result of Jesus's having lived among an allegedly superstitious people who regarded
the "fumes of the most disordered imaginations" as "special communications of the
deity."[59] Instead, he admired Jesus as the preeminent reformer of the Jewish religion
whose extraordinary moral sense had enabled him to enunciate a universally valid
body of moral teachings. In Jefferson's considered judgment, Jesus was the "Herald

of truths reformatory of the religions of mankind in general, but more immediately of that of his own countrymen, impressing them with more sublime and more
worthy ideas of the Supreme being, teaching them the doctrine of a future state of
rewards and punishments, and inculcating the love of mankind, instead of the antisocial spirit with which the Jews viewed all other nations."[60] But since in the end
Jefferson regarded Jesus as human rather than divine, he accepted his moral teachings because he considered them reasonable and socially beneficial, not because he
regarded them as a product of divine revelation.

Belief in the unity of God, acceptance of the moral precepts of Jesus, hope for life
after death, and reverence for Jesus as history's greatest moral reformer—such were
the constituent elements of Jefferson's demythologized Christian faith and, or so he
thought, the faith of primitive Christianity as well. Otherwise he rejected the traditional theological and ecclesiological doctrines of Christian orthodoxy as corruptions of Jesus's original message. He attributed these so-called corruptions to the
machinations of the clergy, whose exaltation of mystery over reason and dogma over
morality was allegedly part of a diabolical plot to subject the laity to clerical power.
Purged of the "artificial constructions" of the clergy, he believed that Christianity
would be the "purest system of morals ever before preached to man."[61] Freed from
clerical power, he predicted, in an epitome of his ideal form of religion, "We should
all then, like the quakers, live without an order of priests, moralise for ourselves, follow the oracle of conscience, and say nothing about what no man can understand,
nor therefore believe; for I suppose belief to be the assent of the mind to an intelligi-
ble proposition."[62] In the end, therefore, Jefferson's demythologized Christianity
remained true to the Enlightenment drive to rationalize and demystify religion.

"A Religion of All Others Most Friendly to Liberty": Demythologized Christianity and Republican Virtue

Jefferson was generally reticent about discussing his personal religious views except
with those he regarded as reasonable men. In part this was because of the heterodox
nature of those beliefs, in part because of his conviction that religion was a private
affair between each person and God, and in part because of his visceral aversion to
public controversy. In fact, Jefferson's eagerness to avoid direct personal involvement in public controversies and his consequent reliance on others to defend his
views before the bar of public opinion are two of the most significant features of his
public career. Witness, for example, the numerous occasions during the 1790s when
he prevailed upon James Madison to respond in print to various Hamiltonian
newspaper sallies against the Republican cause, instead of rebutting Hamilton himself. Given the constraints under which he normally chose to operate, therefore,
Jefferson went to remarkable lengths to promote the cause of demythologized
Christianity in the United States.

To begin with, Jefferson's two inaugural addresses guardedly expressed his preference for demythologized Christianity and his belief in the need to reform what he regarded as the corruptions of Christian orthodoxy. In the first inaugural, for example, he clearly emphasized the primacy he gave to Christian morality over Christian dogma by enumerating as one of the American nation's blessings that it was "enlightened by a benign religion, professed indeed & practiced in various forms, yet all of them inculcating honesty, truth, temperance gratitude & the love of man, acknowledging & adoring an overruling providence, which by all it's dispensations proves that it delights in the happiness of man here, & his greater happiness hereafter." In the second, moreover, in a passage that ostensibly described the deleterious effect of traditionalism among American Indians but was actually meant to be a veiled attack on the conservatism of his Federalist and clerical detractors, Jefferson lashed out at those who "inculcate a sanctimonious reverence for the customs of their ancestors; that whatsoever they did, must be done through all time; that reason is a false guide, and to advance under its counsel, in their physical, moral, or political condition, is perilous innovation; that their duty is to remain as their Creator made them, ignorance being safety, and knowledge full of danger; in short, my friends, among them is seen the action and counteraction of good sense and bigotry; they, too, have their anti-philosophers, who find an interest in keeping things in their present state, who dread reformation, and exert all their faculties to maintain the ascendancy of habit over the duty of improving our reason, and obeying its mandates."[63]

Jefferson was even more pointed in his private correspondence, where he discussed the need to demythologize Christianity on a number of occasions during the last twenty-six years of his life. Christianity, he told a Vermont Republican leader shortly after his election to the presidency, "is a religion of all others most friendly to liberty, science, and the freest expansions of the human mind"—but only "when divested of the rags in which they [the clergy] have inveloped it, and brought to the original purity and simplicity of it's benevolent institutor."[64] Although he usually confined himself to general calls for purging Christianity of its corruptions, in private he believed that rationalizing and demystifying it would eventually entail the rejection of such things as the "immaculate conception of Jesus, his deification, the creation of the world by him, his miraculous powers, his resurrection and visible ascension, his corporeal presence in the Eucharist, the Trinity, original sin, atonement, regeneration, election, orders of Hierarchy &c."[65] Otherwise the need to emphasize the moral teachings of Jesus that united the American people as opposed to the dogmas of the Christian churches that divided them was a recurring refrain in Jefferson's correspondence from 1800 until his death.[66]

Not content with public Aesopian language and private calls for deep religious change in the new American nation, Jefferson twice sought to encourage Unitarian religious thinkers to produce works that were clearly designed to promote public discussion of the merits of demythologized Christianity. In 1803 he encouraged Joseph Priestley to undertake a systematic comparison of classical philosophy, Judaism, and the teachings of Jesus, so as to demonstrate that Jesus's "system of morality was the most benevolent and sublime probably that has ever been taught." Such a work was needed, Jefferson argued, to rescue Jesus from "those who pretend to be his special disciples, and who have disfigured and sophisticated his actions and precepts, from views and special interests, so as to induce the unthinking part of mankind to throw off the whole system in disgust, and to pass sentence as an imposter on the most innocent, the most benevolent the most eloquent and sublime character that ever has been exhibited to man."[67] But Priestley's resultant work, *The Doctrines of Heathen Philosophy, Compared with Those of Revelation,* written during his final illness and published posthumously in 1804, fell far short of Jefferson's hopes, being a long, diffuse, and badly written discussion of often abstruse philosophical and theological differences between classicism and Christianity that failed to highlight the peculiar excellence of Christian morality.

Undaunted by this setback, Jefferson returned to the fray thirteen years later, lending his enthusiastic support to a proposed naturalistic biography of Jesus by Francis Adrian Van der Kemp, a Dutch-born Unitarian minister whose intellectual reach often exceeded his grasp. In fact, Jefferson was so enthused by Van der Kemp's plans for a rationalistic biography of Jesus that he even offered to allow him to include in it two expressions of Jefferson's own demythologized version of Christianity, subject to the concealment of their Jeffersonian authorship—his "Syllabus of an Estimate of the merit of the doctrines of Jesus, compared with those of others" and his *Philosophy of Jesus.* With all three of these works between the covers of one book, Jefferson confidently predicted, his excitement getting the better of his syntax, "the world will see, after the fogs shall be dispelled, in which for 14 centuries he [Jesus] has been inveloped by Jugglers to make money of him, when the genuine character shall be exhibited, which they have dressed up in the rags of an Impostor, the world, I say, will at length see the immortal merit of this first of human Sages."[68] Alas for Jefferson's hopes, Van der Kemp did not turn out to be an American Strauss or Renan, for he never wrote his projected life of Jesus. But if Jefferson was disappointed by these two exponents of Unitarianism, he was heartened by signs of the progress of their creed in America after the War of 1812, seeing in its anti-trinitarianism and emphasis on the moral precepts of Jesus a welcome return to the pristine purity of primitive Christianity which led him to predict that the "present generation will see Unitarianism become the general religion of the United states."[69]

Finally, Jefferson's eagerness to promote a demythologized version of Christianity was so great that he virtually incorporated it into his curriculum for the University of Virginia. To be sure, he omitted a professor of divinity from this state-supported institution in accordance with the imperatives of protecting religious freedom and maintaining separation of church and state. But in his basic blueprint for the university he also noted that there would be no need for such a professorship because "the proofs of the being of a God, the creator, preserver, and supreme ruler of the universe, the author of all the relations of morality, and of the laws and obligations these infer, will be within the province of the professor of ethics; to which, adding the developments of these moral obligations, of those in which all sects agree, with a knowledge of the languages, Hebrew, Greek, and Latin, a basis will be formed common to all sects."[70] The existence of God, the grounding of morality in him, and the principles of morality common to all Christian sects—do these not constitute most of the elements of Jefferson's own demythologized Christianity?

Jefferson's interest in encouraging the spread of a demythologized form of Christianity among the American people can best be understood within the context of his response to what he perceived to be in effect a growing crisis of liberal individualism in the United States. During the half century or so after Jefferson wrote the Declaration of Independence, the United States was gradually transformed from a republican society, in which the operative assumption was that private interests must ultimately be subordinated to the overarching public good, to a liberal society, in which the guiding principle was that the pursuit of private interests would actually achieve the general good. Jefferson was deeply troubled by many features of this transformation, starting as early as the Federalist-Republican party strife of the 1790s, but especially in the aftermath of the War of 1812. At that time incipient signs of accelerated commercialization, urbanization, and manufacturing in the North led Jefferson to fear that the growing dependence of artisans, craftsmen, and farmers on a narrow circle of bankers, merchants, and manufacturers would gradually undermine the personal freedom required for the pursuit of republican virtue in that vitally important section of the nation. The establishment of the Second Bank of the United States and the speculative fever that culminated in the great Panic of 1819 revived Jefferson's apprehensions about an unsavory alliance between the central government and the monied interest that would corrupt and despoil the agrarian majority throughout the country and ultimately destroy the social structure he regarded as absolutely essential for ensuring the success of the American experiment in republican self-government. The invocation of the Hamiltonian doctrine of loose construction of the Constitution by John Marshall's Supreme Court in a series of legal decisions that dealt sharp constitutional blows to the hallowed Republican doctrine of state sovereignty rekindled Jefferson's fears of a new wave of government centralization, which he considered as intrinsically dangerous to local and individual liberty. And the crisis over slavery in Missouri convinced him that the Union he had done so much to create faced two potentially fatal threats to its very existence—the possibility of an irreconcilable sectional conflict between the North and the South over slavery, and a sinister effort by Northern Federalists to exploit antislavery sentiment in order to revive their political fortunes and thereby resurrect their traditional policies of political and economic centralization, which Jefferson ranked as among the gravest threats to republican liberty.

Jefferson responded to the perceived crisis of liberal individualism in a variety of ways. In response to what he regarded as a dangerous decline of the nation's true republican spirit, he advocated the establishment of ward republics on the local level to regenerate the popular commitment to republicanism and led the struggle to create the University of Virginia in order to train a natural aristocracy of merit and virtue according to the tenets of the true republican gospel. In reaction to the centralizing decisions of the Marshall Court and the efforts of the Henry Clay entrepreneurial wing of the Republican party to have the federal government play an active role in promoting American economic development, Jefferson called for a renewed commitment to the traditional Republican principles of strict construction of the Constitution and limited central government. And in the face of mounting sectional tensions over slavery, he advocated a renewal of Republican party unity to preserve the Union and called for the diffusion of slavery beyond its current limits in the curious hope that this would somehow hasten the day when the peculiar institution could be safely abolished and the freed slaves colonized far from America's shores.

Within this framework it seems clear that Jefferson's various efforts after 1800 to promote the moral imperatives of Jesus that united the American people while deemphasizing the dogmas of the Christian churches that divided them was at bottom a hitherto neglected aspect of his encounter with the forces that were transforming the United States from a republican to a liberal society. By encouraging the acceptance of a Christian social ethic that stressed the values of harmony and cooperation among the American people, Jefferson was essentially trying to anchor republican virtue against the rising tide of liberal individualism that was gradually eroding the republican order he had dedicated his career to creating. From the beginning there had been a basic tension in Jefferson's thought between his liberal emphasis on the pursuit of individual happiness and his republican assumption that there was an overriding public good that was greater than the sum total of these pursuits. As the balance in American society shifted from republicanism to liberalism, threatening to destroy Jefferson's ideal of a virtuous agrarian republic, he reacted by reemphasizing the civic humanist features of his republican political ideology. In the process he evidently concluded that a demythologized Christian ethic could be instrumental in tempering the growing liberal pursuit of private interest in America with a classical republican concern for the common good. But in view of the wave of evangelicalism that swept across the land after 1800 during the Second Great Awakening, rolling back the tide of the religious rationalism which Jefferson best exemplified, perhaps it would be more accurate to say that in this particular respect Jefferson's republicanism was less the last act of the Age of the Renaissance than the last gasp of the Age of Enlightenment.[71]

SUZANNE W. MORSE

Ward Republics: The Wisest Invention for Self-Government

"Divide the county into wards of such size as that every citizen can attend, when called on, and act in person . . . and by making every citizen an acting member of the government, and in the offices nearest and most interesting to him, will attach him by his strongest feelings to the independence of his country and its republican constitution . . . ."

Thomas Jefferson to Samuel Kercheval
July 12, 1816

After leaving the presidency and returning to Monticello, Thomas Jefferson focused considerable attention on the implementation of a local form of government called ward republics. Jefferson saw the creation of a system of small republics—wards—as the full realization of republicanism and the only way to protect self-government. These wards, as Jefferson envisioned them, were to be small enough so that citizens could participate *directly* in deciding public issues of importance to the community, but large enough to carry on the functions of local government.

This discussion of Jefferson's theory of ward republics is based on his fundamental belief that the strength of the Republic lay in the capacity of its citizens to participate in the public realm and his dedication to the notion that citizens must decide their own fate. Although the concept of wards came later in Jefferson's life, after he had returned to Monticello from his service as president, the idea was a predictable outcome of his circumstances and experiences. The concept of smaller units in the newly formed democracy was an evolution of Jefferson's earlier thinking, not a departure from it. His early interest in the Greeks, his continuing opposition to the finality of the Constitution, his confidence that citizens must have a role in government, and his commitment to the rural, agrarian way of life forged the ideas that undergird his ward theory. Writing to John Tyler on May 28, 1816, he laid the philosophic groundwork for the ward republics:

> Purely and simply, [republicanism] means a government by its citizens in mass, acting directly and personally, according to rules established by the majority; and that every other government is more or less republican, in proportion as it has its composition more or less of this ingredient of the direct action of citizens.[1]

Jefferson's circumstances before 1816 also give some insight into why the wards became so prominent in his thinking. First, Jefferson had had several decades to observe the new nation at work. He opposed the restrictiveness of the Constitution, but it was not until he had seen the new nation at work that he began to think about the practical antidotes to his fears of representation and its possible outcome, citizen isolation. Second, he was able to draw on his international experience in this reflective period and begin to sort out his objections to large urban areas, primarily in Europe, and think through what a different American scenario might be. Although his opposition to cities yielded to the inevitable demands of economics, he remained leery that city-dwellers could ever participate in public politics or that cities themselves could ever be places for democracy. As the early Greeks referred to those not in civic service as *idotes,* so Jefferson held in contempt inhabitants of cities who did not participate in civic affairs. He came to believe that cities were a certainty in modern times but that they must be modified to create a place for necessary self-governing. Third, his experiences as president, particularly with the failure of the Embargo, convinced him of the importance of maintaining the revolutionary spirit and of keeping citizens from pursuing public interests over private ones. Finally, Jefferson's lack of clarity on precisely how the wards would function is deliberate. He knew fundamentally that the basis of a democracy was citizen participation. At the same time he knew that communities can have many functions. His strategy was to have the idea of the small republics accepted and let their value for different purposes evolve. As this essay will show, the most difficult part of the ward theory is the creation of a framework for how citizens might practice politics. That framework is critical to Jefferson's theory but has been overshadowed by aspects that are easier to implement and alas, understand.

Therefore, because of circumstances and experiences the idea of the ward system and its necessity to the newly formed Republic came late in Jefferson's life and is not part of his formal writings and is only found in personal correspondence. As political philosopher Hannah Arendt points out, the only detailed descriptions of the wards are in Jefferson's letters, written primarily in 1816, and these letters repeat rather than expand the concept.[2] Jefferson, however, does give an indication in his larger writings on his sources for the ward concept. He refers to four primary models of governance in different writings: Native American tribal councils; the ancient

Greek city-state, *polis;* the Anglo-Saxon hundreds which divided territory into composites of a hundred men; and the New England town meeting. Each of these unique civic structures informs Jefferson's concept of ward republics and illuminates his thinking about the role of government and citizen participation.

Jefferson and Citizen Participation in Government

In his *Notes on the State of Virginia,* Jefferson addresses the self-governance of Native Americans. Jefferson greatly admired the fact that Native Americans operated, in his view, without government (this fact could be disputed because of the way tribal law and custom operated), but he admitted that larger populations must have government to exist. The Native American model divided the large tribe down into smaller tribal councils for decision making. Jefferson's observation of the tribal organization of Native American societies informed his vision of ward republics as vehicles for governing in its most basic and perhaps most necessary level.[3]

The Greek *polis* was a place where male citizens of a certain standing could come together to discuss affairs of state. For the early Greeks, each man was a political being and was expected to take an active role in public decisions. Jefferson was attracted to the citizen participation component of the *polis,* but he moderated his design of the ward republics to accommodate a clear separation of public and private life. An admirer of the Greeks, Jefferson drew from Aristotle's notion that citizenship requires direct participation in the affairs of state. Aristotle contended that in order to mete justice and distribute responsibility, it is necessary to have a small democracy—citizens must know each other in order to make those decisions.[4] This idea comes forth in Jefferson's letter to Samuel Kercheval, when he argued that in the ward republics, judges, juries, and sheriffs should be elected by the people. This idea comes in part because of Jefferson's concern over the possible authoritarian perspective of appointed positions and his feeling that citizens should know and be known by those in law enforcement positions.[5] Despite Jefferson's admiration of the *polis,* he did not advocate the symbiotic relationship between the public and private that the Greeks had. For the Greeks, writes Sartori, *man* and *citizen* meant exactly the same thing. The *polis* was sovereign in the sense that the individuals that compose it are completely subject to it.[6] Jefferson's American modification of the Greek *polis* was more in line with Athenian statesman Pericles's idea that average citizens should join the aristocracy in executing the life of the community.[7] These ideas of the reciprocal relationship between citizens and the state and the relationship among citizens were important to Jefferson and influenced his thinking about the importance of self-governing.

Jefferson's reference to the Anglo-Saxon idea of hundreds was expressed in a letter to John Tyler, May 26, 1810, where he discussed dividing the counties into "hundreds." The implication was that the wards were to consist of a hundred men.[8]

Further, he wanted the wards to be geographically concise, perhaps five or six miles square, so that convening would be practical.[9]

Jefferson seemed to speak of ward republics and the New England town meetings as synonymous. He wrote: "These wards, called townships in New England, are the vital principle of their governments, and have proved themselves the wisest invention ever devised by the wit of man for the perfect exercise of self-government, and for its preservation."[10]

Jefferson saw the elements of self-governing, direct participation, and local politics encompassed in the town meetings. They represented both a physical space and a vehicle where every citizen could have a voice. Jefferson viewed the town meetings as a model for the practical implementation of his concept of wards.

Jefferson's commitment to the ward system and his total belief in it were expressed in an 1810 letter to Governor John Tyler, where writes that he does not want to return to the Virginia legislature but rather will devote his time to the "two great measures without which no republic can maintain itself." These were the ward republics and the general education of the citizenry.[11] His commitment to the cause of the wards continued to be a preoccupation, and as he wrote to John Cartwright, "As Cato concluded every speech with the words, *Carthage delenda est* [Carthage must be destroyed] so do I every opinion, with injunction, 'divide the county into wards.'"[12]

Although the idea of ward democracy came late in Jefferson's life and writings, the importance of the message is not diluted. Hannah Arendt was the first political philosopher to recognize the significance of wards to Jefferson's political thought and to analyze what he meant—or what they meant—in the functioning of a democracy. Arendt views the concept of wards not as political hyperbole but as fundamental to Jefferson's philosophy. She contends that Jefferson's reference to Cato was "no idle slip of the tongue" used in Latin quotations; it was meant to emphasize that Jefferson thought the absence of such a subdivision of the country constituted a vital threat to the very existence of the country.[13] This emphasis, claims Arendt, "was an exposition of his most cherished political idea, which, alas turned out to be as incomprehensible to posterity as it had been to his contemporaries."[14]

Writers since Arendt concur that the ward system forms the core of Jefferson's classical republican theory. Political theorist Garrett Sheldon writes: "The center of Jefferson's classical republican theory is his conception of ward democracy, with its educational, political and economic components, and its theory of leadership and representation that leads into Jefferson's idea of federalism."[15] Sheldon is quite right that Jefferson's vision for the wards was broad. Jefferson's preoccupation with ward republics, however, had less to do with geography and economics and more to do with a functioning democracy. On the one hand, he feared the possibilities of representation but on the other he dreaded the passivity that could result from it. He felt that some kind of local governmental unit was necessary to maintain citizen interest and the revolutionary spirit that made the independent America possible and to teach these new citizens the skills of citizenship. Formal education was clearly in Jefferson's mind as one function that the wards could perform, but the *political education* they provided was of even greater concern.

Of all the founders Thomas Jefferson was the only one who saw the necessity for an involved citizenry. James Madison, Alexander Hamilton, and others at the time viewed the mostly uneducated citizenry as prone to forming factions that would promote self-interests at the expense of the common good. They believed that public decision making should be left to the representatives of the people not the people themselves. Jefferson, however, was skeptical of representation as the only way to decide public issues. This skepticism continued in his later years as he called for a system of local democracy through the ward republics. He believed that every generation had both a right and an obligation to determine its own destiny and that participation in the wards could help make that revisitation possible.

The ward republics were to be designated as parts of the community or township, small enough for citizens to make necessary public decisions, where certain appropriate functions of government could take place. This is the extent of the fundamental idea that Jefferson revealed. His writings gave hints and suggestions on ways that wards could function but were not specific as to the implementation. Jefferson provided the most helpful insights for modern-day implementation when he talked about what should happen as a result of the ward system. In them, as he wrote to Samuel Kercheval on July 12, 1816, "the voice of the whole people would be fairly, fully, and peaceably expressed, discussed, and decided by the common reason."[16] An earlier letter to John Tyler, written May 26, 1810, maintained that "these little republics would be the main strength of the great one."[17]

What these two letters suggest is a democratic plan for the new country that placed citizens at its core. Despite his earlier differences with the Constitution, Jefferson's system of wards was to supplement and protect the Constitution—not provide a substitute. Jefferson's concern was that representation would replace the important investment of time, energy, and thought that had been in place before and during the Revolutionary War. Although Jefferson did indeed oppose the Constitution, and said so from Paris, it became almost a metaphor in his writings for the kind of rigidness and stricture that he feared most for the new country.

In Matthews's interpretation of Jefferson's writings on the wards, he cites letters to Governor Tyler (May 26, 1810); to Joseph Cabell (February 2, 1816); and to Samuel Kercheval (September 5, 1816), as revealing a basic outline of the primary functions of the wards. Matthews determined four responsibilities of the ward republics. The first was to ensure the balance and security of power at home, by making wards the headquarters of local militia. Jefferson's experience with the lack of enforcement of the Embargo and his belief that the country needed citizen-soldiers confirmed his view that local militia in the wards would increase the response and readiness should the military be needed. Second, the wards were to preserve and encourage the revolutionary spirit of 1776. Jefferson celebrated the call to arms and the call for common purpose that the Revolution evoked. This spirit provided the citizenry with both the inclination and the challenge to think critically about their government on a regular basis. Whether this is Jefferson's call to redefine government every generation is less certain, but part of the reason for this reaffirmation was his disappointment that the citizenry did not embrace or obey the rules of the Embargo. He felt that the wards should be small enough so that citizens could maintain their commitment to the government and its policies as well as have a voice of their own. Third, the wards would provide a general education for citizens. Schools were to be created in each ward to make them more accessible. In a letter to Joseph Cabell (November 28, 1820), Jefferson states that each ward should establish a school and supply it with teachers. He was adamant about the importance of an educated citizenry and viewed the size of the wards as conducive to allowing more citizens to receive an education. He believed strongly in local support of education. The fourth and final function of the wards was to create and maintain a public space for the daily activity of local politics. This political practice would allow citizens to make the public decisions appropriate to the wards and would strengthen their skills for self-government.[18]

A review of this list of four shows that all of the functions are related directly to Jefferson's republican theory; but two—maintaining the revolutionary spirit and providing a place to practice democratic politics—are at its center. They reflect Jefferson's belief that if American democracy was to survive, let alone flourish, its citizens must be educated, must be willing to question and challenge the system, and must have a place for even the most ordinary citizens among them to practice the art of citizenship. In fact, providing a place and opportunity to practice politics was perhaps the essence of Jefferson's theory of wards. He knew that without the habit and practice of deliberation, Americans might retreat and isolate themselves from each other to such an extent that there would be little common action or thought.

Whether recognized as Jeffersonian or not, the practicality of local governing and oversight is a part of our democratic life. Public education in this country is essentially local. Not withstanding forced busing or rules and regulations handed down by city, county, and state school boards, public education tends to be thought of as part of a community, if not a neighborhood. Although Jefferson would be aghast at the intervention—alas, interference—of higher bodies, it could be said that part of his idea of the wards has been fulfilled: local and universal education does exist.

The need for the second function—local militia—has, of course, changed over time. Although the idea of the citizen-soldier has never been implemented as Jefferson envisioned it, his concerns for readiness and locality have been met in part by an all-volunteer armed forces and the creation of the National Guard.

If two of Jefferson's ideas have essentially been carried out, the two remaining functions, maintaining the revolutionary spirit and providing a place to practice politics, are yet to be fulfilled. Writes Matthews, "The creation of public space is intimately linked with the maintenance of a spirit of revolution in the society at large. Having been in the foreground of several revolutions, Jefferson appears to have found the experiences refreshing. His letters on revolution convey a sense of catharsis, of cleansing, of providing an opportunity to begin again."[19] In Arendt's interpretation of the importance of Jefferson's ideas, she places them in the context of the other revolutionary experiments of the modern world, namely, the French Revolution and the Russian Revolution. Although Jefferson's views exceeded the experiences of the Parisian Commune or the soviets, all were models of kinds of citizen councils and groups that emerged during the nineteenth and twentieth centuries. Arendt observes:

> Each time they appeared, they sprang up as the spontaneous organs of the people, not only outside of all revolutionary parties, but entirely unexpected by them and their leaders. Like Jefferson's proposals, they were utterly neglected by statesmen, historians, political theorists, and most importantly, by the revolutionary tradition itself.... they failed to understand to what extent the council system confronted them with an entirely new form of government, with a new public space for freedom which was constituted and organized during the course of the revolution itself.[20]

Some scholars contend that the concept of the wards was Jefferson's way of emphasizing the "generational revolution" both literally and figuratively; Matthews interprets Jefferson's dedication to the ward idea as a way to "keep the spirit of change alive."[21] For all of Jefferson's resistance to revolution, he wrote James Madison in 1787 saying, "I hold it that a little rebellion now and then is a good thing—"[22]—it was a spirit of stable rebellion that he was really after. As theorist A. J. Beitzinger explains, "Jefferson's remarks were the rhetoric of exaggeration. He was prudent and cognizant of the fact that the general must be understood in terms of the particular. He could extol rebellion but admit that the peaceful making or amending of the Constitution, as well as election served the purpose well."[23]

The American Revolution provided the cause, if not the opportunity, for citizens to unite and express their views. Jefferson's vision for the wards was not to recreate revolution, but to encourage citizens to stay attached and engaged in the affairs of their country. Although Jefferson emphasized the importance of revolution to the health of a democratic society and even conceded that a little blood must be shed, it can be argued that change and reflection were what he sought. One may posit that even the most ardent proponent of rebellion would not have wanted the one that occurred in America in 1861.

At the heart of the theory of wards was that citizens must practice politics regularly and participate in public affairs of state as appropriate to a local level of government. Jefferson carefully spelled this out in his letter to Samuel Kercheval on July 12, 1816: "We should thus marshal our government into, 1, the general federal republic, for all concerns foreign and federal; 2, that of the State, for what relates to our citizens exclusively; 3, the county republics, for duties and concerns of the counties; and 4, the ward republics, for small, and yet numerous and interesting concerns of the neighborhood."[24]

Jefferson was afraid that the transfer of power from the towns, capitals, and states to the federal government would leave citizens with no place to practice politics except on election day. He felt that this would create a vacuum that would encourage, or at least allow, tyranny and corruption to ferment. Further, as he wrote to Kercheval, he believed that it made ultimate sense to organize the country in such a way "that all matters, great and small, can be managed to perfection. And the whole cemented by giving to every citizen, personally, a part in the administration of public affairs."[25]

This four-tiered pyramid of governance—federal, state, county, and ward—was found lacking by Alexis de Tocqueville when he visited America in 1831-32. Rather than the pyramid Jefferson envisioned, Tocqueville observed only two actual systems of government rather than four, "the one fulfilling the ordinary duties and responding to the daily and infinite calls of a community, the other circumscribed within certain limits and exercising an exceptional authority over the general interests of the country."[26] What Tocqueville observed and Jefferson feared was a system of government that lacked a balance of participation and decision making and that was overly reliant on the federal branch.

This imbalance contributes, in part, to Arendt's analysis of Jefferson's fear of governmental corruption. Jefferson disliked the representative system and feared the lack of direct political participation, but he also feared the corruption of the people themselves. It is when "private interests invade the public domain, that is, they spring from below and not above" that corruption occurs.[27] Corruption happens when people have a share of public power and learn how to manipulate it. Jefferson understood this and prescribed through the wards a way to avoid it. Arendt's interpretation embellishes Jefferson's idea: "The only remedies against the misuse of power by private individuals lie in the public realm itself, in the light which exhibits each deed enacted within the boundaries, in the very visibility to which it exposes all those who make it . . . what he perceived as mortal danger was that of the Constitution."[28]

Jefferson's reasoning for the ward republics was to put private citizens in the "light" of the public realm, a critical point that is often overlooked. Jefferson was attempting not only to protect the people from the government but the people from themselves. His emphasis on the practice of political skills came in part from his larger theory about the moral sense of man. Garrett Sheldon analyzes Jefferson's theory using three components:

That theory has three interrelated qualities: (1) the human capacity for moral choice, or the knowledge of good and evil, and the freedom to act on that knowledge in choosing the good; (2) an innate identification with others, a feeling of sympathy for others' concerns and sufferings, and a pleasure in the relief of others' pain and their attaining happiness; and (3) from the combination of these two qualities, a natural sense of justice, making social life possible and beneficial, as this appreciation for justice allows the individual to feel concern for the good of others and for the whole community of which he is a part.[29]

It is this view of human beings and his theories of self-government that ultimately undergird Jefferson's concept of wards. Jefferson continued to assert throughout his writings that there was a compatibility between moral human beings and political ones. Although his faith in mankind wavered somewhat in later years, Jefferson embraced the notion of civic humanism and believed that human beings realize their morality and their potential only after civic participation and public interaction. He believed that any conflict felt by citizens between their moral selves and their political selves could be resolved by providing both the opportunity and place to practice self-governance. Jefferson knew profoundly, as Arendt and others note, that left to their own devices, citizens would allow the obligations and responsibilities of citizenship to give way to the benefits. The important work of citizenship comes between revolutions. Jefferson's call for a revisitation of the Constitution every generation not withstanding, it was this spark of liberty between revolutions—and the encouragement of generational changes—that the wards could encourage and cement. For democratic self-government to work, it was critical, in Jefferson's mind, that there be a citizen balance to the representative form of government. He saw such a balance coming in the graduated responsibilities of the various levels of government with the wards forming the base that would both meet and respond to direct citizen needs.

From Ward Republics to Townships and Beyond

Throughout the nineteenth century and into the twentieth, it became apparent that the idea of the ward republics would be subsumed into counties and municipalities and would not be implemented as Jefferson had imagined. His idea of direct democracy seemed infeasible in all but the very smallest of places. In the 1960s, however, urbanologist Lewis Mumford returned to the issue and wrote of the importance to functioning democracy of smaller political entities, namely townships. He describes a township "as a political organization that encloses a group of towns, villages, hamlets, and the open country that surrounds them: it performs the functions of local government, including providing schools and the care of local roads without accepting the long-established division between town and country."[30] Mumford laments the omission of the township from either the federal or state constitution, saying that it "was one of the tragic oversights of post-revolutionary political development. Thus, the abstract political system of democracy lacked concrete organs."[31] Mumford's townships and Jefferson's wards shared many of the same characteristics and functions. In particular, both were concerned that functions in communities be decentralized as much as practicably possible.

The virtues of citizen participation and decision making were extolled by Jefferson, but almost two hundred years later "we still have virtually no mechanism for permitting the citizen to participate in making policies that directly concern him or her and in influencing decisions that affect the quality of life, except the mildest of actions, the occasional casting of a vote."[32] This statement by political scientist Max Skidmore begs the question of what kind of mechanism would allow a citizen to directly participate.

The modern political world is filled with political practices of which Jefferson and his colleagues could not have conceived. The factionalism that Madison and others feared has found its way into government through the lobbyists and special interests that inundate every level of it, along with systemic gridlock and partisanship. Jefferson's foreboding about democracy not providing a place for citizens to practice politics except at the ballot box has essentially come true. Citizens find their voice through representation and special interests, rarely through any process that allows them to participate directly.

Today, public participation has come to mean tradeoffs, private interests, elections, and power. The view that our political lives are too narrow and confining is displayed in statements by ordinary citizens such as, "I'm staying out of politics" or "Politics is dirty business." The reality is that all citizens have both a part and a stake in public life no matter what their disposition. It is difficult to distinguish, in fact, between our public and private lives.[33] No matter the personal interest or circumstance, citizens are affected by and involved in public decisions regularly. From public taxes to public subsidies to public roads, citizens cannot isolate themselves from the public realm. The lack of distinction between public and private life results from our public lives having become so impoverished that we as citizens have lost the natural political experiences that Jefferson advocated and that would allow us to distinguish between the two.[34] No longer does private life allow individuals to retreat. No matter what the level of civic participation, every person is affected daily by "public" decisions.

The intersection of political and private of which Jefferson was so aware raises the question of what encompasses our public lives. Hannah Pitkin writes:

> Political life is not some leisure-time sport for aristocrats, in which they may cultivate their honor and display their powers. It is the activity through which relatively large and permanent groups settle how they will live together and decide their future to whatever extent that is within human power. Public life in this sense is of utmost seriousness and importance, and potentially of surprising glory. But, it never occurs in the abstract, without content, it always affects the lives of real people.[35]

This notion that public life involves real people working on real problems is exactly what Jefferson had in mind with the ward republics. He came to accept representation, but he was sure that a vital public must have a voice. Jefferson knew that politics at its base is about choice. The ability to make informed, rational decisions in concert with a community of fellow citizens provides a connection among them. Public decision making is not, however, easy; it takes skill, time, and effort to talk and reason through difficult options. Public skills are not presupposed or automatic but must be learned from the practice of citizenship. A strong public life gives us the potential for practicing citizenship which evolves through participative action.[36]

Because issues are rarely one-dimensional, they require discussion and debate about the interrelationship of the consequences of one choice or another. Those discussions of interdependency actually create a public voice. William Sullivan writes that "public discussion aims to bring before the whole civic community an understanding of the 'externalities' of public choices,—"[37] or what these choices will mean for various groups.

Jefferson gave modern-day theorists and practitioners license to take his concept of ward republics and develop an appropriate role and apparatus for them. His own borrowing of ideas from Native American societies, the early Greeks, and the New England town meetings suggests that he realized the need for continual refinement of the practice of democracy. In fact, he made the point clear when he said, "The moment a person forms a theory, his imagination sees in every object only the traits which favor that theory."[38] It is important then to follow Mr. Jefferson's lead and examine the modern application of ward republics.

Today's world gives both opportunities and restrictions for constructing a governmental structure like the ward republics. The scale of both population and geography in the world requires that bold innovative attempts be made toward implementing ways to practice politics. The restrictions on developing ward republics probably are most evident when any kind of boundaries are applied. Even the most fundamental issues exceed geographic and political frontiers. Law and order issues, for instance, cannot be isolated to one particular cluster of individuals or one neighborhood. An advantage of this scale, however, is that a lack of boundaries gives us the flexibility to build relationships in many ways. There are certainly ways in which decision making can be more decentralized in communities. Neighborhood councils, for instance, give citizens opportunities to voice their opinions and to have some say in the allocation of public resources. Other examples include religious organizations, civic organizations, trade unions, and though, less successful, public hearings. What these examples lack, of course, is the benefit of the "externalities" of their choices and conversations. Although the topics they discuss may be general, participants are almost obliged to look at them from their own points of view.

Ward Republics in the Twenty-First Century

How then, in the twenty-first century, can Jefferson's idea of ward republics be implemented? The response can be grouped into three categories: geography, mediating institutions, and new democratic processes. First, geography makes it possible to implement the ward concept that Jefferson proposed. Towns with populations under ten thousand make up 85 percent of all local government, according to the 1987 Census of Governments. Using plat divisions, city blocks, or aggregated neighborhoods, people could assemble in small groups to confer about public issues. In the northeast, town meetings are still quite functional and productive, and the geographical model will also work in most rural areas. In research on the entrepreneurial nature of rural communities, sociologists Cornelia and Jan Flora say clearly that success comes with the community's ability to galvanize around goals and strategies.[39] That galvanization comes from the willingness to decide together about issues in common to the community and to take innovative approaches to social organizations and institutions.

Second, mediating institutions offer practical political opportunities for citizens who live in heavily populated areas. Promoting the private interests of the mediating institution itself presents a risk, however. Mediating institutions, writes political theorist Benjamin Barber, make it possible for great numbers of citizens to participate and thus develop both vertical and lateral ties.[40] As part of their mediating role, institutions must have a general mission and a convening capacity. The term "mediating role" is used to include the mix of institutions such as businesses, social service agencies, or even governments, which can shed most of their traditional role for a broader scope. There are inherent problems in multipurpose organizations such as mediating institutions, but they can play the role in the right circumstances. The best of all worlds, of course, is a separate convening and mediating entity that will bring citizens together to confer and decide, but we must use what is available. If the process is to begin to build the "practice of politics" into everyday lives, then it must start where people are.

Third, new democratic processes in modern society must create opportunities for fundamentally different approaches to civic participation. Clearly, there are barriers in the modern world to having anything resembling a ward republic system. Taking Jefferson's lead that we can learn from the past, there are several directions to explore. The first is the practice of democratic talk. Jefferson believed, as did Aristotle and later, Tocqueville, that civic skills come with practice. Public talk becomes a pedagogy for public participation. Pericles understood the need for public discussion when he said that the Athenians "taught themselves first through talk."[41] There must be opportunities for citizens to talk to each other. The New England town meeting provides a place for such talk, but other forms, broaden the possible opportunities. These include local forums, study circles, and Barber's suggestions in *Strong Democracy* of neighborhood assemblies. Although Barber suggests assemblies in "every rural, suburban, and urban district in America," he understands what a gradual process this could be.[42] These assemblies would not go headlong into the decision-making mode that Jefferson sought but would rather begin with three functions: "to ensure local accountability, to deliberate on issues (and set agendas), and to act as ombudsmen."[43] This, Barber believes, would be a localization of certain levels of decision making. The dispersion of Americans both by geography and by circumstances of work and family responsibilities challenges us to think of ways to include citizens in the public dialogue by using interactive technology, cable-access television, and a range of vehicles called by Christopher Arterton "teledemocracy."[44]

The importance of the access to public discussion was borne out in a provocative study by The Harwood Group for the Kettering Foundation that found that citizens are not apathetic to public life, but impotent; they do not know how or where to make themselves heard.[45] Using the broadest definition of assemblies—town meetings, citizen action groups, neighborhood forums—may allow citizens to be a part of the political system for the first time. Using interactive media, formal educational programs, or a whole host of community opportunities, citizens who do not normally participate can find a niche. One particular area of concern is for those citizens who because of circumstance or situation of birth find themselves left out of the civic infrastructure. These are people in prison, illiterates, new Americans, the socially and economically disenfranchised, and so on—people who can find no place at the table. Although Jefferson's view of citizens was limited, according to modern times, he would have wanted to expand the table. We must find practical ways to include disenfranchised people in public life and actions. An example of this is the program called the National Issues Forums that focuses part of its work on adults who, because of language or reading barriers, are left out of the system. The forums have created both materials and opportunities for low level readers and new Americans to participate in the discussion of critical national issues emphasizing the choices citizens have about the issues. Jefferson knew that this process of "informing their discretion" was the only way to ensure an educated, participating public.[46]

Finally, the formation of a system of democracy that includes the smallest divisions of our republic can begin in local libraries, historical associations, public schools, or town halls—in any organization that can provide information and a public space for people to practice politics. Citizens must know how to talk, think, judge, and ultimately act as a public. To begin the process this requires first and foremost that they convene.

These ideas suggest avenues to create modern versions of ward republics. If Jefferson's prediction was correct, that without such a structure, citizens become more separate from government and from each other, they must have opportunities to confer and decide. Part of that structure, however, can be provided by government at all levels. The notion of "reinventing government" put forward by David Osborne and Ted Gaebler underscores Jefferson's idea of a different kind of government. They write, "The ultimate form of ownership is not ownership simply of problem solving or of services, but of government. . . . What Americans *do* hunger for is more control over matters that directly affect their lives: public safety, their children's schools, the developers that want to change their neighborhoods."[47]

The challenge for a twenty-first century world is to invent a system that puts citizens where Jefferson thought they should be—at the center. Jefferson's notion was not so much direct democracy as it was citizen democracy. The ward system would be one that celebrated the importance of self-governance and simultaneously defined the work that citizens must do. This invention would be, in Michael Ignatieff's words, "small enough so that each person would know his neighbor and could play a part in the governance of the city, large enough so that the city could feed itself and defend itself; a place of intimate bonding in which the private sphere of the home and the family, and the public sphere of civic democracy would be but one easy step apart."[48]

V

An International Perspective

RALPH KETCHAM

The Education of Those Who Govern

If we are to achieve good government, political thinkers from Plato and Confucius to Erasmus and John Dewey have argued, everything depends on the proper education of those who are to govern. Acceptance of this timeless connection in fact undergirded Thomas Jefferson's persistent interest in widespread education as he contemplated the future of his newly independent and self-governing country. As for all the profound commentators, there was for Jefferson a primary public, or civic dimension in his thought and plans for education: though certain learning and wisdom and skills were useful individually for humans, they were especially important for those who in some way took part in government. The new aspect of Jefferson's thinking was not that he was less concerned than Confucius and Erasmus about the education of rulers, or even that he disagreed very much about the general content and purpose of that education, but rather that he regarded large numbers of people—all the citizens—as the "rulers" in the body politic. He thus asked of citizens the question Plato asked about philosopher-kings, that Confucius asked about Mandarin officials, and that Erasmus asked about Christian princes: how should they be educated in order that they be able to govern well?

We can say, then, that Jefferson differed only quantitatively, not qualitatively, from his eminent predecessors. Indeed, the attention to the education of the female "child-raisers" in Charlotte Perkins Gilman's *Herland* (1915) and Martin Luther King's care in orienting and training civil rights activists, for examples, suggest that the essential connection has near universal applicability. Instead of elaborate educational schemes for a few philosopher kings or a design for rearing Christian princes, or even national examinations to select future government officials, Jefferson had to devise plans both for the primary education of all participants in a self-governing society and for higher education to qualify full time office-holders. But his concern was always to ensure as much as possible that those who would be electing, discussing, consenting, legislating, and administering in a self-governing society would be up to the task.

In this way Jefferson accepted entirely the vital Aristotelian distinction between good and bad government, whatever the number of people involved. Thus there could be good governments by one, a few, or the many (monarchy, aristocracy, or constitutional polity), and there could be bad government by each (tyranny, oligarchy, or democracy). Since to Jefferson and most of his colleagues "just power derived from the consent of the governed" ("inviolable attention due to . . . the republican form," as Madison put it in *Federalist* no. 37), the need then became to make government by the many also be good government. To achieve that, he believed that the governors had to be properly educated for their responsibilities—just as Plato and Erasmus had believed—but for Jefferson the task was all the more complex and arduous because so many more people were involved. In other words, Jefferson remained in the time-honored posture of one seeking enlightenment of the rulers in order to achieve good government while at the same time having vastly enlarged the number of those within his concern.

Jefferson was thus at a creative transition point between an ancient and a modern dictum. The recent, learned work of Paul Rahe and Joseph Levine[1] has clarified for us the profound and pervasive connotations of *ancient* and *modern* in Jefferson's day: the ancient dictum was that good government required wise and public spirited rulers, whereas the modern one was that government should be according to the consent of the governed. The difficult matter he faced, of course, was to effect an accommodation, educate those who governed—the many and eventually all—so that they might be good governors. No task of the founding era was more daunting and compelling, and no founder turned to it with more zeal, persistence, and clarity than Thomas Jefferson.

If we look, then, at the intellectual resources available to Jefferson as he faced this large question, we find rich, yet problematic circumstances. He had read and was aware, of course, of the thorough Greek attention to the education of rulers—though he hearkened more to Aristotle's concern for the education of a considerable group of citizens than to Plato's more intensive training of philosopher-kings. (Recall that Aristotle was one of Jefferson's four sage writers of "elementary books of public right" undergirding American independence, while he scorned Plato's *Republic* for its "whimsies, puerilities, and unintelligible jargon".)[2] Nearly all aspects of classical political culture, though, carried with it an emphasis on the character and education of rulers that Jefferson referred and recurred to throughout his life, though he tended always to take into account as well the condition of all the people. He wrote to John Adams in 1819, for example, that "I have been amusing myself latterly with reading the voluminous letters of Cicero." These letters of the "exalted patriot," Jefferson thought, left the ideas of "the parricide Caesar" in "odious contrast." Given the "corruption, vice, and venality [of] the whole nation," and the tyranny of Roman government, though, not even the virtue of "Cicero, Cato, Brutus" or the good intentions of "their Titusses, their Trajans and Antoninuses,"

Jefferson thought, could have given it good government. The only answer, taking many generations, would have been to recognize that Rome, like all others, was "a nation entitled to self-government." Then the people would need to be improved so that "their minds were to be informed by education, what is right and what wrong, to be encouraged in habits of virtue, and deferred from those of vice by the dread of punishments, proportioned indeed, but irremissible." Only this would "render the people a sure basis for the structure of order and good government."[3] Jefferson moved, then, from the traditional problem of educating a prince or a small elite to educating "the whole nation" to achieve "order and good government." But this move sustains in a central place the timeless equations that only wise rulers can provide good government and that such rulers, of whatever number, require thorough and deliberate education.

Virtually all the Greek and Latin authors whom Jefferson read all his life and to whom he returned so joyously upon his retirement showed some preoccupation with the question of educating rulers. In addition to the insistent focus on good government and wise rulers in Plato, Aristotle, and Cicero, Jefferson found the same message in Xenophon, Seneca, Plutarch, and Marcus Aurelius. That Cicero and Marcus Aurelius had had major roles in Roman government, that Plutarch had used biographies of famous statesmen to convey his message, and that Aristotle had been the teacher of Alexander the Great all heightened a sense of intimate relationship between learning, training for public life, and the practice of government. Indeed, it is unlikely that anyone of Jefferson's profound classicism would be other than deeply impressed with those linkages.

With the conversion of the emperor Constantine and the writings of St. Augustine, of course, the emphasis shifted from seeing a direct connection between proper political education of the ruler(s) and the "good life" in the state, to assuring that the prince was a faithful Christian who understood how to live out that faith in ruling the earthly city. Good princes, according to Augustine, would "fear, love, worship God . . . [and] make their power the handmaid of His majesty by using it for the greatest possible extension of His worship."[4] Like other medieval thinkers, Augustine then supposed that Christian faith required rulers to be merciful, benevolent, just, disciplined in their own desires, and altogether mindful of the peace, good order, and welfare of the earthly city.

St. Thomas Aquinas gave systematic expression to the Christian view of educating rulers in his *On the Training of Princes* (1266) where he also emphasized the duty of the Christian prince not only to sustain directly the Holy Church, but to see that secular affairs were conducted in accord with God's will. But since men achieved their highest end, salvation, "not by human but by divine virtue," it was God's officers, not the earthly state, that presided over man's highest functions. Thus though under a Christian prince Aquinas saw earthly justice "rather confirmed than removed by the faith of Christ," and therefore sanctioning obedience to secular rulers, he nonetheless asserted the essential subordination of all to God's will, "If the Emperor bids one thing and God another, the Emperor is to be neglected and God obeyed."[5] In another way, then, Christian philosophers (and, in theory, Christian practice in the Holy Roman Empire) emphasized the spiritual and moral education and condition of rulers as essential to the proper conduct of the state. Though Jefferson did not pay particular attention to these patterns of thought, he would have appreciated their agreement with the basic equation that rightful government in any state depended on the proper orientation and education of the earthly ruler.

Much more relevant for Jefferson and for other postmedieval thinkers, though, was the synthesis of classical and Christian thought on the subject of educating rulers found in Erasmus's *The Education of a Christian Prince* (*Institutio principis Christiani*), written for the guidance of the youthful future Hapsburg emperor Charles V in 1516 and translated and reprinted dozens, perhaps hundreds, of times subsequently. Though we do not have specific evidence that Jefferson ever read the *Institutio,* he did have three volumes of Erasmus in his library and could scarcely have avoided a general knowledge of a book and even genre much in vogue in the sixteenth to the eighteenth centuries. Along with the books by Plato, Cicero, Plutarch, and Thomas Aquinas about educating rulers, Erasmus's little volume, written in his elegant and lively Latin, became a standard on the subject, used as a model in English, for example, from Sir Thomas Elyot's *The Book Named The Governor* (1531) to Bolingbroke's *Idea of a Patriot King* (1738). Though the work is conventional in seeing monarchy as the best form of government and, following Aristotle, tyranny as the worst form, and hence focuses on training and precepts for princes, the argument is that the character of the state depends on that of the ruler, and that deliberate nurture and education is necessary to prepare the ruler.

Erasmus emphasizes, for example, that the right "seeds . . . should be sown in the young heart by . . . parents, nurses, and tutor" in order that the prince be properly nurtured. In this way good habits and attitudes can be encouraged from infancy, but "the main hope lies in sound ideas." The young prince, then, should not be reared on "wild and impetuous" stories of warriors such as "Achilles, Alexander the Great, Xerxes, or Julius Caesar," or even of King Arthur and Lancelot, "which are not only about tyrants, but are very poorly done, stupid, and fit to be 'old wives' tales.'" Instead, the young prince should read, in order, the Proverbs of Solomon ("to hear what the wisest king of all teaches his own son"), the Gospels (to "kindle a love" of Jesus and His precepts), Plutarch (including his *Lives,* "preferred to those of anyone else"), Seneca ("to excite one to a life of moral integrity"), the *Politics* of Aristotle, Cicero's *On Duty,* and Plato as "the most venerable source" of right ideas about good government. After warning about reading uncritically the histories of the Greeks, the Romans, and the Hebrews, full of "butcheries, barbarity toward . . . enemies," and stories of "great raging robbers," Erasmus nonetheless insists that "from no source is the truth more honestly and advantageously gained than from books."[6] Altogether, then, those who were to rule needed to be nourished on the great moral and practical teaching of the Greco-Roman and Judeo-Christian traditions in order that they form good character. (One feels sure, by the way, that had Erasmus known of other, non-Western moral teaching, such as that of Islam or Confucius, it would have been made part of the prince's study.)

For the most part Erasmus is content to urge that young princes simply be inculcated with the conventional benevolent and humane virtues of the Christian and classical traditions. The two traditions overlap and converge in Erasmus's mind all the time—Solomon, Pericles, Trajan, and Philip the Good, for example—are all extolled as model rulers. Quoting a Roman moralist, Erasmus urged that a prince be "mild, peaceful, lenient, foresighted, just, humane, magnanimous, frank, . . . rational, of keen judgment, clear thinking, circumspect," and so on. Thus, he concluded, "there can be no good prince who is not also a good man." More pointedly, though, Erasmus emphasized the *essential, peculiar* virtue of the prince was public-spiritedness—for him "no concern is of longer standing or more dear than the state . . . . [He] considers his wealth to lie in the advantages of his country; [he] is ever on the watch so that everyone else may sleep deeply; [he] grants no leisure to himself so that he may spend his life in the peace of his country; [he] worries himself with continual cares so that his subjects may have peace and quiet." "The one idea," Erasmus insists, "which should concern a prince in ruling, which should likewise concern the people in selecting their prince: the public weal, free from all private interests. . . . His mind must be divested of all private emotions. . . . Only those who govern the state not for themselves but for the good of the state itself, deserve the title of 'prince.'" Erasmus summarized by noting that "in his *Politics* Aristotle differentiates between a prince and a tyrant on the basis that one is interested in his own pursuits and the other is concerned for the state."[7] For Erasmus as for virtually all political thinkers in the classical and Christian traditions, there was really only one, essential public virtue: preeminent concern for the good of the whole, and consequent subordination of personal or factional interests. The metaphors used again and again by Erasmus were those of the father, the shepherd, and the sea captain, whose sense of responsibility and concern for the whole, set the paradigm for the political leader. Jefferson would have agreed that this was a proper standard for office holders from president to citizen, and would have thought nourishment of such virtue to be the heart of proper civic education.

Two further emphases in *The Education of a Christian Prince* help us discern the background for Jefferson's understanding of education for good government. First, Erasmus repeatedly sees the prince as needing not only to be wise and public-spirited enough to know what is good for the whole, but active and efficient to "gain that which the prince desires."[8] The prince, on the model of Pericles and Augustus and Solomon, must beautify the capital, defend and administer the realm, build the edifices of national devotion and purpose, and attend to the welfare of all the people. In the same spirit, two seventeenth-century Puritan writers condemned "*lukewarm neuter-passive* Magistrates, . . . scarecrow Constables, and mealemouthed under officers . . . resembling Ostriches, which have great feathers, but no flight." Instead, they called for Magistrates who were "*men of activitie . . .* requiring *Moses* his spirit, *Phineas* his zeale."[9] This activeness, moreover, was to reflect, after the prince had looked beyond the "factions, . . . strife, . . . and chance animosities" of the kingdom, "the harmonious agreement of good men and of cities."[10] The classical and Christian traditions available to Jefferson would each have emphasized for rulers an education pointed not only toward practical and effective action, but also embodying "the harmonious agreement of good men."

Second, though there is nothing in Erasmus's advice to Charles V about moving toward democracy (in fact, monarchy is assumed to be the best form of government, and the people are often scorned as vulgar, narrow-minded, and ignorant), there is a constant theme of attentiveness toward listening and responding to the needs and desires of the people. The young prince is counseled to be present at the deliberations of the court, but to be schooled in not making any decisions "unless they are approved by the judgment of many men." The prince, moreover, should remember his "common relation" with the people wherein their "taxes, allegiance and honor" are given to the prince in return for his goodness and care.[11] Then, with this willing bond, the state will have a strength and vigor impossible when obedience rests on fear and force—a theme Jefferson picked up in his first inaugural address (1801) when he declared American government to be "The strongest government on earth" because citizens would willingly "fly" to its defense.[12] As in the famous maxim of the Confucian scholar Mencius that rulers "see with the eyes of all, and listen with the ears of all," Erasmus had in mind a government attentive to the people, open to their sentiments, and resting on their willing consent and obedience—government for the people, if not yet by or even of the people. Hence his advice on civic education agreed in intention with that necessary in a polity ruled by the many.

The emphasis then, in Erasmus's advice on the education of those who would govern, is on the vital connection between the wisdom and virtue of the decision-maker and the quality of good government the realm would thus experience. If government itself was to pursue the public good, then those conducting it would have to be public-spirited. For Erasmus the basic understanding both of what good government itself consisted and of what qualification this required in the governors came from his revered classical sages: Plato, Aristotle, Plutarch, Cicero, Seneca, and so on. He insisted as well, of course, that the prince be Christian, though he did not suppose that insofar as government was concerned, this in any way contradicted or even introduced any serious tension with the ancient wisdom. In the time-honored way, rulers were to be wise, learned, open-minded, molders of harmony, worthy models, fair, active, and, above all virtuous, or public-spirited. That Erasmus direct-ed his advice toward the young prince rather than to the people at large simply acknowledged who, in his time and place, would do the ruling. In his thought noth-ing suggests that qualitative advice would be any different if a larger number, or even the whole number, of people were of the ruling body. Hence, when Jefferson faced the question of educating large numbers of rulers in a more democratic poli-ty, he had available a time-tested pattern of schooling, still appropriate in its sub-stantial intentions but requiring, of course, pervasive administrative and pedagogi-cal adjustment to make it relevant and effective for wider and more complex deci-sion-making processes. Even Erasmus's presumption that both the prince and the realm would be Christian, though not compatible with Jefferson's insistence on a secular polity, would not have been morally or generally troublesome to him because he much admired Christian ethical teachings.

Though Erasmus was probably the most influential Renaissance "mentor of rulers," Jefferson would also have had available to him many English works in the same tradition, including Sir Thomas More's *Utopia* (1516), and perhaps more prac-tically, Sir Thomas Elyot's *The Book Named the Governor* (1531). This frequently reprinted work deliberately patterned itself on Erasmus (and, of course, Plato), and was addressed to Henry VIII and to "the education of them that hereafter may be deemed worthy to be governors of the public weal under your highness."[13] After agreeing with Erasmus that the best form of government was monarchy, because rule by a large number was "a monster with many heads, . . . never certain nor sta-ble. . . . Virtue is not constant in a multitude, . . . whereby [vain] glory, . . . ambition, . . . and covetousness . . . [cause them] to fall into contention," Elyot outlines a care-fully graded pattern of study for those destined for public service. Beginning at age seven a child should study the Ancient languages, first being read "Aesop's Fables in Greek," and then the epic stories of Homer and Virgil, for their vivid moral lessons and evocation of character. After reading other carefully selected poets, mainly to train the ear for impressive language, the great orations of Demosthenes and Cicero would be read, and then the histories of Livy, Xenophon, Caesar, and Tacitus, all emphasizing the classical preoccupation with the connection between good charac-ter in the ruler and good government for the realm. Finally, by age seventeen, came the study of philosophy, especially the *Ethics* of Aristotle, Cicero's *De officiis* (*On Duty*), Plato's *Republic,* and the proverbs of Solomon. Insisting once again upon the vital need for good teachers ("Lord God, how many good and clean wits of children be nowadays perished by ignorant schoolmasters!"), Elyot advocated instruction in sports, music, dancing, hunting, and use of the crossbow to complete an education "whereby noblemen may attain to be worthy to have authority in a public weal."[14]

Notable here, as in all the two-thousand-year tradition of educating rulers, is emphasis on the deliberate nourishment of qualities vital to public life. Good char-acter is to be instilled through vivid stories for children. The ear is to be trained to hear and love language: the sometimes puzzling emphasis on rhetoric in classical education had much to do with the need for clear and forceful language in public discourse. The study of history is preeminently to learn the records of previous governments so their lessons can be applied to the present. Finally, philosophy is understood in largely practical terms, with emphasis on ethics and on the need to understand public life as a basically moral enterprise. Jefferson's frequent plans of education for young men (and even young women) and proposals for university curricula do not deviate from this basic pattern, though of course he would not agree in all particulars. For instance, he had a low opinion of Plato, and always added the need to study modern languages, science, literature, philosophy, and history. "The statesman," Jefferson declared, "will find in [Greek and Latin] history, politics, mathematics, ethics, eloquence, love of country"—the perspective and principles that were the indispensable guides for good government.[15]

We do not know that Jefferson ever read Elyot's *The Book Named the Governor* (only one work by him was in Jefferson's library, according to Sowerby), but the very conventionality of the work, and its obvious place in an ancient and honored genre of books to instruct those who would rule, would make it part of the intellectual milieu of anyone interested in that topic in the eighteenth century. Bolingbroke's *Idea of a Patriot King* (1738), for example, at once repudiating Machiavelli's *Prince*, patterned on Erasmus's *Christian Prince*, and echoing Elyot's idea of a book for governors, gathers the mingled precepts of Renaissance and Enlightenment thought that were the context for Jefferson's lifelong interest in forming the minds of those who would rule.[16] Bolingbroke recurs repeatedly to the successes and limitations in the education of rulers from Alexander the Great to Louis XIV, all emphasizing the critical importance of the examples and precepts set before the fledgling princes: it made all the difference whether there had been an Aristotle in the tutor's room, or, in Bolingbroke's opposite example, a Cardinal Mazarin training the boy king Louis XIV in cunning, arrogance, and absolutism.[17]

Another important tradition in the nourishment of good rulers that may have crossed Jefferson's intellectual path, at least indirectly, is that of Confucius. Jefferson cannot have been unaware of the wave of Sinophilia that swept across Europe in the seventeenth and eighteenth centuries. He probably knew Sir William Temple's *Upon Heroick Virtue* (1683), Leibniz's *Novissima Sinica* (1699), and, above all, Voltaire's article "De la Chine" in the *Dictionnaire Philosophique*. Leibnitz asserted that though Europe might surpass the Chinese in logic, metaphysics, astronomy, geometry, and military science, "we are beaten by them . . . in the principles of Ethics and Politics. . . . Everything in the laws of the Chinese . . . is directed to the achievement of public tranquillity, to . . . the good order in the relations of men to one another." Among the points particularly emphasized in the "Sinomania" was that the highest state offices below the emperor were "open to all men, without any respect of degree or parentage" and that "admission to the public service required definite and exacting educational qualifications, tested by examinations, and evidence of personal character and competence."[18]

The particular use made of the Chinese-Confucian example is illustrated by a work of Christian Wolff (or Wolfius) published in English translation in 1757: *The Real Happiness of a People under a Philosophical King Demonstrated: Not Only from the Nature of Things, but from the Undoubted Experience of the Chinese* . . . (London, 1750). ("Wolfius's *Law of Nature*" was on the list of works Jefferson and Madison recommended Congress purchase in 1783; Jefferson had Wolfius's *Institutions du Droit de la Nature et des Gens* in his own library, and the two men agreed in 1784 that Wolfius would be "worth having" in a collection of books "on Law of Nature and Nations.")[19] Wolfius was an enthusiastic logician and rationalist who believed a law of nature and other universal propositions and principles could be arrived at through logic and philosophical reasoning. Wolfius sought the implications of "the well known . . . saying of Plato that . . . a Community will be happy when either Philosophers rule, or they that rule are Philosophers," when one also accepted the common Enlightenment (post-Lockean) dictum "that men came together to form a Society with no other View but to be in a Condition with joint Powers to promote a Common Good, and to defend themselves against any Assaults of an Enemy." Understanding that "the common Good comprises the highest Good which every Individual can attain to in this World, according to the different State he is in," and that this "common Good" consisted in happiness (variously defined), Wolfius thought it possible "to deduce the Connection of civil Happiness with the government of a Philosopher." The philosopher-king would discern the general principles, the forms of government, and the administrative practices conducive to the "common Good" of the people.[20]

After showing, rather conventionally, that wisdom, moral rectitude, political understanding, and "Recourse to the other Disciplines or Sciences" were the requisite qualities of the good ruler, Wolfius found in the writings of the Sinophiles the embodiment of his ideal: "the ancient Chinese Emperors, who were Philosophers too, not only reasoning about good Government, but exercising their Genius on other subjects, to enable them to get an Insight into the obstruser Parts of Good Government." The early emperors described in the Confucian *Annals* were thus skilled with musical instruments, contemplaters of nature, inventors of agricultural equipment, and knowledgeable about "the medicinal virtues of plants" (the comparison with Jefferson is striking, of course). With this broad knowledge and wisdom, the emperors who founded the Chinese state (beginning in 2697 B.C. according to a date accepted by Wolfius) over three or more generations were able "to frame a model of Government, which exceeds all others, that have hitherto appeared in the world." Wolfius was especially impressed with the gradual enlargement of "notions of good Government" from the proper regulation of the ruler's "own Conduct and Actions, . . . especially his own Body," to that of the family, then to "a Province or Kingdom," and finally, continuing the paternal analogy, to "a whole Empire consisting of several Kingdoms under the same figure."[21] The point was to infuse morality, wisdom, and public spirit throughout the whole society, culminating in the good and harmonious government of the whole realm.

In recounting how the Chinese were able to sustain this philosophically guided government, Wolfius emphasized the education and apprenticeship of the ruler, a dependence on sage advice, learning from experience, and openness to the needs and views of the subjects. Confucius himself was "a close reader of the *Annals*," and had "often acted the Part of a Governor of a Province, and Minister of State, in order to gain clearer Notions of Government." The first Chinese emperors, Yao and Xun, had passed over their own sons in order to choose wise, well-educated successors, and then made them "Partners of the Empire," one for twenty-eight years and the other for seventeen years, before extending to them the full powers of government. Following the custom of Confucius and Mencius, in "Things of an arduous Nature" the emperor was to "consult the Philosophers, who were the Council of the petty Princes." Finally, the emperor Xun "was so great a Lover of Truth, that distrusting his own abilities, he would know the opinions of others both about himself and his Actions. He therefore set up to publick View a Table, in which he would have anyone put down any Misconduct of his he observed, that upon any Examination he might seasonably rectify what might prove detrimental to the Community." Thus rulers would "by their own Example both teach the Subjects their Duty, and . . . oblige than to act up to what Reason and the Publick Welfare required."[22]

The point in noting the Chinese example so widely praised in the eighteenth century is to see how it entirely reenforced the general notions, both of the Ancients from Plato onward and of those concerned for the education of Christian princes, that good government came from good and wise rulers, and that such rulers had to be carefully educated for their duties and tasks. There was as well an utter agreement on the proposition that the critical qualifications of the ruler were first to be able to discern a higher wisdom that would guide judgment and conduct, and then to apply it in a way mindful of the common good; that is, "to act up to what Reason and the Publick Welfare required." This was the conventional wisdom, gathered from across time and around the world, about rulers, education, and good government—and it was a wisdom Jefferson entirely absorbed and accepted. The point was put directly in an Elizabethan chronicle Jefferson may have had among his piles and shelves of Tudor and Stuart era tracts: "The goodness and badnes of any realm, lyeth in the goodness or badnes of the rulers . . . . For in dede the welth and quiet of everye common weale, the disorder also and miseries of the same, cum specially through them."[23]

What was new and different for Jefferson, of course, was his need to bring this pattern of thought to bear on his own situation in a post-Lockean, self-governing nation where, ultimately, all the people (including, theoretically, even slaves, women, the propertyless, and others excluded at the time) would, as holders of the office of citizen, be among the rulers. But in devising and proposing plans of education for the new republican circumstances, Jefferson's own deeply Classical, liberal, and humanistic frame of mind left him no starting place but the conventional wisdom just traced. Finding Plato and Cicero, Aquinas and Erasmus, Thomas Elyot and the Chinese tradition in basic agreement about the principles and even processes of educating rulers, about the substance to be inculcated and the qualities to be nourished, Jefferson could scarcely have had any other foundation for thinking about the equations linking rulers, education, and good government. This would explain, for example, why Jefferson was always provisional in his endorsement of self-government, and in his sense of the prospects for it: it would be a blessing for humankind *if* the people (who ruled ultimately) could "have their discretion so informed" that they could make wise and public-spirited contributions as participants in the process of government. If not, then one could expect no more of a democratic regime than the likes of Alcibiades, Caligula, Richard III, and all the bashaws, eunuchs, tyrants, and traitors who had disgraced the idea of government throughout most of human history. The trick, as always, was to see that the reins of government were in the hands of those properly qualified to rule—and that could only be the case where the utmost care was taken in the education and training of the rulers.

Even if one turns to more modern ideas and experiments in education, such for example as Locke's *Some Thoughts Concerning Education* (1693) and plans by Benjamin Franklin for a college in Philadelphia in 1750, the same emphasis persists on what Locke termed "the great Business of . . . Vertue and Wisdom." Though Locke was also concerned to attune education to the new epistemological and psychological insights of his *Essay concerning Human Understanding,* he by no means abandoned traditional precepts. While proposing, for example, that French be learned before Latin, and that modern science and literature be part of the curriculum, Locke still peppered his treatise with examples and quotations from Classical authors, especially Cicero's canonical guide to moral obligation, *De officiis* (written in the form of a letter of guidance for his son). The object of Locke's educational plans, as his editor put it, was "the *Governour,* the gentleman who protected English life and liberty, and guided the affairs of the nation."[24] Attention, that is, still focused on those who would rule—for Locke not so much the monarch as the Whig and Tory oligarchs in power after the Revolution of 1689. Another student has argued that the seventeenth-century revolutions in England substituted for the personal loyalty to the king a "public consciousness and civic loyalty" as the basis of the state—moving toward a broader conception of nationhood.[25] Jefferson's further extension, of course, was to give *all* citizens a part in a self-governing polity, even as he retained the traditional emphasis on the education of those who rule.

The plans of Benjamin Franklin and others for an academy and college in Pennsylvania sustained Locke's thrust toward a more "modern" and broadly based education (Franklin quoted extensively from Locke's *Thoughts* in his "Proposals Relating to the Education of Youth in Pennsylvania," 1750). At the same time, though, he continued to emphasize Classical studies as the foundation for moral and public education. Franklin believed that with the demise of men educated in Europe who had migrated to Pennsylvania, it was urgent that an academy be established "as might supply the succeeding Age with Men qualified to serve the Publick with Honour to themselves, and to their country." "Impressions of the Beauty and Usefulness of Virtue of all Kinds, Publick Spirit, Fortitude, etc.," needed to be inculcated among students who should also learn "the Advantages of Civil Orders and Constitutions. . . the Advantages of *Liberty*, Mischiefs of *Licentiousness*, Benefits arising from good Laws and a due Execution of Justice. . . [and] the first Principles of sound Politicks."[26] Franklin noted particularly the importance of training young men living in North America "to bear Magistracies, and execute other Offices of Trust," especially since "vast Numbers of Foreigners are yearly imported among us, totally ignorant of our Laws, Customs, and Languages." In a curriculum for an English School (as opposed to one emphasizing Greek and Latin) Franklin proposed the study of history begin at about age ten to acquaint students with public affairs and improve "the Morals as well as the Understanding." Reading the best English authors ("Tillotson, Milton, Locke, Addison, Pope, Swift") would further "qualify [students] to pass thro' and execute the several Offices of civil Life, with Advantage and Reputation to themselves and Country."[27] The charter granted to the Academy by Thomas and Richard Penn in 1753, noting that it should be open to poor and indigent children as well as to "the Opulent," stated among its purposes to instruct "tender minds . . . in the several dutys they owe to the Society in which they live, and one towards another . . . . in order to render them serviceable in the several Publick Stations to which they may be called."[28]

The point is not that there was anything exceptional about the Philadelphia Academy, nor do we have record that Jefferson paid any particular attention to it (though he surely knew of it, and doubtless talked often with Franklin about it). Rather, the plans for it, whatever the new (and controversial) proposals about "modern" studies or emphasis on the English language, retained the conventional focus on the need to properly prepare those who would exercise the various offices of government—in order that Pennsylvania, in its new status as a distant and partially self-governing part of the British Empire, be well governed. The Pennsylvania proposals sustain, too, the growing (since Erasmus's entire focus on the education of the young prince-emperor) breadth and ambiguity about the circumstances and numbers of those to be prepared for various participations in public life. There is no evidence, though, in the writings of Locke or Franklin, that either abandoned at all the ancient equation that good government required the proper education of those who govern.

When Jefferson faced the implications of this equation for the new United States, then, he accepted, as Benjamin Rush put it in 1786, that "the form of govern-

ment we have assumed, has created a new class of duties to every American," but he
also was still deeply heir to the ancient idea that careful, public-spirited education
would be required to enable fulfillment of those duties. Rush insisted further than
in order to "fit [citizens] more easily for uniform and peaceable government," they
would have to be nourished in the virtue that came with religious instruction. Rush,
of course, believed Christianity best provided this foundation, but said "I had rather
see the opinions of Confucius or Mahomed inculcated upon our youth, than see
them grow up wholly devoid of a system of religious principles." Though Jefferson
would not have put the matter quite that way, Rush's implication that proper citizen education required a foundation in a universal system of moral precepts would
not have been uncongenial to the founder of the University of Virginia. In fact, Rush
and Jefferson, long colleagues in science, philosophical inquiry, and republicanism
(if not religious faith), agreed that the essence of education for public office (including that of citizen) was to inculcate "a SUPREME REGARD TO THEIR COUNTRY,
. . . . that a pupil does not belong to himself but that he is public property, . . . [that]
he must shun the rage, and acrimony of party spirit, . . . [and] must be taught to
love his fellow creatures in every part of the world, but he must cherish with a more
intense and peculiar affection, the citizens of Pennsylvania and of the United
States."[29] Cicero or Erasmus of Locke would not have put differently the matter of
educating those who govern.

When Jefferson wrote the famous passages about education in *Notes on Virginia*,
in letters to Peter Carr, George Wythe, John Adams, and others, and in the Rockfish
Gap Report, then, he had always in view the "new class of duties" created for citizens in a republic: they were to be "qualified to understand their rights, to maintain
them, and to exercise with intelligence their parts in self-government." And, if anyone questioned their capacity to do this, he insisted the answer was not to bar them
from governing, but rather to "inform their discretion through education."[30] In eras
where different ideas of legitimacy obtained, Confucius would have agreed so far as
qualification for the mandarincy was concerned and Erasmus would have agreed in
the case of the fledgling prince about to become emperor. Jefferson even once put
forth a republican version of the Confucian requirement that those admitted to
public office pass an examination. He proposed that, once a system of free and universal public schools was in operation, no person "shall, after the age of fifteen years,
be a citizen of this commonwealth [Virginia] until he or she can read readily in
some tongue, native or acquired."[31] Jefferson's intention was not at all to *restrict* the
right of citizenship, but rather to encourage all young people (and their parents) to
take advantage of the public school system in order to achieve what seemed a reasonable qualification for "exercising with intelligence their parts in self-government." Again Jefferson was holding explicitly to the time-honored dictum that good
government required the careful preparation of those who would govern.

Jefferson put the whole matter, as was his remarkable gift, concisely and eloquently in the first of his many plans and proposals for education, in 1778: "where-

as it is generally true that the people will be happiest whose laws are best, and are best administered, and that laws will be wisely formed, and honestly administered, in proportion as those who form and administer them are wise and honest; whence it becomes expedient for promoting the publick happiness that those persons whom nature hath endowed with genius and virtue, should be rendered by liberal education worthy to receive, and able to guard the sacred deposit of the rights and liberties of their fellow citizens, and that they should be called to that charge without regard to wealth, birth, or other accidental condition or circumstance." Though Jefferson here has reference to the purposes of the grammar school (secondary) level of a proposed Virginia educational system, the same principle applied, in lesser or greater degree, to elementary and university education. The elementary schools (for "all the free children, male and female") would teach "reading, writing, and common arithmetick, . . . [and be] acquainted with Graecian, Roman, English, and American history," while the University would teach all branches of learning, ancient and modern.[32] Throughout the assumption was that from ordinary citizen to president an appropriate level of education would be necessary if government was to be "wise and honest" and directed toward "the publick happiness." All of Jefferson's voluminous, incessant, and earnest writings and plans on education make that same, simple, time-honored point.

This understanding of Jefferson's *purpose* (achieving good government) in seeking suitable education for all people possessed of political obligation in a self-governing society (including citizens) provides another clear illustration of the creative impact of his standing between the "Ancients" and the "Moderns." From the Ancients from Plato and Cicero to Erasmus, Elyot, and others who revived their influence in early modern Europe, Jefferson absorbed an understanding of the need for serious, comprehensive attention to the nurture and education of those who would govern. No aspect of his thought or conduct ever gives reason to doubt his commitment to that dictum. He retained especially the entire emphasis on the need to develop and inculcate intelligence, virtue, and public spirit in those who had a role in public affairs. From the "Moderns" from Bacon and Locke to Franklin and Benjamin Rush (all of whom, of course, remained themselves "Ancients" in basic ways) he absorbed the dictum that just government derived from the consent of the governed, which as theory and practice increasingly would acknowledge and require, meant all those in a given polity. The need, of course, was to bring the two dicta together in a system that would achieve for all, in some degree, the nurturing in wise, thoughtful, well-informed, and public-spirited attention to public affairs that good government required. As Jefferson knew, and as we perhaps know even more poignantly today, this is a very tall order indeed. Yet, there is no avoiding the force of the equations, and we are fortunate that Jefferson's powerful legacy as theorist of education and government bears the stamp of *both* the ancient wisdom on the preparing of rulers and the modern wisdom on the need to include all in that category.

LIU ZUOCHANG

Thomas Jefferson and His Conception of Happiness

In American history, no one has surpassed Thomas Jefferson in the rich diversity of his achievements. No one, except Benjamin Franklin, played so notable a part in the spheres of both activity and thought. And although Jefferson's thoughts on democracy were broad and profound, they were also complex and paradoxical. It follows that the themes that can be explored on Thomas Jefferson's thought will never be exhausted. Jefferson's conception of the happiness of men occupies a noteworthy position in his political philosophy, and it can provide valuable enlightenment to mankind as we are about to cross the threshold into the twenty-first century.

Let us begin with the Declaration of Independence. In this world-famous paper, Jefferson listed the "pursuit of happiness" as one of natural rights of men, to the exclusion of property rights. Thirteen years later, when the French Revolution broke out, the French revolutionaries drafted a declaration of rights of men in which were enumerated many natural rights, including property rights. When asked by Lafayette for his opinion of the declaration, Jefferson urged him to substitute "pursuit of happiness" for "property." Hence, we can see how deeply Jefferson concerned himself with the happiness of men.

It is well-known that the theory of natural rights formulated by the Enlightenment thinkers of the seventeenth century saw property rights as one of the natural rights of men. In substituting pursuit of happiness, Jefferson indeed made an innovation in the theory of natural rights. This is not simply a change of words, but a change in a major issue of principle, because it shows that Jefferson was concerned about the happiness of the great mass of people instead of the property of the rich. More importantly it also indicates that Jefferson put pursuit of happiness above all other things, regarding property and even government merely as a means of realizing the happiness of men. In the last analysis, what Jefferson valued most was the human being.

Moreover, Jefferson more than once asserted that the purpose for instituting government was to secure happiness to the people. In the Declaration of

Independence, he explicitly declared that it was for the purpose of securing the nat-ural rights of men, including the right of the pursuit of happiness, that "govern-ments are instituted among men." In 1812, he reiterated this principle in a letter to a friend: "The only orthodox object of the institution of government," he said, "is to secure the greatest degree of happiness possible to the general mass of those associ-ated under it." On another occasion he claimed that "the care of human life and happiness, and not their destruction, is the first and only legitimate object of good government."

Here, Jefferson uttered an important principle in political science. From his words it can be inferred that for the sake of the happiness of men, government interference in the economy or the institution of a social security policy can be jus-tified. Unwittingly Jefferson provided a theoretical basis for the New Deal of Franklin D. Roosevelt.

Now, how to secure happiness to the people? He pondered such an immense problem tirelessly almost all his life. What came first into his mind was the better-ment of the condition of men, because he perceived sharply that bettering the con-dition of the people would be a precondition of securing happiness to them. So, a good government, he thought, ought to take some proper measures to improve the living conditions of the people.

Jefferson believed that the best way to improve the condition of people was to encourage and develop the sciences and the arts. He was deeply convinced that these would greatly benefit mankind. In a Memorial to the U. S. Congress, he called its attention to "the value of science to a republican people, the security it gives to liberty, by enlightening the minds of its citizens; the protection it affords against foreign power; . . . in short, its identification with power, morals, order, and happiness."[1]

In 1818, he analyzed the functions of science and technology, saying:

> Indeed, we need look back half a century, to times which many now living remem-ber well, and see the wonderful advances in the sciences and arts which have been made within that period. Some of these have rendered the elements themselves subservient to the purposes of men, have harnessed them to the yoke of his labors, and effected the general blessings of moderating his own, of accomplishing what was beyond his feeble force, and extending the comforts of life to a much enlarged circle, to those who had before known its necessaries only.[2]

Jefferson not only valued science and the arts, but he did his best to promote them. During his residence in France he sent quantities of books and journals regu-larly to his friends in America, conveying to them the latest information on science and new discoveries. And he was anxious to establish a "System of Agricultural Societies," the purpose of which was "to promote . . . the diffusion of this skill, and thereby to procure with the same labor now employed, greater means of subsistence and of happiness to our fellow citizens." He devoted himself to the activities of invention and innovation in tools. He improved the moldboard of the plow; and for his design for the iron blade, he won a prize from the French Institute.

Jefferson was far-sighted too when he saw education to be the key to the betterment of men's condition. "What, but education," he asked, "has advanced us beyond the condition of our indigenous neighbour?" His reply was that, if the condition of men should be improved step by step, education ought to be the chief instrument to attain this goal.

Why could education promote the betterment of human livelihood? Jefferson replied that this was because men could obtain knowledge through education. He placed universal education in an important position. "I look," he said, "to the diffusion of light and education as the resource most to be relied on for ameliorating the condition, promoting the virtue, and advancing the happiness of man. . . . And I do hope that, in the present spirit of extending to the great mass of mankind the blessings of instruction, I see a prospect of great advancement in the happiness of the human race; and that this may proceed to an indefinite, although not to an infinite degree."

In Jefferson's eyes, improvement in the condition of men ought to be guaranteed as well by some measure of social justice, which might moderate the extreme inequality of property among men. Quite simply, if wealth was concentrated in the hands of the rich, it would be very difficult for the poor to ameliorate their condition.

Jefferson felt sympathy for the poor and was anxious to improve their lives. In a letter addressed to Bishop James Madison, he portrayed, with a sentimental touch, the scenes of his conversation with a poor woman:

> As soon as I had got clear of the town, I fell in with a poor woman walking at the same rate with myself and going the same course. Wishing to know the condition of the laboring poor I entered into conversation with her, which I began by enquiries for the path which would lead me to the mountain: and thence proceeded to enquiries into her vocation, condition and circumstances. She told me she was a day laborer at 8 sous or 4d sterling the day: that she had two children to maintain, and to pay a rent of 30 livres for her house (would consume the hire of 75 days), that often she could get no employment and of course was without bread. . . . I gave her, on parting, 24 sous. She burst into tears of a gratitude which I could perceive was unfeigned because she was unable to utter a word. She had probably never before received so great an aid.[3]

He had advised his young friends to "Take every possible occasion for entering into the houses of the laborers, and especially at the moments of their repast; see what they eat, how they are clothed, whether they are obliged to work too hard, whether the government or their landlord takes from them an unjust proportion of their labor; on what footing stands the property they call their own, their personal liberty, etc."[4]

His regard for the poor propelled him to devise a project of bettering their conditions. Writing to Bishop James Madison about France in 1785, he expounded his reform plan as follows:

> The property of this country is absolutely concentrated in a few hands. . . . I am conscious that an equal division of property is impracticable, but the consequences of this enormous inequality producing so much misery to the bulk of mankind, legislators cannot invent too many devices for subdividing property, only taking care to let their subdivisions go hand in hand with the natural affections of human mind. The descent of property of every kind therefore to all the children, or to all the brothers and sisters, or other relations in equal degree, is a politic measure and a practicable one. Another means of silently lessening the inequality of property is to exempt all from taxation below a certain point, and to tax the higher portions or property in geometrical progression as they rise. Whenever there are in any country uncultivated lands and unemployed poor, it is clear that the laws of property have been so far extended as to violate natural right. The earth is given as a common stock for man to labor and live on.[5]

Here, Jefferson proposed a taxation policy that foreshadowed the progressive taxation pursued by modern industrial countries, and justified it by the theory of natural rights. His reform plan shows that he was a moderate, for he avoided radical reform measures, such as equal division of property. A practician as well as a theorist, Jefferson tried to put his plan into practice after he entered the White House. Earlier, when Alexander Hamilton had been secretary of the treasury, he had collected excise duties, putting a financial burden on the shoulders of the poor. But Jefferson abolished these excise duties and at the same time took two other measures: enforcing fiscal economy and limiting taxation to customs. The latter step shifted the financial burden to the rich, because objects of customs duties were solely luxury items. Thus, Jefferson's financial measures helped to moderate the gap between rich and poor to some extent.

Jefferson also demanded a stop to the plundering of the majority of the people by the few, an attitude clearly shown in his struggle against Hamilton's financial system, which enriched capitalists, speculators, and security brokers at the expense of the great mass of the people. Jefferson, working to root out speculative activities, was averse to "licentious commerce and gambling speculations for a few, with eternal war for the many." He would not tolerate "a few citizens, infested with the mania of rambling and gambling, to bring danger on the great mass in innocent and safe pursuits at home."

Thus, Jefferson stood consistently and energetically for the betterment of the condition of men. But he also believed that happiness consisted in more than a comfortable life, because being different from beasts, men demand something beyond mere material comforts. In his eyes, happiness had a dual constitution, having its spiritual as well as its physical aspect, the former being more essential to men than the latter. When comparing Paris with his beloved Monticello, he preferred the spiritual satisfaction he would usually enjoy in his native place to the physical pleasures he experienced in the glittering capital of France. "I am", he said, "savage enough to prefer the woods, the wilds, and the independence of Monticello, to all the brilliant pleasures of this gay capital. I shall therefore rejoin myself to my native country with new attachments, with exaggerated esteem for it's advantages, for tho' there is less wealth there, there is more freedom, more ease and less misery."[6]

Apparently, Jefferson found much more happiness in mental satisfaction than in wealth or any physical pleasure. Writing to Madison, he told him that he found "happiness in the lap and love of my family, in the society of my neighbours and my books, in the wholesome occupations of my farm and my affairs, in an interest or affection in every bud that opens, in every breath that blows around me, in an entire freedom of rest or motion, of thought or incogitancy, owing account to myself alone of my hours and actions."[7]

Besides, Jefferson could list among the spiritual enjoyments various facets of human life such as pleasures resulting from "innocent and safe pursuits," mental comforts in helping others, pleasure from appreciating works of art, and pleasures generated by a struggle for one's ideal. And all these spiritual satisfactions, he thought, could be gained by everyone who chose, though these could not be bought with money. "We have," he said, "most abundant resources of happiness within ourselves, which we may enjoy in peace and safety." In his "Dialogue between my Head and my Heart," he (as Head) wrote, "the most effectual means of being secure against pain is to retire within ourselves, and to suffice for our own happiness. Those, which depend on ourselves, are the only pleasures a wise man will count on: for nothing is ours which another may deprive us of. Hence the inestimable value of intellectual pleasures."[8]

It seems to me that Jefferson attaches primary importance to family love, and considers happiness deriving from harmonious family life as the core of a sound and healthful spiritual enjoyment. This can be attested by the address he delivered to his native inhabitants after he left the presidency and came home in 1809. What he longed for most of all, he said, were the "endearments of family love, which nature has given us all as the sweetener of every hour."[9]

And his statements in a letter to Charles Bellini show how profoundly he comprehended the pleasure of family love: In Europe, "Intrigues of love," he wrote, "occupy the younger, and those of ambition, the elder part of the great. Conjugal love having no existence among them, domestic happiness, of which that is the basis, is utterly unknown. In lieu of this, are substituted pursuits which nourish and invigorate all our bad passions, and which offer only moments of ecstacy, amidst days and months of restlessness and torment. Much, very much inferior, this, to the tranquil, permanent felicity with which domestic society in America, blesses most of its inhabitants; leaving them to follow steadily those pursuits which health and reason approve, and rendering truly delicious the intervals of those pursuits."[10] That is to say, being different from the Parisians, Americans enjoy a true family love and true family happiness.

Here, I remember a brilliant poet in ancient China, whose name was T'ao-hua-shan. What striking similarities there are between Jefferson and T'ao-hua-shan! Like Jefferson, T'ao-hua-shan considered his family and relatives as the chief source of happiness for him. In his verses we can read words to the effect that to watch his child playing around him gave him the greatest joy in the universe. While ambitious men aspire to go far away from their native place, in order to seek fame and gain, he would rather seek happiness by staying at home, living with his children and other relatives.

Jefferson also found happiness in society. Writing to Madison in 1784, he noted that, "Agreeable society is the first essential in constituting the happiness and of course the value of our existence: Weigh well the value of this against the difference in pecuniary interest, and ask yourself which will add most to the sum of your felicity through life."[11] This statement reflected his values: he preferred harmonious relationships to the conflict or competition fed by pecuniary interest. It also indicated his intention of ameliorating the general mood of society, in the hope that friendship might supersede differences in wealth or property. The spirit of venality pervading the whole society caused Jefferson the greatest concern, for if men forget "themselves" but dwell "in the sole faculty of making money," the result will be their "eating one another" as in Europe. Here Jefferson hopes, perhaps naively, to exclude forever the spirit of venality from America.

Last, Jefferson finds the foundation of happiness in morality. To him, morality is essential not only to social peace but also to personal happiness. He claimed that the greatest happiness of men depended not on casual living conditions, but on kind-heartedness and good health. Only a virtuous man can enjoy genuine happiness. Writing to Peter Carr, he admonished him that morality, learning, and good health would secure his happiness. He believed in the Epicurean axiom: "Virtue is the foundation of happiness."[12]

It seems to me that Jefferson's proposition can be justified psychologically. Apparently Jefferson himself experienced much pleasure in his own moral behavior. He was a man of strict morals. As a public servant, he had no lust for power, still less any desire to use his office for his private interest. Almost all he did and thought in the arena of politics was for the welfare of the people and for safeguarding democracy. He was honest and incorruptible, turning away any kind of bribery. Never in his life did he disgrace himself by taking part in speculation. In the sphere of private life, he was a good husband, a good father, and a good friend. No doubt such altruistic deeds gave him much happiness, attaining a sublime level unknown to ordinary men.

He was not satisfied with this, however, and he hoped that all his fellow citizens might become virtuous and enjoy pleasure resulting from moral deeds. He devoted himself to the cause of education almost all his life, one of his objects being to make men virtuous through education. He introduced the cultivation of morality into the curriculum of educational institutions of every level.

Not only did Jefferson have a deep regard for the happiness of men, but he also had a profound understanding of the conception of happiness. He not only richly delineated the substance of happiness but also distinguished its material aspect from its spiritual aspect. More significantly, he put the spiritual aspect of happiness above its material or physical aspect, and believed that the former was within everyone's reach. He regarded the pleasure derived from familial love as the core of the spiritual aspect of happiness. And it is characteristic of him that he believed morality to be the foundation of happiness. Thus, Jefferson endowed the conception of happiness with a noble and elegant nature, and therefore elevated it to an ideal and sublime realm.

In Jefferson's deepest thinking, however, the happiness of men could be realized to the utmost extent only in an agricultural society. He pictured the truest happiness for men in a republic of small farmers. As early as the revolutionary years, Jefferson had already envisioned a bucolic arcadia in an agrarian republic. He had naively dreamed that America would remain an agricultural country, to the exclusion of manufacturing. In his *Notes on the State of Virginia*, written in 1781, he for the first time recommended this vision to the public. "While we have land to labour there, let us never wish to see our citizens occupied at a work-bench, or twirling a distaff. . . . let our workshop remain in Europe." And again, "Were I to indulge my own theory, I should wish them to practise neither commerce nor navigation, but to stand with respect to Europe precisely on the footing of China. We should thus avoid wars, and all our citizens would be husbandmen."[13]

And this ideal society was to be a society of small farmers. On many occasions Jefferson expressed a strong desire to set up a small land-holding system. His draft constitution for Virginia stipulated that, "Every person of full age neither owning nor having owned 50 acres of land, shall be entitled to an appropriation of 50 acres." Why did he hanker for a society of small farmers? The reasons are, first, that he considered that small farmers were the most virtuous people. "Those who labour in the earth are chosen people of God, if ever he had a chosen people, whose breasts he has made his peculiar deposit for substantial and genuine virtue. It is the focus in which he keeps alive that sacred fire, which otherwise might escape from the face of the earth. Corruption of morals in mass of cultivators is a phenomenon of which no age nor nation has furnished an example," Moreover, "Cultivators of the earth are the most valuable citizens. They are the most vigorous, the most independent, the most virtuous."

On the other hand, he thought city life and industrial community would corrupt the morality of man. City life, he said, "begets subservience and venality, Suffocates the germ of virtue, and prepares fit tools for the designs of ambition." About the urban population, he said, "The mobs of great cities add just so much to the support of pure government, as sores do to the strength of the human body."

Second, small farmers were closely connected with the maintainance of democracy. Farmers, he said, "are tied to their country and wedded to its liberty and interest by the most lasting bonds." And, "Here every one may have land to labour for himself if he chooses; Every one, by his property, or by his satisfactory situation, is interested in the support of law and order. And such men may safely advantageously reserve to themselves a wholesome control over their public affairs."[14]

Third, the occupation of husbandry would beget social stability. Writing to Washington in 1787, he noted that "the wealth acquired by speculation and plunder is fugacious in its nature and fills society with the spirit of gambling. The moderate and sure income of husbandry begets permanent improvement, quiet life and orderly conduct."

In explaining the reasons for which he pursued an agrarian republic, Jefferson actually gave us a key to his ideal society. As he saw it, in this society, everyone behaved in accordance with moral norms, mutual love and mutual help being the order of the day. Even a shadow of plunder, speculation, gambling, or corruption disappeared from sight. People enjoyed political as well as socioeconomic freedom and equality in such a small land-holding system. As C. B. MacPherson remarked, "With one's own small property one could not be made subservient. And small property was the great guarantee against government tyranny as well as against economic oppression. It was to secure individual liberty, and all the virtues that can flourish only with sturdy independence, that Jefferson wanted America to remain a country of small proprietors. . . . This justification of property rests, in the last analysis, on the right to life at a more than animal level: freedom from coerced labour and arbitrary government are held to be part of what is meant by a fully human life."[15] And it is for this reason that, in this republic of small farmers, men can work leisurely and rhythmically. No wonder people lead a carefree and happy life here. Such a social order and its pastoral atmosphere naturally offered a satisfactory cosummation for the deepest yearning of the human spirit, and thereby greatly added to the happiness of men.

In my opinion, what attracted Jefferson most of all to the economy of the family-sized farm was that it keeps family members living and working together, and thereby fosters love and happiness in family life, something Jefferson cherished most.

Therefore, in this realm of harmony, beauty, and peace, men would truly experience the pleasure of human life, human dignity would be best maintained, and human fulfillment would be fully realized. In essence, such a society has sociological, ethical, and aesthetic value rather than an economic value. A. Whitney Griswold grasped the quintessence of Jeffersonian agrarianism when he said: "Agriculture, to him, was not primarily a source of wealth but [of] human virtues and traits most congenial to popular government. It had a sociological rather than an economic value. This is the dominant note in all his writings on the subject."

It is no wonder that Jefferson saw a "good life" full of "friendship, felicity, and freedom" in the agrarian republic he envisioned. And it is exactly this "ideal of a good society" that impassioned him day and night, even to his last days. His agrarianism thoroughly reflects his inner world.

It is interesting that Jefferson's vision of agrarian society had its counterpart in ancient China. The well-known "Notes on Peach Blossom Nest," composed by T'ao-hua-shan, whom I mentioned above, is wonderfully similar in its theme to the Jeffersonian agrarian vision. In this short narrative, with a verse attached to it, T'ao-hua-shan told a story, as follows. A fisherman one day unexpectedly discovered a tranquil and secluded retreat totally separated from the outer world by a mountain range and inhabited by a people whose ancestors had moved to that place to escape the despotic rule of the first emperor of the Chin dynasty. The fisherman was infatuated with the scenery with its enchanting beauty. Nature was here a series of wonders, and a fund of delight, beautifully colored, elegantly shaped, and charmingly flavored. The green plain was checked with farms, ponds, woods, houses, and lanes. Men and women labored on the farms with delight, the old men and women enjoying leisure at home and children playing happily nearby. To all appearances, they were free politically as well as economically, because no taxation or oppression tormented them, as they told the fisherman. In such a bucolic habitation, in a word, people enjoy a carefree and happy life. Nevertheless, both Jefferson's agrarian republic and T'ao-hua-shan's "Peach Blossom Nest" are fantasy utopias, running counter to the general trend of human development. The small farm system hinders both industrialization and modernization.

Jefferson, however, was a realist as well as an idealist. For well-known reasons he abandoned his agrarianism in the 1790s, giving it up altogether after he entered the White House in 1801. Yet, it was with reluctance that he did so. He always retained his predilection for agriculture and rural life. An agrarian strain runs through his life, and his preference for farm life remained latent in his inner world, finding expression at the earliest opportunity. It can be said that idealism and realism coexist in Jefferson and constitute one of the paradoxes in him, which give his political enemies a pretext for denouncing him as a hypocrite.

Jefferson's conceptions and his agrarian vision have their theoretical values that can be reduced to the following principles:

(1) He attributed a central and ultimate importance to man, subordinating to this value all other things, including property. Mankind's welfare itself is the end, property and even government being merely the means to that end.

(2) As for man himself, although Jefferson did not neglect his material comforts, he claimed that his spiritual life should take precedence over his material well-being.

(3) He considered morality as an integral part and even the backbone of man's spiritual life.

These principles, I think, may be epitomized under the term *humanism*, which I reluctantly borrow from the Renaissance. Humanism, as a product of the Renaissance and as an antithesis of medieval theology, puts the emphasis upon man instead of God and upon this life instead of a life after death. Humanism places value on the physical condition and happiness of man.

But Jeffersonian humanism is far in advance of Renaissance humanism in its connotations, the former having much more profound, profuse, and far-reaching implications than the latter. It is a credit to Renaissance humanists that they diverted men's attention from the other life to this life and therefore accelerated man's exploitation of the physical world, but Renaissance humanism fails to address problems of how to construct a reasonable and just society or how to arrange human life more reasonably. It is to Jefferson's credit that he made up for what Renaissance humanists lacked: he tried to elaborate a project for a reasonable and just society in this life and taught men how to live a reasonable life and how to pursue a reasonable happiness.

Jefferson's humanism is surprisingly consonant with Confucianism, though he had no opportunity to read the *Analects* of Confucius. First, Confucius attached primary importance to man. His whole theory was dedicated to the cause of the advancement of man's position. This is attested by an episode. In the *Analects* it is recorded: "The stable was burned to ashes. Confucius came home from the Court, and asked, 'Was any one injured?' instead of enquiring about the horses" (*Analects*, chapter 10). Second, Confucius had a deep concern for the living conditions of the people, claiming that governors should improve them. But, he was even more concerned about the people's cultural life, claiming that governors should educate them. Third, Confucius deemed morality to be the most substantial part of human life. He advocated brotherhood among men, considering family love as the core of human love. These similarities between Jefferson and Confucius are meaningful phenomena in cultural and philosophical history and indicate that Eastern and Western civilizations hold something in common.

Although it seems that both Confucian principles and Jeffersonian humanism are out of date and incompatible with today's industrial society, they could still provide an effective cure for the social maladies of the modern world. Such social ills as the enormous gulf between the rich and the poor, lives given up to pleasure, a wild spirit of venality, the family crisis, rampant social crimes, and widespread moral corruption could someday precipitate man's descent into an abyss of disaster.

Such social maladies can be said to have their source in a lack of legal or moral restraint encouraged by the overabundance that industrialization produces. The only remedy is to change mankind's values and outlook on life. Here, either Jeffersonian humanism or the Confucian doctrine could serve as one prescription.

The theories and principles of Confucius and Jefferson may be as essential as technology and industrialism to the future of mankind.

Notes

CITIZENS AND FAMILIES: A JEFFERSONIAN VISION OF DOMESTIC RELATIONS AND GENERATIONAL CHANGE

MICHAEL GROSSBERG

1. Jefferson to James Madison, September 6, 1789, in Julian P. Boyd et al., eds., *The Papers of Thomas Jefferson*, 27 vols. to date (Princeton: Princeton University Press 1950-), 15:395-96, hereafter cited as Boyd, *Papers*.

2. For a compelling discussion of Jefferson's attitudes toward the state, see Christopher Tomlins, *Law, Labor, and Ideology in the Early Republic* (New York: Cambridge University Press, 1993), 84-89.

3. For examples of the debate over Jefferson's political beliefs, see Lance Banning, *The Jeffersonian Persuasion* (Ithaca, N.Y.: Cornell University Press, 1978); Banning, "Jeffersonian Ideology Revisited," *William and Mary Quarterly*, 3rd ser., vol. 43 (1986): 3-19; Drew McCoy, *The Elusive Republic: Political Economy in Jeffersonian America* (Chapel Hill: Published for the Institute of Early American History and Culture, Williamsburg, Va., by the University of North Carolina Press, 1980); Richard K. Matthews, *The Radical Politics of Thomas Jefferson, Revisionist View* (Lawrence, Kans.: University Press of Kansas, 1984); Joyce Appleby, "What Is Still American in the Political Philosophy of Thomas

Jefferson," *William and Mary Quarterly*, 3rd ser., vol. 39(1982): 287-309; Appleby, *Capitalism and a New Social Order: The Republican Vision of the 1790s* (New York, 1984); Appleby, "Republicanism in Old and New Contexts," *William and Mary Quarterly*, 3rd ser., 43(1986):3-34; Isaac Kramnick, "Republicanism Revisionism Revisited," *American Historical Review* 87(1982): 629-64; and Garrett Ward Sheldon, *The Political Philosophy of Thomas Jefferson* (Baltimore: Johns Hopkins University Press, 1991).

4. Willi Paul Adams, *The First American Constitutions: Republican Ideology and the Making of the State Constitutions in the Revolutionary Era* (Chapel Hill: Published for the Institute of Early American History and Culture, Williamsburg, Va., by the University of North Carolina Press, 1980), 188.

5. Appleby, "What Is Still American in the Political Philosophy of Thomas Jefferson," 297.

6. Paul L. Ford, ed., *The Works of Thomas Jefferson*, 12 vols. (New York: G.P. Putnam's Sons, 1904-5), 1:48.

7. Jeffrey Barnouw, "The Pursuit of Happiness in Jefferson and Its Background

in Bacon and Hobbes," *Interpretation: A Journal of Political Philosophy* 11(1983):229; and see Stanley N. Katz, "Republicanism and the Law of Inheritance in the American Revolutionary Era," *Michigan Law Review* 76(1977):17-18.

8. In this context, *telos* means end or goal.

9. Matthews, *Radical Politics of Thomas Jefferson,* 122.

10. *Testamentary* means issues pertaining to a will.

11. Intestate refers either to a person who died without making a will or to the process of disposing of property without the guidance of a will.

12. Frederick Pollock and Frederic Maitland, *The History of English Law,* ed. S. Milsom, 2nd ed., 2 vols. (Cambridge: Cambridge University Press, 1968), 2:363.

13. Ibid.

14. William Blackstone, *Commentaries on the Law of England,* 2nd ed., 4 vols. (London: Clarendon Press, 1766-69), 1:455.

15. Theodore Plunkett, *A Concise History of the Common Law,* 5th ed. (1956), 711-46; Carol Shammas, Marylynn Salmon, and Michele Dahlin, *Inheritance in America: From Colonial Times to the Present* (New Brunswick, N.J., 1987), 39.

16. See Richard Morris, *Studies in the History of American Law,* 2nd ed. (New York; 1930; Philadelphia: J.M. Mitchell Co., 1959), 69-125.

17. Shammas et al., *Inheritance in America,* 38.

18. Keim, "Primogeniture and Entail in Colonial Virginia," *William and Mary Quarterly,* 3rd ser., 25(1968):545.

19. "After the Revolution: 'Reform' of the Law of Inheritance," *Law and History Review* 10(1992):42.

20. Kenneth A. Lockridge, *On the Sources of Patriarchal Rage: The Commonplace Books of William Byrd and Thomas Jefferson and the Gendering of Power in the Eighteenth Century* (New York: New York University Press, 1992),

see esp. 86-90.

21. Boyd, *Papers,* 1:562.

22. Ford, *Works,* 1:57-58.

23. To Skelton Jones, July 28, 1809, in Andrew A. Lipsomb and A. Ellery Berg, eds., *The Writings of Thomas Jefferson,* 20 vols. (Washington: Issued under the auspices of the Thomas Jefferson Memorial Association, 1903-4), 12:298-300. He wrote a similar version several years later in his autobiography. Jefferson recalled that the revisers had first considered whether "to abolish the whole existing system of laws, and prepare a new and complete Institute, or preserve the general system, and only modify it to the present state of things." Surprisingly, Pendleton, "contrary to his usual disposition in favor of antient things, was for the former proposition, in which he was joined by Mr. Lee." Wythe, Mason, and Jefferson took the opposition view: "that to abrogate our whole system would be a bold measure, and probably far beyond the views of the legislature" which probably intended that the revisers should follow the customary practice of "omitting the expired, the repealed and the obsolete [laws], amending only those retained" except that the process should in this case be applied to "the British statutes as well as our own." The objection was also made that "to compose a new Institute like those of Justinian and Bracton, or that of Blackstone, would be an arduous undertaking," requiring extensive research and deliberation. Moreover, when completed every word of the text agreed upon would become the subject of litigation and "render property uncertain until, like the statutes of old, every word had been tried, and settled by numerous decisions, and by new volumes of reports and commentaries." In addition, such a work "to be systematical, must be the work of one hand," and none of the revisers would probably be willing to undertake such a task." Ford, *Works,* 1:67-68. For a listing of the committee's guidelines see Boyd, *Papers,* 2:325.

24. To Jones July 28, 1809, in Lipscomb and Berg, *Writings* 12:298-300. For a different version, see Boyd, *Papers,* 2:316.

25. Ford, *Works,* 3:243.

26. Even the text of the revisions has proven difficult to reassemble, see Boyd, *Papers,* 2:308-13. Boyd also argues that the "actual scope of the revision seems to lie somewhere between the two extremes of a complete codification or institute advocated by Pendleton and a compilation of laws in force, 'omitting the expired, the repealed and the obsolete,' that the majority of the Committee, according to Jefferson's remembered account, agreed upon. Its scope was also much less comprehensive than Jefferson asserted in *Notes on the State of Virginia* and Madison repeated in 1826." Ibid., 315.

27. Ford, *Works,* 1:68.

28. Boyd, *Papers,* 1:330.

29. Ibid., 1:344.

30. Ibid., 1:352, 353, 362, 363.

31. *Allodial* refers to land free from the tenurial rights of a feudal overlord.

32. To Edmund Pendleton, August 13, 1776, in Merrill D. Peterson, ed., *Writings [of] Thomas Jefferson* (New York: Literary Classics of the United States, 1984), 751.

33. Boyd, *Papers,* 1:331.

34. *Fee-tail* refers to inherited land limited to a particular class of heirs.

35. *Fee simple* refers to inherited land held without limitation to any particular class of heirs.

36. Ibid., 1:561; and see Dumas Malone, *Jefferson, the Virginian* (Boston, 1948), 251-57.

37. Boyd, *Papers,* 1:561, 562, and see notes for full analysis of the legislation. In a similar vein, Blackstone had used his *Commentaries* to catalog the evils of entail: "Children grew disobedient when they knew they could not be set aside: farmers were ousted of their leases made by tenants in tail . . . creditors were defrauded of their debts. . . ." *Commentaries,* 2:116.

38. Ford, *Works,* 1:49-50.

39. Act of 1776, chap. 26, sec. 1, reprinted in W. W. Hening, ed. *The Statutes at Large,* 13 vols.(Richmond, 1809-23), 9:226. In fact, sensing broad support for the elimination of entail, Jefferson had substituted a bolder measure completely outlawing the property device in place of his initial bill that had paralleled Pendleton's.

40. Quotes cited from Malone, *Jefferson, the Virginian,* 255.

41. In a revision plan agreed on January 13, 1777, the committee laid out the general outlines of a republican inheritance law, Boyd, *Papers,* 2:326-27.

42. Boyd, *Papers,* 2:391.

43. Ford, *Works,* 1:59.

44. Boyd, *Papers,* 2:393.

45. Madison to Jefferson, January 22, 1786, in Boyd, *Papers,* 9:195; Madison to Jefferson, December 4, 1786, ibid., 10:575.

46. Uncertainties over the wording of Jefferson's 1776 bill abolishing entail also led to the passage of a second measure. It won easy enactment along with the other changes. Act of 1785, chap. 62, reprinted in Hening, *Statutes at Large,* 12:156-57.

47. Boyd, *Papers,* 2:308.

48. Jefferson to Madison, October 28, 1785, in Peterson, *Jefferson, Works,* 841-42.

49. For a useful discussion of this point, see Jennifer Nadelsky, *Private Property and the Limits of American Constitutionalism: The Madisonian Framework and Its Legacy* (Chicago: University of Chicago Press, 1990), 32-33.

50. Matthews, *Radical Politics,* 88-89.

51. Katz, "Republicanism and the Law of Inheritance," 15-16.

52. Malone, *Jefferson, the Virginian,* 256.

53. July 12, 1816, in Peterson, *Writings,* 1,401.

54. *Howell v. Netherland* (Virginia, April 1770) in Thomas Jefferson, ed., *Reports of Cases Determined in the General Court of Virginia, from 1730 to 1740, and from 1768 to 1772* (Charlottesville: F. Carr & Co., 1829), 90.

55. For an important rereading of the issue of republican motherhood, see Jan Lewis, "Motherhood and the Construction of the Male Citizen in the United States, 1750-1850," in George Levine, ed., *Constructions of the Self* (New Brunswick, N.J.: Rutgers University Press, 1992), 143-63.

56. For a comparison between the French and American approaches, see Katz, "A Republican Law of Inheritance," 21-28.

57. Ibid., 18.

58. Malone, *Jefferson, the Virginian*; Shammas et al., *Inheritance in America*, 63-67.

59. Lawrence M. Friedman, *A History of American Law*, 2nd ed. (New York: Simon & Schuster, 1985), 250; Adams, *First Constitutions*, 196.

60. Sir Henry Maine, *Ancient Law*, Everyman's Library (1917; London: J.H. Dent & Sons, 1972), 140.

61. For an elaboration of these points see Michael Grossberg, *Governing the Hearth* (Chapel Hill: University of North Carolina Press, 1985), chap. 1.

62. For a discussion of Madison's views, see Nadelsky, *Private Property*, 33-34; Matthews, *The Radical Politics of Thomas Jefferson*, 23-24, and more generally chap. 6; Christopher Tomlins, *Law, Labor, and Ideology* (Cambridge: Cambridge University Press, 1993), 88; and Adrienne Koch, *Jefferson and Madison, the Great Collaboration* (New York: Knopf, 1950), chap. 4.

63. Isaac Kramnick, *Republicanism and Bourgeois Radicalism, Political Ideology in Late Eighteenth-Century England and America* (Ithaca: Cornell University Press, 1990), 5-18.

64. For the most comprehensive analysis of Tucker's career, see Charles T. Cullen, *St. George Tucker and Law in Virginia, 1772-1804* (New York: Garland, 1987).

65. Jefferson to Madison, February 17, 1826, Ford, *Works*, 12:456. And see Julian S. Waterman, "Thomas Jefferson and Blackstone's Commentaries," *Illinois Law Review* 27(1933):629-59.

66. For a discussion of Tucker's efforts to publish the project see Cullen, *St. George Tucker*, 157-62.

67. Robert Cover, "Tucker's Blackstone," *Columbia Law Review* 70(1970):1475.

68. St. George Tucker, ed., *Blackstone's Commentaries, on English Law*, 5 vols. (Philadelphia, 1803; reprinted, South Hackensack, N.J.: Rothman Reprint Co., 1969), 1:iv, iv-v. vi. Italics in the original.

69. Ibid., 1:x-xi, xvii. Italics in the original.

70. Ibid., 3:105, n1; 169, n2; 191, n16; 214, n5; 223, n9; 2:445, n1; 449, 457, n13.

71. Ibid., 3:119, n14, and see 125, n7; 114, n10.

72. Ibid., 3:212, n4.

73. Ibid., 2:468, n16.

74. Ibid., 2:451, n450.

75. Ibid., 3: appendix 19.

76. Cullen, *St. George Tucker*, 162-63; Edward Dumbauld, *Thomas Jefferson and the Law* (Norman: University of Oklahoma Press, 1978), 8-9. In fact, Cover argues that "[n]o other commentator of such pure Jeffersonian pedigree ever wrote." "Tucker's Blackstone," 1,476.

77. *Stones v. Keeling*, 5 Call 143, 146-47 (Va. 1804).

78. For a general review of the adoption of bastardy law reforms, see Grossberg, *Governing the Hearth*, 203-12.

79. *Stevenson's Heirs v. Sullivan*, 5 Wheaton 260, 262 (U.S 1820).

80. Grossberg, *Governing the Hearth*, 213-14.

81. Quoted in Jan Lewis, *The Pursuit of Happiness: Family and Values in Jefferson's Virginia* (New York: Cambridge University Press, 1983), 154. Italics in the original.

82. Lewis, "Motherhood," and see Lockridge, *On the Sources of Patriarchal Rage* (New York: New York University, 1992), 111-14.

83. *Garland v. Harrison,* 8 Leigh 368, 369, 372 (Va. 1837).

84. *Neblett v. Smith,* 142 Va. 840, 128 S.E. 247, 249 (1925); and see *Copenhaven, et al. v. Pendleton, et al.,* 155 Va. 463, 155 S.E. 802, 812 (1930).

85. "On the Education of Youth in America," in *A Collection of Essays and Fugitive Writings* (Delmar, New York: Scholars' Facsimiles and Reprints, 1977), 24.

86. James W. McIntyre, ed., *The Writing and Speeches of Daniel Webster* (Boston: Little, Brown and Co., 1903), 1:215.

87. James Kent, *Commentaries on America Law,* 4 vols. (New York: O. Halsted, 1826-30), 4:20.

88. Alexis de Toqueville, *Democracy in America,* trans. Henry Reeve, rev. Francis Bowen, ed. Phillips Bradley, 2 vols. (New York: Knopf, 1945), 1:47, 48-49.

89. Lewis, *The Pursuit of Happiness,* 154, and see her discussion of the consequences of the household privatism individualism encouraged, 174.

90. Kramnick, *Republicanism and Bourgeois Radicalism,* 14.

91. Quoted in ibid., 12.

92. Jefferson to Adams, October 28, 1813, in Ford, *Works,* 9:425.

93. Salter's poem is printed in the *New Republic* 208, no. 5 (February 1, 1993): 58.

BINDING TIES: THE PUBLIC AND DOMESTIC SPHERES IN JEFFERSON'S LETTERS TO HIS FAMILY

FRANK SHUFFELTON

1. *New York Times,* August 21, 1992, A1; August 23, 1992, section IV, 2.

2. Christopher Lasch, *Haven in a Heartless World: The Family Besieged* (New York: Basic Books, 1977); quoted from *The American Family in Social-Historical Perspective,* ed. Michael Gordon (New York: St. Martin's Press, 1983), 82-83.

3. Lasch, *Haven,* 83. Such readers, alarmed by what they saw as a peculiarly contemporary crisis, could also overlook Lasch's historical argument that the bourgeois family system had been slowly decaying throughout the twentieth century, a phenomenon that had been decried as early as the 1890s.

4. Carl N. Degler, *At Odds: Women and the Family in America from the Revolution to the Present Time* (New York: Oxford University Press, 1980), 8-9. Lasch more generally locates in this period the first appearance of the conception of the family as a "haven in a heartless world [taking] for granted a radical separation between work and leisure and between public life and private life." Gordon, 82. Stephanie Coontz similarly situates the emergence of "the domestic family" in "about the 1820s," but like Lasch and unlike Degler sees this family system as undergoing significant change in the early twentieth century. See Stephanie Coontz, *The Social Origins of Private Life: A History of American Families, 1600-1900* (New York: Verso, 1988), 34-35.

5. For an excellent account of the transformation of American society, see Gordon Wood, *The Radicalism of the American Revolution* (New York: Knopf, 1992).

6. See Douglas L. Wilson, "Jefferson and the Character Issue," *Atlantic Monthly* 270 (November 1992): 57-74, for an account of contemporary difficulties with Jefferson.

7. Coontz, *Social Origins of Private Life,* 15.

8. See Glen H. Elder, Jr., on "The Life Course Perspective" in "History and the Family: The Discovery of Complexity," *Journal of Marriage and the Family,* August 1981, 508-14. Also, Tamara K. Hareven, ed., *Transitions: The Family and the Life Course in Historical Perspective* (New York: Academic Press, 1978).

9. Jan Lewis, *The Pursuit of Happiness: Family and Values in Jefferson's Virginia* (New York: Cambridge University Press, 1983), 74.

10. Thomas Jefferson to Chastellux, November 26, 1783. In *The Papers of Thomas Jefferson,* ed. Julian Boyd et al., 27 vols. to date (Princeton: Princeton University Press, 1950-), 6:203. See also Martha Jefferson Randolph's account of her father's grief, pp. 199-200.

11. Boyd, *Papers,* 6:186. Famous because circulated and its contents fairly well known.

12. Boyd, *Papers,* 6:198.

13. Jan Lewis, "'The Blessings of Domestic Society': Thomas Jefferson's Family and the Transformation of American Politics," in *Jeffersonian Legacies,* ed. Peter Onuf (Charlottesville: University Press of Virginia, 1993), 111-12, notices this peculiar relationship between Jefferson's setbacks in public life and his affirmation of the value of family relationships. She however, contends that Jefferson's correspondence with his family discovers a realm of happiness not engaged by his political philosophy. I would like to argue for a closer relationship in which he in effect politicized his family and tried to sentimentalize civic society.

14. Boyd, *Papers,* 6:253. One indication of a changing attitude toward letter writing might lie in Jefferson's beginning to keep his "Summary Journal of Letters" on November 11, 1783. See "Foreword," Boyd, *Papers,* 6:vii-x.

15. For Jefferson's copy of the *Legacy,* see E. Millicent Sowerby, *Catalogue of the Library of Thomas Jefferson,* 5 vols. (Washington: Library of Congress, 1952-59), 2:50; letter from Thomas Jefferson to Mary Jefferson, February 16, 1791, in *The Family Letters of Thomas Jefferson,* ed. Edwin Morris Betts and James A. Bear, Jr. (1966; reprint, Charlottesville: University Press of Virginia, 1986), 72. Further quotations of Jefferson's letters to his children and grandchildren will be from this edition and identified parenthetically in the text by page number.

16. Locke, *Some Thoughts Concerning Education* in *John Locke on Politics and Education,* ed. Howard R. Penniman (New York: D. Van Nostrand, 1947), 211. John Gregory, *A Father's Legacy to His Daughters* (Boston, 1791), 18-19, 21, 32, 35, 33. In his study of the influence of Locke's rationalist pedagogy in America, Jay Fliegelman shows Gregory's popularity: *Prodigals and Pilgrims: The American Revolution against Patriarchal Authority, 1750-1800* (New York: Cambridge University Press, 1982), 39, 44-45.

17. Locke, 242. See also Jay Fliegelman, *Declaring Independence: Jefferson, Natural Language, and the Culture of Performance* (Stanford: Stanford University Press, 1993) 9-35, for a discussion of strategies of pedagogic discipline.

18. For example, seven-year-old Mary Jefferson was told "not to go out without your bonnet because it will make you very ugly and then we should not love you so much."

19. Fliegelman, *Declaring Independence,* 38-66, suggests both the prevalence and the complexity of the disciplinary use of emotion to ensure moral behavior. Despite some objections, Jefferson's reliance on moral sense theory is now a critical commonplace since Garry Wills, *Inventing America: Jefferson's Declaration of Independence* (New York: Doubleday, 1978).

20. D. D. Raphael, "Introduction" to Adam Smith, *The Theory of Moral*

Sentiments (Oxford: Oxford University Press, 1979), 15. The Skipwith letter is in Boyd, *Papers,* 1:76-81.

21. Adam Smith, *Theory of Moral Sentiments* (London: A Strahan, T. Cadell, 1792), 41, 113. Thomas Jefferson to Thomas Jefferson Randolph, Betts and Bear, *Family Letters,* 363. Jefferson's recognition of the moral significance of letter writing in the early years of his correspondence with his children seems to have developed over time. Compare the advice in this 1808 letter to consult the imagined moral presences of Small, Wythe, and Peyton Randolph with the more traditional description in his 1783 letter to daughter Martha of conscience as a "faithful internal Monitor" given to all by "Our maker" (21).

22. Smith, *Moral Sentiments,* 112. Richard Matthews in making a point to which mine is related, that Jefferson thought men "must be encouraged to pursue happiness in both" the public and the private realms, points to the influence of the Stoic Epictetus. *The Radical Politics of Thomas Jefferson* (Lawrence: University Press of Kansas, 1984), 94-95. It seems worth noting that D. D. Raphael observes, "it is not too much to say that Adam Smith's ethics and natural theology are predominantly Stoic" (10). The Stoic modulation of Jefferson's Epicureanism thus resonates with Smith's moral sense theory and enhances its power to make theatricalized internal voices stand against "the censure of the world."

23. Smith, *Moral Sentiments,* 110.

24. On the republic of letters, see Norman S. Fiering, "The Transatlantic Republic of Letters: A Note on the Circulation of Learned Periodicals to Early Eighteenth-Century America," *William and Mary Quarterly* 33(1976): 642-60.

25. Jürgen Habermas, *The Structural Transformation of the Public Sphere,* trans. Thomas Burger (Cambridge: MIT Press, 1989), 30. Habermas uses the term police not in its modern institutionalized sense, e.g., a police force, but in the earlier, more abstract sense of the state's oversight, or supervision, of the welfare and behavior of its subjects.

26. Jefferson, *Notes on the State of Virginia,* ed. William Peden (Chapel Hill: University of North Carolina Press, 1954), 159.

27. Pierre Eugène du Simitière taught art to Martha and other young ladies.

28. This was a basic feature of Lockean pedagogy. See Fliegelman, *Declaring Independence,* 14-15. Jefferson sent each of his daughters a letter that redefined their new relationship; in the case of his younger daughter, he responded to her account of problems in the Bolling family with a "sermon" on the importance for her of maintaining the affection of her husband. Jefferson to Mary Jefferson Epes, January 7, 1798, 151-53.

29. Thomas Jefferson to Nathaniel William Burwell, March 14, 1818. *The Writings of Thomas Jefferson,* ed. Andrew A. Lipscomb and Albert Ellery Bergh, 20 vols. (Washington: Thomas Jefferson Memorial Association, 1903–4), 15:165-66.

30. See William H. Gaines, Jr., *Thomas Mann Randolph: Jefferson's Son-in-Law* (Baton Rouge: Louisiana State University Press, 1966), 142-62, for an account of Randolph's melancholy and alienation in Jefferson's last years.

31. Letters of May 16 and 23, in Betts and Bear, *Family Letters,* 56, 57. Letter to Randolph in Lipscomb and Bergh, *Writings,* 8:29-33. The editors of *The Family Letters of Thomas Jefferson* leave out correspondence between Jefferson and his sons-in-law, presumably for reasons of space, but in doing so, they perhaps unintentionally misrepresent Jefferson's family. He wished to include his sons-in-law within the family circle and scheduled regular letters to them in ways in which he did not for his own brother and sisters.

32. See Smith, *Theory of Moral Sentiments,* 39.

33. Thomas Jefferson to Martha Jefferson Randolph, *Family Letters,* 146; Smith, *Moral Sentiments,* 23.

34. Jefferson to Priestley, Lipscomb and Bergh, *Writings,* 10: 142; on Trist and Bache, see Jane Flaherty Wells, "Thomas Jefferson's Neighbors: Hore Browse Trist of 'Birdwood' and Dr. William Bache of 'Franklin,'" *Magazine of Albemarle County History* 47(1989): 1-13. Jefferson's attempts to lure friends to settle near him was not merely philosophical, since he also extended his blandishments to political allies like Monroe and Madison. On his early efforts to surround Monticello with a congenial society, see Rhys Isaac, "The First Monticello," in *Jeffersonian Legacies,* 77-108.

35. See Michel Baridon, "Les méthodes d'observation de Jefferson," in *Voyage et Tourisme en Bourgogne à l'èpoque de Jefferson,* ed. Baridon and Bernard Chevignard (Dijon: Éditions universitaires de Dijon, 1988), 117-30, for a discussion of Jefferson's evolving attitude about observation and the value of fact.

36. Jefferson had set Ellen to breeding Bantam chickens; see his letter to her of November 30, 1806: "I propose on their subject a question of natural history for your enquiry: that is whether this is the Gallina Adrianica, or Adria, the Adsatick cock of Aristotle? For this you must examine Buffon, etc." (291).

37. See Jan Lewis, *Pursuit of Happiness,* "The Blessings of Domestic Society," and "The Republican Wife: Virtue and Seduction in the Early Republic," *William and Mary Quarterly* 44(1987): 689-721;

Rhys Isaac, *The Transformation of Virginia, 1740-1790* (Chapel Hill: University of North Carolina Press, 1982); Melvin Yazawa, *From Colonies to Commonwealth: Familial Ideology and the Beginnings of the America Republic* (Baltimore: Johns Hopkins University Press, 1985). Both Lewis in *Pursuit* and Isaac link the sentimentalization of society with the absence of successors to the great Virginia leaders of the revolutionary generation.

38. "Report of the Commissioners Appointed to Fix the Site of the University of Virginia" in Roy Honeywell, *The Educational Work of Thomas Jefferson* (Cambridge: Harvard University Press, 1931), 257; Harold Hellenbrand, *The Unfinished Revolution* (Newark: University of Delaware Press, 1990), has extensively discussed Jefferson's projects for affectionate education.

39. See Thomas Jefferson to the Trustees of East Tennessee College, May 6, 1810, Lipscomb and Bergh, *Writings,* 386-88.

40. For a masterly analysis of the changes in Virginians' self-understanding in the later eighteenth century, culminating in a triumph of sentiment, see Isaac, *The Transformation of Virginia.* For the sentimental transformation of the family in Jeffersonian Virginia, see Lewis, *The Pursuit of Happiness,* 209-30.

41. Thomas Jefferson to Joseph Coolidge, Jr., *Writings,* 18:343; Jefferson to Destutt Tracy, in Paul Leicester Ford, ed., *The Writings of Thomas Jefferson,* 10 vols. (New York: G.P. Putnam Sons, 1892-99), 10: 174; Jefferson to George Ticknor, Lipscomb and Bergh, *Writings,* 455.

BEYOND EDUCATION: THOMAS JEFFERSON'S "REPUBLICAN" REVISION OF THE LAWS REGARDING CHILDREN

HOLLY BREWER

I would like to thank Ruth Bloch, Joyce Appleby, and the members of EATS (the Early American Thesis Seminar at UCLA) for their encouragement and advice. The ideas presented here were elaborated in my dissertation, "Constructing Consent: How Children's Status in Political Theory Shaped Public Policy in Virginia, Pennsylvania, and Massachusetts before and after the American Revolution" (Ph.D. diss., University of California at Los Angeles, 1994), now in press.

1. Both passages are quoted in Julian P. Boyd, ed., *The Papers of Thomas Jefferson*, 27 vols. to date (Princeton: Princeton University Press, 1950), 2:308. The first passage was taken from a letter dated October 13, 1785, and the second from Jefferson's autobiography. See Paul Leicester Ford, ed., *The Writings of Thomas Jefferson* (New York: G.P. Putnam's Sons, 1892-99), 1:68-69.

2. For a good summary of the debate on this issue, see J. R. Pole's "Reflections on American Law and the American Revolution," *William and Mary Quarterly*, 3rd series, 50 (1993): 122-59, and the responses in the same volume by Peter Charles Hoffer, "Custom as Law: A Comment on J. R. Pole's 'Reflections,'" 160-67; and Bruce H. Mann, "The Evolutionary Revolution in American Law: A Comment on J. R. Pole's 'Reflections,'" 168-75. Bruce Mann, following his book *Neighbors and Strangers: Law and Community in Early Connecticut* (Chapel Hill: University of North Carolina Press, 1987) and an earlier article, "Legal Reform and the Revolution," in Jack P. Greene and J. R. Pole, eds., *The Blackwell Encyclopedia of the American Revolution* (Cambridge, Mass.: Blackwell Reference, 1991), 437-42, denies most strongly the relevance of the revolution to American law. It should be remembered, however, that Mann's work is focused on legal prosecutions for debt in Connecticut, and that there might have been less change during and after the revolution with respect to this issue than others. Certainly, as I acknowledge at the end of this essay, some of the changes in the laws that affected the legal status of children in Virginia were evolutionary as well as revolutionary: many of these evolutionary changes related to political thought as well, however. A persuasive argument for how the political and moral thought of late seventeenth- and early eighteenth-century England affected rules of legal evidence and procedure is made by Barbara J. Shapiro in *"Beyond Reasonable Doubt" and "Probable Cause": Historical Perspectives on the Anglo-American Law of Evidence* (Berkeley: University of California Press, 1991). Also see note 65, below.

3. Jefferson to Thomas Mann Randolph, Jr., Paris, July 6, 1787, Boyd, *Papers*, 11:557-58. The comment refers to Jefferson's suggestion that Randolph study politics and history together.

4. I define "republican" political theory in its broadest meaning as the group of political theories that were read and promulgated by those who justified the American revolution. I do not refer merely to the narrower group of writers designated as "Classical Republican" by such scholars as J. G. A. Pocock in his *The Machiavellian Moment: Florentine Political Thought and the Atlantic Republican Tradition* (Princeton, N.J.: Princeton

University Press, 1975) and about which there has appeared a voluminous literature over the past twenty years. As will be clear below, I explicitly include John Locke's writings, which have been described as being part of a separate tradition of liberalism.

5. Filmer, *Patriarcha,* report in Thomas Cook, ed., *Two Treatises of Government by John Locke with a Supplement Patriarcha by Robert Filmer* (New York: Hafner Publishing Co., 1947), 260.

6. See David Wootton, ed., *Divine Right and Democracy: An Anthology of Political Writing in Stuart England,* (New York: Penguin Books, 1986), 99, 105.

7. See Ernst H. Kantorowicz, *The King's Two Bodies: A Study in Medieval Political Theology* (Princeton, N.J.: Princeton University Press, 1957), 8, 18-19, and J. H. Burns, *Lordship, Kingship, and Empire: The Idea of Monarchy 1400-1525* (New York: Oxford University Press, 1992).

8. Obviously, there are other political theorists whom Jefferson admired. In emphasizing Locke and Sidney, I chose two authors whom he referred to consistently over the course of his political development. On this, see particularly, Ronald Hamowy, "Jefferson and the Scottish Enlightenment: A Critique of Garry Wills's *Inventing America: Jefferson's Declaration of Independence,*" in *William and Mary Quarterly,* 3rd ser., 36 (1979): 503-23, and Houston, on Algernon Sidney, cited below. Jefferson's 1771 letter to Robert Skipwith, in which he recommends reading Skipwith in order to receive a good education, included Locke, Sidney, Montesquieu, and a few other political authors (Boyd, *Papers,* 1:79).

In 1825, Jefferson claimed that the "authority" of the Declaration of Independence had come from "the harmonizing sentiments of the day, whether expressed in conversation, in letters, in printed essays, or in the elementary books of public right, as Aristotle, Cicero, Locke,

Sidney, &c." Also in 1825, Jefferson proposed that all law students at the University of Virginia, which he had founded, be given, in addition to distinctively American political texts such as the Constitution and the Federalist Papers, John Locke's *Second Treatise* and Sidney's *Discourses concerning Government,* which would provide "the general principles of liberty and the rights of man, in nature and in society." Both passages are quoted in Alan Craig Houston, *Algernon Sidney and the Republican Heritage in England and America* (Princeton, N.J.: Princeton University Press, 1991), 269.

9. This is not to imply that it is not useful to distinguish between the political ideas of James Harrington and John Locke, for example. It is merely to note that Jefferson did not see Sidney and Locke as having contradictory ideas and that there were many commonalities between the various "classical republican" and "liberal" thinkers: their theories are not necessarily distinguishable except by individual comparisons.

Garrett Ward Sheldon sees Jefferson as torn between these two schools of thought in *The Political Philosophy of Thomas Jefferson* (Baltimore: Johns Hopkins University Press, 1991). For more information on this debate see Gordon S. Wood, *The Creation of the American Republic, 1776-1787* (New York: Norton, 1972), Pocock, *The Machiavellian Moment* and *Three British Revolutions,* Lance Banning, *The Jeffersonian Persuasion* (Ithaca: Cornell University Press, 1978), Robert Shalhope, "Toward a Republican Synthesis: The Emergence of an Understanding of Republicanism in American Historiography," *William and Mary Quarterly,* 3rd ser., 29 (January 1972): 49-80, and "Republicanism and Early American Historiography," *William and Mary Quarterly,* 3rd ser., 39 (April 1982):334-56. Many scholars have recently pointed out that Locke's thought is not as distinct from that of classical republicanism as it has sometimes been portrayed and that classical republicanism itself has been so attractive because it was so protean. See Daniel T. Rogers, "Republicanism: The Career of a Concept," *Journal of American History* 79 (1992): 11-38, and Houston, *The Republican Heritage,* 8, 225. See also Isaac Kramnick, *Republicanism and Bourgeois Radicalism: Political Ideology in Late Eighteenth-Century England and America* (Ithaca: Cornell University Press, 1990) and Joyce Appleby's collection of essays in *Liberalism and Republicanism in the Historical Imagination* (Cambridge, Mass.: Harvard University Press, 1992). Bernard Bailyn, although credited with being one of the authors of the "Republican Synthesis," never distinguished Locke's thought as different from the other authors. See Bailyn, *The Ideological Origins of the American Revolution* (Cambridge, Mass.: Harvard University Press, 1967).

10. See, for example, Jefferson's letter to Robert Skipwith of 1771, cited above, where Jefferson encourages Skipwith to read Locke on education as well as Locke on government.

11. See, particularly, Samuel F. Pickering, *John Locke and Children's Books in Eighteenth-Century England* (Knoxville: University of Tennessee Press, 1981).

12. This is not to argue that Locke and Harrington, for example, had the same ultimate vision of the common good. The social ends of education emphasized self-sacrifice for the public weal more in Harrington's discussion. Shelley Burtt's *Virtue Transformed: Political Argument in England, 1688-1740* (Cambridge: Cambridge University Press, 1992), has an excellent discussion of the different meanings of civic virtue in early eighteenth-century England. She differentiates between a "publicly-oriented" and a "privately-oriented" definition of virtue,

where the first focuses on self-sacrifice for the public good (such as military service) and the second focuses on morally developing the self, especially "the dispositions which contributed most importantly to the preservation of public liberty [such as] personal honesty, industry, [and] frugality in one's personal affairs" (p. 10). Lockean virtue and much of what Pocock has described as public virtue fall into the second category. Burtt acknowledges the latter, but strangely neglects any discussion of Locke except to summarize the received interpretation of his political ideas: that he promoted self-interest. Yet Locke begins his *Thoughts Concerning Education* (1693) with a discussion of how education leads to virtue, and teaches a child to deny simple self-interest. "The great Principle and foundation of all virtue and worth is placed in this: That a man is able to deny himself his own Desires, cross his own Inclinations, and purely follow what reason directs as best tho' the appetite lean the other Way." Locke, *Thoughts Concerning Education,* ed. John W. Yolton and Jean S. Yolton (Oxford, U.K.: Oxford University Press, 1989), 21. For a subtle discussion of different meanings of virtue in America in the late eighteenth century, along with its intellectual roots, see Ruth Bloch, "The Gendered Meanings of Virtue in Revolutionary America," in *Signs* 13 (1987): 37-58.

13. John Locke, *Second Treatise of Government,* C. B. McPherson, ed. (Indianapolis: Hackett, 1980), 31-32.

14. See Locke, *An Essay Concerning Human Understanding,* Peter H. Nidditch, ed. (Oxford: Oxford University Press, 1975), esp. 127- 32, 163-66.

15. Locke was not the only seventeenth- or eighteenth-century political writer to create a distinctive political space for children. James Harrington, who wrote thirty years earlier during the English civil war and was the main exponent of what J. G.

A Pocock distinguished as "republican" ideas that differed from Locke's, would have agreed with Locke on the essential point about a just government being based on the consent of those who have reason. According to Harrington, "the liberty of a man consists in the empire of his reason." In Harrington's *Oceana* the ones who make decisions are the wise and those who vote for these "Fathers" are those men who are above the age of thirty and who have "paternal power" and wisdom.

Harrington sought in a way to compromise between Filmer's emphasis on fatherly power and an authority based on consent by claiming that those who should elect and be elected should be wise but were also "fathers" and bore fatherly authority. Thus Harrington did not separate parental power from state power, as did Locke, but he did recognize the same link that those who should have power should have the most reason. See J. G. A. Pocock, *The Machiavellian Moment: Florentine Political Thought and the Atlantic Republican Tradition,* (Princeton: Princeton University Press, 1975), 424, and James Harrington, "The Commonwealth of Oceana," in *The Political Works of James Harrington,* ed. J. G. A. Pocock, (Cambridge: Cambridge University Press, 1977), 170, 212-13, 349, also 358, where "Lord Archon," the founder of the mythical kingdom of "Oceana," has his tombstone inscribed with "pater patriae."

16. A member of the long parliament who had actively participated in the civil war, Sidney was executed for treason in 1683 largely because of his *Discourses concerning Government.* His writings were popular in eighteenth-century America, where he was considered a martyr for liberty. See Houston, *Algernon Sidney.*

17. Locke did not emphasize this aspect of Filmer's work to the same extent as Sidney. He did, however make the same point as Sidney when he criticized primo-

geniture for illogically promoting some to authority over others, particularly when an "infant" was promoted over "a man and able." "I go on then to ask whether in the inheriting of this paternal power, this supreme fatherhood, the grandson by a daughter hath a right before a nephew by a brother? Whether the grandson by the eldest son, being an infant, before the younger son, a man and able? . . ." John Locke, "First Treatise of Government," in Thomas I. Cook, ed., *Two Treatises of Government by John Locke with a Supplement Patriarcha by Robert Filmer* (New York: Hafner Publishing Co., 1947), 89.

18. Filmer, "Patriarcha," 258.

19. Sidney, *Discourses Concerning Government,* ed. Thomas G. West (Indianapolis: Liberty Classics, 1990), 6.

20. For other explicit references to a child-king who lacks reason, a situation that Sidney regards as neither "reasonable nor just" see Sidney, *Discourses,* 81, 119, 248, 279-80, 299, 300-301, 389, 390, 392, 393, 400, 404, 464, 532-34, 549, 552. Sidney acknowledged that a particularly wise child might not be the worst choice for king. Citing Solomon's dictum that "*a wise child is better than an old and foolish king*" (Ecclesiastes 4:13), he argued that power should not simply be based on the right of the eldest—but it should be based on who is the worthiest. See page 38.

Tom Paine, in *Common Sense,* a pamphlet that sold more copies than any other book except the Bible in eighteenth-century America (most in 1776) made an attack on primogeniture the centerpiece of his criticisms. As with Sydney, he made a strong point that qualifications for government in a monarchy were by birth, not by wisdom or the ability to exercise reason or to represent the interests of the people. Not only was many a king foolish but also, "[a]nother evil which attends hereditary succession is, that the throne is subject to be possessed by a minor at any age." Paine, "Common Sense," reprinted in Michael Foot and Isaac Kramnick, eds., *Thomas Paine Reader* (Harmondsworth, Middlesex, Eng.: Penguin Books, 1987).

21. Edmund S. Morgan has argued that we must see the use of the term *equality* as a fiction used by members of powerful political factions to gain legitimacy for their groups, a term which ultimately became self-fulfilling, but almost by accident. Morgan has claimed that it was a fiction since it was obviously not true. Morgan is clearly correct in the broader sense. Yet if the emphasis on equality is contextualized within the other emphases in the political discourses of the eighteenth century, notably the emphasis on reason, it is clear that contemporaries did not regard equality merely as a fiction and that many held it out as a goal. See Morgan's *Inventing the People: The Rise of Popular Sovereignty in England and America* (New York: Norton, 1988).

22. See Boyd, *Papers,* 1:135.

23. Boyd, *Papers,* 2:545. Most of this passage was cut in the version of the bill that was finally passed.

24. See "Jefferson's Third Draft of the Virginia Constitution, 1776," in Boyd, *Papers,* 1:358. Jefferson restricted the suffrage to "male persons of *full age and sane mind,*" [my italics] who had a quarter acre in a town or twenty-five acres of land in the country or who had paid taxes for two years. The implications of "reasonability" and property restrictions will be more fully discussed below.

25. Boyd, *Papers,* 2:545.

26. "To Robert Pigott" Paris, June 3, 1788, Boyd, *Papers,* 13:235.

27. Locke, *Second Treatise of Government,* chap. 34, para. 61.

28. Virginians had "the first legislature who has had the courage to declare that the reason of man may be trusted with the formation of his own opinions." Paris, December 16, 1786, Boyd, *Papers,* 10:604

29. See, for example, Jefferson's letter to James Madison dated October 28, 1785 (Boyd, *Papers,* 8:682). "Whenever there is in any country, uncultivated lands and unemployed poor, it is clear that the laws of property have been so far extended as to violate natural right. The earth is given as a common stock for man to labour and live on. If, for the encouragement of industry we allow it to be appropriated, we must take care that other employment be furnished to those excluded from the appropriation. If we do not the fundamental right to labour the earth returns to the unemployed." Jefferson does not specifically mention that the unemployed (and the unpropertied) should be taught a trade, but that is the clear implication.

30. "To George Wythe," Paris, August 13, 1786, Boyd, *Papers,* 10:244.

31. "To Edward Carrington," Paris, January 16, 1787, Boyd, *Papers,* 11:49.

32. That suffrage restrictions and electability restrictions derived from children's lack of reason is clear from a comment by Gouverneur Morris of Pennsylvania in the constitutional debates over suffrage qualifications. By the time that Morris was speaking, suffrage restrictions based on age had been in place for almost a century in all regions of the colonies/states. "Children do not vote. Why? Because they want prudence, because they have no will of their own. The ignorant and the dependent can be as little trusted with the public interest." Cited in Wilbourn E. Benton, ed., *1787: Drafting the U.S. Constitution* (College Station: Texas A & M Press, 1986), 2:228. Morris was here using the exclusion of children from the suffrage as a basis for excluding others. Yet he was also making a larger, very strong argument that children could not consent, that their consent was in fact irrelevant, because "they have no will of their own," and are dependent.

John Adams made the same argument in a letter debating the limits that should be placed on the "consent of the people."

"It is certain in Theory," he begins, "that the only moral Foundation of Government is the consent of the People. But to what Extent Shall We carry this Principle? . . . Children have not Judgment or Will of their own. True. But will not these reasons apply to others? Is it not equally true, that Men in general in every Society, who are wholly destitute of Property, are also too little acquainted with public Affiars to form a Right Judgment, and too dependent upon other Men to have a Will of their own?" For Adams, children, like poor men and women, servants and slaves, were dependent on those who fed, clothed, and employed them, and thus for Adams were in critical ways incapable of making independent, rational decisions and incapable of citizenship. This letter continues at great length in the same vein. Adams to James Sullivan. See Robert J. Taylor, ed., *Papers of John Adams,* 4:208-13, (Cambridge, Mass.: Harvard University Press, 1979). Also see, on this, *Federalist* number 79, by Hamilton. "A power over a man's subsistence amounts to a power over his will."

33. Quoted by Shannon C. Stimson, *The American Revolution in the Law: Anglo-American Jurisprudence before John Marshall* (Princeton: Princeton University Press, 1990), 101. The emphasis on the importance of reason in granting authority to a just government is repeated in political writings in the American colonies at the time of the American Revolution and afterward. Madison, in *Federalist* number 49 wrote that "[I]t is the reason, alone, of the public that ought to control and regulate the government."

34. There is considerable debate about whether Locke was more conservative or radical in his political vision, and thus whether Locke believed that all male adults possessed the requisite qualities for the franchise. See, particularly, Richard Ashcraft, *Revolutionary Politics and Locke's "Two Treatises of Government"* (Princeton:

Princeton University Press, 1986), chap. 4, and C. B. MacPherson, *The Political Theory of Possessive Individualism* (Oxford: Clarendon Press, 1962).

35. "To John Banister" Paris, February 7, 1787, Boyd, *Papers,* 11:120.

36. For an examination of these issues in detail, see Jan Lewis, *The Pursuit of Happiness: Family and Values in Jefferson's Virginia* (Cambridge: Cambridge University Press, 1983).

37. Annapolis, December 11, 1783, Jefferson, *Papers,* 6:379-80. The context of the quote is the following: ". . . I hope you have restored yourself perfectly to the esteem of Mr. Maury. I have so much confidence in his justice and prudence as to be satisfied he will always make your good the object of what he does. Were it to happen however that in the exercise of that strict discipline which a large school requires, that he should be harsher with you than you suppose to be necessary, yet you must have resolution enough to bear it, and to bear it with resignation."

38. See, for example, "To Martha Jefferson," Annapolis, November 28, 1783, Boyd, *Papers,* 6:359-60 or "To Mary Jefferson," Paris, September 29, 1785, *Papers,* 8:532-33, where he used the word "love" at least eight times in a letter where he encouraged her, in exchange for his love, among other things to learn "to play on the harpsichord, . . . to read and talk French, . . . [to be] a very good girl, . . . never suffer yourself to be angry with any body, . . . give your playthings to those who want them . . . mind your book and your work when your aunt tells you, never play but when she permits you, nor go where she forbids you."

39. From Jefferson's account book for 1774. Boyd, *Papers,* 1:495.

40. See [Hening], *Statutes at Large,* 9:226.

41. Brewer, "Entailing Aristocracy in Colonial Virginia: 'Ancient Feudal Restraints' and Revolutionary Reform,"

William and Mary Quarterly, 3rd ser., 54, no. 2 (April 1997): 307-46.

42. See Bills 20 and 21 of the revisal of the laws, in Boyd, *Papers,* 2:391-92, 394. Also see Bill 60, where it is directed that "any father, even if he be not twenty one years old, may, by deed, or last will and testament, either of them being executed in presence of two creditable witnesses, grant or devise the custody and tuition of his child, which had never been married, although it be not born during any part of the infancy of such child, to whomsoever he will."

43. Boyd, *Papers,* 2:477.

44. "Notes on British and American Alienage" [1783], Boyd, *Papers,* 6:433-34. [I think this is misdated by the editors, who guessed at 1783 because it must have occurred after peace with England. Yet this same argument is expressed, in detail, in a letter to John Adams dated February 7, 1786, *Papers,* 9:259.] This letter makes it clear that Jefferson differed from others on the question of whether adult American citizens could inherit English property.

> *Qu. 1:* *Can an American citizen, adult, now inherit lands in England?*
>
> Natural subjects can inherit. Aliens cannot.
>
> There is no middle character. Every man must be the one or the other of these.
>
> A natural subject is one born within the king's allegiance and still owing allegiance. No instance can be produced in the English law, nor can it admit the idea of a person's being a natural subject and yet not owing allegiance.
>
> An alien is the subject or citizen of a foreign power.
>
> The treaty of peace acknowledges we are no longer to owe allegiance to the king of G.B. It acknowledges us no longer as Natural subjects then.
>
> . . . it makes us aliens then . . .

> *Qu. 2.* *The father a British subject; the son in America, adult, and within the description of an American citizen, according to their laws. Can the son inherit?*
>
> . . . He owes allegiance to the states. He is an alien then and cannot inherit . . .

> *Qu. 3* *The father is a British subject. The son as in Qu. 2, but an infant. Can be inherit?*
>
> As long as the infant were born in Britain . . . or "within the king's obedience . . ." the infant can inherit.

Linda Kerber has written a fascinating analysis of whether women were citizens in the New Republic, concluding from a situation remarkably similar to the one that Jefferson outlined above that there was tension and it was unresolved. See Kerber, "The Paradox of Women's Citizenship in the Early Republic: The Case of *Martin vs. Massachusetts,* 1805," *American Historical Review* 97 (1992): 349-78.

45. See Bills 116, 48, and 27, the last two probably written by Jefferson, in Boyd *Papers,* 2: 631, 465, 415.

46. Care, *English Liberties: or, The Freeborn Subject's Inheritance . . .* (London, 1680), 103. This pamphlet was reprinted in Boston in 1721 and in Providence in 1774.

47. The Virginia Constitution gave twenty-five as the minimum age. See [Hening], *Statutes at Large,* 9:114 (1776). For Jefferson's suggestions, see "Jefferson's Third Draft of the Virginia Constitution" [1776], in Boyd, *Papers,* 1:359.

48. The version of the militia law that came out of the revision of the laws actually set the minimum age limit at sixteen, which matched the extant law. This particular bill was probably not written by Jefferson, but he probably approved it, on some level, since he, Wythe, and Pendleton discussed their revisions. When the bill was actually passed in 1784, however, the

minimum age was set at eighteen. See Bill
5, Boyd, *Papers,* 2:350.

49. See Morgan, *Inventing the People,*
and Richard Bushman, *King and People in
Provincial Massachusetts* (Chapel Hill:
Published for the Institute of Early
American History and Culture by the
University of North Carolina Press, 1985).

50. For Jefferson's suffrage restrictions,
see "Jefferson's Third Draft of the Virginia
Constitution" [1776] in Boyd, *Papers,*
1:358. "All male persons of full age [twen-
ty-one] and sane mind and [some minimal property or residence requirements]."
"To Edmund Pendleton" August 26, 1776,
in Boyd, *Papers,* 1:503, where he recommends "having resided a certain time, or
having a family, or any or all of them."
Age and gender were probably implicit.
Also see "A Bill concerning the Election of
Members of the General Assembly" in the
Revisal of the Laws (Bill 2) in Boyd,
Papers, 2:337, which allowed "Every free
male person, aged twenty one years" and
who was possessed of property or a long-
term lease to vote. The assembly, when
passing this bill into law, specifically
excluded "free negroes or mulattos" and
added residency requirements.

Also see his "Report of the Committee
[to prepare a plan for the temporary government of the Western Territory] March
1, 1784, in Boyd, *Papers,* 6:603-4. The creation of temporary governments would
come from settlers who were "free males
of full age."

51. See above, note 32.

52. Bill 86 of the Revisal of the Laws,
Boyd, *Papers,* 2:557. Any clerk who issued
a marriage license without the father's or
guardian's consent to the marriage of a
person under twenty-one would be liable
for damages.

53. Bill 86 was brought up by Madison
in 1785. It was postponed to 1786 and
passed a "second reading" but was never
formally passed. In [Hening], *Statutes at
Large,* 12:688 (1788), a similar law that

prohibits marriages is passed but the
clause that marriages of minors without
parental consent are "null" or void was
not part of the law.

54. See particularly [Henry Stebbing],
*An Enquiry into the Force and Operation
of the Annulling Clauses in a Late Act for
the Better Preventing of Clandestine
Marriages* . . . (London, 1754), which
apparently began the controversy, and
also his *A Dissertation on the Power of
States to Deny Civil Protection to the
Marriages of Minors made without the
Consent of their Parents or Guardians* . . .,
(London, 1754). At least seven other pamphlets appeared between 1754 and 1756 on
this subject. It is not clear whether they
were read in the colonies. I have found
no evidence that any of them were actually published in the colonies, but they
might well have been available, and
excerpts might well have appeared in
newspapers.

55. This is elaborated in my disserta-
tion, "Constructing Consent," chapter 3.
On English marriage law, see Lawrence
Stone, *Broken Lives: Separation and
Divorce in England, 1660-1857* (Oxford:
Oxford University Press, 1993, 55-57.

56. See Jefferson's comments on his
revisal of the laws, Bill 64, Boyd, *Papers,*
2:497. He concluded that "the offence of
carnally knowing a girl under 12 (the age
of consent) or 10 years of age will not be
distinguished from any other." Rape was
defined under the common law as having
carnal copulation with a woman without
her consent. See, for example, Michael
Dalton, *The Country Justice* (Amsterdam:
N. Israel, 1975), 248. Dalton's *Justice* was
originally published in 1619 and was recommended for the use of Virginia justices of the peace by an act of 1666 for
"the better conformity of the proceedings
of the courts of this country." See
Hening, *[Virginia] Statutes,* 2:246. "[T]o
ravish a woman, where she doth neither
consent before nor after; or to ravish any

woman with force, though she do consent after, is felony."

57. Thanks to Ruth Bloch for this insight.

58. Both laws were based on earlier English statutes. These various laws are cited by Hening, *[Virginia] Statues.* These issues are fully discussed in my dissertation, "Constructing Consent," chapter 6, which concerns limits on the custody of parents and masters, especially as they pertain to physical abuse.

59. See, for example, Dalton, *Countrey Justice,* 204-6, which discusses the crime of petty treason and the punishment. "The childe maliciously killeth the father, or mother; this is Pettie treason (although the father or mother at the same time give neither meate, drinke, nor wages to such childe:) But it is Trason in the child, in respect of the duetie of nature violated." How interesting that for Jefferson, to be dissected by anatomists after death was that extra punishment beyond death. It displays Jefferson's attachment to science.

60. From Bill 64, on crimes, of the revisal of the laws. Boyd, *Papers,* 2:494. Indeed, the evidence I have from Frederick County, Virginia, shows that prosecution of "murders" of bastard children dropped precipitously between the 1750s and the 1810s, probably in part, at least, because this presumption of guilt was dropped.

61. The origins of pension plans in Virginia has not yet received thorough treatment. The act of October 1779 in fact replaced earlier, partial pension plans. The first pension plan included benefits only for the families of soldiers maimed or wounded in the French and Indian war and was passed in 1755. [Hening], *Statutes at Large,* 6:527. In 1775, at the beginning of the Revolutionary War, partly to encourage more to enlist, the legislature promised that it would provide financial support for all those maimed in the war (*Statutes,* 9:14).

In 1777, for the first time, temporary support was to be provided to widows whose husbands had died while soldiers in the Continental or Commonwealth armies (*Statutes,* 9:344-45). In October 1778 that was substantially reinforced by giving pensions to all widows of soldiers for the remainder of their natural lives "equal to half the pay that her husband was entitled to when in the service" (*Statutes,* 9:566). The purpose of this law was explicitly to "provid[e] for the family of such officers and soldiers."

In October 1779 these earlier plans were abrogated for widows who did not have financial need, but provided for additional family members who could demonstrate poverty. The new plan gave county courts the power "to grant allowances to the wives, parents, and families of any soldier now in actual service, upon proof to them made, that such wives, parents, or families are so poor that they cannot maintain themselves; such allowance not to exceed one barrel of corn and fifty pounds of nett port for each person, annually." Earlier acts which gave pensions to all widows were disallowed, but special, and broader provisions were made for indigent families: these would have been the families most likely to fall upon poor relief and the children in these families would have been the most likely to have been bound out (*Statutes,* 10:212). In 1782 the provisions for the families of soldiers were made easier to obtain and in 1785 pensions for the maimed soldiers and for the families of soldiers killed in the Revolutionary War were upheld and the process simplified (*Statutes,* 11:11, 11:146, and 12:102-6). My examination of the records of Frederick County, Virginia, reveals that substantial provision was made for many different families under this law during the 1780s.

62. The analysis and data about apprenticeships are presented in chapter 6 of my dissertation. Significant changes in

the ability of illigitimate children to remain with their mothers are not evident until the 1810s. My study looked at only these three decades (1750s, 1780s, and 1810s) so the change with regard to provision for illigitimate children may have begun as early as the 1790s.

63. Bill 60, Boyd, *Papers,* 2:487. Also Bill 32, "A bill for the support of the Poor," 2:420. Also see Bill 51, "A bill concerning slaves," where it was directed that mulatto children should be bound out just as were poor orphans, 2:471, and Bill 17, "A bill concerning seamen," which allowed poor boys over age ten to be bound apprentices to the masters of ships, 2:383.

64. See Bill 79, "A Bill for the more General Diffusion of Knowledge," Boyd, *Papers,* 2:526-27.

65. This problem has been persuasively illuminated recently by James Q. Whitman and David Lieberman in terms of the tension between "custom" and "reason" in eighteenth-century legal thought. Precedent was not merely custom: it sifted the past for appropriate precedents. Whitman, "Why Did the Revolutionary Lawyers Confuse Custom and Reason?" *University of Chicago Law Review* 58 (1991): 1321-68. David Lieberman, *The Province of Legislation Determined: Legal Theory in Eighteenth-Century Britain*

(Cambridge: Cambridge University Press, 1989), delineates some of the profound ways in which Blackstone's influential version of the common law was shaped by the Enlightenment. For a discussion of how legal tradition could be used to legitimate opposing points of view, see J. G. A. Pocock, *The Ancient Constitution and the Feudal Law: A Study of English Historical Thought in the Seventeenth-Century, a Reissue with Retrospect* (Cambridge: Cambridge University Press, 1987). Jefferson himself, while not denying that a common law, as such, existed, castigated Blackstone for differing from Coke in his interpretation of the common law. Coke's Whig principles were clear in his *Institutes,* but Blackstone's *Commentaries on the Common Law* created "Tories of all those young Americans whose native feelings of independence do not place them above the wily sophistries of a Hume or a Blackstone." See Julius S. Waterman, "Thomas Jefferson and Blackstone's Commentaries," in David Flaherty, ed., *Essays in the History of Early American Law* (Chapel Hill: University of North Carolina Press, 1969), 451-88, 458-59. See also note 2, above.

66. See my dissertation, "Constructing Consent," chapters 3 and 4.

JEFFERSON, THE FAMILY, AND CIVIC EDUCATION

JAN LEWIS

1. Thomas Jefferson, *Writings,* ed. Merrill D. Peterson (New York: Library of America, 1984); Thomas Jefferson, *The Life and Selected Writings of Thomas Jefferson,* ed. Adrienne Koch and William Peden (New York: Modern Library, 1944).

2. See for example Jay Fliegelman, *Prodigals and Pilgrims: The American Revolution against Patriarchal Authority,*

1750-1800 (New York: Cambridge University Press, 1982); Edwin G. Burrows and Michael Wallace, "The American Revolution: The Ideology and Psychology of National Liberation," *Perspectives in American History* 6 (1972): 167-306; Winthrop D. Jordan, "Familial Politics: Thomas Paine and the Killing of the King, 1776," *Journal of American History* 60

(1973): 294-308; and Melvin Yazawa, *From Colonies to Commonwealth: Familial Ideology and the Beginnings of the American Republic* (Baltimore: Johns Hopkins University Press, 1985).

3. Garry Wills, *Imagining America: Jefferson's Declaration of Independence* (New York: Doubleday, 1978), 312.

4. Despite the problems inherent in some of its psychoanalytic interpretations, the best work on Jefferson's family is Fawn M. Brodie, *Thomas Jefferson: An Intimate History* (New York: W.W. Norton, 1974). Also valuable is Dumas Malone, *Jefferson the Virginian* (Boston: Little, Brown, and Co., 1948). For family life in Jefferson's Virginia, see Daniel Blake Smith, *Inside the Great House: Planter Family Life in Eighteenth-Century Chesapeake Society* (Ithaca: Cornell University Press, 1980), and Jan Lewis, *The Pursuit of Happiness: Family and Values in Jefferson's Virginia* (New York: Cambridge University Press, 1983).

5. See Jan Lewis, "The Republican Wife: Virtue and Seduction in the Early Republic," *William and Mary Quarterly,* 3d ser., 44 (1987): 689-721.

6. Jefferson's son-in-law's sister would later be implicated in the killing of her own illegitimate infant. Jefferson believed the young woman to be innocent, and he would counsel his daughter Martha to be charitable: "Never throw off the best affections of nature in the moment when they become most precious to their object; nor fear to extend your hand to save another, less you should sink yourself." Jefferson to Martha Jefferson Randolph, April 28, 1793, in *The Family Letters of Thomas Jefferson,* ed. by Edwin Morris Betts and James A. Bear, Jr. (Columbia, Mo.: University of Missouri Press, 1966; Charlottesville: Published for the Thomas Jefferson Memorial Foundation by the University Press of Virginia, 1986), 116.

7. Daniel J. Boorstin, *The Lost World of Thomas Jefferson* (Boston: Beacon Press, 1948; 1960).

8. See, for example, Boorstin, *Lost World of Thomas Jefferson;* Joyce Appleby, *Liberalism and Republicanism in the Historical Imagination* (Cambridge, Mass.: Harvard University Press, 1992); and *Capitalism and a New Social Order* (New York: New York University Press, 1984); and John P. Diggins, *The Lost Soul of American Politics: Virtue, Self-interest, and the Foundations of Liberalism* (New York: Basic Books, 1984).

9. Alexis de Tocqueville, *Democracy in America,* translated by Henry Reeve, rev. Francis Bowen, ed. Phillips Bradley, 2 vols. (New York: Alfred A. Knopf, 1945); Nancy F. Cott, *The Bonds of Womanhood: "Woman's Sphere" in New England, 1780-1865* (New Haven: Yale University Press, 1977); Kathryn Kish Sklar, *Catharine Beecher: A Study in American Domesticity* (New Haven: Yale University Press, 1973); and Steven Mintz and Susan Kellogg, *Domestic Revolutions: A Social History of American Family Life* (New York: Basic Books, 1988).

10. Jay Fliegelman, *Declaring Independence: Jefferson, Natural Language, and the Culture of Performance* (Stanford: Stanford University Press, 1993). See also Smith, *Inside the Great House;* Philip Greven, *The Protestant Temperament: Patterns of Religious Experience and the Self in Early America* (New York: Alfred A. Knopf, 1977); and Lewis, *Pursuit of Happiness.*

11. The question of children's rights has been brought to the public's attention recently by several highly publicized child custody cases and by the work of Hillary Rodham Clinton. Clinton has suggested that the law should presume the competence of minors, rather than presuming their incompetence, as is now the case. See Garry Wills, "H. R. Clinton's Case," *New York Review of Books* 39 (March 5, 1992): 3-5.

12. See also Fliegelman, *Prodigals and Pilgrims.*

13. See Lewis, "'The Blessings of Domestic Society': Thomas Jefferson's Family and the Transformation of American Politics," in Peter S. Onuf, ed., *Jeffersonian Legacies* (Charlottesville: University Press of Virginia, 1993), 109-46.

14. "First Inaugural Address," March 4, 1801, in Thomas Jefferson, *Writings,* ed. Merrill D. Peterson (New York: Library of America, 1984), 494.

15. Joyce Appleby, "Jefferson and His Complex Legacy," in Onuf, ed., *Jeffersonian Legacies,* 1-16.

16. Jürgen Habermas, *The Structural Transformation of the Public Sphere,* trans. by Thomas Burger (Cambridge, Mass.: MIT Press, 1989).

17. Thomas Paine, *Common Sense,* ed. by Isaac Kramnick (New York: Penguin Books, 1986), 65.

18. "First Inaugural Address," in Peterson, *Writings,* 493.

19. Jefferson to Martha Jefferson, May 31, 1798, in Betts and Bear, *Family Letters,* 164.

20. Martha Jefferson Randolph to Jefferson, January 31, 1801; Jefferson to Martha Jefferson Randolph, February 5, 1801, ibid., 192-96.

21. Jefferson to James Madison, February 20, 1784, in Malone, *Jefferson the Virginian,* 409. See also Rhys Isaac, "The First Monticello," in Onuf, ed., *Jeffersonian Legacies,* 87-88.

22. See Wills, *Inventing America.*

23. Jefferson to Martha Jefferson Randolph, May 17, 1798, in Betts and Bear, *Family Letters,* 161.

24. Jefferson to Martha Jefferson Randolph, February 5, 1801, in Betts and Bear, *Family Letters,* 195-96.

25. Kenneth A. Lockridge, *On the Sources of Patriarchal Rage: The Commonplace Books of William Byrd and Thomas Jefferson and the Gendering of Power in the Eighteenth Century* (New York: New York University Press, 1992).

26. Frank Shuffelton, "In Different Voices: Gender in the American Republic of Letters," *Early American Literature* 25 (1990): 289-304. "It is notable that Jefferson's letter [to Abigail Adams] about politics and friendship, public differences and private bonds, creates an enlarged family circle, a kind of town meeting in the republic of letters which recognizes that the world of print needs to be balanced by the consenting heart" (301).

27. Jefferson to Anne Willing Bingham, May 11, 1788, in Peterson, *Writings,* 922-23.

28. See Lewis, " 'Blessings of Domestic Society.'"

29. Jefferson to Nathaniel Burwell, March 14, 1818, in Peterson, *Writings,* 1:411.

30. In Peterson, *Writings,* 367.

31. Ellen W. Coolidge to Mr. [Henry] Randall, 185[ ], in Sarah N. Randolph, *The Domestic Life of Thomas Jefferson* (Charlottesville: Thomas Jefferson Memorial Foundation, 1939; 1947), 294.

32. Dumas Malone, *The Sage of Monticello* (Boston: Little Brown & Co., 1977; 1981), 294-95.

33. *Collected Papers of the Monticello Association of the Descendants of Thomas Jefferson,* ed. George Green Shackelford (Charlottesville: Monticello Association, 1984), 35.

34. Jefferson to Burwell, March 14, 1818, in Peterson, *Writings,* 1:411.

35. Jefferson to Martha Jefferson Randolph, August 31, 1817, in *Family Letters* ed. Betts and Bear, 419.

JEFFERSON AND LITERACY

DOUGLAS L. WILSON

1. Merrill D. Peterson, "The American Scholar: Emerson and Jefferson," in *Thomas Jefferson and the World of Books: A Symposium held at the Library of Congress, September 21, 1976* (Washington: Library of Congress, 1977), 29.

2. This view is expressed by the Head in the famous dialogue Jefferson composed for Maria Cosway between his Head and his Heart. Jefferson to Maria Cosway, October 12, 1786, in Thomas Jefferson, *Writings,* ed. Merrill D. Peterson (New York: Library of America, 1984), 872.

3. David D. Hall, *Worlds of Wonder, Days of Judgment: Popular Religious Belief in Early New England* (Cambridge: Harvard University Press, 1990 [1989]), 38.

4. Charles Francis Adams, ed., "A Dissertation on the Canon and Feudal Law," *The Works of John Adams,* 10 vols. (Boston: Little, Brown, 1850-56), 3:448.

5. Ibid., 3:456.

6. Peterson, *Writings,* 365.

7. Quoted in William Gribbin, "Rollin's Histories and American Republicanism," *William and Mary Quarterly,* 3d series 29 (October 1972): 616.

8. Peterson, *Writings,* 1308-9.

9. Thomas Jefferson to John Wythe, May 19, 1809, Peterson, *Writings,* 1207-8.

10. See his letter to P. S. Dupont de Nemours, April 24, 1816, Peterson, *Writings,* 1387-88.

11. Carl F. Kaestle, "The History of Literacy and the History of Readers," *Review of Research in Education,* vol. 12, ed. Edmund W. Gordon (Washington: American Educational Research Association, 1985), 12.

12. Kaestle, "The History of Literacy and the History of Readers," 14, 13.

13. Ibid., 29. A study making the case for colonial American schools as conservative and constraining is Kenneth A. Lockridge, *Literacy in Colonial New England: An Enquiry into the Social Context of Literacy in the Early Modern West* (New York: Norton, 1974).

14. Cathy N. Davidson, *Revolution and the Word: The Rise of the Novel in America* (New York: Oxford University Press, 1986), 58.

15. Ibid., 64.

16. Jefferson to Edward Carrington, January 16, 1787, in Julian P. Boyd, ed., *The Papers of Thomas Jefferson,* 27 vols. to date (Princeton: Princeton University Press, 1950-), 11:48-49.

17. E. D. Hirsch, Jr., *Cultural Literacy: What Every American Needs to Know* (Boston: Houghton Mifflin, 1987), 13.

18. Jefferson to John Adams, May 17, 1818, *The Adams-Jefferson Letters,* ed. Lester J. Cappon, 2 vols. (Chapel Hill: Published for the Institute of Early American History and Culture at Williamsburg, Va., by the University of North Carolina Press, 1959), 524.

19. See my exposition of this matter in "Thomas Jefferson's Library and the Skipwith List," *Harvard Library Bulletin,* new series 3, no. 4 (Winter 1992-93), 65-68.

20. Jefferson to William Duane, August 12, 1810, Peterson, *Writings,* 1:228. For an account of Jefferson's view of Hume's history, see Douglas L. Wilson, "Jefferson vs. Hume," *William and Mary Quarterly,* 3d series 46 (January 1989): 49-70.

21. See Douglas L. Wilson, ed., *Jefferson's Literary Commonplace Book, The Papers of Thomas Jefferson,* 2d series, ed. Charles T. Cullen (Princeton: Princeton University Press, 1989), 24-38, 40-55, 155-57.

22. Jefferson to Peter Carr, August 10,

1787, Peterson, *Writings,* 904.

23. Kaestle, "The History of Literacy and the History of Readers," 13.

24. Jefferson to John Adams, October 28, 1813, Peterson, *Writings,* 1:309.

25. Frederick Douglass, *Narrative of the Life of Frederick Douglass, an American Slave, Written by Himself,* ed. Benjamin Quarles (Cambridge, Mass.: Belknap Press, 1960), 58-59.

26. Ibid., 67

27. Dana Nelson Salvino, "The Word in Black and White: Ideologies of Race and Literacy in Antebellum America," in Cathy N. Davidson, ed., *Reading in America: Literature and Social History* (Baltimore: Johns Hopkins University Press, 1989), 140.

28. The most detailed study of Lincoln's reading is David C. Mearns, "'The Great Invention of the World': Mr. Lincoln and the Books he Read," in *Three Presidents and Their Books: The Reading of Jefferson, Lincoln, and Franklin D.*

Roosevelt (Urbana: University of Illinois Press, 1955), 45-83. See also Douglas L. Wilson, *Lincoln before Washington: New Perspectives on the Illinois Years* (Urbana and Chicago: University of Illinois Press, 1997), 3-17.

29. Jefferson to John Adams, September 4, 1823, Peterson, *Writings,* 1, 478.

30. Joseph Gillespie to W. H. Herndon, December 8, 1866, (Herndon-Weik Collection, Library of Congress), published in Douglas L. Wilson and Rodney O. Davis, eds. *Herndon's Informants: Letters, Interviews, and Statements about Abraham Lincoln* (Urbana and Chicago: University of Illinois Press, 1997), 506.

31. Roy Basler et al., eds., *The Collected Works of Abraham Lincoln* (New Brunswick: Rutgers University Press, 1953), 3:360.

32. Ibid., 3:362.

33. Ibid., 3:362-63.

BULWARK OF REVOLUTIONARY LIBERTY: THE RECOGNITION OF THE INFORMED CITIZEN

RICHARD D. BROWN

Richard D. Brown, *The Strength of a People: The Idea of an Informed Citizenry in America, 1650-1870* (Chapel Hill, N.C.: University of North Carolina Press, 1996), chapter 3, presents a more fully developed version of issues presented here.

1. A 1646 Scots statute required landowners to pay for the creation of schools and to provide salaries for teachers in their own locales. Although this law was repealed in 1662, a 1696 law compelled heritors and burgh councils to fund the capital cost of schools and the salaries of teachers. R. A. Houston, *Scottish Literacy and the Scottish Identity:*

Illiteracy and Society in Scotland and Northern England, 1600-1800 (Cambridge and New York: Cambridge University Press, 1985), 112-14.

2. "A Dissertation on the Canon and Feudal Law," *Boston Gazette,* September 30, 1765, in Robert J. Taylor, et al., eds., *Papers of John Adams,* 8 vols. (Cambridge: Belknap Press of Harvard University Press, 1977-89), 1:120.

3. *New York Post-Boy,* 1756. Quoted in Jeffrey A. Smith, *Printers and Press Freedom: The Ideology of Early American Journalism* (New York: Oxford University Press, 1988), 130.

4. Quoted in Lawrence A. Cremin's

American Education: The Colonial Experience, 1607-1783 (New York: Harper and Row, 1970), 517.

5. Ibid., 531.

6. Ibid., 544-45.

7. "A Dissertation on the Canon and Feudal Law," *Boston Gazette*, September 30, 1765, Taylor, et al., eds., *Papers of John Adams*, 1:120.

8. Harvey J. Graff, *The Legacies of Literacy: Continuities and Contradictions in Western Culture and Society* (Bloomington: Indiana University Press, 1987), chap. 6, especially pp. 246-57; Houston, *Scottish Literacy and the Scottish Identity,* especially pp. 162-92; and Carl F. Kaestle et al., *Literacy in the United States: Readers and Reading since 1880* (New Haven: Yale University Press, 1991), 3-32.

9. Jon Teaford, "The Transformation of Massachusetts Education, 1670-1780," *History of Education Quarterly* 10 (1970): 287-307, especially 295; Robert Middlekauff, *Ancients and Axioms: Secondary Education in Eighteenth-Century New England* (New Haven: Yale University Press, 1963), 40.

10. Quoted in Merrill D. Peterson, *Thomas Jefferson and the New Nation* (New York: Oxford University Press, 1970), 151.

11. Thomas Jefferson, "A Bill for The More General Diffusion of Knowledge," late 1778, as reported by the Committee of Revisions, January 6, 1779, *The Papers of Thomas Jefferson*, ed. Julian P. Boyd, 27 vols. to date (Princeton: Princeton University Press, 1950-), 2:526-27.

12. Ibid., 2:526-27.

13. Ibid., 2:530-31.

14. Ibid., 2:531.

15. Ibid., 2:532.

16. Ibid., 2:533.

17. "A Bill for Amending the Constitution of the College of William and Mary . . . June 18, 1779," in Boyd, *Papers*, 2:540-42.

18. *Notes on the State of Virginia*, in

Paul Leicester Ford, ed., *The Works of Thomas Jefferson,* vol. 4 (New York: G.P. Putnam's Sons, 1904), 61, 64.

19. To Jonathan Dickinson Sergeant, Philadelphia, July 21, 1776. J. Taylor et al., eds., *Papers of John Adams*, 4:397.

20. John Adams to Joseph Hawley, Philadelphia, August 25, 1776, in Taylor et al., eds. *Papers of John Adams*, 4:495-97.

21. Gordon S. Wood, *The Creation of the American Republic, 1776-1787* (Chapel Hill: University of North Carolina Press, 1969), chap. 12, "The Worthy against the Licentious."

22. John Adams to Joseph Hawley, Phila., August 25, 1776, in Taylor et al., eds., *Papers of John Adams*, 4:495-97.

23. Phillips Payson, Massachusetts Election Sermon, 1778, in Hyneman and Lutz, eds., *American Political Writing*, vol. 1, (Indianapolis: Liberty Press, 1983), 526-27.

24. Ibid., 1:527.

25. Massachusetts Constitution of 1780 in *The Popular Sources of Political Authority: Documents on the Massachusetts Constitution of 1780,* Oscar and Mary F. Handlin (Cambridge: Harvard University Press, 1966), 442-43.

26. Ibid., 446.

27. Ibid., 446.

28. Ibid., 465.

29. Ibid., 467.

30. Nathan O. Hatch, *The Sacred Cause of Liberty: Republican Thought and the Milennium in Revolutionary New England* (New Haven: Yale University Press, 1977), and his *The Democratization of American Christianity* (New Haven: Yale University Press, 1989), 9-11.

31. Quoted in Howard Miller, *The Revolutionary College: American Presbyterian Higher Education, 1707-1837* (New York: New York University Press, 1976), 119, 118.

32. Ezra Stiles, *The United States Elevated to Glory and Honor* (New Haven: Printed by Thomas and Samuel Green,

1783), 34; Rush to John Armstrong, Philadelphia, March 19, 1783, *Letters of Benjamin Rush,* ed. L. H. Butterfield, 2 vols. (Princeton, N.J.: Published for the American Philosophical Society by Princeton University Press, 1951), 1:294.

33. In Samuel Eliot Morison, ed., *Sources and Documents Illustrating the American Revolution, 1764-1788, and the Formation of the Federal Constitution,* 2d ed. (New York: Oxford University Press, 1972), 207.

THOMAS JEFFERSON AND LEGAL EDUCATION IN REVOLUTIONARY AMERICA

HERBERT A. JOHNSON

1. Felix Frankfurter and James M. Landis, *The Business of the Supreme Court: A Study of the Federal Judicial System* (New York: Macmillan, 1928), 128

2. In commenting upon the work of a lawyer, Jefferson's friend and contemporary John Adams indicated that legal education was complicated by the American attorney's need to be attorney, counselor, solicitor, and scrivener, as the case and occasion demanded. Marian C. McKenna, *Tapping Reeve and the Litchfield Law School* (New York: Oceana Publications, 1986), 12.

3. Roy J. Honeywell, *The Educational Work of Thomas Jefferson* (Cambridge: Harvard University Press, 1931; reprint edition, New York: Russell & Russell, 1964), 121; there is a useful chart concerning Jefferson's curriculum proposals from 1779 through 1824 at pp. 110-11.

4. Frank L. Dewey suggests that only two of the five years were spent in concentrated study, and that there were frequent interruptions or diversions from law study in the first three years. *Thomas Jefferson, Lawyer* (Charlottesville: University Press of Virginia, 1986), 9-11.

5. Ibid. 1-4. Some lawyers practiced in the county courts for several years before moving up to the central higher courts; Dewey indicates that a busy county court lawyer might make considerably more in fees than his more prestigious General Court contemporaries. Ibid., 6. For the

colonial General Court's jurisdiction, see 18-19. Dumas Malone dates Jefferson's college training from 1760 to 1762, and his legal clerkship from 1762 to 1767. *Jefferson the Virginia* (Boston: Little, Brown & Co., 1948), 49, 65.

6. Robert B. Kirtland, *George Wythe: Lawyer, Revolutionary, Judge* (New York: Garland Publishing, 1986), 48

7. Ibid., 119-22

8. Ibid., 45

9. See, generally, Paul M. Hamlin, *Legal Education in Colonial New York* (New York: New York University Law Quarterly Review, 1939; reprint edition, New York: DaCapo Press, 1970); for a more detailed picture of John Jay's clerkship, see Herbert A. Johnson, *John Jay: Colonial Lawyer* (New York: Garland Publishing, 1989), 12-28.

10. Johnson, *Jay,* 46-58

11. Henry C. Van Schaack, *Life of Peter Van Schaack* (New York: D. Appleton & Co., 1842), 9.

12. Jefferson to John Garland Jefferson, June 11, 1790, Julian P. Boyd et al., eds., *The Papers of Thomas Jefferson,* 27 vols. to date (Princeton: Princeton University Press, 1950-), 16: 480-82. Of clerkship Jefferson wrote, "It is a general practice to study the law in the office of some lawyer. This indeed gives to the student the advantage of his instruction. But I have ever seen that the services expected in return have been more than the instruc-

tions have been worth. All that is necessary for a student is access to a library, and directions in what order the books are to be read." Ibid., 480.

13. Jefferson to Thomas Turpin, February 5, 1796, quoted in Edward Dumbauld, *Thomas Jefferson and the Law* (Norman: University of Oklahoma Press, 1978), 7

14. See discussion at ibid., 9. Joseph Story as a clerk reportedly shed tears of frustration while reading *Coke upon Littleton*. R. Kent Newmyer, *Supreme Court Justice Joseph Story: Statesman of the Old Republic* (Chapel Hill: University of North Carolina Press, 1985), 41.

15. Van Schaack, *Life of Peter Van Schaack,* 14

16. See Malone, *Jefferson the Virginian,* 65-74

17. Matthew Bacon, *A New Abridgment of the Law,* 5 vols. (London: E. and R. Nutt, 1736-66), and Charles Viner, *A General Abridgment of Law and Equity, alphabetically digested under proper titles . . .* 1st ed., 24 vols. (Aldershot: Charles Viner, 1742-53)

18. See the introductory comments in Herbert A. Johnson, *Imported Eighteenth Century Law Treatises in American Libraries, 1700-1799* (Knoxville: University of Tennessee Press, 1978), ix-xxvi.

19. See lists of New York lawyers with their educational background in Hamlin, *Legal Education,* 151-54; and Herbert A. Johnson, *John Jay* (New York: Garland Publishing, 1989), 166-69.

20. Dumbauld, *Jefferson and the Law,* 4-7.

21. To Thomas Mann Randolph, Jr., August 27, 1786, Boyd, *Papers,* 10:305-9, at 306.

22. Ibid., 307.

23. There is a short, but perceptive, discussion of the English Inns of Court in McKenna, *Reeve and Litchfield,* 1-7. Paul M. Hamlin discusses the English Inns from the largely critical perspective of the

New York colonial bar, *Legal Education,* 12-34.

24. "The Myth of Jefferson's County Court Practice," Appendix B, Dewey, *Thomas Jefferson, Lawyer,* 122-26; Malone, *Jefferson the Virginian,* 113-14.

25. Dewey, *Jefferson, Lawyer,* 29; he did gain some revenue from the filing of petitions against unoccupied patented land, and caveats against surveyed land not patented. Ibid., 30-34.

26. Ibid., 83-93

27. Ibid., 65-72

28. This case involved the claim of Edward Livingston to some land accreted to the shoreline of the Mississippi River, which had been contested during Jefferson's term as president. Following Jefferson's orders the United States marshal evicted Livingston and his workmen from the batture, precipitating the commencement of civil litigation against Jefferson. Of his printed brief, Jefferson observed, "It is merely a law argument, and a very dry one." Dumbauld, *Jefferson and the Law,* 36. Delving into the complexities of French and Spanish law as applicable to Louisiana, Jefferson turned to French treatises and Roman law back to the Twelve Tables. This supplemented extensive discussion of English law concerning alluvial lands. Ibid., 54-70.

29. As a member of the committee to revise the statutes in Virginia which began its work in 1776, but failed to have any bills approved, Jefferson had prepared a bill to bring the College of William and Mary within state control, and which would have established a professorship of law and police. "A Bill for Amending the Constitution of the College of William and Mary . . .," Boyd, *Papers,* 2: 535-43, at 540, 541.

30. See editorial note and an extract of Marshall's law notes in *The Papers of John Marshall,* edited by Herbert A. Johnson, Charles T. Cullen, et al., 6 vols. to date (Chapel Hill: University of North

Carolina Press, 1974-), 1:37-87. Young Marshall was perhaps more intent upon his courtship of Mary Willis Ambler than he was on Bacon's *Abridgment,* for her name appears throughout the law note-book. Ibid., 45; see also Frances Norton Mason, *My Dearest Polly* (Richmond: Garret & Massie, 1961), 7.

31. *Marshall Papers,* 1:40; Boyd, *Papers,* 7:112.

32. *The Works of James Wilson,* edited by Robert Green McCloskey, 2 vols. (Cambridge: Belknap Press of Harvard University Press, 1967).

33. Ibid., 1:91-94

34. Ibid., 1:181-84.

35. Ibid., 369-98.

36. Ibid., 2:585-610.

37. Ibid., 2:600-602.

38. Ibid., 2:611-707.

39. Ibid., 1:37.

40. Ibid., 72.

41. Ibid., 200.

42. Charles T. Cullen, *St. George Tucker and the Law in Virginia, 1772-1804* (New York: Garland Publishing, 1987), 116-17.

43. Ibid., 121.

44. Ibid., 121, 126.

45. Ibid., 145.

46. The list is printed as Appendix E, ibid., 205-6. Blackstone's *Commentaries* precedes *Coke upon Littleton* on the sec-tion dealing with treatises; since the list is not in alphabetical order, this possibly indicates the order in which the works were to be read.

47. Ibid., 132.

48. Quoted in ibid., 133-34.

49. With the possible exception of Selden, as an antiquarian, and Coke, as a candidate for antiquarianism and perhaps guilty of some civilian leanings, the iden-tification of these great common law authors as being civilians, i.e., continental writers, is puzzling. Possibly Minor would have profited from a bit more theory in his truncated education.

50. Ibid., 134-35.

51. John Theodore Horton, *James Kent: A Study in Conservatism, 1763-1847* (New York: D. Appleton-Century Company, 1939), 86-96 provides details of Kent's appointment and inaugural lecture.

52. "Kent's Introductory Lecture," *Columbia Law Review* 3 (1903): 330-43, at 330, 331.

53. Ibid., 334-35. This included, of course, the concept of judicial review, and the principle of separation of powers.

54. Ibid., 338.

55. Ibid., 338-39.

56. Ibid., 341.

57. McKenna, *Reeve and Litchfield,* 123, lists nineteen private law schools estab-lished by 1835, including those of Reeve and Van Schaack. Included within the list is the professorship of George Wythe at William and Mary from 1779 to 1789.

58. Ibid., 63, 85.

59. Ibid., 59-60, 64, 65.

60. Ibid., 64.

61. Professor McKenna indicates that the Kinderhook, New York, law school operated by Peter Van Schaack, paralleled the course offerings at Litchfield, but that Van Schaack had an obsession with prac-tice, and had his students read the full record of important cases. Ibid., 139. He also wrote *An Analysis of the Practice of the Supreme Court,* praised by Chancellor James Kent for being "clear, methodical and perfectly correct." Van Schaack, *Life of Peter Van Schaack,* 445.

62. McKenna, *Reeve and Litchfield,* 122. McKenna is correct in observing that none of the university lectureships attempted to offer a complete technical education to law students (p. 59).

63. See George L. Haskins and Herbert A. Johnson, *Foundations of Power, John Marshall, 1801-15,* vol. 2, *History of the Supreme Court of the United States* (New York: Macmillan Publishing Co., 1981), 381; Newmyer, *Joseph Story,* 80-81, 176.

64. McKenna, *Reeve and Litchfield,* 67.

65. Ibid., 174.

66. *Early History of the University of Virginia as Contained in the Letters of Thomas Jefferson and Joseph C. Cabell, . . .* (Richmond: J.W. Randolph, 1856), pp. 385-387. It is something of an unusual distinction to be made by one who considered himself a "man of the people," but the second class which did not intend to practice is not unlike the citizens seen as the beneficiaries of instruction by professors of law and police.

67. Ibid., 339; Philip A. Bruce comments on "how keenly interested, if not fanatical, Jefferson was in prescribing the text-books to be taught on the political side of that school." *History of the University of Virginia 1819-1919,* vol. 1 (New York: Macmillan Company, 1920), 102.

68. *Early History,* 338, 377. Concerning the possibility of appointing Judge Dade, Cabell commented, "I am truly gratified to think that we shall have so faithful an expositor of the admirable text books on government selected by yourself and Mr. Madison" (p. 353).

69. Virginius Dabney, *Mr. Jefferson's University: A History* (Charlottesville: University Press of Virginia, 1981), 7; Bruce, *History of the University of Virginia,* vol. 2 (New York: Macmillan Company, 1920), 31, 105.

70. Bruce, *History of the University of Virginia,* 2:102, 105.

71. Newmyer paints an exciting picture of Story's law classes that is "must reading" for the student of legal education. *Joseph Story,* 237-70.

72. Joseph Story, *A Discourse Pronounced upon the Inauguration of the Author as Dane Professor of Law in Harvard University on the Twenty-Fifth Day of August, 1829* (Boston: Hilliard, Gray, Little and Wilkins, 1829), 28.

73. Ibid., 15, 16.

74. Ibid., 34.

75. Ibid., 7.

76. Ibid., 10, 35.

77. Julius Goebel, "Learning and Style: A Historian's Lament," *Columbia Law Review* 6 (1961): 1393, 1398-99.

"THAT KNOWLEDGE MOST USEFUL TO US"

JENNINGS L. WAGONER, JR.

1. Thomas Jefferson to John Banister, Jr., October 15, 1785, in Andrew A. Lipscomb and Albert Ellery Bergh, eds., *The Writings of Thomas Jefferson,* 20 vols. in 10 (Washington: Thomas Jefferson Memorial Foundation, 1905), 5:186, emphasis added. Although at this point in time Jefferson thought Rome superior to other seats of learning, a few years later he considered Edinburgh the best in the world. See Thomas Jefferson to Mr. M'Alister, December 22, 1791, ibid., 8:274-75.

2. Thomas Jefferson to Charles Bellini, September 30, 1785, in Lipscomb and

Bergh, *Writings,* 5:151-54.

3. See, for example, Thomas Jefferson to George Wythe, August 13, 1786, in Lipscomb and Bergh, *Writings* 5:396 and Thomas Jefferson, First Inaugural Address, [March 4, 1801], in Adrienne Koch and William Peden, eds., *The Life and Selected Writings of Thomas Jefferson* (New York: Modern Library, 1944), 323.

4. Jefferson to Banister, Jr., October 15, 1785, in Lipscomb and Bergh, *Writings,* 5:186-87. A provocative inquiry into Jefferson's sexual life is provided by Fawn M. Brodie, *Thomas Jefferson: An Intimate History* (New York: W.W. Norton, 1974).

For an opposing view, see Virginius Dabney, *The Jefferson Scandals: A Rebuttal* (New York: Dodd, Mead, 1981).

5. Jefferson to Banister, Jr., October 15, 1785, in Lipscomb and Bergh, *Writings*, 5:185-88. Only two months earlier, Jefferson had written to Walker Maury, who was tutoring Jefferson's nephew, Peter Carr: "Of all the errors which can possibly be committed in the education of youth, that of sending them to Europe is the most fatal." Two years later Jefferson thought it necessary to remind his nephew: "There is no place where your pursuit of knowledge will be so little obstructed by foreign objects, as your own country, nor any, wherein the virtues of the heart will be less exposed to be weakened." Thomas Jefferson to Walker Maury, August 19, 1785, in Julian P. Boyd, ed., *The Papers of Thomas Jefferson*, 27 vols. to date (Princeton: Princeton University Press, 195-), 8(1953):409-10; Thomas Jefferson to Peter Carr, August 10, 1787, in Lipscomb and Bergh, *Writings*, 6:262. For variations on this theme, see Thomas Jefferson to Charles Thompson, November 11, 1784, in Paul Leicester Ford, ed., *The Writings of Thomas Jefferson*, 10 vols. (New York: G.P. Putnam's Sons, 1892-99), 4(1899):14-15; Thomas Jefferson to Ralph Izard, July 17, 1788, in Lipscomb and Bergh, *Writings* 7:70-73.

6. Dumas Malone, *Jefferson the Virginian* (Boston: Little, Brown & Co., 1948), xiv; Merrill D. Peterson, ed., *The Portable Thomas Jefferson* (New York: Penguin Books, 1975), xxi; Thomas Jefferson to George Washington, January 4, 1785 [i.e., 1786] in Boyd, *Papers*, 9:150-52.

7. George Wythe was Jefferson's primary collaborator in this undertaking, although the original committee consisted of five members. Also named to the Committee of Revisors were George Mason, who asked to be excused from the arduous task, Thomas Ludwell Lee, who died soon after the committee began its work, and Edmund Pendleton. Pendleton remained a member of the committee, but his contributions were not significant. The final report, submitted two and a half years after the revision was initiated, contained 126 bills. Among the most important bills that clearly bear Jefferson's stamp were the ones dealing with citizenship, crime and punishment, religion, and education. See Malone, *Jefferson the Virginian*, 261ff; Thomas Jefferson to Skelton Jones, July 28, 1809, in Lipscomb and Bergh, *Writings*, 12:297-303.

8. Jefferson to Wythe, August 13, 1786, in Lipscomb and Bergh, eds., *Writings*, 5:396.

9. Thomas Jefferson, A Bill for the More General Diffusion of Knowledge, June 18, 1779, in Roy J. Honeywell, *The Educational Work of Thomas Jefferson* (New York: Russell & Russell, 1964), 199-205; Thomas Jefferson, *Notes on the State of Virginia* [1787], ed. William Peden (Chapel Hill: University of North Carolina Press, 1954), 146; Malone, *Jefferson the Virginian*, 280; Jefferson to Wythe, August 13, 1786, in Lipscomb and Bergh, *Writings*, 5:394-98.

10. Thomas Jefferson to James Madison, December 20, 1787, in Koch and Peden, *Life and Selected Writings*, 436-41.

11. Jefferson, Bill for the More General Diffusion of Knowledge, in Honeywell, *The Educational Work*, 199; Thomas Jefferson to William C. Jarvis, September 28, 1820, in Ford, ed., *Writings*, 10: 160-61. Over time, Jefferson's specific curricular recommendations varied in some details. In a letter written more than thirty years after he drafted his initial proposal, for example, Jefferson recommended geography as an elementary level subject and moved history (to be taught in conjunction with the ancient and modern languages) into the secondary and tertiary tiers. See Thomas Jefferson to Peter Carr, September 7, 1814, in Koch and Peden, *Life and Selected Writings*, 642-49.

12. [Thomas Jefferson], "Report of the Commissioners Appointed to Fix the Site of the University of Virginia, &c.," August 4, 1818, in Honeywell, *The Educational Work*, 249-50. Again making slight adjustments in the ordering of elementary subjects, in addition to "reading, writing and numerical arithmetic," Jefferson specified "the elements of mensuration" [basic geometry] and "the outlines of geography and history."

13. Thomas Jefferson to Colonel Charles Yancey, January 6, 1816, in Ford, *Writings*, 10:1-4.

14. Jefferson to Carr, August 10, 1787, in Lipscomb and Bergh, *Writings*, 6:258.

15. Benjamin Rush, "Thoughts upon the Mode of Education Proper in a Republic," [Philadelphia, 1786], in Frederick Rudolph, ed., *Essays on Education in the Early Republic* (Cambridge: Harvard University Press, 1965), 10-12.

16. Thomas Jefferson to Matthew Carey, November 11, 1816, in Ford, *Writings*, 10:67-68; Thomas Jefferson to James Fishback, September 27, 1809, in Lipscomb and Bergh, *Writings*, 12:314-16.

17. Jefferson to Carr, August 10, 1787, in Lipscomb and Bergh, *Writings*, 6:258-61. Jefferson's views on the role of religion in education has been explored in Robert M. Healey, *Jefferson on Religion in Public Education* (New Haven: Yale University Press, 1962). See also Charles B. Sanford, *The Religious Life of Thomas Jefferson* (Charlottesville: University Press of Virginia, 1984).

18. Thomas Jefferson to John Adams, May 5, 1817, in Lipscomb and Bergh, *Writings*, 15:427; Thomas Jefferson to Thomas Law, Esq., June 13, 1814, ibid., 14:139-41; Jefferson to Carr, August 10, 1787, ibid., 6:257; Healey, *Jefferson on Religion*, 159-60. See also Garry Wills, *Inventing America: Jefferson's Declaration of Independence* (New York: Vintage Books, 1978), 181-206. In his letter to Carr,

Jefferson gave classic form to the idea of the equality of the moral sense by asserting: "State a moral case to a ploughman and a professor. The former will decide it as well, and often better than the latter, because he has not been led astray by artificial rules" (pp. 257-58).

19. Thomas Jefferson to Nathaniel Burwell, Esq., March 14, 1818, in Koch and Peden, *Life and Selected Writings*, 688; Thomas Jefferson to Robert Skipwith, August 3, 1771, in Boyd, *Papers*, 1:76-77.

20. Jefferson, *Notes on the State of Virginia*, 147.

21. Jefferson to Carr, August 10, 1787, in Lipscomb and Bergh, *Writings*, 6:258, emphasis added. In an earlier letter to Carr, Jefferson had warned that loss of honor and integrity "can never be made up by all the other acquirements of body and mind." Morality, then, should be the first object of education. "Give up money, give up fame, give up science, give the earth itself and all it contains, rather than do an immoral act." Jefferson to Carr, August 19, 1785, ibid., 5:83.

22. Martha Wayles Skelton Jefferson died on September 6, 1782, when the youngest Jefferson daughter, Lucy Elizabeth, was only a few months old. Lucy Elizabeth (the second Jefferson daughter so named) died at the age of two; two other infant sisters and an unnamed brother had preceded her in death. The two daughters who lived to adulthood, Mary and Martha, were four and ten when their mother died. The girls passed much of their youth in the care of their aunt and uncle, Elizabeth and Francis Eppes.

23. Jefferson to Burwell, March 14, 1818, in Koch and Peden, *Life and Selected Writings*, 687-89; Thomas Jefferson to Maria [Mary] Jefferson, April 11, 1790, in Edwin Morris Betts and James Adam Bear, Jr., eds., *The Family Letters of Thomas Jefferson* (Charlottesville: University Press of Virginia, 1966), 52;

Thomas Jefferson to Martha Jefferson, March 28, 1787, ibid., 35.

24. Jefferson to Burwell, March 14, 1818, in Koch and Peden, *Life and Selected Writings,* 687-89; Jefferson to Marbois, December 5, 1783, in Boyd, *Papers,* 6: 373-74.

25. Jefferson to Burwell, March 14, 1818, in Koch and Peden, *Life and Selected Writings,* 687; Thomas Jefferson to Martha Jefferson, January 15, 1784, in Betts and Bear, *Family Letters,* 23; Thomas Jefferson to Martha Jefferson, November 28, 1783, ibid., 20; Thomas Jefferson to Martha Jefferson, December 22, 1783, ibid., 22; Thomas Jefferson to Martha Jefferson, March 28, 1787, ibid., 35.

26. Jefferson to Burwell, March 14, 1818, in Koch and Peden, *Life and Selected Writings,* 688-89.

27. Thomas Jefferson to Martha Jefferson, May 21, 1787, in Betts and Bear, *Family Letters,* 41.

28. This discussion of education for republican citizenship has made no mention of Jefferson's ideas concerning the education of noncitizens: Native and African Americans, slave or free. He did advocate a scheme for the education of slaves as part of a plan for the gradual emancipation and deportation of the African American population and at various times expressed views concerning the education and assimilation of the Native American population. These concerns, although vital in terms of a complete understanding of Jefferson's educational and social philosophy, are beyond the scope of this essay. See, in addition to Jefferson's comments on the differences among the races and his deep misgivings over slavery as expressed in his *Notes,* the assessment of John Chester Miller, *The Wolf by the Ears: Thomas Jefferson and Slavery* (Charlottesville: University Press of Virginia, 1991). A brief commentary may be found in Jennings L. Wagoner, Jr., "Jefferson, Justice, and the Enlightened Society," in *Spheres of Justice in Education,*

edited by Deborah A. Verstegen and James Gordon Wood (New York: HarperCollins, 1991), 20-23.

29. Jefferson, *Notes,* 147; Thomas Jefferson to Peter Carr, September 7, 1814, in Lipscomb and Bergh, *Writings,* 19:213; Jefferson, Bill for the More General Diffusion of Knowledge, in Honeywell, *The Educational Work,* 199.

30. The precise structural details of Jefferson's educational plans are not of immediate concern in this essay. See, among others, Honeywell, *The Educational Work;* Charles F. Arrowood, *Thomas Jefferson on Education in a Republic* (New York: McGraw Hill, 1930); Gordon C. Lee, ed., *Crusade against Ignorance: Thomas Jefferson on Education* (New York: Teachers College, Columbia University, [1961], 1967); James B. Conant, *Thomas Jefferson and the Development of American Public Education* (Berkeley and Los Angeles: University of California Press, 1962); Joseph F. Kett, "Education," in Merrill D. Peterson, *Thomas Jefferson: A Reference Biography* (New York: Charles Scribner's Sons, 1986), 233-51; and Harold Hellenbrand, *The Unfinished Revolution: Education and Politics in the Thought of Thomas Jefferson* (Newark: University of Delaware Press, 1990).

31. Jefferson, Bill for the More General Diffusion of Knowledge, in Honeywell, *The Educational Work,* 199-200. Cf. Jefferson's 1817 bill and his detailed letter of September 7, 1814, to Peter Carr, both available in ibid., 233-43, 222-27.

32. Merle Curti, *The Social Ideas of American Educators* (Totowa, N.J.: Littlefield, Adams and Co., [1935], 1974), 42.

33. Jefferson, *Notes on the State of Virginia,* 148; Jefferson, "Bill for the More General Diffusion of Knowledge," in Honeywell, *The Educational Work,* 200.

34. Thomas Jefferson to John Adams, October 28, 1813, in Lester J. Cappon, ed., *The Complete Adams-Jefferson Letters* (Chapel Hill: University of North

Carolina Press, [1959], 1987), 387-92, at 388-90, emphasis added.

35. Merrill D. Peterson, *Thomas Jefferson and the New Nation* (New York: Oxford University Press, 1970), 971. See, for example, Thomas Jefferson to John Adams, July 5, 1814, in Cappon, *Adams-Jefferson Letters,* 430-34, at 434; Jefferson to Carr, September 7, 1814, in Lipscomb and Bergh, *The Writings,* 19:211-21, at 211, emphasis added.

36. Thomas Jefferson to Dr. Joseph Priestley, January 18, 1800, in Honeywell, *The Educational Work,* 215, emphasis in original.

37. Ibid., 215-16; Jefferson to Carr, September 7, 1814, ibid., 222-27; [Thomas Jefferson], A Bill for Establishing A System of Public Education [October 24, 1817], ibid., 233-43; [Jefferson], "Report of the Commissioners," [August 4, 1818], ibid., 248-60.

38. [Jefferson], "Report of the Commissioners," August 4, 1818, in Honeywell, *The Educational Work,* 251, emphasis in original.

39. Ibid., 250.

40. Jefferson's proposed curriculum included: Ancient Languages (Latin, Greek, Hebrew); Modern Languages (French, Spanish, Italian, German, and Anglo-Saxon); Pure Mathematics (algebra, fluxions [calculus], geometry, and military and naval architecture); Physico-Mathematics (mechanics, statics, dynamics, pneumatics, acoustics, optics, astronomy, and geography); Natural Philosophy (physics, chemistry, and mineralogy); Natural History (botany and zoology); Anatomy and Medicine; Government (political economy, the law of nature and nations, and history interwoven with politics and law); Law; and Ideology (the science of thought, embracing grammar, ethics, rhetoric, belles lettres, and the fine arts). See [Jefferson], "Report of the Commissioners," in Honeywell, *The Educational Work,* 252-53.

Jefferson expected candidates for diplomas in any of the schools of the university to be able to read the highest Latin classics with ease. His hopes for high scholarship were such that no provision was made for the bachelor of arts degree; diplomas were to be of two grades, doctor and graduate. Jefferson met with disappointment in terms of the actual level of proficiency, ability, and deportment of some of the early students, however. See, for example, Philip A. Bruce, *History of the University of Virginia, 1819-1919,* vol. 2 (New York: Macmillan, 1920); Dumas Malone, *The Sage of Monticello,* 418-25; Jennings L. Wagoner, Jr., "Honor and Dishonor at Mr. Jefferson's University: The Antebellum Years," *History of Education Quarterly* 16 (Summer 1986):155-79.

41. [Jefferson], "Report of the Commissioners," in Honeywell, *The Educational Work,* 254-55. See also Thomas Jefferson, "An Essay towards Facilitating Instruction in the Anglo-Saxon and Modern Dialects of the English Language for the Use of the University of Virginia," pamphlet enclosed in letter to Herbert Croft, Esq, LL.B., October 30, 1798, in Lipscomb and Bergh, *Writings,* 18:361-411.

42. Ibid., 255; Peterson, *Jefferson and the New Nation,* 973.

43. Ibid., 256; Peterson, *Jefferson and the New Nation,* 973-74.

44. Thomas Jefferson to Thomas Cooper, November 2, 1822, in Ford, *Writings,* 10:242-44.

45. [Thomas Jefferson, Rector], Report to the President and Directors of the Literary Fund, October 7, 1822, in [Nathaniel Francis Cabell, ed.], *Early History of the University of Virginia as Contained in the Letters of Thomas Jefferson and Joseph C. Cabell* (Richmond: J.W. Randolph, 1856), 475; Joseph C. Cabell to Thomas Jefferson, February 3, 1823, ibid., 272-73. See also Dumas

Malone, *The Sage of Monticello* (Boston: Little, Brown and Company, 1981), 392-93; Peterson, *Jefferson and the New Nation,* 979-80.

46. Thomas Jefferson to William Roscoe, December 27, 1820, in Lipscomb and Bergh, *Writings,* 15:303.

47. Daniel J. Boorstin, *The Lost World of Thomas Jefferson* (Boston: Beacon Press, 1948), 222-23.

48. Boorstin, *Lost World,* 238.

49. Stephen K. Bailey, "The Purposes of Education," in Edith K. Mosher and Jennings L. Wagoner, Jr., eds., *The Changing Politics of Education* (Berkeley: McCutchan Publishing Co., 1978), 12.

50. Thomas Jefferson to Marc-Antoine Julien, July 23, 1818, in Lipscomb and Bergh, *Writings,* 15:172.

EDUCATION AND DEMOCRACY

Benjamin R. Barber

This essay, originally written for the Library of Congress symposium in *1993,* also appears in Benjamin R. Barber, *A Passion for Democracy: American Essays* (Princeton: Princeton University Press, 1998).

1. "There is no safe depository of the ultimate powers of the society but the people themselves . . . and if we think them not enlightened enough to exercise their control with a wholesome discretion, the remedy is not to take it from them, but to inform their discretion by education." Thomas Jefferson to William C. Jarvis, September 28, 1820, in Paul Leicester Ford, ed., *The Writings of Thomas Jefferson,* 10 vols. (New York: G.P. Putnam's Sons, 1892-99), 12:161.

2. Cited by Hannah Arendt, *On Revolution* (New York: Viking Press, 1963), 236. See Robert Michels, *Political Parties: A Sociological Study of the Oligarchical Tendencies of Modern Democracy,* trans. by Eden and Cedar Paul (New York: Collier Books, 1962).

3. Jefferson to John Adams, August 1, 1816; note that this was later in his life when some claim his revolutionary ardor had cooled! Andrew A. Lipscomb and

Albert E. Bergh, eds., *The Writings of Thomas Jefferson,* 20 vols. (Washington: Thomas Jefferson Memorial Foundation, 1903-4), 15:50.

4. Jefferson to Samuel Kercheval, July 12, 1816, ibid., 12:3.

5. Jefferson to Colonel William Stephens Smith, November 13, 1787, in Ford, *Writings,* 6:371.

6. "I know also that laws and institutions must go hand in hand with the progress of the human mind. . . . We might as well require a man to wear still the coat which fitted him when a boy, as civilized society to remain ever under the regimen of their barbarous ancestors." Jefferson to Kercheval, July 12, 1816.

7. Jefferson to James Madison, 1789.

8. "I hold it that a little rebellion now and then is a good thing, and as necessary in the political world as storms in the physical." Jefferson to James Madison, January 30, 1787, in Lipscomb and Bergh, *Writings,* 6:63.

9. Recent Jefferson skeptics like Joseph Ellis have argued that Jefferson was ashamed of his early enthusiasm for the revolution and had accordingly doctored early correspondence to modulate its zealotry. But they misread a temperamen-

tal preference for ongoing popular participation in the affairs of government that
persisted throughout Jefferson's career as
a sometime and quite contingent enthusiasm for France supposedly born of his
first-hand acquaintance with the country
immediately before the revolution. See
Joseph J. Ellis, *American Sphinx: The
Character of Thomas Jefferson* (New York:
Alfred A. Knopf, 1997).

10. "Paradoxical as it may sound,"
wrote Arendt, "it was in fact under the
impact of the Revolution that the
Revolutionary spirit in this country began
to wither away, and it was the
Constitution itself, this greatest achievement of the American people, which
eventually cheated them of their proudest
possession." *On Revolution,* 242.

11. Jefferson to Joseph Cabell, February
12, 1815, in Ford, *Writings,* 11:446.

12. Gordon Wood, *The Radicalism of
the American Revolution* (New York:
Vintage, 1991) and Bruce Ackerman, *We
the People: Foundations* (Cambridge,
Mass.: Harvard University Press, 1991).

13. Ackerman, *We the People,* 27.

14. Wood, *The Radicalism,* 8.

15. James MacGregor Burns and
Stewart Burns, *A People's Charter: The
Pursuit of Rights in America* (New York:
Alfred A. Knopf, 1991).

16. Besides O'Brien and Ellis Leonard
Levy's *Jefferson and Civil Liberties: The
Darker Side* (New York: Quadrangle/The
New York Times Book Company, 1963)

and Paul Finkelman, "Jefferson and
Slavery: 'Treason against the Hopes of the
World,'" in his *Slavery and the Founders:
Race and Liberty in the Age of Jefferson*
(Armonk, N.Y.: M.E. Sharpe, 1996),
105–37.

17. In his *Notes on Virginia* (1787), he
treats the Native American tribes with
seeming affection as a feature of the New
World's flora and fauna rather than as a
part of the distinctively human race.

18. Michael Oakeshott, *Rationalism in
Politics* (New York: Basic Books, 1962), 32.

19. Jefferson to Colonel William Smith,
November 13, 1787, in Ford, *Writings,*
6:371.

20. Douglas Wilson, "Jefferson and
Literacy," in this volume, 79–90.

21. The most recent contribution to the
debate about Jefferson's democratic character, especially as it is impacted by slavery and Jefferson's own relationship to his
slaves, is *Thomas Jefferson and Sally
Hemings: An American Controversy*
(Charlottesville: University Press of
Virginia, 1997), by Annette Gordon-Reed,
who makes a careful case for the still contentious claim that Jefferson fathered
Hemings's children even as he maintained
despicably racist views.

22. Robert G. McCloskey, ed., *The
Works of James Wilson,* 20 vols.
(Cambridge: The Belknap Press of
Harvard University Press, 1967), 1:37.

23. See Gordon-Reed, *Thomas Jefferson
and Sally Hemings.*

THOMAS JEFFERSON AND THE OLD WORLD

Elizabeth Wirth Marvick

I am indebted for support for this
study to the Virginia Foundation for the
Humanities and Public Policy and to the
Virginia Historical Society. I owe thanks
to Dorothy Twohig, Editor, *The George*
Washington Papers, The University of
Virginia, and to Lucia C. Stanton,
Director of Research, The Jefferson
Memorial Foundation, Monticello, for
valuable advice and assistance.

1. It has been pointed out that although he spent fewer than twenty years away from his home during his lifetime, Jefferson claimed that he had been absent forty years. Maude H. Woodfin, "Contemporary Opinion in Virginia of Thomas Jefferson," in *Essays in Honor of William E. Dodd,* ed. Avery Craven (Chicago: University of Chicago Press, 1935), 30-85.

2. He had seen no city of size except Philadelphia until, with his appointment in 1784, he had ventured up the coast from Annapolis as far as Portsmouth. Frank Shuffelton, "Traveling in the Republic of Letters," in *Voyage et tourisme en Bourgogne à l'époque de Jefferson,* ed. Michel Baridon and Bernard Chevignard (Dijon: Publications de l'université de Bourgogne, 1988), 1-16.

3. A study analyzing that performance in the light of Jefferson's interests as a Virginian is Jacob M. Price, *France and the Chesapeake: A History of the French Tobacco Monopoly, 1674-1791, and of Its Relationship to the British and American Tobacco Trades* (Ann Arbor: University of Michigan Press, 1973) 2: 750-87.

4. Bernard Bailyn, "Boyd's Jefferson: Notes for a Sketch," *New England Quarterly* 33 (1960): 400.

5. Gilbert Chinard, *Thomas Jefferson, the Apostle of Americanism,* 2nd ed. (Boston: Little Brown, 1939), 212.

6. Robert W. Tucker and David C. Hendrickson, *Empire of Liberty: The Statecraft of Thomas Jefferson* (New York: Oxford University Press, 1990), 4.

7. Short was sixteen years Jefferson's junior. Both he and Jefferson used this term, or one like it, at various times. See below, and Marie Goebel Kimball, "William Short, Jefferson's Only 'Son,'" *North American Review* 223 (1926-27): 471-86.

8. George Green Shackelford, ed., "To Practice Law: Aspects of the Era of Good Feelings Reflected in the Short-Ridgely Correspondence, 1816-1821," *Maryland Historical Magazine* 64 (1969): 354-55. December 11, 1816.

9. Bailyn, "Boyd's Jefferson," 399.

10. The layout of the pavilions and château is supposed to have been one of the inspirations for the design of the University of Virginia. Olivier Choppin de Janvry, "Thomas Jefferson au Désert de Retz," *Voyage et tourisme en Bourgogne,* 141-50. On this subject, see note 120, below.

11. The Account Books of Thomas Jefferson, 1785-93, transcribed by James A. Bear. Mimeo., Alderman Library, University of Virginia.

12. *The Papers of Thomas Jefferson,* ed. Julian P. Boyd et al., 27 vols. to date (Princeton: Princeton University Press, 1950-), 7:508.

13. Martha Jefferson to "My dearest friend," n.d. [1785], Edgehill-Randolph Papers, Alderman Library, University of Virginia. Boyd identifies the correspondent as Eliza Trist. See Boyd, *Papers,* 8:436-38.

14. Throughout his stay in Europe he was on the alert for species inferior to the American varieties. Having listened to a nightingale in the garden of a friend, he wrote, "In America it would be deemed a bird of the third rank only." To John Adams, June 21, 1785. Gilbert Chinard, *Les Amitiés américaines de Madame d'Houdetot, d'après sa correspondance inédite avec Benjamin Franklin et Thomas Jefferson* (Paris: Champion, 1924), 32.

15. Jean Gaulmier, "L'Idéologue Volney (1757-1820), contribution à l'histoire de l'Orientalisme en France" (Thesis for the Faculty of Letters, University of Paris, Beyruth, 1951), 347-48.

16. J. Bayard H. Smith to his mother, July 29, 1839, in Margaret Bayard Smith, *First Forty Years of Washington Society,* ed. Gaillard Hunt (New York: Scribner's, 1906), 382-83.

17. August 1, 1824, in *The Family Letters*

of *Thomas Jefferson,* ed. Edwin M. Betts and James A. Bear, Jr. (Columbia: University of Missouri Press, 1966), 454-55.

18. To Monroe, June 17, 1785; to Eliza H. Trist, August 18, 1785, Boyd, *Papers,* 8:233; 403-4.

19. "Notes of a Tour into the Southern Parts of France &c.," Boyd, *Papers,* 11:415-64.

20. On his trip to England he wrote to a Virginian friend, "Their architecture is in the most wretched style I ever saw, not meaning to except America where it is bad, nor even Virginia where it is worse than in any other part of America, which I have seen." What can the untraveled friend conclude from this and Jefferson's further pronouncement, "The city of London, tho' handsomer than Paris, is not so handsome as Philadelphia," unless that it is more worthwhile to stay home in America than to visit either of those European cities? (To John Page, May 4, 1786, Boyd, *Papers,* 9:445.)

21. Nice, April 11, 1787. *The Letters of Lafayette and Jefferson,* ed. Gilbert Chinard (Baltimore: Johns Hopkins University Press, 1929), 110-12. His credit to the English for their pleasure gardens is in the letter to John Page cited above.

22. To Mme de Tessé, Nîmes, March 20, 1787. Boyd, *Papers,* 11:226.

23. I am grateful to Lucia C. Stanton for letting me study the manuscript of her annotated edition of Jefferson's Account Books. She has supplied the full name of the sculptor of the statue Jefferson admired. See Boyd, *Papers,* 11:420.

24. Boyd, *Papers,* 11:246. March 27, 1787. See Bear, "Account Books," for Jefferson's itinerary.

25. Howard C. Rice, "Thomas Jefferson à Strasbourg," (Strasbourg: Société pour la conservation des monuments historiques d'Alsace, 1958). Offprint from *Cahiers alsaciens d'archéologie, d'art et d'histoire.* In Strasbourg, again, Jefferson admired the neoclassic palais de Rohan.

26. *Apostle,* 163-65.

27. Marie Kimball, "Thomas Jefferson's Monticello Collection," *Antiques* 59 (1951): 297-99.

28. Anna Brodeau Thornton wrote of the discomfort of Jefferson's guest accommodations in 1802. "Journal of Anna Maria Brodeau, wife of Dr. Wm Thornton of Washington," cited by Shuffelton, *Voyage et tourisme,* 8. In 1793 Jefferson wrote Madison from Philadelphia, "I have scribbled . . . notes on the plan of a house you inclosed" (for Madison's brother). "I have done more." He had completely revised the architect's plan, throwing it "into another form." The new design was "varied . . . with alcove bed rooms, to which I am much attached." May 19, 1793. *The Papers of James Madison,* ed. William T. Hutchinson, Robert A. Rutland, et al., 17 vols. to date (Chicago: University of Chicago Press, and Charlottesville: University of Virginia Press, 1962-), 15:18.

29. Alexander Hamilton was nearer to the facts when he later described Jefferson as one of those "rulers who love to loll in the lap of epicurean ease." *The Papers of Alexander Hamilton,* ed. Harold C. Syrett, 27 vols. (New York: Columbia University Press, 1961-87), 25:467.

30. One trace of an earlier taste for gothic design exists—a sketch made by him in 1771, apparently for a cemetery monument to his late sister Jane. Frank H. Sommer, "Thomas Jefferson's First Plan for a Virginia Building," in *Papers on American Art,* ed. John C. Milley (New Jersey: Maple Shade, 1976), 87-112.

31. Jefferson urged Madison to wait for the plans he was sending for the Virginia capitol, copied after the Maison Carrée: "It will be superior in beauty to any thing in America, and not inferior to anything in the world." He added, "It is very simple." Paris, September 1, 1785, in Boyd, *Papers,* 8:462.

32. Aix, to William Short, March 27, 1787, in Boyd, *Papers,* 11:246.

33. To Mme de Tott, Marseilles, April 5, 1787, in Boyd, *Papers,* 11:251; to Maria Cosway, Paris, October 12, 1786, in Sarah N. Randolph, *The Domestic Life of Thomas Jefferson* (Charlottesville: University of Virginia Press, 1978), 88.

34. The term is used by Howard C. Rice, *L'Hôtel de Langeac, 1785-1789* (Paris: Henri Lefebre, 1947), 15.

35. Memoir of Martha Jefferson, Edgehill-Randolph Papers, Alderman Library, University of Virginia.

36. Rice, *L'Hôtel de Langeac,* 20, 23n4; Frederick Doveton Nichols, *Thomas Jefferson's Architectural Drawings* (Boston: Massachusetts Historical Society, 1961), 3, 5.

37. To James Buchanan and William Hay, August 12, 1785, in Boyd, *Papers,* 8:367.

38. The landlord protested that retaining this gardener was a term of the lease and assured Jefferson that he himself was entirely satisfied with his services. Boyd, *Papers,* 11:81. January 27, 1787.

39. On the several mutations of Monticello before the French trip, see Gene Waddell, "The First Monticello," *Journal of the Society of Architectural Historians* 46 (March 1987):5-29.

40. To Lafayette, Monticello, August 4, 1781. Lafayette had offered him a hospitable reception in France. "That I cannot avail myself of [the offer] has given me more mortification than almost any occurrence of my life." Chinard, *Lafayette-Jefferson Letters,* 49.

41. To John Trumbull, February 15, 1789. Millicent E. Sowerby, *Catalogue of the Library of Thomas Jefferson,* 5 vols. (Washington: Library of Congress, 1952-59), 2:52.

42. "A Bill for the more General Diffusion of Knowledge" [1778], in Boyd, *Papers,* 2:528.

43. A school exercise in translation of a simple German love poem contains mistakes and omissions. See Henry S. Randall, *The Life of Thomas Jefferson,* 3

vols. (New York: Derby and Jackson, 1858), 1:25. It is characteristic of Jefferson, however, that in a note of thanks for the gift of a new German grammar he recommends proposals he jotted down years before, when studying such a book in college, for reforming the German language in the direction of orthographical consistency and grammatical simplification. Jefferson to Sir Herbert Croft, October 30, 1798. Millicent E. Sowerby, *Catalogue of the Library of Thomas Jefferson,* 5 vols. (Washington: Library of Congress, 1952-59), 5:112-13.

44. Thomas Jefferson, *Notes on the State of Virginia,* ed. William Peden (New York: Norton, 1972), 64. Since Jefferson returned his responses quite soon after receiving Barbé Marbois's queries, it is possible that some of the words stressing this theme were not inserted until after he arrived in France. However, he considered the manuscript ready for publication by the spring of 1784, before he left for France. In reply to Chastellux's letter thanking him for a copy of the *Notes* and appreciating the way in which he had "combatted our great naturalist," Jefferson partially acquits Buffon of having said that European man degenerates in the United States but condemns Raynal. June 7, 1785, Boyd, *Papers,* 8:184-85.

45. In this attitude, too, Jefferson was of distinctly two minds. As governor of Virginia he was so devoted to d'Alembert's and Diderot's *Encylopédie,* then appearing periodically, that he had subscribed in the name of the state, borrowed it for personal use, and had to be reminded by the legislature to return it. See Douglas L. Wilson, "Jefferson and the Republic of Letters," in *Jeffersonian Legacies,* ed. Peter S. Onuf (Charlottesville: University Press of Virginia, 1993), 55-56.

46. To Eliza H. Trist, August 18, 1785, Boyd, *Papers,* 8:403-4.

47. "Letters from Mrs. Ralph Izard

(Alice De Lancey of New York) to Hannah Philippa [Ludwell] Lee," *Virginia Magazine of Biography and History* 8 (1900): 16-28. February 10, 1782.

48. To T. M. Randolph, Jr., August 27, 1786, Boyd, *Papers,* 10:307.

49. *George Washington as the French Knew Him: A Collection of Texts,* ed. and trans. Gilbert Chinard (Princeton: Princeton University Press, 1940), passim.

50. "Soyez bien persuadé que quoique vous ne soyez pas roy, vous serez aussi bien reçu qu'eux [sic]," W. W. Abbot and Dorothy Twohig, eds., *Papers of George Washington,* Confederation Series (Charlottesville: University Press of Virginia, 1987-), 1:455.

51. Duc de Noailles, *Anne-Paule-Dominique de Noailles, marquise de Montagu* (Paris: Lainé et Havard, 1864), 20.

52. Alfred O. Aldridge, *Franklin and His French Contemporaries* (Westport: Greenwood Press, 1976 [1957]), 9-17.

53. Much of Jefferson's interest in mechanical and other devices, specially constructed furnishings, and idiosyncratic architectural strategies had the effect of concealing or minimizing the role of servants. For instance, at his house Poplar Forest he had "two artificial mounds placed on either side for the purpose of concealing outbuildings." Norma B. Cuthbert, "Poplar Forest," *Huntington Library Quarterly* 6 (May 1943): 348. Other examples are the various kinds of dumb-waiters he acquired and installed, pulleys for removing clothes from sight, and "self-opening" doors.

54. George G. Shackelford, "William Short: Diplomat in Revolutionary France, 1785-1793," American Philosophical Society, *Proceedings* 102 (1958): 596-612; Jefferson to Francis Eppes, August 30, 1785, Boyd, *Papers,* 8:451.

55. Fontainebleau, October 28, 1785, *Papers of Madison,* 8:385-86. On his southern trip fifteen months later he suggests

he has an ear for the French of Languedoc and is able to express himself in it, by way of his knowledge of Italian rather than French. To William Short, March 29, 1787, Boyd, *Papers,* 11:254. His report that he learned Spanish from a fellow passenger on the crossing from New York apparently met with some skepticism in his family. See Randall, *Jefferson,* 1:24-25.

56. Paris, May 9, 1788, Boyd, *Papers,* 13:149-50.

57. Emile Rousse, *La Roche-Guyon, châtelains, château et bourg* (Paris: Hachette, 1892), 294-311. On some of the intellectual activities of these La Rochefoucaulds, see Louis-Alexandre d'Enville de La Rochefoucauld, *Correspondance avec George Louis Le Sage,* (Paris, 1918), 5-28.

58. Abigail Adams Smith, *Journal & Correspondence of Miss Adams,* ed. Caroline A. S. De Windt (New York, 1841), 15.

59. Boyd, *Papers,* 8:270.

60. Jefferson to Williamos, July 7, 1785. Boyd relates the circumstances under which Williamos, who had been almost an alter ego for Jefferson, was suddenly cut off by him, under suspicion of conflicting loyalties. Boyd, *Papers,* 8:270-71.

61. Barry Shapiro, "Revolutionary Justice in 1789-90: The Comité des Recherches, the Châtelet, and the Fayettist Coalition," *French Historical Studies* 17 (1992): 656-69.

62. John Adams to James Warren, April 16, 1783), *Warren-Adams Letters* (1778-1814), Massachusetts Historical Society Collections 72-73, 2 vols. (Boston, 1925), 2:213-15.

63. October 17, 1784, Boyd, *Papers,* 7:451n.

64. January 30, 1787, Chinard, *Lafayette-Jefferson Letters,* 69.

65. Louis Gottschalk, *Lafayette between the American and the French Revolution (1783-1789)* (Chicago: University of Chicago Press, 1950), 142-60.

66. May 1784, *Papers of George Washington,* Confederation Series, 2: 292n, 352.

67. After receiving one of Short's increasingly alarmed letters detailing and deploring the progress of the Terror in France, Jefferson, as secretary of state, warned the younger man against expressing such counterrevolutionary thoughts and claimed that he had been asked to do so by Washington. Short to Thomas Jefferson, August 31, 1792, Shackelford, "Short Diplomat," 596-612. Jefferson to Short, January 3, 1793, Boyd, *Papers,* 24:155-56.

68. After his second election to the presidency, Jefferson contends "from intimate knowledge" that Washington, thin-skinned as he was, would never have exposed himself to the calumny of the campaign that Jefferson was then enduring. May 21, 1805. Cited from Ford, 8: 354-56 by Dumas Malone, *Jefferson the President: Second Term, 1805-1809* (Boston: Little, Brown, 1974), 13. Malone himself disagrees.

69. April 11, 1787. Chinard, *Lafayette-Jefferson Letters,* 110-12. Kenneth Lockridge has called to my attention that some of the words used here by Jefferson can be traced to Lawrence Sterne's *Tristram Shandy,* one of Jefferson's favorite works. Jefferson often depicts himself in such easy familiar contact with the poor in France. There is rarely testimony to such encounters from third persons. His reports, moreover, contrast with his well-known aloofness in his journeys in the United States. There seem to be ingredients of invention in these stories.

70. Boyd, *Papers,* 15:166-68.

71. Ibid.

72. To Lafayette, May 6, 1789, Boyd, *Papers,* 15:97-98.

73. Lafayette was alone, among the other nobility of Riom, in advocating a joint commission to determine credentials for the États. Louis Gottschalk and

Margaret Maddox, *Lafayette in the French Revolution: Through the October Days* (Chicago: University of Chicago Press, 1969), 51. On the other hand, he may have been less suspicious of the motives of the "ancient nobility" of Auvergne, to which he belonged, than Jefferson was. He wrote to him on August 27, 1787: "There is a Very Good Understanding Betweeen the Ancient Noblesse and the last order." Boyd, *Papers,* 12:59.

74. E.g., it concludes, "I love you, your wife and children. Tell them so, and adieu. Yours Affectionately." April 11, 1787, in Chinard, *Lafayette-Jefferson Letters,* 111-12. Such expressions did not usually come naturally to Jefferson, but it is a style in which Washington often expressed open affection.

75. Chinard, *Lafayette-Jefferson Letters,* 151. March 19, 1791. It is also Chinard's "third ear" that hears another example of the medley in Jefferson's mind between himself, Washington, and Lafayette. Following Washington's instructions, Jefferson drafted a letter on Lafayette's behalf, to be sent in the president's name to Gouverneur Morris. "Amusingly enough," Chinard notices, he wrote at the end of his draft of this letter the initials "G. W." (ibid, p. 158).

76. Gottschalk and Maddox, *Through the October Days,* 58-59.

77. Chinard was the first to publish Jefferson's mysogynistic writings. See Gilbert Chinard, *The Literary Bible of Thomas Jefferson* (Baltimore: Johns Hopkins Press, 1928), 159. An interesting recent analysis of these is Kenneth A. Lockridge, *On the Sources of Patriarchal Rage* (New York: New York University Press, 1992), 47-73.

78. Jefferson to Girardin, January 15, 1815. Edith Philips, ed., *Louis Hue Girardin and Nicholas Gouin Dufief and Their Relations with Thomas Jefferson* (Baltimore: Johns Hopkins University Press, 1926), 54.

79. Noailles, *Marquise de Montagu,* 40.

80. Introduction to Renée-C.-Victoire de Froulay, marquise de Créquy, *Lettres inédites de la marquise de Créqui à Sénac de Meilhan (1782-1789)* (Paris: L. Potier, 1856), xcix-cv.

81. Gabriel-Paul-Othenin de Cléron, vicomte d' Haussonville, *Le Salon de Madame Necker, d'après des documents tirés des Coppet,* 2 vols. (Paris: C. Lévy, 1882).

82. Claude-Anne Lopez, *Cher Papa: Benjamin Franklin and the Ladies of Paris* (New Haven: Yale University Press, 1960), 243-71.

83. Gilbert Chinard, *Trois amitiés françaises de Jefferson (avec Mme de Bréhan, Mme de Tessé, et Mme de Corny)* (Paris: Société d'édition Les Belles Lettres, 1927), 2.

84. June 21, 1785, Boyd, *Papers,* 8:586. To Benjamin Franklin Jefferson spoke of "the good old countess." Cited by Chinard, *Amitiés américaines,* 1-10.

85. Créquy, *Lettres inédites,* xli.

86. *Souvenirs de la marquise de Créquy de 1710 à 1803,* 3 vols. (Paris: H.L. Delloye, 1842), 2:80-100. These memoirs, though "apocryphal," were compiled by one Maurice Cousen who had mingled in émigré circles in Germany, where Madame de Tessé established herself with an extended retinue in 1790. Edouard Vellay, "Les sources des mémoires apocryphes de Madame de Créqui," *L'Intermédiaire des chercheurs et curieux* (1960), 10:675-81. The remark cited is entirely consistent with others about her relative that the marquise confided to Sénac de Meilhan and represents views that were probably known to Tessé herself. Vellay himself chooses "authentic" extracts from the supposedly false memoirs.

87. Chinard, *Trois amitiés françaises,* 100-135.

88. To Eliza H. Trist, August 18, 1785, in Boyd, *Papers,* 8:403-4.

89. Jefferson to Anne Willing Bingham, February 7, 1787; Anne Bingham to Thomas Jefferson, June 1, 1788; in Randolph, *Domestic Life,* 96-98. See also Robert C. Alberts, *The Golden Voyage: The Life and Times of William Bingham, 1752-1804* (Boston: Houghton Mifflin Co., 1969).

90. August 26, 1788, in Chinard, *Trois amitiés américaines,* 44.

91. Mme d'Enville to Jefferson, La Rocheguyon, December 30, 1792, Boyd, *Papers,* 24:798.

92. Tessé to Thomas Jefferson, February 22; Jefferson to Tessé, March 20, 1787; Boyd, *Papers,* 11:206-7, 227.

93. Chinard, *Amitiés américaines,* 32-38.

94. Jefferson to Anne Willing Bingham, February 7, 1787; Anne Bingham to Jefferson, June 1, 1787, Boyd, *Papers,* 11:122-24; 392-94. Before receiving Mrs. Bingham's reply Jefferson made another blunder. In a second letter to her he rejoices that "our good ladies" are "too wise to wrinkle their foreheads with politics," but are "contented to soothe and calm the minds of their husbands returning ruffled from political debate." May 11, 1788. Boyd, 13:152.

95. Hippolyte Buffenoir, *La Comtesse d'Houdetot, une amie de J.-J. Rousseau* (Paris: Calmann Lévy, 1901), 77.

96. Charles de Pougens, *Mémoires et souvenirs* (Paris: Fournier, 1834), 298.

97. Créquy, *Lettres inédites,* 298.

98. December 4, 1788, in Boyd, *Papers,* 13:227.

99. Mme d'Enville to Thomas Jefferson, La Rocheguyon, December 30, 1792. She ingeniously suggests that the one-legged Gouverneur Morris, who has the appointment, would be better off in The Hague, where Short is serving, because it would be easier for him to get around on canals than in the streets of Paris. Boyd, *Papers,* 24:798.

100. To Lafayette, February 28; to Tessé, March 20; to Madison, June 20, 1787,

Boyd, *Papers,* 11:186, 227, 482. To Washington, December 4, 1788, in *Papers of Washington,* Presidential Series, 1:154.

101. Thomas Jefferson to Short, January 3, 1793, in Boyd, *Papers,* 24:155-56.

102. Autobiography, in *The Writings of Thomas Jefferson,* ed. Henry Augustine Washington, 9 vols. (New York: Riker, 1857), 1:101.

103. May 11; September 1, 1785, in Boyd, *Papers,* 8:147-48, 462.

104. Jefferson to Brissot, February 10, 1788, in Sowerby, *Catalogue,* 3:374.

105. The loan was made on November 21, 1796. The earlier lenders were Wakelyn Welsh, Henderson McCaul & Co., Filippo Mazzei, and William Short. Van Staphorst himself took seventeen more. Jefferson Papers, Library of Congress. Short wrote Jefferson on December 27, 1797, that he did not intend to acquire slaves when he returned to settle in the United States. See "The Papers of William Short," 8 vols. (typescript, Cornell University, 1900), vol. 1.

106. Correspondence between Jefferson and Abigail Adams, January 29, 1787; February 22, 1787; in Boyd, *Papers* 11:174.

107. Jefferson to John Adams, November 13, 1787, in Boyd, *Papers,* 12:351. For a discussion of Jefferson's position see Chinard, *Apostle,* 194-21.

108. Jefferson to Francis Hopkinson, Paris, March 13, 1789, in Boyd, *Papers,* 14:651.

109. Lafayette to Thomas Jefferson, (1788?), *Lafayette-Jefferson Letters,* 123.

110. *Papers of George Washington,* Presidential Series, 1:152-53.

111. As soon as he received news of the passage of this bill by the Virginia legislature he had copies bound in with copies of the *Notes on Virginia* that he was distributing to French friends at the time. See Peden, *Notes,* 297.

112. Thomas Jefferson to Mrs. Bolling, July 23, 1787, in Randolph, *Domestic Life,* 130.

113. Chastellux to Jefferson, August 24, 1784, in Boyd, *Papers,* 7:41.

114. Samia I. Spencer, "Women and Education," in *French Women and the Age of Enlightenment,* ed. Samia I. Spencer (Bloomington: Indiana University Press, 1984), 86. This and other points concerning Jefferson's relations with French women are developed in my "Thomas Jefferson and the Ladies of Paris," *Proceedings of the Western Society for French History* 21 (1994): 84-94.

115. Miss Adams, *Journal,* 27.

116. She adds that she is glad no one else in the school understands English. Julia Annesley to Martha Jefferson, April 20, 1786. Edgehill Randolph Papers, Alderman Library, University of Virginia.

117. Account Books, transcribed by Bear, Alderman Library.

118. Piganiol de La Force, *Description historique de la ville de Paris et de ses environs,* vol. 7 (Paris: Desprez, 1765), 245-46. Chinard follows Martha Jefferson in confounding Mount Calvaire with the Chartreuse. *Trois amitiés françaises,* 74.

119. Jefferson's selection of paintings for Monticello favored religious subjects which, of course, predominated at the Chartreuse de Paris.

120. To the various candidates for having inspired the design of the University of Virginia might be added the cloister of this monastery with individual cells surrounding its green enclosure and its domed building at one end. See *La Chartreuse de Paris* (Paris: Les Musées de la Ville de Paris, 1987), plate 45. On other candidates (the château de Marly, the gallery of the Palais Royal, etc.), see Frederick D. Nichols, "Architecture," in *Thomas Jefferson: A Reference Biography,* ed. Merrill D. Peterson (New York: Scribner's, 1986), 215-32.

121. Autobiography, in Washington, ed., *Works,* 1:107.

122. Short to Thomas Jefferson, Paris, November 30, 1789, Boyd, *Papers,* 15:564.

123. March 24, 1789, Boyd, *Papers,* 14:694-97.

124. To Charles Thomson, November 11, 1784, in Boyd, *Papers,* 8:519.

125. Jefferson to Jonathan Trumbull, June 1, 1789, in Boyd, *Papers,* 15:164.

126. To Charles Thomson, November 12, 1784, in Boyd, *Papers,* 8:519.

127. To John Banister, Jr., October 15, 1785, in Boyd, *Papers,* 8:636.

128. "When I returned from France, after an absence of six or seven years . . .," Jefferson to William Short, October 3, 1801, in H. A. Washington, *Writings,* 4:413.

129. To Monroe, June 17, 1785, in Boyd, *Papers,* 8:233.

130. C. Vann Woodward, "The Southern Ethic in a Puritan World," *William and Mary Quarterly* 25 (1968):343-70.

131. September 2, 1785, in Boyd, *Papers,* 8:468.

132. To Martha Jefferson, March 28, 1787, in Betts and Bear, *Family Letters,* 34-35.

133. The acute French minister to the United States, Louis-Guillaume Otto, who had known Jefferson in his pre-Parisian days, must have been surprised at changes in him when he returned. Otto informed his government that although Jefferson had been offered the position most likely to lead to the presidency, he expected him to decline it because "les habitudes qu'il a contractées en France lui présentent plus de ressources et d'agréments dans ses fonctions de Ministre Plénipotentiaire." Otto to Montmorin, December 10, 1789, in Boyd, *Papers,* 15:557n.

WHY SLAVES CAN'T READ

James Oakes

1. David Walker, *Walker's Appeal in Four Articles,* ed. William Loren Katz (New York: Arch Press, 1969), 38-39.

2. Ibid., 11, 17, 20.

3. Ibid., 44.

4. This essay was written before the publication of Ronald Hamony's excellent edition of *Cato's Letters,* by John Trenchard and Thomas Gordon, 2 vols. (Indianapolis: Liberty Fund, 1995). Here I rely on David Louis Jacobson, ed., *The English Libertarian Heritage* (Indianapolis, Indiana: Bobbs-Merrill, 1965), 94, 189. The influence of the radical Whig tradition, in particular Trenchard and Gordon, is demonstrated in Clinton Rossiter, *Seedtime of the Republic: The Origin of the American Tradition of Political Liberty* (New York: Harcourt Brace: 1953), 224ff.; and confirmed in Bernard Bailyn, *The Ideological Origins of the American Revolution* (Cambridge, Mass.: Belknap Press of Harvard University Press, 1967), 35-37. J. G. A. Pocock, *The Machiavellian Moment: Florentine Political Thought and the Atlantic Republican Tradition* (Princeton: Princeton University Press, 1975), places Trenchard and Gordon within the "republican" tradition, whereas Ronald Hamowy, "Cato's Letters, John Locke, and the Republican Paradigm," *History of Political Thought* 2, no. 2 (summer 1990): 273-94, makes a more persuasive case that they were part of a Lockean liberal tradition.

5. Herbert Aptheker, ed., *A Documentary History of the Negro People in the United States,* vol. 1 (New York: Citadel Press, 1951), 11.

6. Ibid., 52.

7. Aptheker, *Documentary History,* 1:228.

8. Frederick Douglass, *Narrative of the Life of Frederick Douglass* (Boston, 1845; Garden City, N.Y.: Anchor Books, 1963), 36.

9. Kenneth M. Stampp, *The Peculiar Institution: Slavery in the Antebellum South* (New York: Vintage Books, 1956), 208.

10. Janet Duitsman Cornelius, *When I Can Read My Title Clear: Literacy, Slavery, and Religion in the Antebellum South* (Columbia: University of South Carolina Press, 1991).

11. Thomas L. Webber, *Deep like the Rivers: Education in the Slave Quarter Community, 1831-1865* (New York: Norton, 1978), p. 29.

12. Thomas Jefferson, *Notes on the State of Virginia,* in Adrienne Koch and William Peden, eds., *The Life and Selected Writings of Thomas Jefferson* (New York: Modern Library Press, 1944), 259-60.

13. Ibid., 260, 257.

14. On this point, see Winthrop D. Jordan, *White over Black: American Attitudes toward the Negro, 1550-1812* (Chapel Hill: Published for the Institute of Early American History and Culture by the University of North Carolina, Press, 1968), 429-81.

15. I am concerned in this essay with the political significance of Jefferson's belief that blacks were *intellectually* inferior to whites. But a similar argument can be made about the claims of bodily (or aesthetic) inferiority. Here I can only hint at what such an argument might look like.

Simply put, where intellectual inferiority rendered blacks unfit to participate in the *public* sphere as the equals of whites, their physical/aesthetic inferiority rendered them unfit to participate equally with whites in the *private* sphere. Sentiment, sexual attraction, and even passion played a role in the private sphere analogous to the place of reason in public life. Hence Jefferson's insistence that

blacks' sensibilities were brutish, their sexual appetites crude, their emotions transient and indelicate.

This was nothing if not a political argument. Peter Laslett pointed out some years ago that Locke's major point in the *Two Treatises of Government* was to distinguish the rules governing the public from those governing the private life. More recently, Don Herzog, *Happy Slaves: A Critique of Consent Theory* (Chicago: University of Chicago Press, 1989), has suggested that liberal ideology prevailed over its rivals because it offered a better explanation for the pattern of social differentiation that characterizes the modern world. Thus Jefferson's sharp distinction between public and private is among the clearest marks of his deep-seated liberalism. His claim that blacks were inferior in the endowments of body and mind coincided neatly with his liberal ideology. Intellectual inferiority forever precluded racial equality in public life; bodily inferiority foreclosed the possibility of racial equality in private life.

16. Garry Wills, *Inventing America* (New York: Doubleday, 1978). Morton White, *The Philosophy of the American Revolution* (New York: Oxford University Press, 1978). See Jefferson to Thomas Law, June 13, 1814, Merrill Peterson, ed., *Writings of Thomas Jefferson* (New York: Literary Classics, 1984), 1337-38: "The want or imperfection of the moral sense in some men, like the want or imperfection of the senses of sight and hearing in others, is no proof that it is a general characteristic of the species. When it is wanting, we endeavor to supply the defect by education, by appeals to reason and calculation, by presenting to the being so unhappily conformed, other motives to do good and to eschew evil, such as the love, or the hatred, or rejection of those among whom he lives, and whose society is necessary to his happiness and even existence; demonstrations by sound calcula-

tion that honesty promotes interest in the long run; the rewards and penalties established by the laws; and ultimately the prospects of a future state of retribution for the evil as well as the good done while here. These are the correctives which are supplied by education, and which exercise the functions of the moralist, the preacher, and legislator. . . ." Here Jefferson accepts that the moral sense is not equally well developed in all individuals, and that "appeals to reason and calculation" can compensate for this inequality whenever the "disparity is not too profound to be eradicated."

17. Koch and Peden, *Life*, 264. See also Thomas Jefferson to Thomas Mann Randolph, Jr., August 27, 1786, in Julian Boyd, et al., eds., *The Papers of Thomas Jefferson*, 27 vols. to date (Princeton: Princeton University Press, 1950-), 10:305.

18. Jefferson thought women similarly deficient in their capacity for rational maturity, hence his proposals for female education emphasized the study of French along with dancing, music, drawing, and "household economy." See Thomas Jefferson to Martha Jefferson, November 28, 1783, Peterson, *Writings*, 782; Thomas Jefferson to Nathaniel Burwell, March 14, 1818, ibid., 1411-13.

19. Thomas Jefferson to Peter Carr, August 19, 1785, Boyd, *Papers*, 8:406.

20. Thomas Jefferson to Peter Carr, August 10, 1787, Boyd, *Papers*, 12:17.

21. Thomas Jefferson, autobiography, Peterson, *Writings*, 37.

22. Thomas Jefferson to Peter Carr, August 10, 1787, Boyd, *Papers*, 12:15.

23. Thomas Jefferson to Thomas Law, June 13, 1814, Peterson, *Writings*, 1337.

24. Daniel Boorstin, *The Lost World of Thomas Jefferson* (Boston: H. Holt, 1948).

25. Thomas Jefferson to John Adams, October 28, 1813, in Lester Cappon, ed., *The Adams-Jefferson Letters* (Chapel Hill: University of North Carolina Press, 1959), 388.

26. Thomas Jefferson to Governor John Langdon, March 5, 1810, in Peterson, *Writings*, 1,221.

27. Thomas Jefferson to Robert Skipwith, August 3, 1771, Boyd, *Papers*, 1:76-77.

28. Jefferson, *Notes on the State of Virginia*, in Peden and Koch, *Life*, 264-65.

29. Jefferson to George Wythe, August 13, 1786, in Boyd, *Papers*, 10:244.

30. Thomas Jefferson to Caesar Rodney, February 10, 1810, in Peterson, *Writings*, 1,217.

31. Thomas Jefferson, "Response to the Citizens of Albemarle," February 12, 1790, ibid., 491.

32. Thomas Jefferson to Diodati, August 3, 1789, in Boyd, *Papers*, 15: 326.

33. Jurgen Habermas, *The Structural Transformation of the Public Sphere: An Inquiry into a Category of Bourgeois Society*, trans. Thomas Burger(Cambridge, Mass: MIT Press, 1989). For a sampling of the rapidly multiplying commentaries, see Craig Calhoun, ed., *Habermas and the Public Sphere* (Cambridge, Mass.: MIT Press, 1992).

34. Thomas Jefferson to John Tyler, June 28, 1804, in Peterson, *Writings*, 1,147.

35. Ibid., 120.

36. Thomas Jefferson to François D'Ivernois, February 6, 1795, ibid., 1,023.

37. Thomas Jefferson to Joseph Willard, March 24, 1789, Boyd, *Papers*, 14:699.

38. Thomas Jefferson to John Adams, January 11, 1816, in Cappon, *Adams-Jefferson Letters*, 458.

39. Thomas Jefferson to John Adams, September 4, 1823, ibid., 596.

40. Thomas Jefferson to William Green Munford, June 18, 1799, in Peterson, *Writings*, 1,065-66.

41. "A Bill for Establishing Religious Freedom," ibid., 346.

42. Thomas Jefferson to Richard Price, January 8, 1789, in Boyd, *Papers*, 14:420.

43. Thomas Jefferson, autobiography, in Peterson, *Writings*, 39-45.

44. Thomas Jefferson to George Wythe, August 13, 1786, in Boyd, *Papers,* 10:244, 245.

45. Thomas Jefferson to John Wyche, May 19, 1809, in Peterson, *Writings,* 1,207-8.

46. Thomas Jefferson to John Adams, October 28, 1813, in Cappon, *Adams-Jefferson Letters,* 390.

47. See, for example, Thomas Jefferson to Mann Page, August 30, 1795, in Andrew A. Lipscomb and Albert E. Bergh, eds., *The Writings of Thomas Jefferson,* 20 vols. (Washington: Issued under the auspices of the Thomas Jefferson Memorial Association, 1903-4), 9:306.

48. Thomas Jefferson to Littleton Waller Tazewell, January 5, 1805, ibid.

49. The "Report . . ." is in Peterson's edition of Jefferson's *Writings,* 459-62, and is the basis for this paragraph and the one following.

50. Jefferson, *Notes on the State of Virginia,* Koch and Peden, *Life,* 258.

51. Ibid., 259.

52. Ibid., 258-59.

53. Ibid., 258.

54. Ibid., 259-61.

55. Thomas Jefferson to Henri Gregoire, February 25, 1809, in Peterson, *Writings,* 1,202.

56. Thomas Jefferson, Autobiography, ibid., 44.

57. Walker, *Appeal,* 56-84.

58. Ibid., 84-85.

THOMAS JEFFERSON'S DUALISTIC PERCEPTIONS OF NATIVE AMERICANS

DONALD A. GRINDE, JR.

1. Thomas Jefferson to James Madison, January 30, 1787, Julian P. Boyd, ed., *The Papers of Thomas Jefferson,* 27 vols. to date (Princeton: Princeton University Press, 1950-), 11:92-93.

2. I am referring to Vernon L. Parrington, *Main Currents in American Thought* (New York: Harcourt, Brace, 1927, 1930); Merrill D. Peterson, *The Jeffersonian Image in the American Mind* (New York: Oxford University Press, 1960); Leonard W. Levy, *Jefferson and Civil Liberties: The Darker Side* (Cambridge: Harvard University Press, 1963); and Dumas Malone's multivolume study, *Jefferson and His Time,* 6 vols. (Boston: Little Brown & Company, 1962).

3. Winthrop D. Jordan, *White over Black: American Attitudes toward the Negro, 1550-1812* (Chapel Hill: University of North Carolina Press, 1968).

4. See Bernard Sheehan, *Seeds of Extinction: Jeffersonian Philanthropy and the American Indian* (New York: W.W. Norton, 1974) for a fuller discussion of these themes in Jeffersonian America.

5. Richard K. Matthews, *The Radical Politics of Thomas Jefferson: A Revisionist View* (Lawrence: University Press of Kansas, 1984), 17-18.

6. Ibid., 122.

7. Ibid., 54.

8. Julian P. Boyd, "Dr. Franklin: Friend of the Indian," in Ray Lokken, Jr., ed., *Meet Dr. Franklin* (Philadelphia: Franklin Institute, 1981), 240.

9. Ibid. See also Jean Jacques Rousseau, "A Discourse on the Origin of Inequality," in G. D. H. Cole, trans., *The Social Contract and Discourses* (New York: E.P. Dutton, 1950), 242-44. As early as 1540, Michel Eyquem de Montaigne in his "Essay on Cannibals," in Donald France, ed., *Complete Works of Montaigne*

(Stanford: Stanford University Press, 1958), 153, makes similar observations about the nature of American Indian people.

10. Felix Cohen, "Americanizing the White Man," *American Scholar* 21, no. 2 (spring 1952): 179-80.

11. See Neal Salisbury, "American Indians and American History," in Calvin Martin, ed., *The American Indian and the Problem of History* (New York: Oxford University Press, 1987), 46.

12. Lester J. Cappon, ed., *The Adams-Jefferson Letters,* 2 vols. (Chapel Hill: University of North Carolina Press, 1959), 2:307.

13. Thomas Jefferson to Martha Jefferson Randolph, Philadelphia, December 31, 1792, in Edwin M. Betts and James A. Bear, Jr., eds., *The Family Letters of Thomas Jefferson* (Columbia: The University of Missouri Press, 1966), 108.

14. Thomas Jefferson to Martha Jefferson Randolph, Philadelphia, March 22, 1792, ibid., 96.

15. Thomas Jefferson to the marquis de Chastellux, June 7, 1785, Boyd, *Papers,* 8:186.

16. Thomas Jefferson to John Adams, June 11, 1812, Cappon, *Adams-Jefferson Letters,* 2:308.

17. Sheehan, *Seeds of Extinction,* passim.

18. For a fuller discussion of this subject, see Stephen Jay Gould, *The Mismeasure of Man* (New York: W.W. Norton, 1981), chapters 3 and 4.

19. Thomas Jefferson, *Notes on the State of Virginia,* ed. William Peden (Chapel Hill: University of North Carolina Press, 1955), 63.

20. Paul L. Ford, ed., *The Works of Thomas Jefferson,* 12 vols. (New York: G.P. Putnam's Sons, 1904-5), 3:458.

21. Charles Thomson to Samuel Rhodes, Easton, July 28, 1757, *Pennsylvania Magazine of History and Biography* 20, no. 3 (October 1896): 421-22.

22. Andrew A. Lipscomb and Albert Ellery Bergh, eds., *The Writings of Thomas Jefferson,* 20 vols. (Washington: Thomas Jefferson Memorial Association, 1903-4), 11:345-46.

23. Ibid., 11:346.

24. Ibid., 16:426-27.

25. Thomas Jefferson to William Henry Harrison, February 27, 1803, in ibid., 10:370.

26. Saul K. Padover, *The Complete Jefferson* (New York: Duell, Sloan and Pearce, 1943), 503-5.

27. See Donald A. Grinde, Jr., *The Iroquois and the Founding of the American Nation* (San Francisco: Indian Historian Press, 1977) for a more detailed analysis of these themes.

28. Sheehan, *Seeds of Extinction,* 7.

29. Thomas Jefferson to Benjamin Hawkins, February 18, 1803, in Lipscomb and Bergh, *Writings of Thomas Jefferson,* 10:363.

30. Thomas Jefferson to John Adams, Monticello, July 11, 1812, in Cappon, *Adams-Jefferson Letters,* 2:305

31. Ibid., 2:305-6.

32. Ibid., 2:306.

33. I am referring to Joseph F. Lafitau, *Customs of the American Indians Compared with the Customs of the Primitive Times,* ed. William N. Fenton and Elizabeth L. Moore, 2 vols. (Toronto: Champlain Society, 1974-77).

34. Cappon, *Adams-Jefferson Letters,* 2:306. Jefferson is referring to: Thomas Hariot's *Admiranda Narratio* (Frankfort: Published by Theodor de Bry, 1590), Jacques Le Moyne de Morgues, *Brevis Narratio eorum quae in Florida Americae* (Frankfort: Published by Theodor de Bry, 1591), and *Americae nona & postrema pars* (Frankfort: Published by Theodor de Bry, 1602).

35. Cappon, *Adams-Jefferson Letters,* 2:305.

36. Ibid., 2:306.

37. Ibid., 2:306. See also James Adair,

The History of the American Indians (New York: Arno Press, n.d.), particularly chapters 1-7.

38. Thomas Jefferson to John Adams, May 27, 1812, in Cappon, *Adams-Jefferson Letters,* 2:323-24.

39. Boyd, *Papers,* 11:683.

40. See "Unquahog tribe, Pushpatuck Settlement, Brookhaven, Long Island, N.Y. taken by Thomas Jefferson, June 13, 1791 in the presence of James Madison and General Wm. Floyd," in Indian Boxes, Box 1, Manuscript Division, New York Public Library.

41. See Thomas Jefferson, "A Manuscript Comparative Vocabulary of Several Indian Languages," class 497, no. J35, American Philosophical Society Library. See also Thomas Jefferson to Benjamin Barton Smith, September 21, 1809, in Lipscomb and Bergh, *Writings of Jefferson,* 12:312-13; Thomas Jefferson to Peter S. Deponceau, November 7, 1817, ibid., 15:153; and Boyd, *Papers,* 20:451-52.

42. Thomas Jefferson to Peter Wilson, January 20, 1816, Lipscomb and Bergh, *Writings of Jefferson,* 14:402. Jefferson, however, was never fully convinced that American Indians were the source of Asian populations. See Peden, *Notes on the State of Virginia,* 282, and more specifically, Jefferson additions after p. 162 of his personal rebound copy of *Notes* (Stockdale edition), Alderman Library, University of Virginia, Charlottesville, Virginia.

43. Peden, *Notes on the State of Virginia,* 97-100.

44. Charles Thomson to Thomas Jefferson, April 28, 1787, Boyd, *Papers,* 11:323-24; and Thomas Jefferson to Charles Thomson, September 20, 1787, ibid., 12:159.

45. Thomas Jefferson to Ezra Stiles, September 1, 1786, ibid., 10:316.

46. Julian P. Boyd, "Dr. Franklin: Friend of the Indian," in Ray Lokken, Jr., ed., *Meet Dr. Franklin* (Philadelphia:

Franklin Institute, 1981), 240.

47. Thomas Jefferson to Charles Bellini, Paris, September 30, 1785, in Boyd, *Papers,* 8:568.

48. See Carl Binger, *Thomas Jefferson: A Well-Tempered Mind* (New York: W.W. Norton Company, 1970), 309. For a similar observation of the poverty and injustice among the poor of France, see Jefferson to Madison, Fountainebleau, October 28, 1785, in Boyd, *Papers,* 8:681-83.

49. Thomas Jefferson to John Adams, Monticello, January 21, 1812, in Cappon, *Adams-Jefferson Letters,* 2:291.

50. "Letter to Abbé Raynal on the Affairs of North America," in Moncure D. Conway, ed., *Writings of Thomas Paine,* 4 vols. (New York: G. P. Putnam's Sons, 1894-96), 2:105.

51. Quoted from Malone, *Jefferson and His Time,* vol. 3, *Jefferson and the Ordeal of Liberty* (Boston: Little Brown, 1962).

52. Thomas Jefferson to Edward Carrington, January 16, 1787, in Boyd, *Papers,* 11:49.

53. Ibid., 11:49.

54. Paul L. Ford, ed., *The Writings of Thomas Jefferson,* 10 vols. (New York: G.P. Putnam Sons, 1892-99) 3:198-99.

55. Ibid.

56. Ibid.

57. See Donald A. Grinde, Jr., and Bruce E. Johansen, *Exemplar of Liberty: Native America and the Evolution of Democracy* (Los Angeles: UC Regents and UCLA American Indian Studies Center, 1991), chapter 2.

58. Ford, *Writings,* 3:441. Jefferson also reported that birth control was used by American Indian women: "[T]hey have fewer children that we do" and "have learned the practice of procuring abortion by use of some vegetable." He also noted that such abortion practices prevented "conception for a considerable time after." Ibid.

59. See "Law of the Woman Chief," J.N.B. Hewitt Collection, mss. 1586,

National Anthropological Archives, Smithsonian Institution, Washington, D.C., and Judith K. Brown, "Economic Organization and the Position of Women among the Iroquois," *Ethnohistory* 17, no. 3-4 (Summer-Fall 1970): 151-67.

60. Malone, *Jefferson's Time,* 1:267.

61. Binger, *Well-Tempered Mind,* 100.

62. Ford, *Writings,* 3:189-90.

63. See Grinde and Johansen's *Exemplar of Liberty* for a fuller treatment of these themes.

64. Peden, *Notes on the State of Virginia,* 93.

65. Ford, *Writings,* 3:195.

66. Ibid., 3:317-19.

67. Ibid., 3:341.

68. Peden, *Notes on the State of Virginia,* 93. See also Thomas Jefferson to Francis W. Gilmer, June 7, 1816, in Ford, *Writings,* 10:32-33.

69. Adrienne Koch and William Peden, eds., *The Life and Selected Writings of Thomas Jefferson* (New York: The Modern Library, 1944), 408.

70. Thomas Jefferson to John Rutledge, August 6, 1787, in Boyd, *Papers* 11:701.

71. Chevalier de Chastellux to General Philip Schuyler, February 18, 1782, in Philip Schuyler Papers, Box 35, New York Public Library.

72. "Speech of Hon. Charles Pinckney," May 14, 1788, *American Museum* 4, no. 3 (September 1788): 157. Indeed, Pinckney was merely reinforcing a significant sentiment at the Constitutional Convention. James Wilson, delegate to the Constitutional Convention from Pennsylvania, stated at the convention that: "The British government cannot be our model. We have no materials for a similar one. Our manners, ours laws, the abolition of entails and primogeniture, the whole genius of the people are opposed to it." James Wilson, June 7, 1787, in Adrienne Koch, ed., *Notes on Debates in the Federal Convention of 1787 Reported by James Madison* (Athens, Ohio: Ohio State University Press, 1966), 85.

A few weeks later, Franklin would echo a similar sentiment: "We have gone back to ancient history for models of Government, and examined different forms of those Republics which having been formed with the seeds of their own dissolution now no longer exist. And we have viewed Modern States all round Europe, but find none of their Constitutions suitable to our circumstances." Benjamin Franklin, June 28, 1787, ibid., 209.

At the Constitutional Convention, an interesting image of Native Americans was invoked by Gouverneur Morris (delegate from Pennsylvania), who made this crucial statement about American Indians and private property: "Men do not enter into Society to protect their Lives or Liberty—the Savages possess both in perfection—they unite in Society for the Protection of Property." According to notes of Rufus King, July 5, 1787, in Charles B. King, ed., *The Life and Correspondence of Rufus King,* 6 vols. (New York: Da Capo Press, 1971), 1:613.

73. New York *Journal,* August 10, 1790.

74. Ibid.

75. Ibid.

76. David Ramsay, *History of the American Revolution,* 2 vols. (London: J. Stockdale, 1793), 1:29.

77. David Ramsay, "Dissertation on the Manner of Acquiring the Character and Privileges of a Citizen of the United States" [1802], MS 34-297, South Carolina Historical Society, Charleston.

78. Peden, *Notes on the State of Virginia,* 62.

79. *The New Cambridge Modern History,* vol. 7, *The Old Regime,* 1713-63, ed. J. O. Lindsay (Cambridge: Cambridge University Press, 1970), 65.

80. Jack Forbes, "Americanism Is the Answer," *Akwesasne Notes* 6 (1975):37. See

also Grinde and Johansen, *Exemplar of Liberty.* Native American scholars are painfully aware of the dualistic standards that operate in the historical profession today with regard to American Indian history. American Indian history is the only branch of the discipline in which practicing research historians are not required to know the language, culture, philosophy, and religion of the people they are studying. Indeed, some non-Indian scholars who do research on American Indian history such as James Axtell revel in this ignorance as proof of their "objectivity." See Grinde, "Iroquoian Political Concept and the Genesis of American Government: Further Research and Contention," *Northeast Indian Quarterly* 6(winter 1989):10-21. See also Bruce Trigger's review of Axtell's *Beyond 1492: Encounters in Colonial North America* (New York: Oxford University Press, 1992) in *Ethnohistory* 40, no. 3 (summer 1993) for further criticism of Axtell's flawed objectivist position. One wonders how far French historians in the profession would get by proclaiming their ignorance of French language, culture, and so on as proof of their objectivity!

81. See Grinde, "Iroquoian Political Concept," 10-21.

82. Thomas Jefferson to William Ludlow, September 6, 1824, in Lipscomb and Bergh, *Writings,* 16:74-75.

83. Ibid.

84. Ibid. See also Sheehan, *Seeds of Extinction,* chapter 8, and Matthews, *Jefferson,* chapter 4. Ronald Takaki argues that the Jeffersonians' motives in dealing with American Indians and African Americans were to create an "ideology for bourgeois acquisitiveness and modern capitalism" (see Ronald Takaki, *Iron Cages: Race and Culture in the 19th Century* [New York: Oxford University Press, 1990], 9). Takaki does not deal extensively with the nature and consequences of the conquest and settler states that Jefferson aimed at creating in the name of progress, but he does point out that Jefferson and others saw the frontier as a place of vacant lands where settlers could engage in "regeneration" (ibid., 15).

THE OLD AND THE NEW WORLDS: SUMMARY AND COMMENT

C. VANN WOODWARD

1. Quotations in the summary of the papers will be found in the papers being summarized.

2. Thomas Jefferson to Maria Cosway, October 12, 1786, Julian Boyd, ed., *The Papers of Thomas Jefferson,* 27 vols. to date (Princeton: Princeton University Press, 1950-), 10:444-51. Dumas Malone, *Jefferson and His Time,* 6 vols. (Boston: Little, Brown, 1951), 2:70-78.

3. *Notes on the State of Virginia* (London: Stockdale, 1787), 239-40.

4. Richard Matthews, *The Radical Politics of Thomas Jefferson* (Lawrence:

University of Kansas, 1984), 70-73.

5. Simon Schama, *Citizens, a Chronicle of the French Revolution* (New York: Vintage Books, 1989), 615, 631.

6. Gordon S. Wood, *The Radicalism of the American Revolution* (New York: Knopf, 1991), 231-34.

7. Richard Matthews, *Radical Politics,* 85-87.

8. In the Lincoln-Douglas debates, October 16, 1854, Roy P. Basler, ed., *The Collected Works of Abraham Lincoln,* 8 vols. (New Brunswick, N.J.: Rutgers University Press, 1953), 2:249.

CITIZENSHIP AND CHANGE IN JEFFERSON'S CONSTITUTIONAL THOUGHT

DAVID N. MAYER

1. For a comprehensive treatment of Jefferson's thought, see David N. Mayer, *The Constitutional Thought of Thomas Jefferson* (Charlottesville: University Press of Virginia, 1994; paperback edition, 1995). This paper is adapted largely from chapter 10, " 'Hand in Hand with the Progress of the Human mind': Constitutional Change and the Preservation of Republicanism."

2. Julian P. Boyd, "The Chasm that Separated Thomas Jefferson and John Marshall," in *Essays on the American Constitution,* ed. Gottfried Dietze (Englewood Cliffs, N.J.: Prentice-Hall, 1964), 10. This favorable attitude toward change in the forms of government, along with the more general impulse toward reform and innovation that Boyd associates with Jefferson, are among the key differences between Jefferson and Marshall that Boyd cites.

3. My book *The Constitutional Thought of Thomas Jefferson* seeks to provide a fresh perspective on Jefferson's thought, free from the "liberalism" versus "civic republicanism" debate that has so dominated early American scholarship in recent years—and which, I have argued, has been a false and misleading debate with respect to early American constitutional thought. See David N. Mayer, "English Radical Whig Origins of American Constitutionalism," *Washington University Law Quarterly* 70 (1992): 131-208. Rather than trying to force it into either of these paradigms, I instead seek to explain comprehensively Jefferson's constitutional thought on its own terms.

4. These radical Whigs were the three generations of "Commonwealthmen" whom Caroline Robbins has described. Robbins, *The Eighteenth-Century Commonwealthman: Studies in the Trans-mission, Development, and Circumstance of English Liberal Thought* (Cambridge, Mass.: Harvard University Press, 1959). For a summary of the three generations of radical Whigs, within the context of the development of Anglo-American constitutional thought, see Mayer, "English Radical Whig Origins of American Constitutionalism."

5. Jefferson to Samuel Kercheval, July 12, 1816, in *The Writings of Thomas Jefferson,* ed. Paul L. Ford, 10 vols. (New York: Putnam's, 1892-99), 10:43; Algernon Sidney, *Discourses concerning Government* (London, 1698), 16. On Jefferson's recommendation of Sidney's treatise, along with Locke's, as "elementary books of public right," see, for example, Jefferson to John Norvell, June 14, 1807, to Henry Lee, May 8, 1825, Ford, *Writings,* 9:71, 10:343.

6. James Burgh, *Political Disquisitions,* 3 vols. (London; E. and C. Dilly, 1774-75), 1:3-4.

7. Sidney, *Discourses,* 134; Burgh, *Political Disquisitions,* 1:6.

8. Sidney, *Discourses,* 117, 365. "There is no disorder or prejudice in changing the name or number of Magistrates, whilst the root and principle of their Power"—the sovereignty of the people—"continues," Sidney observed, with specific reference to constitutional change in ancient Rome. This is the context of his statement that all human constitutions are subject to corruption and must perish unless timely renewed and reduced to first principles.

9. Machiavelli, in his *Discourses,* had advised that "to insure a long existence . . . republics, it is necessary frequently to bring them back to their original principles." This could result from either extrinsic accident or intrinsic prudence, he further observed, making clear that the lat-

ter—through "either good laws or good men"—was the preferable mode. See Niccolò Machiavelli, *The Prince and the Discourses,* ed. Max Lerner (New York: Modern Library, 1950), 397-402 (book 3, chap. 1).

10. Jefferson to Edward Carrington, January 16, 1787, to James Madison, January 30, 1787, in Julian P. Boyd, ed., *The Papers of Thomas Jefferson,* 27 vols. to date (Princeton: Princeton University Press, 1950-), 11:48-49, 92-93.

11. He defined rotation in office as "the obligation on the holder of [an] office to go out at a certain period" (Jefferson to Sarsfield, April 3, 1789, Boyd, *Papers,* 15:25). The general history of the idea is ably discussed in Mark P. Petracca, "Rotation in Office: The History of an Idea," in *Limiting Legislative Terms,* ed. Gerald Benjamin and Michael J. Malbin (Washington: Congressional Quarterly, 1992), 19-51. As noted below, the office that most concerned Jefferson at this time was that of the president of the United States; he bemoaned the fact that the Constitution had no limits on presidential terms.

12. "Sentiments of the Town of Roxbury on the Constitution of Civil Government proposed by Conventions," May 1780, in *The Popular Sources of Political Authority, Documents on the Massachusetts Constitution of 1780,* ed. Oscar and Mary Handlin (Cambridge, Mass.: Harvard University Press, 1966), 793.

13. Merrill D. Peterson, *Thomas Jefferson, the Founders, and Constitutional Change* (Claremont, Calif.: Claremont Institute, 1984), 5-6. Peterson notes in addition that the idea of change by way of the amendment process was particularly slow to catch on, despite the example of Article V of the United States Constitution. The constitutions of all five of the new states down to 1812—Vermont, Kentucky, Tennessee, Ohio, and

Louisiana—contained convention provisions but no amendment provisions. Not until the 1830s and 1840s did the amendment article become a fixture of state constitutions (ibid., 7).

14. Third Draft of a Constitution for Virginia, [before June 13, 1776], Boyd, *Papers,* 1:364.

15. Under Jefferson's provision, a convention could be authorized by "any two of the three branches of government concurring in opinion, each by the voices of two thirds of their whole existing number"; writs would then by sent to every county for the election of so many delegates as they send to the General Assembly; the convention thus specially called would have "equal powers" with the original Convention that adopted the constitution (Jefferson's Draft of a Constitution for Virginia, [May-June 1783], Boyd, *Papers,* 6:304). The Massachusetts precedent-making experience with both a constitutional convention and popular ratification is discussed in Willi Paul Adams, *The First American Constitutions: Republican Ideology and the Making of State Constitutions in the Revolutionary Era* (Chapel Hill: University of North Carolina Press, 1980), 86–93.

16. Jefferson, *Notes on the State of Virginia* (1787 Stockdale ed.), in Thomas Jefferson's *Writings,* ed. Merrill D. Peterson (New York: Library of America, 1984), 251 (Query XIII).

17. Madison, *Federalist* no. 49, [February 2, 1788], in *The Federalist,* ed. Jacob E. Cooke (Middletown, Conn.: Wesleyan University Press, 1961), 339-40.

18. Merrill D. Peterson, *Jefferson and Madison & the Making of Constitutions* (Charlottesville: University Press of Virginia, 1987), 12. In his written observations on Jefferson's 1783 draft constitution, Madison did not mention the provision for constitutional change although he did discuss Jefferson's provision for a council

of revision to pass on the constitutionality of laws (Boyd, *Papers,* 6:315).

19. As he later put it, Jefferson wrote "strongly" to Madison, urging the addition of a bill of rights; Madison drew upon many of Jefferson's arguments when he introduced the amendments in the first session of Congress (Jefferson to Dr. Joseph Priestley, June 19, 1802, Ford, *Writings,* 8:159; Mayer, *The Constitutional Thought of Jefferson,* 148-57).

20. Jefferson to James Madison, December 20, 1787, to Edward Carrrington, May 27, 1788, Boyd, *Papers,* 12:440-41, 13:208-9.

21. Jefferson to Alexander Donald, February 7, 1788, Boyd, *Papers,* 12:571. See also Jefferson to William Carmichael, December 15, 1787, ibid., 12:425.

22. Jefferson to Edward Carrington, May 27, 1788, Boyd, *Papers,* 13:208-9.

23. Jefferson to James Madison, September 6, 1789, Boyd, *Papers,* 15:392.

24. Ibid., 392-95.

25. Ibid., 395-96.

26. Ibid., 397.

27. James Madison to Jefferson, February 4, 1790, ibid., 16:147-49.

28. Ibid., 149-50; Jefferson to James Madison, September 6, 1789, ibid., 15:396.

29. For example, in 1791 Jefferson argued that the prosperity of the United States showed "the advantage of the changeableness of a constitution," here referring to the replacement of the Articles of Confederation with the Constitution (Jefferson to Benjamin Vaughan, May 11, 1791, Boyd, *Papers,* 20:392). Jefferson's devotion to the idea of change at about the time of his return to the United States can also be assessed by his frustrating correspondence with Noah Webster in 1790. Webster had misread Jefferson's criticisms of the Virginia constitution of 1776 in *Notes on the State of Virginia* as arguments for a perpetual and unalterable constitution. Jefferson explained to Webster that he had sought

to prove that the constitution *was* alterable by the ordinary legislature and to criticize it on this ground, not to argue that it *ought not to be* alterable; Webster, however, continued to misunderstand the point (Jefferson to Noah Webster, Jr., December 4, 1790, Boyd, *Papers,* 18:133 and editorial note on 134).

30. Jefferson, Opinion on the Constitutionality of the Bill for Establishing a National Bank, February 15, 1791, Boyd, *Papers,* 19:275-80.

31. Jefferson to James Monroe, February 15, 1801, to Dr. Joseph Priestley, March 21, 1801, Ford, *Writings,* 7:491, 8:22. Discussing this episode, Merrill Peterson observes that change by way of convention "held no terrors for Jefferson," although, citing Jefferson's letter to Monroe, Jefferson said that the very word convention "gave [the Federalists] the horrors." Although Jefferson's willingness to call a convention in this context might be regarded as "partisan taunts and maneuvers," the crisis was real and the expediency of calling a convention was a logical solution (Peterson, *Thomas Jefferson, the Founders, and Constitutional Change,* [Claremont, Calif.: Claremont Institute, 1984], 12-13).

32. John Randolph to Joseph H. Nicholson, July 26, 1801, cited in Richard E. Ellis, "The Persistence of Antifederalism after 1789," in *Beyond Confederation: Origins of the Constitution and American National Identity,* ed. Richard Beeman et al. (Chapel Hill: University of North Carolina Press, 1987), 303.

33. Dumas Malone, *Jefferson the President: First Term, 1801-1805* (Boston: Little, Brown, 1970), 118-19; Harry Ammon, "James Monroe and the Election of 1808 in Virginia," *William and Mary Quarterly,* 3d ser., 20 (1063): 33, 35-36. The Old Republicans' persistent demands for substantial reform during Jefferson's second term led to the schism in the Republican party, and particularly

in Virginia, where the Old Republicans supported Monroe rather than Madison in the election of 1808. A fine statement of the Old Republican position may be found in a letter written by John Taylor to Wilson Cary Nicholas, June 10, 1806, which is published in David N. Mayer, "Of Principles and Men: The Correspondence of John Taylor of Caroline with Wilson Cary Nicholas, 1806-1808," *Virginia Magazine of History and Biography* 96 (1988): 345-88. Taylor notes that he had "constantly thought that our policy could not be saved, except by amending the federal constitution" and bemoans the fact that Republicans, who in the 1790s had complained of "the paper systems, the Sedition & alien laws precedents, the executive patronage, & the influence on congress by contracts," after they came to power neglected to provide against these evils by constitutional amendments.

34. As I discuss in chapter 8 of my book, the chief practical consideration was the possibility of the loss of the Louisiana Purchase itself, if Jefferson were to press the constitutional difficulty and insist on an amendment.

35. Jefferson to Wilson Cary Nicholas, September 7, 1803, Ford, *Writings*, 8:247-48.

36. Jefferson to John Melish, January 13, 1813, Ford, *Writings*, 9:374-75.

37. For a brief discussion of the civic republican tradition and its historiography, see Mayer, "English Radical Whig Origins," 131.

38. Jefferson to A. Coray, October 31, 1823, in *The Writings of Thomas Jefferson*, ed. Andrew A. Lipscomb and Albert Ellery Bergh, 20 vols. (Washington: Thomas Jefferson Memorial Association, 1904), 15:480. By "the people," Jefferson meant no particular class but rather "the mass of individuals composing the society" (Jefferson to P. S. Du Pont de Nemours, April 24, 1816, Ford, *Writings*, 10:22-23).

39. Jefferson to Samuel Kercheval, July 12, 1816, to P. S. DuPont de Nemours, April 24, 1816, Ford, *Writings*, 10:24, and to John Taylor, May 28, 1816, Ford, *Writings*, 10:37-39, 24, 28-29.

40. Jefferson to Isaac H. Tiffany, August 26, 1816, Lipscomb and Bergh, *Writings*, 15:66.

41. Jefferson to Samuel Kercheval, July 12, 1816, Ford, *Writings*, 10:37-45, especially 42-43. Kercheval's pamphlet was written under a fictitious name, H. Tomkinson, the name to which Jefferson's famous letter was actually addressed (Dumas Malone, *The Sage of Monticello* [Boston: Little, Brown, 1981], 348, n.11).

42. Jefferson to John Taylor, May 28, 1816, Ford, *Writings*, 10:29-30.

43. Jefferson to Samuel Kercheval, July 12, 1816, Ford, *Writings*, 10:39-41.

44. Ibid., 43. Jefferson expressed the principle of the sovereignty of the living generation this way: "It is now forty years since the constitution of Virginia was formed," he noted. Mortality tables show that within that period, two-thirds of the adults then living were now dead. "Have then the remaining third, even if they had the wish, the right to hold in obedience to their will, and to laws heretofore made by them, the other two-thirds, who, with themselves, compose the present mass of adults? If they have not, who has? The dead? But the dead have no rights." Ibid., 44.

45. Ibid., 47.

46. The circumstances of the 1816 letters to Kercheval, and Jefferson's relationship to the movement to call a constitutional convention in Virginia in 1816 are discussed in Malone, *Sage of Monticello*, 349-50. When the movement was revived in 1824, Jefferson again was supportive but continued to decline Kercheval's request that he permit the publication of his 1816 letter. His son-in-law and eldest grandson, however, were actively involved in the movement (ibid., 441-43).

47. Jefferson to Robert J. Garnett, February 14. 1824, Ford, *Writings,* 10:295.

48. Jefferson Autobiography, [January 6, 1821], Ford, *Writings,* 1:111-12.

49. See Jefferson to William T. Barry, July 2, 1822, Lipscomb and Bergh, *Writings,* 15:389; Jefferson to James Pleasants, December 26, 1821, Ford, *Writings,* 10:198.

50. Jefferson to Thomas Earle, September 24, 1823, to John Cartwright, June 5, 1824, Lipscomb and Bergh, *Writings,* 15:470-71, 16:42.

51. This was a campaign of rhetoric conducted by a group of Virginia "Old Republicans" in response to a series of decisions handed down by the Supreme Court, including *McCulloch v. Maryland* (1819) and, most importantly, *Cohens v. Virginia* (1821). The Virginia campaign, and Jefferson's involvement in it, are discussed in the last section of chapter 9 of Mayer, *The Constitutional Thought of Thomas Jefferson.*

52. Jefferson to Judge William Johnson, June 12, 1823, Ford, *Writings,* 10:231-32.

53. Jefferson to William Charles Jarvis, September 28, 1820, Lipscombs and Bergh, *Writings,* 15:277-78.

54. Jefferson, "Fair Copy" Draft of the Kentucky Resolutions, [November 1798], Ford, *Writings,* 7:304-5.

55. Jefferson to James Madison, January 30, 1787, to David Hartley, July 2, 1787, to William S. Smith, November 13, 1787, to James Madison, December 20, 1787, Boyd, *Papers,* 11:92-93, 526, 12:356-57, 442. The letter to Smith also contains his famous statement, often quoted out of context, that "the tree of liberty must be refreshed from time to time with the blood of patriots & tyrants. It is it's natural manure."

56. Jefferson to Madison, January 30, 1787, to Edward Carrington, January 16, 1787, Boyd, *Papers,* 11:92-93, 48-49.

57. The uniqueness of Jefferson's political philosophy, in this regard, has been noted by Jean Yarbrough, who has argued that "of the Founders, only Jefferson seems to have recognized from the beginning that lethargy posed an equal if not greater danger to the preservation of republican government, especially a *representative* republic. Accordingly, while his colleagues were devising means to dampen political enthusiasm, Jefferson was thinking about how this political spirit might be sustained" (Yarbrough, "Republicanism Reconsidered: Some Thoughts on the Foundation and Preservation of the American Republic," *Review of Politics* 61 [1979]: 61-95, 88).

58. Jefferson to Dr. Joseph Priestley, June 19, 1802, Ford, *Writings,* 8:158-59.

59. Jefferson to George Wythe, August 13, 1786, Boyd, *Papers,* 10:245.

60. Jefferson to Col. Charles Yancy, January 6, 1816, Ford, *Writings,* 10:4.

61. Jefferson to P. S. Du Pont de Nemours, April 24, 1816, Ford, *Writings,* 10:24-25. In this letter he expressed his approbation of a provision, supposedly in the Spanish constitution, that no person could acquire the rights of citizenship until he could read and write. "It is impossible sufficiently to estimate the wisdom of this provision," he observed, calling it the "most effectual" means of preserving constitutional government.

62. Jefferson, *Notes on the State of Virginia,* in Peterson, *Writings,* 274 (Query XIV).

63. Ibid.; Jefferson, A Bill for the More General Diffusion of Knowledge, Boyd, *Papers,* 2:526-27.

64. Jefferson, Sixth Annual Message, December 2, 1806, Ford, *Writings,* 8:494: "Education is here placed among the articles of public care, not that it would be proposed to take its ordinary branches out of the hands of private enterprise, which manages so much better all the concerns to which it is equal; but a public institution can alone supply those sciences which, though rarely called for, are yet necessary to complete the circle, all the

parts of which contribute to the improvement of the country, and some of them to its preservation."

65. Jefferson to Governor John Tyler, May 26, 1810, Lipscomb and Bergh, *Writings,* 12:391.

66. Jefferson to Samuel Kercheval, July 12, 1816, Ford, *Writings,* 10:41. The division of powers between the federal government and the states—with "foreign" concerns only allocated to the federal government, and all "domestic" concerns allocated to the states—was what Jefferson regarded as "the true theory of the Constitution." His understanding of federalism and its implications, particularly regarding his theory for interpreting the Constitution, are discussed in chapters 7 and 9 of my study of Jefferson's constitutional thought.

67. Jefferson to Joseph Cabell, February 2, 1816, in Peterson, *Writings,* 1,380-81.

68. Jefferson to John Adams, October 28, 1813, in *The Adams-Jefferson Letters,* ed. Lester J. Cappon (Chapel Hill: University of North Carolina Press, 1959; reprint, New York: Clarion, 1971), 390.

69. Jefferson to Joseph C. Cabell, January 31, 1814, Ford, *Writings,* 9:451.

70. Jean Yarbrough observes that what set Jefferson apart from his colleagues was his rather low opinion of all political activity. His heroes were not the classical lawgivers but rather the philosopher-scientists Bacon, Newton, and Locke. "Not even the glorious activities of founding a republic could alter his essentially negative view of politics" (Yarbrough, "Republicanism Reconsidered," 91).

71. Dumas Malone, "The Great Generation," *Virginia Quarterly Review* 23 (1947): 108-22.

72. Jefferson to Samuel Kercheval, July 12, 1816, Ford, *Writings,* 10:39.

73. Jefferson to John Taylor, May 28, 1816, Ford, *Writings,* 10:30.

LIBERTY AND VIRTUE: RELIGION AND REPUBLICANISM IN JEFFERSONIAN THOUGHT

Eugene E. Sheridan

I wish to thank John Fleming, William C. Jordan, Jean-Yves Le Saux, John M. Murrin, J. G. A. Pocock, Daniel T. Rodgers, Sylvia A. Sheridan, Sean Wilentz, and John Wilson for their comments on this essay.

1. Peter Gay, *The Enlightenment: An Interpretation,* vol. 1, *The Rise of Modern Paganism* (New York: Knopf, 1966), 207-419. See also Henry F. May, *The Enlightenment in America* (New York: Oxford University Press, 1976); and Donald H. Meyer, *The Democratic Enlightenment* (New York: Putnam, 1976).

2. Jefferson to J. P. P. Derieux, July 25, 1788, Julian P. Boyd et al., eds., *The Papers of Thomas Jefferson,* 27 vols. to date (Princeton: Princeton University Press, 1950-), 13:418, hereafter cited as Boyd, *Papers.*

3. Jefferson to Peter Carr, August 10, 1787, ibid., 12:15.

4. Douglas L. Wilson, ed., *Jefferson's Literary Commonplace Book* (Princeton: Princeton University Press, 1989), 24-25, 214; Walter M. Merrill, *From Statesman to Philosopher: A Study in Bolingbroke's Deism* (New York: Philosophical Library, 1949); Merrill D. Peterson, "Thomas Jefferson and the Enlightenment: Reflections on Literary Influence," *Lex et Scientia* 11 (1975):103-7.

5. Wilson, *Jefferson's Literary Commonplace Book*, 24-25, 55.

6. Ibid., 33, 52-55; Jefferson to Peter Carr, August 25, 1787, Boyd, *Papers,* 12:15-17.

7. Wilson, *Jefferson's Literary Commonplace Book,* 30-33, 42-43.

8. Ibid., 33, 35-36.

9. Jefferson to Peter Carr, August 25, 1787, Boyd, *Papers,* 12:16.

10. William Peden, ed. *Notes on the State of Virginia* (Chapel Hill: University of North Carolina Press, 1955), 160.

11. Jefferson to John Adams, April 11, 1823, Dickinson W. Adams, ed., *Jefferson's Extracts from the Gospels* (Princeton: Princeton University Press, 1983), 410, hereafter cited as *Extracts.*

12. Robert M. Healey, *Jefferson on Religion in Public Education* (New Haven: Yale University Press, 1962), 27.

13. Wilson, *Jefferson's Literary Commonplace Book,* 30, 34, 50; *Notes on the State of Virginia,* 163; Jefferson to Peter Carr, August 25, 1787, Boyd, *Papers,* 12:15-17; First Inaugural, March 4, 1801, Paul L. Ford, ed., *The Works of Thomas Jefferson,* 12 vols. (New York, 1904-5), 9:197; Jefferson to John Adams, August 15, 1820, Lester Cappon, ed., *The Adams-Jefferson Letters,* 2 vols. (Chapel Hill, 1959), 2:567-69; Jefferson to Adams, April 11, 1823, Adams, *Extracts,* 410-13.

14. Jefferson to Thomas Law, June 13, 1814, *Extracts,* 356-57.

15. Wilson, *Jefferson's Literary Commonplace Book,* 35; Adrienne Koch, *The Philosophy of Thomas Jefferson* (New York: Columbia University Press, 1943), 15-22; Garry Wills, *Inventing America: Jefferson's Declaration of Independence* (Garden City, N.Y.: Doubleday, 1978), 200-206; Charles A. Miller, *Jefferson and Nature: An Interpretation* (Baltimore: Johns Hopkins University Press, 1988), 91-117; Lee Quinby, "Thomas Jefferson: The Virtue of Aesthetics and the Aesthetics of Virtue," *American Historical Review* 87

(1982):337-56; Charles L. Griswold, Jr., "Rights, and Wrongs: Jefferson, Slavery, and Philosophical Quandaries," in Michael J. Lacey and Knud Haakonssen, eds., *A Culture of Rights: The Bill of Rights in Philosophy, Politics, and Law—1791 and 1991* (New York: Cambridge University Press, 1991), 154-69.

16. Gilbert Chinard, ed., *The Commonplace Book of Thomas Jefferson: A Repertory of His Ideas on Government* (Baltimore: Johns Hopkins Press, 1926), 351-56, 359-63; Jefferson to Joseph Priestley, March 21, 1801, Ford, *Works,* 9:217; Jefferson to William Baldwin, January 19, 1810, *Extracts,* 345; Jefferson to Margaret Bayard Smith, August 6, 1816, ibid.; Sarah N. Randolph, *The Domestic Life of Thomas Jefferson* (New York: Harper, 1871), 427; Peter Byrne, *Natural Religion and the Nature of Religion: The Legacy of Deism* (London: Routledge, 1989), 79-92.

17. Outline of Argument, [November 1776], Boyd, *Papers,* 1:537-39; Notes on Locke and Shaftesbury, [1776], ibid., 544-48; *Notes on the State of Virginia,* 159-61; Jefferson to James Fishback, September 27, 1809, *Extracts,* 343-45.

18. Bill for the More General Diffusion of Knowledge, Boyd, *Papers,* 2:527; Response to Albemarle Address, February 12, 1790, ibid., 16:179; Jefferson to Thomas Paine, July 29, 1791, ibid., 20:308; ibid., 1:x; Jefferson to Samuel Knox, February 12, 1810, Andrew A. Lipscomb and Albert E. Bergh, eds., *The Writings of Thomas Jefferson,* 20 vols. (Washington: Thomas Jefferson Memorial Association, 1903-4), 12:361; *Notes on the State of Virginia,* 165.

19. Jefferson to James Madison, May 9, 1791, *Jefferson Papers,* 20:293; Jefferson to Joseph Priestley, June 19, 1802, Ford, *Works,,* 9:382; Jefferson to Archibald Thewat, December 24, 1821, ibid., 12:197.

20. *Notes on the State of Virginia,* 163; see also Boyd, *Papers,* 1:121, 135, 193, 197, 423, 429; and Thomas E. Buckley, "The

Political Theology of Thomas Jefferson,"
Merrill D. Peterson and Robert C.
Vaughan, eds., *The Virginia Statute for
Religious Freedom: Its Evolution and
Consequences in American History*
(Cambridge: Cambridge University Press,
1988), 75-108.

21. First Inaugural, March 1, 1801, Ford,
Works,, 9:197.

22. Report of the Commissioners for
the University of Virginia, August 4, 1818,
Merrill D. Peterson, ed., *Thomas Jefferson:
Writings* (New York: Library of America,
1984), 461, hereafter cited as Peterson,
Writings; Garrett W. Sheldon, *The Political
Philosophy of Thomas Jefferson* (Baltimore:
Johns Hopkins University Press, 1991), 41-
52; Joyce Appleby, "What Is Still American
in the Political Philosophy of Thomas
Jefferson?" *William and Mary Quarterly,*
3d ser., 39 (1982):287-309; Appleby,
"Republicanism in Old and New
Contexts," ibid., 43 (1986):20-34.

23. *Notes on the State of Virginia,* 164-
65; Jefferson to George Washington, May
23, 1792, Boyd, *Papers,* 23:536-38; Gordon
S. Wood, *The Creation of the American
Republic* (Chapel Hill: University of North
Carolina Press, 1969), 46-69; Drew
McCoy, *The Elusive Republic: Political
Economy in Jeffersonian America* (Chapel
Hill: University of North Carolina Press,
1980); Robert E. Shalhope, "Thomas
Jefferson's Republicanism and Antebellum
Southern Thought," *Journal of Southern
History,* 42 (1976):529-56; Lance Banning,
"Jeffersonian Ideology Revisited: Liberal
and Classical Ideas in the New American
Republic," *William and Mary Quarterly,*
3d ser., 43 (1986):3-19; Banning, "Some
Second Thoughts on Virtue and the
Course of Revolutionary Thinking,"
Terence Ball and J. G. A. Pocock, eds.,
Conceptual Change and the Constitution
(Lawrence: University of Kansas Press,
1988), 194-212.

24. Paul A. Rahe, *Republics Ancient &
Modern* (Chapel Hill: University of North

Carolina Press, 1992), 698-725.

25. Jefferson to Edward Carrington,
January 16, 1787, Boyd, *Papers,* 11:49.

26. Bill for the More General Diffusion
of Knowledge, ibid., 2:526-27; *Notes on the
State of Virginia,* 121; Bernard Bailyn, *The
Ideological Origins of the American
Revolution* (Cambridge, Mass.: Harvard
University Press, 1967), 55-93; Lance
Banning, *The Jeffersonian Persuasion:
Evolution of a Party Ideology* (Ithaca, N.Y.:
Cornell University Press, 1978); Sheldon,
Political Philosophy of Thomas Jefferson,
53-82.

27. John C. Miller, *Wolf by the Ears:
Thomas Jefferson and Slavery* (New York:
Free Press, 1977); Edmund S. Morgan, *The
Meaning of Independence: John Adams,
George Washington, Thomas Jefferson*
(Charlottesville: University Press of
Virginia, 1975), 60-61; *Notes on the State of
Virginia,* 84-85.

28. Minutes of University of Virginia
Board of Visitors, October 7, 1822,
Peterson, *Writings,* 478.

29. Boyd, *Papers,* 1:536.

30. *Notes on the State of Virginia,* 161.

31. Ibid., 159.

32. Boyd, *Papers,* 1:537.

33. *Notes on the State of Virginia,* 159.

34. Boyd, *Papers,* 1:537-38.

35. *Notes on the State of Virginia,* 160.

36. Jefferson to the Danbury Baptists,
January 1, 1802, Lipscomb and Bergh,
Writings, 16:281-82.

37. Boyd, *Papers,* 2:545-47.

38. Jefferson to James Madison,
December 16, 1786, ibid., 10:604.

39. Bill for the More General Diffusion
of Knowledge, ibid., 2:526-33; *Notes on the
State of Virginia,* 146-49; Lorraine Smith
Pangle and Thomas L. Pangle, *The
Learning of Liberty: The Educational Ideals
of the American Founders* (Lawrence:
University of Kansas Press, 1993), 106-24.

40. Albert Schweitzer, *The Quest of the
Historical Jesus: A Critical Study of Its
Progress from Reimarus to Wrede* (1910;

New York: Macmillan, 1950).

41. For fully annotated texts of these three key documents, see *Extracts*, 45-314, 332-36. See also Susan Bryan, "Reauthorizing the Text: Jefferson's Scissor Edit of the Gospels," *Early American Literature* 22 (1987): 19-42.

42. Jefferson to Francis Adrian Van der Kemp, April 25, 1816, *Extracts*, 369.

43. Banning, *Jeffersonian Persuasion*, chaps. 5-9.

44. Jefferson to Edward Rutledge, June 24, 1797, Ford, *Works*, 8:318-19.

45. Jefferson to Martha Jefferson Randolph, April 25, 1803, Edwin M. Betts and James A. Bear, eds., *The Family Letters of Thomas Jefferson* (Columbia: University of Missouri Press, 1966), 244; Jefferson to John Adams, August 22, 1813, *Extracts*, 348.

46. Joseph Priestley, *An History of the Corruptions of Christianity*, 2 vols. (Birmingham: Printed by Piercy and Jones, for J. Johnston, London, 1782), esp. 2:440-66; E. Millicent Sowerby, comp., *Catalogue of the Library of Thomas Jefferson*, 5 vols. (Washington: Library of Congress, 1952-59), 2:120; Ira T. Brown, "The Religion of Joseph Priestley," *Pennsylvania History* 24 (1957):85-100; Caroline Robbins, "Honest Heretic: Joseph Priestley in America," American Philosophical Society, *Proceedings* 106 (1962):60-76.

47. Benjamin Rush to Jefferson, August 22, October 6, 1800, *Extracts*, 317-19, 321-24; Jefferson to Rush, September 23, 1800, April 21, 1803, ibid., 319-21, 331; Rush to Granville Sharp, March 31, 1801, John A. Woods, ed., "The Correspondence of Benjamin Rush and Granville Sharp, 1773-1809," *Journal of American Studies* 1 (1967):34; George W. Corner, *The Autobiography of Benjamin Rush* (Princeton, 1948), 152; Donald J. D'Elia, "The Republican Theology of Benjamin Rush," *Pennsylvania History* 33 (1966):187-204; D'Elia, "Jefferson, Rush, and the Limits of Philosophical Friendship,"

American Philosophical Society, *Proceedings* 117 (1973):333-43.

48. Anonymous to George Washington, January 3, 1792, Washington Papers, Library of Congress; William L. Smith, *The Pretensions of Thomas Jefferson to the Presidency Examined; and the Charges against John Adams Refuted*, part 1 (Philadelphia, 1796), 14, 36-40; Charles O. Lerche, Jr., "Jefferson and the Election of 1800: A Case Study in the Political Smear," *William and Mary Quarterly*, 3d ser., 5 (1948):467-91; Fred Leubke, "The Origins of Thomas Jefferson's Anti-Clericalism," *Church History* 30 (1963):344-56; Constance B. Schulz, "'Of Bigotry in Politics and Religion': Jefferson's Religion, the Federalist Press, and the Syllabus," *Virginia Magazine of History and Biography* 91 (1983):73-91.

49. John M. Mason, *The Voice of Warning, to Christians, on the Ensuing Election of a President of the United States* (New York: Printed and sold by G.F. Hopkins, 1800), 9-14.

50. Ibid., 17.

51. Ibid., 17-18; William Linn, *Serious Considerations on the Election of a President: Addressed to the Citizens of the United States* (New York, 1809), 14-16; *Notes on the State of Virginia*, 159.

52. Linn, *Serious Considerations*, 19. *Notes on the State of Virginia*, 159.

53. Jefferson to William Short, August 4, 1820, *Extracts*, 396.

54. Jefferson to John Adams, August 22, 1813; Jefferson to William Canby, September 18, 1813; Jefferson to James Smith, December 8, 1822, ibid., 347, 350, 409.

55. Jefferson to William Short, October 31, 1819, ibid., 388.

56. "Syllabus of . . . the doctrines of Jesus," ibid., 332.

57. Ibid., 334.

58. Ibid., 334; Jefferson to Francis Adrian Van der Kemp, May 1, 1817, Jefferson Papers, Library of Congress;

Jefferson to John Adams, November 13, 1818, March 14, 1820, January 8, 1825, Cappon, *Adams-Jefferson Letters,* 2:529, 562-63, 606; Jefferson to Martha Jefferson Randolph, [July 2, 1826], Jefferson Papers, Massachusetts Historical Society.

59. Jefferson to William Short, August 4, 1820, *Extracts,* 397.

60. Jefferson to George Thacher, January 26, 1824, ibid., 414.

61. Jefferson to William Baldwin, January 19, 1810, ibid., 345.

62. Jefferson to John Adams, August 22, 1813, ibid., 347.

63. Ford, *Works,* 9:197, 10:127-28, 132-33.

64. Jefferson to Moses Robinson, March 23, 1801, *Extracts,* 325.

65. Jefferson's note to his October 31, 1819 letter to William Short, ibid., 391.

66. Jefferson to Jeremiah Moor, August 14, 1800, Ford, *Works,* 9:143; Jefferson to Joseph Priestley, March 21, 1801, ibid., 217; Jefferson to Elbridge Gerry, March 29, 1801, ibid., 242–43; Jefferson to Isaac Story, December 5, 1801, *Extracts,* 325–26; Jefferson to Joseph Priestley, April 9, 1803, ibid., 327–28; Jefferson to Edward Dowse, April 19, 1803, ibid., 329–30; Jefferson to Thomas Leiper, January 21, 1809, Ford, *Works,* 11:89–90; Jefferson to James Fishback, September 27, 1809, *Extracts,* 343; Jefferson to William Canby, September 18, 1813, ibid., 350; Jefferson to Miles King, September 26, 1814, ibid., 360–61; Jefferson to George Logan, November 12, 1816, ibid., 381; Jefferson to Ezra Stiles Ely, June 25, 1819, ibid., 386–87; Jefferson to Thomas Whittemore, June 5, 1822, ibid., 404; Jefferson to George Thacher, January 26, 1824, ibid., 414–15.

67. Jefferson to Joseph Priestley, April 9, 1803, *Extracts,* 328; see also Jefferson to Priestley, April 24, 1803, January 29, 1804,

ibid., 336–37, 340; Priestley to Jefferson, May 7, 1803, ibid., 338–40; and Jefferson to Benjamin S. Barton, ibid., February 14, 1805.

68. Jefferson to Francis Adrian Van der Kemp, April 25, 1816, ibid., 369; see also Van der Kemp to Jefferson, March 24, June 4, July 14, and November 1, 1816, ibid., 366–68, 370–74, 377–80; Jefferson to Van der Kemp, July 30 and November 24, 1816, ibid., 374–75, 383; and Henry F. Jackson, *Scholar in the Wilderness: Francis Adrian Van der Kemp* (Syracuse, N.Y.: Syracuse University Press, 1963), 246–52.

69. Jefferson to James Smith, December 8, 1822, ibid., 409.

70. Report of the Commissioners for the University of Virginia, August 4, 1818, Peterson, *Writings,* 467; see also Healey, *Jefferson on Religion in Public Education,* 202–26.

71. Gordon S. Wood, *The Radicalism of the American Revolution* (New York: Knopf, 1992), brilliantly charts the transition from a classical republican to a liberal democratic America in the half century or so after the Revolution. Shalhope, "Thomas Jefferson's Republicanism and Antebellum Southern Thought," analyzes Jefferson's reaction to the various manifestations of this transition in the aftermath of the War of 1812. This essay's suggested link between Jefferson's demythologized Christian beliefs and his concern to preserve republican virtue is intended to call attention to a neglected dimension of this problem. For the American Revolution and the republicanism it spawned as "the last great act of the Renaissance," see J. G. A. Pocock, "Virtue and Commerce in the Eighteenth Century," *Journal of Interdisciplinary History* 3 (1972):120.

WARD REPUBLICS: THE WISEST INVENTION FOR SELF-GOVERNMENT

S U Z A N N E   W .   M O R S E

1. Thomas Jefferson to Governor John Tyler, May 26, 1810, Paul Leicester Ford, ed., *Works of Thomas Jefferson*, 12 vols. (New York: G.P. Putnam's Sons, 1904-05), 5:524.

2. Hannah Arendt, *On Revolution* (New York: Viking Press, 1963), 253-54.

3. Garrett Ward Sheldon, *The Political Philosophy of Thomas Jefferson* (Baltimore: Johns Hopkins University Press, 1984), n. 61.

4. Ibid., 12.

5. Richard Matthews, *The Radical Politics of Thomas Jefferson* (Lawrence: University Press of Kansas, 1984), 82.

6. Giovanni Sartori, *The Theory of Democracy Revised* (Chatham: Chatham House, 1987), 284-86.

7. Werner Jaeger, *Paideia: The Ideal of Greek Culture,* 3 vols. (New York: Oxford University Press, 1939), 111-12.

8. Arendt, *On Revolution,* n. 323.

9. Sheldon, *Political Philosophy,* 62.

10. Thomas Jefferson to Samuel Kercheval, July 12, 1816, Ford, *Works*, 12: 8-9.

11. Thomas Jefferson to Governor John Tyler, May 26, 1810, ibid., 5:524-26.

12. Thomas Jefferson to Joseph C. Cabell, February 2, 1816, ibid., 6:544.

13 Arendt, *On Revolution,* 252.

14. Ibid., 252.

15. Sheldon, *Political Philosophy,* 61.

16. Thomas Jefferson to Samuel Kercheval, September 12, 1816, Ford, *Works,* 12:8.

17. Thomas Jefferson to Governor John Tyler, May 26, 1812, ibid., 5:525-26.

18. Matthews, *Radical Politics,* 83.

19. Ibid., 85.

20. Arendt, *On Revolution,* 252-53.

21. Matthews, *Radical Politics,* 85.

22. Thomas Jefferson to James Madison, January 30, 1787, *Papers of Thomas Jefferson,* ed. Julian P. Boyd, 27 vols. to date (Princeton, N.J.: Princeton University Press, 1950-), 11:93.

23. A. J. Beitzinger, "Political Theorist," in *Thomas Jefferson: A Reference Bibliography,* ed. Merrill D. Peterson (New York: Charles Scribner's Sons, 1986), 96.

24. Thomas Jefferson to Samuel Kercheval, September 12, 1816, Ford, *Works,* 12:8.

25. Ibid.

26. Cited in Thomas Bender, *Community and Social Change in America* (Baltimore: Johns Hopkins University Press, 1978), 84-85.

27. Arendt, *On Revolution,* 256.

28. Ibid., 256.

29. Sheldon, *Political Philosophy,* 55-56.

30. Lewis Mumford, *The City in History* (New York: Harcourt, Brace & World, 1961), 332.

31. Ibid.

32. Max J. Skidmore, *American Political Thought* (New York: St. Martin's Press, 1978), 72.

33. Suzanne Morse, *Renewing Civic Capacity: Preparing College Students for Service and Citizenship,* ASHE-ERIC Higher Education Report, no. 8 (Washington: School of Human Development, George Washington University, 1989), 19.

34. Hannah Arendt, *The Human Condition* (Chicago: University of Chicago Press, 1958), 28.

35. Hannah Pitkin, "Justice: On Relating Public and Private," *Political Theory* 9, no. 3 (1981):343.

36. Morse, *Renewing Civic Capacity,* 23.

37. William M. Sullivan, *Reconstructing Public Philosophy* (Berkeley: University of

California Press, 1982), 166.

38. Thomas Jefferson to Joseph C. Cabell, February 2, 1816, Ford, *Works,* 6:423.

39. Cornelia and Jan Flora, "Developing Entrepreneurial Rural Communities," *Sociological Practice* 8(1990):203.

40. Benjamin Barber, *Strong Democracy* (Berkeley: University of California Press, 1984), 235.

41. David Mathews, "Teaching Politics as Public Work: An Alternative Theory of Civic Education," paper presented at annual meeting of Citizenship for the 21st Century, Washington, D.C., October 1988, 306-7.

42. Barber, *Strong Democracy,* 269.

43. Ibid., 270.

44. F. Christopher Arterton, *Teledemocracy: Can Technology Protect Democracy?* (Newbury Park, Calif.: Sage Publications, 1987).

45. The Harwood Group, *Citizens and Politics: A View from Main Street* (Dayton, Ohio: Kettering Foundation, 1991).

46. *National Issues Forums Literacy Programs, 1988-1991,* project report to the John D. and Catherine T. MacArthur Foundation.

47. David Osborne and Ted Gaebler, *Reinventing Government* (New York: Penguin Books USA, 1992), 74.

48. Michael Ignatieff, *The Needs of Strangers* (New York: Viking Penguin, 1984), 107.

THE EDUCATION OF THOSE WHO GOVERN

RALPH KETCHAM

1. Paul Rahe, *Republics Ancient and Modern: Classical Republicanism and the American Revolution* (Chapel Hill: University of North Carolina Press, 1992); Joseph M. Levine, *The Battle of the Books: History and Literature in the Augustan Age* (Ithaca, N.Y.: Cornell University Press, 1991).

2. Thomas Jefferson to Henry Lee, May 8, 1825, in Adrienne Koch and William Peden, eds., *The Life and Selected Writings of Thomas Jefferson* (New York: The Modern Library, 1944), 719; and Jefferson to John Adams, July 5, 1814, in Lester Cappon, ed., *The Adams-Jefferson Letters,* 2 vols. (Chapel Hill: Published for the Institute of Early American History and Culture by the University of North Carolina Press), 2:432-33.

3. Jefferson to John Adams, December 10, 1819, ibid., 2:549-50.

4. *City of God,* 5:24, quoted in Lester K.

Born, ed., *The Education of a Christian Prince by Desiderius Erasmus* (New York: Octagon Books, 1965, c1936), 92.

5. *De Regimine principum,* 1:14, and "Whether subjects are bound to obey their superiors in all things," *Summa Theologica,* Secunda Secundae, Quaest. CIV, Art. V, in Michael B. Foster, *Masters of Political Thought,* vol. 1, *Plato to Machiavelli* (Boston, Houghton Mifflin, 1941), 265-67.

6. Born, ed., *Christian Prince,* 199-203.

7. Ibid., 171, 189, 162-163, 140, 182.

8. Ibid., 187.

9. Richard Carpenter and Alexander Leighton, quoted in T. H. Breen, *The Character of the Good Ruler: A Study of Puritan Political Ideas in new England, 1630-1730* (New York: Norton, 1974, c1970), 23, 25.

10. Born, ed., *Christian Prince,* 164.

11. Ibid., 183, 180.

12. Koch and Peden, eds., *Writings of Jefferson*, 323.

13. John M. Major, ed., *Sir Thomas Elyot's The Book Named The Governor* (New York: Teachers College Press, 1970, c1969), 30.

14. Ibid., 129, 101.

15. Jefferson to John Brazier, August 24, 1819, in H. A. Washington, ed., *The Works of Thomas Jefferson*, vol. 7 (Washington, 1853-54), 133.

16. Isaac Kramnick, ed., *Lord Bolingbroke: Historical Writings* (Chicago, 1972), xxiv, l-lii.

17. Jeffrey Hart, ed., *Political Writings of Eighteenth Century England* (New York, 1964), 208-9, 246-54.

18. A. O. Lovejoy, "The Chinese Origins of a Romanticism" in his *Essays in the History of Ideas* (Westport, Conn.: Greenwood Press, 1978; New York, 1948), 104-10.

19. "Report on Books for Congress," January 23, 1783, Madison to Jefferson, March 16, 1784, and Jefferson to Madison, May 5, 1784, in W. T. Hutchinson et al., eds., *The Papers of James Madison*, 17 vols. (Chicago: University of Chicago Press, 1962-91), 6:66, 8:11, 42.

20. Wolfius, *The Real Happiness of a People under a Philosophical King Demonstrated* (London, 1750), 1-5.

21. Ibid., 12-16, 23-24.

22. Ibid., 31-32, 67-70.

23. Lily B. Campbell, ed., *The Mirror for Magistrates* (New York: Barnes & Noble, 1960; Cambridge, 1938), 64; quoted in Breen, *Good Ruler*, 7.

24. James Axtell, ed., *The Educational Writings of John Locke* (London:

Cambridge University Press, 1968), 268, 60.

25. Donald W. Hanson, *From Kingdom to Commonwealth: The Development of Civic Consciousness in English Political Thought* (Cambridge, Mass.: Harvard University Press, 1970), 14-40.

26. "Proposals Relating to the Education of Youth in Pennsylvania," 1750, in L. W. Labaree et al., eds., *The Papers of Benjamin Franklin*, 32 vols.(New Haven: Yale University Press, 1996), 3:397-413.

27. "Memorandum on the Academy," July 31, 1750, and "Idea of the English School," 1751, ibid., 4:36 and 4:105-8.

28. "Charter of the Academy of Philadelphia," July 13, 1753, ibid., 5:8.

29. "A Plan for the Establishment of Public Schools . . . in Pennsylvania, to which are added Thoughts on the Mode of Education," 1786; reprinted in S. A. Rippa, ed., *Educational Ideas in America: A Documentary History* (New York: D. McKay, 1969), 119-20.

30. Jefferson, "Autobiography," 1821, in Koch and Peden, eds., *Life and Selected Writings*, 52; and Jefferson to W. C. Jarvis, September 28, 1820, in E. Dumbold, ed., *Thomas Jefferson: Political Writings* (New York, 1955), 93.

31. Proposed in a bill for education in Virginia, 1817, but dropped for political reasons. Washington, ed., *Works of Jefferson*, 9:494.

32. "A Bill for the More General Diffusion of Knowledge," 1778, in Thomas Jefferson: *Writings,* ed. Merrill D. Peterson (New York: Library of America, 1984), 365, 367.

THOMAS JEFFERSON AND HIS CONCEPTION OF HAPPINESS

Liu Zuochang

The editors would like to thank Ralph Ketcham for help in documenting the works quoted in this paper.

1. Memorial to Congress on the Book Duty, November 30, 1821, in Thomas Jefferson, *Writings*, ed Merrill D. Peterson (New York: Library of America, 1994), 476.

2. Report of the Commissioners for the University of Virginia, August 4, 1818, in Peterson, *Writings* (1994), 461.

3. Thomas Jefferson to Reverend James Madison, October 28, 1785, in Thomas Jefferson, *The Life and Selected Writings*, ed. Adrienne Koch and William Peden (New York: Random House, 1993), 361.

4. Travelling Notes for Mr. Rutledge and Mr. Shippen, June 3, 1788, in Koch and Peden, *Life and Selected Writings*, 139.

5. Jefferson to Reverend Madison, October 28, 1785, ibid., 361-62.

6. Jefferson to Geismar, September 6, 1785, in *The Papers of Thomas Jefferson*, ed. Julian P. Boyd et al., 27 vols. to date (Princeton: Princeton University Press, 1950-), 8:500.

7. Jefferson to James Madison, June 9, 1793, ibid., 26:240.

8. Jefferson to Maria Cosway, October 12, 1786, in Koch and Peden, *Life and Selected Writings*, 367-77.

9. Jefferson to the Inhabitants of Albermarle County, in Virginia, April 3, 1809, in Koch and Peden, *Life and Selected Writings*, 546.

10. Jefferson to Charles Bellini, September 30, 1785, in Koch and Peden, *Life and Selected Writings*, 355.

11. Jefferson to James Madison, May 8, 1784, in Boyd, *Papers*, 7:233.

12. Jefferson to Peter Carr, August 10, 1787, in Koch and Peden, *Life and Selected Writings*, 398.

13. *Notes on Virginia*, in Koch and Peden, *Life and Selected Writings*, 259.

14. Jefferson to John Jay, July 12, 1785, in Boyd, *Papers*, 8:284.

15. See C. B. MacPherson, *The Political Theory of Possessive Individualism: Hobbes to Locke* (Oxford: Clarendon Press, 1962).

Contributors

BENJAMIN BARBER

Benjamin Barber is Walt Whitman Professor of political science at Rutgers University and director of the Walt Whitman Center for the Culture and Politics of Democracy. He is the author of many articles, essays, and reviews in a broad range of scholarly and popular journals and magazines and the author of twelve books, including *Education for Democracy: Citizenship, Community, Service; Jihad vs. McWorld;* and, most recently, *A Place for Us: How to Make Society Civil and Democracy Strong* and *A Passion for Democracy.*

HOLLY BREWER

Holly Brewer is assistant professor of history at North Carolina State University. Her numerous awards include a fellowship from the National Endowment for the Humanities and an award for best article from the *William and Mary Quarterly.* Her forthcoming book *Constructing Consent: The Legal Status of Children and American Revolutionary Ideology* will be published by the Institute of Early American History and Culture and the University of North Carolina Press.

RICHARD D. BROWN

Currently professor of history at the University of Connecticut, Richard D. Brown has won grants from the American Antiquarian Society, American Philosophical Society, National Endowment for the Humanities, and American Council of Learned Societies, among others. He has written widely about early American society, in *Knowledge Is Power: The Diffusion of Information in Early American Society* and, most recently, *The Strength of a People: The Idea of an Informed Citizenry in America, 1650-1870.*

JOHN Y. COLE

A librarian and historian, John Cole has been the director of the Center for the Book in the Library of Congress since it was created in 1977. His major research interest is the history of the Library of Congress and his most recent book is *On These Walls: Inscriptions and Quotations in the Buildings of the Library of Congress* (1995).

JAMES GILREATH

James Gilreath was American history specialist for the Rare Book and Special Collections Division in the Library of Congress from 1980 to 1996. He was responsible for interpreting, acquiring new material for, and preserving the Library's rare Americana collections. He has written about the history of the book in America, the history of American copyright, Mark Twain, and Abraham Lincoln. With Douglas L. Wilson, he wrote *Thomas Jefferson's Library*. He edited *Federal Copyright Records, 1790-1800*.

DONALD GRINDE, JR.

At the time of the conference, Donald Grinde was Rupert Costo Professor of American Indian History at the University of California at Riverside, and he is now professor of history at the University of Vermont. Much of his writing has focused on political theory and Native American tribal organization and the relationship between American Indians and African Americans.

MICHAEL GROSSBERG

Michael Grossberg is professor of history at Indiana University and editor of the *American Historical Review*. He has published numerous articles in legal and social history as well as *A Judgment for Solomon: The d'Hauteville Case and Legal Experience in Antebellum America* and *Governing the Hearth: Law and Family in Nineteenth Century America*, for which he won the American Historical Association's Littleton-Griswold Prize in the history of American law and society.

HERBERT A. JOHNSON

Herbert A. Johnson is Hollings Professor of Constitutional Law at the University of South Carolina. A specialist in colonial and early national legal history, he was editor of *The Papers of John Marshall*. His most recent book is *The Chief Justiceship of John Marshall*.

RALPH KETCHAM

Ralph Ketcham is Maxwell Professor Emeritus of Citizenship and Public Affairs at Syracuse University. He has been a visiting professor at universities in England, Japan, China, India, Korea, the Netherlands, New Zealand, Hawaii, Virginia, and Texas, and has lectured elsewhere throughout the world. His *James Madison, a Biography* was nominated for the National Book Award.

JAN LEWIS

A pioneering historian of the family in America, Jan Lewis teaches in the History Department at Rutgers University at Newark, New Jersey. The author of *Pursuit of Happiness: Family and Values in Jefferson's Virginia* (Cambridge University Press), she is currently completing her book "Women, Slaves, and the Creation of a Liberal Republic." She is a member of numerous advisory panels including several for Monticello, and among her awards is one for independent study and research granted by the National Endowment for the Humanities (NEH).

LIU ZUOCHANG

Liu Zuochang is professor of history at Shandong Normal University in the People's Republic of China. His biography of Thomas Jefferson, *Chieh-fei-hsun chuan,* was published in Beijing in 1990 by the Chinese Academy of Social Sciences Press. He is currently translating Jefferson's writings into Chinese, the first time such an attempt has been made.

ELIZABETH MARVICK

Elizabeth Marvick is now an independent writer who has taught political science at the University of California at Los Angeles and American civilization and politics at the University of Bordeaux. Her *Louis XIII: The Making of a King* was published by Yale University Press and her book *The Young Richelieu: A Psychoanalytic Approach to Leadership* by the University of Chicago Press. Her articles have appeared in such journals as *Psychohistory Review, Journal of Psychohistory,* and *International Political Science Review.*

DAVID N. MAYER

David Mayer is professor of law and history at Capital University in Columbus, Ohio. His work *The Constitutional Thought of Thomas Jefferson* was published by the University Press of Virginia in 1994. He has written for various journals, including *Washington University Law Quarterly,* the *Missouri Law Review, Cato Journal, Virginia Magazine of History and Biography*, and *Perspectives on Political Science.*

SUZANNE W. MORSE

Suzanne Morse is executive director of the Pew Partnership for Civic Change, a national community-building initiative established by The Pew Charitable Trusts in 1992, and Visiting Professor at the University of Richmond. Before joining the Pew Partnership, she was with the Charles F. Kettering Foundation as director for programs. She has written extensively on ways to increase civic participation, including *Renewing Civic Capacity: Preparing College Students for Service and Citizenship.*

JAMES OAKES

James Oakes holds the Graduate School Chair in the Humanities at the Graduate Center of the City University of New York. He is one of the leading scholars and authors writing about American slavery. His *Slavery and Freedom: An Interpretation of the Old South* and *The Ruling Race: A History of American Slaveholders,* both published by Knopf, are his major works. He has been a Fellow at the Institute for Advanced Study at Stanford and received an NEH grant for independent study and research.

EUGENE R. SHERIDAN

Eugene R. Sheridan was a member of the Princeton University History Department and senior associate editor of *The Papers of Thomas Jefferson* when he died in an automobile accident in May 1996. He is the author of *Lewis Morris, 1671-1746; A Study in Early American Politics* and editor of *The Papers of Lewis Morris.* He was a frequent contributor to historical journals and was working on a study of Thomas Jefferson's quest for the historical Jesus at the time of his death.

FRANK SHUFFELTON

Frank Shuffelton is a professor at the University of Rochester where he was director of graduate studies from 1981 to 1986. His *Thomas Jefferson: A Comprehensive Annotated Bibliography of Writings about Him, 1826-1980* and *Thomas Jefferson, 1981-1990* are standard sources in the field.

JENNINGS WAGONER, JR.

Jennings Wagoner, Jr., is a professor at the Curry School of Education at the University of Virginia, specializing in the history of higher education in America. He has written *Thomas Jefferson and the Education of a New Nation,* "Jefferson, Justice, and the Enlightened Society" in D. A. Verstegen's *Spheres of Justice in Education,* and "Honor and Dishonor at Mr. Jefferson's University: The Antebellum Years," for the *History of Education Quarterly.*

DOUGLAS L. WILSON

Douglas L. Wilson is Saunders Director of the International Center for Jefferson Studies at the Thomas Jefferson Memorial Foundation (Monticello). At the time of the conference, he was professor of English at Knox College in Galesburg, Illinois. He has edited *Jefferson's Literary Commonplace Book* and, with James Gilreath, *Thomas Jefferson's Library.* He has published articles on Jefferson in the *Atlantic Monthly,* the *William and Mary Quarterly,* and the *Harvard Library Bulletin.*

C. VANN WOODWARD

One of the most distinguished historians of the South, C. Vann Woodward has written extensively about southern culture, including *Origins of the New South,* which won the American Historical Society's Bancroft Prize. He is Sterling Professor Emeritus at Yale University, where he taught for many years. Dr. Woodward has lectured throughout the world and was the Harmsworth Professor at Oxford University in England.

Index

A

Ackerman, Bruce, 138, 139
Adair, James, 198, 199
Adams, Abigail, 167, 173
Adams, John
    and citizenship restrictions, 55
    drafting Massachusetts constitution, 98-
        100
    on Lafayette's ambitions, 164
    letters from Jefferson
        on American Indians, 195, 196, 198
        on aristocracy, 127
        on corruption in English government,
            200-201
        effects of printing on culture, 88
        on letters of Cicero, 282
        love of reading, 85
        on natural aristocracy, 27, 86
        on public opinion, 187
        on universal education, 81
        while in France, 167
    and need for men of learning as leaders,
        97-98
    private tutorial, 95
    program for an informed citizenry, 92-102
    on universal literacy in America, 80, 83, 93,
        94, 100, 188, 293
Adams, Willi-Paul, 5, 64
African Americans
    abolition of slavery, 171-72, 211, 213, 249,
        262
    colonization of freed slaves, 191, 249
    equality of, 177-92, 193
    and Jefferson's racism, 139-40, 151, 177-92,
        193, 213, 216, 347 n15
    literacy and slaves, 86-87, 92-93, 142, 144,
        178-80
agrarianism, 303-4

allodial land, 10, 20, 309 n31
American Indians. *See* Native Americans
American Philosophical Society, 198, 200, 212
Anglo-Saxon hundreds, 266
Anglo-Saxon language, 130
antistatism, 4, 65
Appeal (Walker), 177, 179, 192
Appleby, Joyce, 5, 71
Arendt, Hannah, 138, 148, 265, 267, 270, 271,
    338 n10
aristocracy
    artificial vs. natural aristocracy, 27, 86, 127,
        132, 136, 150, 238, 252, 263
    of republican representatives, 135
    vs. republican government, 27, 65
Aristotle, 266, 282, 283, 284, 285, 286, 287
Arterton, Christopher, 276
Articles of Confederation, 139
Assembly of Notables, 168, 169
Auld, Sophia, 178-79

B

Bache, William, 41
Bacon, Matthew, 108, 109
Bailyn, Bernard, 141, 155, 156
Banister, John, Jr., 55, 115, 116, 117, 149, 175
Bankhead, Charles, 47
Banneker, Benjamin, 181
Barbé-Marbois, François, 161, 341 n44
Barber, Benjamin R., 368
    on education and democracy, 134-52
    on neighborhood assemblies, 275-76
    notes, 337-38
bastardy law. *See* illegitimate children
Beitzinger, A. J., 270
Bellini, Charles, 201, 299
Bible, Jefferson's rejection of, 244

Bill for Establishing Religious Freedom (Virginia), 53, 80, 101-2, 173, 251
Bill for the More General Diffusion of Knowledge (Virginia), 54, 56, 61, 73, 80-81, 95-97, 118, 119, 125, 136, 143-44, 145-46, 150, 238, 252
Billington, James H., x
Bingham, Anne Willing, 73, 168, 169
black inferiority, Jefferson's racist views on, 177, 180-89, 193, 213, 216, 347 n15
Blackstone, Sir William, 6, 7, 19, 59, 64, 106, 107, 109
Bloom, Allan, 135
Bolingbroke, Lord, 86, 243, 245, 284, 288
The Book Named the Governor (Elyot), 284, 287, 288
Boorstin, Daniel J., ix, 65, 132, 133, 184
Boyd, Julian P., ix, 10, 11, 166, 193, 194, 200, 221
Brewer, Holly, 368
    on laws regarding children, 48-62
    commentary, 63-75
    notes, 314-24
Brown, Richard D. , 368
    on informed citizenry, 91-102
    commentary, 144-47
    notes, 328-29
Bry, Theodor de, 199
Buffon, Georges Louis Leclerc, comte de, 193, 195, 196, 207, 209, 341 n44
Bultmann, Rudolph, 253
Burgh, James, 222-24
Burns, James MacGregor, 139
Burwell, Nathaniel, 73, 124
Bushman, Richard, 58
Business of the Supreme Court (Frankfurter), 103

C
Cabell, Joseph C., 113, 131, 239, 268
Calvin, John, 245
Care, Henry, 58
Carr, Peter, 55, 86, 125, 127, 175, 184, 293, 300, 333 n5
Carrington, Edward, 54, 83-84, 135, 202, 224, 236
Carter, Landon, 12
Cartwright, John, 222, 235, 267
Cary, Archibald, 31
Cato, 267, 282
Chase, Samuel, 234
Chastellux, marquis de, 205, 216, 341 n44

children
    age requirements for citizenship, 57-58
    apprenticeships, 60-61, 62
    incapable of reason, 49, 52
    independence vs. discipline, 55
    intrafamilial murder law, 60, 64
    laws regarding, 48-62, 315 n2
    legal reform to limit, 56-62
    literature written for, 50
    Locke's views on, 50-51
    need for formal education, 53-54
    relations with parents, 51, 53, 64
    relations with tutor/teacher, 36, 55, 320 n37
    in republican political thought, 49-56
    rights of illegitimate, 3, 7, 13, 16, 17, 23-24, 60, 64-65, 324-25 n6
    statutory rape, 59-60
    as witnesses, 56, 62
    See also education; public education
children's rights movement, 67, 325 n11
Chinard, Gilbert, 155-56, 159, 166, 168, 209, 210, 343-44
Chinese philosophy of government, 288-90, 291
church and state, separation of, 92, 101, 242, 249-52, 253
Cicero, 282, 283, 284, 286, 287, 291
citizen participation. See ward republics
citizenship, requirements of, 58
civic humanism, 247, 248, 263, 272, 304
civic virtue. See under moral behavior
classical republicanism, 50, 224, 225, 316 n9, 363 n71
Clay, Henry, 263
Cohen, Felix, 194
Coke, Sir Edward, 9, 19, 105, 106
Cole, John Y. , 368
    preface, ix-x
College of Philadelphia
    law school curriculum, 108, 110, 148
    plans for, 291
College of William and Mary
    access to, 118
    curriculum reform, 104, 127
    legal education curriculum, 104, 107, 109, 110, 148
    professorship of law and police, 108
    scholarship students, 126
    Tucker as professor of law, 18
    Virginia bill for improvements to, 96, 331 n29
    Wythe as first professor of law, 108

Columbia College, legal education, 110-11
Commentaries on the Laws of England
(Blackstone), 6-7, 19-20, 59, 109
common law, 9, 56, 59-60, 62, 64, 111, 114
Confucius, 288, 293, 304-5
consent of the governed, 53, 54, 67, 224, 282
Constitution (U.S.)
amendment proposals, 230, 234, 355 n13
defects, 227, 355-56 n18, n19
ratification of, 172-73
constitutional change
generational change theory, 3, 26-27, 228,
235, 240, 357 n44
Jefferson's views on, 137, 221-241, 356 n29,
n31
Old Republicans' position, 356-57 n33
constitutional conventions, 224-26, 355 n15
constitutions, amendment process, 224-25
Coolidge, Ellen Randolph, 173
Coontz, Stephanie, 30
Coray, A., 136
corruption in government, 200-201, 223, 271
Cosway, Maria, 160, 184, 214, 326 n2
Cover, Robert, 19
Curti, Merle, 126

D
Davidson, Cathy N., 82-83, 144
Dearborn, Gen. Henry, 197
Declaration of Independence, 52, 63, 120, 139,
247, 262, 295-96, 316 n8
*The Declaration of Independence: The Evolution
of a Text* (Boyd), ix
Degler, Carl N., 29, 36
Deism, 92, 243-44, 246, 257
Democracy in America (Tocqueville), 25-26
Dewey, Frank L., 107, 329-30 n4, n5
Discourses (Machiavelli), 354-55 n9
Discourses Concerning Government (Sidney),
52, 222
Dissertation on Canon and Feudal Law
(Adams), 99
*The Doctrines of Heathen Philosophy,
Compared with Those of Revelation*
(Priestley), 261
domestic relations law. *See* family law
Douglass, Frederick, 86-87, 142, 179
Duché, Jacob, 93

E
Edgeworth, Maria, 42

education
foreign study for American youth, 115-17,
175, 333 n5
inequality, 133
and informed citizenry, 91-102, 136, 144-47
linked to liberty, 118
of noncitizens, 335 n28
private tutorials, 95
privately funded, 92, 95
for republican citizens, 115-34
of republican leaders, 125-31, 281-94
role of history in basic education, 81, 119
self-education, impact of, 86-90, 144
seminary schools, 131
universal education, 81-83, 125, 187, 188,
281-94
utility in education, 115-34, 149-51
Virginia bills, 54, 56, 61, 73, 80-81, 95-97,
118, 119, 125, 136, 143-44, 145-46, 150, 238,
252
vocationalism, 132
See also legal education; literacy; public
education
The Education of a Christian Prince (Erasmus),
284, 285, 288
elected officials
minimum age requirements, 56
term limits, 222, 227, 230, 240
Elements of Criticism (Kames), 85
Elyot, Sir Thomas, 284, 287, 288, 291
English common law. *See* common law
English inheritance law, 6-7
Enlightenment beliefs
children as nonrational, 49
in conflict with Christian orthodoxy, 242-
43
and constitutional reform, 222
faith in reason and knowledge, 91, 95
of methodical inquiry, 187
Enville, Marie Louise Nicole Elisabeth de La
Rochefoucauld de Roye, duchesse d', 163, 169
environmental degeneracy thesis, 193-97, 207,
208
Eppes, Elizabeth Wayles (Jefferson's sister-in-
law), 31
Eppes, Francis (Jefferson's brother-in-law), 32
Eppes, Francis Wayles (Jefferson's grandson),
33, 45-46
equal opportunity, 18, 26
equality
of African Americans, 177-92, 193
of all men, 192, 212-13

equality *(continued)*
        as a fictional term, 318 n21
        Jefferson's views on, 52-53, 64
        limits to, 53
        of Native Americans, 193-208
Erasmus, 281, 282, 284-87, 288, 291, 293
Essay Concerning Human Understanding
        (Locke), 50, 51
European culture, Jefferson's views on, 115-17

F
family law
        impact of inheritance law reform, 17-26
        intrafamilial murder, 60, 64, 322 n59
        pension plans, 60-61, 64, 322-23 n61
family life
        Jefferson's experience, 63
        Jefferson's ideas about, 68-69, 313 n28, n31
        letters of Jefferson, 28-47, 312 n13
        and public culture, 63-64
A Father's Legacy to His Daughters (Gregory),
        32
Fauquier, Francis (British governor), 167
federalism
        division of powers, 358-59 n66
        and Native American self-governance
                model, 202-3, 205
Filmer, Sir Robert, 49-52, 67
Fliegelman, Jay, 66
Floyd, Gen. William, 199
Forbes, Jack, 207
foundationalism, 138, 140
Frankfurter, Felix, ix, 103
Franklin, Benjamin, 162, 163, 167, 196, 204, 291-
        92
free press, 92, 99
free speech, 92
free will, 52
freedom
        Jeffersonian limits to, 53
        natural freedom of children, 53
French Declaration of Rights, 166, 210
French Revolution, 137, 141, 216-17, 338 n9, 343
        n67
French salons and social life, 167-71

G
Gaebler, Ted, 277
Garnet, Henry Highland, 178
Gay, Peter, 242, 243, 246
Gillespie, Joseph, 88
Gilman, Charlotte Perkins, 281

Gilreath, James, 369
        introduction, xiii-xv
Girardin, Louis Hue, 44
Glorious Revolution (1688-89), 223
Goff, Frederick R., ix
Gordon, Thomas, 178
Gottschalk, Louis, 165, 166
Gould, James, 112
Gregory, John, 32
Grinde, Donald A., Jr. , 369
        on perceptions of Native Americans, 193-
                208
        commentary, 211-12, 214
        notes, 349-53
Griswold, A. Whitney, 302
Grossberg, Michael, 368
        on domestic relations and generational
                change, 3-27
        commentary, 63-75
        notes, 307-11

H
Habermas, Jürgen, 36, 46, 69, 71, 186
Hall, David D., 80
Hamilton, Alexander, 268, 298
Hamiltonian economics, 248, 254, 262
happiness
        Jefferson's concept of, 295-305
        pursuit of, 5, 15
Harrington, James, 316 n9, 317 n12, 317-18 n15
Harrison, William Henry, 197
Harvard University
        constitutional provisions for, 99
        funding for, 95
        law school curriculum, 113-14
        mission statement, 99
Hawkins, Benjamin, 199
Head and Heart dialogue, 184, 214, 299, 326 n2
Hendrickson, David, 156
Henry, Patrick, 12
Herland (Gilman), 281
Hirsch, E. D., Jr., 84
History of American Indians (Adair), 199
An History of the Corruptions of Christianity
        (Priestley), 254
Home, Henry, Lord Kames. *See* Kames, Henry
        Home, Lord
Houdetot, Sophie de Lalive d', 167, 169, 170
Hopkinson, Mrs. Thomas, 36
humanism. *See* civic humanism
Hume, David, 34, 85
Hutcheson, Francis, 34, 63

I

Idea of a Patriot King (Bolingbroke), 284, 288
illegitimate children (filius nullius)
    death of, 60, 64, 324-25 n6
    rights, 3, 7, 13, 16, 17, 23-24, 65
individualism, origin of word, 26
inequality
    for citizenship rights, 249
    denial of natural rights, 139-40
    in educational opportunity, 133
    environmental degeneracy thesis, 193-97
informed citizenry. *See* education; literacy;
    public education
inheritance law reform, 3-27
    American vs. English law, 19-23
    dower rights for widows, 6
    entail defined, 56
    entail provisions abolished, 3, 7-8, 10, 11-12,
        16, 20, 25, 52, 56-57, 65, 309 n37, n39, n46
    fee simple tenure, 10, 11, 309 n35
    illegitimate children, 3, 7, 13, 16, 17, 23-24,
        65
    incorporation and limits of, 17-26
    intestate, defined, 308 n11
    intestate succession, 6, 7, 57
    Jefferson legacy, 26-27
    law of descent, 3, 10, 17
    primogeniture revisions, 3, 6, 7, 10, 12-13,
        16, 20, 24, 52, 56, 57, 318 n17, n20
    revising Virginia laws, 5-17, 65
    testamentary, defined, 308 n10
    testamentary disposition, 6, 12-13
    testamentary rights for women, 6, 7, 10, 21
Institutes and Reports (Coke), 106
Iroquois Confederacy, political system, 204-6

J

James I (king of England), 49
Jefferson, Lucy (daughter), 31
Jefferson, Martha (*called* Patsy, daughter)
    at Panthemont (convent school in France),
        173
    education of, 74, 123-24
    friendship with American Indians, 195
    impressions of France, 157
    life at Monticello, 71
    relationship with father, 31-34, 42, 69
Jefferson, Martha Wayles Skelton (wife), 29, 31,
    335 n22
Jefferson, Mary (daughter), 31, 37, 40, 41, 123,
    312 n18

Jefferson, Peter (father)
    death of, 63
    relationship with American Indians, 195
Jefferson, Thomas
    death of, 29
    duality of mind and personality, 209-17
    family life, 28-47
    as a father, 31-35
    as governor of Virginia, 31-32
    grief over wife's death, 31, 312 n10
    health of, 39
    inaugural addresses, 55, 71, 260
    as law clerk with George Wythe, 104-7, 147
    marriage, 63
    as minister to France, 13, 39, 115-17, 155-76,
        209-11
    as president, 42-43, 55, 237
    as president of American Philosophical
        Society, 198, 212
    presidential election, 229-30
    as a rascist, 139, 141, 177-84
    as secretary of state, 37, 174
    as slave owner, 171-72, 338 n21
    as vice president, 40
    as Virginia legislator, 3-27, 48, 57-58
*Jefferson's Legacy: A Brief History of the Library
    of Congress*, x
Jesus Christ, as a historical figure, 244, 253, 256,
    258-59, 261
Johnson, Herbert A., 369
    on legal education in America, 103-14
    commentary, 147-49
    notes, 329-32
Jordan, Winthrop, 193, 208
jury service, age requirements, 58, 62

K

Kaestle, Carl, 82
Kames, Henry Home, Lord, 85, 245
Katz, Stanley, 17
Kent, James, 25, 66, 110
Kercheval, Samuel, 16, 141, 232, 233, 264, 266,
    268, 271
Ketcham, Ralph, 369
    on education of those who govern, 281-94
    notes, 365-66
Kimball, Marie, 159
king
    as political father, 49-50, 63
    power by primogeniture, 49
King, Martin Luther, 281
Kirtland, Bob, 104-5

Kramnick, Isaac, 18, 26

L
La Rochefoucauld, François de, 163
Lafayette, Adrienne, 168
Lafayette, Marie-Joseph-Paul-Yves-Roch-
    Gilbert du Motier, marquis de, 141, 158, 162,
    164-66, 168, 170, 195, 204, 210
Lafitau, Joseph François, 198-99
Landis, James, 103
languages, study of, 129-30, 199-200
Lasch, Christopher, 28
leadership, educating republican leaders, 125-
    31, 281-94
Lee, Thomas Ludwell, 8, 9, 333-34 n7
legal education
    bar exam preparation, 111
    for citizenship training, 112
    clerkships, 103, 329-30 n4, n12, n13
    clinical legal education, 103
    college curriculums, 108-11
    in context of arts and sciences, 108-11
    Jefferson's advice concerning, 106-7
    private law schools, 111, 112, 148, 332 n61
    professionalism in, 111-14
    in Revolutionary America, 103-14, 147-49
    and role of attorney, 329 n2
    vs. technical training, 149
    Wilson lectures, 108-9
Leibniz, Gottfried Wilhelm, 288
Levine, Joseph, 282
Levy, Leonard W., 193
Lewis, Jan, 369
    on family and civic education, 63-75
    on Jefferson as a transitional figure, 30
    notes, 324-26
Lewis, Meriwether, 199
liberal individualism, 66, 242, 262, 263
liberty
    Jefferson's view on, 137
    Rousseau's view on, 137
Library of Congress
    anniversaries of Jefferson's birth, ix
    and Jefferson's personal library, ix, 217
The Life and Morals of Jesus (Jefferson), 253
Lincoln, Abraham, and self-education, 87-90,
    144
literacy
    debate over purpose of, 82-83
    historical significance of, 82
    Jefferson's views on, 79-90, 143-44
    liberating power of, 86-90

link to religion, 80
and self-government, 83-84
and slavery, 86-87
study of race, 87
See also public education
Literary Commonplace Book (Jefferson), 243
Liu Zuochang, 370
    on Jefferson's concept of happiness, 295-
        305
    notes, 367
Locke, John
    comparison with Harrington, 316 n9, 317
        n12
    on education, 291-92
    influence on Jefferson, 55, 63, 67, 184
    on natural rights, 5
    reasoning adults vs. children, 50-51
Lockean Liberalism, 50, 247
Lockridge, Kenneth, 8
Logan (Mingo chief), 196
Lomax, John T., 113
The Lost World of Thomas Jefferson (Boorstin),
    65, 132

M
Machiavelli, 354-55 n9
MacLeish, Archibald, ix
MacPherson, C. B., 302
Maddox, Margaret, 166
Madison, James
    on citizenship restrictions, 268
    on constitutional conventions, 226
    friendship with Jefferson, 164
    on good government, 282
    on Lafayette's ambitions, 164
    letters from Jefferson
        on education, 119
        on formal education to nurture reason,
            53-54
        on generational change, 3, 228-29
        on happiness, 300
        on majority rule, 227
        on Native Americans, 193, 204
        on rebellion, 270
        on Shay's rebellion, 217, 224, 236
    opposed to constitutional change, 234
    relationship with Hamilton, 259
    on slavery, 171
    study of American Indian languages, 199
    Virginia constitutional reform, 176
    Virginia education bill, 95, 119
    Virginia inheritance bills, 13-14

Madison, James (bishop), 108, 297, 298
Maine, Sir Henry, 17
Maitland, Frederic, 6
Malone, Dumas, ix, 16, 118, 134, 184, 193, 240
marriage law
    intermarriage with native peoples, 197, 212
    interracial marriages, 23
    parental consent requirement, 56, 58-59, 60
    published banns, 59
Marshall, John, 108, 109, 112, 148, 234, 262, 263, 354 n2
Marvick, Elizabeth Wirth, 370
    on Jefferson and the Old World, 155-76
    commentary, 209-11, 214
    notes, 339-46
Mason, George, 8, 9
Massachusetts
    Constitution, 98-100, 146, 225
    free schools for free boys, 93
    public education, 97-98, 145-46
Matthews, Richard, 5, 15, 193, 194, 216, 217, 268, 270
Maury, Walker, 55, 320 n37, 333 n5
Mayer, David N., 370
    on constitutional change, 221-41
    notes, 354-359
McCloskey, Robert, 109, 148
Michels, Robert, 138
Mill, John Stuart, 186
Minor, Garritt, 110, 331 n49
Monroe, James
    letter from Jefferson on "private life," 31-32
    letters from France, 157, 158
Monticello
    architectural design, 159
    family life, 71-72, 299
    society of Jefferson's neighbors, 40-41, 299, 313-14 n34
moral behavior
    and civic virtue, 50, 99, 317 n12
    foundation of happiness, 300
    from theological doctrine, 246
    Golden Rule and, 121
    guided by our conscience, 34-35, 313 n21
    Jefferson's views on, 30, 32-35
    of Native Americans, 204
    and religious instruction, 120-22
    and reputation, 335 n21
    utility of reading moral fiction, 85, 122, 124
moral sense theory, 34-35, 79, 183, 184, 216, 245, 258, 271, 312 n19, 313 n22, 334 n18, 347-48 n16
Moral Tales for Young People (Edgeworth), 42

More, Sir Thomas, 287
Morgan, Edmund S., 58, 318 n21
Morris, Gouverneur, 55, 345 n99, 352 n72
Morse, Suzanne W., 370
    on ward republics, 264-77
    notes, 363-65
Mumford, Lewis, 272

N
Narrative (Douglass), 87
Native Americans
    assimilation of, 151
    birth control, 351 n58
    historians for, 352-53 n80
    Jefferson's condescension toward, 193-208, 211-12, 338 n17
    Jefferson's study of languages, 199-200
    models of governance and political thought, 200-208, 265, 266, 352 n72
    rights denied to, 140
natural rights, 5, 49, 227, 247, 250, 298, 391 n29
New Abridgment of the Law (Bacon), 108, 109
New England town meetings, 266-67
Nicholas, Wilson Cary, 231
Notes on the State of Virginia (Jefferson), 9, 13, 110, 122, 157, 161, 171, 177, 178, 181, 182, 191-92, 196, 197, 198, 200, 204, 209, 212, 216, 225, 233, 238, 244, 247, 250, 256, 266, 293, 301
Novissima Sinica (Leibniz), 288

O
Oakes, James, 370
    on Jefferson and African Americans, 177-92
    commentary, 212-14, 215
    notes, 346-49
Oakeshott, Michael, 140
O'Brien, Connor Cruse, 139
On the Training of Princes (St. Thomas Aquinas), 283
Orth, John, 8
Osborne, David, 277
Otto, Louis-Guillaume, 346 n133

P
Paine, Thomas, 201
Parrington, Vernon L., 193
paternal authority
    children's independence from, 57-58
    and relationship with children, 51, 53, 55, 64
    vs. political authority, 50-51

patriarchal absolutism, 50
patriarchal theory, 49-50, 51
Pendleton, Edmund, 8-13, 48, 57, 230, 308 n23, 333-34 n7
Pericles, 266, 275, 285
Peterson, Merrill
    biographer of Jefferson, 80
    on constitutional change, 226
    index of Jefferson's writings, 63
    on Jefferson and education, 118
    and Jefferson symposium, ix
    on Jefferson's faith in book learning, 85, 144
    on Jefferson's ideas, 127, 134
Philadelphia Academy, 292
Philosophical Works (Bolingbroke), 86
The Philosophy of Jesus (Jefferson), 253, 261
Pinckney, Charles, 205
Pitkin, Hannah, 273
Plato, 281, 282, 285, 286, 287, 289, 291
Pocock, J. G. A., 50
police, defined, 313 n25
polis (Greek city-state), 266
Political Disquisitions (Burgh), 222
Politics (Aristotle), 284, 285
poor
    Jefferson and the, 297-98
    law policy, 60-61
    pension plans, 60-61, 64, 322-23 n61
    scholarship students, 96, 125-26, 145-46
Pricstley, Joseph, 41, 128, 254-55, 261
primogeniture
    inheritance laws and, 3, 6, 7, 10, 12-13, 16, 20, 24, 52, 56
    with respect to kings, 49, 51-52
printing, impact on human culture, 88, 144, 187
property rights
    age requirements, 58
    and individual rights, 4
    and inheritance law, 57, 320-21 n44
    ownership responsibilities, 14-15
    redistribution of property, 65
public education
    British model, 94
    of children, 32-33, 48
    elementary curriculum, 12, 119-20, 334 n11
    funding for, 94, 145-46, 328 n1
    gratis, for the poor, 96, 125-26, 145-46
    for informed consent, 54-55
    institutions of, 94-101
    New England model, 94-95, 145
    programs for, 91-102

religious instruction, 120-21, 252, 257
    Virginia bills, 54, 56, 61, 73, 80-81, 95-97, 118, 119, 125, 136, 143-44, 145-46, 150, 237-38, 252
    for women, 73-74, 95, 123-25
    See also education; literacy
public libraries, 81, 118, 188
public life
    of Jefferson children and grandchildren, 43-44
    vs. private life, 28-47, 40-41, 273-74, 311 n4
public virtue. *See* moral behavior, and civic virtue
Puritan legacy, 93

Q
The Quest of the Historical Jesus (Schweitzer), 253

R
racial prejudices, 139-40, 177-92, 212-14, 256-57
Radical Whigs
    and an informed citizenry, 91-102, 354 n4
    and free speech and press, 92
The Radicalism of the American Revolution (Wood), 138
Rahe, Paul, 248, 282
Ramsay, David, 206
Randolph, Anne Cary (Jefferson's granddaughter), 41-42
Randolph, Cornelia (Jefferson's granddaughter), 42
Randolph, Ellen Wayles (Jefferson's granddaughter), 42
Randolph, Jefferson (Jefferson's grandson), 35, 44, 46
Randolph, John, 230
Randolph, Mary (Jefferson's granddaughter), 39
Randolph, Thomas Mann, Jr., 37-39 , 47, 106
Raynal, Abbé, 196, 207, 209
reading
    Jefferson on reading fiction, 85
    Jefferson's life-long experiences with, 84-86
The Real Happiness of a People under a Philosophical King Demonstrated (Wolff), 289
reason, adult men alone capable of, 49
Reeve, Tapping, 111, 112
religious beliefs
    "Holy Cause of Freedom," 246-49

religious beliefs *(continued)*
  Jefferson's personal beliefs, 130-31, 243-46
  rejection of the Trinity, 243, 255
  and republicanism, 242-63
religious freedom, 53, 242
  Jefferson's views on, 249-53
  and literacy, 80, 91-92, 93
  for moral instruction, 98-99
  Virginia bill, 53, 80, 101-2, 173, 251
Report of the Commissioners for the
  University of Virginia (August 4, 1818),
  44-45, 120, 128, 150, 188, 293
republic of letters, 35-36, 45, 46, 326 n26
Republic (Plato), 287
republicanism, defined, 231-32
revolution, as good for democracy, 137-38, 270,
  338 n8, 358 n55
Roane, Spencer, 22-23
Rochambeau, Jean-Baptiste-Donatien de
  Vimeur, comte de, 162, 210
Rockfish Gap report. *See* Report of the
  Commissioners for the University of
  Virginia (August 4, 1818)
Rodney, Caesar, 186
Rollin, Charles, 81
Rousseau, Jean-Jacques, 137, 138, 194, 198
Rush, Benjamin, 100, 120-21, 137, 255-56, 292-93
Rutledge, John, 250

S
Salisbury, Neal, 194
Salter, Mary Jo, 27
Salvino, Dana Nelson, 87
Sancho, Ignatius, 181, 190
Schaack, Peter Van, 105, 106, 111, 332 n61
Schweitzer, Albert, 253
seal of the United States, Jefferson's concept of,
  56
The Second Treatise of Government (Locke), 50
Shay's rebellion (Massachusetts), 54, 83-84, 141,
  144, 172, 217, 224, 236
Sheldon, Garrett, 267, 271, 316 n9
Sheridan, Eugene R., 371
  on religion and republicanism, 242-63
  notes, 359-63
Short, William, as Jefferson's secretary, 156, 158,
  159, 163, 165, 166, 170, 174-75, 343 n67
Shuffelton, Frank, 371
  on Jefferson family letters, 28-47
  commentary, 63-75
  notes, 311-14

Sidney, Algernon, 50-52, 55, 63, 67, 222-24,
  318 n16
Skelton, Martha Wayles. *See* Jefferson, Martha
Skipwith, Robert, 34, 85, 185
slave literacy, 86-87, 92-93, 142, 144, 178-80
slave societies, 180, 190
slavery
  abolition of, 171-72, 211, 213, 249, 262
  colonization of freed slaves, 191, 249
  and literacy, 178-80
Small, William, 167
Smith, Adam, 34-35, 63
Smith, Col. William, 141
Smith, William L., 256
social contract, 137-39
Social Contract (Rousseau), 194
Society of the Cincinnati, 165
Some Thoughts Concerning Education (Locke),
  50, 51, 291-91
Stamp Act crisis, 80
statutory rape, 59-60, 322 n56
Stiles, Ezra, 100
Stoicism, 313 n22
Story, Joseph, 112, 113, 148, 330 n14
Strong Democracy (Barber), 276
suffrage. *See* voting rights
Sullivan, William, 274

T
taxation
  of churches, 92
  policy, 298
  for public education, 94-95, 145
Taylor, John, 141
Temple, Sir William, 288
term limits
  for elected officials, 222, 230, 240
  for the presidency, 227, 230, 355 n11
Tessé, Madame de, 167-68, 169, 170, 210
Theory of Moral Sentiments (Smith), 34
Thomas Aquinas, Saint, 283-84, 291
Thomson, Charles, 197, 198
Tocqueville, Alexis de, 25-26, 66, 271, 275
Tott, Brigitte de, 160
townships, 272-73
Trenchard, John, 178
The Trew Law of Free Monarchies (James I), 49
Trist, Eliza, 168, 237
Trist, Hore Browse, 41
Trumbull, Jonathan, 174-75
Tucker, Henry St. George, 24, 65-66
Tucker, Nathaniel Beverly, 105

Tucker, Robert, 156
Tucker, St. George
    his Americanized version of Blackstone's *Commentaries*, 19-22
    inheritance law cases, 22-24
    legal career, 18
    as professor of law at College of William and Mary, 109-10, 148
Turner, Nat, 179
Turner's rebellion, 179
Two Treatises of Government (Locke), 50-51
Tyler, John, 265, 266, 267, 268

U
University of Pennsylvania. *See* College of Philadelphia
University of Virginia
    academical village, 45, 131
    creation and establishment of, 67, 120, 136, 263
    curriculum, 45-46, 127-31, 261, 336 n40
    legal education, 113
    medical studies, 130
    purposes of, 129
    religious and ethical studies, 261-62
    student disorders, 45
    theological studies, 130-31
Upon Heroick Virtue (Temple), 288
usufruct, laws of, 3, 136, 165
Utopia (More), 287

V
Van der Kemp, Francis Adrian, 261
Virginia
    constitutional change, 225, 232-33
    constitutional drafts, 10, 48
    education bills, 54, 56, 61, 73, 80-81, 95-97, 118, 119, 125, 136, 143-44, 145-46, 150, 237-38, 252
    law revision committee, 8-9, 11, 308 n23, 309 n26, 333-34 n7
    literacy laws, 93-94
    religious liberty law, 53, 80, 101-2, 173, 251
virtue. *See* moral behavior, and civic virtue; moral sense theory
Volney, Count, 157
Voltaire, 288
voting rights
    for adult males, 318-19 n24, 320 n34
    age requirements, 58
    restrictions, 319 n32, 321-22 n50

W
Wagoner, Jennings L., Jr., 371
    on utility of civic education, 115-34
    commentary, 149-51
    notes, 333-37
Walker, David, 177-80, 191-92
Walpole, Robert, 91
ward republics, 138, 238-40, 263, 264-77
    in the twenty-first century, 275-77
    four responsibilities of, 268-69
Washington, Bushrod, 23, 25, 112
Washington, George, 12, 118, 162, 165, 172-73, 206, 210, 256
Watkins, Thomas, 110
Watson, Joseph S., 110
We the People (Ackerman), 138
Webster, Daniel, 25, 66
Wheatley, Phillis, 181
Whiskey rebellion, 254
William and Mary College. *See* College of William and Mary
Williamos, Charles, 163-64
Williams, David, 26-27
Wills, Garry, 183
Wilson, Douglas L., 371
    on literacy, 79-90
    commentary, 143-44
    notes, 326-27
Wilson, E. O., 181
Wilson, James, law school lectures, 108-9, 111, 148
Wirt, William, 113
Wolff, Christian, 289-90
women
    in American Indian societies, 203, 212
    "domestic sphere"/domestic skills, 32-33, 123, 125, 249
    dower rights for widows, 6
    education of, 38, 73-74, 123-25, 150, 281, 348 n18
    in French society, 167-71
    gender roles, 37-38, 73
    in political life, 73, 170-71, 210
    rights denied to, 140, 249
    statutory rape of girls, 59-60
    testamentary rights, 6, 7, 21
    university admission denied, 47
Wood, Gordon, 138, 139, 141, 217
Woodward, C. Vann, 175, 371
    on Old and New Worlds, 209-17
    notes, 353

Wythe, George
    education of legal apprentices, 104-5
    as Jefferson's mentor, 104-6, 147, 167, 243
    letters from Jefferson, 54
    as professor of law at College of William
        and Mary, 108-9, 148
    Virginia education bill, 95, 118, 187-88, 237,
        293
    as Virginia judge, 12
    and Virginia law revision committee, 8-9,
        12, 48, 57

Y
Yale University, funding for, 95

Book design: Gerard A. Valerio, Bookmark Studio

Composed in Minion by Sherri Ferritto, Typeline